Human Rights and
the Environment

Human Rights and the Environment

Cases, Law, and Policy

Svitlana Kravchenko

PROFESSOR OF LAW
LL.M. PROGRAM DIRECTOR
UNIVERSITY OF OREGON SCHOOL OF LAW

John E. Bonine

PROFESSOR OF LAW
UNIVERSITY OF OREGON SCHOOL OF LAW

CAROLINA ACADEMIC PRESS
Durham, North Carolina

ISBN 13: 978-1-59460-413-3
LCCN: 2008929634

Carolina Academic Press
700 Kent Street
Durham, North Carolina 27701
Telephone (919) 489-7486
Fax (919) 493-5668
www.cap-press.com

Printed in the United States of America

To all our parents,
to daughter Maria,
and to our professional families
at ELAW and EPL.

Summary of Contents

Preface   xxi

Acknowledgments   xxv

Chapter 1 · Why Human Rights and the Environment?   3
   I.   Environmental Human Rights   3
   II.   Linkages between Human Rights and the Environment   12
   III. Human Rights Instruments and Institutions   20

Chapter 2 · Substantive Environment Rights in International Law   23
   Introduction   23
   I.   Environmental Rights under the European Convention   23
     A. European Convention on Human Rights   24
     B. Right to Private and Family Life   26
       1. Origin of the Article 8 Right   26
       2. Weakening of Article 8?   37
       3. Reestablishing Rights, Providing Remedies, Enforcing Precedents   43
     C. Right to Life   48
   II.   Environmental Rights under the African Charter   52
     A. African Charter on Human and Peoples' Rights   52
     B. Finding an Environmental Right   55
   III. Environmental Rights under the American Declaration and Convention   60
     A. American Declaration of the Rights and Duties of Man   60
     B. American Convention on Human Rights   62
     C. San Salvador Protocol   63

Chapter 3 · Substantive Environment Rights in National Law   67
   Introduction   67
   I.   Substantive Rights in National or State Constitutions   68
   II.   Challenging Government Action and Inaction   72
     A. Overturning Legislation   73
     B. Overturning Executive Action   79
     C. Requiring Affirmative Government Programs   93
   III. Challenging Actions by Private Parties   100
     A. Enforcement against Private Actors by Attorneys General   100
     B. Enforcement by Citizens against Private Defendants   105
   IV. Evaluating the Role of the Courts   110

Chapter 4 · Right to Water 113
Introduction 113
   I. A Right to Water in International and Regional Instruments 114
      A. Soft and Hard Law Sources 114
      B. General Comment 15: Private or Public Good? 119
   II. A Right to Water in National Instruments 129
      A. Examples of the Right to Water at a National Level 129
      B. Quantity, Affordability, and Procedure:
         Implementing South Africa's Constitution 134
      C. Quality: Interpreting India's Constitution 139

Chapter 5 · Indigenous Rights and Environment 147
Introduction 147
   I. United Nations Instruments and Institutions 149
      A. International Covenant on Civil and Political Rights 149
      B. Declaration on the Rights of Indigenous Peoples 157
      C. ILO Convention No. 169 on Indigenous and Tribal Peoples 160
         1. Text of Convention 161
         2. International Remedies 164
         3. National Remedies 168
      D. Convention on Biological Diversity 170
   II. Regional Human Rights Instruments and Institutions 171
      A. American Convention on Human Rights 172
      B. African Charter on Human and Peoples' Rights 188
      C. European Convention on Human Rights 191
   III. National Jurisprudence and Legal Systems 193
      A. Indigenous Property Rights under National Jurisprudence 193
      B. U.S. Courts, Indian Treaties, and the Environment 202
         1. The Right to Fish, and the Right to Insist on the
            Survival of Fish 202
         2. The Tribes' Environmental Right: The *"Culverts Case"* 210

Chapter 6 · Right to Information 219
Introduction 219
   I. The Right to Request Information 221
      A. Europe, Caucasus, Central Asia—International Rights 221
      B. Latin America—Statutory and International Rights 233
      C. Asia—Constitutional and Statutory Rights 244
      D. United States—Statutory Rights 249
   II. The Right to Insist on Dissemination of Information 251

Chapter 7 · Public Participation 259
Introduction 259
   I. Public Participation as a Right 260
   II. Public Participation: Europe, Caucasus, Central Asia 265
      A. The Ladder of Public Participation 265
      B. Participation for Specific Projects 267
      C. Participation in Plans, Programs, Policies and Executive Regulations 275
         1. Aarhus Convention 275
         2. Strategic Environmental Assessment 285

III. Public Participation in Other Regions 287
    A. Latin America 287
    B. Africa 293
    C. Asia and Pacific 300
    D. United States 306
       1. Participation for Specific Projects: EISs and EAs 306
       2. Executive Regulations and Public Participation Rights 309

Chapter 8 · Access to Justice: Compliance, Enforcement, and Remedies 311
Introduction 311
    I. Regional Courts and Tribunals 311
   II. Committees and Mechanisms 312
    A. U.N. Human Rights Committee 312
    B. Compliance Committees 313
  III. National Courts 316
    A. Standing to Sue 316
       1. Standing in Various Jurisdictions 316
       2. New International Law on National Standing 340
    B. Financial Barriers to Access to Justice 356

Chapter 9 · Corporate Accountability 367
Introduction 367
    I. International Standards, Liability, and Aspirations 367
    A. From Soft Law to Norms? 367
    B. Analysis 374
   II. Litigating in National Courts for Harms Abroad 380
    A. Corporate Liability for Crimes Abroad 380
    B. Corporate Liability for Torts Abroad 382
       1. Enforcing the Law of Nations in U.S. Courts 382
       2. Do Environmental Abuses Violate the "Law of Nations"? 398
    C. The Issue of *Forum non Conveniens* 410
    D. Ordinary Tort Liability in an Age of *Forum non Conveniens* 421
       1. Litigating Multinational Liability in the Country of Damage 421
       2. Anti-*Forum non Conveniens* Legislation 425
       3. The U.S. DBCP Litigation 437

Chapter 10 · Human Rights and International Financial Institutions 445
Introduction 445
    I. Multilateral Development Banks 445
    A. History of MDBs 445
    B. Critiques of MDBs 446
    C. Information and Participation Rights in MDB Projects 453
   II. The World Bank Inspection Panel 457
    A. Overview 457
    B. Recourse and Remedies 459
    C. The Chad-Cameroon Pipeline 461
  III. IFC/MIGA Compliance Advisor and Ombudsman 475

Chapter 11 · Protecting Environmental Advocates and Defenders 483
Introduction 483

I. International Protections for Defenders   484
   A. The United Nations Declaration and Special Representative   484
   B. European Union Guidelines   489
II. Criminal Charges against Advocates   492
   A. Treason and Disclosure of Official Secrets   492
   B. Sedition   496
   C. Insult and Defamation   500
      1. Insult   500
      2. Defamation   504
III. Civil Charges and Remedies—SLAPPs   508
   A. Introduction to SLAPPs   508
   B. Legal Claims Against Appeals and Litigation   510
   C. Demonstrations and Economic Boycotts   513
   D. Campaigns, Criticisms, Defamation   521
      1. European and Inter-American Courts of Human Rights   521
      2. Australia   522
   E. Judicial Remedies in the U.S. and Europe   527
      1. U.S. "SLAPPback"   527
      2. Fair Trial and Disproportionate Damages   529
   F. Legislative Remedies in the U.S. and Australia   537
      1. Anti-SLAPP Legislation   537
      2. Changes in Australian Legislation   540

Chapter 12 · Human Rights and Climate Change   549
 Introduction   549
  I. Climate Change, Its Effects, and International Obligations   550
  II. Human Rights Litigation and Climate Change   554
   A. Litigation Theories   554
   B. Litigation in International Human Rights Bodies—The Inuit Petition 557
      1. Background   557
      2. Does Climate Change Violate Recognized Human Rights Law? 560
      3. The Next Step?   572
   C. International Court of Justice   573
   D. Substantive Rights in National Courts   575
   E. Procedural Rights in International and National Fora   583
      1. Access to Information   584
      2. Public Participation   585
  III. United Nations Security Council: Right to Security   593

Table of Authorities   597

Index   627

Contents

Preface   xxi

Acknowledgments   xxv

Chapter 1 · Why Human Rights and the Environment?   3
  I. Environmental Human Rights   3
    Günther Handl, *Human Rights and the Protection of the Environment*   6
    Michael R. Anderson, *Human Rights Approaches to Environmental*
      Protection: An Overview   10
    Dinah Shelton, *Environmental Rights*   11
  II. Linkages between Human Rights and the Environment   12
    Draft Principles on Human Rights and the Environment 13
    Meeting of Experts on Human Rights and the Environment 16
  III. Human Rights Instruments and Institutions   20

Chapter 2 · Substantive Environment Rights in International Law   23
  Introduction   23
  I. Environmental Rights under the European Convention   23
    A. European Convention on Human Rights   24
    Convention for the Protection of Human Rights and
      Fundamental Freedoms   24
    B. Right to Private and Family Life   26
      1. Origin of the Article 8 Right   26
      López Ostra v. Spain   26
      Guerra v. Italy   31
      Mariana T. Acevedo, *The Intersection of Human Rights and*
        Environmental Protection in the European Court of Human Rights 35
      2. Weakening of Article 8?   37
      Hatton v. United Kingdom   37
      David Hart QC, *Comment*   41
      3. Reestablishing Rights, Providing Remedies, Enforcing Precedents 43
      Fadeyeva v. Russia   43
    C. Right to Life   48
    Öneryildiz v. Turkey   49
  II. Environmental Rights under the African Charter   52
    A. African Charter on Human and Peoples' Rights   52
    African Charter on Human and Peoples' Rights   53
    B. Finding an Environmental Right   55
    Social and Economic Rights Action Center v. Nigeria   55

III. Environmental Rights under the American Declaration and Convention   60
   A. American Declaration of the Rights and Duties of Man   60
      American Declaration of the Rights and Duties of Man   60
      Resolution 12/85 [Yanomami Case]   61
   B. American Convention on Human Rights   62
      American Convention on Human Rights   62
   C. San Salvador Protocol   63
      Additional Protocol to the American Convention on Human Rights
         in the Area of Economic, Social and Cultural Rights   63
      Jorge Daniel Taillant, *Environmental Advocacy and the Inter-American*
         Human Rights System   63

Chapter 3 · Substantive Environment Rights in National Law   67
   Introduction   67
   I.   Substantive Rights in National or State Constitutions   68
        Barry E. Hill, Steve Wolfson, & Nicholas Targ, *Human Rights*
           and the Environment: A Synopsis and Some Predictions   68
   II. Challenging Government Action and Inaction   72
        A. Overturning Legislation   73
           Montana Environmental Information Center v.
              Dep't of Environmental Quality (USA)   73
        B. Overturning Executive Action   79
           Oposa v. Factoran (Philippines)   79
           Shehla Zia v. WAPDA (Pakistan)   87
           Senih Özay v. Ministry of the Environment and
              Eurogold Madencilik (Turkey)   90
        C. Requiring Affirmative Government Programs   93
           M. C. Mehta v. Union of India (India)   94
           Dhungel v. Godawari Marble Industries (Nepal)   96
   III. Challenging Actions by Private Parties   100
        A. Enforcement against Private Actors by Attorneys General   100
           Pennsylvania v. National Gettysburg Battlefield Tower (USA) 100
        B. Enforcement by Citizens against Private Defendants   105
           Pedro Flores v. Corporación del Cobre-Division Salvador (Chile) 105
   IV. Evaluating the Role of the Courts   110
        Dr. Parvez Hassan & Azim Azfar, *Securing Environmental Rights*
           through Public Interest Litigation in South Asia   110
        Shubhankar Dam & Vivek Tewary, *Is a "Polluted" Constitution*
           Worse Than a Polluted Environment?   110

Chapter 4 · Right to Water   113
   Introduction   113
   I.   A Right to Water in International and Regional Instruments   114
        A. Soft and Hard Law Sources   114
           John Scanlon, Angela Cassar, & Noémi Nemes,
              Water as a Human Right? (2004)   114
        B. General Comment 15: Private or Public Good?   119
           Stephen C. McCaffrey, *The Human Right to Water*   119
           James Salzman, *Thirst: A Short History of Drinking Water*   123

II. A Right to Water in National Instruments 129
    A. Examples of the Right to Water at a National Level 129
        Erik B. Bluemel, *The Implications of Formulating a
            Human Right to Water* 129
    B. Quantity, Affordability, and Procedure:
        Implementing South Africa's Constitution 134
        *Residents of Bon Vista Mansions v.
            So. Metropolitan Local Council (South Africa)* 134
    C. Quality: Interpreting India's Constitution 139
        AP Pollution Control Board-II v. Prof. MV Nayudu (Retd) (India) 139
        Shajimon Joseph v. State of Kerala (India) 142

Chapter 5 · Indigenous Rights and Environment 147
    Introduction 147
    I. United Nations Instruments and Institutions 149
        A. International Covenant on Civil and Political Rights 149
            International Covenant on Civil and Political Rights 149
            Bernard Ominayak and the Lubicon Lake Band v. Canada 149
            Länsman v. Finland (I) 154
        B. Declaration on the Rights of Indigenous Peoples 157
            Declaration on the Rights of Indigenous Peoples 157
        C. ILO Convention No. 169 on Indigenous and Tribal Peoples 160
            1. Text of Convention 161
            *Convention (No. 169) Concerning Indigenous and
                Tribal Peoples in Independent Countries* 161
            2. International Remedies 164
            Linda A. Malone & Scott Pasternack , *Defending the Environment:
                Civil Society Strategies to Enforce International Environmental
                Law (2006)* 164
            The Ecuador Oil Consultation 166
            3. National Remedies 168
            Unconstitutionality of the General Forestry Act (Colombia) 168
        D. Convention on Biological Diversity 170
            Convention on Biological Diversity 170
    II. Regional Human Rights Instruments and Institutions 171
        A. American Convention on Human Rights 172
            Peter McManus, *Sovereignty, Self-Determination, and
                Environment-Based Cultures: The Emerging Voice of
                Indigenous Peoples in International Law* 172
            American Convention on Human Rights 172
            Mayagna (Sumo) Awas Tingni Community v. Nicaragua 174
            Moiwana Community v. Suriname (I) 180
            Moiwana Community v. Suriname (II) 181
            Saramaka People v. Suriname 186
        B. African Charter on Human and Peoples' Rights 188
            African Charter on Human and Peoples' Rights 188
            Social and Economic Rights Action Center v. Nigeria 189
        C. European Convention on Human Rights 191
            Rainer Grote, *On the Fringes of Europe: Europe's Largely
                Forgotten Indigenous Peoples* 191

III. National Jurisprudence and Legal Systems   193
   A. Indigenous Property Rights under National Jurisprudence   193
     Aurelio Cal v. Atty. Gen. of Belize   193
     Haida Nation v. British Columbia (Minister of Forests) (Canada)   201
   B. U.S. Courts, Indian Treaties, and the Environment   202
     1. The Right to Fish, and the Right to Insist on the Survival of Fish   202
     Treaty with the Nisqualli, Puyallup, etc.   202
       a. U.S. v. Washington, Phase I (Fair Share, 1970s)   203
       b. U.S. v. Washington, Phase II (False Start at Conservation, 1980s) 204
     Lewis Kamb, *Boldt Decision 'Very Much Alive' 30 Years Later*   205
     2. The Tribes' Environmental Right: The "Culverts Case"   210
     U.S. v. Washington (Phase II, Culverts)   210

Chapter 6 · Right to Information   219
  Introduction   219
   I. The Right to Request Information   221
     A. Europe, Caucasus, Central Asia—International Rights   221
     Convention on Access to Information, Public Participation in
      Decision-Making and Access to Justice in Environmental Matters
      (Aarhus Convention)   221
     Stephen Stec & Susan Casey-Lefkowitz, with Jerzy Jendroska,
      The Aarhus Convention: An Implementation Guide (2000)   223
     Svitlana Kravchenko, *The Aarhus Convention and Innovations in*
      Compliance with Multilateral Environmental Agreements   227
     Findings and Recommendations with Regard to
      Compliance by Kazakhstan   228
     B. Latin America—Statutory and International Rights   233
     Eric Heyer, *Latin American State Secrecy and Mexico's*
      Transparency Law   233
     Benjamin Fernandez Bogado, Emilene Martinez-Morales,
      Bethany Davis Noll, & Kyle Bell, *The Federal Institute for Access*
      to Information & A Culture of Transparency—Follow Up Report   237
     Claude Reyes v. Chile   239
     C. Asia—Constitutional and Statutory Rights   244
     Forests Survey Inspection Request Case (Korea)   244
     The Right to Information Act, 2005 (India)   249
     D. United States—Statutory Rights   249
     David Banisar, *Freedom of Information Around the World 2006*   249
   II. The Right to Insist on Dissemination of Information   251
     Guerra v. Italy   251
     Convention on Access to Information, Public Participation in
      Decision-Making and Access to Justice in Environmental Matters
      (Aarhus Convention)   254
     Stephen Stec & Susan Casey-Lefkowitz, with Jerzy Jendroska,
      The Aarhus Convention: An Implementation Guide (2000)   255

Chapter 7 · Public Participation   259
  Introduction   259
   I. Public Participation as a Right   260

George (Rock) Pring & Susan Y. Noé, *The Emerging International Law of Public Participation Affecting Global Mining, Energy and Resources Development*   260

John E. Bonine, *The Construction of Participatory Democracy in Central and Eastern Europe*   262

International Norms for Public Participation   263

II. Public Participation: Europe, Caucasus, Central Asia   265

A. The Ladder of Public Participation   265

Stephen Stec & Susan Casey-Lefkowitz with Jerzy Jendroska, *The Aarhus Convention: An Implementation Guide (2000)*   266

B. Participation for Specific Projects   267

Convention on Access to Information, Public Participation in Decision-Making and Access to Justice in Environmental Matters (Aarhus Convention)   267

Jurisprudence of the Aarhus Compliance Committee   270

Findings and Recommendations with Regard to Compliance by Ukraine 270

C. Participation in Plans, Programs, Policies and Executive Regulations   275

1. Aarhus Convention   275

Convention on Access to Information, Public Participation in Decision-Making and Access to Justice in Environmental Matters (Aarhus Convention)   276

Stephen Stec & Susan Casey Lefkowitz, with Jerzy Jendroska, *The Aarhus Convention: An Implementation Guide (2000)*   276

Findings and Recommendations with Regard to Compliance by Albania 278

2. Strategic Environmental Assessment   285

Protocol on Strategic Environmental Assessment to the Convention on Environmental Impact Assessment in a Transboundary Context   286

III. Public Participation in Other Regions   287

A. Latin America   287

Jorge Caillaux, Manuel Ruiz, & Isabel Lapeña, *Environmental Public Participation in the Americas*   288

B. Africa   293

Collins Odote & Maurice O. Makoloo, *African Initiatives for Public Participation in Environmental Management*   293

Earthlife Africa (Cape Town) v. Dept. of Envt'l Affairs & Tourism & Eskom Holdings (South Africa)   297

C. Asia and Pacific   300

Roda Mushkat, *The Principle of Public Participation: An Asia-Pacific Perspective*   300

Jesse L. Moorman & Zhang Ge, *Promoting and Strengthening Public Participation in China's Environmental Impact Assessment Process: Comparing China's EIA Law and U.S. NEPA*   300

Note on Thailand's 1997 Constitution   303

Policy Responses—Asia and Pacific   304

D. United States   306

1. Participation for Specific Projects: EISs and EAs   306

National Environmental Policy Act of 1969   306

Regulations for Implementing NEPA   307

2. Executive Regulations and Public Participation Rights   309

Administrative Procedure Act   310

Chapter 8 · Access to Justice: Compliance, Enforcement, and Remedies   311
    Introduction   311
        I.   Regional Courts and Tribunals   311
        II. Committees and Mechanisms   312
             A. U.N. Human Rights Committee   312
                 Introduction to the Human Rights Committee   312
             B. Compliance Committees   313
                 Svitlana Kravchenko, The Aarhus Convention and Innovations in
                     Compliance with Multilateral Environmental Agreements   313
        III. National Courts   316
             A. Standing to Sue   316
                 1. Standing in Various Jurisdictions   316
                 Oposa v. Factoran (Philippines)   317
                 M. C. Mehta v. Union of India   322
                 Truth About Motorways v. Macquarie Infrastructure Management
                     (Australia)   324
                 Hon Justice Peter McClellan, Access to Justice in Environmental Law:
                     An Australian Perspective   327
                 Kellas v. Department of Corrections (USA)   332
                 John E. Bonine, The Public's Right to Enforce Environmental Law   334
                 2. New International Law on National Standing   340
                 Convention on Access to Information, Public Participation in
                     Decision-Making and Access to Justice in Environmental Matters
                     (Aarhus Convention)   341
                 Findings and Recommendations with Regard to
                     Compliance by Belgium   343
                 Esther Pozo Vera, Nathy-Rass Masson, & Ludwig Krämer,
                     Summary Report on the Inventory of EU Member States' Measures
                     on Access to Justice in Environmental Matters   351
             B. Financial Barriers to Access to Justice   356
                 Nicolas de Sadeleer, Gerhard Roller, & Miriam Dross,
                     Access to Justice in Environmental Matters (2003)   356
                 John E. Bonine, Removing Barriers and Providing Incentives for
                     Citizen Enforcement of Environmental Laws   357
                 Access to Justice as a Guarantee of Economic, Social, and
                     Cultural Rights   361
                 Steel & Morris v. United Kingdom: Legal Aid in the
                     European Court of Human Rights   363

Chapter 9 · Corporate Accountability   367
    Introduction   367
        I.   International Standards, Liability, and Aspirations   367
             A. From Soft Law to Norms?   367
                 Olivier de Schutter, Challenge of Imposing Human Rights Norms
                     on Corporate Actors   367
                 U.N. Global Compact   369
                 OECD Guidelines For Multinational Enterprises   369
                 ILO Tripartite Declaration of Principles Concerning
                     Multinational Enterprises and Social Policy   371

    (Draft) Norms on the Responsibilities of Transnational Corporations
       and Other Business Enterprises with Regard to Human Rights   372
   B. Analysis   374
    John Ruggie, *Mapping International Standards of Responsibility*
       and Accountability for Corporate Acts   374
  II. Litigating in National Courts for Harms Abroad   380
   A. Corporate Liability for Crimes Abroad   380
    John Ruggie, *Mapping International Standards of Responsibility*
       and Accountability for Corporate Acts   380
   B. Corporate Liability for Torts Abroad   382
    1. Enforcing the Law of Nations in U.S. Courts   382
    Harold Hongju Koh, *Transnational Public Law Litigation*   382
    Sosa v. Alvarez-Machain   388
    Doe I v. Unocal   393
    2. Do Environmental Abuses Violate the "Law of Nations"?   398
    Richard L. Herz, *Litigating Environmental Abuses under the Alien*
       Tort Claims Act: A Practical Assessment   398
    Beanal v. Freeport-McMoran   399
    Flores v. Southern Peru Copper   401
    Sarei v. Rio Tinto   407
    Sarei v. Rio Tinto   408
   C. The Issue of *Forum non Conveniens*   410
    Judith Kimerling, *Transnational Operations, Bi-National Injustice—*
       Chevrontexaco and Indigenous Huaorani and Kichwa in the
       Amazon Rainforest in Ecuador   410
    Aguinda v. Texaco   415
    Englebert Ngcobo v. Thor Chemicals (United Kingdom)   417
   D. Ordinary Tort Liability in an Age of *Forum non Conveniens*   421
    1. Litigating Multinational Liability in the Country of Damage   421
    William Langewiesche, *Jungle Law*   421
    2. Anti-*Forum non Conveniens* Legislation   425
    Winston Anderson, Forum Non Conveniens *Checkmated?—*
       The Emergence of Retaliatory Legislation   425
    Henry Saint Dahl, Forum Non Conveniens, *Latin America*
       and Blocking Statutes   426
    E.E. Daschbach, *Where There's a Will, There's a Way*   429
    Law No. 364 Nicaragua   430
    Consultation on Law 364 (Nicaragua)   432
    2007 National Trade Estimate Report on Foreign Trade Barriers   436
    3. The U.S. DBCP Litigation   437
    Dow v. Calderon   437
    Tellez v. Dole   438
    Noaki Schwartz, *$2.5 Million in Punitive Damages Awarded*
       to Banana Workers   442

Chapter 10 · Human Rights and International Financial Institutions   445
  Introduction   445
  I. Multilateral Development Banks   445
   A. History of MDBs   445

B. Critiques of MDBs 446
John W. Head, *For Richer or for Poorer: Assessing the Criticisms
Directed at the Multilateral Development Banks* 446
C. Information and Participation Rights in MDB Projects 453
Nathalie Bernasconi-Osterwalder & David Hunter,
Democratizing Multilateral Development Banks 453
II. The World Bank Inspection Panel 457
A. Overview 457
Nathalie Bernasconi-Osterwalder & David Hunter,
Democratizing Multilateral Development Banks 457
B. Recourse and Remedies 459
Dana L. Clark, *The World Bank and Human Rights:
The Need for Greater Accountability* 459
C. The Chad-Cameroon Pipeline 461
Korinna Horta, *Rhetoric and Reality:
Human Rights and the World Bank* 462
Genoveva Hernández Uriz, *To Lend or Not to Lend: Oil,
Human Rights, and the World Bank's Internal Contradictions* 463
Ngarlejy Yorongar, *Request for Investigations by the World Bank
Inspection Panel* 465
World Bank, *Chad-Cameroon Petroleum and Pipeline Project* 468
III. IFC/MIGA Compliance Advisor and Ombudsman 475
Nathalie Bernasconi-Osterwalder & David Hunter,
Democratizing Multilateral Development Banks 475
LEAT, *Bulyanhulu Complaint to IFC/MIGA
Compliance Advisor/Ombudsman* 477
CAO, *MIGA's Guarantee of the Bulyanhulu Gold Mine, Tanzania* 479
The Yanacocha Mine, Peru 481

Chapter 11 · **Protecting Environmental Advocates and Defenders** 483
Introduction 483
I. International Protections for Defenders 484
A. The United Nations Declaration and Special Representative 484
Hina Jilani, *Report of the Special Representative of the
Secretary-General on Human Rights Defenders* 487
B. European Union Guidelines 489
*Ensuring Protection—European Union Guidelines on
Human Rights Defenders* 489
II. Criminal Charges against Advocates 492
A. Treason and Disclosure of Official Secrets 492
Nikitin v. Russia 492
B. Sedition 496
Tundu Lissu, *View from the Accused* 497
Alloyce Komba, *Environment Lawyer in Court* 498
C. Insult and Defamation 500
1. Insult 500
Dr. R. Panji Utomo, Petitioner (Indonesia) 500
Marilyn J. Greene, *It's a Crime:
How Insult Laws Stifle Press Freedom* 504

2. Defamation   504
Towards Decriminalisation of Defamation, Resolution 1577 (2007)   505
III. Civil Charges and Remedies—SLAPPs   508
  A. Introduction to SLAPPs   508
    George Pring & Penelope Canan, *SLAPP: Getting Sued for
    Speaking Out (1996)*   508
  B. Legal Claims Against Appeals and Litigation   510
    George Pring & Penelope Canan, *SLAPP: Getting Sued for
    Speaking Out (1996)*   510
  C. Demonstrations and Economic Boycotts   513
    Tom Price, *Fighting the Big Gunns in Tasmania*   513
    Daishowa, Inc. v. Friends of the Lubicon (Canada)   515
  D. Campaigns, Criticisms, Defamation   521
    1. European and Inter-American Courts of Human Rights   521
    2. Australia   522
    Chapman v. Conservation Council of South Australia   522
  E. Judicial Remedies in the U.S. and Europe   527
    1. U.S. "SLAPPback"   527
    George Pring & Penelope Canan, *SLAPP: Getting Sued for
    Speaking Out (1996)*   527
    2. Fair Trial and Disproportionate Damages   529
    Steel & Morris v. United Kingdom   529
  F. Legislative Remedies in the U.S. and Australia   537
    1. Anti-SLAPP Legislation   537
    Baker v. Parsons (USA)   537
    2. Changes in Australian Legislation   540
    Greg Ogle, *Gunning for Change: The Need for Public Participation
    Law Reform*   540
    NSW Defamation Act (2005)-Sect 9   546

Chapter 12 · Human Rights and Climate Change   549
  Introduction   549
  I. Climate Change, Its Effects, and International Obligations   550
    Climate Change 2007: Synthesis Report (4th Assessment Report)   550
    International Agreements and Climate Change   553
  II. Human Rights Litigation and Climate Change   554
    A. Litigation Theories   554
    Sara C. Aminzadeh, *A Moral Imperative: The Human Rights
    Implications of Climate Change*   554
    B. Litigation in International Human Rights Bodies—The Inuit Petition   557
    1. Background   557
    Donald M. Goldberg & Martin Wagner, *Petitioning for Adverse
    Impacts of Global Warming in the Inter-American
    Human Rights System*   557
    2. Does Climate Change Violate Recognized Human Rights Law?   560
    Sheila Watt-Cloutier, *Petition to the Inter-American Commission on
    Human Rights*   560
    3. The Next Step?   572
    C. International Court of Justice   573
    Rebecca Elizabeth Jacobs, *Treading Deep Waters*   573

D. Substantive Rights in National Courts   575
  Jonah Gbemre v. Shell Petroleum (Nigeria)   575
  Eric A. Posner, *Climate Change and International Human Rights
    Litigation: A Critical Appraisal*   581
E. Procedural Rights in International and National Fora   583
  U.N. Framework Convention on Climate Change   584
  1. Access to Information   584
  2. Public Participation   585
  Gray v. Minister for Planning (Australia)   585
III. United Nations Security Council: Right to Security   593

Table of Authorities   597

Index   627

Preface

Courts, legislatures, and experts increasingly recognize *environmental* rights—both substantive and procedural—as enforceable *human* rights. Environmental law can no longer be viewed only as something for legislatures to consider as a matter of policy choices. It is time for new thinking and new teaching. It is time also to view this developing field not as one exclusively of international law, nor national law, nor comparative law. All three are important.

A new casebook

This new casebook provides, for the first time, primary case law and other legal materials edited for study in classes and seminars on the protection of environmental rights. We include international and national court cases from Europe, Africa, Asia, and the Americas that interpret treaties, constitutions, and human rights legislation in light of environmental imperatives. We seek to prepare students to think creatively about human rights instruments when asked by clients to evaluate or take action regarding an environmental problem. In this book, we also ask them to consider the development of the law in countries and cultures other than their own, in hopes that they may gain useful insights.

There is no reason to be coy about our own beliefs. We believe that a human rights approach to environmental protection brings advantages to both fields. Robust and established human rights instruments can help protect the environment. In a clean and safe environment, human rights can be fully enjoyed and realized. We also believe in environmental democracy and the increasing role of non-state actors in international environmental and human rights law. At the same time, in this book we offer materials and ask questions that challenge these and other points of view and encourage students to reach their own conclusions.

Two converging fields of law

The notion that environmental degradation can lead to violations of human rights, first broached nearly 40 years ago, has grown apace in the last two decades. A human right to a safe or healthy environment has appeared not only in scholarly articles and several books, but increasingly in treaties and multilateral environmental agreements and in national constitutions. "Rights" are of limited value if they cannot be enforced by courts or other independent and impartial bodies. That is why development of case law in this field is so important, as well as citizen enforcement in domestic courts and individual complaints in international human rights courts and compliance mechanisms. The jurisprudence of human rights courts, commissions, and committees, as well as that of domestic courts in some countries, has endorsed and expanded environmental rights in various ways. Lawyers have worked to fuse environmental concerns with protection of fundamental rights—rights to life, health, property, private and family life, freedom of expression, petition, self-determination, and culture.

Authors' backgrounds

As professors in the former Soviet Union, Ukraine, and the United States for more than thirty years, the authors have moved from viewing environmental law as a domestic legal discipline to viewing it also in its comparative and international law dimensions. One of this book's authors has been teaching a class titled Human Rights and the Environment for the last six years, which has led to stimulating discussions with numerous students in those classes and has provided the genesis for many of the ideas in this book. The other has been teaching Comparative Environmental Law with a special focus on access to justice.

The authors have worked for national and international governmental and non-governmental organizations. Each co-founded the first environmental law clinic in his or her home country, plus the public interests law firms Ecology-People-Law (EPL) in Ukraine and the Western Environmental Law Center (WELC) in the United States. Both have been involved in drafting and negotiating multinational environmental agreements and helping oversee their implementation, one of us in the capacity of the Vice Chair of the Compliance Committee under the UN ECE Aarhus Convention. One co-founded the Environmental Law Alliance Worldwide (ELAW) and the other started its Ukraine office. ELAW is a network of public interest environmental lawyers in seventy countries, whose lawyers bring cases both in national courts and before international human rights and environmental institutions and support one another with ideas and consultations across national borders. Several lawyers involved in ELAW have offered advice in the preparation of this casebook.

Thanks to many

This book could not have happened without the help of many people. We are especially grateful to the following law students (many of them now lawyers and the others soon to be) who toiled long hours as our heroic and skilled research assistants: Jia Min Cheng, Marianne Dellinger, Rebecca Kammerling, Genevieve LeBlanc, Brook Meakins, Ryan Orr, Kevin Parks, Mark Reece, Erin Roach, Mae Sader, Paul Tassin, Brian Walker, Casey Whelan, and Dinara Ziganshina. They did excellent work under sometimes pressing deadlines, finding cases and scholarly articles, helping to edit them, suggesting ideas, formulating the first drafts of some questions and discussion materials, proofreading, and obtaining copyright permissions. We are also thankful to law students Michael Borges, Judson Brehmer, Betsy Bridge, Morgan Dethman, and Amanda Freeman for their assistance. For specialized translation or substantive help, we appreciate the contributions of our colleagues Astrid Puentes of Colombia, Isabela Figueroa of Ecuador, Su Jeong Suh of Korea, Carla Garcia Zendeja of Mexico, Meche Lu of Peru, and Hanna Khomechko and Elizaveta Aleksyeyeva of Ukraine. We also appreciate invaluable comments on the manuscript and information provided by Professor Donald Anton of Australian National University. Despite the wonderful help from all these bright minds, we assume responsibility for any errors that remain.

An undertaking such as this book would not have been possible without the aid of the University of Oregon's skillful and truly committed administrative assistant, Debby Warren. We thank her for her tremendous help, often at night and on weekends, and also Jill Forcier for initial help on formatting. Invaluable support was provided by Debby Thurman by organizing the work of our wonderful administrative staff. We are also thankful to Dean Margie Paris and other members of the law school staff for organizational support.

Excerpts and stylistic matters

Despite our intention to give reasonably comprehensive and reliably accurate coverage to the major issues in the field of human rights and the environment, this book is designed for teaching, not for research. Therefore, in editing the cases, treaties, guidelines, articles (including book chapters), and other materials, we have strived to make them readable. To that end, we have changed fonts, deleted paragraph numbering, and omitted most citations and footnotes. Our own footnotes are indicated by letters instead of numbers. We have shown deletions of paragraphs or words with small ellipses (triple dots). For deletions of entire paragraphs or of words at a paragraph's beginning, we appended ellipses to a preceding paragraph. We have left British spelling if used in cases, articles, or legal instruments. We have changed all punctuation to American style. We have used periods in the names of the U.S. and U.N., but omitted periods for other organizations (such as UNEP or ILO).

Some final words

Good advocates are those whose eyes are wide open—not only to alternative legal arguments but to the humanity of those around them. A now-deceased human rights and environmental lawyer and law professor—himself a *desaparecido* in Argentina in the late 1970s—remarked to one of us and to his own students, "In this life, once you have opened your eyes, you can never close them again." We hope to contribute to that process.

Svitlana Kravchenko and John Bonine
Eugene, Oregon, July 2008

Acknowledgments

Aminzadeh, Sara C., *A Moral Imperative: The Human Rights Implications of Climate Change*, 30 Hastings Int'l & Comp. L. Rev. 231 (2007), (c) 2007 by the University of California, Hastings College of the Law. Reprinted from Hastings International and Comparative Law Review, Volume 30, Number 2, Winter 2007, 231, by permission

Anderson, Winston, *Forum Non Conveniens Checkmated?—The Emergence of Retaliatory Legislation*, 10 J. Transnat'l L. & Pol'y 183 (2001)

Avicedo, Mariana T., *The Intersection of Human Rights and Environmental Protection in the European Court of Human Rights*, 8 N.Y.U. Envtl. L.J. 437 (2000)

Bernasconi-Osterwalder, Nathalie, & David Hunter, *Democratizing Multilateral Development Banks* in THE NEW "PUBLIC": THE GLOBALIZATION OF PUBLIC PARTICIPATION, Copyright The Environmental Law Institute (2002)

Bluemel, Eric B., *The Implications of Formulating a Human Right to Water*, 31 Ecology L.Q. 957 (2004), (c) 2004 Regents of the Univ. of California, reprinted by permission

Bonine, John E., *The Construction of Participatory Democracy in Central and Eastern Europe* in HUMAN RIGHTS IN NATURAL RESOURCE DEVELOPMENT, Oxford Univ. Press (2002) (c) The International Bar Association

Bonine, John E., *The Public's Right to Enforce Environmental Law* in HANDBOOK ON ACCESS TO JUSTICE UNDER THE AARHUS CONVENTION, Regional Environmental Center (2001)

Caillaux, Jorge, Isabel Lapeña, & Manuel Ruiz, *Environmental Public Participation in the Americas* in THE NEW "PUBLIC": THE GLOBALIZATION OF PUBLIC PARTICIPATION, Environmental Law Institute (2002)

Ciorciari, John D., *Lawful Scope of HR Criteria in World Bank Decisions: An Interpretive Analysis of the IBRD and IDA Articles of Agreement*, 33 Cornell Int'l L.J. 331 (2000).

Clark, Dana L., *The World Bank and Human Rights: The Need for Greater Accountability*, 15 Harv. Hum. Rights J. 205 (2002)

Dam, Shubhankar & Vivek Tewary, *Is a "Polluted" Constitution Worse Than a Polluted Environment?*, 17 J. of Envtl. L. 383 (2005), by permission of Oxford Univ. Press

Daschbach, Emma E., *Where There's a Will, There's a Way: The Cause for a Cure and Remedial Prescriptions for Forum Non Conveniens as Applied in Latin American Plaintiffs' Actions Against U.S. Multinationals*, 13 L. & Bus. Rev. Am. 11 (2007)

de Schutter, Olivier, *Challenge of Imposing Human Rights Norms on Corporate Actors* in TRANSNATIONAL CORPORATIONS AND HUMAN RIGHTS, NYU Global Law Working Paper (2005)

Goldberg, Donald M. & Martin Wagner, *Petitioning for Adverse Impacts of Global Warming in the Inter-American Human Rights System*, CIEL/Earthjustice (2002)

Grote, Rainer, *On the Fringes of Europe: Europe's Largely Forgotten Indigenous Peoples,* 31 Am. Indian L. Rev. 425 (2006-7)

Handl, Günther, *Human Rights and the Protection of the Environment* in ECONOMIC, SOCIAL AND CULTURAL RIGHTS, Kluwer Law Int'l (2nd ed., 2001)

Hart, David, *Comment* (July 2003)

Hassan, Parvez, & Azim Azfar, *Securing Environmental Rights through Public Interest Litigation in South Asia,* 22 Va. Envtl. L. J. 215 (2004).

Head, John W., *For Richer or for Poorer: Assessing the Criticisms Directed at the Multilateral Development Banks,* 52 U. Kan. L. Rev. 241 (2004)

Hector, Mireille, *Protecting Human Rights Defenders: Analysis of the newly adopted Declaration on Human Rights Defenders,* Human Rights First (1999)

Hernández Uriz, Genoveva, *To Lend or Not To Lend: Oil, Human Rights, and the World Bank's Internal Contradictions,* 14 Harv. Hum. Rts. J. 197 (2001), Copyright 2001, The President & Fellows of Harvard College and the Harvard Human Rights Journal

Herz, Richard L., *Litigating Environmental Abuses Under the Alien Tort Claims Act: A Practical Assessment,* 40 Va. J. Int'l L. 545 (2000)

Heyer, Eric, *Latin American State Secrecy and Mexico's Transparency Law,* 38 Geo. Wash. Int'l L. Rev. 437 (2006), (c) 2006 The George Washington International Law Review

Hill, Barry E., Steve Wolfson, & Nicholas Targ, *Human Rights and the Environment: A Synopsis and Some Predictions,* 16 Geo. Int'l Envtl. L. Rev. 359 (2004), reprinted by permission of the publisher, Georgetown International Environmental Law Review (c) 2004

Horta, Korinna, *Rhetoric and Reality: Human Rights and the World Bank,* 15 Harv. Hum. Rights J. 227 (2002), Copyright 2002, The President & Fellows of Harvard College and the Harvard Human Rights Journal

Compliance Advisor/Ombudsman, *CAO Assessment Report Summary (Bulyanhulu, Tanzania),* International Finance Corportation/MIGA (2002)

Inspection Panel, World Bank, *The Inspection Panel Investigation Report, Chad-Cameroon Petroleum and Pipeline Project (Loan No.4558 CD), Executive Summary,* World Bank (2002)

Jacobs, Rebecca Elizabeth, *Treading Deep Waters Substantive Law Issues in Tuvalu's Threat to Sue the United States in the International Court of Justice,* 14 Pac. Rim L. & Pol'y 103 (2005)

Lamb, Lewis, *Boldt Decision 'Very Much Alive' 30 Years Later,* Seattle Post-Intelligencer (February 12, 2004)

Kimerling, Judith, *Transnational Operations, Bi-National Injustice—Chevrontexaco and Indigenous Huaorani and Kichwa in the Amazon Rainforest in Ecuador,* 31 Am. Indian L. Rev. 445 (2006)

Koh, Harold Hongju, *Transnational Public Law Litigation,* 100 Yale L.J. 2347 (1991)

Kravchenko, Svitlana, *The Aarhus Convention and Innovations in Compliance with Multilateral Environmental Agreements,* 18 Colo. J. Int'l Envtl. L. & Pol'y 1 (2007)

Langewiesche, William, *Jungle Law,* Vanity Fair (May 2007)

Lissu, Tundu, *View from the Accused,* Email letter (2002)

Malone, Scott, & Linda A. Pasternack, DEFENDING THE ENVIRONMENT: CIVIL SOCIETY STRATEGIES TO ENFORCE INTERNATIONAL ENVIRONMENTAL LAW, Island Press (2006)

McCaffrey, Stephen C., *The Human Right to Water* in FRESH WATER AND INTERNATIONAL ECONOMIC LAW (2005)

McClellan, Justice Peter, *Access to Justice in Environmental Law: An Australian Perspective* (2005)

McManus, Peter, *Sovereignty, Self-Determination, and Environment-Based Cultures: The Emerging Voice of Indigenous Peoples in International Law,* 23 Wis. Int'l L.J. 553 (2005), Copyright by The Board of Regents of the University of Wisconsin System; Reprinted by permission of the Wisconsin International Law Journal

Moorman, Jesse L., & Zhang Ge, *Promoting and Strengthening Public Participation in China's Environmental Impact Assessment Process: Comparing China's EIA Law and U.S. NEPA,* 8 Vt. J. Envtl. L. 281 (2007)

Odote, Collins, & Maurice O. Makoloo, *African Initiatives for Public Participation in Environmental Management* in THE NEW "PUBLIC": THE GLOBALIZATION OF PUBLIC PARTICIPATION, Environmental Law Institute (2002)

Ogle, Greg, *Gunning for Change: The Need for Public Participation Law Reform,* The Wilderness Society, Inc., Australia (2005)

Philippines, Supreme Court of, *Oposa v. Factoran,* G.R. No. 101083, 224 SCRA 792 (July 30, 1993), 33 I.L.M. 173 (1994)Posner, Eric A., *Climate Change and International Human Rights Litigation: A Critical Appraisal,* 155 U. Pa. L. Rev. 1925 (2007)

Price, Tom, *Fighting the Big Gunns in Tasmania,* CorpWatch (March 14, 2005)

Pring, Geoge (Rock), & Penelope Canan, SLAPP: GETTING SUED FOR SPEAKING OUT, Temple Univ. Press (1996)

Pring, George (Rock), & Susan Y. Noé, *The Emerging International Law of Public Participation Affecting Global Mining, Energy and Resources Development* in HUMAN RIGHTS IN NATURAL RESOURCE DEVELOPMENT, Oxford Univ. Press (2002) (c) The International Bar Association

Saint Dahl, Henry, *Forum Non Conveniens, Latin America and Blocking Statutes,* 35 U. Miami Inter-Am. L. Rev. 21 (2003)

Salzman, James, *Thirst: A Short History of Drinking Water,* 18 Yale J.L. & Humanities 94 (2006), reprinted by permission of The Yale Journal of Law & the Humanities

Scanlon, John, Angela Cassar, & Noémi Nemes, WATER AS A HUMAN RIGHT?, International Union for Conservation of Nature and Natural Resources (2004)

Stec, Stephen, & Susan Casey-Lefkowitz, THE AARHUS CONVENTION: AN IMPLEMENTATION GUIDE, UNECE (2000)

Taillant, Jorge Daniel, *Environmental Advocacy and the Inter-American Human Rights System* in LINKING HUMAN RIGHTS AND THE ENVIRONMENT (2003)

Watt-Cloutier, Sheila, *Inuit Petition to the Inter American Commission on Human Rights* (2005)

Human Rights and
the Environment

Chapter 1

Why Human Rights and the Environment?

I. Environmental Human Rights

We live in an era of human rights. This is no less true of environmental matters than of any other field. The harm caused to individuals and communities by degraded environments—from unsafe drinking water to disappearing wildlife—is increasingly seen by many people as a question of their "rights" being violated. This book seeks to examine the myriad ways in which environmental issues have come to be viewed as human rights issues. Protection of the environment can no longer be seen as simply a policy choice.

The modern human rights movement owes much to the adoption of the 1948 Universal Declaration of Human Rights in 1948. But one cannot find explicit environmental rights in that document. Similarly, the 1966 International Covenant on Civil and Political Rights and the International Covenant on Economic, Social and Cultural Rights, adopted the same year, seem to be oblivious to environmental concerns, much less environmental rights. At the time of their adoption environmental problems were not yet on the international human rights agenda or very high on most national agendas. For the same reasons, explicit environmental rights were not included in the 1950 European Convention for the Protection of Human Rights and Fundamental Freedoms, nor in the 1969 American Convention on Human Rights. The environmental movement had been growing for several years worldwide by the end of the 1960s, but many of its adherents had not yet conceived of their efforts as a movement for human rights. A conspicuous exception was the famed American scientist, Rachel Carson, who exposed the dangers of pesticides to a wide audience and insisted that one of the most basic of human rights was the "right of the citizen to be secure in his own home against the intrusion of poisons applied by other persons." She wrote eloquently about the "right to know." Rachel Carson, SILENT SPRING (1962).

Everything was starting to change by the arrival of the first Earth Day in April 1970. No longer satisfied with treating pollution and destruction of landscapes as just a policy dispute, many turned to the concept of rights. Within two years, the right to a quality environment was proclaimed at the United Nations Conference on the Human Environment, in the Stockholm Declaration, June 16, 1972, in Principle 1:

> Man has the fundamental right to freedom, equality, and adequate conditions of life, in an environment of a quality which permits a life of dignity and well-being, and he bears a solemn responsibility to protect and improve the environment for present and future generations.

3

U.N. Doc. A/Conf.48/14, 11 I.L.M. 1416 (1972).

The African Charter on Human and Peoples' Rights, adopted in 1981, states in its Article 24:

> All peoples have the right to a generally satisfactory environment favourable for their development.

O.A.U. Doc. CAB/LEG/67/3 rev. 5; 21 I.L.M. 58 (1982)

The Additional Protocol to the American Convention on Human Rights in the Area of Economic, Social, and Cultural Rights (San Salvador Protocol), signed in 1988 and subsequently ratified by 14 nations in the Americas (although not the United States, Canada, and numerous other countries), provides in its Article 11:

> Everyone shall have the right to live in a healthy environment and to have access to basic public services.

O.A.S. Treaty Series No. 69, Inter-Am. C.H.R., OEA/Ser.L.V/II.82 doc.6 rev.1 (1992).

By 1990, the United Nations General Assembly had adopted a resolution by consensus stating that "all individuals are entitled to live in an environment adequate for their health and well-being." G.A. Res. 45/94 (1990), U.N. Doc. A/Res/45/94 (14 December 1990). The environmental right was subsequently characterized as an "entitlement" in Principle 1 of the Rio Declaration at the conclusion of the United Nations Conference on Environment and Development (UNCED) in 1992:

> Human beings are at the center of concerns for sustainable development. They are entitled to a healthy and productive life in harmony with nature.

U.N. Doc. A/Conf.151/26 (Vol. I) (12 August 1992), 31 I.L.M. 874 (1992). In addition, specific procedural rights were proclaimed in Principle 10 of the Rio Declaration:

> ... At the national level, each individual shall have appropriate access to information concerning the environment that is held by public authorities, including information on hazardous materials and activities in their communities, and the opportunity to participate in decision-making processes. States shall facilitate and encourage public awareness and participation by making information widely available. Effective access to judicial and administrative proceedings, including redress and remedy, shall be provided.

Of course, international declarations and resolutions do not by themselves make international law; they are considered "soft law." At the level of international "hard law" (treaties, conventions, and customary international law) some legal instruments have also stated that the right to a healthy environment exists. In addition to the African Charter and the San Salvador Protocol mentioned above, the Aarhus Convention on Access to Information, Public Participation in Decision-Making, and Access to Justice in Environmental Matters, ratified by more than 40 nations in Europe, the Caucasus region, and Central Asia, as well as the European Community, states in both its Preamble and Article 1 that "every person" has the "right" to live in an "environment adequate to his or her health and well-being." The entire convention, furthermore, is devoted to the procedural rights proclaimed in Principle 10 of the Rio Declaration. U.N. Doc. ECE/CEP/43 (1998).

Questions and Discussion

1. *Declarations and rights.* Consider how many of the sources listed above amount to declarations rather than binding conventions. Declarations are sometimes considered to reflect norms that have become accepted as part of customary international law. Does

the right to a healthy or safe environment rise to that level? Might the answer be different in various regions, in light of the regional agreements listed above? Even in those regions, is it realistic to view the environmental rights to be more than generalized but unenforceable statements?

2. *Mere aspiration?* Apparently determined to discourage an environmental right from gaining a foothold in British law, the United Kingdom of Great Britain and Northern Ireland, alone among the nations gathered in 1998 to sign the Aarhus Convention in the Danish city of Aarhus, made this limiting "declaration":

> The United Kingdom understands the references in article 1 and the seventh preambular paragraph of this Convention to the "right" of every person "to live in an environment adequate to his or her health and well-being" to express an aspiration which motivated the negotiation of this Convention and which is shared fully by the United Kingdom. The legal rights which each Party undertakes to guarantee under article 1 are limited to the rights of access to information, public participation in decision-making and access to justice in environmental matters in accordance with the provisions of this Convention.

http://www.unece.org/env/pp/ctreaty_files/ctreaty_2007_03_27.htm. The United Kingdom confirmed this declaration at the time of ratification in 2005, while not formally characterizing it as a "reservation." *Id.*

No other country signing or ratifying the Convention has characterized the right as being limited to the status of an "aspiration." (Among the major countries in Europe, the Caucasus, and Central Asia, however, Russia and Uzbekistan also stand out as not having ratified the Convention at all.)

In addition to clearly stated *environmental* rights, all international human rights instruments proclaim a right to *"life"* in various manners. These include Article 3 of the Universal Declaration of Human Rights, Article 6 of the International Covenant on Civil and Political Rights, Article 4 of the American Convention on Human Rights, Article 2 of the European Convention for the Protection of Human Rights and Fundamental Freedoms, and Article 4 of the African Charter on Human and Peoples' Rights. In most instances, the right appears as a procedural right, in the context of prohibitions against arbitrary deprivations of life and in the requirements for fair criminal trials.

Some attempts have been made, particularly in regional human rights institutions, however, to give this right to "life" a substantive content. Such a right might include a right to clean water and air, adequate food, and shelter; at a minimum it includes a right not to die from an explosion at a poorly operated waste dump, as held in a European Court of Human Rights case that is discussed in Chapter 2. In addition to the right to life, Article 8, section 1, of the European Convention on Human Rights states, "Everyone has the right to respect for his private and family life, his home and his correspondence." Could this amount to a right to a healthy environment in some circumstances? See Chapter 2.

In the Americas, the 1948 American Declaration on the Rights and Duties of Man asserts that "[e]very human being has the right to life" and "the right to the preservation of his health." The Inter-American Commission on Human Rights has invoked the right to life in this Declaration in at least one instance of environmental and cultural injury, involving the Yanomami Indians in Brazil, discussed in Chapter 2. The 1969 American Convention on Human Rights similarly provides: "Every person has the right to have his life respected."

Some human rights become so widely accepted as a matter of international law that they attain the status of customary international law. Such law is evidenced by generally accepted state practices that most nations believe to be required by law. If nations consider a particular norm, or rule of behavior, to be so fundamental that it does not even require the consent of individual states and to be one from which no treaty can derogate, that norm is considered "peremptory" (the Latin term is *jus cogens*, meaning "compelling law"). Norms of those levels may be enforceable in the United States by federal courts as part of the "law of nations." As we will see in Chapter 9, however, two U.S. Courts of Appeals have ruled that the international "right" to a healthy environment has not risen to that level. Other skeptics exist as well.

Human Rights and the Protection of the Environment
Günther Handl
(A. Eide, C. Krause & A. Rosas, eds.)
ECONOMIC, SOCIAL AND CULTURAL RIGHTS: A TEXTBOOK (2nd ed., 2001)

[The] relationship between protection of the environment and protection and promotion of human rights ... is a complex one that is often misunderstood.... [C]ontrary to frequently voiced opinion, it is far from clear that the objectives underlying human rights and environmental protection norms are either fully complementary or truly indivisible....

[A] description of specific human rights characteristics to a given environmental claim and recourse to established human rights processes for vindication of such a claim would, it is suggested, make a difference in outcome. However, ... the underlying assumption that such a right provides a "complementary alternative to traditional international environmental law," is not self-evidently correct....

In short, the core controversy in the long-standing debate over human rights and the environment relates to the existence and utility of environmental human rights proper....

2. IS THERE A SUBSTANTIVE ENVIRONMENTAL HUMAN RIGHT IN CONTEMPORARY INTERNATIONAL LAW? ...

[E]vidence of actual supportive state practice ... remains an essential element of any argument that a given human rights claim is recognized by general [i.e. customary] international law. When analysed from this perspective, the case for a substantive environmental human right at the international level is a weak one.

At a global level, neither the Universal Declaration of Human Rights (1948) nor the 1966 International Covenant on Economic, Social and Cultural Rights (CESCR) readily lends support to the idea of an existing substantive human right to a clean environment.... Article 25 of the Declaration is not generally deemed to have come to reflect today customary international law [and] merely refers to everybody's "right to a standard of living adequate for the health and well-being of himself and of his family." Article 12, paragraph 2(b) of the CESCR commits States Parties to improve "all aspects of environmental and industrial hygiene." But this reference is ... "so narrow that it scarcely addresses environmental protection at all."

One of the earliest characterizations of an entitlement that truly sounds like an environmental human right can be found instead in Principle 1 of the 1972 Stockholm Declaration on the Human Environment.... However, at the time of its adoption, Principle 1 ... was understood not to reflect customary law....

The issue of [a human right to the environment] was brought into sharp focus again in 1994 [with the Ksentini Report; see page 13]. With the aim of facilitating consolidation at United Nations level of "the right of a satisfactory environment," the report included a set of draft Principles on Human Rights and the Environment that postulated the existence of a generic human right to a "secure, healthy, and ecologically sound environment." While the draft Principles have since been the subject of various procedural resolutions by the United Nations Commission on Human Rights, ... the fact remains that the Commission has thus far taken no substantive action on them. Today, the outlook for its formal adoption remains cloudy.

At the regional level, the European human rights system does not recognize — either expressly or implicitly — a substantive environmental human right. Proposals of such an entitlement have yet to find acceptance as an operational normative concept. There are, however, other regional human rights treaties that do endorse the concept of a substantive environmental human right [(i.e. The African Charter on Human and Peoples' Rights and the American Convention on Human Rights). The African] formulation ... has been criticized for latent ambiguities concerning the entitlement's meaning and scope, one of them stemming from the inherent potential for conflict between its environmental protection and development objectives. Operationally, the right is conceptualized not as a programmatic entitlement, but as one that would be effective immediately.... Given the socio-economic realities of Africa, this stipulation is clearly an implausible one....

The other regional regime of interest is the Inter-American system.... It is by no means certain ... that the institutions involved in supervising domestic implementation and international protection of [San Salvador Protocol Article 11's right to live in a healthy environment] might be willing or able to use Article 11 effectively as a vehicle for pushing an environmental protection agenda....

Notwithstanding an exceedingly slim evidentiary basis in international practice ... for a general acceptance of a substantive right to a clean, healthy or satisfactory environment, in her final report, Special Rapporteur Ksentini optimistically concludes that "[a]t the regional and universal level, recognition of the right to a satisfactory environment as a human right is reflected ... in the related normative developments." ... In the final analysis, what is required is evidence of unequivocal support by states. Such evidence, however, is lacking. Evidence of this kind is also unlikely to be forthcoming in the near future....

The credibility of the claim that a generic, substantive — as against procedural — environmental human right could be an effective vehicle for the protection of the environment is based on two premises. One, it assumes that because they would be couched in human rights terms, environmental protection objectives would be accorded priority over other competing socio-economic objectives. Two, it assumes that, if necessary, such human rights-based objectives could also be vindicated through recourse to established human rights processes and institutions. Tested against these implicit assumptions, it is difficult to see, how a substantive environmental human right, if viewed as a third-generation ... right, could be an effective tool in the above sense. Such a "right" would commonly be understood to imply a corresponding commitment of states, international organizations, and others to work cooperatively towards the realization of the environmental objectives concerned. By definition such a "right" hardly evinces the quality of a truly normative concept that would determine priorities among competing social, economic or political goals. For the same reason, namely its inherently defective normative quality, and quite apart from the problem that such an environmental entitlement's contents is non-specific, it would not be routinely invokable in any international human rights *fora*....

If, on the other hand, the proposed substantive environmental human right is understood to represent aspects of a first generation, a second generation right, or to represent a mix thereof, its application in practice would be intrinsically problematical because of the notion's latent ambiguity, that is, indeterminacy of its contents.... [A]ny ad hoc attempt at establishing criteria for the evaluation of states' compliance with their obligations flowing from the generic environmental human right would be fraught with political and technical difficulties. It would raise questions about the proper division of labour between human rights and environmental institutions, as well as the appropriate *locus* of decision-making, at the international as against the national level. In other words, such an entitlement, if recognized, could lead to a redrawing of traditional demarcation lines between domestic and international jurisdiction by turning the right into a platform for "internationalizing" national decision-making in sensitive core areas of traditional state sovereignty. By the same token, such a generic right offers a powerful tool for socio-economic engineering by human rights decision-making bodies, thus raising justified concerns about the technical adequacy and, indeed, democratic legitimacy of a human rights-based approach to vindicating collective environmental interests....

Rejection of the present-day utility of a generic, substantive environmental human right does not, however, imply a denial of the fact that human rights instruments have significant operational implications for environmental protection purposes. The opposite is true, of course. Environmental concerns are routinely being redressed incidentally—*par ricochet*, so to speak—by application of established human rights norms....

Questions and Discussion

1. *Evidence of an environmental human right.* Professor Handl contends that there is not sufficient "evidence of actual supportive state practice" for us to conclude that any environmental human rights claims were part of customary international law and thus reflected by the statements in the Universal Declaration of Human Rights at the time of its issuance in 1948, the International Covenant on Economic, Social and Cultural Rights when signed in 1966, or the Stockholm Declaration on the Human Environment adopted in 1972. As for treaties, he dismisses the explicit environmental rights language in the African Charter as "implausible" and containing "latent ambiguities and expresses doubt that institutions will be willing to use the environmental rights language in the San Salvador Protocol effectively. Finally, he rejects the position of Special Rapporteur Ksentini (see page 7 of this chapter) as lacking in evidence of "unequivocal support by states."

You may want to consider some of the detailed responses in Luis E. Rodriguez-Rivera, *Is the Human Right to Environment Recognized under International Law? It Depends on the Source* 12 Colo. J. Int'l Envtl. L. & Pol'y 1, 29–37 (2001). In response to the evidence objections raised by Professor Handl, Professor Rodriguez-Rivera writes:

The strongest objection raised ... is that the proponents of the human right to environment have failed to support their claims by producing solid positive evidence....

This evidentiary objection is built on the following assumptions: (1) the ... *right to environment* has not found any express affirmation in any binding or effective international legal instrument; (2) the ... *right to environment* finds its support in *indirect, normatively "soft," or limited in scope* evidence; (3) the incorporation of the ... *right to environment* in national constitutions and legislation is irrelevant absent evidence of actual domestic practice consistent with the same; and (4) current state practice does not support the ... *right to environment*. These assumptions are consistent with the traditionalist proposition that international norms are required to evince state consent, be it through binding treaties or state practice. However, … the sources of international norms are the object of debate among international legal scholars. Thus, in order to respond to [the] evidentiary objection, the sources which should be considered in evaluating the existence of new human rights, particularly that of the human right to environment, must be examined.

Id. at 36–37. This chapter and succeeding ones consider in detail the evidence for the existence, at both international and national levels, of a number of legal environmental rights, including the general human right to a healthy environment, the right to life, and others. At the end of studying the cases, ask yourself whether you agree with Professor Handl or Professor Rodriguez-Rivera, or have a third view.

2. *Disadvantages of a right to environment.* Professor Handl contends that a human right to the environment has a number of disadvantages: that states and others would have to work toward environmental objectives but that such a right is not capable of determining priorities among competing societal goals, that implementation would be "fraught with political and technical difficulties" including incursions on state sovereignty, and that human rights bodies lack the democratic legitimacy that they should have in order to impose their will on nations. What is your evaluation of these arguments?

3. *Other drawbacks.* Another list of asserted drawbacks is provided by Professor Anderson, namely: (1) a right to environment will not guarantee that disadvantaged groups will benefit from this strategy as it does not include economic and political reform; (2) a right to environment can displace other forms of legal remedy which are better suited to environmental issues, such as national tort and administrative laws; and (3) a right to environment will likely attract overt opposition from polluters and national governments. Michael R. Anderson, *Human Rights Approaches to Environmental Protection: An Overview,* in Alan Boyle & Michael R. Anderson, eds., HUMAN RIGHTS APPROACHES TO ENVIRONMENTAL PROTECTION 22–23 (1996).

On the other hand, Daniel Taillant has argued:

International as well as national jurisprudence that address the environment and human rights have focused on these legal arenas through separate frameworks, separating inextricably linked issues, even though the links between environmental abuses and human rights abuses are unarguably evident. By maintaining this rift between the areas, we duplicate efforts, thin available resources, and miss the opportunity to leverage our actions…. The human rights advocacy community simply does not communicate with their environmental counterpart, and the same is true in the other direction.

Jorge Daniel Taillant, *Environmental Advocacy and the Inter-American Human Rights System,* in LINKING HUMAN RIGHTS AND THE ENVIRONMENT (R. Picolotti & J. D. Taillant, eds., 2003).

4. *Aarhus Convention.* The right to a healthy environment was explicitly (if indirectly) recognized, as mentioned on page 4, in the Convention on Access to Information, Public Participation in Decision-making and Access to Justice in Environmental Matters (1998) (Aarhus Convention). The preamble of the Aarhus Convention recognizes that that "every person has the right to live in an environment adequate to his or her health and well-being." Article 1 of the convention under "Objective" provides:

In order to contribute to the protection of the right of every person of present and future generations to live in an environment adequate to his or her health and well-being, each Party shall guarantee the rights of access to information, public participation in decision-making, and access to justice in environmental matters in accordance with the provisions of this Convention."

An interesting interpretation of this provision is given by Professor Marc Pallemaerts:

> The explicit recognition of the right to a healthy environment in the Aarhus Convention adds weight to its operative provisions for the implementation of procedural rights.... It does not, however, have immediate consequences, as the provisions of Article 1 do not, as such, impose on parties any specific obligations beyond those laid down in the other provisions of the convention. Indeed, the protection of the right to a healthy environment is presented as an *objective* to which the Aarhus Convention is intended to contribute, not as a substantive obligation distinct from the specific obligations with respect to access to information, participation and access to justice which it imposes on its contracting parties. It is striking that the fundamental right to live in a healthy environment, at the very moment of its legal recognition, finds itself, as it were, immediately reduced to its mere procedural dimension....

Marc Pallemaerts, *The Human Right to a Healthy Environment as a Substantive Right* in M. Dejeant-Pons & M. Pallemaerts, eds., HUMAN RIGHTS AND THE ENVIRONMENT (2002).

Do you agree that the "right of every person of present and future generations to live in an environment adequate to his or her health and well-being" in the Aarhus Convention, stated in the "Objective" article, is merely to be obtained by *procedural* rights in the Convention and does not itself infer any *substantive* legal obligations for the Parties? Compare this with Article 24 of the African Charter, which simply asserts "a right to a generally satisfactory environment favourable for development," and Article 11 of the San Salvador Protocol, which simply proclaims a "right to live in healthy or satisfactory environment" (see Chapter 2). Compare this also with the simple, unadorned assertions of environmental rights found in numerous national constitutions (see Chapter 3). Do these provisions result in no "immediate consequences" and impose no "substantive obligations"? Consider whether the argument about the lack of additional "specific obligations" and "operative provisions" in Aarhus is similar to the arguments that constitutional provisions cannot be "self-executing."

Apart from the evidentiary and normative debate in the preceding materials, it is useful to consider the various ways in which existing human rights may be used or reformulated in support of environmental rights, and whether the creation of recognition of an entirely separate environmental human right would be appropriate. The following two excerpts illustrate these choices.

Human Rights Approaches to Environmental Protection: An Overview
Michael R. Anderson
HUMAN RIGHTS APPROACHES TO ENVIRONMENTAL PROTECTION
(A. Boyle & M. Anderson, eds., 1996)

2. Human Rights Approaches to Environmental Protection ...

[T]here appear three main approaches: first, mobilizing existing rights to achieve environmental ends; secondly, reinterpreting existing rights to include environmental concerns; and thirdly, creating new rights of an explicitly environmental character....

(a) Mobilizing Existing Rights ...

[H]uman rights norms which are already protected under international instruments and domestic constitutions play an important role in environmental protection. It may even be argued that existing rights, if fully realized, are so robust in themselves that proposals for new environmental rights are at best superfluous and at worst counter-productive. The body of existing rights at the international level is detailed and comprehensive. An argument may be made out that if activists devoted their attentions to securing additional ratifications and campaigning for effective implementation of existing international instruments, rather than dreaming up and promoting new standards, then environmental protection will follow automatically. Whether this argument stands or falls depends upon the scope of existing rights....

(b) Reinterpretation of Existing Rights

While existing human rights standards do provide some weapons which can be used in environmental protection, there is an argument that they are inadequate so long as conventional means of interpreting and applying such rights are followed. On this argument, the mere mobilization of existing rights norms will not satisfy environmental needs. Instead, existing rights must be reinterpreted with imagination and rigour in the context of environmental concerns which were not prevalent at the time existing rights were first formulated.

(c) New Human Rights [for] Environmental Protection

Although existing human rights, if fully mobilized, may offer a great deal to global and local environmental protection, there are good reasons to suspect that they will fall short of meeting desired ends. Established human rights standards approach environmental questions obliquely, and lacking precision, provide clumsy tools for urgent environmental tasks. It may be argued that a comprehensive norm, which relates directly to environmental goods, is required.... [Scholars] are divided on whether new environmental rights, if desirable, should be mainly procedural or substantive in character.

Environmental Rights

Dinah Shelton

PEOPLES' RIGHTS (Philip Alston, ed., 2001)

Human rights law and environmental protection interrelate at present in four different ways. First, those primarily interested in the environment utilize or emphasize relevant human rights guarantees in drafting international environmental instruments. They select from among the catalogue of human rights those rights that can serve the aims of environmental protection, independent of the utility of such protection for the enjoyment of other human rights. Recognizing the broad goals of environmental protection, the emphasis is placed on rights such as freedom of association for members of non-governmental environmental organizations and the right to information about potential threats to the environment, which may be used for nature protection nor necessarily related to human health and well-being. The weakness of compliance mechanisms in nearly all international environmental agreements raises questions about the short-term effectiveness of this method in achieving the goals of environmental protection, at least when compared with recourse to the more developed human rights supervisory machinery.

A second approach invokes existing human rights law and institutions, recasting or applying human rights guarantees when their enjoyment is threatened by environmental harm. This method is unreservedly anthropocentric. It seeks to ensure that the environment does not deteriorate to the point where the human right to life, the right to health, the right to a family and private life, the right to culture, the right to safe drinking water, or other human rights are seriously impaired. Environmental protection is thus instrumental, not an end in itself.... With a focus on the consequences of environmental harm to existing human rights, this approach can serve to address most serious cases of actual or imminently-threatened pollution. The primary advantage it offers, compared to pursuing the environmental route, is that existing human rights complaint machinery may be invoked against those states whose level of environmental protection falls below that necessary to maintain any of the guaranteed human rights. From the perspective of environmental protection, however, this human rights approach is deficient because it generally does not address threats to non-human species....

The third approach aims to incorporate the environmental agenda fully into human rights by formulating a new human right to an environment that is not defined in purely anthropocentric terms, an environment that is not only safe for humans, but one that is ecologically-balanced and sustainable in the long term. Various international efforts have been undertaken in this direction ... and some have proved successful. Nonetheless, despite the inclusion of ecological concerns in various formulations of the right, strict environmentalists continue to object to the anthropocentrism inherent in taking a human rights approach to environmental protection....

Finally, a fourth approach questions claims of rights in regard to environmental protection, preferring to address the issue as a matter of human responsibilities.

Questions and Discussion

1. *Mobilize, reinterpret, or create new rights?* Which is the most effective way of using human rights for environmental protection: to mobilize existing human rights, to reinterpret them, or to create new environmental rights?

2. *Advantages and disadvantages of the human rights approach.* Do you agree with the argument of some that including new environmental rights into existing human rights doctrine will diminish the importance of fundamental human rights, taking focus and efforts away from rights issues such as genocide, torture, extra-judicial executions, and forced labor? What do you think of the argument that human rights doctrine is too human-centered and does not reflect the intrinsic values of nature?

II. Linkages between Human Rights and the Environment

Some human rights violations cause or contribute to environmental degradation. At the same time, deterioration of the environment can affect the enjoyment of human rights (including the right to life, health, self-determination, development, property, information, participation, and justice). The connection between the two fields had been discussed and established in a number of different United Nations activities, initiatives, and meetings.

In 1989, Mrs. Fatma Zohra Ksentini, the U.N. Special Rapporteur on human rights and the environment, was asked to study the relation between human rights and environmental rights. One of her tasks was to examine the possible need for a human right to a healthy environment. U.N. Doc. E/CN.4/Sub.2/1989/C23 (1989). As mentioned in the excerpt above by Prof. Handl, in 1994 the resultant "Ksentini Report" was finalized and presented to the Commission. Its opening statement asserts a connection between human rights and the environment in modern society:

> The environment, development, democracy, human rights: these are the key issues which characterize the close of this century and pose a continuing challenge to the establishment of an order in which, in conformity with the Universal Declaration of Human Rights, the rights set out therein can be fully realized....

> For the particular purposes of this study of human rights and the environment, it is equally important to establish the legal framework for pursuing what have become the essential demands of this century, in order to take up the legitimate concerns of our generation, to preserve the interests of future generations and mutually to agree upon the components of a right to a healthy and flourishing environment.

The Report concluded that environmental rights are a part of existing human rights. Since adoption of the Stockholm Declaration, it said,

> large numbers of national, regional and international instruments have been drawn up which have strengthened the legal bases of environmental rights and stressed the intrinsic link that exists between the preservation of the environment, development and the promotion of human rights.... This research has revealed universal acceptance of the environmental rights recognized at the national, regional and international levels.

U.N. Doc. E/CN.4/Sub.2/1994/9 (6 July 1994). Attached to the report as Annex I were "Draft Principles on Human Rights and the Environment," prepared by a group of academic and NGO experts meeting in Geneva at Mrs. Ksentini's invitation. It provides a succinct statement of claimed linkages.

Draft Principles on Human Rights and the Environment
U.N. Doc. E/CN.4/Sub.2/1994/9, Annex I (6 July 1994)[a]

Preamble

Guided by the Charter of the United Nations, the Universal Declaration of Human Rights, the International Covenant on Economic, Social and Cultural Rights, the International Covenant on Civil and Political Rights, ... and other relevant international human rights instruments,

Guided also by the Stockholm Declaration of the United Nations Conference on the Human Environment, the World Charter for Nature, the Rio Declaration on Environment and Development, Agenda 21: Programme of Action for Sustainable Development, and other relevant instruments of international environmental law....

Reaffirming the universality, indivisibility and interdependence of all human rights....

[We] Declare the following principles:

---

a. Report by Mrs. Fatma Zohra Ksentini, Special Rapporteur, Sub-Commission on Protection of Discrimination and Protection of Rights of Minorities. Full title: *Review of Further Developments in Fields with Which the Sub-Commission Has Been Concerned: Human Rights and the Environment.*

Part I

1. Human rights, an ecologically sound environment, sustainable development and peace are interdependent and indivisible.

2. All persons have the right to a secure, healthy and ecologically sound environment. This right and other human rights, including civil, cultural, economic, political and social rights, are universal, interdependent and indivisible....

4. All persons have the right to an environment adequate to meet equitably the needs of present generations and that does not impair the rights of future generations to meet equitably their needs.

Part II

5. All persons have the right to freedom from pollution, environmental degradation and activities that adversely affect the environment, threaten life, health, livelihood, well-being or sustainable development within, across or outside national boundaries.

6. All persons have the right to protection and preservation of the air, soil, water, sea-ice, flora and fauna, and the essential processes and areas necessary to maintain biological diversity and ecosystems.

7. All persons have the right to the highest attainable standard of health free from environmental harm.

8. All persons have the right to safe and healthy food and water adequate to their well-being.

9. All persons have the right to a safe and healthy working environment.

10. All persons have the right to adequate housing, land tenure and living conditions in a secure, healthy and ecologically sound environment....

14. Indigenous peoples have the right to control their lands, territories and natural resources and to maintain their traditional way of life. This includes the right to security in the enjoyment of their means of subsistence.

Indigenous peoples have the right to protection against any action or course of conduct that may result in the destruction or degradation of their territories, including land, air, water, sea-ice, wildlife or other resources.

Part III

15. All persons have the right to information concerning the environment. This includes information, howsoever compiled, on actions or courses of conduct that may affect the environment and information necessary to enable effective public participation in environmental decision-making. The information shall be timely, clear, understandable and available without undue financial burden to the applicant.

16. All persons have the right to hold and express opinions and to disseminate ideas and information regarding the environment.

17. All persons have the right to environmental and human rights education.

18. All persons have the right to active, free and meaningful participation in planning and decision-making activities and processes that may have an impact on the environment and development. This includes the right to a prior assessment of the environmental, developmental and human rights consequences of proposed actions.

19. All persons have the right to associate freely and peacefully with others for purposes of protecting the environment or the rights of persons affected by environmental harm.

20. All persons have the right to effective remedies and redress in administrative or judicial proceedings for environmental harm or the threat of such harm....

Questions and Discussion

1. *Universal acceptance?* The Ksentini Report itself stated that "environmental rights are a part of existing human rights" and that the Special Rapporteur's research "has revealed universal acceptance of the environmental rights recognized at the national, regional and international levels." Can you envisage that some human rights or other experts might argue with that statement? What would their arguments be? Come back to this question repeatedly as you progress through this course and ask yourself whether the statement of universality contains at least a grain of truth—or more than a grain.

2. *Definition of the environmental right.* The Draft Principles use various definitions of the environmental right: a right to a "healthy and flourishing environment" or a "satisfactory environment" in the Report and a right to "a secure healthy and ecologically sound environment" in the Draft Principles. Different terminology was used in the Stockholm Declaration—"environment of a quality that permits a life of dignity and well-being"—and in the Rio Declaration—the right "to live in harmony with nature." The African Charter of Human and Peoples' Rights talks of all peoples having "the right to a generally satisfactory environment favourable for their development." The Protocol of San Salvador proclaims a "right to live in healthy or satisfactory environment." In the Aarhus Convention it is a person's right to live in "environment adequate to his or her health and well-being." National constitutions of more than 100 states contain variations of this right—including the right to an ecologically safe or decent environment, the right to a balanced ecology, and so forth.

Would it be productive to try to unify these definitions and to choose the clearest and most definite wording? Or is diversity better in this matter? Is it realistic to try to agree upon one definition for the entire world, considering its different cultures and traditions?

4. *Background and commentary.* A thorough analysis is provided by one of those involved in the drafting. Neil Popovic, *In Pursuit of Environmental Human Rights: Commentary on the Draft Declaration of Principles on Human Rights and the Environment*, 27 Colum. Hum. Rts. L. Rev. 487 (1996).

––––––––––

Another U.N. event that explored the connections between human rights and the environment was an Expert Seminar on Human Rights and the Environment that took place in Geneva in 2002. Organized jointly by the United Nations High Commissioner for Human Rights (OHCHR) and the Executive Director of the United Nations Environment Programme (UNEP), the gathering, in which one of the co-authors participated, reviewed progress made at the international level since the U.N. Conference on Environment and Sustainable Development in Rio de Janeiro in 1992. The experts—half of them from the field of human rights and half from the environmental field—examined multilateral environmental agreements developed since 1992, considered the jurisprudence of global and regional human rights bodies, and studied reports of national implementation of environmental human rights through constitutional law, legislation, administrative practices, and decisions of domestic courts. At the end of their seminar, they agreed upon a document of "Conclusions."

Meeting of Experts on Human Rights and the Environment
U.N. High Commissioner for Human Rights
14–15 January 2002
http://www.unhchr.ch/environment/conclusions.html

CONCLUSIONS

REVIEW

The experts noted in particular that the linkage of human rights and environmental concerns, approaches and techniques is reflected in developments relating to procedural and substantive rights, in the activities of international organizations, and in the drafting and application of national constitutions....

The experts found that at the national and international levels Principle 10 of the Rio Declaration (on access to information, participation and effective remedies) has played an important role in fostering connections between human rights and environmental approaches. The experts observed that multilateral agreements at the global and regional level have developed Principle 10 of the Rio Declaration by establishing mechanisms for the exercise of procedural rights, in particular the right to environmental information and to public participation in decision-making. This was reflected, for example, in the 1998 Aarhus Convention on Access to Information, Public Participation [in Decision-Making] and Access to Justice in Environmental Matters, which aims to provide effective means for the exercise of procedural rights in the field of the environment....

At the global level, some human rights treaties include the value of the environment in their systems of protection, such as the Convention on the Rights of the Child and ILO Convention 169 concerning Indigenous and Tribal Peoples in Independent Countries. The experts noted that, at the regional level, the African Charter on Human and Peoples' Rights and the Protocol of San Salvador to the American Convention on Human Rights expressly recognize the right to live in a healthy or satisfactory environment. Similarly, a number of environmental treaties embody human rights approaches.

From a review of the decisions of international treaty bodies (including courts and commissions), the experts noted that in the last decade a substantial body of case law and decisions has recognized the violation of a fundamental human right as the cause, or result, of environmental degradation. A significant number of decisions at the national and international levels have identified environmental harm to individuals or communities, especially indigenous peoples, arising as a result of violations of the rights to health, to life, to self-determination, to food and water, and to housing. Particularly in the European system, a clear connection has been made between a violation of the right to privacy and home life and the right not to be subject to pollution, including the right to know whether pollution is likely to affect a particular individual or community....

At the national level, the right to a healthy environment (or a related formulation) has been formally recognized in most national constitutions enacted since 1992. In many constitutions this right permits individuals or groups to file legal actions to protect the environment or fight against pollution. Over the past ten years there has been a growing domestic case law indicating the potential role that environmental rights may play in achieving practical protections. That case law may also be relevant for international jurisprudence....

ASSESSMENT ...

In relation to procedural matters, the experts noted that broad recognition of the linkage between human rights and the environment since UNCED has come through the development of Principle 10 of the Rio Declaration on Environment and Development. States and international organizations are increasingly recognizing the rights of access to information, public participation and access to justice.... The experts recognized the need for further developments in this regard, including through the adoption of new international legal instruments (at the regional level or, some suggest, the global level) to provide effectively for rights of access to information, public participation in decision-making and access to justice.

In relation to substantive matters, a growing body of case law from many national jurisdictions is clarifying the linkages between human rights and the environment, in particular by: (1) recognizing the right to a healthy environment as a fundamental human right; (2) allowing litigation based on this right and facilitating its enforceability in domestic law by liberalizing provisions on standing; (3) acknowledging that other human rights recognized in domestic legal systems can be violated as a result of environmental degradation. The experts recognized the important role that the judiciary (national and international) can play in this regard, and emphasized the need to sensitize and provide further training for judges, lawyers and public officials.

The experts noted the particular lessons that may be learned from the experiences of indigenous peoples, which appear particularly relevant to a broader understanding of the relationship between human rights and the environment. In this regard the experts noted the particular importance of the principle of self-determination and the rights associated with the ownership, possession and use of traditional lands, territories and resources.

VIEWS OF THE EXPERTS

During the course of the two-day meeting, the experts put forward suggestions for future developments....

With regard to institutional arrangements, the linkage between human rights and the environment is in need of reinforcement. This could be achieved by:

- Coordinating efforts between OHCHR and UNEP and operational and financial institutions in appropriate aspects of their respective activities, including by: ...

- Promoting programmes to sensitize decision makers, including public officials, legislators and members of the judiciary, as to the need to develop a sense of commitment to the protection of human and environmental rights....

- Enhancing mechanisms for receiving and addressing citizens' complaints in the field of human rights and the environment....

Questions and Discussion

1. *Two types of rights.* The conclusions of the Meeting of Experts on Human Rights and the Environment make an analytical distinction between "substantive" and "procedural" environmental human rights. What rights would you consider to be substantive? Which of them would you consider procedural? Does it help to think of the former as leading to a particular policy outcome and the latter as empowering the citizen but not necessarily dictating a particular decisionmaking result?

2. *Substantive environmental rights?* What substantive human rights can be reinterpreted and used to lead to greater protection of the environment? Pollution of the environment by toxic substances can causes long-term health or mortality problems or even immediate deaths (for example, the infamous disaster in Bhopal, India, when a subsidiary of the Union Carbide Company released 40 tons of methyl isocyanate gas, killing 3,800 people). Can the right to life be mobilized or interpreted to guard against, or compensate for, the consequences of such events? Does the right to life, in other words, include the right to live in a healthy environment, and free of harmful pollution? Can this right be enforced in court in the case of environmental degradation? What other human rights might be used? The right to health? Right to property? Right to freedom of expression? Right to privacy and family life?

3. *Procedural environmental rights?* Which rights would you classify as procedural? In what way might they be considered to be environmental rights? Are they easier to enforce and use for the protection of the environment than substantive rights? In what way might a right of access to information help protect the environment or human health? Is there a necessary correlation between public participation and decisions that are more environmentally favorable? Is the procedural right to go to court essential for the implementation of substantive environmental rights, or can they be adequately recognized and protected by actions of executive and legislative branches alone, or by influencing individuals to change their behavior?

4. *Indigenous people and environments.* Many would assert that the experience of indigenous peoples is particularly relevant to a broader understanding of the relationship between human rights and the environment. Do you agree and why, or why not? Does the style of life and culture of indigenous peoples who maintain a closer connection to the environment and natural resources make them natural allies for those whose main concern is the protection of nature? Is such an alliance assured? If both indigenous rights and environmental rights are respected by a society, which should prevail if they come into conflict, such as when indigenous peoples want to cut trees and sell them, or want to hunt for animal, bird, or fish species that may be endangered?

5. *Sensitization of decisionmakers.* Among other suggestions, the 2002 Meeting of Experts in Geneva proposed that efforts be made to sensitize decisionmakers, including public officials, legislators and members of the judiciary. The goal is to develop in them a sense of commitment to the protection of human and environmental rights. Why would they use term "sensitize" rather than "educate" or "train"? Does the judiciary have a special role in establishing linkages between human rights and the environment? Should those advocating such linkages encounter judges only in litigation, or seek other ways to influence them?

6. *Viewpoint of Justice Weeramantry.* Justice Christopher Weeramantry, a former Vice-President of the International Court of Justice, in a separate opinion concerning a project to divert some waters of the famed Danube River, saw no need to separate human rights and the environment. He wrote:

> The protection of the environment is ... a vital part of contemporary human rights doctrine, for it is a *sine qua non* for numerous human rights such as the right to health and the right to life itself. It is scarcely necessary to elaborate on this, as damage to the environment can impair and undermine all the human rights spoken of in the Universal Declaration and other human rights instruments.

Case Concerning the Gabčíkovo-Nagymaros Project (Hungary/Slovakia), [1997] ICJ Rep. 7, 91–92.

7. *Sources of case law.* Two significant sets of publications collect cases that are otherwise hard to find: HUMAN RIGHTS AND ENVIRONMENT (International Environmental Law Reports, Volumes 1–4, edited by Cairo A.R. Robb, 2001–4) and COMPENDIUM OF JUDICIAL DECISIONS ON MATTERS RELATED TO ENVIRONMENT: NATIONAL DECISIONS (UNEP, Volumes 1–3, edited by Prof. Charles Okidi, 1998–2001). In addition, a COMPENDIUM OF SUMMARIES OF JUDICIAL DECISIONS IN ENVIRONMENT RELATED CASES, SACEP/UNEP/NORAD Publication Series on Environmental Law and Policy No. 3 (1997) can be found at http://www.unescap.org/drpad/vc/document/compendium/index.htm.

8. *ELAW.* The Environmental Law Alliance Worldwide (ELAW), co-founded by one of the authors of this book, maintains a collection of court decisions collected by its members and in some instances found nowhere else, See http://www.elaw.org/resources.

———————

Some have argued that human rights consist of three generations. The first "generation" of rights consists of civil and political rights and includes the right to life, freedom of speech, freedom of assembly, and so forth. These rights are sometimes called "negative" because they are said to exist as long as nobody interferes with them. The second generation of rights is often considered to be more recent. It includes economic, social and cultural rights, such as the right to health, culture, and family life. They are said to be "positive" rights, requiring governmental action for their full realization. At the time of preparation and negotiation of the Universal Declaration of Human Rights after the Second World War, the Soviet-bloc countries were reluctant to recognize civil and political rights, while some Western countries, including the United States, contended that the government had no obligation to guarantee economic, social and cultural rights. This controversy was one of the reasons that the Universal Declaration was adopted in a non-binding form, and the human rights field was divided in two. It required another eighteen years of difficult diplomatic efforts to accommodate and bridge fundamental differences and political divisions between Western democratic and socialist states to conclude and adopt two human rights treaties—the International Covenant on Civil and Political Rights and the International Covenant on Economic, Social and Cultural Rights. Both were signed in 1966 and entered into force a decade later, after obtaining enough ratifications. Both have been ratified by approximately 160 countries, but the United States has not ratified the latter covenant. Together with the Universal Declaration these covenants are called the "International Bill of Rights."

A third "generation" of rights—so-called solidarity or group rights—emerged later. The generational labels were coined by the former Director of the Division of Human Rights and Peace of the United Nations Educational, Scientific, and Cultural Organization (UNESCO), building on the work of Senegalese jurist Keba M'Baye. Karel Vasak, *A 30-Year Struggle*, UNESCO Courier (Nov. 1977). According to the theory of generations of rights, these rights are not held by individuals but by groups in society or even by the entire society. This analytical distinction has been used by some to question the validity of the use of the term "rights" for this category. In this book we shall make no such distinctions, but it is worth keeping the concepts in mind and raising questions about enforceability and appropriateness as you progress through the course.

Some would classify environmental rights in the third generation. In terms of time, that would be correct. Environmental concerns increased dramatically in the 1960's. As the extent of air, water, and pesticide contamination became more evident, ship accidents led to massive oil spills, the last wild areas were discovered and made accessible, and the first photographs of Earth taken from humankind's first trip to the Moon revealed both its wholeness and its fragility, international and domestic environmental law started to respond. It was not long before people were discussing the problems in the language of rights. Today it is widely accepted that human rights, including the right to continued and satisfactory life itself, cannot be fully enjoyed and realized in a polluted and degraded environment. At the same time, violations of other human rights often appear to go hand-in-hand with careless government or private actions that lead to dramatic degradation of the environment.

III. Human Rights Instruments and Institutions

In this book we will look at several legal instruments and institutions in action as we study and discuss various cases. Here we give a brief description of the main ones.

We have already mentioned that the International Bill of Rights is considered to include the Universal Declaration of Human Rights (1948) and two covenants—the International Covenant on Civil and Political Rights and the International Covenant on Economic, Social and Cultural Rights (1966). The main body of international human rights law also includes the Convention on the Prevention and Punishment of the Crime of Genocide (1948), the first post-war human rights agreement, the Convention on the Elimination of all Forms of Racial Discrimination (1965), the Convention on the Elimination of all Forms of Discrimination Against Women (1979), the Convention against Torture and other Cruel, Inhuman, or Degrading Treatment or Punishment (1984), the Convention on the Rights of the Child (1989), and others.

Regional human rights treaties include the European Convention on Human Rights and Fundamental Freedoms (1950) and the European Social Charter (1961), the American Declaration on the Rights and Duties of Man (1948), the American Convention on Human Rights (1969), and the African Charter on Human and Peoples' Rights (1981). In addition, a number of protocols and covenants implementing these are important.

Not all of the human rights instruments have been used for the protection of the environment. In this book you will encounter the two Covenants, the regional human rights treaties, and certain protocols.

One international convention stands out as a unique instrument at the intersection of the two fields—the Aarhus Convention on Access to Information, Public Participation in Decision-Making and Access to Justice in Environmental Matters (1998). It includes the right to live in an environment adequate to health and well-being and procedural rights to information, participation and access to justice. Other multilateral environmental agreements also provide various kinds of rights, particularly procedural rights.

All six main global human rights conventions have relevant committees—"treaty-based organs"—that are intended to monitor compliance by states with their obligations under those treaties. These organs have similar structure and functions. They consist of independent experts who serve in their personal capacity rather than as representatives of states. They base their monitoring on examination of periodical reports filed by states. In case of a committee's concern about non-compliance in a particular country, it can invite a representative of the party whose report is being examined to its session to answer questions. Then the committee can draft concluding observations and make suggestions and recommendations to the reporting state. Notable among these bodies is the U.N. Human Rights Committee, which exists under the International Covenant on Civil and Political Rights, and the U.N. Committee on Economic, Social and Cultural Rights (ESC Committee). We include some of the cases of the Human Rights Committee particularly in Chapter 5, and activity of the ESC Committee in Chapter 4. The Human Rights Committee and the Committee on Elimination of Racial Discrimination (CERD) can receive and consider communications from one party about alleged non-compliance by another party with obligations under the treaty. Only three treaty-based organs—the Human Rights Committee, the Committee Against Torture (CAT), and the CERD—accept complaints from individual persons. Treaty-based organs also adopt "General Comments" which are

> in a sense the Committee's jurisprudence, and which provide … authoritative interpretation of the general obligations and rights embodied in the different treaties. General Comments are intended to indicate to states how they can promote implementation of human rights norms. General Comments often give substance and clarity to vague or inadequately defined human rights provisions. General Comments can also serve to give substance and clarity to issues that are not specifically covered by, but which arise in the context of, the human rights treaties.

Caroline Dommen, *Claiming Environmental Rights: Some Possibilities Offered by the United Nations' Human Rights Mechanism,* 11 Geo. Int'l. L. Rev. 1, 8 (1998). We will discuss General Comment 15 of the U.N. Committee on Economic, Social, and Cultural Rights in Chapter 4.

Another group of bodies are called "Charter-based organs," whose creation is mandated by the U.N. Charter. These are the General Assembly, the Economic and Social Council, and the Human Rights Council. The Human Rights Council was created by General Assembly Resolution 60/251 on March 15, 2006, and replaced the Commission on Human Rights, which had been created in 1946. A recent example of Human Rights Council activity is its Resolution of March 26, 2008, "Human rights and climate change." The resolution emphasized that "climate change poses an immediate and far-reaching threat to people and communities around the world and has implications for the full enjoyment of human rights." The Resolution's preamble took into account the findings of the Fourth Assessment Report of the Intergovernmental Panel on Climate Change, the "right to development as a universal and inalienable right and as an integral part of fundamental human rights," and the "Commission on Human Rights resolution 2005/60 of 20 April 2005 on human rights and the environment as part of sustainable development." The Human Rights Council decided to undertake "a detailed analytical study of the relationship between climate change and human rights … and thereafter to make available the study … to the Conference of Parties to the United Nations Framework Convention on Climate Change for its consideration." U.N. Doc. A/HRC/7/L.21/Rev.1 (26 March 2008).

The Human Rights Council from time to time establishes various "special procedures," including special rapporteurs, representatives, or experts and working groups that investigate, discuss, and report on specific human rights issues under a country mandate or thematic mandate. These procedures can be used for the protection of the environment. For example, a Special Rapporteur on Human Rights and the Environment was appointed to study the relation between human rights and environmental rights. The work resulted in the report and Draft Principles on Human Rights and the Environment discussed earlier in this chapter.

The High Commissioner for Human Rights is the highest U.N. official responsible for human rights. He or she is appointed by the Secretary General, with the approval of the

General Assembly. The office of the High Commissioner has a headquarters staff in Geneva, Switzerland, plus field operations in more than 60 countries.

We will study the jurisprudence of regional human rights commissions and courts in various chapters. They are separate from the United Nations and are established under regional human rights conventions. The European human rights system now consists of only the European Court of Human Rights. A previous Commission on Human Rights was abolished as a result of a reform in 1999. As a result, citizens now have direct access to the Court, whereas previously they were required to go through the Commission first. Several cases from the European Court are discussed in this book, particularly in Chapters 2 and 6. The Inter-American human rights system consists of the Inter-American Commission on Human Rights and the Inter-American Court of Human Rights. The Commission is in charge of states' reporting, monitoring, and individual complaints. It serves as a filter for the Court. If it cannot resolve a complaint and the case is important, the Commission will present the case to the Court. Individuals do not have direct access to the Court on their own. Matters involving the Commission are presented in Chapters 2 and 12, while cases from this Court are included particularly in Chapters 5 and 6. A similar structure exists in the African human rights system. It consists of the African Commission and the African Court on Human and Peoples' Rights. We present an important case from the African Commission in Chapter 2. The African Court was created quite recently—in 2006—and did not yet have cases at the time of publication.

Although the multilateral environmental agreements (MEAs) generally have compliance mechanisms, the mechanisms are usually not directly available to the public, even when procedural rights are provided. The Aarhus Compliance Committee is an exception, accepting communications from the public (individuals and non-governmental organizations). In Chapters 6, 7, and 8 we will look at several cases of alleged non-compliance with environmental procedural rights that have come in recent years from the unique compliance mechanism created under the Aarhus Convention.

International financial institutions, such as the World Bank, have established review bodies and have granted procedural rights to individuals and NGOs complaining that the institutions' activities will harm human rights and the environment. We include cases brought before these bodies in Chapter 10.

The International Labour Organization, a U.N. specialized body, oversees various agreements, including one of particular interest to indigenous peoples, ILO Convention No. 169. ILO procedures are generally available to representatives of workers but this convention may also be enforced in national courts. This is discussed in Chapter 5.

A number of non-binding guidelines relating to corporate responsibility have been promulgated in recent years but none has an effective enforcement institution. Lawyers representing injured people or NGOs have focused their efforts to enhance corporate accountability on various legal theories in national court litigation.

A great deal of law of all kinds involving environmental human rights exists at the national level. The constitutions of more than 100 nations include a right to a healthy environment in various formulations. Both Supreme and Constitutional Courts enforce those rights, as well as state Supreme Courts in the U.S. In some countries the right to life is interpreted broadly, including various kinds of environmental protection. Several courts have been creative and firm in articulating environmental rights and duties. Cases from national courts are found in nearly every chapter of this book.

Chapter 2

Substantive Environment Rights in International Law

Introduction

A right to a healthy or safe environment has been proclaimed in numerous international declarations, some international treaties and conventions, and many national constitutions. Is it therefore a recognized human right? Two U.S. Courts of Appeals have ruled that a right to a healthy environment is not part of the "law of nations," while one international human rights body at the regional level has ruled that such a right *does* exist for its continent. A right to "life" is found in numerous international instruments as well and has been used in environmental matters. In addition, various human rights conventions contain rights to private and family life or property that human rights courts have pressed into service for environmental protection.

The highest courts in several countries and at least one U.S. state have ruled that such an environmental right is a fundamental and enforceable human right. Courts in at least two of these countries have stated that it is a fundamental right even if it is *not* stated in a national constitution. The next chapter considers the status of environmental rights in national law.

This chapter considers the articulation and judicial or quasi-judicial protection given to substantive environmental rights pursuant to international human rights conventions, protocols, and declarations.

I. Environmental Rights under the European Convention

The European Convention for the Protection of Human Rights and Fundamental Freedoms (often called the European Convention on Human Rights) was signed in 1950 and entered into force in 1953, before environmental problems were recognized and protection of the environment appeared in international law. Therefore, environmental rights cannot be found among rights enshrined in the Convention.

It was first opened to signature in newly liberated Rome in 1950, as a response to the experiences of the World War II. Consequently, its thrust is the provision of core civil and political rights thought necessary to safeguard democracy from the threat of totalitarianism. When, in 1976, the now-defunct European Commission of Human Rights dismissed a claim for an environmental right under the Convention on the basis that it was so manifestly ill-founded in principle as to be inadmissible, *X and Y v. Fed. Rep. of Germany*, No. 7407/76, 5 Decisions and Reports 161 (May 1976), few could have been surprised. Later, Judge Harvey reinforced the difficulty faced by the Commission in that case in his comment that "in the absence of authority," one would have thought that the ECHR had "nothing to do" with the environment. *Marcic v. Thames Water Utilities* [2001] 3 All E.R. 698 at 719; High Court, 2001 WL 720375.

Ben Pontin, *Environmental Rights under the UK's "Intermediate Constitution,"* 17 Nat. Res. & Envir. 21 (2002).

However, as we will see from the cases in this chapter, the European Court of Human Rights has taken a new direction, starting in the 1990s. The Court has derived environmental rights from traditional fundamental rights, such as the right to respect for private and family life, the right to information, the right to life, and the right to effective judicial protection. In particular, the Court's jurisprudence has recognized violations of Article 8—the right to respect for private and family life—and violations of Article 2—the right to life.

The European Convention on Human Rights has been ratified by every nation that is a member of the Council of Europe, from the Atlantic Ocean to the Pacific, from the North Sea to the Mediterranean. In some countries the Convention is directly applicable, meaning that national courts apply it in the same way they apply their own national laws. In such countries it may even be superior to national legislation, giving it quasi-constitutional status. In other countries, the Convention is effectively applied only when cases are taken to the European Court of Human Rights. In both types, decisions of the Court are, once handed down, considered to constitute a legal obligation for the country concerned as well as a matter of precedent to be observed by that member and all other members of the Council of Europe. As a consequence, the jurisprudence of the European Court of Human Rights is central to the question of whether environmental harms have a human rights dimension in this part of the world.

A. European Convention on Human Rights

Convention for the Protection of Human Rights and Fundamental Freedoms

November 4, 1950
213 U.N.T.S. 222

The governments signatory hereto, being members of the Council of Europe,

Considering the Universal Declaration of Human Rights proclaimed by the General Assembly of the United Nations on 10th December 1948; ...

Being resolved, as the governments of European countries which are like minded and have a common heritage of political traditions, ideals, freedom and the rule of law, to take the first steps for the collective enforcement of certain of the rights stated in the Universal Declaration,

Have agreed as follows:

Article 2
Right to life

1. Everyone's right to life shall be protected by law. No one shall be deprived of his life intentionally save in the execution of a sentence of a court following his conviction of a crime for which this penalty is provided by law.

Article 3
Prohibition of torture

No one shall be subjected to torture or to inhuman or degrading treatment or punishment.

Article 8
Right to respect for private and family life

1. Everyone has the right to respect for his private and family life, his home and his correspondence.

2. There shall be no interference by a public authority with the exercise of this right except such as is in accordance with the law and is necessary in a democratic society in the interests of national security, public safety or the economic well-being of the country, for the prevention of disorder or crime, for the protection of health or morals, or for the protection of the rights and freedoms of others.

Article 10
Freedom of expression

1. Everyone has the right to freedom of expression. This right shall include freedom to hold opinions and to receive and impart information and ideas without interference by public authority and regardless of frontiers....

Article 13
Right to an effective remedy

Everyone whose rights and freedoms as set forth in this Convention are violated shall have an effective remedy before a national authority notwithstanding that the violation has been committed by persons acting in an official capacity.

SECTION II — EUROPEAN COURT OF HUMAN RIGHTS

Article 19
Establishment of the Court

To ensure the observance of the engagements undertaken by the High Contracting Parties in the Convention and the Protocols thereto, there shall be set up a European Court of Human Rights, hereinafter referred to as "the Court." It shall function on a permanent basis.

Article 27
Committees, Chambers and Grand Chamber

1. To consider cases brought before it, the Court shall sit in committees of three judges, in Chambers of seven judges and in a Grand Chamber of seventeen judges....

Article 34
Individual applications

The Court may receive applications from any person, non-governmental organisation or group of individuals claiming to be the victim of a violation by one of the High Contracting Parties of the rights set forth in the Convention or the protocols thereto. The High Contracting Parties undertake not to hinder in any way the effective exercise of this right.

Questions and Discussion

1. *Substantive rights.* Although there is obviously no explicit, substantive right to a safe, clean, or healthy environment in the European Convention on Human Rights, could one be constructed from Articles 2, 3, or 8?

2. *Procedural rights.* Are procedural rights of access to information and access to justice implicitly or explicitly contained within Articles 10 and 13?

B. Right to Private and Family Life

Despite the lack of an explicit right to a healthy environment in the European Convention on Human Rights, other rights that are recognized in the Convention have been used to grant remedies in the case of environmental harm. The cases that follow will illustrate such jurisprudence, raise questions about how far these rights extend and just how they are creatively interpreted, and look for trends over the past decades.

1. Origin of the Article 8 Right

López Ostra v. Spain

European Court of Human Rights
Application No. 16798/90, Series A no. 303-C, (1995) 20 E.H.R.R. 277
Judgment of 9 December 1994

The President, Judge RYSSDAL; Judges BERNHARDT, SPIELMANN, PALM, MORENILLA, BIGI, BAKA, LOPES ROCHA, MIFSUD BONNICI

AS TO THE FACTS

Mrs. Gregoria López Ostra, a Spanish national, lives in Lorca (Murcia). At the material time she and her husband and their two daughters had their home in the district of "Diputación del Rio, el Lugarico," a few hundred metres from the town centre....

The town of Lorca has a heavy concentration of leather industries. Several tanneries there, all belonging to a limited company called SACURSA, had a plant for the treatment of liquid and solid waste built with a State subsidy on municipal land twelve metres away from the applicant's home.

The plant began to operate in July 1988 without the licence (licencia) from the municipal authorities required by Regulation 6 of the 1961 regulations on activities classified as causing nuisance and being unhealthy, noxious, and dangerous ("the 1961 regulations"), and without having followed the procedure for obtaining such a licence.

Owing to a malfunction, its start-up released gas fumes, pestilential smells, and contamination, which immediately caused health problems and nuisance to many Lorca people, particularly those living in the applicant's district. The town council evacuated the local residents and rehoused them free of charge in the town centre for the months of July, August, and September 1988. In October the applicant and her family returned to their flat and lived there until February 1992.

On 9 September 1988, following numerous complaints and in the light of reports from the health authorities and the Environment and Nature Agency for the Murcia region, the town council ordered cessation of one of the plant's activities—the settling of chemical and organic residues in water tanks (lagunaje)—while permitting the treatment of waste water contaminated with chromium to continue.

There is disagreement as to what the effects were of this partial shutdown, but it can be seen from the expert opinions and written evidence of 1991, 1992 and 1993, produced before the Commission by the Government and the applicant, that certain nuisances continue and may endanger the health of those living nearby....

[In a lower court proceeding] the judge ordered a number of expert opinions as to the seriousness of the nuisance caused by the waste-treatment plant and its effects on the health of those living nearby....

The investigation file contains several medical certificates and expert opinions concerning the effects on the health of those living near the plant. In a certificate dated 12 December 1991 Dr. de Ayala Sánchez, a pediatrician, stated that Mrs. López Ostra's daughter, Cristina, presented a clinical picture of nausea, vomiting, allergic reactions, anorexia, etc., which could only be explained by the fact that she was living in a highly polluted area. He recommended that the child should be moved from the area.

In an expert report of 16 April 1993 the Ministry of Justice's Institute of Forensic Medicine in Cartagena indicated that gas concentrations in houses near the plant exceeded the permitted limit. It noted that the applicant's daughter and her nephew, Fernando López Gómez, presented typical symptoms of chronic absorption of the gas in question, periodically manifested in the form of acute bronchopulmonary infections. It considered that there was a relationship of cause and effect between this clinical picture and the levels of gas....

As to the Law ...

II. Alleged Violation of Article 8 of the Convention ...

Mrs. López Ostra first contended that there had been a violation of Article 8 of the Convention, which provides:

> 1. Everyone has the right to respect for his private and family life, his home, and his correspondence.

> 2. There shall be no interference by a public authority with the exercise of this right except such as is in accordance with the law and is necessary in a democratic society in the interests of national security, public safety or the economic well-being of the country, for the prevention of disorder or crime, for the protection of health or morals, or for the protection of the rights and freedoms of others....

The [European] Commission [on Human Rights] subscribed to this view, while the Government contested it....

The Audiencia [appellate court] [stated that] ... the nuisances in issue impaired the quality of life of those living in the plant's vicinity, but it held that this impairment was not serious enough to infringe the fundamental rights recognised in the Constitution .

Naturally, severe environmental pollution may affect individuals' well-being and prevent them from enjoying their homes in such a way as to affect their private and family life adversely, without, however, seriously endangering their health.

Whether the question is analysed in terms of a positive duty on the State to take reasonable and appropriate measures to secure the applicant's rights under paragraph 1 of Article 8, as the applicant wishes in her case, or in terms of an "interference by a public authority," to be justified in accordance with paragraph 2, the applicable principles are broadly similar. In both contexts regard must be had to the fair balance that has to be struck between the competing interests of the individual and of the community as a whole, and in any case the State enjoys a certain margin of appreciation. Furthermore, even in relation to the positive obligations flowing from the first paragraph of Article 8, in striking the required balance the aims mentioned in the second paragraph may be of a certain relevance.

It appears from the evidence that the waste-treatment plant in issue was built by SACURSA in July 1988 to solve a serious pollution problem in Lorca due to the concentration of tanneries. Yet as soon as it started up, the plant caused nuisance and health problems to many local people.

Admittedly, the Spanish authorities, and in particular the Lorca municipality, were theoretically not directly responsible for the emissions in question. However, as the Commission pointed out, the town allowed the plant to be built on its land and the State subsidised the plant's construction.

The town council reacted promptly by rehousing the residents affected, free of charge, in the town centre for the months of July, August, and September 1988 and then by stopping one of the plant's activities from 9 September . However, the council's members could not be unaware that the environmental problems continued after this partial shutdown. This was, moreover, confirmed as early as 19 January 1989 by the regional Environment and Nature Agency's report and then by expert opinions in 1991, 1992 and 1993.

Mrs. López Ostra submitted that by virtue of the general supervisory powers conferred on the municipality by the 1961 regulations the municipality had a duty to act. In addition, the plant did not satisfy the legal requirements, in particular as regards to its location and the failure to obtain a municipal license.

On this issue the Court points out that the question of the lawfulness of the building and operation of the plant has been pending in the Supreme Court since 1991. The Court has consistently held that it is primarily for the national authorities, notably the courts, to interpret and apply domestic law.

At all events, the Court considers that in the present case, even supposing that the municipality did fulfill the functions assigned to it by domestic law, it need only establish whether the national authorities took the measures necessary for protecting the applicant's right to respect for her home and for her private and family life under Article 8.

It has to be noted that the municipality not only failed to take steps to that end after 9 September 1988 but also resisted judicial decisions to that effect. In the ordinary administrative proceedings instituted by Mrs. López Ostra's sisters-in-law it appealed against the Murcia High Court's decision of 18 September 1991 ordering temporary closure of the plant, and that measure was suspended as a result.

Other State authorities also contributed to prolonging the situation. On 19 November 1991 Crown Counsel appealed against the Lorca investigating judge's decision of 15 November temporarily to close the plant in the prosecution for an environmental health offence with the result that the order was not enforced until 27 October 1993....

Having regard to the foregoing, and despite the margin of appreciation left to the respondent State, the Court considers that the State did not succeed in striking a fair balance between the interest of the town's economic well-being—that of having a waste-treatment plant—and the applicant's effective enjoyment of her right to respect for her home and her private and family life.

There has accordingly been a violation of Article 8.

III. ALLEGED VIOLATION OF ARTICLE 3 OF THE CONVENTION

[The Court rejected an argument that Article 3, prohibiting inhuman or degrading treatment or punishment, had also been violated.]

IV. APPLICATION OF ARTICLE 50 OF THE CONVENTION ...

Mrs. López Ostra claimed compensation for damage and reimbursement of costs and expenses.

A. Damage ...

The Court accepts that Mrs. López Ostra sustained some damage on account of the violation of Article 8. Her old flat must have depreciated and the obligation to move must have entailed expense and inconvenience.

The applicant, moreover, undeniably sustained non-pecuniary damage. In addition to the nuisance caused by the gas fumes, noise and smells from the plant, she felt distress and anxiety as she saw the situation persisting and her daughter's health deteriorating.

The heads of damage accepted do not lend themselves to precise quantification. Making an assessment on an equitable basis in accordance with Article 50, the Court awards Mrs. López Ostra ESP 4,000,000 [Spanish pesetas].

B. Costs and expenses [for attorneys and court fees] ...

In the light of the criteria laid down in its case-law, the Court considers it equitable to award the applicant 1,500,000 [Spanish pesetas] under this head, less the 9,700 French francs paid by the Council of Europe.

Questions and Discussion

1. *Margin of appreciation.* In interpreting Article 8 of the Convention, the Court states that "regard must be had to the fair balance that has to be struck between the competing interests of the individual and of the community as a whole." In evaluating this balance the Court uses a "margin of appreciation" doctrine. Under this doctrine, the Court allows the state a certain degree of discretion in determining the appropriate balance. Does the Court indicate what factors go into this balance and analysis, or is it entirely up to the judges in each case or to the state?

2. *National jurisprudence and legislation.* In order for Convention-based human rights to become truly embedded in the legal system of a country, the national courts of that country must *also* begin making decisions similar to that of the European Court of Human Rights. What kind of guidance does the European Court of Human Rights' (EHCR's) *López Ostra* decision give to the national courts of Spain and other countries governed by the European Convention? How are they to determine how to handle future claims involving pollution and private homes? Furthermore, in order for such rights to become embedded in the culture, practices, and legislation of a country, legislatures must be able to draw lessons from the ECHR decision. If you were advising a legislator, how would you state the lessons,

or rules, that emerge from the *López Ostra* decision, which should be considered in any future legislation?

3. *Holding.* In order to promote consistency from one person to the next, one country to the next, and one problem to the next similar one, future panels of the ECHR must be able to ascertain the "holding" of the *López Ostra* decision and apply it. Can you state the ECHR's holding?

4. *Exhaustion of Remedies.* Exhaustion of national remedies is a requirement under Article 35 (1) of the Convention that must normally be satisfied before filing a complaint to the European Court of Human Rights. It has proved to be one of the main obstacles to gaining access to the Court (and other international tribunals). In *López Ostra*, however, the ECHR merely required the exploration of special domestic remedies applicable to fundamental human rights and did not require the applicant to exhaust ordinary administrative domestic remedies before challenging the operation of the plant. The Court held:

> [I]t was not necessary for the applicant to institute ordinary criminal and administrative proceedings since the special application for protection of fundamental rights lodged with the Audiencia Territorial was an effective, rapid means of obtaining redress in the case of her complaints relating to her right to respect for her home and for her physical integrity, especially since that application could have had the outcome she desired, namely closure of the waste-treatment plant.

If you were a judge on the ECHR, how would you apply this standard in future cases where the applicant has not exhausted all domestic remedies?

5. *New evidence.* Medical reports (forming the ground for the complaint) were submitted to the ECHR directly. If the administrative or judicial review process lasts long, new facts and evidence can appear while a complaint is being considered in national courts or the European Court of Human Rights. In *López Ostra v. Spain* the ECHR considered government objections to this procedure to be unfounded, saying that "where a situation under consideration is a persisting one, the Court may take into account facts occurring after the application has been lodged and even after the decision on admissibility has been adopted."

6. *Giacomelli v. Italy.* A homeowner complained of pollution from a waste storage and treatment plant about 30 meters from her home. The state authorities had granted permission to operate the plant and increase the quantity of waste processed there without conducting an environmental impact assessment ("EIA") to ensure the plant's compliance with Italy's environmental laws. Eventually, when the plant operator applied for relicensing five years later, an EIA was conducted. Even though the EIA indicated that the plant was in violation of two different Italian environmental laws, the authorities did not suspend operation of the plant as required by law. The ECHR held that the state conduct violated Article 8 because the state authorities deprived the homeowner of her procedural rights by failing to complete an EIA in the first instance and by failing to suspend the plant's operation when the EIA was eventually completed. *Giacomelli v. Italy*, App. No. 59909/00, ECHR 2006, (2007) 45 E.H.R.R. 38, judgment of 2 November 2006. What is the difference between a substantive Article 8 claim and a procedural one? Which one is easier for a court to decide? Which one is easier for the government to rectify?

7. *Kyrtatos v. Greece.* A homeowner lived near a swamp that was a protected bird habitat. The local authorities had redrawn the urban growth boundary to include the swamp and subsequently authorized development in the swamp. The homeowner challenged the development under Article 8 claiming, *inter alia*, that the general degradation of the en-

vironment violated Article 8. The court rejected the contention. It ruled that Article 8 prevents pollution only when it affects an individual's right to private and family life, and as such, challenges to state decisions that cause the general degradation of the environment are not actionable under Article 8. *Kyrtatos v. Greece*, App. No. 41666/98, ECHR 2003-VI (extracts), (2005) 40 E.H.R.R. 16, judgment of 22 May 2003. Do you agree with the Court's analysis? Can you think of any arguments for a reading of Article 8 that would provide relief when an applicant complains of general environmental degradation?

Guerra v. Italy
European Court of Human Rights
Application No. 14967/89, *Reports of Judgments and Decisions*
1998-I, (1998) 26 E.H.R.R. 357
Judgment of 19 February 1998

The President, Judge BERNHARDT; Judges THÓR VILHJÁLMSSON, GÖLCÜKLÜ, MATSCHER, WALSH, MACDONALD, RUSSO, SPIELMANN, PALM, LOIZOU, SIR JOHN FREELAND, LOPES ROCHA, MIFSUD BONNICI, MAKARCZYK, REPIK, JAMBREK, KURIS, LEVITS, CASADEVALL, VAN DIJK

The 40 applicants lived in the town of Manfredonia, approximately 1km from a chemical factory which produced fertilisers and other chemicals. In 1988, the factory was classified as "high risk" according to criteria set out by Presidential Decree. Emissions from the factory were often channeled towards Manfredonia. The applicants complained that the authorities had not taken appropriate action to reduce the risk of pollution by the factory and to prevent the risk of accident. This, they argued, infringed their rights to life and physical integrity under Article 2 of the Convention. They also complained that the State had failed to take steps to provide information about the risks and how to proceed in the event of an accident. They argued that this involved a breach of their right to freedom of information under Article 10 of the Convention. The Commission declared the case admissible only in relation to the complaint under Article 10. Before the Court, the applicants relied not only on Article 10, but also Article 2. In addition, they complained before the Court that their right to respect for family life under Article 8 of the Convention had been infringed, as a result of the authorities' failure to provide them with the relevant information.

THE FACTS

I. THE CIRCUMSTANCES OF THE CASE

A. The Enichem agriculture factory

The applicants all live in the town of Manfredonia (Foggia). Approximately 1km away is the Enichem agriculture company's chemical factory, which lies within the municipality of Monte Sant'Angelo....

In 1988 the factory, which produced fertilisers and caprolactam (a chemical compound producing, by a process of polycondensation, a polyamide used in the manufacture of synthetic fibres such as nylon), was classified as "high risk" according to the criteria set out in Presidential Decree [D.P.R.] No. 175 of 18 May 1988, which transposed into Italian law. Directive 82/501/EEC of the Council of the European Communities on the major-accident hazards of certain industrial activities dangerous to the environment and the well being of the local population....

The applicants said that in the course of its production cycle the factory released large quantities of inflammable gas—a process which could have led to explosive chemical reactions, releasing highly toxic substances—and sulphur dioxide, nitric oxide, sodium, ammonia, metal hydrides, benzoic acid and, above all, arsenic trioxide. These assertions have not been disputed by the Government.

Accidents due to malfunctioning have already occurred in the past, the most serious one on 26 September 1976 when the scrubbing tower for the ammonia synthesis gases exploded, allowing several tonnes of potassium carbonate and bicarbonate solution, containing arsenic trioxide, to escape. One-hundred-and-fifty people were admitted to hospital with acute arsenic poisoning.

In a report of 8 December 1988 a committee of technical experts appointed by Manfredonia District Council established that because of the factory's geographical position, emissions from it into the atmosphere were often channelled towards Manfredonia. It was noted in the report that the factory had refused to allow the committee to carry out an inspection and that the results of a study by the factory itself showed that the emission treatment equipment was inadequate and the environmental impact assessment incomplete.

In 1989 the factory restricted its activity to the production of fertilisers, and it was accordingly still classified as a dangerous factory covered by D.P.R. 175/88....

In 1994 the factory permanently stopped producing fertiliser. Only a thermoelectric power station and plant for the treatment of feed and waste water continued to operate....

D. Steps taken to inform the local population

Articles 11 and 17 of D.P.R. 175/88 require the relevant mayor and prefect to inform local inhabitants of the hazards of the industrial activity concerned, the safety measures taken, the plans made for emergencies, and the procedure to be followed in the event of an accident.

On 2 October 1992 the Co-ordinating Committee for Industrial Safety Measures gave its opinion on the emergency plan that had been drawn up by the Prefect of Foggia, in accordance with Article 17(1) of D.P.R. 175/88. On 3 August 1993 the plan was sent to the relevant committee of the Civil Defence Department. In a letter of 12 August 1993 the under-secretary of the Civil Defence Department assured the Prefect of Foggia that the plan would be submitted promptly to the Co-ordinating Committee for its opinion and expressed the hope that it could be put into effect as quickly as possible, given the sensitive issues raised by planning for emergencies.

On 14 September 1993 the Ministry for the Environment and the Ministry for Health jointly adopted conclusions on the factory's safety report of July 1989, as required by Article 19 of D.P.R. 175/88. Those conclusions prescribed a number of improvements to be made to the installations, both in relation to fertiliser production and in the event of resumed caprolactam production and provided the Prefect with instructions as to the emergency plan for which he was responsible and the measures required for informing the local population under Article 17 of D.P.R. 175/88.

In a letter of 7 December 1995 to the European Commission of Human Rights, however, the mayor of Monte Sant'Angelo indicated ... that he had not received any documents relating to [conclusions of the Ministries of Environment and Health under Article 19]. He pointed out that the District Council was still awaiting direction from the Civil Defence Department before deciding what safety measures should be taken and what procedures should be followed in the event of an accident and communicated to the public. He said that if the factory resumed production, the measures for informing the public would be taken as soon as the conclusions based on the investigation were available....

III. WORK BY THE COUNCIL OF EUROPE

Of particular relevance among the various Council of Europe documents in the field under consideration in the present case is [Council of Europe] Parliamentary Assembly Resolution 1087 (1996) on the consequences of the Chernobyl disaster, which was adopted on 26 April 1996.... Referring not only to the risks associated with the production and use of nuclear energy in the civil sector but also to other matters, it states "public access to clear and full information ... must be viewed as a basic human right." ...

JUDGMENT

III. ALLEGED VIOLATION OF ARTICLE 8 OF THE CONVENTION

The applicants, relying on the same facts, maintained before the Court that they had been the victims of a violation of Article 8 of the Convention....

The Court's task is to determine whether Article 8 is applicable and, if so, whether it has been infringed....

The direct effect of the toxic emissions on the applicants' right to respect for their private and family life means that Article 8 is applicable.

The Court considers that Italy cannot be said to have "interfered" with the applicants' private or family life; they complained not of an act by the State but of its failure to act. However, although the object of Article 8 is essentially that of protecting the individual against arbitrary interference by the public authorities, it does not merely compel the State to abstain from such interference: in addition to this primarily negative undertaking, there may be positive obligations inherent in effective respect for private or family life....

The Court reiterates that severe environmental pollution may affect individuals' well being and prevent them from enjoying their homes in such a way as to affect their private and family life adversely. In the instant case the applicants waited, right up until the production of fertilisers ceased in 1994, for essential information that would have enabled them to assess the risks they and their families might run if they continued to live at Manfredonia, a town particularly exposed to danger in the event of an accident at the factory.

The Court holds, therefore, that the respondent State did not fulfil its obligation to secure the applicants' right to respect for their private and family life, in breach of Article 8 of the Convention.

IV. ALLEGED VIOLATION OF ARTICLE 2 OF THE CONVENTION

[The Court ruled that because it found a violation under Article 8, there was no need to consider an additional claim under Article 2, the right to life.]

V. APPLICATION OF ARTICLE 50 OF THE CONVENTION ...

A. Damage ...

The Court considers that the applicants did not show that they had sustained any pecuniary damage as a result of the lack of information of which they complained. As to the rest, it holds that the applicants undoubtedly suffered non-pecuniary damage and awards them 10,000,000 lire each....

C. Other claims

Lastly, the applicants sought an order from the Court requiring the respondent State to decontaminate the entire industrial estate concerned, to carry out an epidemiological study of the area and the local population, and to undertake an inquiry to identify the possible serious effects on residents most exposed to substances believed to be carcinogenic.

The Government submitted that those claims were inadmissible.

The Delegate of the Commission expressed the view that a thorough and efficient inquiry by the national authorities together with the publication and communication to the applicants of a full, accurate report on all the relevant aspects of the factory's operation over the period in question, including the harm actually caused to the environment and people's health, in addition to the payment of just satisfaction, would meet the obligation laid down in Article 53 of the Convention.

The Court notes that the Convention does not empower it to accede to such a request. It reiterates that it is for the State to choose the means to be used in its domestic legal system in order to comply with the provisions of the Convention or to redress the situation that has given rise to the violation of the Convention. . . .

THE COURT . . .

3. *Holds* unanimously that Article 8 of the Convention is applicable and has been infringed;

4. *Holds* unanimously that it is unnecessary to consider the case under Article 2 of the Convention. . . .

CONCURRING OPINION OF JUDGE WALSH

While bearing in mind that a breach of the Convention can frequently have implications for Articles other than the Article claimed to have been violated, I am fully in agreement that on the particular facts of this case Article 8 is the more appropriate article to examine than Article 10. The Convention and its Articles must be construed harmoniously. While the Court in its judgment has briefly mentioned Article 2, but has not ruled on it, I am of the opinion that this provision has also been violated.

In my view Article 2 also guarantees the protection of the bodily integrity of the applicants. The wording of Article 3 also clearly indicates that the Convention extends to the protection of bodily integrity. In my opinion there was a violation of Article 2 in the present case and in the circumstances it is not necessary to go beyond this provision in finding a violation. . . .

CONCURRING OPINION OF JUDGE JAMBREK

In their memorial the applicants also expressly complained of a violation of Article 2 of the Convention. The Court held that it was not necessary to consider the case under that Article given that it had found a violation of Article 8. I wish, nevertheless, to make some observations on the possible applicability of Article 2 in this case.

Article 2 states that "Everyone's right to life shall be protected by law. No one shall be deprived of his life intentionally save. . . ." The protection of health and physical integrity is, in my view, as closely associated with the "right to life" as with the "respect for private and family life." An analogy may be made with the Court's case law on Article 3 concerning the existence of "foreseeable consequences"; where—mutatis mutandis—substantial grounds can be shown for believing that the person(s) concerned face a real risk of being subjected to circumstances which endanger their health and physical integrity, and thereby put at serious risk their right to life, protected by law. If information is withheld by a government about circumstances which foreseeably, and on substantial grounds, present a real risk of danger to health and physical integrity, then such a situation may also be protected by Article 2 of the Convention: "No one shall be deprived of his life intentionally."

It may therefore be time for the Court's case law on Article 2 (the right to life) to start evolving, to develop the respective implied rights, articulate situations of real and serious risk to life, or different aspects of the right to life. Article 2 also appears relevant and applicable to the facts of the instant case, in that 150 people were taken to hospital with severe arsenic poisoning. Through the release of harmful substances into the atmosphere, the activity carried on at the factory thus constituted a "major-accident hazard dangerous to the environment."

Questions and Discussion

1. *Scope of the Article 8 environmental rights.* How does the European Court of Human Rights interpret Article 8(1)? Does it include only direct measures taken by a public authority against a person's privacy and home, or also indirect unavoidable consequences of measures not specifically directed against individuals? Does the state have a positive obligation not only to respect but also to protect the rights guaranteed by Art. 8(1)? Does the court so hold?

2. *Article 2, right to life.* Are claims under Article 2 merely redundant, or could they provide relief when a claim under Article 8 might not succeed? Should Article 2 claims be available for ordinary pollution claims? Judge Walsh argued that it should be used in preference to Article 8. Does that have any advantages? The Court eventually brought Article 2 into play in a more serious context in *Öneryildiz v. Turkey*, in this chapter at page 49

3. *Article 10, right to expression.* Why do you suppose the Court avoids making a ruling that failure to provide information is a violation of Article 10, choosing Article 8 instead? Is turning Article 10 into an "access to information" right more adventurous than turning Article 8 into such a right? For more on courts interpreting freedom of expression guarantees as access to information rights, see pages 251 to 253 in chapter 6.

The Intersection of Human Rights and Environmental Protection in the European Court of Human Rights
Mariana T. Acevedo
8 N.Y.U. Envtl. L.J. 437 (2000)

Powell & Rayner v. United Kingdom [12 Eur. Ct. H.R. 355 (ser. A)(1990)] was the first case where the [European Court of Human Rights] explicitly recognized the interrelationship of the environment and quality of life. The applicants, owners of residences in the airport vicinity, alleged that the noise pollution generated by Heathrow's air traffic violated their right to privacy under Article 8 of the Convention. It found that noise pollution from Heathrow Airport interfered with the local residents' quality of life; however, the greater economic interest of the community at large justified such an interference....

While finding an impairment of this right, the Court adopted a two-part test to determine whether the interference was excused or justified. First, the Court looked at whether the State had a positive duty to secure the applicants' right to privacy. Then the Court posited a balancing test:

> In both contexts regard must be had to the fair balance that has to be struck between the competing interests of the individual and of the community as a whole; and in both contexts the State enjoys a certain margin of appreciation in determining the steps to be taken to ensure compliance with the Convention....

This interpretation had a significant impact on environmental claims. The standard set forth in *Powell & Rayner* essentially enabled States to set a low threshold for compliance on the assumption that their actions, absent nonfeasance, would be sufficiently within the margin of appreciation to merit a finding of an excused interference....

[I]n *López Ostra v. Spain* [see page 26], the Court held that an illegal operation of a waste treatment plant resulted in a violation of the right to privacy under Article 8 of the Convention. The applicant, who resided in the vicinity of a privately owned and operated solid and liquid waste-treatment facility, petitioned the Court complaining that she had suffered a violation of her right to privacy and freedom from torture....

In finding for the applicant, the Court employed the fair balance test set forth in Article 8(2) and examined whether the local authorities struck "a fair balance between the interest of the town's economic well-being—that of having a waste-treatment plant—and the applicant's effective enjoyment of her right to respect for her home and her private and family life." The Court found that Spanish authorities had failed to enforce domestic law by enabling the facility to operate without a license and without compliance with the appropriate national standards. This amounted to a breach of its affirmative duty to ensure the respect for home and private life under Article 8(1).

López Ostra represents a significant turning point for environmental claims under the Convention regime. It was the first case in which "the organs of the European Convention found a breach of the Convention as a consequence of environmental harm." Moreover, Spain was found to have breached an affirmative duty to act to ensure the respect of a derivative right not explicitly set forth under the Convention regime, the right to live in an environment not adverse to one's health. This finding of direct responsibility for actions for which Spanish authorities may not have been directly responsible had serious implications for environmental cases. It changed the inquiry into the parties that could be found responsible for environmental harm and recognized a right to live in an environment of quality, despite evidentiary difficulties in demonstrating causation. In other words, by couching Spain's nonfeasance as a violation of the applicant's right to the enjoyment of her home and family life, the Court implied that the applicant had a right to live in an environment which would not be actively detrimental to her health....

Finally, the significance of the *López Ostra* decision is evident in the Court's award of compensatory damages for environmental harm.... The finding is extraordinary because it marked a departure from the general practice envisaged by the Convention's drafters, which presumed that determinations of damages were matters to be remanded to the national judicial bodies of the Contracting Parties. However, the Court did not provide any guidance as to how it reached this determination....

Clearly, the organs of the European Convention conceived the relationship between environmental rights and human rights as one in which existing human rights norms could be reinterpreted to address environmental justice issues. Furthermore, it is evident that in applying existing human rights norms to environmental issues the Court accommodated claims brought pursuant to civil and political rights, as claims from which environmental rights can be derived. This accommodation is consistent with the Court's interpretation of the Convention as an evolving document responsive to the changing needs of its intended beneficiaries....

The Court's holding [in *Guerra v. Italy*, see p. 31] is significant for its finding that States must not only refrain from interfering with the rights of its inhabitants, but must also take affirmative steps to ensure the fulfillment of those rights. The potential applications of this holding, if applied consistently, are far-reaching and may have an important impact on environmental litigation before the Court. The Court's finding turns on the identification of a high-risk or unhealthy environment that the applicants should have been able to opt out of, but could not due to the State's failure to provide the applicants with access to information concerning the potential hazards of remaining....

Having found a violation pursuant to Article 8, the Court found it unnecessary to pursue the applicants' claims under Article 2. Accordingly, the Court turned to a valuation of damages under Article 50 and awarded the applicants' just satisfaction in the form of compensatory damages. The Court held that Italy was liable for 400 million lire in non-pecuniary damage; however, as in *López Ostra*, the Court did not explain how it arrived at that figure....

The issue of valuation of damages in environmental law continues to be highly controversial due to the lack of clear rules and procedures.... The questions of who is responsible for how long, for how much, and by what proof are next to impossible to measure accurately. Yet it is precisely for this reason that the Court's award is noteworthy.... In keeping with the Court's attribution of third-party responsibility in *López Ostra*, the Court made clear that nonfeasance was not adequate where an opportunity for action existed. The Court moved away from its past deference to the margin of appreciation doctrine....

In *Guerra*, the Court confirmed its earlier finding in *López Ostra*, that environmental pollution that adversely affects the enjoyment of one's home and family life violates the right to privacy under Article 8 of the Convention, and extended its application to include access to information which might enable individuals to assess the risks of living in proximity to a polluter....

Questions and Discussion

1. *Damages*. The ECHR has never laid out a formula for damages in an Article 8 environmental case. What type of formula or factors would you suggest in determining liability in one of these cases? Is such a formulation possible?

2. *Pre-Hatton Note*. This article was written before the ECHR's decision in *Hatton v. United Kingdom*, an excerpt of which comes next. After reading *Hatton*, below, revisit this article and consider what *Hatton* has done to change or clarify an Article 8 environmental challenge.

2. Weakening of Article 8?

Having seen the creation and flowering of an environmental right in *Guerra* and *López Ostra*, examine the following case. Consider whether the Court's doctrines started to change with this case. Think about whether this case indicates reluctance by the Court to further expand Article 8's implied environmental rights or whether the Court's judgment resulted from certain distinguishable facts particular to the applicants in this case.

Hatton v. United Kingdom
European Court of Human Rights (Grand Chamber)
Application No. 36022/97, ECHR 2003-VIII
Judgment of 8 July 2003

The President, Judge WILDHABER; Judges COSTA, RESS, BONELLO, PALM, CABRAL BARRETO, TÜRMEN, STRÁŽNICKÁ, BUTKEVYCH, ZUPANČIČ, VAJIČ, BOTOUCHAROVA, KOVLER, ZAGREBELSKY, STEINER, PAVLOVSCHI, BRIAN KERR

[The applicant's] house was 11.7 km from the end of the nearest runway at Heathrow and fell within a daytime noise contour where the level of disturbance from aircraft noise was between 57 and 60 dBA Leq. According to the Government, dBA Leq measure the average degree of community annoyance from aircraft noise over a sixteen-hour daytime period and studies have shown that in areas where the daytime noise exposure is below 57 dBA Leq there is no significant community annoyance. The Government state that a daytime noise contour of 57 dBA Leq represents a low level of annoyance; 63 dBA Leq represent a moderate level of annoyance; 69 dBA Leq correspond to a high level of annoyance; and 72 dBA Leq represent a very high level of annoyance.

According to [the applicant] Ms. Hatton, in 1993 the level of night noise increased and she began to find noise levels to be "intolerable" at night. She believed that the noise was greater when aircraft were landing at Heathrow from the east. When this happened, Ms. Hatton was unable to sleep without ear plugs and her children were frequently woken up before 6 a.m., and sometimes before 5 a.m. If Ms. Hatton did not wear ear plugs, she would be woken by aircraft activity at around 4 a.m. She was sometimes able to go back to sleep, but found it impossible to go back to sleep once the "early morning bombardment" started which, in the winter of 1996/1997, was between 5 a.m. and 5.30 a.m. When she was woken in this manner, Ms. Hatton tended to suffer from a headache for the rest of the day. When aircraft were landing from the west the noise levels were lower, and Ms. Hatton's children slept much better, generally not waking up until after 6.30 a.m. In the winter of 1993/1994, Ms. Hatton became so run down and depressed by her broken sleep pattern that her doctor prescribed anti-depressants. In October 1997, she moved with her family to Kingston-upon-Thames in order to get away from the aircraft noise at night.... Heathrow Airport is the busiest airport in Europe, and the busiest international airport in the world. It is used by over 90 airlines, serving over 180 destinations worldwide. It is the United Kingdom's leading port in terms of visible trade....

On 6 July 1993 the Secretary of State for Transport announced his intention to introduce, with effect from October 1993, a quota system of night flying restrictions [the "1993 scheme"], the stated aim of which was to reduce noise at the three main London airports, which included Heathrow....

The British Air Transport Association (BATA) commissioned a report from Coopers & Lybrand into the economic costs of maintaining the restrictions on night flights.... The report concluded that the economic cost of the then current restrictions being maintained during the period 1997/1998 to 2002/2003 was about 850 million pounds sterling (GBP)....

A series of noise mitigation and abatement measures is in place at Heathrow Airport, in addition to restrictions on night flights....

The applicants complained that the government policy on night flights at Heathrow introduced in 1993 violated their rights under Article 8 of the Convention....

Article 8 protects the individual's right to respect for his or her private and family life, home and correspondence. There is no explicit right in the Convention to a clean and quiet environment, but where an individual is directly and seriously affected by noise or other pollution, an issue may arise under Article 8. Thus, in *Powell Rayner v. the United Kingdom*, where the applicants had complained about disturbance from daytime aircraft noise, the Court held that Article 8 was relevant, since "the quality of [each] applicant's private life and the scope for enjoying the amenities of his home [had] been adversely affected by the noise generated by aircraft using Heathrow Airport." Similarly, in *López Ostra v. Spain* the Court held that Article 8 could include a right to protection from severe environmental pollution, since such a problem might "affect individuals' well-being and prevent them from enjoying their homes in such a way as to affect their private and family life adversely, without, however, seriously endangering their health." In *Guerra v. Italy*, which, like *López Ostra,* concerned environmental pollution, the Court observed that "[the] direct effect of the toxic emissions on the applicants' right to respect for their private and family life means that Article 8 is applicable."

At the same time, the Court reiterates the fundamentally subsidiary role of the Convention. The national authorities have direct democratic legitimation and are, as the Court has held on many occasions, in principle better placed than an international court to evaluate local needs and conditions. In matters of general policy, on which opinions within a democratic society may reasonably differ widely, the role of the domestic policy-maker should be given special weight.

Article 8 may apply in environmental cases whether the pollution is directly caused by the State or whether State responsibility arises from the failure to regulate private industry properly. Whether the case is analysed in terms of a positive duty on the State to take reasonable and appropriate measures to secure the applicants' rights under paragraph 1 of Article 8 or in terms of an interference by a public authority to be justified in accordance with paragraph 2, the applicable principles are broadly similar. In both contexts regard must be had to the fair balance that has to be struck between the competing interests of the individual and of the community as a whole; and in both contexts the State enjoys a certain margin of appreciation in determining the steps to be taken to ensure compliance with the Convention....

The Court considers that in a case such as the present one, involving State decisions affecting environmental issues, there are two aspects to the inquiry which may be carried out by the Court. First, the Court may assess the substantive merits of the government's decision, to ensure that it is compatible with Article 8. Secondly, it may scrutinise the decision-making process to ensure that due weight has been accorded to the interests of the individual.

In relation to the substantive aspect, the Court has held that the State must be allowed a wide margin of appreciation....

The Court is ... faced with conflicting views as to the margin of appreciation to be applied: on the one hand, the Government claim a wide margin on the ground that the case concerns matters of general policy, and, on the other hand, the applicants' claim that where the ability to sleep is affected, the margin is narrow because of the "intimate" nature of the right protected. This conflict of views on the margin of appreciation can be resolved only by reference to the context of a particular case.

In connection with the procedural element of the Court's review of cases involving environmental issues, the Court is required to consider all the procedural aspects, including the type of policy or decision involved, the extent to which the views of individuals (including the applicants) were taken into account throughout the decision-making procedure, and the procedural safeguards available....

The case concerns the way in which the applicants were affected by the implementation in 1993 of the new scheme for regulating night flights at Heathrow....

The 1993 Scheme accepted the conclusions of the 1992 sleep study that for the large majority of people living near airports there was no risk of substantial sleep disturbance due to aircraft noise and that only a small percentage of individuals (some 2 to 3%) were more sensitive than others. On this basis, disturbances caused by aircraft noise were regarded as negligible in relation to overall normal disturbance rates. The 1992 sleep study continued to be relied upon by the government in their 1998/99 review of the regulations for night flights, when it was acknowledged that further research was necessary, in particular as regards sleep prevention, and a number of further studies on the subject were commissioned.

The Court has no doubt that the implementation of the 1993 Scheme was susceptible of adversely affecting the quality of the applicants' private life and the scope for their enjoying the amenities of their respective homes, and thus their rights protected by Article 8 of the Convention....

The Court notes at the outset that in previous cases in which environmental questions gave rise to violations of the Convention, the violation was predicated on a failure by the national authorities to comply with some aspect of the domestic regime. Thus, in *López Ostra*, the waste-treatment plant at issue was illegal in that it operated without the necessary licence, and was eventually closed down. In *Guerra*, the violation was also founded on an irregular position at the domestic level, as the applicants had been unable to obtain information that the State was under a statutory obligation to provide.

This element of domestic irregularity is wholly absent in the present case....

In order to justify the night flight scheme in the form in which it has operated since 1993, the Government refer not only to the economic interests of the operators of airlines and other enterprises as well as their clients, but also, and above all, to the economic interests of the country as a whole....

The Court must consider whether the State can be said to have struck a fair balance between those interests and the conflicting interests of the persons affected by noise disturbances, including the applicants. Environmental protection should be taken into consideration by States in acting within their margin of appreciation and by the Court in its review of that margin, but it would not be appropriate for the Court to adopt a special approach in this respect by reference to a special status of environmental human rights. In this context the Court must revert to the question of the scope of the margin of appreciation available to the State when taking policy decisions of the kind at issue....

The Court's supervisory function being of a subsidiary nature, it is limited to reviewing whether or not the particular solution adopted can be regarded as striking a fair balance....

As to the economic interests which conflict with the desirability of limiting or halting night flights in pursuance of the above aims, the Court considers it reasonable to assume that those flights contribute at least to a certain extent to the general economy. The Government have produced to the Court reports on the results of a series of inquiries on the economic value of night flights, carried out both before and after the 1993 Scheme.... One can readily accept that there is an economic interest in maintaining a full service to London from distant airports, and it is difficult, if not impossible, to draw a clear line between the interests of the aviation industry and the economic interests of the country as a whole....

A further relevant factor in assessing whether the right balance has been struck is the availability of measures to mitigate the effects of aircraft noise generally, including night noise. A number of measures are referred to above. The Court also notes that the applicants do not contest the substance of the Government's claim that house prices in the areas in which they live have not been adversely affected by the night noise. The Court considers it reasonable, in determining the impact of a general policy on individuals in a particular area, to take into account the individuals' ability to leave the area. Where a limited number of people in an area (2 to 3% of the affected population, according to the

1992 sleep study) are particularly affected by a general measure, the fact that they can, if they choose, move elsewhere without financial loss must be significant to the overall reasonableness of the general measure.

On the procedural aspect of the case, the Court notes that a governmental decision-making process concerning complex issues of environmental and economic policy such as in the present case must necessarily involve appropriate investigations and studies in order to allow them to strike a fair balance between the various conflicting interests at stake.... The 1993 Scheme had thus been preceded by a series of investigations and studies carried out over a long period of time.... Had any representations not been taken into account, they could have challenged subsequent decisions, or the scheme itself, in the courts.

In these circumstances the Court does not find that, in substance, the authorities overstepped their margin of appreciation by failing to strike a fair balance between the right of the individuals affected by those regulations to respect for their private life and home and the conflicting interests of others and of the community as a whole, nor does it find that there have been fundamental procedural flaws in the preparation of the 1993 regulations on limitations for night flights.

There has accordingly been no violation of Article 8 of the Convention.

Comment
David Hart QC
July 2003
http://www.humanrights.org.uk/200/text.nc

The successful outcome of the government's appeal [in *Hatton*] was generally anticipated in many quarters. Whichever way one looks at this judgment, the conclusion that the Court has opted for a retrograde approach to "environmental rights" is hard to resist.

The reasoning turns on the interpretation of a government's "positive obligations" under the Convention, particularly Article 8. The Court seeks to distinguish the present issue from those at the core of previous environmental cases by stressing that the *Hatton* claimants could not point to any breach of domestic regulation....

[As for balancing individual rights against economic needs, the judges in a previous ruling, before the Grand Chamber issue its ruling] had reached the view that, in the particularly sensitive field of environmental protection, mere reference to the economic well-being of the country was not sufficient to outweigh the rights of others.

The Grand Chamber responded to this with the somewhat startling statement (in the light of all that was said in *Guerra* and *López Ostra*) that:

Environmental protection should be taken into consideration by Governments in acting within their margin of appreciation and by the Court in its review of that margin, but it would not be appropriate for the Court to adopt a special approach in this respect by reference to a special status of environmental human rights.

What do we take this statement to mean? ... [In] the recent case of *Katsoulis v. Greece* ... the kernels of this present anti-environment efflorescence were exposed; there, it will be remembered, the Court concluded that damage caused by industrial development to the natural environment had insufficient impact on the health of neighbouring residents to engage Article 8. So do we take it that the line of cases including *López* and culminating in *Guerra* have reached the end of their particular cul de sac?

Not if the strongly worded dissent by Judges Costa, Ress, Turmen, Zupancic, and Steiner is anything to go by. Read without this dissenting opinion, it might appear from *Hatton* that environmental rights are now regarded as an embarrassing offshoot of the days when such rights seemed so far fetched as to seem positively unthreatening to macro economics, and therefore worth Strasbourg's championship. Not so, say the dissenters, who make a strong case for their argument that the Court should continue to develop environmental rights consistently with other implied rights in the Convention.

As they note at para 2 of their opinion, "In the field of environmental human rights, which was practically unknown in 1950, the Commission and the Court have increasingly taken the view that Article 8 embraces the right to a healthy environment, and therefore to protection against pollution and nuisances caused by harmful chemicals, offensive smells, agents which precipitate respiratory ailments, noise, and so on. At paragraph 5 they state, more pungently, that

> The Grand Chamber's judgment in the present case, in so far as it concludes, contrary to the Chamber's judgment of 2 October 2001, that there was no violation of Article 8, seems to us to deviate from the above developments in the case-law and even to take a step backwards. It gives precedence to economic considerations over basic health conditions in qualifying the applicants' "sensitivity to noise" as that of a small minority of people (para 118). The trend of playing down such sensitivity—and more specifically concerns about noise and disturbed sleep—runs counter to the growing concern over environmental issues, all over Europe and the world. A simple comparison of the above-mentioned (*Powell & Rayner*) with the present judgment seems to show that the Court is turning against the current.

Questions and Discussion

Relevance of domestic law. The Court in *Guerra* relied in part on Italian domestic law in finding a violation of Article 8. In *Hatton v. United Kingdom*, the Court found no violation—noting in part that the noise constituting the alleged interference with private and family life was not in violation of British domestic law. One commentator has observed:

> The existence of parallel domestic standards lessens the concern that the supranational tribunal will trespass onto sovereign territory by insisting that the state live up to an international obligation. Also, the institutional competence problem recedes if a state's legislative body commits a certain course of conduct to judicial supervision by enacting socioeconomic policy into law. The court does not manufacture an obligation out of supranational cloth but rather follows the domestic lead.

David Marcus, *The Normative Development of Socioeconomic Rights Through Supranational Adjudication*, 42 Stan. J. Int'l L. 53 (2006). Should the interpretation of international, treaty-based human rights "follow the domestic lead"? Another author has the following comment on such reasoning:

> There are ... very significant difficulties in [*Hatton's*] re-interpretation of the leading previous cases.
>
> (1) The previous decisions of the Strasbourg Court did not identify this domestic illegality as a necessary element in an environmental human rights complaint.

(2) It seems illogical to attach significant weight to domestic illegality given that Strasbourg caselaw attaches much more importance to their own "autonomous" conceptions of what does or not amount to a breach of a Convention right.

(3) Cases since have confirmed the principles of *López Ostra* and *Guerra* without discerning any such additional principle.

(4) The argument may often be circular, if, as often in countries incorporating the Convention, the Convention interference will amount to domestic illegality.

David Hart QC, *Environmental Rights and the Public Interest: Hatton v. United Kingdom/Dennis v. Ministry of Defence*, Seminar Paper delivered to the British Institute of International And Comparative Law on Thursday 24 July 2003, http://www.humanrights.org.uk/860/.

3. Reestablishing Rights, Providing Remedies, Enforcing Precedents

If the impression left from the *Hatton* case was that the Court's recognition of environmental rights through Article 8 had waned, the following case, two years later, presented a different picture.

Fadeyeva v. Russia

European Court of Human Rights
Application No. 55723/00, ECHR 2005-IV, (2007) 45 E.H.R.R. 10
Judgment of 30 November 2005

The President, Judge LORENZEN; Judges TULKEN, VAJIČ, BOTOUCHAROVA, KOVLER, ZAGREBELSKY

THE FACTS

A. Background

The applicant was born in 1949 and lives in the town of Cherepovets, an important steel-producing centre situated about 300 km north-east of Moscow. In 1982 her family moved to a flat situated at 1 Zhukov Street, about 450 metres from the territory of the "Severstal" steel-plant ("the plant").

The plant is the largest iron smelter in Russia and the main employer of approximately 60,000 people. In order to delimit the areas in which pollution caused by steel production could be excessive, the authorities established a buffer zone around the Severstal premises—"the sanitary security zone." It covered a 5,000 metre-wide area around the territory of the plant. Although this zone was, in theory, supposed to separate the plant from the town's residential areas, in practice thousands of people (including the applicant's family) lived there. The apartment buildings in the zone belonged to the plant and were designated mainly for its workers, who occupied the flats as life-long tenants. A Decree of the Council of Ministers of the RSFSR, dated 10 September 1974, obliged the Ministry of Black Metallurgy to resettle the inhabitants of the sanitary security zone who lived in districts nos. 213 and 214 by 1977. However, this has not been done.

In 1990 the Government of the [Russian Soviet Republic] adopted a programme that stated that "the concentration of toxic substances in the town's air exceeds the acceptable norms many times" and that the morbidity rate of Cherepovets residents was higher than average. It was noted that many people still lived within the steel-plant's sanitary security zone. Under the programme, the steel-plant was required to reduce its toxic emissions to safe levels by 1998. The steel-plant was also ordered to finance the construction of 20,000 square metres of residential property every year for the resettlement of people living within its sanitary security zone.

By municipal decree no. 30 of 18 November 1992 the boundaries of the sanitary security zone around the plant were redefined. The width of the zone was reduced to 1,000 metres.

In 1993 the steel-plant was privatized and acquired by Severstal PLC. In the course of privatisation the apartment buildings owned by the steel-plant and situated within the zone were transferred to the municipality.

On 3 October 1996 the Government of the Russian Federation adopted Decree no. 1161. Implementation of the 1996 programme was funded by the World Bank. The second paragraph of this programme stated as follows:

> The concentration of certain polluting substances in the town's residential areas is 20–50 times higher than the maximum permissible limits (MPLs).…[a] The biggest "contributor" to atmospheric pollution is Severstal PLC, which is responsible for 96 per cent of all emissions. The highest level of air pollution is registered in the residential districts immediately adjacent to Severstal's industrial territory.… The situation is aggravated by an almost complete overlap of industrial and residential areas of the city, in the absence of their separation by sanitary security zones.

The Decree further stated that "the environmental situation in the city has resulted in a continuing deterioration in public health." In particular, it stated that over the period 1991–95 the number of children with respiratory diseases increased from 345 to 945 cases per thousand, those with blood and haematogenic diseases from 3.4 to 11 cases per thousand, and those with skin diseases from 33.3 to 101.1 cases per thousand. The Decree also noted that the high level of atmospheric pollution accounted for the increase in respiratory and blood diseases among the city's adult population and the increased number of deaths from cancer.…

According to the State Report on the Environment for 1999, the Severstal plant in Cherepovets was the largest contributor to air pollution of all metallurgical plants in Russia.

B. The applicant's attempt to be resettled outside the zone

In 1995 the applicant brought a court action seeking resettlement outside the zone. The applicant alleged that the environmental situation in the zone was unfavourable for humans, and that living there was potentially dangerous to health and life.…

On 17 April 1996 the Town Court examined the applicant's action.… However, no specific order to resettle the applicant was given by the court in the operative part of its judgment. Instead, the court stated that the local authorities must place her on a "priority waiting list" to obtain new local authority housing.…

On 10 February 1997 the bailiff discontinued the enforcement proceedings on the ground that there was no "priority waiting list" for new housing for residents of the sanitary security zone.

In 1999 the applicant brought a fresh action against the municipality, seeking immediate execution of the judgment of 17 April 1996. The applicant claimed, inter alia, that

---

a MPLs are the safe levels of various polluting substances, as established by Russian legislation .

systematic toxic emissions and noise from Severstal PLC's facilities violated her basic right to respect for her private life and home, as guaranteed by the Russian Constitution and the European Convention on Human Rights. She asked to be provided with a flat in an ecologically safe area or with the means to purchase a new flat.

On 27 August 1999 the municipality placed the applicant on the general waiting list for new housing. She was number 6,820 on that list.

On 31 August 1999 the Town Court dismissed the applicant's action. The court noted that there was no priority waiting list for the resettlement of residents of sanitary security zones, and no council housing had been allocated for that purpose.... That judgment was upheld by the Vologda Regional Court on 17 November 1999....

THE LAW

I. ALLEGED VIOLATION OF ARTICLE 8 OF THE CONVENTION

The applicant alleged that there had been a violation of Article 8 of the Convention on account of the State's failure to protect her private life and home from severe environmental nuisance arising from the industrial activities of the Severstal steel-plant....

A. *Applicability of Article 8 in the present case*

Both parties agreed that the applicant's place of residence was affected by industrial pollution. Neither was it disputed that the main cause of pollution was the Severstal steel-plant, operating near the applicant's home.

The Court observes, however, that the degree of disturbance caused by Severstal and the effects of pollution on the applicant are disputed by the parties. Whereas the applicant insists that the pollution seriously affected her private life and health, the respondent Government assert that the harm suffered by the applicant as a result of her home's location within the sanitary security zone was not such as to raise an issue under Article 8 of the Convention....

[The Court concluded that because the applicant's health deteriorated as a result of her prolonged exposure to the industrial emissions from the Severstal steel-plant, the actual detriment to the applicant's health and well-being reached a level sufficient to bring it within the scope of Article 8 of the Convention.]

B. *Holding under Article 8 § 2 ...*

(1) The Court's assessment

(i) *The alleged failure to resettle the applicant*

The Court notes at the outset that the environmental consequences of the Severstal steel-plant's operations do not comply with the environmental and health standards established in the relevant Russian legislation. In order to maintain the operation of an important enterprise of this type, the Russian legislation, as a compromise solution, has provided for the creation of a buffer zone around the enterprise's premises in which pollution may officially exceed safe levels. Therefore, the existence of such a zone is a condition *sine qua non* for the operation of a dangerous enterprise—otherwise it must be closed or significantly restructured....

The Government submitted that the pollution levels attributable to the metallurgic industry are the same if not higher in other districts of Cherepovets than those registered near the applicant's home. However, this proves only that the Severstal steel-plant has failed to comply with domestic environmental norms ...

It is material that the applicant moved to this location in 1982 knowing that the environmental situation in the area was very unfavourable. However, given the shortage of housing at that time and the fact that almost all residential buildings in industrial towns belonged to the State, it is very probable that the applicant had no choice other than to accept the flat offered to her family.…

The Court reiterates that the Russian legislation directly prohibits building of any residential property within a sanitary security zone. However, the law does not clearly indicate what should be done with those persons who already live within such a zone.… [T]he Russian legislation as applied by the domestic courts and national authorities makes no difference between those persons who are entitled to new housing, free of charge, on a welfare basis (war veterans, large families etc.) and those whose everyday life is seriously disrupted by toxic fumes from a neighbouring enterprise.

The Court further notes that, since 1999, when the applicant was placed on the waiting list, her situation has not changed. Moreover, as the applicant rightly pointed out, there is no hope that this measure will result in her resettlement from the zone in the foreseeable future.…

(ii) The alleged failure to regulate private industry …

It might be argued that, given the complexity and scale of the environmental problem around the Severstal steel-plant, this problem cannot be resolved in a short period of time. Indeed, it is not the Court's task to determine what exactly should have been done in the present situation to reduce pollution in a more efficient way. However, it is certainly in the Court's jurisdiction to assess whether the Government approached the problem with due diligence and gave consideration to all the competing interests.…

The Court cannot conclude that, in regulating the steel-plant's industrial activities, the authorities gave due weight to the interests of the community living in close proximity to its premises.

In sum, the Court finds the following:

The State authorised the operation of a polluting enterprise in the middle of a densely populated town. Since the toxic emissions from this enterprise exceeded the safe limits established by the domestic legislation and might endanger the health of those living nearby, the State established that a certain territory around the plant should be free of any dwelling. However, these legislative measures were not implemented in practice.

It would be going too far to state that the State or the polluting enterprise were under an obligation to provide the applicant with free housing, and, in any event, it is not the Court's role to dictate precise measures which should be adopted by the States in order to comply with their positive duties under Article 8 of the Convention. In the present case, however, although the situation around the plant called for a special treatment of those living within the zone, the State did not offer the applicant any effective solution to help her move from the dangerous area.… The Court concludes that, despite the wide margin of appreciation left to the respondent State, it has failed to strike a fair balance between the interests of the community and the applicant's effective enjoyment of her right to respect for her home and her private life. There has accordingly been a violation of Article 8.

II. APPLICATION OF ARTICLE 41 OF THE CONVENTION

Article 41 of the Convention provides:

If the Court finds that there has been a violation of the Convention or the Protocols thereto, and if the internal law of the High Contracting Party concerned allows only partial reparation to be made, the Court shall, if necessary, afford just satisfaction to the injured party.

A. *Damage*

1. Non-pecuniary damage ...

In sum, taking into account various relevant factors, such as age, the applicant's state of health and the duration of the situation complained of, and making an assessment on an equitable basis in accordance with Article 41, the Court awards the applicant EUR 6,000 under this head, plus any tax that may be chargeable on this amount.

2. Pecuniary damage

The applicant claimed that the Government should be required to offer her new housing, comparable to her current flat, outside the Cherepovets sanitary security zone.... Alternatively, the applicant claimed an award of damages of EUR 30,000, which was the value of a flat comparable to the applicant's but located outside the Cherepovets sanitary security zone.

The Government argued that this claim should be rejected.

With regard to this claim the Court notes, first of all, that the violation complained of by the applicant is of a continuing nature. Within the period under consideration the applicant lived in her flat as a tenant and has never been deprived of this title. Although during this time her private life was adversely affected by industrial emissions, nothing indicates that she has incurred any expenses in this respect. Therefore, in respect of the period prior to the adoption of the present judgment the applicant failed to substantiate any material loss.

As regards future measures to be adopted by the Government, the resettlement of the applicant in an ecologically safe area would be only one of many possible solutions. In any event, the Court has established the Government's obligation to take appropriate measures to remedy the applicant's individual situation.

[Unanimously held]

Questions and Discussion

1. *Balancing under Article 8.* Assuming that their steel mill is of great importance to the Russian economy, just as night-time flights at Heathrow may be to the British economy, why does the Court find a violation here but no violation in *Hatton*?

2. *Choice of remedies.* What remedy did the Court order in *Fadeyeva*? Why did it not order Russia to clean up the steel plant or move the residents? Is the Court's limitation on its remedies a necessary nod to national sovereignty, a weakness in the enforcement system, both, or neither? Is it clear that monetary compensation will satisfy the Court for future cases? Is it clear that Russia will be obliged to do anything at all in the future for anyone living in polluted areas?

3. *National v. ECHR remedies.* Might more comprehensive remedies be available in the national court system? If so, would it be possible for a litigant in a national court to use the ECHR ruling on a violation of Article 8 but to ask a national court to grant a more sweeping remedy such as an injunction to clean up the steel plant or resettle the residents? Does the history of domestic court actions recited in this case give much cause for hope? If the Russian Federation ignores ECHR precedents and compensation rulings, what can a complainant do? Does it matter whether the European Convention on Human Rights has direct application within the nation's legal system? Does that give hope for achieving a domestic remedy after this ECHR ruling?

4. *Ledyayeva—Fadeyeva's Sequel.* A year later, the Court considered similar claims from several applicants living in the same apartment complex area and within the same "security zone" near the Severstal plant. The Court unanimously found as follows:

> Having examined the materials submitted to it, the Court notes that in the present cases the Government did not put forward any new fact or argument capable of persuading it to reach a conclusion different from that of the *Fadeyeva* case. The Court concludes that, despite the wide margin of appreciation left to the respondent State, the authorities failed to take appropriate measures in order to protect the applicants' right to respect for their homes and private lives against serious environmental nuisances. In particular, the authorities have neither resettled the applicants outside the dangerous zone, nor have they provided for a compensation for those seeking the resettlement. Furthermore, it appears that the authorities failed to develop and implement an efficient public policy which would induce the steel-plant to reduce its emissions to the safe levels within a reasonable time. There has accordingly been a violation of Article 8 of the Convention.

Ledyayeva v. Russia, App. Nos. 53157/99, 53247/99, 53695/00 and 56850/00, Judgment of 26 October 2006.

5. *The necessity of Ledyayeva?* Why should it have been necessary for the *Ledyayeva* case to be decided by the Court after the *Fadeyeva* case? Shouldn't the first case have been a sufficient precedent in the national legal system that additional persons in the same situation could use to obtain at least compensation? Consider the following directive given by the Supreme Court of the Russian Federation:

> The Russian Federation, as a Party to the Convention for the Protection of Human Rights and Fundamental Freedoms, accepts the jurisdiction of the European Court of Human Rights as binding on matters of the interpretation and application of the Convention and its Protocols in the case of a presumed infringement by the Russian Federation of the provision of these treaties documents, when the presumed infringement occurred after the entry into force in relation to Russian Federation ... Therefore use by the courts of the above mentioned Convention must have regard to the practice of the European Court of Human Rights so as to avoid any infringement of the Convention....
>
> Interpretations of the decisions concerning the Russian Federations implies that, should the need arise, the State will adopt special measures aimed at eliminating breaches of the human rights covered by the Convention and the consequences of these breaches. The courts should act within their competence so as to ensure fulfillment of the obligations of the State arising from the participation of the Russian Federation in the Convention ...

No.5 of Oct. 10, 2005 (Plenum), reprinted in 25 Hum. Rts. L. J 108 (2004) and available in Russian at БЮЛЛЕТЄНЬ No. 12 ОТ 31.12.2003, http://www.supcourt.ru/vs-court_detale.php?id=1961.

C. Right to Life

While much of the ECHR judicial activity regarding implied environmental rights has involved Article 8 and it has sometimes appeared that Article 2, involving the right to life, was a non-starter for environmental rights, the following case presents a different picture.

Öneryildiz v. Turkey

European Court of Human Rights (Grand Chamber)
Application No. 48939/99, ECHR 2004-XII, (2005) 41 E.H.R.R. 20
Judgment of 30 November 2004

The President, Judge WILDHABER; Judges ROZAKIS, COSTA, RESS, BRATZA, PALM, LOU-
CAIDES, TÜRMEN, TULKENS, JUNGWIERT, TSATSA-NIKOLOVSKA, GREVE, BAKA, KOVLER,
ZAGREBELSKY, MULARONI

THE FACTS

I. THE CIRCUMSTANCES OF THE CASE

The applicant was born in 1955 and is now living in the district of Şirvan (province
of Siirt), the area where he was born. At the material time he was living with twelve close
relatives in the slum quarter (*gecekondu mahallesi*) of Kazım Karabekir in Ümraniye, a district of Istanbul, where he had moved after resigning from his post as a village guard in
south-eastern Turkey.

A. The Ümraniye household-refuse tip and the area in which the applicant lived

Since the early 1970s a household-refuse tip had been in operation in Hekimbaşı, a slum
area adjoining Kazım Karabekir. On 22 January 1960 Istanbul City Council ("the city
council") had been granted use of the land, which belonged to the Forestry Commission
(and therefore to the Treasury), for a term of ninety-nine years. Situated on a slope over-
looking a valley, the site spread out over a surface area of approximately 35 hectares and
from 1972 onwards was used as a rubbish tip by the districts of Beykoz, Üsküdar, Kadıköy,
and Ümraniye under the authority and responsibility of the city council and, ultimately,
the ministerial authorities.

When the rubbish tip started being used, the area was uninhabited and the closest
built-up area was approximately 3.5 km away. However, as the years passed, rudimen-
tary dwellings were built without any authorisation in the area surrounding the rubbish
tip, which eventually developed into the slums of Ümraniye....

B. Steps taken by Ümraniye District Council ...

On 9 April 1991 Ümraniye District Council applied to the Third Division of the Üsküdar District Court for experts to be appointed to determine whether the rubbish tip complied with the relevant regulations, in particular the Regulations on Solid-Waste Control
of 14 March 1991. The district council also applied for an assessment of the damage it had
sustained, as evidence in support of an action for damages it was preparing to bring
against the city council and the councils of the three other districts that used the tip....

According to the experts' report, drawn up on 7 May 1991, the rubbish tip in question
did not conform to the technical requirements set forth, *inter alia*, in regulations 24 to
27, 30 and 38 of the Regulations of 14 March 1991 and, accordingly, presented a number of dangers liable to give rise to a major health risk for the inhabitants of the valley,
particularly those living in the slum areas: no walls or fencing separated the tip from the
dwellings fifty metres away from the mountain of refuse, the tip was not equipped with
collection, composting, recycling or combustion systems, and no drainage or drainage-
water purification systems had been installed. The experts concluded that the Ümraniye
tip "exposed humans, animals, and the environment to all kinds of risks." In that connection
the report, drawing attention first to the fact that some twenty contagious diseases might
spread, underlined the following:

> In any waste-collection site gases such as methane, carbon dioxide, and hydrogen sulphide form. These substances must be collected and ... burnt under supervision. However, the tip in question is not equipped with such a system. If methane is mixed with air in a particular proportion, it can explode. This installation contains no means of preventing an explosion of the methane produced as a result of the decomposition [of the waste]. May God preserve us, as the damage could be very substantial given the neighbouring dwellings.

On 27 May 1991 the report was brought to the attention of the four councils in question, and on 7 June 1991 the governor was informed of it and asked to brief the Ministry of Health and the Prime Minister's Environment Office ("the Environment Office")....

[T]he Environment Office, which had been advised of the report on 18 June 1991, made a recommendation (no. 09513) urging the Istanbul Governor's Office, the city council and Ümraniye District Council to remedy the problems identified in the present case....

On 27 August 1992 Şinasi Öktem, the mayor of Ümraniye, applied to the First Division of the Üsküdar District Court for the implementation of temporary measures to prevent the city council and the neighbouring district councils from using the waste-collection site. He requested, in particular, that no further waste be dumped, that the tip be closed, and that redress be provided in respect of the damage sustained by his district.

On 3 November 1992 Istanbul City Council's representative opposed that request....

Istanbul City Council had ... issued a call for tenders for the development of new sites conforming to modern standards. The first planning contract was awarded to the American firm CVH2M Hill International Ltd, and on 21 December 1992 and 17 February 1993 new sites were designed for the European and Anatolian sides of Istanbul respectively. The project was due for completion in the course of 1993.

While those proceedings were still pending, Ümraniye District Council informed the mayor of Istanbul that from 15 May 1993 the dumping of waste would no longer be authorised.

C. The accident

On 28 April 1993 at about 11 a.m. a methane explosion occurred at the site. Following a landslide caused by mounting pressure, the refuse erupted from the mountain of waste and engulfed some ten slum dwellings situated below it, including the one belonging to the applicant. Thirty-nine people died in the accident....

I. Alleged Violation of Article 2 of the Convention

The applicant complained that the death of nine of his close relatives in the accident of 28 April 1993 and the flaws in the ensuing proceedings had constituted a violation of Article 2 of the Convention, the relevant part of which provides:

> Everyone's right to life shall be protected by law. No one shall be deprived of his life intentionally save in the execution of a sentence of a court following his conviction of a crime for which this penalty is provided by law....

1. The Chamber judgment

[T]he Chamber emphasised that the protection of the right to life, as required by Article 2 of the Convention, could be relied on in connection with the operation of waste-collection sites, on account of the potential risks inherent in that activity. It accordingly held that the positive obligation on States to take appropriate steps to safeguard the lives of those within their jurisdiction, for the purposes of Article 2, applied in the instant case.

2. Submissions of those appearing before the Court

The Government argued that the Chamber's conclusion that "all situations of unintentional death" came within the scope of Article 2 had given rise to an unprecedented extension of the positive obligations inherent in that provision....

At the hearing the Government submitted that the State's responsibility for actions that were not directly attributable to its agents could not extend to all occurrences of accidents or disasters and that in such circumstances the Court's interpretation as to the applicability of Article 2 should be neither teleological nor broad, but rather should remain restrictive. Otherwise, it might be inferred that the mere fact of being near an airport, a nuclear power station or a munitions factory or of simply being exposed to chemicals could give rise to a potential violation of Article 2.

The applicant contended that the negligent omissions on the part of the State authorities undoubtedly came within the ambit of Article 2 of the Convention, seeing that they had resulted in the death of his relatives, and that there was nothing in the Government's submissions to rebut that conclusion.

3. The Court's assessment ...

[T]he Court reiterates that Article 2 does not solely concern deaths resulting from the use of force by agents of the State but also, in the first sentence of its first paragraph, lays down a positive obligation on States to take appropriate steps to safeguard the lives of those within their jurisdiction.

The Court considers that this obligation must be construed as applying in the context of any activity, whether public or not, in which the right to life may be at stake, and *a fortiori* in the case of industrial activities, which by their very nature are dangerous, such as the operation of waste-collection sites.

Where the Convention institutions have had to examine allegations of an infringement of the right to the protection of life in such areas, they have never ruled that Article 2 was not applicable. The Court would refer, for example, to cases concerning toxic emissions from a fertiliser factory or nuclear tests.

In this connection, contrary to what the Government appear to be suggesting, the harmfulness of the phenomena inherent in the activity in question, the contingency of the risk to which the applicant was exposed by reason of any life-endangering circumstances, the status of those involved in bringing about such circumstances, and whether the acts or omissions attributable to them were deliberate are merely factors among others that must be taken into account in the examination of the merits of a particular case, with a view to determining the responsibility the State may bear under Article 2....

To sum up, it considers that the applicant's complaint undoubtedly falls within the ambit of the first sentence of Article 2, which is therefore applicable in the instant case....

THE COURT

1. *Holds* unanimously that there has been a violation of Article 2 of the Convention in its substantive aspect, on account of the lack of appropriate steps to prevent the accidental death of nine of the applicant's close relatives.

Questions and Discussion

1. *Right to life and environment.* In this case, the Court focuses on the violation to life, which in this case was caused by environmental pollution. Does this case's interpretation

of Article 2 have the potential for greater protection of the environment in future cases that do not involve actual death?

2. *The "margin of appreciation" doctrine.* According to one commentator, "'margin of appreciation' is a somewhat nebulous concept borrowed from French law. In essence, the concept is that there is room for countries to differ in what is acceptable under the terms of the Convention based on cultural differences. Thus, using the 'margin of appreciation' concept, the Court has discretion under the Convention to find a law or practice violative of the Convention in one member country, but acceptable in another—even though both ratified the Convention." Paul L. McKaskle, *The European Court of Human Rights: What it is, how it works, and its future,* 40 U.S.F. L. Rev. 1, 49 (2005).

3. *The requirement of overlapping domestic law.* One commentator has observed:

> The ECHR [European Court of Human Rights] has acted aggressively in Article 8 cases *when an overlapping domestic law imposes a positive obligation on the respondent state* [emphasis added]. In *López Ostra v. Spain* ... the court twice observed that the tannery operated without a license in violation of municipal law. In *Guerra v. Italy* ... [the court] reached [its] conclusion after it stressed that domestic law also required that the government take [steps to protect the environment.] ...
>
> An opposite result in *Hatton v. United Kingdom* confirms the importance of domestic law in cases where the ECHR must address positive and progressive obligations imposed by interstitial socioeconomic rights. There, the applicant complained that the government permitted unlawful noise pollution by inadequately policing nighttime flights in and out of London's Heathrow Airport. The court ruled in the government's favor. Citing *López Ostra* and *Guerra,* it observed that "in previous cases in which environmental questions gave rise to violations of the Convention, the violation was predicated on a failure by the national authorities to comply with some aspect of the domestic regime." This "element of domestic irregularity [was] wholly absent in [*Hatton*]."

David Marcus, *The Normative Development of Socioeconomic Rights through Supranational Adjudication,* 42 Stan. J. Int'l L. 53, 74–75 (2006).

How does the requirement that a domestic environmental law be violated weaken the environmental protection that Article 8 could otherwise offer? If a litigant can receive protection of environmental rights under Article 8 only when her country provides a domestic environmental law, does Article 8 actually provide any protection of environmental rights? Put another way, what is the importance of an implied environmental right under Article 8 if there is domestic legislation applicable to the complaint? Why couldn't a litigant merely complain of the environmental pollution in her country's national courts? What extra protection does Article 8 offer?

II. Environmental Rights under the African Charter

A. African Charter on Human and Peoples' Rights

Unlike the European Convention on Human Rights, in which environmental rights must be inferred from various provisions indirectly, the African Charter on Human and

Peoples' Rights has quite explicit provisions on both health and the environment. The Charter also contains provisions allowing individual complaints to be made before an African Commission.

African Charter on Human and Peoples' Rights
June 27, 1981
O.A.U. Doc. CAB/LEG/67/3 rev. 5; 21 I.L.M. 58 (1982)

Article 16

1. Every individual shall have the right to enjoy the best attainable state of physical and mental health.

2. State Parties to the present Charter shall take the necessary measures to protect the health of their people and to ensure that they receive medical attention when they are sick.

Article 24

All peoples shall have the right to a general satisfactory environment favorable to their development....

Article 30

An African Commission on Human and Peoples' Rights, hereinafter called "the Commission," shall be established within the Organisation of African Unity [now the African Union] to promote human and Peoples' Rights and ensure their protection in Africa.

Article 45

The functions of the Commission shall be: ...

2. Ensure the protection of human and Peoples' Rights under conditions laid down by the present Charter....

Article 55

1. Before each Session, the Secretary of the Commission shall make a list of the Communications other than those of State Parties to the present Charter and transmit them to Members of the Commission, who shall indicate which Communications should be considered by the Commission.

2. A Communication shall be considered by the Commission if a simple majority of its members so decide.

Article 59

1. All measures taken within the provisions of the present Chapter shall remain confidential until the Assembly of Heads of State and Government shall otherwise decide....

Questions and Discussion

1. *Rights to health and satisfactory environment.* Do Articles 16 and 24 appear to be "enforceable" as a matter of individual rights, or are they merely in the Charter to encourage the states parties to adopt good legislation?

2. *African Commission on Human and Peoples' Rights.* The Commission's procedure rules can be found in Rules of Procedure of the African Commission on Human and Peoples' Rights, *adopted on* October 6, 1995, *available at* http://www1.umn.edu/human-rts/instree/africancomrules.html.

3. *Standing before the African Commission.* Under Article 55 of the African Charter, "communications" may be received by the Commission from "other than those of State Parties"—that is, individuals and organizations.

4. *Confidentiality.* Note that Article 59 requires that measures taken by the Commission are presumptively confidential—not available to the public. Does this serve to protect individuals submitting complaints? Does it also serve to protect governments against whom complaints are filed?

5. *Limitations of the Commission.* Originally, the African Commission was the only body charged with promoting and protecting human rights and collective rights throughout the African continent. It interpreted the African Charter on Human and Peoples' Rights and considered individual complaints of violations of the Charter. Critics charged, however, that because of numerous restrictions, the Commission was a "toothless bulldog" that was never "created to bite." Nsongurua J. Udombana, *Toward the African Court on Human and Peoples' Rights: Better Late Than Never,* 3 Yale Hum. Rts. & Dev. L.J. 45, 63 (2000). Indeed, an empirical study of the 44 cases in which the Commission found human rights violations and issued recommendations found that "in only six of the forty-four communications (or 14 percent) did state parties comply fully and in timely fashion with the recommendations of the African Commission." Frans Viljoen & Lirette Louw, *State Compliance with the Recommendations of the African Commission on Human and Peoples' Rights, 1994–2004,* 101 Amer. J. Int'l L. 1, 5 (2007). In 30 percent of cases, the study found non-compliance and in 32 percent partial compliance, while in another 16 percent of cases a change of government amount to "situational compliance." *Id.* at 5–7. The authors concluded, "Our analysis of cases of full and clear noncompliance suggests that the most important factors predictive of compliance are political, rather than legal." *Id.* at 32.

6. *African Court of Human and Peoples' Rights.* In addition to the Commission, there is now an African Court on Human and Peoples' Rights. Protocol to the African Charter on Human and Peoples' Rights on the Establishment of the African Court on Human and Peoples' Rights, O.A.U. Doc. OAU/LEG/MIN/AFCHPR/PROT (III) (9 June 1998). The Protocol entered into force January 1, 2004, and the Court had its first meeting in 2006. Two years later, it does not yet have its own website. The researchers cited in the previous paragraph caution that:

> the mere fact that the Court will provide legally binding and specific remedies and better formulated judgments will not in itself guarantee improved state compliance. The advent of the Court may coincide with a gradual hardening of human rights commitments and lead to improved human rights adherence, but it would then be on the strength of a stronger domestic and regional political commitment, increased publicity, and greater involvement of civil society.

Frans Viljoen and Lirette Louw, *State Compliance with the Recommendations of the African Commission on Human and Peoples' Rights, 1994–2004,* 101 Amer. J. Int'l L. 1, 33 (2007).

7. *Indirect access to the Court.* The Commission may submit cases to the African Court, including those submitted by individuals or to it under Article 55. Protocol to the African Charter on Human and Peoples' Rights on the Establishment of the African Court on Human and Peoples' Rights, June 9, 1998, O.A.U. Doc. OAU/LEG/MIN/AFCHPR/PROT (III) (8 June 1998).

8. *Direct access to the Court.* In addition to State Parties having the right to bring cases to the Court, nongovernmental organizations that have been granted official observer status before the Commission, as well as individuals, may be permitted to bring cases to the Court. This is true, however, only if a country has specifically accepted the Court's exercise of such jurisdiction. Protocol, *id.,* Article 5.3, Article 34.6. "The provision on individual access was one of the most contentious in the whole Protocol establishing the Court." Rebecca Wright, *Finding an Impetus for Institutional Change at the African Court on Human and Peoples' Rights,* 24 Berkeley J. Int'l L. 463, 475 (2006). Indeed, only one State, Burkina Faso, has made a declaration allowing individuals direct access to the African Court. This differs from access to the European Court of Human Rights, which is completely open to such cases by individuals and NGOs. At the other extreme, the Inter-American Court of Human Rights prohibits them entirely, requiring that cases come only from the Inter-American Commission on Human Rights.

B. Finding an Environmental Right

The Ogoni People are an indigenous community in the Niger Delta region of southeast Nigeria. They call their homeland "Ogoniland." In 1995 their leader, Ken Saro-Wiwa, and eight others who campaigned against the environmental degradation, were executed by the military government that was in control of Nigeria at the time, an action that provoked outrage around the world. In 1999 the military stepped aside and returned the government to civilian rule. Elections in 2003 and 2007 were marked by charges of election fraud. In 2007, a European Union observer mission said the polls "have fallen far short of basic international and regional standards for democratic elections and ... cannot be considered to have been credible." The head of the European Union monitoring team said it was one of the worst elections that the EU had observed.

The Ogoni have suffered a wide variety of human rights abuses that are detailed in the following case, which was filed in 1996 during the period of military rule. Today the condition of the environment in the Niger Delta is reported to be no better than at the time of the case.

Social and Economic Rights Action Center v. Nigeria
African Commission on Human and Peoples' Rights
Case No. ACHPR/Comm/A044/1,
Decision Regarding Comm. No. 155/96 (2001)

Summary of Facts:

The Communication alleges that the military government of Nigeria has been directly involved in oil production through the State oil company, the Nigerian National Petroleum Company (NNPC), the majority shareholder in a consortium with Shell Petroleum Development Corporation (SPDC), and that these operations have caused environmental degradation and health problems resulting from the contamination of the environment among the Ogoni People.

The Communication alleges that the oil consortium has exploited oil reserves in Ogoniland with no regard for the health or environment of the local communities, disposing toxic wastes into the environment and local waterways in violation of applicable international environmental standards. The consortium also neglected and/or failed to maintain its facilities causing numerous avoidable spills in the proximity of villages. The resulting contamination of water, soil, and air has had serious short and long-term health impacts, including skin infections, gastrointestinal and respiratory ailments, and increased risk of cancers, and neurological and reproductive problems.

The Communication alleges that the Nigerian Government has condoned and facilitated these violations by placing the legal and military powers of the State at the disposal of the oil companies. The Communication contains a memo from the Rivers State Internal Security Task Force, calling for "ruthless military operations."

The Communication alleges that the Government has neither monitored operations of the oil companies nor required safety measures that are standard procedure within the industry. The Government has withheld from Ogoni Communities information on the dangers created by oil activities. Ogoni Communities have not been involved in the decisions affecting the development of Ogoniland.

The Government has not required oil companies or its own agencies to produce basic health and environmental impact studies regarding hazardous operations and materials relating to oil production, despite the obvious health and environmental crisis in Ogoniland. The government has even refused to permit scientists and environmental organisations from entering Ogoniland to undertake such studies. The government has also ignored the concerns of Ogoni Communities regarding oil development, and has responded to protests with massive violence and executions of Ogoni leaders.

The Communication alleges that the Nigerian government does not require oil companies to consult communities before beginning operations, even if the operations pose direct threats to community or individual lands.

The Communication alleges that in the course of the last three years, Nigerian security forces have attacked, burned, and destroyed several Ogoni villages and homes under the pretext of dislodging officials and supporters of the Movement of the Survival of Ogoni People (MOSOP). These attacks have come in response to MOSOP's nonviolent campaign in opposition to the destruction of their environment by oil companies. Some of the attacks have involved uniformed combined forces of the police, the army, the airforce, and the navy, armed with armoured tanks and other sophisticated weapons. In other instances, the attacks have been conducted by unidentified gunmen, mostly at night. The military-type methods and the calibre of weapons used in such attacks strongly suggest the involvement of the Nigerian security forces. The complete failure of the Government of Nigeria to investigate these attacks, let alone punish the perpetrators, further implicates the Nigerian authorities.

The Nigerian Army has admitted its role in the ruthless operations which have left thousands of villagers homeless. The admission is recorded in several memos exchanged between officials of the SPDC and the Rivers State Internal Security Task Force, which has devoted itself to the suppression of the Ogoni campaign. One such memo calls for "ruthless military operations" and "wasting operations coupled with psychological tactics of displacement." ...

The Communication alleges that the Nigerian government has destroyed and threatened Ogoni food sources through a variety of means. The government has participated in irresponsible oil development that has poisoned much of the soil and water upon which Ogoni farming and fishing depended. In their raids on villages, Nigerian security forces have destroyed crops and killed farm animals. The security forces have created a state of terror and insecurity that has made it impossible for many Ogoni villagers to return to their fields and animals. The destruction of farmlands, rivers, crops, and animals has created malnutrition and starvation among certain Ogoni Communities.

Complaint:

The communication alleges violations of Articles 2, 4, 14, 16, 18(1), 21, and 24 of the African Charter....

LAW

Admissibility

Article 56 of the African Charter governs admissibility. All of the conditions of this Article are met by the present communication....

The Commission takes cognisance of the fact that the Federal Republic of Nigeria has incorporated the African Charter on Human and Peoples' Rights into its domestic law with the result that all the rights contained therein can be invoked in Nigerian courts including those violations alleged by the Complainants. However, the Commission is aware that at the time of submitting this communication, the then Military government of Nigeria had enacted various decrees ousting the jurisdiction of the courts and thus depriving the people in Nigeria of the right to seek redress in the courts for acts of government that violate their fundamental human rights. In such instances, and as in the instant communication, the Commission is of the view that no adequate domestic remedies are existent.

The Commission therefore declared the communication admissible.

Merits

The Complainants allege that the Nigerian government violated the right to health and the right to clean environment as recognized under Articles 16 and 24 of the African Charter by failing to fulfill the minimum duties required by these rights. This, the Complainants allege, the government has done by:

- Directly participating in the contamination of air, water, and soil and thereby harming the health of the Ogoni population,

- Failing to protect the Ogoni population from the harm caused by the NNPC Shell Consortium but instead using its security forces to facilitate the damage

- Failing to provide or permit studies of potential or actual environmental and health risks caused by the oil operations

Article 16 of the African Charter reads:

(1) Every individual shall have the right to enjoy the best attainable state of physical and mental health.

(2) States Parties to the present Charter shall take the necessary measures to protect the health of their people and to ensure that they receive medical attention when they are sick.

Article 24 of the African Charter reads:

All peoples shall have the right to a general satisfactory environment favourable to their development.

These rights recognise the importance of a clean and safe environment that is closely linked to economic and social rights in so far as the environment affects the quality of life and safety of the individual. As has been rightly observed by [Professor] Alexander Kiss, "an environment degraded by pollution and defaced by the destruction of all beauty and variety is as contrary to satisfactory living conditions and the development as the breakdown of the fundamental ecologic equilibria is harmful to physical and moral health."

The right to a general satisfactory environment, as guaranteed under Article 24 of the African Charter or the right to a healthy environment, as it is widely known, therefore imposes clear obligations upon a government. It requires the State to take reasonable and other measures to prevent pollution and ecological degradation, to promote conservation, and to secure an ecologically sustainable development and use of natural resources. Article 12 of the International Covenant on Economic, Social and Cultural Rights (ICESCR), to which Nigeria is a party, requires governments to take necessary steps for the improvement of all aspects of environmental and industrial hygiene. The right to enjoy the best attainable state of physical and mental health enunciated in Article 16(1) of the African Charter and the right to a general satisfactory environment favourable to development (Article 16(3)) already noted obligate governments to desist from directly threatening the health and environment of their citizens. The State is under an obligation to respect the just noted rights and this entails largely non-interventionist conduct from the State for example, not from carrying out, sponsoring or tolerating any practice, policy or legal measures violating the integrity of the individual.

Government compliance with the spirit of Articles 16 and 24 of the African Charter must also include ordering or at least permitting independent scientific monitoring of threatened environments, requiring and publicising environmental and social impact studies prior to any major industrial development, undertaking appropriate monitoring and providing information to those communities exposed to hazardous materials and activities, and providing meaningful opportunities for the continent's painful legacy, and restore co-operative economic development to its traditional place at the heart of African Society.

Governments have a duty to protect their citizens, not only through appropriate legislation and effective enforcement but also by protecting them from damaging acts that may be perpetrated by private parties (See *Union des Jeunes Avocats /Chad* [African Commission]). This duty calls for positive action on part of governments in fulfilling their obligation under human rights instruments. The practice before other tribunals also enhances this requirement as is evidenced in the case *Velàsquez Rodríguez v. Honduras*. In this landmark judgment, the Inter-American Court of Human Rights held that when a State allows private persons or groups to act freely and with impunity to the detriment of the rights recognised, it would be in clear violation of its obligations to protect the human rights of its citizens. Similarly, this obligation of the State is further emphasised in the practice of the European Court of Human Rights, in *X and Y v. Netherlands*. In that case, the Court pronounced that there was an obligation on authorities to take steps to make sure that the enjoyment of the rights is not interfered with by any other private person.

The Commission notes that in the present case, despite its obligation to protect persons against interferences in the enjoyment of their rights, the Government of Nigeria facilitated the destruction of the Ogoniland. Contrary to its Charter obligations and despite such internationally established principles, the Nigerian Government has given the green light to private actors, and the oil Companies in particular, to devastatingly affect the well-being of the Ogonis. By any measure of standards, its practice falls short of the minimum conduct expected of governments, and therefore, is in violation of Article 21 of the African Charter....

The uniqueness of the African situation and the special qualities of the African Charter on Human and Peoples' Rights imposes upon the African Commission an important task. International law and human rights must be responsive to African circumstances.

Clearly, collective rights, environmental rights, and economic and social rights are essential elements of human rights in Africa. The African Commission will apply any of the diverse rights contained in the African Charter. It welcomes this opportunity to make clear that there is no right in the African Charter that cannot be made effective. As indicated in the preceding paragraphs, however, the Nigerian Government did not live up to the minimum expectations of the African Charter.

The Commission does not wish to fault governments that are labouring under difficult circumstances to improve the lives of their people. The situation of the people of Ogoniland, however, requires, in the view of the Commission, a reconsideration of the Government's attitude to the allegations contained in the instant communication. The intervention of multinational corporations may be a potentially positive force for development if the State and the people concerned are ever mindful of the common good and the sacred rights of individuals and communities. The Commission however takes note of the efforts of the present civilian administration to redress the atrocities that were committed by the previous military administration as illustrated in the Note Verbale [submitted by the government].

For the above reasons, the Commission,

Finds the Federal Republic of Nigeria in violation of Articles 2, 4, 14, 16, 18(1), 21 and 24 of the African Charter on Human and Peoples' Rights;

Appeals to the government of the Federal Republic of Nigeria to ensure protection of the environment, health, and livelihood of the people of Ogoniland by:

- Ensuring adequate compensation to victims of the human rights violations, including relief and resettlement assistance to victims of government sponsored raids, and undertaking a comprehensive cleanup of lands and rivers damaged by oil operations;

- Ensuring that appropriate environmental and social impact assessments are prepared for any future oil development and that the safe operation of any further oil development is guaranteed through effective and independent oversight bodies for the petroleum industry; and

- Providing information on health and environmental risks and meaningful access to regulatory and decision-making bodies to communities likely to be affected by oil operations.

Urges the government of the Federal Republic of Nigeria to keep the African Commission informed of the outcome of the work of:

- The Federal Ministry of Environment which was established to address environmental and environment related issues prevalent in Nigeria, and as a matter of priority, in the Niger Delta area including the Ogoniland;

- The Niger Delta Development Commission (NDDC) enacted into law to address the environmental and other social related problems in the Niger Delta area and other oil producing areas of Nigeria....

Questions and Discussion

1. *The Commission's interpretation of the Articles.* How broadly does the Commission interpret Article 24 of the African Charter? What positive duties does the Commission consider to be imposed on the government with regard to third parties? Is this kind of obli-

gation reasonable? Is it likely to be implemented? Why is Article 16 relevant to environmental conditions?

2. *Enforcement of the Commission's decision.* How is the language in the conclusions of the Commission worded? To what degree does the Commission rely on the good will of the government? Does the change in government between the time of filing the complaint and the time of decision make it more likely that the Commission's recommendations will be implemented?

3. *Precedential effect of the decision.* Even if the Commission has little authority to enforce its decisions, could a litigant use its findings and rulings in Nigerian national courts? To affect the actions of other international bodies? To affect the actions of foreign investors?

4. *Persuasive global authority.* Note how the African Commission cited precedents from human rights courts on other continents. Note, on the other hand, its comment about the "uniqueness of the African situation and the special qualities of the African Charter" and its statement that international law and human rights "must be responsive to African circumstances." Are precedents from other human rights courts relevant in such a situation? In your view, do "African circumstances" require less protection of environmental rights than elsewhere or more?

5. *The effect of government regulation of private parties on the decision.* Does the Commission make it clear which way it would have ruled if the Nigerian government had not directly supported the action of the NNPC Shell Consortium? What if the government had condemned the corporate operations immediately? What if it never commented nor acted to support the corporation?

6. *Compliance.* According to an empirical study of compliance with recommendations of the African Commission, as far as the *Social and Economic Rights Action Center* case is concerned, "Although partial compliance was recorded..., a great many of the recommendations forwarded in this case are still outstanding." Frans Viljoen & Lirette Louw, *State Compliance with the Recommendations of the African Commission on Human and Peoples' Rights, 1994–2004*, 101 Amer. J. Int'l L. 1, 27 n. 119 (2007).

III. Environmental Rights under the American Declaration and Convention

A. American Declaration of the Rights and Duties of Man

American Declaration of the Rights and Duties of Man
1948
O.A.S. Res. XXX, adopted by the Ninth International Conference of
American States (1948), *reprinted in* Basic Documents Pertaining to
Human Rights in the Inter-American System,
OEA/Ser.L.V/II.82 doc.6 rev.1 at 17 (1992)

Article I

Every human being has the right to life, liberty, and the security of his person.

Article VIII

Every person has the right to fix his residence within the territory of the state of which he is a national, to move about freely within such territory, and not to leave it except by his own will.

Article XI

Every person has the right to the preservation of his health through sanitary and social measures relating to food, clothing, housing, and medical care, to the extent permitted by public and community resources.

Resolution 12/85 [Yanomami Case]
Inter-American Commission on Human Rights
IACHR Case 7615 (Brazil) (March 5, 1985), *printed in*
Inter-Am.C.H.R., 1984–1985 Annual Report 24,
OEA/Ser.L/V/II.66, doc. 10, rev. 1 (Oct. 1, 1985)

BACKGROUND:

On December 15, 1980, a petition against the Government of Brazil was presented to the Inter-American Commission on Human Rights, in which the petitioners, Tim Coulter (Executive Director, Indian Law Resource Center) ... and other persons, allege violations of the human rights of the Yanomami Indians....

CONSIDERING: ...

That international law in its present state, and as it is found clearly expressed in Article 27 of the International Covenant on Civil and Political Rights, recognizes the right of ethnic groups to special protection on their use of their own language, for the practice of their own religion, and, in general, for all those characteristics necessary for the preservation of their cultural identity....

That from the careful examination made by the Commission of the facts, including the replies from the Government of Brazil, it finds the following:

a. That on account of the beginning, in 1973, of the construction of highway BR-210 (the Northern Circumferential Highway), the territory occupied for ages beyond memory by the Yanomami Indians was invaded by highway construction workers, geologists, mining prospectors, and farm workers desiring to settle in that territory;

b. That those invasions were carried out without prior and adequate protection for the safety and health of the Yanomami Indians, which resulted in a considerable number of deaths caused by epidemics of influenza, tuberculosis, measles, venereal diseases, and others;

c. That Indian inhabitants of various villages near the route of highway BR-210 (the Northern Circumferential Highway) abandoned their villages and were changed into beggars or prostitutes, without the Government of Brazil's taking the necessary measures to prevent this; and

d. That after the discovery in 1976 of ores of tin and other metals in the region where the Yanomamis live, serious conflicts arose that led to acts of violence between prospectors and miners of those minerals, on one side, and the Indians, on the other. Such conflicts ... affected the lives, security, health, and cultural integrity of the Yanomamis.

That from the facts set forth above a liability of the Brazilian Government arises for having failed to take timely and effective measures to protect the human rights of the Yanomamis....

The Inter-American Commission on Human Rights

Resolves:

1. To declare ... that, by reason of the failure of the Government of Brazil to take timely and effective measures in behalf of the Yanomami Indians, a situation has been produced that has resulted in the violation, injury to them, of the following rights recognized in the American Declaration of the Rights and Duties of Man: the right to life, liberty, and personal security (Article I); the right to residence and movement (Article VIII); and the right to the preservation of health and to well-being (Article XI)....

Questions and Discussion

1. *Right to life.* The Inter-American Commission issued a similarly critical report on violation of rights due to pollution and other environmental harm in Inter-Am.C.H.R., *Report on the Situation of Human Rights in Ecuador*, OEA/Ser.L/V/II.96, doc. 10 rev. 1 (1997). The Commission spoke about the right to life:

> [t]he realization of the right to life, and to physical security and integrity is necessarily related to and in some ways dependent upon one's physical environment. Accordingly, where environmental contamination and degradation pose a persistent threat to human life and health, the foregoing rights are implicated.

Id. at 88.

2. *Other rights.* The American Declaration contains neither a provision on environmental rights nor one on indigenous rights. Does that really matter, in terms of making a human rights argument?

3. *Jurisdiction.* The Inter-American Commission receives complaints and makes findings without regard to whether a country has ratified the American Convention on Human Rights. It considers its jurisdiction to extend to adopting resolutions for what it concludes are human rights violations under the American Declaration.

4. *Climate change.* Even though the United States and Canada are not parties to the American Convention, could the Commission make findings if it concluded that individuals' human rights were being violated by actions or inaction by one of those governments with regard to climate change? Could the Inuit people of the far North do so? See Chapter 12.

B. American Convention on Human Rights

American Convention on Human Rights

O.A.S.T.S. No. 36, 1144 U.N.T.S. 123,
OEA/Ser.L.V/II.82 doc.6 rev.1 at 25 (1992)

Article 1
Obligation to Respect Rights

1. The States Parties to this Convention undertake to respect the rights and freedoms recognized herein and to ensure to all persons subject to their jurisdiction the free and full exercise of those rights and freedoms, without any discrimination....

Article 4
Right to Life

1. Every person has the right to have his life respected. This right shall be protected by law and, in general, from the moment of conception....

———————

Consider whether the "right to life" in Article 4 could be extended by the Inter-American Court of Human Rights to environmental threats to life. Recall that the Inter-American Commission did so in the *Yanomami* and *Ecuador* situations.

C. San Salvador Protocol

As mentioned at the beginning of this chapter, the Additional Protocol to the American Convention on Human Rights in the Area of Economic, Social, and Cultural Rights (San Salvador Protocol), ratified by 14 nations in the Americas (although not the United States, Canada, and numerous other countries), provides in its Article 11: "Everyone shall have the right to live in a healthy environment and to have access to basic public services." Inter-Am. C.H.R., OEA/ser. L./V./II.82, doc. 6 rev. 1 (1992). Compare the specific environmental protections in the San Salvador Protocol to the implied environmental rights discussed earlier in this chapter.

Additional Protocol to the American Convention on Human Rights in the Area of Economic, Social and Cultural Rights
November 17, 1988
O.A.S. Treaty Series No. 69, Inter-Am. C.H.R.,
OEA/Ser.L.V/II.82 doc.6 rev.1 (1992)

Article 11
Right to a Healthy Environment

1. Everyone shall have the right to live in a healthy environment and to have access to basic public services.

2. The States Parties shall promote the protection, preservation, and improvement of the environment.

Environmental Advocacy and the Inter-American Human Rights System
Jorge Daniel Taillant
Linking Human Rights and the Environment
(R. Picolotti & J. D. Taillant, eds., 2003)

The San Salvador Protocol

The SSP [San Salvador Protocol] is an important international step in the consideration of the recognition of the symbiotic links between the environment and human rights. Specifically, the SSP in its preamble makes reference to,

> the close relationship that exists between economic, social and cultural rights, and civil and political rights, in that the different categories of rights constitute an indivisible whole, ... bearing in mind that ... rights [in the Americas] be reaf-

firmed ... on the basis of full respect for the ... right of its peoples to development, self determination, and the free disposal of their wealth and natural resources; ...

Article 11 is especially relevant to the environment and to environmental advocates seeking assistance of international law. It reads:

Article 11: The Right to a Healthy Environment

1. Everyone shall have the right to live in a healthy environment and to have access to basic public services.

2. The States Parties shall promote the protection, preservation, and improvement of the environment.

The SSP delineates certain state and international organization responsibilities with respect to economic, social and cultural rights, which may be especially useful to environmental advocates seeking redress before states for violations of human rights abuses related to environmental degradation. Some of these are: ...

(d) that States, in order to protect these rights, must submit periodic reports on the progressive measures taken to ensure due respect for the rights in the SSP (Article 19 (1));

(e) with respects to Articles 8A and 13 (Trade Unions and Education), the Inter-American Commission on Human Rights may give rise to legal petitions against States for non-compliance with the Inter-American Human Rights System (Article 19 (6));

(f) the Commission may formulate such observations and recommendations as it deems pertinent concerning the status of economic, social and cultural rights established in the SSP (Article 19(7)).

The SSP is a fairly new international legal instrument that has yet to be used or applied. It is however, cited in more recent analysis of international human rights law, and references to the SSP also appears in several precedent setting briefs aiming to link environmental degradation to human rights abuses. The SSP makes a bold step to reaffirm and regulate economic, social and cultural rights. Due to the difficulty and reluctance of most States to ensure economic, social and cultural rights, these rights have been for the most part ignored by international tribunals, although the rising awareness and debate over the importance of achieving sustainable development, as well as the growing importance of human rights to international tribunals (and the ability to enforce them at an international level), has begun to change this deficiency of the international legal arena.

It is important to understand that the SSP is an addendum to the American Convention. The spirit of the SSP, and the specific language it contains, sets out a series of useful and enforceable obligations and duties, while at the same time, limiting the capacity of the system to achieve some of its objectives. Existing Inter-American human rights institutions *may not* use their full powers with respect to the rights outlined in the SSP. The SSP, for example, limits the Commission to very specific powers.

The Commission (and in certain cases the Court) can:

1. Receive petitions against States based on violations of the Rights cited (only) in Articles 8A and 13 (Trade Unions and Education) of the SSP;

2. Receive Annual Reports of the States on the state of observance and protection of economic, social and cultural rights (as submitted to the Secretary General by the States);

3. Formulate observations and recommendations on the status of Economic, Social and Cultural Rights in all states parties in its annual reports or special reports and present these before the General Assembly.

Of the actions it may take, the Commission may file reports, which have served as effective pressure to States to address circumstances in which human rights violations have or are occurring. Although the reporting system does not carry the weight of legal action, it has proven in the past as a deterrent to States that systematically violate human rights....

———————

The San Salvador Protocol has not yet received a sufficient number of ratifications for it to go into effect, as of 2008.

Chapter 3

Substantive Environment Rights in National Law

Introduction

Despite the relative paucity of rulings by international courts on a right to life or a right to a healthy environment, as seen in the previous chapter, several national court systems enforce both rights. Attempts to embed environmental rights in national legal systems started in the U.S. in the late 1960s and accelerated in the 1970s. In 1968, U.S. Senator Gaylord Nelson submitted a proposal in Congress that an "inalienable right to a decent environment" be added to the U.S. Constitution. H.R. J.Res. 1321, 90th Cong., 2d Sess. (1968). Two years later, Congressman (now Professor) Richard Ottinger proposed a constitutional amendment that would have declared, "The right of the people to clean air, pure water, freedom from excessive and unnecessary noise, and the natural, scenic, historic and esthetic qualities of their environment shall not be abridged." H.R. J.Res. 1205, 91st Cong., 2d Sess. (1970). Neither proposal garnered much support. Instead, the U.S. Congress turned its attention to enacting a broad range of strict environmental laws during the period 1970–1974.

In other countries, however, the idea of a broad environmental right started to advance soon after the Stockholm Declaration, adopted at the U.N. Conference on the Environment in 1972. It stated that every person has "the fundamental right" to "an environment of a quality that permits a life of dignity and well-being." Stockholm Declaration of the United Nations Conference on the Human Environment, U.N. Doc. A/CONF.48/14 and Corr.1 (1972), reprinted in 11 I.L.M. 1416. *See* Chapter 1 of this book. By the 21st century, an environmental right of one kind or another had been adopted in the national constitutions of more than 100 countries as well as in several states of the U.S.

Are such constitutional environmental rights only statements of broad aspirations or are they enforceable legal provisions? Normally the defining characteristic of an enforceable "right" is that it will be protected by the judiciary or an international judicial or quasi-judicial body. National courts have given a range of answers to the question whether environmental rights in national constitutions actually give rise to a judicial remedy. If courts do give legal effect to constitutional provisions protecting environmental rights, do they risk treading on ground that should be left to legislatures and executives? Are they capable of giving practical effect to their pronouncements?

As you study the following materials, consider several different roles that the inclusion of an environmental right in a constitution might serve: as a mere statement of aspiration, as a basis for opening up access to the courts, as policy guidance to a legislature and the executive, as a judicially enforceable check on the legislature, as a command for specific actions by the legislature, as a displacement for executive authority, and as the basis for private remedies for damages or injunction similar to those provided by tort or property law. Each of these roles will be examined in this chapter.

I. Substantive Rights in National or State Constitutions

Human Rights and the Environment:
A Synopsis and Some Predictions
Barry E. Hill, Steve Wolfson, & Nicholas Targ
16 Geo. Int'l Envtl. L. Rev. 359 (2004)

C. National Constitutions

Constitutions of numerous countries around the world contain environmental provisions, taking a variety of forms. More than ninety national constitutions recognize a duty owed by the national government to its citizens to prevent harm to the environment. Of these, over fifty recognize the importance of a healthy environment, either as a duty of the state or as a right.

Far fewer national constitutions, however, are self-executing. For example, less than twenty of these constitutions explicitly make those who harm the environment liable for compensation or remediation of the harm, or establish a right to compensation for those suffering environmental injury. Commentators have noted, with respect to environmental provisions recently included in African constitutions, the near-total absence of court cases interpreting these provisions and proposed several possible causes, including the novelty of such provisions, the limited extent of public interest litigation, and "the failure of governments to set up the machinery to implement their constitutional duties."

Moreover, across nations many of the constitutional provisions are found not in a Bill of Rights of Fundamental Rights section, but in a Directive Principles Chapter, and thus are often not justiciable. Thus, justiciability is an issue at the national level, as it is with respect to international instruments and state constitutions. However, even where justiciability is an issue, these provisions are not without weight. They can provide legislative direction and authority and set the tone for legislative and executive policy development. They can also inform interpretation by courts of subsequent legislative enactments if governments follow through with appropriate legislation to protect environmental health.

In an increasingly large number of countries, but still the vast minority, courts are finding environmental constitutional provisions self-executing, conveying both procedural and substantive rights. A few such provisions are reviewed below, selected, in part, to provide geographic diversity, inclusion of both civil and common law traditions.

The Constitution of India

Perhaps more than in any other country, the judiciary of India has taken a proactive role in developing jurisprudence around environmental and other constitutional provisions to help secure a right to a clean and healthy environment for its citizens. The courts' activism, however, is not a barometer of Legislative or Executive Branch's commitment to environmental protection. Indeed, the courts' activity may, in some large part, be spurred by the perceived lack of engagement on the part of the other two branches of government to protect human health and the environment. While the reasons for India's reliance on constitutional provisions are many, Chief Justice B. N. Kirpal of the Supreme Court of India recently observed, "it has frequently fallen to the judiciary to protect environmental interests, due to the sketchy input from the legislature and laxity on the part of the administration." [An interesting example of Supreme Court initiative is found in this chapter at page 94 (mandatory environmental education case).]

While the Constitution of India was amended in 1976 to expressly address environmental quality, the Supreme Court of India has linked human rights to the environment through the older constitutional guarantee to "right to life," under Article 21. This fundamental right ... provides simply, "[n]o person shall be deprived of his life or personal liberty except according to procedure established by law." Despite the simplicity of Article 21, courts have found it to be a basis for sustainable development and intergenerational equity, which the Court described as meaning "what type or extent of development can take place, which can be sustained by nature/ecology with or without mitigation;" and the public trust doctrine.

Moreover, the Supreme Court of India has recently relaxed standing requirements, which has not only increased the number of public interest suits brought under Article 21, but has created the opportunity for India's judiciary to play an active role in addressing environmental conditions.... [Standing will be discussed in Chapter 8 of this textbook.]

The Constitution of the Philippines

Petitioners have been successful in bringing actions under the Constitution of the Philippines, which provides, pursuant to Article II, section 16, that "the state shall protect and advance the right of the people to a balanced and healthful ecology in accord with the rhythm and harmony of nature." In *Minors Oposa v. Secretary of the Department of Environment and Natural Resources*, children, through their parents, brought an action to have all existing timber license agreements on federal lands canceled, based on their constitutional environmental rights.... [See page 79 in this chapter.] Basing its decision on the right to a clean and healthy environment, specified under Article II, section 16, Chief Justice Davide, writing for the Court, opined that:

> ... Such a right, as hereinafter expounded, considers the "rhythm and harmony of nature." Nature means the created world in its entirety.... Needless to say, every generation has a responsibility to the next to preserve that rhythm and harmony for the full enjoyment of a balanced and healthful ecology. Put a little differently, the minors' assertion of their right to a sound environment constitutes, at the same time, the performance of their obligation to ensure the protection of that right for the generations to come.

Therefore, the petitioners were permitted to pursue their claim for equitable treatment and to secure their constitutional right to a clean and healthy environment both for their own benefit and as representatives of generations yet to come.

A concurring opinion, authored by Justice Feliciano, differed substantially from the majority in several major respects. Justice Feliciano noted that while the right to a balanced and healthful ecology is fundamental, he found that it could not be considered specific enough to form the basis of a cause of action and is not self-executing. He cautioned that the courts not venture "into the uncharted ocean of social and economic policy making." ...

The Constitution of Colombia

The courts of Colombia, like the courts of India, have found an enforceable right to a healthy environment under the constitutional guarantee of a right to life. Article 11 of the Constitution of Colombia, enacted in 1991, provides simply, "[t]he right to life cannot be denied." The courts, however, have interpreted the language expansively in a variety of factual contexts. In the same year that Article 11 was adopted, residents represented by a nongovernmental organization (NGO) brought an action, through an *amparo*, to have their Article 11 rights protected from the noxious operation of an asphalt facility. The trial court granted relief. Like the framers of the Stockholm Declaration of 1972, the trial court found that a right to a healthy environment is a derivative right of the right to life. Specifically, the trial court opined that:

> Everyone has the right to enjoy and live in a healthy environment. This should be regarded as a fundamental human right, which is a prerequisite and basis for the exercise of other human, economic and political rights. It should be recognised that a healthy environment is a sine qua non condition for life itself and that no right could be exercised in a deeply altered environment.

The Constitutional Court upheld the lower court's decision on appeal....

The Constitutional Court has continued this line of reasoning in other cases. For example, in *Victor Ramon Castrillon Vega v. Federacio Nacional de Algodoneros y Corporation Autonoma Regional del Cesar*, the Constitutional Court found that toxic fumes from an open pit violated nearby residents' Article 11 rights. In that case, the Court ordered the facility to remediate the site and to pay past and future medical expenses to those who became sick. Similarly, a lower court found a violation of Article 11 rights based on the harm to local indigenous people who suffered as the result of illegal forest clear-cutting. In addition to ordering restoration of the area, the lower court ordered damages based on the constitutional injury.

The Constitution of Chile

The Constitution of Chile, executed in 1980, creates several environmental rights. Article 19 provides for a "right to life" and a "right to live in an environment free of contamination," which apply to individuals. Article 19 also creates affirmative obligations on the Government of Chile to "ensure that the right to live in an environment free of contamination is not violated" and to "serve as a guardian for and preserve nature/the environment." More than aspirational goals, the Constitution of Chile provides a right of action to enforce these rights under "protection actions" pursuant to Article 20.

Although Chile is a civil law country, the courts have created a protective jurisprudence that is enforceable by individuals. In the first of three cases that help define the parameters of the broadly phrased constitutional-environmental provisions, *Comunidad de Chañaral v. Codeco Division el Saldor*, the Supreme Court found that the right to a clean environmental is owed not only to individuals and communities, but to future generations. Specifically, the Court ruled that the claims brought by a farmer to enjoin drainage of Lake Chungará, "... relate to the right to live in an environment free from pollution...." These problems, the Court opined, "affect not only the well being of man but also his own life, and actually not only the [livelihood] of a single community of persons, at present: future generation would claim the lack of prevision of their predecessors if the environment would be polluted and nature destroyed...." Thus, shortly after the enactment of the Constitution, the Court established minimal standing requirements to enforce the constitutional-environmental right.

Three years later, in 1988, the Supreme Court of Chile established that the constitutional-environmental provisions established a substantive right in addition to creating a right of standing. In *Pedro Flores v. Corporacion Del Cobre, Codelco*, residents of the village of Chañaral filed suit against a government run copper mine to restrain the company from continuing to discharge tailings on local beaches and coves. Based on a site visit, the Court found much of the shore and local waters inert. Finding that "the preservation of nature and the conservation of the environmental heritage is an obligation of the State, according to our Fundamental Constitution, and the polluting act which the respondent voluntarily executes is arbitrary from any point of view," the Court enjoined further dumping within one year. [See page 105 in this chapter.]

Finally, in the *"Trillium Case,"* the Supreme Court of Chile ... considering the merits of the case, which involved both a statutory as well as constitutional components, ... found that the necessary environmental impact assessment had not been completed. Therefore, the government could not offer sufficient evidence that the [logging of forests] was sustainable as required....

The Court's understanding of the constitutional-environmental provision in a social and intergenerational context, parallels the Supreme Court of the Philippines' reasoning in *Minors Oposa v. Secretary of the Department of Environment and Natural Resources*....

Questions and Discussion

1. *Litigating a U.S. federal constitutional right.* Attempts to persuade federal courts in the U.S. to interpret existing provisions of the U.S. Constitution as having an implicit environmental right have been unsuccessful. A U.S. District Court in 1971 sidestepped the issue on the ground that it was not "desirable for a lower court to embrace the exhilarating opportunity of anticipating a doctrine which may be in the womb of time, but whose birth is distant." *Environmental Defense Fund v. Corps of Engineers*, 325 F.Supp. 728 (E.D. Ark. 1971). Similarly, the U.S. Court of Appeals for the Fourth Circuit refused to recognize environmental constitutional rights. *Ely v. Velde*, 451 F.2d 1130, 1139 (4th Cir. 1971). The Ninth Circuit was a bit more adventurous, saying:

> [I]t is difficult to conceive of a more absolute and enduring concern than the preservation and, increasingly, the restoration of a decent and livable environment. Human life, itself a fundamental right, will vanish if we continue our heedless exploitation of this planet's natural resources. The centrality of the environment to all of our undertakings gives individuals a vital stake in maintaining its integrity.

Stop H-3 Ass'n v. Dole, 870 F.2d 1419 (9th Cir. 1989). Nonetheless, the court refused to enjoin construction of a highway that plaintiffs alleged would violate their environmental rights.

2. *State constitutions with environmental rights.* Five state constitutions in the United States explicitly recognize a personal right to a protected environment (Hawaii, Illinois, Massachusetts, Montana, Pennsylvania). Many others contain provisions of one sort or another relating to natural resources or the environment. Neil A. Popovic, *Pursuing Environmental Justice with International Human Rights and State Constitutions*, 15 Stan. Envtl. L.J. 338 (1996). We shall consider court cases in two states later in this chapter.

3. *National constitutions with environmental rights.* As the article mentions, a large number of national constitutions contain environmental rights. We shall examine principal court cases from five countries later in this chapter.

4. *Scope of an environmental right.* Before we turn to cases enforcing a constitutional environmental right, consider these different methods that a court might use to apply or enforce a constitutional right to a healthy environment:

Suits against the Government

- To *overturn a statute* as unconstitutional, in a suit brought by an individual citizen.

- To *cancel an administrative action*, in a suit brought by an individual citizen.

- To require a legislature or executive body *to adopt* a new regulatory program or take other affirmative action, in a suit brought by an individual citizen.

- To *uphold a statute or administrative action*, in a suit by a private, regulated party who challenges the constitutional basis of such legislation.

Suits against Private Persons

- To *authorize an Attorney General* to bring suit *parens patriae* (on behalf of citizens) against a private person alleged to be harming the environment.

- To *authorize a private citizen* to bring suit against a private person alleged to be harming the environment, and issue an *injunction* or award *damages*.

- To *invalidate* a private contractual or property decision, in a suit involving an individual citizen claiming violation of rights by such a decision.

Does any of these methods seem easier for a court to use than others? Does any of them seem to take the court out of its normal role? Does any of them raise questions about democratic governance? Does that matter, as long as the constitutional provision itself was adopted democratically?

5. *Environmental duties.* In some countries, the existence of environmental *duties* in national constitutions provides another important source of law that courts have started to draw upon for the protection of environmental rights. We will see some examples in this chapter of the relevance of environmental duties of both the state and its citizens in recent cases.

6. *Standing to sue.* Although it can be difficult, or even impossible in some legal systems, to distinguish between the concepts of a substantive right to relief and the right of standing to sue, standing will be addressed in Chapter 8 on access to justice.

II. Challenging Government Action and Inaction

Constitutional provisions recognizing environmental rights may be enforced against governments or against private individuals. This section of the chapter provides examples of the former, while the next section provides examples of the latter. Lawsuits challenging governments are most likely to be brought by private persons, as shown by each of the examples here. Lawsuits may ask for the annulment of government legislative or executive actions or sometimes for the initiation of legislative or executive action. Each of these variations raises different questions.

A. Overturning Legislation

Montana Environmental Information Center v.
Dep't of Environmental Quality (USA)

Supreme Court of Montana
296 Mont. 207, 988 P.2d 1236 (1999)

Justice TERRY N. TRIEWEILER delivered the Opinion of the Court.

The Plaintiffs [are] Montana Environmental Information Center (MEIC), Clark Fork-Pend Oreille Coalition, and Women's Voices for the Earth....

The Defendant, Montana Department of Environmental Quality is the State agency in charge of protecting water quality and issuing permits to hard rock mines....

Seven-Up Pete Joint Venture has submitted an application for a massive open-pit gold mine in the upper Blackfoot River valley, near the confluence of the Landers Fork and Blackfoot Rivers. Plaintiffs' complaint alleged that in the summer of 1995, DEQ illegally amended SPJV's mineral exploration license to allow for the discharge of groundwater containing high levels of arsenic and zinc into the shallow aquifers of the Blackfoot and Landers Fork Rivers, without requiring nondegradation review pursuant to §75-5-303(3), MCA (1995), and to the extent that it was authorized to do so, pursuant to §75-5-317(2)(j), MCA (1995), the latter statute violates the right to a clean and healthy environment....

Plaintiffs brought this action on October 6, 1995....

In support of their motion for summary judgment, the Plaintiffs contended that pursuant Article II, Section 3 and Article IX, Section 1 of the Montana Constitution and §75-5-303(3), MCA (1995), the State may not allow degradation of high quality waters without making the necessary showings required by the degradation review process set forth in the statute; that "degradation" includes increasing the concentration of arsenic in high quality waters; (both parties agree the waters in question are "high quality" waters) and that to the extent that water well tests are arbitrarily excluded from review, pursuant to §75-5-317(2)(j), MCA (1995), that statute offends Montana's constitution and the government must demonstrate both a compelling state interest for doing so, that the waiver provided for is closely tailored to effectuate only that interest and that it is the least onerous path available....

The District Court ... held that before strict scrutiny applies, Plaintiffs must demonstrate that a right guaranteed by the constitution has been abridged and that in this case they did not do so....

On appeal, Plaintiffs contend that when the legislature amended the Water Quality Act, by enacting §75-5-317(2)(j), MCA (1995), to exclude certain activities from review pursuant to the act's nondegradation policy, the blanket exclusion is unconstitutional when the facts show, as they did here, that degradation will occur. Plaintiffs contend that because Montanans have a fundamental right to a clean and healthful environment pursuant to Article II, Section 3 of the Montana Constitution, the provisions of the amendment must be strictly scrutinized for not only a compelling state interest, but also to assure that the amendment is closely tailored to effectuate the government's interest by the least onerous path available and that the District Court erred by refusing to apply strict scrutiny.... Plaintiffs request that this Court remand to the District Court for a determination of whether exemption from nondegradation review is constitutional....

The DEQ and SPJV ... contend that the constitutional provisions in question were not intended to prohibit all discharges of water which include arsenic but only those which render the receiving water unclean or unhealthy and that neither condition was proven in this case....

Constitutional and Statutory Framework ...

Article II, Section 3 provides in relevant part that:

All persons are born free and have certain inalienable rights. They include the right to a clean and healthful environment....

Article IX, Section 1 provides in relevant part as follows:

(1) The State and each person shall *maintain and improve* a clean and healthful environment in Montana for present and future generations....

(3) The legislature shall provide adequate remedies for the protection of the environmental life support system *from degradation* and provide adequate remedies to *prevent unreasonable depletion and degradation* of natural resources. (emphasis added).

[The] Plaintiffs contend that the nondegradation policy for high quality waters established by § 75-5-303, MCA, of Montana's Water Quality Act is reasonably well designed to meet the constitution's objectives and that it is the minimum requirement which must be satisfied for a discharge which degrades the existing quality of Montana water. The relevant portions of that statute provide: ...

(3) The department may not authorize degradation of high quality waters unless it has been affirmatively demonstrated ... that:

(a) degradation is necessary because there are no economically, environmentally, and technologically feasible modifications to the proposed project that would result in no degradation;

(b) the proposed project will result in important economic or social development and that the benefit of the development exceeds the costs to society of allowing degradation of high quality waters; ...

(d) the least degrading water quality protection practices determined by the department to be economically, environmentally, and technologically feasible will be fully implemented by the applicant prior to and during the proposed activity.

§ 75-5-317, MCA (1995).

Plaintiffs contend that the Constitution's environmental protections were violated by the legislature in 1995, when it amended § 75-5-317(2)(j), MCA to provide a blanket exception to the requirements of nondegradation review for discharges from water well or monitoring well tests.... Section 75-5-317(2)(j), MCA (1995), provides in relevant part as follows: ...

(2) The following categories or classes of activities are not subject to the provisions of 75-5-303: ...

(j) discharges of water from water well or monitoring well tests ... conducted in accordance with department approved water quality protection practices....

Plaintiffs contend that the groundwater discharged into the alluvia of the Landers Fork and Blackfoot Rivers and ultimately to the alluvial aquifers and the surface water of at least the Landers Fork River, degraded high quality waters....

Because discharges containing carcinogenic parameters, (i.e., discharged water containing concentrations of arsenic equal to .009 mg/l) greater than those in the receiving water (i.e., .003 mg/l) were allowed in this case, Plaintiffs contend that the discharges should not have been exempt from nondegradation....

Constitutional Analysis

In order to address the issue raised on appeal, it is necessary that we determine the threshold showing which implicates the rights provided for by Article II, Section 3 and Article IX, Section 1 of the Montana Constitution and the level of scrutiny to be applied to each provision. DEQ and SPJV contend, and the District Court agreed that actual danger to human health or the health of the environment must first be demonstrated. The Plaintiffs contend that Montana's constitutional provisions are intended to prevent harm to the environment; that degradation to the environment is all that need be shown; and that degradation was established in this case based on the DEQ's own adopted standard.

We have not had prior occasion to discuss the level of scrutiny which applies when the right to a clean and healthful environment guaranteed by Article II, Section 3 or those rights referred to in Article IX, Section 1 are implicated.... However, our prior cases which discuss other provisions of the Montana Constitution and the debate of those delegates who attended the 1972 Constitutional Convention, guide us in both respects.

In *Butte Community Union v. Lewis* (1986), 219 Mont. 426, we held that:

> If a fundamental right is infringed or a suspect classification established, the government has to show a "compelling state interest" for its action.... [I]n order to be fundamental, a right must be found within Montana's Declaration of Rights or be a right "without which other constitutionally guaranteed rights would have little meaning." ...

We elaborated on the level of scrutiny for statutes or rules which implicate rights guaranteed in our declaration of rights in *Wadsworth v. State* (1996), 275 Mont. 287. There we held that, "the inalienable right to pursue life's basic necessities is stated in the Declaration of Rights and is therefore a fundamental right." *Wadsworth*, 275 Mont. at 299....

Applying the preceding rules to the facts in this case, we conclude that the right to a clean and healthful environment is a fundamental right because it is guaranteed by the Declaration of Rights found at Article II, Section 3 of Montana's Constitution, and that any statute or rule which implicates that right must be strictly scrutinized and can only survive scrutiny if the State establishes a compelling state interest and that its action is closely tailored to effectuate that interest and is the least onerous path that can be taken to achieve the State's objective.

State action which implicates those rights provided for in Article IX, Section 1 would normally not be subject to strict scrutiny because those rights are not found in Montana's Declaration of Rights. Those rights would normally be subject to a middle-tier of scrutiny because lodged elsewhere in our state constitution. However, we conclude that the right to a clean and healthful environment guaranteed by Article II, Section 3, and those rights provided for in Article IX, Section 1 were intended by the constitution's framers to be interrelated and interdependent and that state or private action which implicates either, must be scrutinized consistently. Therefore, we will apply strict scrutiny to state or private action which implicates either constitutional provision....

[We] look to the records of the [1972 constitutional] convention discussion and debate to determine the showing that must be made before the rights are implicated and strict scrutiny applied.

Article IX, Section 1 was reported to the floor of the constitutional convention by the Natural Resources and Agricultural Committee on March 1, 1972.... The provision, as introduced, was thought by members of the committee to be the strongest environmental protection provision found in any state constitution. Delegate McNeil explained that descriptive adjectives were not included preceding the word environment such as healthful or unsoiled, because the majority felt that the current Montana environment encompassed all of those descriptive adjectives. He further explained that descriptive adjectives were not originally included because:

> The majority felt that the use of the word "healthful" would permit those who would pollute our environment to parade in some doctors who could say that if a person can walk around with four pounds of arsenic in his lungs or SO2 gas in his lungs and wasn't dead, that that would be a healthful environment. We strongly believe [as] the majority does that our provision or proposal is stronger than using the word "healthful."

Montana Constitutional Convention, Vol. IV at 1201, March 1, 1972....

In concluding remarks in opposition to amending the committee majority's proposed Article IX, Section 1, Delegate McNeil gave the following explanation for the language being recommended:

> We did not want the Supreme Court of this state or the Legislature to be able to say that the environment in Montana, as we know right now, can be degraded to a healthful environment. So our purpose in leaving that word out was to strengthen it. I would like also to remind the delegates that the Illinois provision does not contain subparagraph 3 of the majority proposal, [Article IX, Section 1(3)] which speaks precisely to the point that concerned Jerry Cate so much, and that is there is no provision by which the Legislature can prevent and this is anticipatory can prevent unreasonable depletion of the natural resources. I submit if you will read that majority proposal again and again, you will find that it is the strongest of any constitution....

Delegate Foster also gave the following defense of the language as originally proposed:

> I feel that if we, as a Constitutional Convention of Montana, use our line of defense on the environment on the basis of healthful, then we, in fact, might as well forget it, because what I'm concerned about in Montana is not a healthful environment. This country is going to have to address itself to the question of a healthful environment. What I'm concerned about is an environment that is better than healthful. If all we have is a survivable environment, then we've lost the battle....

In the end advocates for adding the descriptive language "clean and healthful" prevailed. However, it was not on the basis that they wanted less protection than articulated by Delegates McNeil and Foster, it was because they felt the additional language was necessary in order to assure the objectives articulated by Delegates McNeil and Foster. *See* Delegate Campbell cmts. (*Montana Constitutional Convention*, Vol. V at 1246, March 1, 1972). It was agreed by both sides of the debate that it was the convention's intention to adopt whatever the convention could agree was the stronger language.

Although Article IX, Section 1(1), (2), and (3) were all approved by the convention on March 1, 1972, the right to a clean and healthful environment was not included in the Bill of Rights until six days later on March 7, 1972. On that date, Delegate Burkhart moved to add "the right to a clean and healthful environment" to the other inalienable rights listed in Article II, Section 3 of the proposed constitution. He explained his intention that it interrelate with those rights provided for and previously adopted in Article IX, Section 1. He also stated that it was his intention through the addition of this right to the Bill of Rights to give force to the language of the preamble to the constitution. Burkhart stated: "I think it's a beautiful statement, and it seems to me that what I am proposing here is in concert with what's proposed in that Preamble...." Delegate Eck concurred that including the additional language in Article II, Section 3, was consistent with the intention of the Natural Resources Committee when it reported Article IX, Section 1. The right to a clean and healthy environment was, therefore, included as a fundamental right by a vote of 79 to 7.

We conclude, based on the eloquent record of the Montana Constitutional Convention that to give effect to the rights guaranteed by Article II, Section 3 and Article IX, Section 1 of the Montana Constitution they must be read together and consideration given to all of the provisions of Article IX, Section 1 as well as the preamble to the Montana Constitution. In doing so, we conclude that the delegates' intention was to provide language and protections which are both anticipatory and preventative. The delegates did not intend to merely prohibit that degree of environmental degradation which can be conclusively linked to ill health or physical endangerment. Our constitution does not require that dead fish float on the surface of our state's rivers and streams before its far-sighted environmental protections can be invoked....

We conclude, therefore, that the District Court erred when it held that Montana's constitutional right to a clean and healthy environment was not implicated, absent a demonstration that public health is threatened or that current water quality standards are affected to such an extent that a significant impact has been had on either the Landers Fork or Blackfoot River.

We conclude that the constitutional right to a clean and healthy environment and to be free from unreasonable degradation of that environment is implicated based on the Plaintiffs' demonstration that the pumping tests proposed by SPJV would have added a known carcinogen such as arsenic to the environment in concentrations greater than the concentrations present in the receiving water and that the DEQ or its predecessor after studying the issue and conducting hearings has concluded that discharges containing carcinogenic parameters greater than the concentrations of those parameters in the receiving water has a significant impact which requires review pursuant to Montana's policy of nondegradation set forth at § 75-5-303, MCA....

We conclude that for purposes of the facts presented in this case, § 75-5-303, MCA is a reasonable legislative implementation of the mandate provided for in Article IX, Section 1 and that to the extent § 75-5-317(2)(j), MCA (1995) arbitrarily excludes certain "activities" from nondegradation review without regard to the nature or volume of the substances being discharged, it violates those environmental rights guaranteed by Article II, Section 3 and Article IX, Section 1 of the Montana Constitution....

Based on these holdings, we reverse the judgment of the District Court and remand to the District Court for strict scrutiny of the statutory provision in question, and in particular for a determination of whether there is a compelling state interest for the enactment of that statute based on the criteria we articulated in *Wadsworth v. State.*

The judgment of the District Court is reversed and this case is remanded for further proceedings consistent with this opinion.

WILLIAM E. HUNT, SR., JAMES C. NELSON, and JIM REGNIER, JJ., concur.

Justice W. WILLIAM LEAPHART, specially concurring.

I concur in the result reached by the Court and specifically with the conclusion that the right to a clean and healthful environment is a fundamental right guaranteed by the Declaration of Rights found at Article II, Section 3 of the Montana Constitution. Having so concluded, the Court goes on to declare that "state or private action which implicates either[Article II, Section 3 or Article IX, Section 1 of the Montana Constitution], must be scrutinized consistently. Therefore, we will apply strict scrutiny to state or private action which implicates either constitutional provision." I agree that state action implicating the rights guaranteed by Article II, Section 3 or Article IX, Section 1, must be subject to strict scrutiny. Although Article IX, Section 1, clearly imposes an obligation on private entities, as well as the state, to maintain and improve a clean and healthy environment, I would not, in the context of this appeal, address the question of private action. In resolving this appeal, we are not addressing private action. Rather, we are addressing state action; that is, the constitutionality of a state statute. The conclusion that we will apply strict scrutiny analysis to private action is dicta which, I submit, may well prove unworkable in the future. As we state in this opinion, strict scrutiny analysis requires that the state demonstrate a compelling state interest and that its action is both closely tailored to effectuate that interest and the least onerous path that can be taken to achieve the State's objective. I am not clear as to how, or whether, private action lends itself to a "compelling state interest" analysis. That is a question that I think would be better left to another day.

Questions and Discussion

1. *Constitutionalism.* What are the institutional implications of courts overturning legislation on the basis of vague constitutional standards? Are courts well suited to make "policy" decisions? Is such a decision necessarily one of "policy"? When a court overturns legislation on the basis of an environmental right is it any different from overturning legislation on the basis of rights such as freedom of speech or structural constitutional doctrines such as federalism or separation of powers?

2. *Human or ecosystem health?* What is a clean and healthful environment? Does "healthful" in the Montana Constitution mean only a survivable environment? Does it include only human health or also the health of ecosystems and animals? In comparison to the *Montana Environmental Information Center* case, consider jurisprudence under Article IX, section 2, of the Illinois Constitution. The Illinois Supreme Court has ruled that the legislative history of the adoption of that State's constitutional provision revealed that "healthful environment" in that constitution refers only to human health and not to non-human elements of the environment. *Glisson v. City of Marion,* 188 Ill. 2d 211, 242 Ill. Dec. 79 (Ill., 1999).

3. *Danger versus degradation.* Is it necessary for a plaintiff to demonstrate actual danger to human health, or it is enough to show degradation of the environment (decline in quality of water)? If degradation is shown, is that enough to block state legislation, or can environmental harm be allowed if counterbalanced by some benefit?

4. *Basis for unconstitutionality.* How does the court find the exclusion of certain activities from review pursuant to the Water Quality Act non-degradation policy (by the 1995 amendment) to be unconstitutional? How does the court interpret the environmental right to be a "fundamental right"?

5. *"Strict scrutiny" of legislation and administrative actions.* The court in *Montana Environmental Information Center* ruled that because the right to a healthy environment was a fundamental right in Montana, "strict scrutiny" should be applied to any legislation that might violate that right. What is the basis for the Montana Supreme Court's use of the strict-scrutiny standard?

In a subsequent case, *Clark Fork Coalition v. DEQ,* a lower court decided that the *MEIC* case required application of the strict-scrutiny standard also for review of administrative actions. The State of Montana had issued a Montana Pollutant Discharge Elimination System (MPDES) permit that allowed an increase of arsenic in the groundwater. The court said:

> [I]nsofar as the MPDES permit authorizes the discharge associated with Outfall 002, it is in violation of the Montana Constitution and the Montana Water Quality Act in Section 75-5-303, MCA. Since the Montana Constitution's protection of the environment is prospective and preventative, Plaintiffs here need not wait until the mine actually goes into operation and the carcinogenic discharge occurs.... As such, the MPDES permit, insofar as it allows an increased arsenic level in the groundwater below Outfall 002, is declared VOID.

Clark Fork Coalition v. DEQ, 2006 Mont. Dist. LEXIS 210, at 13–14 (2006). Is it reasonable to apply a strict-scrutiny standard to one area of review of administrative actions while other administrative actions are reviewed under a more relaxed "arbitrary or capricious" standard?

6. *Standard of review without fundamental rights.* In contrast to the approach of the Montana courts, consider *Illinois Pure Water Committee v. Director of Public Health,* 104 Ill. 2d 243, 251–252 (Ill. 1984), where the Illinois Supreme Court held that a strict scrutiny standard was not appropriate in considering whether the environmental rights provision of the Illinois Constitution has been violated by administrative action, because the environmental right was not a fundamental right:

> Plaintiffs cite no authority for the proposition that sections 1 and 2 of article XI create a "fundamental" right to a healthful environment, and do not explain why we should subject statutes affecting the environment to a higher level of scrutiny. In the absence of more persuasive reasoning, we decline to do so.

7. *Overturning legislation in Hungary.* Montana is not the only jurisdiction willing to strike down legislation as inconsistent with a substantive constitutional environmental right. In *Magyar Kozlony Case* No 1994/No. 55, page 1919 (Hungarian Constitutional Court, 1994), the Constitutional Court of Hungary held that legislation was unconstitutional under Hungary's constitutional right to a protected environment when the legislation attempted to facilitate the selling-off of public forest lands to private interests.

B. Overturning Executive Action

Oposa v. Factoran (Philippines)
Supreme Court of the Philippines
G.R. No. 101083, 224 SCRA 792 (July 30, 1993), 33 I.L.M. 173 (1994)

EN BANC

DAVIDE, JR., J:

[T]his petition bears upon the right of Filipinos to a balanced and healthful ecology which the petitioners dramatically associate with the twin concepts of "inter-generational responsibility" and "inter-generational justice." Specifically, it touches on the issue of whether the said petitioners have a cause of action to "prevent the misappropriation or impairment" of Philippine rainforests and "arrest the unabated hemorrhage of the country's vital life-support systems and continued rape of Mother Earth."

The controversy has its genesis in Civil Case No. 90-777 which was filed before Branch 66 (Makati, Metro Manila) of the Regional Trial Court (RTC), National Capital Judicial Region. The principal plaintiffs therein, now the principal petitioners, are all minors duly represented and joined by their respective parents.... The minors further asseverate that they "represent their generation as well as generations yet unborn." Consequently, it is prayed for that judgment be rendered:

> ... ordering defendant, his agents, representatives and other persons acting in his behalf to
>
> (1) Cancel all existing timber license agreements in the country;
>
> (2) Cease and desist from receiving, accepting, processing, renewing or approving new timber license agreements

and granting the plaintiffs "... such other reliefs just and equitable under the premises."

The complaint starts off with the general averments that the Philippine archipelago of 7,100 islands has a land area of thirty million (30,000,000) hectares and is endowed with rich, lush and verdant rainforests in which varied, rare and unique species of flora and fauna may be found; these rainforests contain a genetic, biological and chemical pool which is irreplaceable; they are also the habitat of indigenous Philippine cultures which have existed, endured and flourished since time immemorial; scientific evidence reveals that in order to maintain a balanced and healthful ecology, the country's land area should be utilized on the basis of a ratio of fifty-four per cent (54%) for forest cover and forty-six per cent (46%) for agricultural, residential, industrial, commercial and other uses; the distortion and disturbance of this balance as a consequence of deforestation have resulted in a host of environmental tragedies, such as (a) water shortages..., (c) massive erosion and the consequential loss of soil fertility and agricultural productivity, ... (d) the endangering and extinction of the country's unique, rare and varied flora and fauna, (e) the disturbance and dislocation of cultural communities, including the disappearance of the Filipino's indigenous cultures, ... and (k) the reduction of the earth's capacity to process carbon dioxide gases which has led to perplexing and catastrophic climatic changes such as the phenomenon of global warming, otherwise known as the "greenhouse effect." ...

As their cause of action, they specifically allege that:

CAUSE OF ACTION ...

> 8. Twenty-five (25) years ago, the Philippines had some sixteen (16) million hectares of rainforests constituting roughly 53% of the country's land mass.
>
> 9. Satellite images taken in 1987 reveal that there remained no more than 1.2 million hectares of said rainforests or four per cent (4.0%) of the country's land area.
>
> 10. More recent surveys reveal that a mere 850,000 hectares of virgin old-growth rainforests are left, barely 2.8% of the entire land mass of the Philippine archipelago and about 3.0 million hectares of immature and uneconomical secondary growth forests....
>
> 12. At the present rate of deforestation, i.e. about 200,000 hectares per annum or 25 hectares per hour—nighttime, Saturdays, Sundays and holidays in-

cluded—the Philippines will be bereft of forest resources after the end of this ensuing decade, if not earlier....

14. The continued allowance by defendant of TLA [Timber License Agreement] holders to cut and deforest the remaining forest stands will work great damage and irreparable injury to plaintiffs—especially plaintiff minors and their successors—who may never see, use, benefit from and enjoy this rare and unique natural resource treasure.

This act of defendant constitutes a misappropriation and/or impairment of the natural resource property he holds in trust for the benefit of plaintiff minors and succeeding generations.

15. Plaintiffs have a clear and constitutional right to a balanced and healthful ecology and are entitled to protection by the State in its capacity as the *parens patriae*....

18. The continued failure and refusal by defendant to cancel the TLA's is an act violative of the rights of plaintiffs, especially plaintiff minors who may be left with a country that is desertified, bare, barren and devoid of the wonderful flora, fauna and indigenous cultures which the Philippines has been abundantly blessed with....

20. Furthermore, defendant's continued refusal to cancel the aforementioned TLA's is contradictory to the Constitutional policy of the State to ...

> d. "protect and advance the right of the people to a balanced and healthful ecology in accord with the rhythm and harmony of nature." (Section 16, Article II, *id.*)

21. Finally, defendant's act is contrary to the highest law of humankind—the natural law—and violative of plaintiffs' right to self-preservation and perpetuation....

On 22 June 1990, the original defendant, Secretary Factoran, Jr., filed a Motion to Dismiss the complaint based on two (2) grounds, namely: (1) the plaintiffs have no cause of action against him and (2) the issue raised by the plaintiffs is a political question which properly pertains to the legislative or executive branches of Government....

On 18 July 1991, respondent Judge issued an order granting the aforementioned motion to dismiss....

Plaintiffs thus filed the instant special civil action for certiorari under Rule 65 of the Revised Rules of Court and ask this Court to rescind and set aside the dismissal order on the ground that the respondent Judge gravely abused his discretion in dismissing the action....

Petitioners contend that the complaint clearly and unmistakably states a cause of action as it contains sufficient allegations concerning their right to a sound environment based on Articles 19, 20 and 21 of the Civil Code (Human Relations), Section 4 of Executive Order (E.O.) No. 192 creating the DENR, Section 3 of Presidential Decree (P.D.) No. 1151 (Philippine Environmental Policy), Section 16, Article II of the 1987 Constitution recognizing the right of the people to a balanced and healthful ecology, the concept of generational genocide in Criminal Law and the concept of man's inalienable right to self-preservation and self-perpetuation embodied in natural law. Petitioners likewise rely on the respondent's correlative obligation, per Section 4 of E.O. No. 192, the safeguard the people's right to a healthful environment....

On the other hand, the respondents aver that the petitioners failed to allege in their complaint a specific legal right violated by the respondent Secretary for which any relief is provided by law. They see nothing in the complaint but vague and nebulous allegations concerning an "environmental right" which supposedly entitles the petitioners to the "protection by the state in its capacity as parens patriae." Such allegations, according to them, do not reveal a valid cause of action. They then reiterate the theory that the question of whether logging should be permitted in the country is a political question which should be properly addressed to the executive or legislative branches of Government. They therefore assert that the petitioners' recourse is not to file an action in court, but to lobby before Congress for the passage of a bill that would ban logging totally....

We do not hesitate to find for the petitioners and rule against the respondent Judge's challenged order for having been issued with grave abuse of discretion....

The complaint focuses on one specific fundamental legal right—the right to a balanced and healthful ecology which, for the first time in our nation's constitutional history, is solemnly incorporated in the fundamental law. Section 16, Article II of the 1987 Constitution explicitly provides:

> Sec. 16. The State shall protect and advance the right of the people to a balanced and healthful ecology in accord with the rhythm and harmony of nature.

This right unites with the right to health which is provided for in the preceding section of the same article:

> Sec. 15. The State shall protect and promote the right to health of the people and instill health consciousness among them.

While the right to a balanced and healthful ecology is to be found under the Declaration of Principles and State Policies and not under the Bill of Rights, it does not follow that it is less important than any of the civil and political rights enumerated in the latter. Such a right belongs to a different category of rights altogether for it concerns nothing less than self-preservation and self-perpetuation—aptly and fittingly stressed by the petitioners—the advancement of which may even be said to predate all governments and constitutions.

As a matter of fact, these basic rights need not even be written in the Constitution for they are assumed to exist from the inception of humankind. If they are now explicitly mentioned in the fundamental charter, it is because of the well-founded fear of its framers that unless the rights to a balanced and healthful ecology and to health are mandated as state policies by the Constitution itself, thereby highlighting their continuing importance and imposing upon the state a solemn obligation to preserve the first and protect and advance the second, the day would not be too far when all else would be lost not only for the present generation, but also for those to come—generations which stand to inherit nothing but parched earth incapable of sustaining life.

The right to a balanced and healthful ecology carries with it the correlative duty to refrain from impairing the environment....

A denial or violation of that right by the other who has the correlative duty or obligation to respect or protect the same gives rise to a cause of action. Petitioners maintain that the granting of the TLAs, which they claim was done with grave abuse of discretion, violated their right to a balanced and healthful ecology; hence, the full protection thereof requires that no further TLAs should be renewed or granted....

The foregoing considered, Civil Case No. 90-777 cannot be said to raise a political question. Policy formulation or determination by the executive or legislative branches of

Government is not squarely put in issue. What is principally involved is the enforcement of a right vis-a-vis policies already formulated and expressed in legislation....

WHEREFORE, being impressed with merit, the instant Petition is hereby

GRANTED, and the challenged Order of respondent Judge of 18 July 1991 dismissing Civil Case No. 90-777 is hereby set aside. The petitioners may therefore amend their complaint to implead as defendants the holders or grantees of the questioned timber license agreements.

CRUZ, PADILLA, BIDIN, GRIÑO-AQUINO, REGALADO, ROMERO, NOCON, BELLOSILLO, MELO and QUIASON, JJ., concur. NARVASA, C.J., PUNO and VITUG, JJ., took no part.

FELICIANO, J., concurring ...

It is ... very difficult to fashion language more comprehensive in scope and generalized in character than a right to "a balanced and healthful ecology." The list of particular claims which can be subsumed under this rubric appears to be entirely open-ended: prevention and control of emission of toxic fumes and smoke from factories and motor vehicles; of discharge of oil, chemical effluents, garbage and raw sewage into rivers, inland and coastal waters by vessels, oil rigs, factories, mines and whole communities; of dumping of organic and inorganic wastes on open land, streets and thoroughfares; failure to rehabilitate land after strip-mining or open-pit mining; *kaingin* or slash-and-burn farming; destruction of fisheries, coral reefs and other living sea resources through the use of dynamite or cyanide and other chemicals; contamination of ground water resources; loss of certain species of fauna and flora; and so on....

My suggestion is simply that petitioners must, before the trial court, show a more specific legal right—a right cast in language of a significantly lower order of generality than Article II (15) of the Constitution—that is or may be violated by the actions, or failures to act, imputed to the public respondent by petitioners so that the trial court can validly render judgment granting all or part of the relief prayed for....

It seems to me important that the legal right which is an essential component of a cause of action be a specific, operable legal right, rather than a constitutional or statutory policy, for at least two (2) reasons. One is that unless the legal right claimed to have been violated or disregarded is given specification in operational terms, defendants may well be unable to defend themselves intelligently and effectively; in other words, there are due process dimensions to this matter.

The second is a broader-gauge consideration—where a specific violation of law or applicable regulation is not alleged or proved, petitioners can be expected to fall back on the expanded conception of judicial power in the second paragraph of Section 1 of Article VIII of the Constitution which reads: ...

> Judicial power includes the duty of the courts of justice to settle actual controversies involving rights which are legally demandable and enforceable, and to determine whether or not there has been a *grave abuse of discretion* amounting to lack or excess of jurisdiction *on the part of any branch or instrumentality of the Government.* (Emphasis supplied.)

When substantive standards as general as "the right to a balanced and healthy ecology" and "the right to health" are combined with remedial standards as broad ranging as "a grave abuse of discretion amounting to lack or excess of jurisdiction," the result will be, it is respectfully submitted, to propel courts into the uncharted ocean of social and economic policy making. At least in respect of the vast area of environmental protection and management, our courts have no claim to special technical competence and experience and professional qualification. Where no specific, operable norms and standards are shown to exist, then the policy making departments—the legislative and executive departments—must be given a real and effective opportunity to fashion and promulgate those norms and standards, and to implement them before the courts should intervene....

I vote to grant the Petition for *Certiorari* because the protection of the environment, including the forest cover of our territory, is of extreme importance for the country. The doctrines set out in the Court's decision issued today should, however, be subjected to closer examination.

Questions and Discussion

1. *Positive rights and political questions.* Note the Court's conclusion that the case did not present a non-justiciable "political question" because it involved not the creation of new policies, but a review of "policies already formulated and expressed in legislation." How can this issue be cast in terms of "negative rights" versus "positive rights"?

2. *Unwritten constitutional rights.* The Court said that basic rights such as the right to a balanced and healthful ecology "need not even be written in the Constitution for they are assumed to exist from the inception of humankind." Can you relate that concept to the concept of "substantive due process" and "unenumerated fundamental rights" under the U.S. Constitution? In *Griswold v. Connecticut*, 381 U.S. 479, 85 S.Ct. 1678 (1965), the Supreme Court ruled that constitution contains an unenumerated right to privacy. Similarly, in *Roe v. Wade*, 410 U.S. 113, 93 S.Ct. 705 (1973), the Supreme Court held that the unenumerated right to privacy includes a woman's choice to have an abortion. The Philippines does not stand entirely alone in finding an unwritten right to a healthy environment:

> In Argentina, the National Constitution recognizes since 1994 the right to a healthy and suitable environment. However, even before the law provided for such explicit recognition, courts had acknowledged the existence of the right to live in a healthy environment.
>
> Already in 1983, and before the formulation of this right was introduced in Argentinean jurisprudence, an administrative court stated that "the right of any citizen to preserve his or her habitat amounts to a subjective right" and that such right would entitle any person to initiate an action for environmental protection [*Kattan, Alberto v. National Government*, Juzgado Nacional de la Instancia en lo Contencioso administrativo Federal. N°2. Ruling of 10.5.1983, La Ley, 1983-D, 576].
>
> In a 1993 case concerning environmental harm to fisheries and wildlife in a lagoon [*Irazu, Margarita v. Copetro SA, Cámara Civil y Comercial de la Plata. Ruling of 10.5.1993]* the court asserted:
>
>> The right to live in [a] healthy and balanced environment is a fundamental attribute of people. Any aggression to the environment ends up becoming a threat to life itself and to the psychological and physical integrity of the person—which is based on ecological balance http://www2.ohchr.org/english/issues/environment/environ/bp6.htm....
>
> After the Constitution's modification, this right has been often recognized by the judiciary and interpreted broadly. In the 1994 case of *Alberto Sagarduy* [Cámara de Apelaciones en lo Civil y Comercial de La Plata, Sala III. Ruling of 15.11.1994. LLBA, 1998-943-RcyS, 1999-530] the court considered the right to

defend everyone's environment as a "natural human right," which allows citizens to place any complaints to government agencies regardless of the existence of a specific administrative procedure. http://www2.ohchr.org/english/issues/environment/environ/bp6.htm.

It is also interesting to note a decision of 1999 in which the court established that the right to live in a suitable environment and to enjoy an adequate standard of living merits an extensive interpretation, covering as a result the broadest possible number of environmental offences, including, as in the case, the right to enjoy the ocean's view—impaired by the construction of a wall [*Sociedad De Fomento Barrio Félix v. Camet, Cámara De Apelaciones y Garantías en lo Penal de Mar Del Plata, Sala I* . Ruling of 9.9.1999. LLBA, 2000-991].

Adriana Fabra and Eva Arnal, *Background Paper No. 6: Review of jurisprudence on human rights and the environment in Latin America,* Joint UNEP-OHCHR Expert Seminar on Human Rights and the Environment, 14–16 January 2002, Geneva.

3. *Aspiration and statutory claims versus self-execution.* Who has the better position on the question of whether the constitutional environmental right in the Philippine Constitution is self-executing or merely aspirational and should require statutory claims to become operational, Justice Davide or Justice Feliciano? Which view is better for the environment? Which view is better for the legal system and for a democratic society?

Under Justice Feliciano's approach, would the constitutional right to a healthy environment have any substantive content, or would it merely give plaintiffs the right to come into the court if the plaintiffs could find a violation of adopted legislation in the country? Under that approach, would the constitutional right be little more than a relaxation of doctrine that might otherwise restrict standing to sue?

Under the position of Justice Davide and the majority of the Philippine Supreme Court, what would the courts use as a measuring stick to determine violations of the constitutional environmental right? What kinds of defenses would an accused government official or company be able to offer?

4. *The scope of self-executory constitutional claims.* One author has stated that the ruling that the constitutional environmental right is self-executing is the most important aspect of *Oposa v. Factoran*:

> *Oposa* is a statement to the effect that: the right to a sound environment is a self-executory constitutional policy. By itself, independent of specific statutory rights, this right is actionable. And it is actionable against the DENR Secretary who is tasked with carrying out the State's constitutional mandate to control and supervise the exploration, development, utilization, and conservation of the country's natural resources.

> This statement is groundbreaking in that constitutional authorities in the Philippines have always believed otherwise....

> The task at hand now seems to be to test the potential of this decision. *Oposa* need not be confined to forest protection. It may be invoked to prevent other forms of environmental degradation. Mining activities, the change of land use to industrial or commercial purposes, quarrying operations, and the emission of toxic medical wastes are only some of the environmental problems facing the country today.

> *Oposa* also might be used to address the forced displacement of communities caused by infrastructure and development projects. Small landowners have been literally bulldozed out of their lands to make way for export processing

zones. Thousands of families are under the threat of displacement because of the construction of government projects such as commercial and sports complexes, cement plants, dams, geothermal plants, mining operations, and the commercial development of land. All these activities necessarily threaten the environment. May *Oposa* be used to stop any of these activities? ... May a citizen challenge all land use conversions as a violation of this right? ... It is highly unlikely that the courts will sanction suits that seek blanket prohibitions against the issuance of natural resources access instruments.... The courts may, instead, find it necessary to fashion a standard under which the challenged action may be declared unconstitutional.

Dante B. Gatmaytan, *The Illusion of Intergenerational Equity: Oposa v. Factoran as Pyrrhic Victory*, 15 Geo. Int'l Envtl. L. Rev. 457 (2003).

5. *Inter-generational equity.* What arguments could be made in favor and against the concept of inter-generational equity as the basis for human rights? Is involving children as plaintiffs a clever public relations strategy or a sound legal strategy? One author has written, "In cases involving the protection of the environment, the distinction between present and future generations is inconsequential—we cannot protect the rights of future generations without protecting the rights of the present." Dante B. Gatmaytan, *The Illusion of Intergenerational Equity: Oposa v. Factoran as Pyrrhic Victory*, 15 Geo. Int'l Envtl. L. Rev. 457 (2003). Another Philippine legal expert has replied that the *Oposa* court's reference to intergeneration equity "should ... be seen as an authoritative and ultimately precedent-setting statement that has significantly advanced the meaning and scope of the constitutional right to a balanced and healthful ecology in ways that may be directly meaningful and useful for present generations in relation to their environmental duty to future generations." Maria Socorro Z. Manguiat and Vicente Paolo B. Yu III, *Maximizing the Value of Oposa v. Factoran*, 15 Geo. Int'l Envtl. L. Rev. 487 (2003). Do you think that talk of future generations adds nothing to the legal debate, or that the magnitude and permanence of environmental destruction affecting future generations might lead more easily to judicial recognition of an environmental right?

A few other countries have recognized the relevance of children and future generations in interpreting and applying their constitutional environmental rights, including Colombia, mentioned in the article by Hill, Wolfson, and Targ, and Costa Rica. The Constitutional Chamber of Costa Rica's Supreme Court of Justice ordered the closing of a municipal waste site due to violations of constitutional rights, in case brought by a child. *Carlos Roberto Mejía Chacón contra el Ministerio de Salud y la Municipalidad de Santa Ana*, Sentencia No. 3705-93, July 30, 1993 (Sala Constitucional de la Corte Suprema de Justicia, Costa Rica). On the other hand, the Supreme Court of Bangladesh specifically refused to follow the *Oposa* case regarding future generations on the ground that, unlike the Philippine Constitution's reference to future generations, saying, "Our Constitution does not contain any analogous provision." *Dr. Mohiuddin Farooque v. Bangladesh*, 17 B.L.D [Bangladesh Legal Decisions] (AD) 1 (1997) (the Flood Action Plan case).

6. *Remedies and strategies.* Consider that the *Oposa* case was brought against the government, not the private timber companies. Recall the possible remedies listed on page 72, *supra*. Which of those remedies did the court grant in this case? What did it want the plaintiff/petitioner to do?

7. *Was constitutional litigation necessary?* One critic has argued that although the number of timber license agreements (TLAs) dropped by over 75% in the years after the case and there was also "a significant drop in the number of TLAs issued by the DENR," there was "no evidence that this reduction is a consequence of the Court's decision in *Oposa*."

Dante B. Gatmaytan, *The Illusion of Intergenerational Equity: Oposa v. Factoran as Pyrrhic Victory*, 15 Geo. Int'l Envtl. L. Rev. 457 (2003). Similarly, another critic asserts that "since the early 1990s—even before *Oposa* was decided—the issuance of TLAs had already been discontinued. Without any new TLAs being issued, the suspension, cancellation, modification, and non-renewal of existing TLAs reduced the number of TLA holders from 159 in 1986, to 26 in 1997 and less than 20 in 1998. Additionally, a logging ban had already been in place since 1991, protecting old-growth forests and areas with more than fifty percent slope or exceeding 1000 meters above sea level." Ma. Socorro Z. Manguiat and Vicente Paolo B. Yu III, *Maximizing the Value of Oposa v. Factoran*, 15 Geo. Int'l Envtl. L. Rev. 487 (2003).

Note, however, that the case was filed in 1990, that attorney Antonio Oposa used it to generate a great deal of publicity about the peril to remaining Philippine old-growth forests, and that the logging ban was issued after Oposa appealed the adverse trial court decision to the Supreme Court. Does this suggest that advocates of environmental rights should restrict themselves to lobbying government officials to achieve their goals, that constitutional litigation is likely to make a difference alone, or that a combination of rights litigation along with public relations and lobbying activities is most likely to be effective?

Shehla Zia v. WAPDA (Pakistan)
Supreme Court of Pakistan
P.L.D. 1994 S.C. 693

Four residents of Street No.35, F-6/1, Islamabad protested to WAPDA [the Water and Power Development Authority] against construction of [an electrical] grid station in F-6/1, Islamabad.... This letter was sent to this Court by Dr. Tariq Banuri of IUCN [World Conservation Union-Pakistan] for consideration as a human rights case raising two questions; namely, whether any Government agency has a right to endanger the life of citizens by its actions without the latter's consent;....

In an information sent by Mark Chernaik, Environmental Law [Alliance Worldwide, ELAW] to Brig. (Rtd.) Muhammad Yasin, Projects Coordinator, Sustainable Development Policy Institute (SDPI), it is stated that

> when electric current passes through high voltage transmission lines (HVTLs), it produces electric and magnetic fields. Although both can affect biological systems, the greatest concern is the health impacts of magnetic fields. A magnetic field can be either static or fluctuating. Magnetic field from HVTLs fluctuates because the electric currents within HVTLs are alternating currents (AC) which reverse direction 50 to 60 times per second (50 to 60 Hz). Magnetic fields pass nearly unimpeded through building materials and earth.

It refers to four recent epidemiological studies which show that the people exposed to relatively strong static and fluctuating magnetic fields have higher rates of leukaemia as compared to general population. It gives the figures that the rate of leukaemia was higher in over 170,000 children who lived within 300 meters of HVTLs in Sweden from 1960:

> Children who were exposed to fluctuating magnetic fields greater than 0.20 µt were 2.7 times more likely to have contracted leukaemia and children who were exposed to greater than 0.3 µt were 3.08 times more likely to have contracted leukaemia than other children (Reference: Feychting, M. & Anlbon, (October 1993) *Magnetic Fields and Cancer in Children Residing in Swedish Higher Voltage Power Lines*: American Journal of Epidemiology, Vol. 138, page 467.

The petitioners have also relied on an article entitled *Regulatory and Judicial Responses to the Possibility of Biological Hazards from Electromagnetic Fields generated by Power Lines* by Sherry Young, Assistant Professor of Law, ... Villanova Law Review, Vol. 36, page 129 in 1991.... After referring to the various studies and the results arrived at the author has summed up as follows:

> ... At present, the scientific evidence regarding the possibility of adverse bio-logical effects from exposure to power-frequency fields, as well as the possibility of reducing or eliminating such effects, is inconclusive. The remaining question is how the legal system, including both the judiciary and the various regulatory agencies, should respond to this scientific uncertainty....

From the afore-stated material produced on record which contains up-to-date studies and research it seems that so far no definite conclusions have been drawn by the scientist and scholars, but the trend is in support of the fact that there may be likelihood of adverse effects of electromagnetic fields on human health.... WAPDA on the other hand insists on executing the plan which according to it is completely safe and risk free ...

Dr. Parvez Hasan, learned counsel for the petitioners [Shehla Zia] contended that the Rio Declaration on Environment and Development has recommended the precautionary approach contained in principle No. 15, which reads as follows:

> Principle 15. In order to protect the environment, the precautionary approach shall be widely applied by States according to their capabilities. Where there are threats of serious or irreversible damage lack of full scientific certainty shall not be used as a reason for postponing cost-effective measures to prevent environ-mental degradation.

The concern for protecting [the] environment was first internationally recognised when the declaration of United Nations Conference on the Human Environment was adopted at the Stockholm on 16-6-1972. Thereafter it had taken two decades to create awareness and consensus among the countries when in 1992 [the] Rio Declaration was adopted.... [I]t would not be out of place to mention that Principle No. 15 envisages rule of pre-caution and prudence. According to it if there are threats of serious damage, effective measures should be taken to control it and it should not be postponed merely on the ground that scientific research and studies are uncertain and not conclusive....

The learned counsel for the respondent [WAPDA] has raised the objection that ... [no] fundamental right is violated.... So far the fundamental rights are concerned, one has not to go too far to find the reply.

Article 9 of the Constitution provides that no person shall be deprived of life or lib-erty save in accordance with the law. The word "life" is very significant as it covers all facts of human existence. The word "life" has not been defined in the Constitution but it does not mean nor can it be restricted only to the vegetative or animal life or mere exis-tence from conception to death. Life includes all such amenities and facilities which a person born in a free country is entitled to enjoy with dignity, legally and constitution-ally. For the purposes of present controversy suffice it to say that a person is entitled to protection of law from being exposed to hazards of electromagnetic fields or any other such hazards which may be due to installation and construction of any grid station, any factory, power station or such like installations....

... Any action taken which may create hazards of life will be encroaching upon the personal rights of a citizen to enjoy the life according to law. In the present case this is the complaint the petitioners have made. In our view the word "life" constitutionally is so wide that the danger and encroachment complained of would impinge fundamental right of a citizen. In this view of the matter the petition is maintainable.

Dr. Parvez Hasan, learned counsel has referred to various judgments of the Indian Supreme Court in which the term "life" has been explained with reference to public interest litigation. In *Kharak Singh v. State of UP* (AIR 1963 SC 1295) for interpreting the word "life" used in Article 21 of the Indian Constitution reliance was placed on the judgment of Field, J. in *Munn v. Illinois* (1876) 94 US 113 at page 142 where it was observed that

> "life" means not merely the right to the continuance of a person's animal exis-
> tence but a right to the possession of each of his organs—his arms and legs etc.

The word "life" in the [Pakistan] Constitution has not been used in a limited manner. A wide meaning should be given to enable a man not only to sustain life but to enjoy it....

Dr. Parvez Hasan has also referred to several judgments of the Indian Supreme Court in which issues relating to environment and ecological balance were raised and relief was granted as the industrial activity causing pollution had degraded the quality of life. In *Rural Litigation & Entitlement Kendra v. State of UP and others* (AIR 1985 SC 652) mining operation carried out through blasting was stopped and directions were issued to regulate it. The same case came up for further consideration and concern was shown for the preservation and protection of environment and ecology....

In *M.C. Mehta v. Union of India* (AIR 1988 SC 1115) and *M.C. Mehta v. Union of India* (AIR 1988 SC 1037) the Court on petition filed by a citizen taking note of the fact that the municipal sewage and industrial effluents from tanneries were being thrown in River Ganges whereby it was completely polluted, the tanneries were closed down. These judgments go a long way to show that in cases where life of citizens is degraded, the quality of life is adversely affected and health hazards are created affecting a large number of people, the Court ... may grant relief to the extent of stopping the functioning of factories which create pollution and environmental degradation....

[B]efore passing any final order, with the consent of both the parties we appoint NES-PAK [National Engineering Services Pakistan (Pvt.) Limited, a Pakistan consultancy] as Commissioner to examine and study the scheme, planning, device and technique employed by WAPDA and report whether there is any likelihood of any hazard or adverse effect on health of the residents of the locality. NESPAK may also suggest variation in the plan for minimizing the alleged danger. WAPDA shall submit all the plans, scheme and relevant information to NESPAK. The petitioners will be at liberty to send NESPAK necessary documents and material as they desire these documents should reach NESPAK within two weeks. NESPAK is authorised to call for such documents or information from WAPDA and the petitioners which in their opinion is necessary to complete their report.... WAPDA is further directed that in future prior to installing or constructing any grid station and/or transmission line, they would issue public notice in newspapers, radio and television inviting objections and to finalise the plan after considering the objections, if any, by affording public hearing to the persons filing objections. This procedure shall be adopted and continued by WAPDA till such time the Government constitutes any commission or authority as suggested above.

Questions and Discussion

1. *International declarations.* The Pakistan Supreme Court briefly mentions the Stockholm Declaration and the Rio Declaration. Is the Court citing the international environmental declarations as mandatory authority or simply dicta? How do the international

declarations affect the outcome of the case? Notice the court only mentions environmental *concern*, not *right*, in the subsequent paragraph.

2. *Self-executing rights — Pakistan and India*. Note that the *Shehla Zia* Court did not
pause to consider the question whether constitutional environmental rights are self-executing or are simply predicates for legislation, as the courts in *Oposa* and *Montana Environmental Information Center* did. There is no separate environmental right in the
Constitution of Pakistan. Instead, the Court simply interpreted the right to life, found in
Article 9 of the Constitution, to include an environmental aspect. Is it harder to argue that
such a right would be non-self-executing? In a similar manner, the Supreme Court of
India in *Subhash Kumar v. State Of Bihar*, 1991 A.I.R. 420, 1991 SCR (1), took a strong
position on what is encompassed within the right to life:

> Right to live is a fundamental right under Art. 21 of the Constitution and it in-
> cludes the right of enjoyment of pollution free water and air for full enjoyment
> of life. If anything endangers or impairs that quality of life in derogation of laws,
> a citizen has right to have recourse to Art. 32 of the Constitution for removing
> the pollution of water or air which may be detrimental to the quality of life. A
> petition under Art. 32 for the prevention of pollution is maintainable at the in-
> stance of affected persons or even by a group of social workers or journalists.

3. *Self-executing? — Hawaii*. Contrary to the jurisprudence of the Philippines, Pakistan, India, and Montana, the courts of some states of the U.S. have found the environmental rights provisions in their state constitutions to be *not* self-executing at the behest
of citizens or at least subject to limitation by legislation. For example, in *Bremner v. City
& County of Honolulu*, 96 Hawai'i 134, 28 P.3d 350 (Hawai'i App., 2001), the court stated:

> Bremner asserts that the omission of an environmental assessment violated his
> environmental rights under article XI, section 9 of the Hawai'i Constitution.
> The manner in which Bremner's rights under article XI may be enforced, how-
> ever, is governed by section 9's qualification that any such legal proceeding be "sub-
> ject to reasonable limitations and regulation as provided by law." Haw. Const.
> art. XI, §9. Because Hawai'i Revised Statutes ch. 343 provides reasonable limi-
> tations and regulations for adjudicating disputes involving environmental as-
> sessments, Bremner's failure to comply with its provisions forecloses further
> consideration of his constitutional claim.

4. *Remedy*. Does the Pakistan Supreme Court's appointment of a Pakistan consultancy
to make a report raise any questions of delegation of judicial power to a private institution? Does this suggest that formulating remedies in constitutional environmental rights
cases is too difficult a task for the judiciary to undertake? Or is this like appointment of
a special master by a court? Does the insistence on future public notice and public participation suggest a broad-based remedy that could be useful in many cases? Is it much
of a remedy for violation of substantive environmental rights?

Senih Özay v. Ministry of the Environment and Eurogold Madencilik (Turkey)

Supreme Administrative Court of Turkey
Ref. No. 1996/5477; Ruling No. 1997/2312
4 Int'l Envtl. L. Reports 452

This lawsuit was filed to request the cancellation of the licence granted to the Eurogold
Mining Corporation by the Ministry of the Environment, i.e. the licence to operate gold

mines in Izmir and the surrounding villages of Bergama, Ovacik and Camköy provided that the terms of the undertaking are fulfilled, that activities are monitored and inspected by a supervisory commission to be headed ... by the Governor of Izmir in order to monitor and inspect the operation and ensure that it is carried out in accordance with the terms of the agreement, that environmental regulations are being complied with and that other precautions are taken by relevant authorities and institutions ... until the company's obligations have ended. Following the on-site examination and evaluation of the expert, ... the Administrative Court came to the conclusion that the company, i.e. the second respondent, received an exploration permit on 16 August 1989, that the total taxes and State levies for this project would amount to approximately 40 million US dollars in unit prices for 1995, that exporting the entire gold to be produced would provide the country with 320 million US dollars of foreign exchange proceeds, that the investment cost for this project is estimated at 35 million US dollars, that the opinion of the Ministry of the Environment was requested by a letter ... from the Department of Public Housing and Settlement in Izmir, that this matter was examined by the Ministry within the scope of the powers and obligations granted to it by law, that such evaluation was made in terms of the development of the country, the protection of the environment with regard to public health and safety, that the measures to be taken in this respect were determined and that compliance with such obligations was undertaken by the company, i.e. the second respondent, that the conditions to provide for the inspection of the company in every phase of the operation were determined and necessary precautions were taken, that additional work deemed necessary by the experts would be carried out during the operation period, that the company Eurogold Mining Corporation would fulfil the conditions defined in. the agreement dated 18 October 1994 regarding human and environmental health, and relying on the fact that central and local authorities would fulfil their obligations of monitoring and inspection during and after commissioning and that based on such trust, the granting of the licence constituting the subject-matter of this lawsuit does not contravene public safety, natural plant life, historical and cultural resources, olive groves and other agricultural products in respect of public safety and existing regulations. As the licensing act constituting the subject-matter of the lawsuit did not violate existing regulations, the lawsuit was dismissed. The plaintiffs have filed an appeal against this ruling.

Article 17 of Law No. 2709, the Constitution of the Republic of Turkey, states the following:

> Each individual has the right to live, as well as to protect and develop its material and spiritual existence.

Under Article 56 it is stated that:

> Each individual has the right to live in a healthy and balanced environment. It is the duty of the State and citizens to develop the environment, protect environmental health and prevent environment pollution. The State must provide centralised health institutions and organise related services, so that people's lives are protected, people can continue to live in physical and mental health, saving human and material energy, increasing efficiency and developing cooperation....

Article 1 of the Law on the Environment No. 2872 states that the objective of this law is to protect and develop our shared property, i.e. the environment, optimum use and protection of land and natural resources in rural and suburban areas for the prevention of water, soil and air pollution, to protect plants. and animals as well as historic and cultural resources, to set forth the regulations and measures to ensure the development of standards of health, civilisation and life of present and future generations in accordance with economic and social progress goals as well as certain legal and technical principles.

The Environmental Impact Assessment Report and expert reports examined the effects of cyanide treatments to the atmosphere, groundwater, flora-fauna, noise and vibration as well as use of land.... It was determined thereby that the potential erosion of ground soil in the area by water (surface floods) and wind is comparatively high, ... that the degree of erosion of forest soil is classified in classes 2 and 3, whereas it is in class 1 in the other areas, that the forest greatly contributes to society in respect of erosion and public health, that the soil is of permeable nature, that this area is situated in a First Degree Earthquake Zone, that the groundwater is fed by filtration of rainfall and surface waters, ... that rainfalls on the project site would cause flooding, that the quantity and intensity of rainfall in this area is very high in winter and spring, ... and that this leads to flooding of catchment areas during these seasons, that the locals use this groundwater, that poisonous waste/substances could trickle into the groundwater in case of a leakage, that the pH-value with regard to cyanide is important and that this value is affected by rainfall, ... that cyanide is transformed into the extremely dangerous HCN (hydrogen cyanide) gas in the event that the pH-value falls, that HCN has a low boiling point (25.7"C) and, therefore, there is a great risk that it could find its way into the atmosphere, that even if the cyanide is greatly removed by big layers of earth, it will flow back into the water in the course of time for reasons such as hydrolysis, ... that heavy metals produced as a result of the operation should be monitored, that possible effects on the groundwater of substances in the waste dam may last from twenty to fifty years, that the operating company has undertaken to maintain a monitoring period for five years following commissioning, that it is necessary to carry out a detailed hydrogeological study in this region, that leaks can occur in the waste dam due to the permeability of the lining of the dam as well as holes and defects in the lining, that therefore, construction of the waste dam and the lining process is very important, ... that, in the event of a leakage into the atmosphere or groundwater, the environment and flora-fauna will be exposed to negative effects. Relying on the company's goodwill and the fact that it shall fulfil the requirements set out in the undertaking with utmost care, that the central and local authorities will fulfil without exceptions their obligations to examine and monitor, it has been[claimed] the licensing and constituting the subject-matter of this lawsuit does not contravene the public interest or violate existing legal regulations.

The above-mentioned reports reveal that gold mining by "heap leaching" with cyanide, as well as other heavy metals produced thereby presents a risk and danger factor that have a negative effect on human and environmental health, and that, particularly if the cyanide— which is very poisonous—finds its way into the soil, water and air, it constitutes a danger to all living creatures. Therefore, the waste materials containing cyanide that are pumped into waste dams as part of the operation could enter water sources and other areas of use due to leaks in waste dams, which were originally intended to be impermeable, that, consequently, the risk element in connection with the use of cyanide in the operation of gold mines has become a primary concern, that such risk poses a threat of damage to the flora and fauna in this area, that cyanide compounds present a very great risk to human health and the environment and that, therefore, one must be very sensitive in this respect.

The environment continues its existence through maintenance of an equilibrium and comprises natural and artificial elements as well as a variety of human activities....

Based on the above determinations, the method of operation of the gold mine, which is the subject matter of the lawsuit, is unsafe and has a direct and indirect effect on human life. In the judicial review of the administrative act constituting the subject-matter of the lawsuit, public interest and the priorities embodied by this term in particular should be examined taking into account the Constitutional Law and legal regulations.

If one compares the economic gains to be obtained upon completion of the mining activities with the damage that will be caused to the environment and to human life directly or indirectly, relying solely on concepts such as "the goodwill of the company" or "careful monitoring of relevant precautions," it is only natural that public interest will primarily be interpreted in favour of human life. Therefore, with regard to the operation of it gold mine using the heap leaching method with cyanide, one cannot argue that the probability of risk will be reduced based on a feeling of trust towards the company or the monitoring measures to be taken by the same.

Within the framework of the above-mentioned technical and legal determinations, and in light of the fact that people have the right to live, and the State has the duty to protect the environment, to avoid environmental pollution and to ensure that each individual continues to live in physical and mental health, the licence granted for gold mining using cyanide in the heap leaching process, which is the subject matter of the lawsuit, would not be in the public interest, since it is also stated in the Environmental Impact Assessment Report and in the expert report that such gold mining would operate at a risk which, if materialised, would certainly directly or indirectly impair human life due to the resulting damage to the environment.

For this reason, the ruling of the Administrative Court at first instance, by which the lawsuit was dismissed, is deemed incorrect.

For reasons explained above, it is unanimously decided on 13 May 1997 that the ruling of the 1st Chamber of the Administrative Court of Izmir, dated 2 July 1996, under reference number 1994/644 and ruling number *19961539,* is reversed, that court charges totalling 503.500-TL and charges paid in excess totalling 376.200-TL will be reimbursed to the party that filed the appeal and that the file will be sent to the said court.

Questions and Discussion

1. *Courts versus expert agencies.* Who is in the best position to make judgments like the one made by this court and the courts in the *Oposa* and *Shehla Zia* cases—a judicial body like this, or an expert governmental agency? If a governmental agency makes a decision to allow a gold mine using cyanide to go ahead, after evaluating environmental as well as economic factors, what role should a court play in reviewing such a decision?

2. *Constitutional law or standard of review?* Are these primarily cases interpreting constitutional rights (to a healthy environment or to life), or cases using an intensive "arbitrary or capricious" standard of judicial review in evaluating administrative action? Does it seem likely that government agencies will pay more attention to cases cast in one term or the other?

C. Requiring Affirmative Government Programs

Some scholars distinguish between "negative rights" and "positive rights." *See* Seth F. Kreimer, *Allocational Sanctions: The Problem of Negative Rights In A Positive State*, 132 U.

Pa. L. Rev. 1293 (1984). The former require someone to *stop* interfering with another person's actions. The latter are those that require someone to *take action* so that the other person's rights are implemented. The protection of human rights sometimes does require affirmative action on the part of government. Certainly the control of pollution ultimately requires that vast government programs be established to regulate discharges into air and water, if such programs do not already exist. Other types of affirmative government programs may also be important. What is the role of litigation in requiring that such programs be established? How far should a court be able to go in ordering governments to take action? Consider the following cases.

M. C. Mehta v. Union of India (India)
Supreme Court of India
AIR 1992 SC 382

G.N. RAY, A.S. ANAND, Justices

The reliefs claimed in this application under Article 32 of the Constitution are for issuing appropriate directions to cinema exhibition halls to exhibit slides containing information and messages on environment free of cost; directions for spread of information relating to environment in national and regional languages and for broadcast thereof on the All India Radio and exposure thereof on the television in regular and short term programmes with a view to educating the people of India about their social obligation in the matter of the upkeep of the environment ... and making them alive to their obligation not to act as polluting agencies or factors. There is also a prayer that [the] environment should be make a compulsory subject in schools and colleges in a graded system so that there would be a general growth of awareness.

Until 1972, general awareness of mankind to the importance of environment for the well-being of mankind had not been appropriately appreciated, though over the years for more than a century there was a growing realisation that mankind had to live in tune with nature if life was to be peaceful, happy and satisfied. In the name of scientific development, man started distancing himself from nature and even developed an urge to conquer nature. Our ancestors had known that nature was not subduable and, therefore, had made it an obligation for man to surrender to nature and live in tune with it. Our Constitution underwent an amendment in 1976 by incorporating an article (51A) with the heading "Fundamental Duties." Clause (g) thereof requires every citizen to protect and improve the natural environment including forests, lakes, rivers and wildlife, and to have compassion for living creatures....

In this backdrop if the laws are to be enforced and the malaise of pollution has to be kept under control and the environment has to be protected in an unpolluted state it is necessary that people are aware of the vice of pollution and its evil consequences.

We are in a democratic polity where dissemination of information is the foundation of the system. Keeping the citizens informed is an obligation of the Government. It is equally the responsibility of society to adequately educate every component of it so that the social level is kept up. We, therefore, accept on principle the prayers made by the petitioner....

We dispose of this writ petition with the following directions:

(1) Respondents 1, 2 & 3 shall issue appropriate directions to the state Governments and Union Territories to invariably enforce as a condition of license of all cinema halls, touring cinemas and video parlours to exhibit free of cost at least two slides/messages on

environment in each show undertaken by them.... Failure to comply with our order should be treated as ground for cancellation of the licence by the appropriate authorities....

(2) The ministry of Information and broadcasting of the Government of India should without delay start producing information films of short duration as is being done now on various aspects of environment and pollution bringing out the benefits for society on the environment being protected and the hazards involved in the environment being polluted. Mind catching aspects should be made the central theme of such short films. One such film should be shown, as far as practicable, in one show every day by the cinema halls and the Central Government and the State Governments are directed to ensure compliance of this condition from February 1, 1992.

(3) Realising the importance of the matter of environment and the necessity of protecting it in an unpolluted [state,] we had suggested to learned Attorney General to have a dialogue with the Ministry of Information and Broadcasting as to the manner the All India Radio and Doordarshan [the India state television network] can assist this process of education. We are happy to indicate that learned Attorney General has told us that five to seven minutes can be devoted every day and there could be, once a week, a longer programme.... The national network as also the State Doordarshan Centres should immediately take steps to implement this direction so that from February 1 1992, regular compliance can be made.

(4) We accept on principle that through the medium of education awareness of the environment and its problems related to pollution should be taught as a compulsory subject. Learned Attorney General pointed out to us that the Central Government is associated with education at the higher levels and the University Grants Commission can monitor only the under graduate and post graduate studies. The rest of it, according to him, is a State subject. He has agreed that the University Grants Commission will take appropriate steps immediately to give effect to what we have said, i.e., requiring the Universities to prescribe a course on environment. They would consider the feasibility of making this a compulsory subject at every level in college education. So far as education up to the college level is concerned, we would require every State Government and every Education Board connected with education up to the matriculation or stage even intermediate colleges to immediately take steps to enforce compulsory education on environment in a graded way. This should be done that in the next academic year there would be compliance of this requirement....

We dispose of the matter with the aforesaid direction but give liberty to Mr. Mehta to apply to the Court from time to time for further direction, if necessary.

Questions and Discussion

1. *Duties.* Observe how the court used neither environmental rights nor the correlative duties on the part of governments to reach its result, but the duties imposed on individuals. Could the same result be reached in a jurisdiction that did not impose duties on citizens but did recognize that they had environmental rights?

2. *Ordering an executive to act.* Is this environmental education case an easy one for requiring a government to take affirmative steps? Do easy cases make good law? Would an order requiring a government body to create an entire regulatory program pose more problems? The courts of India have ordered a number of affirmative programs by governments, in pursuance of protecting the right to life in Article 21. For example, the

Supreme Court of India ordered the city of Jaipur to "clean the entire Jaipur City" in *L.K. Koolwal v. Rajasthan,* 1988 A.I.R. (Raj.) 2.

3. *Limits to ordering affirmative steps?* If the courts should not require a government body to take affirmative steps on the ground that this transgresses the proper bounds of judicial action, does it mean that the courts should be powerless in the face of massive violations of environmental rights? If they should be able to order affirmative steps by governments, how far may a court go in ordering a government to take action? Could it also order the *legislative* branch of government to take action? Consider the next case.

Dhungel v. Godawari Marble Industries (Nepal)

Supreme Court of Nepal (Full Bench)
WP 35/1992 (31 October 1995)

Hon'ble Trilok Pratap Rana

Hon'ble Laxman Prasad Aryal

Hon'ble Gobinda Bahadur Shrestha

The petitioner in his writ petition dated B.S. 2046/2/30 (June 12, 1989) under the Articles 2, 10, 11(1) (2), 15 of the then Constitution of Nepal has alleged, inter alia, that since the environmental degradation produced due to the presence and the activities of the respondents have violated the public interest including the petitioner's constitutional and legal right, the environmental degradation and its untoward impact on the public life, health and property shall immediately be abandoned....

While summing up the demand of the petitioner, it is appeared mainly that the respondent industry has degraded the environment and from the negative effect of which has infringed the right to live is the healthy environment of the person, and among the respondents, the governments' authorities have not prohibited the works of the respondent Marble Industry and not made surveillance which caused such environmental degradation and therefore helped the same. It is seen to be requested to issue an order that the environmental degradation activity caused by the respondent Marble Industry shall be controlled as per the Constitution and other Laws and Regulations....

Article 11(1) of the Constitution of Nepal 2019 has guaranteed the right to life save in accordance with law.... It is the legitimate right of an individual to be free from a polluted environment. As the protection of environment is directly related with life of human being, it should be accepted that this matter is included in Article 11(1) of the Constitution of the Kingdom of Nepal 2047 (1990).

Since a clean and healthy environment is an indispensable part of a human life, the right to clean, healthy environment is undoubtedly embedded within the Right to Life. It is clear that the constitutional perimeter in which the applicant had filed the writ petition has been substantively changed from the commencement of Article 26(4) of the Constitution of the Kingdom of Nepal 1990, because this Article has taken environmental conservation as one of the basic Directive Principles of the State. Thus, as the environmental conservation is one of the objectives of the applicant "LEADERS Inc.," it needs to be accepted that the applicant has the *locus standi* for the prevention of the environmental degradation.

Since the Industrial Enterprises Act 2049-B.S. requires assessment of the likely untoward effects to the environment before providing the license for the establishment of an industry, not only the government policy but a clear legal provision has been developed to this end. Thus one of the contentions made by the petitioner that adequate measures regarding protection of the environment should be undertaken before providing the license for the establishment of an industry has been converted into a legal procedure.... The applicant has not categorically asked for the closure of the marble industry in the writ petition but rather has emphasized on the regulatory and remedial side for adoption of effective measures to stop or reduce negative environmental effects.

After the Stockholm Conference of 1972 everyone's attention is on environmental degradation. In developed countries including the United Sates, separate legislation has been enacted for environment conservation since the seventies.... In our country also, there has not yet been a separate environmental law but all the necessary frameworks for this goal have been drafted. To declare environmental conservation as a state policy, under Article 26(4) of the Constitution, to form the environmental conservation commission led by the prime minister on 2049/9/27 B.S. (Jan 11,1993); environmental impact evaluation law has prepared on 2050/2/4 B.S.(May 17 1993) by the aforesaid environment Conservation Commission; the Ministry of Environment is established, the matters of the environmental reforms are incorporated in its 8th 5-year plan of the planning commission; among the committees of the parliament an environmental committee is in existence in the house of representatives; and participated in the world environmental conference in Rio de Janeiro, 1992 and has signed the same are some of the instances indicating a deep concern of His Majesty's Government towards the conservation of the environment....

But still the lack of a specific law has hindered the dynamism needed in this regard. [There is] no doubt [that] an appropriate law is indispensable. Without law it is not possible to issue an order for punishment and closure of the industry. As the present laws are currently in scattered forms and also inadequate and ineffective, an appropriate, a separate law encompassing all aspects of the environment is deemed necessary to be formulated and promulgated as soon as possible....

[I]t appears that the executive has shown keen interest in petty things but overlooked the constitutional beckoning and national-international public interest; Henceforth it is revealed that the time has came to mitigate the uncertainty prevailing presently and to fulfill national and international responsibilities towards the environment by promulgating a separate environmental law.

Since after the respondent Marble Industry in the present case got permission on 2024/7/2 B.S. (Oct. 19, 1967) with the conditions of modernization and expansion, various reports published by different governmental and non-governmental organizations have indicated that the complaint about the negative impact to the environment of Godawari area has surfaced and this controversy has been gradually proceeding towards the explosive stage. But no official scrutiny has ever been undertaken despite so many reports and controversies. So far as the environmental degradation of Godawari area is concerned, its extent is yet to be explored in a scientific and official manner. The respondents in their discussions and submission have mentioned various remedy measures like forestation, silt satelliting construction, distribution of masks to the workers during working period in order to curb the environmental degradation. It appears quite essential to investigate the effectiveness of those regulatory and remedy measures as well as the ratio between the pollution rate and the permissible limit....

It is beyond doubt that industry is the foundation of development of the country. Both the country and society need development; however it is essential to maintain an environmental balance along with industry. It is essential to establish balance between the need to provide continuity to developmental activities and priority to the protection of the environment.... There has always been ... adverse impact on the environment from industries.... First remedial and then regulatory measures need to be adopted to mitigate such negative effects. If these measures are unable to protect the environment, the activity that is causing environmental pollution needs to be closed....

[T]he remedy measures shall be adopted at first and if it fails then the extensive measures like closure of the Mines shall be adopted....

In relation to the submission of the applicant that lease can be cancelled based on public interest ... [t]he petitioner has not been able to clearly point out a specific section of the law that has not been obeyed or followed. Where someone claims that a legal duty has not been fulfilled, such person needs to specifically indicate that such and such agency or official did not fulfill such and such legal duty. For the purpose of mandamus, the legal duty must be definite and fixed. Therefore mandamus cannot be issued on the basis of a general claim that public interest has not been fulfilled in the absence of a clear statement of respondents' legal duty. Taking into account the sensitive, humanitarian issue of national and international importance such as the protection of the environment of Godawari area, we found that effective and satisfactory corrective activity has not taken place. Therefore, it is appropriate to issue this directives in the name of respondents to enforce the Minerals Act 2042 (1985), enact necessary legislation for protection of air, water, sound and environment and to take action for protection of the environment of Godawari area.

Be certain to send a copy of the order to the respondent His Majesty's Government also for implementation of the order.

Done on the 14th day of the month of Kartik, 2052 (Oct. 31, 1995)

Questions and Discussion

1. *Ordering a legislature to take action.* Is it reasonable for a Supreme Court to order a national legislature to enact legislation, as happened in Nepal? Does it matter that the legislature is bound by the Constitution? Is ordering a legislative program to be adopted likely to be successful? Does the answer depend on any societal or historical factors?

2. *Ordering the executive branch to take action.* In *Dr. Mohiuddin Farooque v. Bangladesh*, 17 B.L.D [Bangladesh Legal Decisions] (AD) 1 (1997) (the Flood Action Plan case), the Supreme Court of Bangladesh interpreted the right to life provision in the Constitution of Bangladesh to grant legal standing to the Bangladesh Environmental Lawyers Association (BELA).

After *Farooque v. Bangladesh*, various cases in Bangladesh have used the right to life provision as the basis for substantive relief. For example, one author notes:

> In a public interest litigation concerning air and noise pollution, the Dhaka High Court ordered the Government to convert petrol and diesel engines in government-owned vehicles to gas-fueled engines; the same order also calls for the withdrawal of hydraulic horns in buses and trucks by 28 April 2002. Another far reaching decision of the Dhaka High Court has called for the withdrawal of two-stroke engine vehicles from Dhaka City by December 2003, the cancellation of licenses for nine-year-old three-wheelers, the provision of adequate numbers of compressed natural gas stations, and the establishment of a system for issuing fitness certificates for cars through computer checks.

Parvez Hassan & Azim Azfar, *Securing Environmental Rights through Public Interest Litigation in South Asia*, 22 Va. Envtl. L.J. 215 (2004).

3. *Ordering private parties to take action.* If the courts issue orders only directly against polluters, will they become more involved in the minutiae of setting environmental policy than if they are able to issue orders to the other branches of government in order to have them create the necessary programs? Consider these and other problems in the next part of this chapter.

4. *Judicial creativity and the Nepal Constitution.* Although the case was brought under the "right to life" provision of Nepal's 1962 Constitution, the Constitution was changed in 1990 while the case was pending. The new Constitution lacked "right to life" language. Nonetheless, the Supreme Court said above, "As the protection of environment is directly related with life of human being, it should be accepted that this matter is included in Article 11(1) of the Constitution of the Kingdom of Nepal 2047 (1990)." An examination of Article 11 will reveal no use of the word "life." Then how did the Supreme Court find that harm to the environment violated the right to life? Perhaps the Court found the concept implicit in the concept of constitutionalism. Recall the statements by the Philippine Supreme Court in the *Oposa* case to the effect that some concepts were so fundamental that they must be applied as constitutional principles even if not written into the Constitution.

After a peace settlement, Nepal adopted Interim Constitution 2007. This constitution contains a right to environment and health (Article 16), a right to constitutional remedy (Article 107), an obligation on the State to protect the environment (Article 35.5), and specific jurisdiction for public interest cases (Article 207). Article 115 states that the government has a duty to assist the judiciary in delivering justice, while Article 116 states that the government has a duty to comply with the orders and decisions of the courts and has a specific duty to follow precedents on interpretations of law and legal principle. Furthermore, Article135(3)(b) provides that the Attorney General has a duty to monitor compliance. The Interim Constitution of Nepal, 2063 (2007): As Amended by the First, Second and Third Amendments (http://www.undp.org.np/constitutionbuilding/constitutionnepal/contitutionfile/Interim_Constitution_bilingual.pdf (English and Nepali); http://www.supremecourt.gov.np/ic.pdf (Nepali).

5. *Implementation in Nepal.* To help achieve compliance, the Nepalese NGO, Pro Public (which brought the case), has adopted a comprehensive strategy for obtaining compliance, from field monitoring and building up of partnerships with local communities to issuing reminders to agencies and asking courts to issue more specific instruction (including time lines and report-back requirements) to filing motions for contempt of court against government inaction. Presentation by Pro Public, 26th Annual Public Interest Environmental Law Conference, Eugene, Oregon (2008).

6. *Implementation of constitutional decisions.* Without implementation, court decisions purporting to protect human rights may be of interest primarily to scholars, not to people affected by human rights violations. After the case of *Farooque v. Bangladesh* and other cases, the Bangladesh Environmental Lawyers Association concluded that winning a court case is only the first step. As a consequence, they engage in comprehensive activities involving the news media, political efforts, involving government officials in various programs, monitoring, and filing of subsequent applications with the court. Ultimately, they have considered, but not yet adopted, the tactic of filing motions against government officials for contempt of court. The Nepalese case, *Dhungel v. Godawari Marble Industries,* excerpted above, has continued for years since it was first filed. The Nepalese NGO, Pro Public, has both returned to court and used administrative lobbying to address the problem.

III. Challenging Actions by Private Parties

Most rights jurisprudence in the United States concerns alleged governmental violations of rights. The "state action doctrine" usually prohibits lawsuits against private parties alleging deprivation of constitutional rights. *Jackson v. Metropolitan Edison Co.*, 419 U.S. 345 (1974) (state's approval of utility company's business practices did not signify state action). In some instances, however, private actors are also prohibited from violating constitutional rights and cases may be brought against them. Such cases can be brought either by government authorities or, in some jurisdictions, by other private parties. The first of these has something of the character of a tort action sounding in "public nuisance." The second involves a private right of action or "citizens suit" for enforcement. This final part of the chapter will consider both kinds of cases.

A. Enforcement against Private Actors by Attorneys General

Pennsylvania v. National Gettysburg Battlefield Tower (USA)

Supreme Court of Pennsylvania
454 Pa. 193 A.2d 588 (1973)

Before, JONES, C.J., and EAGEN, O'BRIEN, ROBERTS, POMEROY, NIX and MANDERINO, JJ.

O'BRIEN, Justice.

On July 3, 1971, National Gettysburg Battlefield Tower, Inc. (the Tower Corporation) and Thomas R. Ottenstein, two of the appellees, negotiated an agreement with the United States Government, acting through the Director of the National Park Service, in which the Tower Corporation conveyed certain land to the government and agreed to abandon construction of an observation tower near the Gettysburg Battlefield, at an area found objectionable to the Park Service, in exchange for the government's cooperation and permission to build the tower in another area near the battlefield....

What the National Park Service was originally willing to permit, the Commonwealth of Pennsylvania, appellant herein, sought to enjoin. On July 20, 1971, the Commonwealth brought an action in the Court of Common Pleas of Adams County, to enjoin construction of the proposed 307-feet tower, alleging that the proposed construction was "a despoilation of the natural and historic environment," because, in the words of one critic:

> The tower as proposed ... would disrupt the skyline, dominate the setting from many angles, and still further erode the natural beauty and setting which once was marked by the awful conflict of a brothers' war.

At the trial, the Commonwealth produced a number of witnesses who generally agreed that they found the tower, in their opinion, to be detrimental to the historic, scenic, and aesthetic environment of Gettysburg. Appellees, on the other hand, produced experts who found the geometric form of the tower to be aesthetically pleasing and its design, while unobtrusive, to be of great educational value because it would provide "the full sweep or overview of a landscape where a significant event in American history took place." ...

[T]here is no statute of the Pennsylvania Legislature, which would authorize the Governor and the Attorney General to initiate actions like the law suit in the instant case.

Rather, authority for the Commonwealth's suit is allegedly based entirely upon Article 1, § 27 of the State Constitution, ratified by the voters of Pennsylvania on May 18, 1971, which reads as follows:

> The people have a right to clean air, pure water, and to the preservation of the natural, scenic, historic and esthetic values of the environment. Pennsylvania's public natural resources are the common property of all the people, including generations yet to come. As trustee of these resources, the Commonwealth shall conserve and maintain them for the benefit of all the people.

It is the Commonwealth's position that this amendment is self-executing; that the people have been given a right "to the preservation of the natural, scenic, historic and esthetic values of the environment," and "that no further legislation is necessary to vest these rights in the people." ...

It should be noted that § 27 does not give the powers of a trustee of public natural resources to the Governor or to the Attorney General but to the Commonwealth. Article 4 of the State Constitution, which provides in § 1 that:

> The Executive Department of this Commonwealth shall consist of a Governor, Lieutenant Governor, Attorney General, Auditor General, State Treasurer, and Superintendent of Public Instruction and such other officers as the General Assembly may from time to time prescribe,

defines the duties of an executive generally, in § 2, to mean that the Governor: "shall take care that the laws be faithfully executed." ...

Under a constitution providing for a balance of powers, such as Pennsylvania's State Constitution, when power is given simply to the Commonwealth, it is power to be shared by the government's three co-equal branches. The governor cannot decide, alone, how or when he shall exercise the powers of a trustee. It is not for him alone to determine when the "natural, scenic, historic, and esthetic values of the environment" are sufficiently threatened as to justify the bringing of an action. After all, "clean air," "pure water" and "the natural, scenic, historic and esthetic values of the environment," have not been defined. The first two, "clean air" and "pure water," require technical definitions, since they depend, to some extent, on the technological state of the science of purification. The other values, "the natural, scenic, historic and esthetic values" of the environment are values which have heretofore not been the concern of government. To hold that the Governor needs no legislative authority to exercise the as yet undefined powers of a trustee to protect such undefined values would mean that individuals could be singled out for interference by the awesome power of the state with no advance warning that their conduct would lead to such consequences.

If we were to sustain the Commonwealth's position that the amendment was self-executing, a property owner would not know and would have no way, short of expensive litigation, of finding out what he could do with his property. The fact that the owner contemplated a use similar to others that had not been enjoined would be no guarantee that the Commonwealth would not seek to enjoin his use. Since no executive department has been given authority to determine when to move to protect the environment, there would be no way of obtaining, with respect to a particular use contemplated, an indication of what action the Commonwealth might take before the owner expended what could be significant sums of money for the purchase or the development of the property....

The Commonwealth also argues that the Pennsylvania environmental protection amendment is self-executing by comparing it with similar constitutional amendments enacted in Massachusetts, Illinois, New York, and Virginia, all of which are obviously not self-executing. The Commonwealth seeks to put great store in the fact that Pennsylvania's amendment, alone, does not specifically provide for legislative implementation. However, we find it more significant that all of these other states, which expanded the powers of their governments over the natural environment in the same way as Article 1, § 27 expanded the powers of the Commonwealth, recognized that legislative implementation was necessary before such new power could be exercised.

[Opinion joined by POMEROY, J.]

ROBERTS, Justice (concurring).

I agree that the order of the Commonwealth Court should be affirmed; however, my reasons for affirmance are entirely different from those expressed in the opinion by Mr. Justice O'Brien (joined by Mr. Justice Pomeroy).

I believe that the Commonwealth, even prior to the recent adoption of Article I, Section 27 possessed the inherent sovereign power to protect and preserve for its citizens the natural and historic resources now enumerated in Section 27. The express language of the constitutional amendment merely recites the "inherent and independent rights" of mankind relative to the environment which are "recognized and unalterably established" by Article I, Section 1 of the Pennsylvania Constitution.

Prior to the adoption of Article I, Section 27, it was clear that as sovereign "the state has an interest independent of and behind the titles of its citizens, in all the earth and air within its domain...." *Georgia v. Tennessee Copper Co.*, 206 U.S. 230, 237, 27 S.Ct. 618, 619, 51 L.Ed. 1038 http://www.westlaw.com/Find/Default.wl?rs=dfa1.0&vr=2.0&DB=708&FindType=Y&ReferencePositionType=S&SerialNum=1907100408&ReferencePosition=619(1907). The proposition has long been firmly established that

> [i]t is a fair and reasonable demand on the part of a sovereign that the air over its territory should not be polluted..., that the forests on its mountains, be they better or worse, and whatever domestic destruction they have suffered, should not be further destroyed or threatened..., that the crops and orchards on its hills should not be endangered....

Parklands and historical sites, as "natural resources" are subject to the same considerations.

Moreover, "it must surely be conceded that, if the health and comfort of the inhabitants of a state are threatened, the state is the proper party to represent and defend them...." *Missouri v. Illinois*, 180 U.S. 208, 241, 21 S.Ct. 331, 344, 45 L.Ed. 497 (1901). Since natural and historic resources are the common property of the citizens of a state, see *McCready v. Virginia*, 94 U.S. 391, 24 L.Ed. 248 (1876), the Commonwealth can — and always could — proceed as parens patriae acting on behalf of the citizens and in the interests of the community, or as trustee of the state's public resources.

However, in my view, the Commonwealth, on this record, has failed to establish its entitlement to the equitable relief it seeks, either on common-law or constitutional (prior or subsequent to Section 27) theories. The chancellor determined that

> [t]he Commonwealth has failed to show by clear and convincing proof that the natural, historic, scenic, and aesthetic values of the Gettysburg area will be irreparably harmed by the erection of the proposed tower at the proposed site.

I believe that the chancellor correctly denied equitable relief. The Commonwealth Court concluded that the chancellor's findings should not be disturbed and that the Commonwealth was not entitled to relief.

I am unable, on this record, to find any error in either the chancellor's determination or that of the Commonwealth Court. Moreover, I entertain serious reservations as to the propriety of granting the requested relief in this case in the absence of appropriate and articulated substantive and procedural standards. See *Just v. Marinette County*, 56 Wis.2d 7, 201 N.E.2d 761 (1972).

MANDERINO, J., joins in this opinion.

JONES, Chief Justice (dissenting).

This Court has been given the opportunity to affirm the mandate of the public empowering the Commonwealth to prevent environmental abuses; instead, the Court has chosen to emasculate a constitutional amendment by declaring it not to be self-executing. I am compelled to dissent.

Article I, Section 27, of the Commonwealth's Constitution was passed by the General Assembly and ratified by the voters on May 18, 1971.[1]

Its provisions are clear and uncomplicated:

> The people have a right to clean air, pure water, and to the preservation of the natural, scenic, historic and esthetic values of the environment. Pennsylvania's public natural resources are the common property of all the people, including generations yet to come. As trustee of these resources, the Commonwealth shall conserve and maintain them for the benefit of all the people.

As part of the declaration of rights embraced by Article I, the amendment confers certain enumerated rights upon the people of the Commonwealth and imposes upon the executive branch a fiduciary obligation to protect and enforce those rights.

If the amendment was intended only to espouse a policy undisposed to enforcement without supplementing legislation, it would surely have taken a different form. But the amendment is not addressed to the General Assembly. It does not require the legislative creation of remedial measures. Instead, the amendment creates a public trust. The "natural, scenic, historic and aesthetic values of the environment" are the trust Res; the Commonwealth, through its executive branch, is the trustee; the People of this Commonwealth are the trust beneficiaries. The amendment thus installs the common law public trust doctrine as a constitutional right to environmental protection susceptible to enforcement by an action in equity.

The majority relies on constitutional amendments of Massachusetts, Illinois, New York and Virginia to support its holding that Section 27 is not self-executing. The Court finds it "significant that all of these other states, which expanded the powers of their governments over the natural environment in the same way as Article I, Section 27 expanded the powers of the Commonwealth, recognized that legislative implementation was necessary before such new power could be exercised." I find no significance in the fact that the constitutional provisions of these several jurisdictions are not self-executing for it is evident to me that each of the cited amendments is materially distinguishable from Article I, Section 27. Each of these amendments purports to establish a policy of environmental protection, but either omits the mode of enforcement or explicitly delegates the responsibility for implementation to the legislative branch. The Pennsylvania amendment defines enumerated rights within the scope of existing remedies. It imposes a fiduciary duty upon the Commonwealth to protect the people's "right to clean air, pure water, and to the preservation of the natural, scenic, historic and esthetic values of the environment." That the

---

1. The amendment received 1,021,342 votes: more than any candidate seeking state-wide office.

language of the amendment is subject to judicial interpretation does not mean that the enactment must remain an ineffectual constitutional platitude until such time as the legislature acts.

Because I believe Article I, Section 27 is self-executing, I believe that our inquiry should have focused upon the ultimate issue of fact: does the proposed tower violate the rights of the people of the Commonwealth as secured by this amendment? ...

The Commonwealth presented compelling evidence that the proposed observation tower at Gettysburg would desecrate the natural, scenic, aesthetic and historic values of the Gettysburg environment....

Pulitzer prize-winning Civil War historian Bruce Catton testified that the historical integrity of the area was delicate, and that the proposed tower would shatter the visitor's vicarious historical involvement in Gettysburg best experienced by a ground level observation of the area.

The facts presented, even as construed in a light most favorable to the appellees, permit me only one conclusion: the proposed structure will do violence to the "natural, scenic, historic and aesthetic values" of Gettysburg. This Court's decision today imposes unhappy consequences on the people of this Commonwealth. In one swift stroke the Court has disemboweled a constitutional provision which seems, by unequivocal language, to establish environmental control by public trust and, in so doing consequently sanctions the desecration of a unique national monument. I would enjoin the construction of this tower by the authority of Article I, Section 27 of the Pennsylvania Constitution.

I dissent!!

EAGEN, J., joins in this dissent.

Questions and Discussion

1. *Self-execution by the Attorney General.* After the *Gettysburg Battlefield Tower* case, is the right to clean air, pure water and preservation of the natural, historic and esthetic values of the environment in Pennsylvania "self-executing" in a suit brought by a government body, or is further legislation required? You must count the votes of individual Supreme Court justices to determine whether there is a majority view on this issue. Compare this kind of lawsuit to actions by attorneys general filed to abate a "public nuisance."

2. *Comparison to other states' constitutions.* Who has the better argument, the court or the dissent, regarding the relevance of constitutional provisions in four other states that are clearly not self-executing?

3. *Legal uncertainty.* How strong is the court's argument that Pennsylvania's environmental rights provision should not be considered to be self-executing in part because property owners would be uncertain about what they could do with their property, even if they abided by all relevant legislation? Would that situation be any different from having statutes and regulations while, at the same time, allowing the continuance of common law tort litigation? Would it be any different from the continued existence of "public nuisance" cases in an age of regulation?

4. *Technical definition.* The main court opinion asserted that "clean air" and "pure water" require a "technical definition," presumably by a body other than the court. If this is so, who should provide that technical definition? Can a court itself find a way to provide such definitions? Is this more difficult for a court than to define terms like "freedom of speech" in a constitution?

5. *Who are the experts?* Another court considered who should have the responsibility of defining violations of a constitutional environmental rights provision and reached the opposite conclusion. *Merlin Myers Revocable Trust v. Yellowstone County*, 2002 Mt. 201, 311 Mont. 194, 53 P.3d 1268 (Mont., 2002). County commissioners refused to comply with a state law on the ground that in their view the law violated the right to a healthy environment in Montana's Constitution. The Montana Supreme Court ruled, however, over a dissenting judge, that only a court can make such a judgment of constitutional violation). On the other hand, in *Laguna Lake Development Authority v. Court of Appeals*, G.R. No. 110120 (Supreme Court of the Philippines, 1994), a court upheld local enforcement action based on the Philippine Constitution's right to a healthy environment.

6. *Public trust doctrine.* In what way does the public trust doctrine give content to a generalized right to environmental protection? What would the trustee's responsibilities be toward the trust "res"? Should the executive branch of government be considered to be the "trustee," as the dissent argues? If not, who should fulfill that role? What implications would that have?

B. Enforcement by Citizens against Private Defendants

Pedro Flores v. Corporación del Cobre-Division Salvador (Chile)

Corte de Apelaciones, Copiacó

Recurso de Protección

Rol. 2.052 (23 June 1988)[a]

Signed by Ministers JORGE PIZARRO, LUIS HUGO FUENZALIDA

Affirmed by the Chilean Supreme Court on 28 July 1988; injunction issued.

Mr. Pedro Flores San Martin … brought an appeal for protection against Codelco [Corporación del Cobre]-Chile, Division Salvador.… [Mr. Flores] alleges that respondent employs the method of "flotation" which requires the use of great quantities of water, adding that since the beginning of the mineral development, [respondent] decided to do away with the copper tailings containing great amounts of poisonous and highly toxic substances by depositing the copper tailings into the bed of the Salado River, which for decades has been polluting Chañaral's coast. The petitioner maintains that faced with the embankment of the ocean floor, and consequently the inability of the Port of Chañaral to bring in ships of great tonnage, conscious only of her commercial spirit, the respondent, artificially diverted the course of the Salado River leading it to disembogue in the beautiful Caleta Palito (Palito Cove), in Pan de Azúcar National Park. In the petitioner's opinion, it seems grotesque that while on the one hand the State creates in the shores of the sea and in the coastal belt north of the city of Chañaral, a privileged zone, declaring it Pan de Azúcar National Park, to preserve the irreplaceable riches composed of its flora and fauna, on the other hand the marine and surface habitat be destroyed by way of the discharge of toxic waste expedited by the working of respondent's mines.…

---

a Translation by Claudia C. Bohorquez. The Court of Appeals decision was affirmed by the Supreme Court of Chile on July 28, 1988. Another English translation of this decision can be found at 2 Geo. Int'l Envtl. L. Rev. 251 (1989) and another in Alice Palmer and Cairo Robb (eds), INTERNATIONAL ENVIRONMENTAL LAW REPORTS-VOLUME 4: INTERNATIONAL ENVIRONMENTAL LAW IN NATIONAL COURTS (2005).

[A]ccording to technical reports, [these substances] are nonbiodegradable, will not settle on the ocean floor, and layers of variable thickness impede the photosynthesis of surface plankton and cause erosion of the rocks, stripping them of marine plants and algaes, making all life impossible, including the death of abundant and diverse quantities of fish that inhabited what is today a marine desert.

The petitioner concludes by stating that article 19 of the Political Constitution establishes a right to live in an environment free of pollution and an obligation by the State to guard this right from being adversely affected and to teach preservation of nature. As such, the Court can and must set specific restrictions that abate the abusive illegal and antiregulatory exercise that the respondent, a state company, produces, and in this way protect the environment, health, nature and, in general, life itself. The petitioner seeks an order demanding that Division Salvador of Codelco-Chile put an end to the pollution of the Salado River, under warning of closing of the company, payment of damages and, finally, all measures in the judgment of the Court conducive to the reestablishment and protection of [petitioner's] rights, with costs....

Joined to this appeal of protection was the appeal initiated by the "Citizens' Committee for the Protection of the Environment and Development of Chañaral" brought by the director, Julio R. Palma Vergara, ... four other directors of said organization, and seventy-two leading citizens from various institutions of Chañaral, who in synthesis also appeal for protection. The appeal was brought so that the Court will protect their guaranteed Constitutional right to live in an environment free of pollution as established in article 19, No. 8 of the Political Constitution of the Republic which has been arbitrarily and illegally affected by the activities promoted by Division Salvador of Codelco-Chile....

The effects of the passage of almost 20 tons of waste per minute, produced by the emptying of the tailings into the ocean, signify the burial of bays and the environment, of life and the future, because of the daily accumulation of thousands of tons of contaminants by whose fast and silent chemical action the ecology, along the coast, is destroyed, producing the ecological destruction of all forms of marine life in hundreds of square kilometers in Palitos Cove, Tinejas, Rio Seco and Playa Blanca; a devastation that blossoms over the whole coastal area of the National Park Pan de Azúcar, with which dies a piece of Chile....

From a legal point of view, this appeal maintains that a set of legal norms exists which supports the right to live in an environment free of pollution founded in the Constitution..., not to mention the Fundamental Constitution, regulation 3 133 of 191 6, concerning "Neutralization of the Residuals of Industrial Establishments," whose enforcement belongs to the National Service of Sanitation Works; [A list of statutes and legal principles supporting the petitioners' position followed].... [The petitioners] ask that the necessary ruling be adopted to put an end to the contamination of the beaches and waters of Chañaral, reestablishing the right [to live in an unpolluted environment] and assuring its proper protection, with costs.... Joined to this appeal for protection were 1200 citizens [of Chañaral]....

Answering both appeals, the Copper Corporation of Chile, Division Salvador, represented by its General Manager Raúl Poblete de la Cerda, entered pleadings ... asking that the claims be rejected in all of their parts....

In count IV the respondent undertakes what it calls the facts of the appeal and tries to downplay, if not the polluting effect of the tailings on the marine life and coast at the mouth of the tailing canal and its surroundings, then the magnitude of it....

Findings of Fact and Conclusions of Law:

FIRST: That ... the pollution of the coast of Chañaral ... violates the right of the inhabitants of the city of Chañaral to live in an unpolluted environment, a guarantee of constitutional rank, codified by article 19, No. 8 of the Political Constitution of the Republic, granting in article 20, clause 2, the appeal of protection to protest when said right or guarantee is affected by an arbitrary and illegal act imputable to a specific authority or person, in this case the respondent....

FOURTH: That the present appeals of protection are imbued with unique importance by being related to the protection of the right to live in an environment free of pollution and to the preservation of nature. These problems affect not only the well-being, but also the life of man, and not only of a specific community of present men. Future generations will protest the lack of foresight of their ancestors if the environment is contaminated and nature destroyed, exhausting the renewable resources, and if the ecosystem loses its capacity to regenerate or fulfill its principal functions in biophysical processes. From these principal ideas spring the importance of these appeals for protection.

FIFTH: ... [T]he Supreme Court, in a decision rendered on 19 December, 1985 in an appeal for protection on "*Pollution of Irrigation Water and Illegal Extraction of Water from Lake Chungará*," in its tenth [legal] reason, stated precisely:

> that the environment, environmental heritage and preservation of nature, of which the Constitution speaks and which it secures and protects, is everything which naturally surrounds us and that permits the development of life, and it refers to the atmosphere as it does to the land and its waters, to the flora and fauna, all of which comprise nature, with its ecological systems of balance between organisms and the environment in which they live.

The environment and the environmental heritage are negatively affected and nature is not preserved when they are polluted, putting in danger, by breaking the natural equilibrium of the ecosystem, the environmental element that serves as the sustenance of existence itself. The evolution and development of all humanity are precisely what is secured by our Political Constitution....

EIGHTH: That ... it is necessary now to explain if indeed the respondent carries out the arbitrary and illegal act with which it is charged, upsetting and threatening the right of the petitioners to live in an environment free of pollution, thus violating the constitutional guarantee of article 19, No. 8 of the Fundamental Constitution....

ELEVENTH: The evidence at trial ... permit[s] the following fact to be taken as proven:

> That the tailings, produced by the respondent, with its content of water, various minerals—copper, molybdenum, arsenic, etc., and various chemical reagents, form chemical and physical pollutants which, upon discharge directly into the Pacific Ocean-Caleta Palitos—has caused on the northern coast of Chañaral ecological injury by pollution of the seawater, the creation of artificial beaches of sterile solids issuing from the tailings. [This] pollution includes, especially, Caleta Palitos—the place of the tailing discharge—and adjacent coves, extending northward into the boundaries of Pan de Azúcar National Park....

FOURTEENTH: That the act which the respondent performs is illegal, inasmuch as the respondent has relied on the water rights for industrial use granted by Decree No. 565 of the Ministry of Public Works on 11 March, 1963 ... to the Andes Copper Mining Company [respondent's legal predecessor] ... modified in the name of the respondent by resolution No. 74 of 29 February, 1984, authorizing [the respondent] to restore the water, without purifying it, in a specific part of the bed of the Salado River. Such authorization cannot be understood to mean the restoration of the aforementioned polluted water because upon restoring it in that form, the respondent commits an illegal act which surpasses the authorization granted.

FIFTEENTH: Moreover, the orders of authority referred to which permit the restoration of the water without purification to a place from which the tailings naturally drain into the ocean, causing pollution, violate Decree with Force of Law [D.F.L.] No. 208, published in the Official Newspaper, which created the Consultative Council of Fishing and Hunting, where at article 8 it states that

> it shall be illegal to throw into the ocean, rivers and lakes, the residues or tailings of the agricultural, manufacturing and mining industries that could be harmful to the life of fish or shellfish, without first having been purified or diluted.

Likewise, the respondent's acts violate that ordered by the current Sanitation Code in article 73.... Violated also is that commanded by article 142, clause 1 of the Decree Law 2222 of 1978, which states under the title On Pollution:

> It is absolutely prohibited to throw rubble, debris or trash and spill oil or its derivatives or residue, mineral tailings or other harmful or dangerous substances of any type which cause damage or harm into waters under national jurisdiction, and into ports, rivers, and lakes.

Finally, in this respect, we must mention as infringed article 43, clause 3 of D.F.L. No. 5 of 1983....

SIXTEENTH: The environment-polluting act that the respondent executes, besides being illegal, is arbitrary by its very nature.... Never will it be said that a person or authority has the right to pollute the environment, in which a community of people live and grow, by a voluntary act of its own, as is occurring in this case. Moreover, said act, by affecting nature itself, is violating all civilized norms of cohabitation of man with his environment. The preservation of nature and conservation of the environmental heritage is an obligation of the State, according to our Fundamental Constitution, and the polluting act which the respondent voluntarily executes is arbitrary from any point of view....

For these legal reasons, legal decrees cited and that ordered by article 19, Nos. 8 and 20, clause 2, of the Political Constitution of the Republic ... IT IS HELD:

> That the appeals for protection are accepted ... and it is ordered that within a maximum time of one year from the time this ruling becomes final, the respondent, Division Salvador of Codelco-Chile, State Enterprise, must proceed to put a definitive end to the deposition of the tailings issuing from the mine development industry of El Salvador into the Pacific Ocean.

Questions and Discussion

1. *Supreme Court decision.* In *Pedro Flores v. Corporacion del Cobre*, Supreme Court of Chile Rol.12.753.FS. 641 (1988), the Supreme Court of Chile upheld the appellate decision.

2. *The Trillium case.* Nine years after *Pedro Flores*, the Supreme Court of Chile overturned, on constitutional grounds, a logging plan that had no environmental impact assessment. *Trillium Case*, Decision No. 2.732-96, Sup. Ct. of Chile (Mar. 19, 1997).

3. *Use of constitution, statutes, or both?* Note that in granting relief against a private company in *Pedro Flores* the court concluded that not only were constitutional rights of Chilean citizens infringed, but also that specific statutes were violated. Does this mean that the constitutional rights were only window-dressing for what was otherwise a simple case of permitting citizen enforcement against polluters? The earlier *Lago Chungará* case, cited in *Pedro Flores*, held that the Chilean Constitution's environmental right served to abolish previous restrictions on standing-to-sue, so that any Chilean citizen could file environmental lawsuits. Does *Pedro Flores* suggest that the courts might be reluctant to give substantive meaning to an environmental rights provision if a statute were not also being violated?

4. *Citizen suits in the United States.* In the United States, several environmental statutes provide a specific right to individual persons to enforce the statutes against others, such as companies. The first of these "citizen suit" provisions for federal courts was adopted in the Clean Air Act of 1970, 42 U.S.C. § 7604. It was modeled upon a similar provision in the Michigan Environmental Protection Act of 1970, Mich. Stat. Ann. § 14.528(201)-(207), Mich. Comp. Laws § 324.1701 (1994). Issues of access to the courts by citizens, including standing to sue, are discussed in more detail in Chapter 8.

5. *Using environmental rights not to clean up but to get away.* Recall that Judge Leaphart, concurring in the *Montana Environmental Information Center* case, wrote, "I would not, in the context of this appeal, address the question of private action." However, the issue arose in the Montana Supreme Court in *Cape-France Enterprises v. Estate of Peed*, 2001 MT 139, 305 Mont. 513, 29 P.3d 1011 (Mont. 2001). A buyer of land wanted to subdivide the land for homes. To obtain a permit for the subdivision, the buyer was required to show that water was available, but in fact a "pollution plume" was spreading through underground water toward the land. The court allowed the buyer to cancel the contract of sale, saying:

> In light of [the] two provisions of Montana's Constitution, it would be unlawful for Cape-France, a private business entity, to drill a well on its property in the face of substantial evidence that doing so may cause significant degradation of uncontaminated aquifers and pose serious public health risks. As already noted, a contract may be rescinded where the object of the contract is unlawful.

> Moreover, for a court to mandate specific performance of the contract at issue on the record here, would not only be to require a private party to violate the Constitution—a remedy that no court can provide—but, as well, would involve the state itself in violating the public's Article II, Section 3 fundamental rights to a clean and healthful environment, and in failing to maintain and improve a clean and healthful environment as required by Article IX, Section 1.

Three Justices dissented, saying that the constitutional issue had not been squarely presented by the case, one of them writing:

> Montana constitutional rights relating to the environment are hugely important and impactful to the citizens of Montana and should not be dallied with by this Court in the absence of issues being raised in the District Court and fully briefed in this Court.

> For the reasons stated above, I dissent from the Court's opinion on the issue actually before us and strenuously dissent from its inappropriate insertion of the "clean and healthful" discussion, which will unnecessarily fan the flames of controversy in Montana.

IV. Evaluating the Role of the Courts

The preceding cases have shown a variety of ways that the highest courts of various countries (and one U.S. state) have used constitutional provisions to strike down legislation, overturn executive actions, and demand affirmative action from legislatures, executive branches of government, and private individuals. Consider these two differing perspectives on whether the courts should be engaged in such work.

Securing Environmental Rights through Public Interest Litigation in South Asia
Dr. Parvez Hassan & Azim Azfar
22 Va. Envtl. L.J. 215 (2004)

[I]n the three decades since Stockholm, the developing world has reached an impressive sophistication in its environment-related legal regimes. In South Asia in particular, Pakistan, India, Bangladesh, and Sri Lanka all possess integrated and robust framework laws that feature the essential tools noted above. To this end, notable mention should be made of the Environment Protection Act of 1997 (Pakistan), the Environment Protection Act of 1986 (India), the Environment Conservation Act of 1995 (Bangladesh), and the National Environmental Protection Act (Sri Lanka).

Unfortunately, in what has been the biggest disappointment with regard to these impressive legislative structures, the symmetry between the making of laws and their implementation has not progressed to anyone's satisfaction....

Perhaps it was overly optimistic to place lofty hopes upon laws that are ultimately implemented by poorly trained bureaucracies rooted in cultures of corruption and inefficiency. Rather than having law for its own sake, we clearly need effective law if we are to move forward towards our goal of sustainable development....

The failure of governments in the region threaten the environment not only through acts of omission and habitual neglect of their duties. Quite often, they also threaten the environment in the planning and execution of development projects such as dams, mining operations, and energy projects launched without adequate forethought for the consequent damage to the ecology and to human settlements. Naturally, in a situation where the policing authorities are the culprits themselves, recourse to the administration becomes pointless and the affected people turn to the defensive mechanisms afforded by the courts.

Fortunately, the courts of South Asia have traveled a long way in meeting the challenges of environmental decay. Where they have not found support in the framework legislation, the courts have delved deeply into the constitutional principles of human rights to develop a jurisprudence that attempts to balance the need for economic progress with humanity's desire—perhaps duty would be a better term—to protect and preserve the environment for present and future generations.

Is a "Polluted" Constitution Worse Than a Polluted Environment?
Shubhankar Dam & Vivek Tewary
17 J. of Envtl. L. 383 (2005)

While some regard the Court as a "saviour," "champion" or "pioneer," more recently, there are references to its role as a "usurper" in environmental matters. This environmental activism (or usurpation) may be studied in three indistinct phases. The first phase was remarkable for the creativity exhibited by the Court when it ventured to provide a new rights' jurisprudence inspired by the social justice philosophy of the Indian Constitution. The second phase, beginning late 1980s, marked a period of judicial lawmaking when the Court strained legal principles, either to develop new jurisprudence or to incorporate principles into India's existing environmental jurisprudence that until then was part of international law. The involvement of the Court in the third phase, however, has been the most controversial. Increasingly, the Court has begun to act as the executive in environmental matters, making policies and creating institutions for their implementation....

The third phase, beginning in the late 1990s, has been by far the most controversial. Rather than judicial interpretation, the Supreme Court has concentrated on matters that arguably are strictly within the dominion of policymaking.... The process that began with a series of M.C. Mehta cases, more popularly known as the Ganga Pollution cases, found newer manifestation of executive authority in the murky issue of European norms and more lately in the matter of introduction of compressed natural gas (CNG) fuel in New Delhi....

The rigor of the formal court procedures and statutory requirements are diluted in favour of a summary, result oriented approach. The main thrust is to substitute the ineffective administrative directives issued by the pollution control boards under the Water Act and the Environment (Protection) Act, with judicial orders, the disobedience of which invites contempt of court action and penalties.

The directions given in the Calcutta Tanneries case were more invasive of the executive authority. Amongst others, the Court set a deadline for the closure of polluting tanneries, imposed a deposit fee on the price of the land, ordered the State Government to set up a unified single agency consisting of all departments concerned to act as a nodal agency, directed the State Government to appoint an authority to assess the ecological loss to the region and asked the same to frame scheme in consultation with National Environmental Engineering Research Institute (NEERI) and the Central Pollution Control Board (CPCB) for reversing the ecological loss.

These were orders passed nearly a decade after the Court had rebuked in the strongest possible words the Kanpur tanneries. For those who believed that the Court could effectively function as an administrative body exercising executive powers, the failures are too glaring to be overlooked. More important, is industrial relocation policy the province of the Court? ...

The administrative role of the Court reached new heights of controversy while introducing CNG as the alternative fuel in New Delhi. In *M.C. Mehta v. Union of India*, noting the harmful consequences of vehicular pollution on the general health of people, the Court ordered the implementation of directions to restrict plying of commercial vehicles including taxis that were fifteen years old and restriction on plying of goods vehicles during the daytime. This was followed by a relentless spate of executive directives. The Court ordered the conversion of the city bus fleet in New Delhi to a single mode of CNG, directed all private vehicles to conform to the Euro-I and Euro-II norms and prohibited registration of diesel-driven vehicles after 4 January 2000, unless those conformed to Euro-II norms....

Most of these orders were passed in pursuance of the report of the Bhure Lal Committee set up under the Environmental Protection Agency (EPA). Even though inspired by the urge to protect public health against the carcinogenic effects of suspended particles in the air, implementation of such norms cannot be achieved without the active and willing participation of the executive. The failure of this activism of the judicial administration was evident when the Court observed in *M.C. Mehta v. Union of India* that it was distressed by certain reports appearing in the print and electronic media, exhibiting a defiant attitude of the Delhi Administration to comply with the orders. That attitude, the Court noted, "if correct, was wholly objectionable and not correct in law." It almost pleaded that its concern "in passing various orders since 1986 has been only one, namely to protect the health of the people...." To the plea of the Central Government that there was shortage of CNG to ensure a complete conversion of all vehicles, the Court responded with the following words:

If there is short supply of an essential commodity, then the priority must be of public health, as opposed to the health of the balance sheet of a private company. To enable industries to cut their losses, or to make more profit at the cost of public heath, is not a sign of good governance, and this is contrary to the constitutional mandate....

While the same may be true, it does not necessarily follow that anything that affects public health is within the jurisdiction of the Court. It is unlikely that any of these decisions have sensitised the executive to act with greater alacrity in environmental matters. The only effect may have been to retard the possible evolution of responsible bureaucracy....

If the weakened institutional balance is to be saved from further depletion, the Supreme Court must withdraw itself from the alchemist role. All problems of life or conflicts of interests are not problems of law. The Court would do well to acknowledge that "ills of governance" are best resolved when they are resolved by the conflicting interest holders themselves.... One may live in a polluted environment but not in a polity that has a "polluted" Constitution. Is not a "polluted" Constitution worse than a polluted environment?

Questions and Discussion

1. *Stimulus or delay?* Dr. Hassan asserts that governments are guilty of "acts of omission and habitual neglect of their duties" as well as projects "launched without adequate forethought" and argues that judicial intervention is necessary. Authors Dam and Tewary argue such interventions "cannot be achieved without the active and willing participation of the executive" and that it is "unlikely" that court decisions "have sensitised the executive to act with greater alacrity." Indeed, the latter two authors assert that judicial action can actually "retard the possible evolution of responsible bureaucracy." Which author's view seems more correct?

2. *When and where?* Is judicial interpretation of the Constitution, as a tool to force laggard governments to protect the environment, likely to be more useful in some societies than in others? More useful in some political situations more than in others? If environmental legislation exists, is there a role for constitutional adjudication on environmental issues, or should matters be left entirely to the legislature and executive?

3. *Are environmental rights different?* Is there a difference between constitutional environmental rights and other constitutional rights that suggests that courts should be less alert to enforce the former? Does adjudicating environmental rights move courts more into policy areas than does adjudicating other constitutional rights?

Chapter 4

Right to Water

Introduction

There has been a lot said about the sacredness of our land which is our body; and the values of our culture which is our soul; but water is the blood of our tribes, and if its life-giving flow is stopped, or it is polluted, all else will die and the many thousands of years of our communal existence will come to an end.[a]

In the developed world, people take for granted the ability to walk a few feet in their houses or offices, turn a knob, and have fresh, clean water pour out. The ability to wake up in the morning and wash your face, make a cup of tea, or take a shower is one that most people in developed countries take for granted, but it is rarely considered a fundamental human right.

In the developing world, women may walk miles each day to obtain water for their families' daily needs. As the temperature of the planet increases in coming years, glaciers melt, and snows disappear, it is estimated that hundreds of millions of people will lose their current supplies of fresh water. In numerous countries, the water available for domestic use is contaminated with illness-inducing bacteria and toxic chemicals.

The following materials examine whether or not *access* to drinking water, and further the provision of *clean* drinking water, is or should be a fundamental right under international law or national constitutions.

---

a Governor Frank Tenorio of the San Felipe Pueblo, New Mexico. Quoted in *A Dwindling Water Supply and the Indian Struggle to Retain Aboriginal and Winters Doctrine Water Rights*, Am. Indian J., Dec. 1978, at 35.

I. A Right to Water in International and Regional Instruments

A. Soft and Hard Law Sources

Water as a Human Right? (2004)

John Scanlon, Angela Cassar, & Noémi Nemes

II. Does international law recognise a human right to water? ...

B. Customary International Law

The development of environmental law as a recognized body of law has created an additional source of law for analysis of the existence of a right to water. This is because uniform State practice may provide evidence of *opinio juris*. It is appropriate to consider national constitutions as a source of an emerging right to water and court interpretations of fundamental rights contained in those constitutions. Whilst over 60 constitutions refer to environmental obligations, less than one-half expressly refer to the right of its citizens to a healthy environment. Only the South African Bill of Rights enshrines an explicit right of access to sufficient water. In view of the foregoing, a position that a uniform constitutional practice has emerged is rather doubtful, especially considering the fact that despite the increasing prevalence of constitutional environmental norms, most countries have yet to interpret or apply such norms.

In many countries, particularly those with a civil law tradition, traditionally constitutional rights were not regarded as being self-executing; legislation was required to implement a constitutional provision and to empower a person to invoke protections. However, with the rise of constitutionalism globally, courts increasingly view the constitution as an independent source of rights, enforceable even in the absence of implementing legislation. Thus, courts could and do rely on the environmental provisions of their constitutions when protecting water from pollution or ensuring access to water to meet basic human needs. Where constitutions lack environmental provisions, reliance has been placed on the right to life, a provision contained in most constitutions worldwide. Constitutions many times incorporate "penumbral rights," rights that are not explicitly mentioned in the constitution, but are consistent with its principles and existing rights. These rights could easily adopt emerging fundamental human rights.

Both civil and common-law countries have incorporated the "Public Trust Doctrine" in their constitutions. The doctrine dates back to the Institutes of Justinian (530 A.D.) and requires governments to protect certain resources, like water, that the government holds in trust for the public. Many of the U.S. state constitutions have incorporated this doctrine, and courts in at least five states have used them to review state action. Similarly, Indian and Sri Lankan courts have relied on the doctrine to protect the environment. In the *M.C. Mehta v. Kamal Nath Case* (1977), which concerned the diversion of a river's flow, the Supreme Court held that the government violated the public trust by leasing the environmentally sensitive riparian forest land to a company....

In many cases, courts have applied the provisions of the right to life, environment, etc. where an environmentally destructive activity directly threatened people's health and life....

C. Judicial Decisions

Recent decisions show that recognition of a human right to water, though not recognized within the law of nations per se, is an emerging trend. In the *Gabčíkovo-Nagymaros Case* (1997), Judge Weeramantry wrote that "[t]he protection of the environment is ... a vital part of contemporary human rights doctrine, for it is a sine qua non for numerous human rights such as the right to health and the right to life itself ... damage to the environment can impair and undermine all the human rights spoken of in the Universal Declaration and other human rights instruments." While there is a no express recognition, human rights courts have been prepared to be creative and liberally interpret existing provisions in there decisions. The following shows how water has been recognized as an integral part of several fundamental human rights.

Right to life, liberty and personal security

In the *Port Hope Case* (1980), the complainant alleged that dumping of nuclear wastes within Port Hope, Ontario, was causing large-scale pollution of residences thus threatening the lives of people. Though the U.N. Human Rights Committee ultimately declared the complaint inadmissible due to failure to exhaust local remedies, it observed that the case "raises serious issues under Art. 6(1)" of the ICCPR, with regard to a State's obligation to protect human life.

The [Inter-]American Commission on Human Rights has the authority to study the human rights situations in the member states of the OAS. In its *Report on the Human Rights Situation in Ecuador* (1997), it found that inhabitants were exposed to toxic byproducts of oil exploitation in their drinking and bathing water, which jeopardized their lives and health. The court stated that "where environmental contamination and degradation pose a persistent threat to human life and health, the foregoing rights (right to life, to physical security and integrity) are implicated."

Right to property

The *Zander v. Sweden Case* (1993) concerned potential pollution of a drinking water well from a nearby dump. The applicants' claim was directly concerned with their ability to use the water in their well for drinking purposes. Such ability was one facet of their right of property, thus Art. 6(1) of the European Convention on Human Rights was applicable. The European Court held in this case that there had been a violation of Art. 6(1).

In 2001, the Inter-American Court on Human Rights explicitly recognized the link between human rights and the environment in the *Awas Tingni Case*. The court ruled that Nicaragua violated the indigenous community's rights to its property (Art. 21 of the American Convention on Human Rights), natural resources and environment when it granted concessions to a Korean logging company to harvest timber on the community's land without the latter's consent.... [This case can be found in Chapter 5 at page 174.]

Right to respect for one's private life and home

In its judgement *López Ostra v. Spain* (1994), the European Court of Human Rights recognised that certain environmental impairment with severe harmful consequences for individuals—though without the need to seriously endanger health—constitute a violation of other human rights, such as the right to respect for one's private life and home. The case concerned a waste treatment plant, which caused health problems and nuisance to many local people, forcing them to relocate. [This case can be found in Chapter 2 at page 26.]

Right to culture

The U.N. Human Rights Committee issued a decision in the *Lubikon Lake Band Case* (1990), that oil and gas exploration deprived the Band of its right to live its traditional way of life and culture and thus violated Art. 27 of the ICCPR. [This case can be found in Chapter 5 at page 149.]

Right to health

In the *Communications 25/89, 47/90, 56/91, 100/93 (Joined) against Zaire*, the African Commission [on Human and Peoples' Rights] argued that "the failure of the Government to provide basic services such as safe drinking water and electricity and the shortage of medicine as alleged in communication 100/93 constitutes a violation of Art. 16" of the African Charter, which states that every individual shall have the right to enjoy the best attainable state of physical and mental health, and that States Parties should take the necessary measures to protect the health of their people.

D. Conclusion: The human right to water is not yet explicitly recognized

The human right to water does exist, as water is the most essential element of life. However, as the overview of the present instruments indicated, this right has not been clearly defined in international law and has not been expressly recognised as a fundamental human right. Rather, a right to water is interpreted as being an implicit component of either existing fundamental human rights, or is expressly included in non-binding instruments that are designed to achieve specific ends. Following both the Millennium Declaration and WSSD [World Summit on Sustainable Development], the possibility has arisen for the creation of stronger linkages between all these instruments in recognition of their common objectives. The meaningful implementation of sustainable development can now be further advanced to help link social development and human rights aspects of sustainable development with the environment, as well as ensuring economic well-being through the benefits that adequate supplies of water can provide. This is important to ensure there is access to water of adequate quality and quantity to meet the needs of all societies, both now and in the future.

If we are to consider the possibility of formulating a human right to water as a separate notion, then consolidation and clear definition of scope will be necessary, particularly as it will potentially relate to present international environmental principles and conventions.

III. Why link water and human rights? ...

... Human rights are formulated in terms of rights of individuals, not in terms of rights and obligations of states vis-à-vis other states as international law provisions generally do. Thus by making water a human right, it could not be taken away from the people. Through a rights-based approach victims of water pollution and people deprived of necessary water for meeting their basic needs are provided with access to remedies. In contrast to other systems of international law, the human rights system affords access to individuals and NGOs. The explicit recognition of water as a human right could thus represent one tool for civil society to hold governments accountable for ensuring access to sufficient, good-quality water. ...

If the right to water were to be recognized within a legally binding human rights instrument, not only would the obligations arising from such a right become more clear-cut, but the violations of this right would also be evident. Injurious deprivation or pollution of an individual's water supply, or denial of his/her access to sufficient and safe water would enable him/her to seek redress through the court system of the state concerned. In the event of failure at national level, aggrieved individuals would still have an international avenue of redress through human rights institutions....

Questions and Discussion

1. *Human rights or environmental rights.* Scanlon suggests looking to environmental law as "an additional source of law for analysis of the existence of a right to water." Would Scanlon's environment-oriented approach elevate ecosystem water needs above human water needs? One study argues:

> As expected for a human rights approach, the U.N. concept for water as a human right is characterized as a sole people-centred approach to development, not recognising the "water rights" of environment in an equal manner.

> A people-centred approach is preferable to a top-down approach which was traditionally in place with water systems imposed on the people by governmental and professional sectors. It is more effective, efficient and less costly. But water is also needed to maintain and recreate nature and environment. The amount of water for peoples' use needs to be balanced with the needs of the environment.

Assaf, K.; Attia, B.; Darwish, A.; Wardam, B; Klawitter, S. *Water as a Human Right: The Understanding of Water in Arab Countries of the Middle East—A Four Country Analysis.* Global Issues Papers. No. 11. September 2004. Berlin: Heinrich Böll Foundation, 2004. Compare that assessment with this one:

> The problem with the environmentally oriented approach towards the human right to water is the inherent conflicts that have not been resolved when considering the needs of the person versus those of the environment, as well as the lack of normative clarity which leads towards an ambiguous and uncertain practical applicability of the human right to water.

Water Resources and International Law, Hague Academy of International Law, Centre for Studies and Research in International Law and International Relations, 101–104 (Report of the 2001 Session by Salman M.A. Salman and Laurence Boisson de Chazournes) (Martinus Nijhoff Publishers 2002), cited from Salman M.A. Salman & Siobhan Mcinerney-Lankford, THE HUMAN RIGHT TO WATER, at ix (2004).

2. *Explicit recognition of water as a human right.* Are Scanlon's arguments for an explicit and separate recognition of water as a human right persuasive? Is it not enough to put emphasis on more effective implementation of existing rights that contain elements of a right to water? In this regard, consider Peter H. Gleick's arguments provided below.

> Even if the human right to water is formally accepted, what is the advantage of such an acknowledgment? After all, despite the declaration of a formal right to food, nearly a billion people remain undernourished. Let me offer five reasons for acknowledging a human right to water:

> 1. Acknowledging a right to water would encourage the international community and individual governments to renew their efforts to meet basic water needs of their populations.

> 2. By acknowledging a right to water, pressures to translate that right into specific national and international legal obligations and responsibilities are much more likely to occur. As Richard Jolly of the United Nations Development ment Programme noted:

To emphasize the human right of access to drinking water does more than emphasize its importance. It grounds the priority on the bedrock of social and economic rights, it emphasizes the obligations of states parties to ensure access, and it identifies the obligations of states parties to provide support internationally as well as nationally.

3. Acknowledging a right to water maintains a spotlight of attention on the deplorable state of water management in many parts of the world.

4. Acknowledging a right to water helps focus attention on the need to more widely address international watershed disputes and to resolve conflicts over the use of shared water by identifying minimum water requirements and allocations for all basin parties.

5. Explicitly acknowledging a human right to water can help set specific priorities for water policy. In particular, meeting a basic water requirement for all humans to satisfy this right should take precedence over other water management and investment decisions.

Gleick, Peter. *The Human Right to Water.* (May 2007). Available at www.pacinst.org/reports/human_right_may_07.pdf.

3. *More Sources.* Professor Stephen McCaffrey suggests these additional sources might be consulted:

While a human right to water must be inferred from the general human rights instruments [if it is to be found], an obligation to provide an adequate domestic or drinking water supply is expressly provided for in several human rights and humanitarian treaties of a more specialized character. These include such agreements as the 1989 Convention on the Rights of the Child, the 1979 Convention on the Elimination of All forms of Discrimination Against Women, and the 1949 Geneva Convention relative to the Treatment of Prisoners of War. However, none of these agreements casts the corresponding entitlement in human rights terms. Instead, they place a duty on governments to ensure that water, among other things necessary to life and good health, is provided to members of groups that have been identified as requiring special protection....

The European Parliament declared in September 2003 that "access to drinking water is a basic human right." ...

Meetings held under the auspices of the United Nations and other organizations have recognized the importance of access to water of adequate quality and quantity for drinking and other domestic uses. But the fact that neither the Plan of Implementation adopted at the World Summit for Sustainable Development held in Johannesburg, 2–11 September 2002, nor—perhaps more importantly— the final Ministerial Declaration of the Third World Water Forum held in Kyoto, 16–23 March 2003, included a reference to a right to water, has aroused controversy. This failure was apparently due to political hesitation regarding the idea, which does not auger well for a general recognition of the right by States....

The 1999 Protocol on Water and Health to the 1992 ECE [Economic Commission for Europe] Convention on the Protection and Use of Transboundary Watercourses and International Lakes requires the parties to take "all appropriate measures for the purpose of ensuring ... [a]dequate supplies of wholesome drinking water" and provides that the parties "shall pursue the aims of ... [a]ccess to drinking water for everyone...."

[A fine example is] the new Water Charter of the Senegal River. In establishing principles and mechanisms for distributing water between different sectors, or uses, the Water Charter provides that any distribution of the River's water will aim at guaranteeing to the populations of the riparian States the full enjoyment of the resource, respecting the safety of persons and works as well as "the fundamental human right to healthful water," in the perspective of sustainable development....
Stephen McCaffrey. The Human Right to Water (2005)

B. General Comment 15: Private or Public Good?

The Human Right to Water
Stephen C. McCaffrey
FRESH WATER AND INTERNATIONAL ECONOMIC LAW (E. B. Weiss,
L. B. DeChazournes & N. Bernasconi-Osterwalder, eds., 2005)

1. Introduction ...

It seems almost axiomatic ... that there should be a human right to water—especially since some 1.1 billion people lack access to potable supplies, according to the World Health Organization. Indeed, it is not uncommon to encounter references to "*the* human right to water," implying that such a right incontrovertibly exists. But while a case can certainly be made for such a right, it is not explicitly recognized in any of the instruments comprising the International Bill of Human Rights—notably, the Universal Declaration of Human Rights of 1948 and the two human rights treaties of 1966 that grew out of the Universal Declaration: the International Covenants on Civil and Political Rights (CP Covenant), and on Economic, Social and Cultural Rights (ESC Covenant)....

Of course, the fact that water is not mentioned in the International Bill of Human Rights does not mean that humans do not have a right to it. In fact, the United Nations Committee on Economic, Social and Cultural Rights [(ESC Committee)] ... has recently declared in a General Comment that a right to water exists as an independent right, by necessary implication from Articles 11 and 12 of the Covenant.... [However,] no doubt a highly authoritative interpretation of the Covenant, the Committee's finding does not bind the 147 States that are parties to it, let alone other States. States would have to accept this interpretation through their practice for it to have binding effect upon them.... [W]hat precisely States are required to do in order to fulfill their obligations in relation to a human right to water ... is the subject of the new General Comment....

[I]t is difficult to identify evidence of State practice on which to base such a customary right to water. Yet it is entirely possible, perhaps even probable, that the action of the ESC Committee in adopting General Comment 15 will attract sufficient State practice over time that a customary norm will be formed on the basis of that practice....

3. The New General Comment and Its Implications

At its twenty-ninth session in 2002, [the ESC Committee] adopted General Comment No. 15 (2002) on "The right to water (Articles 11 and 12 of the International Covenant on Economic, Social and Cultural Rights)." This is the first recognition by a United Nations human rights body of an independent and generally applicable human right to water. As such, it is deserving of attention and examination. First, some background regarding the ESC Committee will help to place General Comment 15 in context.

3.1 Background: The ESC Committee ...

The Committee was established by a 1985 resolution of the Economic and Social Council (ECOSOC) and began functioning in 1987....

The Committee was not authorized to adopt General Comments that would be binding on the States parties to the ESC Covenant.... The General Comment reflects the Committee's interpretation of Articles 11 and 12 of the ESC Covenant.... The fact that States have not yet accepted explicitly a general human right to water suggests that the ESC Committee's General Comment may be somewhat ahead of State practice and therefore may be more in the nature of a statement *de lege ferenda* rather than *lex lata*....

3.2 General Comment 15: Overview and General Features ...

a. Water as a "Public Good"

Interestingly, the Comment begins by characterizing water as a "public good." ... In view of the contemporary controversy over the privatization of water supply systems, the ESC Committee may have intended by using this term to send the message that governments must ensure that the human right to water is safeguarded if they place management of water services in private hands....

The ESC Committee ... seems to have intended to use the expression "public good" not the way an economist would, but more generally, perhaps to convey the notion that water belongs to the public at large. Indeed, Roman law considered perennial streams to be common or public, *rei publicae jure gentium*, things whose use is common to all, a doctrine carried over into Spain's 13th century Siete Partidas and France's *Code Napoleon*.... In any event, the General Comment addresses the relationship between a human right to water and privatization of water systems ... [and] [i]t states that as part of the obligation to "protect," States parties to the ESC Covenant must prevent any third parties that operate or control water services from "compromising equal, affordable, and physical access to sufficient, safe and acceptable water." ...

b. The Sources of the Human Right to Water ...

[T]he General Comment bases the human right to water principally upon Articles 11 and 12 of the ESC Covenant.... It notes that Article 11(1) refers to a number of rights relating to the right to an adequate standard of living, "including adequate food, clothing and housing," and reasons that "[t]he use of the word 'including' indicates that this catalogue of rights was not intended to be exhaustive." The General Comment continues: "The right to water clearly falls within the category of guarantees essential for securing an adequate standard of living, particularly since it is one of the most fundamental conditions for survival." These arguments are not new, but had not previously come from an official source. As to Article 12, the General Comment states that the right to health under paragraph 2(b) of that article requires parties to take steps "on a non-discriminatory basis to prevent threats to health from unsafe and toxic water conditions." ...

There is no doubt that the need for access to sufficient and safe water supplies, particularly for groups in special need of protection, has been repeatedly recognized in international instruments. But this does not necessarily mean that States have recognized a human right to water, with all of its implications, either generally or in those specific instruments....

II. Water for Personal and Domestic Use

As indicated previously, the ESC Committee states in the General Comment: "The human right to water entitles everyone to sufficient, safe, acceptable, physically accessible and affordable water for personal and domestic uses." ... Significantly, the Committee further explains that, in addition to personal and domestic uses, "[p]riority should also be given to the water resources required to prevent starvation and disease, as well as water required to meet the core obligations of each of the Covenant rights." ...

The Committee finds in General Comment No. 15 that there are "a number of core obligations in relation to the right to water," and, crucially, that they are of immediate effect"—despite the fact that parties to the Covenant are generally required only to "achiev[e] progressively the full realization of the rights" it recognizes....

The Committee identifies ... nine core obligations in relation to the right to water [such as access to "minimum essential" levels; sufficient, safe, and regular water within a reasonable distance; equitable distribution; low-cost water programs for vulnerable and marginalized groups; and adequate sanitation]....

It seems inevitable that many States will be hard pressed to guarantee immediately even "minimal essential levels" of the corresponding rights, given the cost involved and capacity required to do so....

III. Water to Produce Food

In addition to water for personal and domestic use, the General Comment points to the "importance of ensuring sustainable access to water resources for agriculture to realize the right [under Article 11] to adequate food." ...

[T]he virtue of this requirement is undeniable. However, it may well be less expensive for some countries—especially those in arid regions—to import food than to use precious water resources to grow it. The General Comment does not allow for the use of such "virtual water" when it would be more economical to do so than to develop potentially expensive infrastructure and management systems....

4. Conclusions ...

No one disputes that every human being on the planet should have a right to "sufficient, safe, acceptable, physically accessible and affordable water for personal and domestic uses." The action of the ESC Committee ... in adopting General Comment No. 15 on the right to water is therefore an important step in the right direction. The status of the human right to water should be evaluated with some care, however....

The foregoing examination of General Comment 15 in its legal and political context leads to several conclusions. First, the ESC Committee's finding that a human right to water may be inferred from Articles 11 and 12 of the ESC Covenant is sound.... The Committee does not have law-making power; its interpretations will have to be accepted by the States parties to the Covenant, to say nothing of those States that are not parties.... [T]he ESC Committee's solution to the problem created by its identification of a range of "core obligations" that must be implemented immediately may do more harm than good, because it makes unrealistic demands and creates lofty expectations that many aspects of the right to water will be discharged immediately. The result may be that these components of the right, and possibly even the right itself, will not be taken seriously.... [L]ast, the Committee is to be commended for addressing "international" aspects of the right to water.... Growing water shortages, coupled with the large portion of Earth's freshwater that is shared by two or more States, suggest that attention should be devoted to this problem....

Questions and Discussion

1. *Actions by human rights commissions.* What were the occasions for the statements by the Inter-American Commission on Human Rights and the African Commission on

Human and Peoples' Rights, mentioned in Prof. McCaffrey's article, on the obligations that governments to take appropriate measures to provide safe drinking water? Do those appear to be significant events, or off-hand declarations?

2. *A right to water under ICCPR or ICESCR.* General Comments adopted by the Human Rights Committee in 1989 urge a broad interpretation of the right to life. How is the argument framed that this might include a right to water? Why does it matter whether a right to water is derived from provisions of the ICCPR or the ICESCR?

3. *Legal basis of the right to water.* How do you understand the General Comment's definition: "The human right to water entitles everyone to sufficient, safe, acceptable, physically accessible and affordable water for personal and domestic uses"? What does each of those terms mean in practical terms? Does this sound like a right that might be enforced in court? Should the same criteria or standard be applied to developed and developing countries?

4. *Water for food production or "virtual water" through food import.* Should the human right to water include access to water for food production? McCaffrey refers to "virtual water" as an economically preferable concept for arid countries—importing food rather than using precious water resources to grow it. Does the General Comment allow for such a use of "virtual water" as satisfying the right to water? Consider the excerpt below and evaluate the advantages and disadvantages of the "virtual water" concept and its implications on the human right to water for developed and developing countries.

> Virtual water is the amount of water that is embedded in food or other products needed for its production. For example, to produce one kilogram of wheat we need about 1,000 litres of water, *i.e.,* the virtual water of this kilogram of wheat is 1,000 litres. For meat, we need about five to ten times more. Trade in virtual water allows water-scarce countries to import high water-consuming products while exporting low water-consuming products and in this way making water available for other purposes. On the other hand, virtual water trade has geo-political implications: it induces dependencies between countries.... Making water available for different purposes by reducing local food production and importing virtual water through food imports may result in loss of employment in agriculture and the quality of livelihoods. In a country like South Africa, which suffers from upwards of 30% unemployment, and where the majority of farm labour has little or no schooling at all there, there is a little prospect of this group finding alternative employment. The livelihoods of these people would be seriously compromised unless the implementing authorities could adequately cater for them. The same counts for the international community with its subsidies and tariffs in agricultural products and trade, which are a serious obstacle to initiate the crop change to overcome poverty in some poor countries.

Source: World Water Council. http://www.worldwatercouncil.org/virtual_water.shtml

5. *Advocacy.* How do you expect General Comment 15 to be used by advocates of a right to water? In litigation? In lobbying for legislative or executive action at a national level?

6. *Human Rights Council.* In 2006 the U.N. Human Rights Council requested the Office of the United Nations High Commissioner for Human Rights (OHCHR) to conduct a study on obligations related to equitable access to safe drinking water and sanitation under international human rights instruments. The OHCHR submitted its report on August 16, 2007. U.N. Doc. A/HRC/6/3 (16 August 2007). On March 20, 2008, the Human Rights Council asserted that various legal instruments "entail obligations in relation to access to safe drinking water and sanitation" and appointed an independent expert to iden-

tify, promote and exchange views on best practices related to access to safe drinking water and sanitation. The expert is also to undertake a study leading to "further clarification of the content of human rights obligations, including non-discrimination obligations, in relation to access to safe drinking water and sanitation." U.N. Doc. A/HRC/7/L.16 (20 March 2008). Do these studies and reports appear to be wheel-spinning—or are they essential steps in developing and promoting the existence of a human right to water? The study's focus is on drinking water and sanitation, so it will not address the question of access to water for other uses or goals, such as economic production, irrigation for farming, industrial use, indigenous territories use, or the protection of ecosystems. Is it important or relevant for a "human" right to water to encompass these issues as well? Is it politically feasible or unwise?

7. *Free access to all?* Does a right to water have to be absolute in order to be effective? Is it inevitable that a right to water must encompass free water to all? Is a right to water likely to advance or retard the provision of adequate drinking water to those who have no easy access? Would it be better to use economic incentives to attract foreign investments for adequate water supplies by declaring water to be a commodity that can be bought and sold?

Thirst: A Short History of Drinking Water

James Salzman
18 Yale J.L. & Humanities 94 (2006)

Nestled in the Andes, the Bolivian city of Cochabamba lies in a fertile valley astride the banks of the Rocha River. Bolivia is the poorest country in South America, with two-thirds of its population below the poverty line. As in many developing countries, over forty percent of Cochabamba's 800,000 residents lack access to a water supply network. And even those who do have pipes cannot depend on reliable service. The poor often live in squatter settlements on the outskirts of town, relying for their drinking and domestic water supplies on private vendors. In a cruel irony, the poorest end up paying much more for their water than wealthier citizens connected to the city's water mains.

As part of a nationwide project to improve provision of municipal services, the government of Bolivia launched a major privatization reform effort in the late 1990s. Prompted by financial institutions such as the International Monetary Fund and World Bank, the Bolivian government actively sought out private investor management for Cochabamba's water and sewage services. Treating drinking water as a priced good under private management, it was widely argued, would improve the water supply system infrastructure and delivery by injecting much-needed capital, greater efficiencies, and increased attention to customer needs. A forty-year concession for water and wastewater services in Cochabamba was granted to an international private consortium headed by Bechtel and known as Aguas del Tunari. In the national law passed to facilitate this transaction, water was declared the property of the state, available for licensing to private companies for distribution.

To cover the costs of laying new pipe, digging a new reservoir, and building a hydroelectric dam, Aguas del Tunari immediately raised the price of water and waste services charged to consumers, with some residents soon spending in excess of twenty percent of their household income on water. Just four months after the privatization scheme commenced in 2000, protests began and soon mushroomed into street demonstrations and violence. In the face of property damage approaching twenty million dollars, dozens of injuries, and mass unrest, the government terminated the privatization concession and resumed control over the water supply system in Cochabamba.

During the heady days of protest, grassroots organizations met and jointly issued the Cochabamba Declaration. Their view of the conflict was clear—drinking water should not be a market commodity. As the Declaration stated, "Water is a fundamental human right and a public trust to be guarded by all levels of government, therefore, it should not be commodified, privatized or traded for commercial purposes."[13]

This ringing prose contrasted starkly with an international statement, the Dublin Statement, published just a few years earlier. The first major recognition of water as a market commodity, the governments represented at the 1992 International Conference on Water and the Environment declared that "water has an economic value in all its competing uses and should be recognized as an economic good."[14]

Cochabamba was not a unique event. Similar protests over drinking water have played out in Paraguay, South Africa, the Philippines, and elsewhere. Cochabamba, however, remains the best-known example and rallying point for opponents of water supply privatization in developing countries. According to the popular recounting of the story, the conflict in Cochabamba served as a globalization morality play of rights versus markets, human need versus corporate greed. This simple dichotomy sounds in the Declaration's ringing prose and echoes in many other fora, from international statements to popular demands.

While making for sharp rhetoric, this facile dichotomy of rights versus markets is terribly limited, shedding only a dim light on the powerful tensions unleashed on the streets in Bolivia. Nor should this be surprising, for drinking water is a dauntingly complex resource to manage. Indeed, the conflicts in Cochabamba are drawn from the pages of a much larger, much older story. From earliest times, human societies have faced the challenge of supplying adequate quality and quantities of drinking water. Whether limited by arid environments or urbanization, provision of clean drinking water is a prerequisite of any enduring society, but it is a multi-faceted task....

Drinking water is most obviously a physical resource, one of the few truly essential requirements for life. Regardless of the god you worship or the color of your skin, if you go without water for three days in an arid environment your life is in danger. And water's physical characteristics confound easy management. Water is heavy—it is difficult to move uphill. Water is unwieldy—it cannot be packed or contained easily. And drinking water is fragile—it easily becomes contaminated and unfit for consumption.

Drinking water can also be regarded as a cultural resource, of religious significance in many societies. A social resource—in some societies access to water reveals much about relative status. A political resource—the provision of water to citizens can help justify a regime. And finally, when scarce, water can become an economic resource.

As the Cochabamba experience makes clear, managing and mediating these many facets of drinking water is no easy matter....

IV. Drinking Water in the Developing World ...

The facts of drinking water in the developing world are both straightforward and daunting. Over one billion people do not have access to even a basic water supply. Well over two billion people lack adequate sanitation. As a result, approximately half of the developing world's inhabitants suffer from illnesses caused by contaminated water supplies. Many environmental ministers consider this the single greatest threat to their people.

---

13. The Cochabamba Declaration, available at http:// www.sierraclub.org/cac/water/human_right/.

14. The Dublin Statement on Water and Sustainable Development, available at http://www.wmo.ch/web/homs/documents/english/icwedece.html [hereinafter The Dublin Statement].

To understand the problem of drinking water in much of the developing world, one must consciously step outside our daily experience. In developed countries, with rare exception we do not even think about drinking water. It is plentiful, clean and easily available. Nor do we give a second thought to the quality or quantity of drinking water. We simply turn on the tap to take a drink or open a bottle of water. Water supply is seen as a government or corporate responsibility.

The contrast with developing countries could not be starker. Neither water quality nor quantity can be assumed. Because water supply infrastructure is not provided in the poorest urban or in many rural areas, obtaining water is regarded as an individual or domestic responsibility. In contrast to the ease of turning on a faucet, lack of infrastructure means a high labor input as someone from the household (generally women and girls) must collect each day's water, whether from a communal pond or well, a tanker, or a kiosk. One billion people do not have water within a fifteen-minute walk of where they live. The daily average time spent on water gathering in 1997 across East Africa was 91.7 minutes daily, triple the time spent three decades earlier. And in the West African country of Senegal, women spend on average 17.5 hours per week gathering water.

Where communal or free water sources are too far away or contaminated, the poor purchase their water from street vendors or tanker trucks. Forty percent of those surveyed in an East African study used water vendors. These prices are always higher than the price of water from municipal supply systems, often twelve times as much, with the tragic irony of the poorest in society paying the most for their water.

The resulting social and economic impacts are immense. With a significant proportion of women's time and family income dedicated to domestic water supply, opportunity for productive activities such as education or other employment get squeezed. It is no exaggeration to say that introduction of piped water can transform the social and economic fabric of a community. Yet the trend is worsening. From 1950 to 1985, the percent of the world's urban population doubled. The U.N. estimates that now over half of all people on earth live in urban rather than rural settings. As a result of growing urbanization, the number of clean communal water sources is decreasing as water and sanitation are put under increasing pressure.

In recognition of these pressing issues, in its Millennium Development Goals the U.N. has pledged by 2015 to "reduce by half the proportion of people without sustainable access to safe drinking water." Given the poor state of water provision in the developing world and the small likelihood of debt-burdened governments making significant public monies available for infrastructure any time soon, what can be done? …

Estimates of the capital investment needed for adequate water infrastructure and sanitation over the next twenty-five years approach $100 billion per year, yet the weak financial resources of developing country governments prevent them from absorbing the costs of water provision upgrades. The private sector, by contrast, could mobilize the necessary capital.…

The failure to treat water as a scarce commodity only ensures its inefficient distribution and use. A basic axiom of resource economics is that we over-consume goods that are underpriced. Since the market is more efficient than governments at allocating scarce goods, the argument goes, market prices should be charged for water. Indeed, the fact that the very poor do pay for water, and pay quite a bit in relative terms, suggested that they both can and will pay for piped water. Thus the principle of "full cost recovery"—charging a price to cover costs and profit—has seemed both possible and desirable.

These arguments became official international policy with adoption in 1992 of the Dublin Statement. As described in the Introduction, the Statement served as the first intergovernmental recognition of water as a market good. This strategy was adopted in policies of international financial institutions, particularly in the Structural Adjustment Programs pursued by the IMF and World Bank in debtor countries. In Bolivia and other countries, privatization of water supply systems was made a prominent lending condition.

Spurred by the Dublin Statement and facilitated by international financial institutions, there has been an unprecedented expansion of private sector participation in water supply over the last two decades. Water supply services have been privatized across the globe, from the United Kingdom, Poland and Morocco to Argentina, Indonesia and the Philippines....

Turning a profit, however, is far from assured. Water supply generally operates as a natural monopoly. Large-scale delivery of water requires large-scale infrastructure. The initial sunk costs can be massive, not to mention the continuing costs of maintenance and upgrade. This creates a significant barrier to entry for competition and requires amortization periods that can run several decades. A return on investment also requires general economic, political, and social stability over that period; yet, in many developing countries, this is far from a given. Hence the difficult challenge—privatization may hold its greatest social potential in developing countries because it can inject needed capital, yet it is in precisely such settings where investment returns are least certain.

Seeking a competitive return on investments in developing countries, privatization has often been followed by efforts at full cost recovery. The immediate problem that can arise is one of inequity. If water access is based on ability-to-pay rather than willingness-to-pay, then what are the implications for poor and marginalized communities? Does changing the management regime effectively deny them access to adequate clean drinking water?

Alert to these concerns and as part of the larger anti-globalization wave, a vocal movement has arisen to challenge the growing pressure for water privatization. Its primary demand lies in recognition of a right to water. We saw such a demand expressed in the Introduction to this article in the grassroots Cochabamba Declaration and its statement that "[w]ater is a fundamental human right and a public trust." Similar calls for a human right to water may be found in over a dozen international documents and proposed federal legislation.

Fleshing out the proper scope of a human right to water, or whether it even exists under customary international law, lies beyond the scope of this paper. For our purposes, it is enough to recognize that the enormous challenge of improving developing country water supplies remains unmet while vigorous accusations and equally strident defenses of water privatization continue to rage. Five years since the celebrated uprising in Cochabamba, its residents still suffer from severe deficiencies in water supply and distribution while Aguas del Tunari, the spurned consortium, has pursued a twenty-five million dollar claim against the Bolivian government in international arbitration.

Conclusion ...

A rights-based water management regime is clearly not a new idea. The Right to Thirst in Jewish and Islamic Law, sharing norms in parts of Africa and India, and the "always ask" custom among Aborigines all depend on a universal norm of access to drinking water by right in times of need. The ... practice in ancient Rome of free water was rights-based, as well—a right of provision from the Emperor.

Treating drinking water supply as a priced resource is by no means a new idea, either....

Turning to the public/private debate, skeptics are right to doubt whether purely private markets can adequately address the different natures of drinking water, but purely private markets are far and few between. Public management remains the dominant source of drinking water today and takes a wide range of forms, whether through municipally-owned waterworks, regulated private water utilities, or public/private ventures. Put simply, the fact of privatization does not, in itself, tell us whether access to water will be based on full cost recovery rates, targeted subsidies, or some other scheme. Thus the privatization question turns on the more practical questions of how water supply should be supervised, how the transition should be managed, and how access to water should be provided.

These obviously are questions that can only be answered in the specific context of particular cities and cultures. A key point worth keeping in mind, however, and perhaps the most consistent finding of my research to date, is the significance of a right to drinking water. While there will surely be exceptions, it is striking that in every water management scheme I have come across to date one finds explicit norms for providing the essential drinking water to those in need, even if they are from outside the community or are unable to pay. It may well be that a core feature of any privatization scheme must be an explicit provision for this right of thirst.

Moving beyond the simplistic discourse of rights versus markets, public versus private provision, it is striking how little attention has been paid to the more fundamental issue—the natures of drinking water, itself. Drinking water has served as a physical resource, and an economic resource, and a social resource far more often than any one of these alone. Yet much of the current debate seems to assume the necessity of choosing one identity to the exclusion of others. Effectively managing access to drinking water necessarily requires management across multiple dimensions—expressly recognizing the natures of the natural resource.

When viewed from such a vantage, understanding the complex stability of the Roman drinking water system becomes much clearer. For several centuries, drinking water was consciously managed as a physical resource (the aqueduct and distribution system within Rome), a social resource (free water in the communal gathering places of the *lacus*), an economic resource (charging the *vectigal* to underwrite maintenance costs), and a political resource (as a justification of imperial rule). Considering how the different natures of drinking water were deliberately managed reveals much more than asking whether access to Roman drinking water was by market or by right....

Questions and Discussion

1. *Economic good or public good.* Dublin Principle No. 4, adopted by governmental and non-governmental persons attending the International Conference on Water and the Environment, at the invitation of the World Meteorological Organization, in 1992, stated:

> Water has an economic value in all its competing uses and should be recognized as an economic good. Within this principle, it is vital to recognize first the basic right of all human beings to have access to clean water and sanitation at an affordable price. Past failure to recognize the economic value of water has led to wasteful and environmentally damaging uses of the resource. Managing water as an economic good is an important way of achieving efficient and equitable use, and of encouraging conservation and protection of water resources.

Dublin Statement on Water and Sustainable Development (1992).

General Comment No. 15 (2002) starts with recognition that "[w]ater is a limited natural resource and a public good fundamental for life and health." U.N. Doc. E/C.12/2002/11 (20 January 2003) What differences for realization of human right to water, if any, might create treating water as a purely economic good? Can social, cultural and environmental values of water be measured in monetary terms and be administrated according to market rules?

2. *Privatization.* What is the relationship between a human right to water and privatization of water systems? Does privatization of water services constitute a violation of the human right to water? What lessons might be learned from the Cochabamba water supply system privatization experience? Can the risks of water privatization be managed? Compare the Bolivian experience with New Zealand's approach that imposes restrictions on public and private water services providers with regard to contract terms, disconnection policies and cost recovery.

> New Zealand's *Local Government Act* stipulates that any local authority considering a partnership with the private sector must develop a formal policy on such partnerships. Such a policy must address how the local authority will assess, monitor and report on the extent to which community outcomes are furthered by a partnership with the private sector. Any contracting-out of water services to the private sector may not be for a term longer than 15 years, and the local government must retain control over pricing, management of water services, and development of policy related to their delivery.

COHRE, *Legal Resources for the Right to Water: International and National Standards* (2004) available at http://www.cohre.org/downloads/water_res_8.pdf and New Zealand Local Government Act 2002, No. 84, 24 December 2002.

3. *Subsequent arbitration.* Salzman mentions that Aguas del Tunari (a subsidiary of Bechtel Corporation) filed an arbitration claim of $25 million against Bolivia for canceling its water privatization contract. In 2005 the International Centre for Settlement of Investment Disputes ruled 2–1 that the case could proceed. *Aguas del Tunari v. Republic of Bolivia,* ICSID Case No. ARB/02/3 (Oct. 11, 2005). In 2006 Bechtel dropped its claim, in return for Bolivia absolving the foreign investors of any potential liability. Investment Treaty News (ITN), Jan. 20, 2006. http://www.iisd.org/pdf/2006/itn_jan20_2006.pdf. Assume that Bechtel did not drop its claim and the Bank panel granted Bechtel's demand. What consequences might it have? Who would bear those costs?

4. *Responsibilities of States and Corporations.* It is recognized that States have the primary responsibility to promote, secure the fulfillment of, respect, ensure respect of, and protect human rights. Are transnational corporations and other business enterprises also responsible for promoting and securing the human rights as a whole and a right to water in particular? See discussion of corporate responsibility and accountability in Chapter 9.

5. *Responsibilities of individuals.* Does a right to water, especially as an element of a right to healthy environment, impose responsibilities on governments alone, or do some duties fall on individuals? Consider the opinion of Amy Hardberger on this matter.

> The duty to provide water cannot lie entirely with government. As the human right to water evolves, the role of individual citizens must also play a part in the realization of these goals. Although this topic is rarely discussed, some ideas can be deduced from existing documents. Human rights provide a mechanism for a citizen to enforce a violation of a right against a state; however, this does not negate the responsibilities citizens have towards themselves and each other....

Although Comment 15 does not specifically list the duties of those benefiting from the right to water, both the UDHR and ICESCR's preambles extend obligations to individuals by stating that everyone must take progressive steps towards the realization of human rights. In the realm of water, private citizens must conserve and contribute to their access of water before attempting to levy a claim against their government.... Although the government is ultimately responsible for their citizens, individuals should share some of the responsibility. One way that citizens can contribute is to pay for their access to water. This payment should be affordable and based on local economies; however, individual contribution is an important part of investing the citizen in their water source. Another way to involve people in their water resources is by adopting participatory management. The inclusion of the public in water decisions achieves many of the goals postulated in social as well as political rights. Citizens also need to be equally responsible for the protection of their water resources through conservation and safe practices. This collective action by a community empowers them to be, at least partially, in control of their water supply.... Although, all the details have yet to be discovered, it is clear that with citizens working together with their governments, the human right to water can be realized and reach the status of customary international law that it deserves.

Hardberger, Amy. *Whose Job Is It Anyway?: Governmental Obligations Created by the Human Right to Water*, 41 Tex. Int'l L.J. 533 (2006)

II. A Right to Water in National Instruments

A. Examples of the Right to Water at a National Level

The Implications of Formulating a Human Right to Water
Erik B. Bluemel
31 Ecology L.Q. 957 (2004)

II. IMPLEMENTING A RIGHT TO WATER: DOMESTIC EXPERIENCES

Although international human rights law has not yet created legally binding obligations on States to recognize a human right to water, it has served to pressure some States into more fully developing a human right to water. The water-stressed countries of South Africa, India, and Argentina all provide a right to water, derived from constitutions, statutes, judicial interpretations, and, in some instances, international human rights instruments.... [T]he experiences of South Africa, India, and Argentina offer unique lessons for the development and definition of an international right to water.

A. South Africa

The 1996 South African constitution recognizes a right to sufficient water[91] and explicitly requires the consideration of international law in interpreting its Bill of Rights.[92] ... The South African Commission on Human Rights indicates that the right does not oblige

---

91. Rep. of S. Afr. Const. (Act 108 of 1996) ch. II, § 27(1)(b). The State assumes an obligation to take reasonable legislative or other measures, within its available resources, to realize the right progressively. *Id.* at § 27(2).
92. *Id.* at § 39(1)(b).

the State to provide free water, but requires it "to create mechanisms that enable people to have access to sufficient water." Nevertheless, the right to water in South Africa has been interpreted to require a free minimum level of water necessary for survival, above which a progressive pricing scheme is used for cost recovery. The South African Department of Water Affairs and Forestry instituted such a scheme for basic water needs in December of 2000.

In 1994, approximately thirty-seven and a half percent of South Africa's population, eighty percent of whom lived in rural areas, lacked access to basic water supplies. The populations most suffering from a lack of access were blacks and other marginalized households. South Africa took enormous steps to reduce this disparity: between the introduction of the constitutional provision in 1996 and 2002, free basic water supplies were provided to approximately twenty-seven million people, or approximately sixty percent of the population. It is believed that such free water supplies can be realized for the entire population by 2009.

However, South Africa's implementation of the right to water is not typical. South Africa already had substantial institutional and technical capacities to implement such a right, capacities that other countries without universal water access may lack. Additionally, "[t]he policy of free access to basic water was made possible by the level of economic development in South Africa. This is not applicable to less-developed countries, unless they benefit from new and creative funding from external sources...." ...

B. India

India has also recognized a right to water in its constitution, although the right is not stated explicitly as is done in the constitution of South Africa. The right to water is implicit, derived from the constitutional right to life,[112] which the Indian courts have interpreted to include the right to clean and sufficient water.[113] The Indian Ministry of Water Resources has therefore called for the provision of water to the entire population, with drinking water having the highest priority.

Despite the right to clean and sufficient water, seventeen percent of the population does not have access to water, including thirty-eight percent of urban residents. Eighty percent of children suffer from water-borne diseases, and a total of forty-four million people have illnesses related to poor water quality. In addition to these water quality issues, India also suffers from water shortage problems and is well on its way to becoming a water-stressed country. Between 1985 and 1996, the number of villages without an adequate water source increased from 750 to 65,000. These problems are caused, in significant part, by the legal system of regulating water, the pressure to develop, and urban migration.

The legal system for regulating surface and ground water in India may hamper the achievement of the human right to water implied in its constitution. Despite the implied right to water in the constitution, no Indian law establishes an explicit right to water, while some laws actually abolish pre-existing use and customary rights to water. India regulates surface water use through riparian law and a public trust doctrine, which limits the amount of usage. Riparian rights are water rights granted to owners of property

---

112. See India Const. art. 21 ("No person shall be deprived of his life or personal liberty except according to procedure established by law.")....

113. *S.K. Garg v. State*, AIR 1999 All 41 (India 1999); *M.C. Mehta v. Union of India*, AIR 1998 SC 1037 (India 1998); *Subhash Kumar v. State of Bihar*, AIR 1991 SC 420 (India 1991) (noting that the right to live includes the right to pollution-free water necessary for the full enjoyment of life); *Attakoya Thangal v. Union of India*, 1990 KLT 580 (Kerala, India 1990).

adjacent to watercourses for their reasonable use, so long as their use does not interfere with either the flow of the water itself or with the use of downstream riparians. These riparian rights provide both access and quality protections to those adjoining waterways. However, the Irrigation Acts place rights to watercourses in the hands of the State, superceding the rights of communities to manage their water resources under the Indian constitution. The State can thus divert water resources and otherwise obstruct traditional water sources and collection methods, a seeming violation of ICESCR. Thus, the Irrigation Acts may hamper the effective realization of the right to water for some less prosperous communities who utilize traditional methods of water collection and supply. Finally, groundwater is minimally regulated, controlled primarily by those who own the land above it.

Development pressures also undermine the right to water in India....

Industrial activities and urban migration further undermine water rights in India. Groundwater mining for commercial purposes in India has significantly depleted water resources and polluted the remaining water, reducing rice yields and making the remaining water unfit for direct human consumption and use. Similarly, textile and other industrial and commercial ventures have been charged with violating the Indian right to water through pollution and groundwater mining. Additionally, large-scale migration to the cities has led New Delhi to seek greater extraction of groundwater—a feat accomplished through significant, inter-regional transfers. Such transfers reduce the water supplies of those living in other districts and nearby farmlands....

C. Argentina

Like South Africa, Argentina has an explicit right to water in its constitution, which recognizes a right to a healthy environment.[131] Similar to India, Argentinean states have dominion over the natural resources in their territories. Argentina's national water management law partly preempts state regulation. This law, however, does little to advance the constitution's human right to water, as the terms and obligations imposed by this right remain undefined and the law deals primarily with interjurisdictional waters rather than freshwater sources wholly located within any single jurisdiction.

Argentina regulates most of its water under a public trust doctrine whereby waters are owned by the State, with allowances for riparian and other users. Some common law ownership principles, however, have lingered or been incorporated by statute and serve to undermine the equitable realization of a right to water. For instance, the Civil Code states that "[s]treams that are born and die within a state belong in property, use and enjoyment, to the owner of it." Additionally, "[w]aters that arise in lands of individuals belong to their owners, who can freely make use of them and change their natural direction." This ownership structure, and ability to alter watercourse paths leaves riparian users highly vulnerable to upstream users and thus without a secure right to water.

Despite these legal drawbacks, Argentina has been able to provide water and sewage services to seventy-nine percent of the country. Unfortunately, due to transmission and other supply costs, only thirty percent of the rural population has access to water, thirty percent lower than the Latin America and Caribbean combined average. An attempt at privatization during the 1990s failed to service fifty percent of potential clients despite rate increases of over one hundred percent designed to recover costs not properly accounted for in the initial tariff agreement. Like in Cochabamba, this focus on cost recovery undoubtedly affected access to the water resources, given that the area of the concession contained significant numbers of impoverished persons. More interesting,

---

131. Const. Arg. ch. VI, §§ 75(22), 41(1).

however, is the focus on cost recovery in the face of constitutional provisions that require expenditures on water management, which is linked to the right to water. The statutory and administrative regime of Argentina has resulted in highly inequitable distributions of water supplies with disproportionate cost burdens imposed upon the urban and rural poor.

While Argentina has not sufficiently modified its legal structure to effectuate an equitable right to water, it has taken significant steps within the court system to protect the right to water. For instance, Argentinean courts have held that failure to remediate pollution of waters essential to community survival is a violation of the right to water.[143] In the *Menoris Comunidad Paynemil* case, the Argentinean courts required a company to provide 250 liters of water per day for an entire indigenous community whose traditional water source was polluted by the company's operations. This figure, however, does not seem grounded in the human right to water, since the WHO indicates that fifty to one hundred liters per person per day is sufficient for normal needs, with an absolute minimum of twenty liters per day in some circumstances. Similar to South Africa, Argentinean courts have held that states must expedite hearings regarding suspension of access to drinking water, and that states must ensure all citizens' access to water regardless of ability to pay. Argentinean courts have thus rather boldly detailed the contours of a human right to water, providing those rights to all community residents, regardless of whether they possess legal title to the water.

Legal decisions from the Argentinean courts, however, have done little to effect change at the legislative and administrative levels. Distribution continues to impose costs disproportionately on the poor. Argentina's legal regime, based on a riparian scheme with minimal duties to ensure reasonable use for downstream users, is partly to blame for this inequitable outcome, because downstream users must pay to ensure a constant water supply in times of low flow. The legal regime in Argentina also leaves resolution of most of its disputes to the courts by failing to define the terms and obligations of the right to water adequately. This failure to clearly define the obligations resulting from the right to water resembles problems with the current status of the right to water advanced by the General Comment. Without providing clearer guidance to administrative agencies, Argentinean law fails to ensure progressive realization of the right to water or equitable distribution of the water supply, two central tenets of a human right to water.

Questions and Discussion

1. *Social policy implications.* Do the problems of implementation of a right to water in India and Argentina call into question the efficacy of basic social policy on such a right except, perhaps, in South Africa? Or are the problems the same that arise with implementation of any right declared by a court?

2. *Implementation in South Africa: success or failure?* Do the successes of implementation in South Africa appear to be due to its infrastructure, as the author argues, or to a political commitment at the national level? For different perspectives, consider the following critical comments from Rose Francis on doubtful water justice in the National Water Act provisions, and from Julie A. Smith and J. Maryann Green on the implementation of the free basic water policy in South Africa.

---

143. See *Menoris Comunidad Paynemil/s accion de amparo*, Expte. 311-CA-1997, Sala II, Cámara de Apelaciones en lo Civil, Neuquen (Arg., May 19, 1997), discussed in Juan Miguel Picolotti, *The Right to Water in Argentina* (2003), available at http://www.cedha.org.ar/docs/doc175-eng.doc.

The National Water Act of 1998 transformed South Africa's laws governing water resources. The Act creates a seemingly progressive framework for water resource management, most notably by abolishing private ownership of water, placing all water resources in a public trust, and establishing a compulsory licensing system with the potential to redistribute water supply more equitably among the populace. The Act contains some important compromises, however, that undermine its capacity for redistribution. It also adopts or facilitates a number of neoliberal policies, including decentralization, cost recovery, and privatization. The implementation of these policies thwarts the government's stated objective to achieve equitable and universal access to clean water....

One of the quintessential features of the NWA is decentralization. Unfortunately, decentralized water management is unlikely to lead to more equitable access, because many local communities do not have the capacity or the funding to manage the resource effectively. In this decentralized regime, the NWA fails to provide guidance or secure funding for local governments who are now responsible for water service provision. In an attempt to address this shortcoming, subsequent water policy documents have emphasized the importance of national grants, which are constitutionally guaranteed sources of funding for local governments, and which water policymakers hope can significantly alleviate the gap in funding for local water resource management. Nonetheless, the financing of water service extension remains a serious problem nationwide, and the process of decentralizing water management and service provision exacerbates current water problems in poverty-stricken localities....

The NWA embraces the policy of cost recovery, in which the dispensation of water pays for itself through fees. Cost recovery has had devastating effects on the majority of the populace, leading to substantially increased household debt, widespread water service cutoffs, citizen unrest, and a nationwide cholera epidemic. As implemented in South Africa, the policy of cost recovery operates at a net economic loss and continues to deny the most impoverished South Africans access to a basic quantity of clean water....

Equity aside, decentralization and cost recovery lay the groundwork for privatization of the water service sector, in which local governments relinquish state-owned water operations to private companies. The NWA and subsequent national policy documents welcome private investment as a partial solution to the nation's water crisis, but in fact, the trend of privatizing water services in South Africa threatens to reinforce apartheid-era patterns of unequal water service provision.

Rose Francis, *Water Justice in South Africa: Natural Resources Policy at the Intersection of Human Rights, Economics, and Political Power*, 18 Geo. Int'l Envtl. L. Rev. 149 2005.

South Africa's past apartheid inequities create unique challenges in achieving water delivery goals. The South African government implemented the free basic water (FBW) policy in July 2001 to ensure all South Africans had access to a basic amount of safe water by 2004. The FBW policy entitles all people to a free lifeline supply of 6000 ls/6 kilolitres (kl) (1 kl = 1000 l) of water per household per month. Despite being heralded as a way of ensuring access of lifeline water services to low-income households, fundamental policy flaws exist. The FBW allocation does not meet the basic water requirements and special water requirements of the majority of low-income households. Low-income households require more than the 6 kl allocation and are thereby expected to pay the full cost for their water service. The affordability crisis has not been addressed as tariff structures and cross-subsidisation mechanisms remain inadequate. The financial sustainability of the FBW policy is reliant on the equitable share, an unconditional grant from national government and user-fees, which the extensive low-income sector cannot afford to pay.

Julie A. Smith & J. Maryann Green, *Free basic water in Msunduzi, KwaZulu-Natal: is it making a difference to the lives of low-income households?* 7 Water Policy 443–467 (2005).

B. Quantity, Affordability, and Procedure: Implementing South Africa's Constitution

Residents of Bon Vista Mansions v. So. Metropolitan Local Council (South Africa)

High Court, Witwatersrand Local Division
2002 (6) BCLR 625 (W); 2001 SACLR LEXIS 103 (9 May 2001)

Judgment by: BUDLENDER AJ ...

The applicants' case was that the respondent had unlawfully discontinued its municipal water supply late on the afternoon of 21 May 2001. They had for three days attempted to seek redress through the manager of the premises, but without any success. In desperation, they turned to the court for relief. They asked for interim relief in the form of an order on the respondent to restore their water supply, pending the final determination of an application for similar relief.

I granted an order in which the City of Johannesburg (alternatively the Southern Metropolitan Local Council) was ordered to restore the water supply to Bon Vista Mansions, pending the final determination of the application. I indicated that I would give my reasons in due course. These are my reasons....

The constitutional foundation

Section 27(1)(a) of the Constitution provides that everyone has the right of access to water. The State must take reasonable legislative and other measures, within its available resources, to achieve the progressive realisation of this right. In terms of section 7, the State must respect, protect, promote and fulfil the rights in the Bill of Rights.

The Council is an organ of State, and plainly bears the duties set out in section 7.

Each of the words used in section 7 has a particular meaning. For example, in this matter we were not concerned—at least at this stage—with the duty on the Council to fulfil the right of access to water. That plainly involves a positive duty to provide access to water services, in the manner required by section 27(2). However, for the reasons set out below, this matter does relate very directly to the duty to respect the right of access to water.

A court is obliged, when interpreting the Bill of Rights, to consider international law. [§39(1)(b) of the Constitution] As has been explained by Chaskalson P:

In the context of §35(1) [of the interim Constitution], public international law would include non-binding as well as binding law. They may both be used under the section as tools of interpretation. International agreements and customary international law accordingly provide a framework within which chap 3 can be evaluated and understood, and for that purpose, decisions of tribunals dealing with comparable instruments, such as the United Nations Committee on Human Rights, the Inter-American Commission on Human Rights, the European Commission on Human Rights, and the European Court of Human Rights and, in appropriate cases, reports of specialised agencies such as the International Labour Organisation, may provide guidance as to the correct interpretation of particular provisions....

[*S. v. Makwanyane* 1995 (3) SA 391 (1995 (6) BCLR 665) (CC) at para 35]

International law is particularly helpful in interpreting the Bill of Rights where the Constitution uses language which is similar to that which has been used in international instruments. The jurisprudence of the International Covenant on Economic, Social and Cultural Rights, which is plainly the model for parts of our Bill of Rights, is an example of this. It assists in understanding the nature of the duties placed on the State (including the Council) by section 7 of the Constitution.

In his analysis of the Covenant, Craven describes the content of the duty to respect a right as follows: in order to respect a right, the State must refrain from action which would serve to deprive individuals of their rights.

This analysis is supported by the United Nations Committee on Economic, Social and Cultural Rights, which has issued General Comments on the International Covenant on Economic, Social and Cultural Rights. The General Comments have authoritative status under international law.

In its General Comment 12, issued in 1999, the Committee explained the duty to respect rights of access as follows, in relation to the right to food:

> The obligation to respect existing access to adequate food requires State parties not to take any measures that result in preventing such access....

On the facts of this case, the applicants had existing access to water before the Council disconnected the supply. The act of disconnecting the supply was prima facie in breach of the Council's constitutional duty to respect the right of access to water, in that it deprived the applicants of existing access. In accordance with what is sometimes called the two-stage approach, that places a burden or an onus on the Council to justify the breach.

The Water Services Act

The Water Services Act 108 of 1997 seeks to create a statutory framework within which such breaches may be justified. The Preamble to the Act recognises the right of access to basic water supply and basic sanitation necessary to ensure sufficient water and an environment not harmful to health or well-being.

Section 4(1) of the Act provides that a water service provider must set conditions in terms of which water services are to be provided. These include:

(c) (iv) the circumstances under which water services may be limited or discontinued

    (v) procedures for limiting or discontinuing water services.

Section 4(3) of the Act provides that procedures for the limitation or discontinuance of water services must:

(a) be fair and equitable

(b) provide for reasonable notice of intention to limit or discontinue water services and for an opportunity to make representations, unless—

    (i)   other consumers would be prejudiced;

    (ii) there is an emergency situation; or

    (iii) the consumer has interfered with a limited or discontinued service; and

(c) not result in a person being denied access to basic water services for non-payment, where that person proves, to the satisfaction of the relevant water services authority, that he or she is unable to pay for basic services.

Mr. Bester accepted that in this case, the Council is the water service provider. He informed me that conditions relating to the termination of water services had been prescribed before the enactment of the Act, in Administrators Notice 21 of 5 January 1977, which was amended on 6 July 1983 and 27 July 1983....

I was advised by Mr. Bester that when a consumer is in arrears in respect of payments for water services, the account sent out by the Council contains a standard printed section informing him or her that if the arrears are not paid, the service will be discontinued. Again, it is not necessary to decide whether such notices comply with the requirements of the Act. Without deciding the matter, however, I must express my doubts about whether such a standard notice, if it does not inform the consumer of his or her statutory right to make representations, meets the requirements of the Act. The right is not likely to have real meaning unless the service provider informs consumers of its existence, which it could easily do.[14]

A genuine opportunity to make representations is particularly important in the light of the provision that water supply may not be discontinued if it results in a person being denied access to basic water services for non-payment, where that person proves, to the satisfaction of the relevant water services authority, that he or she is unable to pay for basic services.

Conclusion

The effect of section 27(1)(a) (read with section 7) of the Constitution, and of section 4 of the Water Services Act is as follows:

27.1 If a local authority disconnects an existing water supply to consumers, this is prima facie a breach of its constitutional duty to respect the right of (existing) access to water, and requires constitutional justification.

27.2 The Water Services Act requires that:

    27.2.1 the water service provider must set conditions which deal with the circumstances under which water services may be discontinued, and the procedures for discontinuing water services.

    27.2.2 those conditions and procedures must meet the requirements of section 4(3) of the Act. In particular, the procedures must be fair and equitable. In the context of a case such as this, they must provide for reasonable notice of termination and for an opportunity to make representations. They must not result in a person being denied access to basic water services for non-payment where that person proves, to the satisfaction of the water services authority, that he or she is unable to pay for basic services.

---

14. Compare *Memphis Light, Gas & Water Division v. Craft*, 436 U.S. 1, 15 & 22 (1978), where it was held that the requirements of due process placed such a duty on the provider of essential services, even though there was no specific statutory provision requiring an opportunity to make representations.

That is a demanding set of requirements. One would assume that the Constitution-makers and Parliament imposed such demanding requirements because of the potentially serious human and health consequences of terminating water services.

It is not necessary to decide, at least at this stage of this case, whether the provisions of Administrators Notice of 1977 meet the requirements of either the Constitution or the Water Services Act.

What is clear is that at this stage of this case, the Council has not produced evidence to show that its actions met the requirements of the Constitution and the Act. It may well be able to do so in due course. On the facts as they stood at the hearing of the application for an interim interdict, however, the applicants had proved that the Council had discontinued their water supply. They averred, in effect, that there was no valid reason for this—although as Mr. Bester pointed out, their allegation that they had honoured their obligations to pay for water was couched in somewhat bald and sweeping terms.

That being the case, in my view the onus rested on the Council to show either that it had not discontinued the water supply (which did not appear to be its case), or that it had legally valid grounds for doing so, and had acted in compliance with the Constitution and the Act....

This should not be a difficult onus for the Council to discharge, if in fact it acted lawfully. One assumes that the Council does not assert a right to disconnect people's water supply without good cause, or without following fair procedures. If that assumption is correct, the Council should have no difficulty in proving the reason for termination, and what procedure it followed in disconnecting the water supply. That reason, and those procedures, can then be tested against the Constitution and the Act....

Under the circumstances, the applicants had shown at least a prima facie right to a continuing supply of water. That right was being infringed in that they had been deprived of access to water, and the deprivation was continuing. They had no other satisfactory remedy. And as Mr. Bester fairly conceded, the balance of convenience weighed heavily in their favour. That being so, they satisfied the requirements for the granting of an interim interdict.

I therefore exercised my discretion to grant an interim order in terms of which the Council was ordered to restore the water supply to Bon Vista Mansions, where the applicants live. The Council was given leave to anticipate the return day on the usual terms.

Questions and Discussion

1. *The Court's interpretation of the Bill.* The Court utilizes international law to interpret the South Africa Bill of Rights on the issue of right to water. Is that an acceptable jurisprudential method? Is the date of the adoption of the South African Constitution relevant? Is the lack of precedents under the new Constitution relevant? Would a South African court be equally justified in referring to developments in international law that take place after the adoption of the Constitution, or only those occurring before?

2. *Substantive or procedural.* To what degree is the result in the case procedural, rather than substantive? Does the decision offer support for the principle that a South African has a right to at least the minimum needed for survival, regardless of ability to pay? Or does it only require adequate notice before such a person can have water disconnected? Note the reference to a case from the U.S. Supreme Court in this regard.

3. *New service.* This case discusses the right to continued provision of water to the occupants. If the right is substantive, can it be extended to mean that the municipal not

only has an obligation to continue service, but to begin it as well? If so, where does the funding come from? How would a priority list be designed?

4. *Whose responsibility?* The municipality is involved in this case, but not the national government. Does the constitutional responsibility to provide access to water lie with the local government or the national? Both? Has the national government in fact undertaken the responsibility?

5. *Interpretations of Constitution.* Section 27 of the South African Constitution states that "Everyone has the right to have access to (a) health care services, including reproductive health care; (b) sufficient food and water...," but it fails to define the pivotal term "access." How would you define the term, taking into consideration the realities of the living situations in this context? In this regard, consider two different interpretations of Section 27 of the Constitution made by the High Court and the Constitutional Court discussed in the following excerpt from Professor Kidd.

> Given §7 of the Constitution's requirement that the state must respect the rights in the Bill of Rights, disconnection of an existing water supply does amount to a limitation of the right of access to water in §27 of the Constitution, as held in *Bon Vista*. Section 27(2) provides that the state must take reasonable legislative and other measures within its available resources, to achieve the progressive realisation of each of these rights. This could be seen as allowing less than full realisation of the right, but it is submitted that this subsection applies only to the state's positive duty to promote and fulfil the right in §27, in other words, the duty of the state to provide access to water to those who do not yet have such access. It would be unrealistic to expect the state to provide such services overnight, and hence the reasonable and progressive realisation of such rights is appropriate. The failure to respect existing rights, on the other hand, is not subject to the qualifier in subsec (2).
>
> A possible problem with this interpretation is that the Constitutional Court has expressed a view that could be seen as contrary to this. In *Minister of Health v. Treatment Action Campaign* [2002 (5) SA 721 (CC)] the court stated that "section 27(1) of the Constitution does not give rise to a self-standing and independent positive right enforceable irrespective of the considerations mentioned in section 27(2)." A careful reading of this portion of the judgment, however, indicates that the court was concerned with an argument relating to the "minimum core" of a right that had yet to be realised and that it was not referring to a right that had already been realised. It is submitted that §27(1) does give rise to a self-standing and independent positive right where that right has already been realised, and it is unlikely that the Constitutional Court's dictum in the Treatment Action Campaign would have been the same had this been the issue there. As Pieterse has suggested, the approach taken in *Bon Vista*—the "conglomerate reading of §§27 and 7(2), and [the] distinction between the different duties imposed by §7(2) is more in line with the position under international law and more consistent with a textual, contextual and purposive interpretative approach to the Bill of Rights than the narrower stance adopted by the Constitutional Court."

Michael, Kidd, *Not a Drop to Drink: Disconnection of Water Services for Nonpayment and the Right of Access to Water.* 20 S. Afr. J. Hum. Rts. 119 (2004).

6. *Building precedents.* For an interesting analysis of how South African courts could build up jurisprudence for positive rights under the South African Constitution in the

absence of precedent, see Pierre de Vos, *Pious Wishes or Directly Enforceable Human Rights?: Social and Economic Rights in South Africa's 1996 Constitution*, 13 S. Afr. J. on Hum. Rts. 67 (1997). For a more recent view, applying the public trust doctrine to interpretation of the right to water in South Africa, see Robyn Stein, *Water Law in a Democratic South Africa: A Country Case Study Examining the Introduction of a Public Rights System*, 83 Tex. L. Rev. 2167 (2005).

7. *Grootboom.* In *Gov't of the Republic of South Africa v. Grootboom*, 2000 (2) SA 46 (CC), (11) BCLR 1169 (SA) (Constitutional Court of South Africa, 2000), the Constitutional Court interpreted the right of housing in the Constitution to require some affirmative steps by the government, in a case brought by squatters who had been dispossessed from their "informal settlement" on another person's private property. A commentary on the *Grootboom* case can be found in Ramin Pejan, *The Right to Water: The Road to Justiciability*, 36 Geo. Wash. Int'l L. Rev. 1181 (2004).

8. *How to make the right effective.* Is a "right to water" most likely to be secured through an international treaty among nations, the development of customary international law, continued declarations of international bodies, interpretation of national constitutions by national courts, or advocacy in legislative or executive forums using the language of rights?

C. Quality: Interpreting India's Constitution

The courts in India have declared that a right to water exists and have worked to implement it, regarding both quantity and quality of water. Of course, if water quality is poor enough that water becomes unfit to drink, the quality issue becomes a quantity issue. The following cases—one from the Supreme Court of India, one from the High Court of the State of Kerala—illustrate the use of the right to water with regard to water quality in India. The first involves a negative obligation—the duty of a government not to allow an industry to contaminate drinking water. The second involves a positive obligation—the duty of a government to install adequate water supplies for its citizens.

AP Pollution Control Board-II v. Prof. MV Nayudu (Retd) (India)
Supreme Court of India (Civil Appellate Jurisdiction)
(2001) 4 LRI 657
(1 December 2000)

JUDGMENT BY: M Jagannadha Rao J

Drinking water is of primary importance in any country. In fact, India is a party to the resolution ... passed during the United Nations Water Conference in 1977 as under:

> All people, whatever their stage of development and their social and economic conditions, have the right to have access to drinking water in quantum and of a quality equal to their basic needs.

Thus, the right to access to drinking water is fundamental to life and there is a duty on the state under art.21 to provide clean drinking water to its citizens.

Adverting to the above right declared in the aforesaid resolution, in *Narmada Bachao Andolan v. Union of India* 2000 (7) Scale 34 (at page 124), Kirpal J observed:

> Water is the basic need for the survival of human beings and is part of right of life and human rights as enshrined in art.21 of the Constitution of India....

Our Supreme Court was one of the first courts to develop the concept of right to healthy environment' as part of the right to life' under art.21 of our Constitution. [See *Bandhua Mukti Morcha v. Union of India* (1984) 3 SCC 161]. This principle has now been adopted in various countries today....

In *López Ostra v. Spain* (303-C, Eur Ct HR (Ser A) 1994), the European Court [of Human Rights] at Strasbourg has held that the result of environmental degradation might affect an individual's well being so as to deprive him of enjoyment of private and family life. Under art.8 of the European Convention, everyone is guaranteed the right to respect for his private and family life.... The Inter-American Commission on Human Rights has found a similar linkage (*Yanomami Indians v. Brazil*) Inter-Amer CHR OEA/SerLV/II/66 Doc 10 rev 1. The commission found that Brazil had violated the Yanomani Indians' rights to life by not taking measures to prevent the environmental damage. The Philippine Supreme Court dealt with the action against Government not to continue licensing agreements permitting deforestation so that the right to a balanced and healthful ecology "in accordance with the rhythm and harmony of nature" is not affected. (*Minors Oposa v. [Factoran]*, [1994] 33 ILM 173. The judgment was based on "intergenerational responsibility." In *Fundepublico v. Mayor of Bugalagrande*, the Constitutional Court of Colombia (17 June 1992) held in favour of the right to healthy environment as a fundamental human right and treated the right as part of customary international law.... About 60 nations since 1990 have recognised in their constitutions a right to a healthy environment as a corollary duty to defend the environment.

Thus, the concept of a healthy environment as a part of the fundamental right to life, developed by our Supreme Court, is finding acceptance in various countries side by side with the rights to development....

The question is whether in the event of the seventh respondent[a company planning to produce castor oil derivatives] being permitted to establish its industry within 10 kms of the lakes [used for drinking water for the cities Hyderabad and Secunderabad in Andhra Pradesh State] ... there is likelihood of serious pollution to the drinking water in these lakes. This court in its judgment dated 27 January 1999 referred the said question to the National Environmental Appellate Authority for its opinion.... The report went against the seventh respondent industry. The industry filed objections to the said report....

Even though, on 31 May 1996 the Commissioner of Industries, specifically informed the industry that it should better select an alternative site, instead of heeding to the said advice, the industry obtained permission of the district collector on 7 September 1996 for change of land use from agricultural to non-agricultural use....

On 1 June 1997, the appellant board wrote to the Commissioner of Industries that the industry would be generating nickel catalyst and other pollutants which could find their way to the lakes either directly or indirectly. Even the solid waste such as activated carbon bleaching earth and sodium sulphate might find entry during rainy season from the storage yard resulting in polluting to lakes....

In spite of the said opinion of the appellant board, the Commissioner of Industries, in his letter dated 6 June 1997 stated that there would be no liquid effluent or acidic fumes and that the limited aqueous effluent was totally bio-degradable and the solid wastes were disposable.

On 25 June 1997, the appellant board once again rejected the application of the industry....

Confronted with the above problems, the industry approached the state government on 24 June 1996 seeking exemption from the 10 km rule.... The state government, in spite of the prohibitory directions issued by it earlier, issued GO [General Order] 153

dated 3 July 1997 granting exemption … on the ground that … there would be no liquid effluents and that the solid wastes would be disposable.…

Meanwhile, the Society for Preservation of Environment and Quality Life (SPEQL)
filed WP 16969 of 1997 for quashing the exemption order in GO 153 dated 3 July 1997
and obtained stay on 25 July 1997.…

The question is whether [the] exemption can be valid?

Coming to the provisions of the Water Act 1974, it is clear that in view of sub-§ 2(e),
2(k) read with §§ 17 and 18 of the Water Act, the fundamental objective of the statute is
to provide clean drinking water to the citizens. Having laid down the policy prohibiting
location of any industries within 10 kms under GO 111 dated 8 March 1996, the state
could not have granted exemption to the seventh respondent industry, nor to any other
industry.… Exercise of such a power in favour of a particular industry must be treated
as arbitrary and contrary to public interest and in violation of the right to clean water
under art.21 of the Constitution of India.…

Such an order of exemption carelessly passed, ignoring the precautionary principle,
could be catastrophic.…

In our earlier judgment in *AP Pollution Control Board (I) v. Prof. MV Nayudu* (1999)
2 SCC 718, this court had occasion to refer to the basis of the precautionary principle
and to explain the basis and content of the very principle. This court also explained the
new principle of burden of proof.

Therefore, it was for the seventh respondent industry to establish that there would be
no danger of pollution to the two reservoirs even if the industry was established within
10 km radius of the said reservoirs. In the present proceedings, the seventh respondent
has failed to discharge the said onus.…

The state of Andhra Pradesh is therefore directed hereby to identify these industries located within 10 km radius of these two lakes and to take action in consultation with
[Andhra Pradesh] pollution control board to prevent pollution to the drinking water in
these two reservoirs. The state and the board shall not permit any polluting industries
within the 10 km radius. A report shall be submitted to this court by the state of Andhra
Pradesh in this behalf within four months from today, in regard to the pollution or pollution potential of industries, if any, existing within 10 km of the lakes. After the report
is received, the matter may be listed.…

Questions and Discussion

1. *International and comparative soft and hard law sources.* How many different sources
of international law did the Supreme Court of India use in its decision? Note how some
are quite soft, while others are hard law jurisprudence from regional human rights courts
and commissions that interpreted regional treaties or conventions. How relevant are these
in national court decisions? Would you say that they are more relevant in the world's
largest democracy, India, than in some other countries? What is the relevance of national
court decisions from other countries (such as the Philippines)? Does the Court treat them
as merely persuasive authority or something more?

2. *Law or ornament.* To what degree does the Supreme Court of India base its decision
on a right to water in international or national instruments, versus merely using the discussion of such a right as ornament to a decision based on statutory grounds? If it does
the latter, does it nevertheless use the right as a canon of statutory interpretation?

3. *Precautionary principle to prevent water pollution.* If the Supreme Court has imported the precautionary principle into the right to life in the Constitution of India, does this give the courts general supervisory power over government decisions on the basis of whether the government can document and justify its decisions on a factual basis as being protective of water? Was the Court's decision made easier by the continued refusal of a pollution appellate board to go along with the exemption provided by the state government?

4. *Backsliding.* The Court rules that the exemption provided by General Order 153 is "arbitrary and contrary to public interest and in violation of the right to clean water under art. 21 of the Constitution of India" and that the general prohibition in the earlier General Order 111 must stand. Why cannot a state countermand one General Order with another one? Is it because the newer one is less protective of water than the earlier one?

5. *Positive or negative obligation.* Does the Supreme Court decision contain any positive obligation on the State to provide clean drinking water to all citizens? Does it rule out courts taking that step next?

Shajimon Joseph v. State of Kerala (India)
Kerala High Court
W. P. (C) No. 16681 of 2006 (S), 2007 (1) KHC 1
2006 KHC 275 : 2006 (1) KLT 919 : ILR 2006 (1) Ker. 705 : 2006 (1) KLJ 498
(4 December 2006)

Hon'ble Mr. Chief Justice V. K. BALI & Hon'ble Mr. Justice S. SIRI JAGAN

The Judgment of the Court was delivered by S. SIRI JAGAN, J.

Kerala is widely known all over the world as a land of backwaters. In fact, the backwaters are important tourist attraction in Kerala. Alappuzha, one of the districts of Kerala, is also rich in that sense, since the district has backwaters in abundance. However, Alappuzha is a place which makes the old saying "water, water everywhere, but not a drop to drink," true to its real sense. In spite of water in such abundance all over the district, the inhabitants of Alappuzha do not get clean drinking water, despite the water supply system in existence operated by the Kerala Water Authority.

The water which comes through the taps of the Kerala Water Authority at Alappuzha is *so* rich in all kinds of organic and inorganic impurities that no person who values his health would dare to drink the same.... This situation has been continuing for several decades....

The people of Alappuzha go on suffering this misery while they go on paying for the dirty water which comes through the water supply system given by the Kerala Water Authority.

It is in the above backdrop that two residents of Alappuzha have approached this Court with this writ petition with very serious allegations against the Government and the Kerala Water Authority not only regarding the apathy of the Government and the Water Authority towards their drinking water problem, but also complaining of corruption in the matter of putting into execution a project for supply of clean drinking water to the people of Alappuzha, which was envisaged as early as in the year 2000....

A scheme known as "Alappuzha Water Supply Scheme" was envisaged by the Kerala Water Authority to cater to the drinking water needs of the people of the entire Alappuzha Municipality and the neighbouring eight Panchayat[b] areas. Although the scheme was envisaged for immediate implementation, it is a sad fact that nothing concrete has happened yet from the side of the Water Authority and the Government who are to implement the project.

It is stated that the Kerala Water Authority had conducted detailed scientific studies for two years in 2001 and 2002 and originally selected an intake water well site or collection center for the project at Kuriath kadavu in the banks of Pamba river. Later on, that site was abandoned as unworkable. Thereafter, a site at a place called "Veeyapuram" was selected, after prolonged study and investigation. The said place is stated to be a river bed having water in abundance as three major rivers of Kerala, namely, Pamba river, Manimala river and Achankovil river converges at Veeyapuram....

[Later], the Water Authority suddenly found it necessary to shift the collection center from Veeyapuram to a place called "Pannai kadavu" which is very near to the earlier abandoned collection center....

On the above allegations, the petitioners have approached this Court through this public interest litigation seeking the following reliefs:

i.   Issue a writ in the nature of mandamus or such other appropriate writ or order or direction calling for the production of all the records and files relating to the Alappuzha Water Supply Scheme....

ii.   Command the 2nd and 3rd respondents to execute and complete the Alappuzha Water Supply Scheme as per the Ext. P4 tender notification dated 15/11/2002 within a time frame fixed by this Hon'ble Court or in the alternative to call for a new workable project report from the 2nd and 3rd respondents....

Counter affidavit has been filed on behalf of respondents 2 and 3 who are the Kerala Water Authority and the Superintending Engineer of Kerala Water Authority.... [They] put the blame on the Government stating that it is because the Government refused to give guarantee for the HUDCO [Housing and Urban Development Corporation of India] loan citing financial constraints, that the project did not take off.... Since the Government guarantee was not sanctioned, the HUDCO also did not sanction loan for the scheme....

We are more distressed to find that neither the 1st respondent—State of Kerala—nor the Alappuzha Municipality, including the concerned block panchayat have not cared to respond to the writ petition. We find from [Exhibit] P20 photographs that the Kerala Water Authority had put up a huge plaque showing the foundation stone laid by the then Chief Minister, on 30/08/2002 with the "HUDCO aided augmentation water supply scheme to Alappuzha Municipality and adjoining villages-Phase I" inscribed thereon. The plaque contains the names of the Minister of Water Resources, Member of Parliament of Alappuzha, four MLAs, District Panchayat President, Alappuzha and Chairperson of Alappuzha Municipality, in addition to the managing director of the Kerala Water Authority. We wonder whether these projects are intended only for inscription of names of these political personalities in the foundation stone for posterity.

We had, sometime back, in our decision in *Vishala Kochi Kudivella Samrakshana Samithi v. State of Kerala* reported in 2006 (1) KLT 919, reminded the Government of the responsibility of the Government in the matter of supply of drinking water to the citizens. We would quote the relevant passage from the same herein:

---

b Editor's note: A "panchayat" is a unit of government at the village level in India and Nepal.

Water is one of the primary needs of man, second only to air. Water is in fact the elixir of life. Any Government whether proletarian or bourgeois and certainly a Welfare State committed to the cause of the common man, is bound to provide drinking water to the public which should be the foremost duty of any Government. When considering the priorities of a Government, supply of drinking water should be on the top of the list.

However, for the past more than three decades, successive Governments who have ruled this State have given scant attention to the need for potable drinking water of the residents of West Kochi. This is indeed a callous and deplorable attitude of the Government, which needs to be deprecated in very strong terms. We have no hesitation to hold that failure of the State to provide safe drinking water to the citizens in adequate quantities would amount to violation of the fundamental right to life enshrined in Article 21 of the Constitution of India and would be a violation of human rights.

Therefore, every Government, which has it is priorities right, should give foremost importance to providing safe drinking water even at the cost of other development programmes. Nothing shall stand in its way whether it is lack of funds or other infrastructure....

In fact in that case, we had directed the State Government to complete all steps necessary for supplying drinking water to the people of the West Kochi within six months.... In spite of the fact that the same was the bounden constitutional duty of the Government to provide drinking water to the citizens of the State, the Government as well as the Kerala Water Authority had the temerity to file review petitions against the judgment challenging the competence of this Court to issue such peremptory directions....

In spite of the above direction and the experience, we are sorry to say that the present Government also continues the apathy towards the drinking water problems of the people of Kerala....

By constituting the Water Authority, the responsibility of the State to supply clean drinking water to the people of Kerala does not end there, since the Water Authority cannot on its own without sufficient funds to carry out that obligation. It has to come from the Government to do what is needed for finding funds for the projects in such cases....

Besides, the right to have clean drinking water supplied in sufficient quantities also forms part of the right to life guaranteed under Article 21 of the Constitution of India to citizens....

In the above circumstances, we issue the following directions to the Kerala Water Authority and the Government:

(1) The Water Authority shall once again make a detailed study of whatever sites that are available for water intake including Veeyapuram site and with the help of scientific data so collected take a final decision on the site to be selected for water intake for the Alappuzha Water Supply project. This shall be done within one month from the date of receipt of a copy of this judgment.... Tender proceedings shall be completed within a further period of one month from the date of finalisation of the water intake site as directed above.

(2) On finalising the tender proceedings, the Government of Kerala shall ensure that the Water Authority gets finance necessary for implementing the project either by providing guarantee for HUDCO loan or by providing finance from other sources or by themselves.... Within two years thereafter, the entire project for sup-

plying drinking water to the people of Alappuzha Municipality and the surrounding 8 panchayats shall be completed and it must be ensured that the people of these localities get clean drinking water in sufficient quantities through
an efficient water supply system without fail, within the above said period.

We also take this opportunity to remind the officers of the Water Authority of Section
30 of the Kerala Water Supply and Sewerage Act which reads thus:

> 30. Surcharge—(1) The Chairman or the Managing Director or any other mem-
> ber, officer or employee of the Authority shall be liable to surcharge for the loss,
> waste or mis-application of any money or property of the Authority if such loss,
> waste' or mis-application is a direct consequence of his neglect or mis-conduct
> while acting as such Chairman or Managing Director or other member or offi-
> cer or employee....
>
> (4) Nothing ... shall prevent the Authority from deducting any amount referred to
> therein from any sum payable by the Authority on account of remuneration or oth-
> erwise to such Chairman or Managing Director or other member, officer or employee.

We make it clear that although we are leaving the expert decisions to be made by the
Water Authority as per our directions, if their decisions prove to cause any damage of
loss, proving the petitioners' allegations correct, it would be open to the petitioners or other
persons of the affected area to bring this fact to the attention of this Court so as to see that
appropriate action under Section 30 as above is initiated against the individual officers responsible for the same....

Questions and Discussion

1. *Inferred constitutional right.* There is no explicit "right to water" in the Constitution
of India. How did the courts find such a right?

2. *Remedies.* Does the presence of a constitutional right make much apparent difference in the face of bureaucratic intransigence, as revealed in this case? The court stresses
the gravity of the situation, identifies problems of lack of implementation, and issues
time-specific orders. What do you think about the potential of the "surcharge" remedy that
it mentions at the end?

3. *Goal of case.* In comparing the two cases from India, which problem appears to be
more difficult—preventing a government from granting permission for the establishment of new industrial sources of pollution, or forcing a government to make investments to provide sources of clean water?

4. *Access to water—duty of the local government?* What kinds of obligations should
local governments bear in order to ensure access to clean drinking water for their citizens? Consider excerpts from a Ukrainian case, *Stanovych v. Drohobych City Council* (22-
a-181/072007). The Appellate Administrative Court of the Lviv region upheld a decision
of the court of first instance, finding:

> Articles 3, 16, and 50 of the Constitution of Ukraine proclaim that the human
> being and his or her life and health are recognized in Ukraine as the highest so-
> cial value, and that the State has a duty to ensure ecological safety and to main-
> tain the ecological balance on the territory of Ukraine, as well as everyone's right
> to an environment that is safe for life and health.
>
> According to provisions of the Law On Local Government in Ukraine bodies
> of local government [resolve] ... issues concerning water supply, sewerage and

purification of wastewater and executing control of the quality of drinking water....

[T]he defendant and its executive bodies, contrary to the stated provisions of the laws, have not provided residents of the "Mlynky" neighborhood with drinking water of the proper quality, have not provided transportation of water to this neighborhood, and no evidences of execution of this duty have been brought to the court. This directly indicates inaction by the defendant....

Does the constitutional status of a right to clean water make it likely that courts will treat the statutory provisions on the matter more seriously? What remedies can a court require? Could it require expensive engineering steps that must be paid by public funds? If a city council refuses to appropriate tax money from its budget, is there anything a court may do? Must citizens who bring such a case be prepared to launch political campaigns, not only court suits, to implement a favorable court ruling?

5. *Right.* After reading this chapter, does a right to water exist either internationally or as a constitutional right in some nations? If so, does it appear that it can lead to results favorable for citizens?

Chapter 5

Indigenous Rights and Environment

Introduction

Indigenous rights are not simply another way for members of the dominant society to protect the environment. Instead, they provide specific legal arguments that are uniquely available to indigenous people.

While the recognition and protection of indigenous peoples' rights may help protect the environment, they may also lead to use and management of that environment in ways to which some people, including environmentalists, might object. Understanding principles of native self-determination is central to understanding the relationship between indigenous rights and the environment. Furthermore, as we shall see, the human rights of indigenous peoples are often those of communities as a whole, rather than only individual indigenous persons.

The United Nations has estimated that there are over 300 million indigenous peoples living in over 70 countries. Indigenous peoples can use various international instruments to protect their rights. These include the International Labour Organization's Convention No. 169 on Indigenous and Tribal Peoples in Independent Countries, the International Covenant on Civil and Political Rights, the African Charter on People's Rights and Freedoms, the American Convention on Human Rights, and the recently adopted United Nations Declaration on the Rights of Indigenous Peoples. In addition, treaties negotiated between indigenous peoples and the U.S. Government have had a significant impact on national law in the United States. Furthermore, in Canada, Australia, and elsewhere national courts have recognized the validity of indigenous rights apart from treaties. Each of these sources of law has been used in some way in attempts to protect the environment in which indigenous peoples live or to recognize the right of indigenous peoples to use and manage natural resources. This chapter discusses these efforts in various judicial and quasi-judicial systems.

As for the term "indigenous people," settling upon the meaning itself has proved difficult. Professor Wiessner has proposed:

> Indigenous communities are ... best conceived of as peoples traditionally regarded, and self-defined, as descendants of the original inhabitants of lands with which they share a strong, often spiritual bond. These peoples are, and desire to be, culturally, socially and/or economically distinct from the dominant groups in society, at the hands of which they have suffered, in past or pre-

sent, a pervasive pattern of subjugation, marginalization, dispossession, exclusion and discrimination.

Siegfried Wiessner, *Rights and Status of Indigenous Peoples: A Global Comparative and International Legal Analysis*, 12 HARV. HUM. RTS. J. 57, 115 (1999).

Unlike other human environmental rights discussed in this book, specific indigenous rights are not universal to *all* persons, as is also the case with women's and children's rights. That is, they can be claimed by only a portion of the world's peoples, and exclusively by them. They are rooted in specific places and environments. Finally, they are often not individual, but belong to a group of indigenous people collectively. These aspects of exclusivity, locality, and collectivity are also those that are often associated with nation-states. National governments are loathe to concede what they may perceive as a quest for sovereignty, because that could and sometimes does challenge the very nature of the modern nation-state. However, indigenous peoples are increasingly recognized as possessing some attributes of self-determination, even while residing within a nation-state dominated by others. Thus, both international and national legal systems now use the term "self-determination" to describe these attributes when applied to indigenous and tribal peoples. Professor James Anaya has noted the importance of the self-determination concept:

> No discussion of indigenous Peoples' Rights under international law is complete without a discussion of self-determination, a principle of the highest order within the contemporary international system. Indigenous peoples have repeatedly articulated their demands in terms of self-determination, and, in turn, self-determination precepts have fueled the international movement in favor of those demands.

> Affirmed in the United Nations Charter and other major international legal instruments, self-determination is widely acknowledged to be a principle of customary international law and even *jus cogens*, a peremptory norm.... [T]he *concept* underlying [self-determination] entails a certain nexus of widely shared values. These values and related processes of decision can be seen as a stabilizing force in the international system and as foundational to international law's contemporary treatment of indigenous peoples....

S. James Anaya, INDIGENOUS PEOPLES IN INTERNATIONAL LAW 97–98 (2004). Professor Anaya observes, however, that self-determination does not necessarily include a demand for independent statehood. As we examine the environmental rights of indigenous people to the use, management, and protection of their environment in this chapter, keep in mind that the issue of self-determination lies at the heart of many of the other issues.

We study indigenous environmental rights by looking at legal sources and systems in three contexts: international covenants and conventions along with the United Nations system for complaints; regional legal instruments in Africa and the Americas and the human rights bodies set up to deal with them; and cases from national courts in Canada, Colombia, Belize, and the United States involving treaties, constitutions, and international instruments.

I. United Nations Instruments and Institutions

A. International Covenant on Civil and Political Rights

International Covenant on Civil and Political Rights
G.A. Res. 2200A (XXI), 21 U.N. GAOR Supp. (No. 16) at 52,
U.N. Doc. A/6316 (1966), 999 U.N.T.S. 171

Article 27

In those States in which ethnic, religious or linguistic minorities exist, persons belonging to such minorities shall not be denied the right, in community with the other members of their group, to enjoy their own culture, to profess and practise their own religion, or to use their own language.

The International Covenant on Civil and Political Rights entered into force in 1976. Currently, 160 nations are parties to the Covenant. The Covenant is enforced by the Human Rights Committee, pursuant to procedures under the Optional Protocol to the Covenant. The Human Rights Committee is a body distinct from the former U.N. Commission on Human Rights or present Human Rights Council. The Committee consists of 18 experts who meet three times a year to review compliance with the Covenant. Complaints are called "communications" and the complainants are called "authors" in the jargon of the Committee. The Committee's disposition of the complaints are called "Views."

The Committee has considered various complaints by indigenous peoples for alleged harm to their environment under Article 27 of the Covenant. Many of the complaints have been unsuccessful, while some have met with moderate success.

The Lubicon Lake Band is part of the Cree First Nation residing in Northern Alberta, Canada. The Band, consisting of approximately 500 members, once lived in a very isolated community. However, completion of an all-weather road in 1979 ushered in an era of oil exploration that the Band claims caused a disintegration of their society. The Band first brought suit in Canadian courts before appealing to the United Nations Human Rights Committee.

Bernard Ominayak and the Lubicon Lake Band v. Canada
U.N. Human Rights Committee
Communication No. 167/1984
U.N. Doc. CCPR/C/38/D/167/1984 (26 March 1990)

VIEWS UNDER ARTICLE 5. PARAGRAPH 4. OF THE OPTIONAL PROTOCOL

The author of the communication is Chief Bernard Ominayak (hereinafter referred to as the author) of the Lubicon Lake Band, Canada. The author alleges violations by the Government of Canada of the Lubicon Lake Band's right of self-determination and by virtue of that right to determine freely its political status and pursue its economic, social and cultural development, as well as the right to dispose freely of its natural wealth and resources and not to be deprived of its own means of subsistence. These violations allegedly contravene Canada's obligations under article 1, paragraphs 1 to 3, of the International Covenant on Civil and Political Rights.

Chief Ominayak is the leader and representative of the Lubicon Lake Band, a Cree Indian band living within the borders of Canada in the Province of Alberta. They are subject to the jurisdiction of the Federal Government of Canada, allegedly in accordance with a fiduciary relationship assumed by the Canadian Government with respect to Indian peoples and their lands located within Canada's national borders. The Lubicon Lake Band is a self-identified, relatively autonomous, socio-cultural and economic group. Its members have continuously inhabited, hunted, trapped and fished in a large area encompassing approximately 10,000 square kilometres in northern Alberta since time immemorial. Since their territory is relatively inaccessible, they have, until recently, had little contact with non-Indian society. Band members speak Cree as their primary language. Many do not speak, read or write English. The Band continues to maintain its traditional culture, religion, political structure and subsistence economy.

It is claimed that the Canadian Government, through the Indian Act of 1970 and Treaty 8 of 21 June 1899 (concerning aboriginal land rights in northern Alberta), recognized the right of the original inhabitants of that area to continue their traditional way of life. Despite these laws and agreements, the Canadian Government has allowed the provincial government of Alberta to expropriate the territory of the Lubicon Lake Band for the benefit of private corporate interests (e.g., leases for oil and gas exploration). In so doing, Canada is accused of violating the Band's right to determine freely its political status and to pursue its economic, social and cultural development, as guaranteed by article 1, paragraph 1, of the Covenant. Furthermore, energy exploration in the Band's territory allegedly entails a violation of article 1, paragraph 2, which grants all peoples the right to dispose of their natural wealth and resources. In destroying the environment and undermining the Band's economic base, the Band is allegedly being deprived of its means to subsist and of the enjoyment of the right of self-determination guaranteed in article 1....

Right of self-determination

The Government of Canada submits that the communication, as it pertains to the right of self-determination, is inadmissible for two reasons. First, the right of self-determination applies to a "people" and it is the position of the Government of Canada that the Lubicon Lake Band is not a people within the meaning of article 1 of the Covenant. It therefore submits that the communication is incompatible with the provisions of the Covenant and, as such, should be found inadmissible under article 3 of the Protocol. Secondly, communications under the Optional Protocol can only be made by individuals and must relate to the breach of a right conferred on individuals. The present communication, the State party argues, relates to a collective right and the author therefore lacks standing to bring a communication pursuant to articles 1 and 2 of the Optional Protocol....

In a detailed reply, dated 8 July 1985, to the State party's submission, the author summarized his arguments as follows.... [T]he Government of Canada alleges that the concept of self-determination is not applicable to the Lubicon Lake Band. The Lubicon Lake Band is an indigenous people who have maintained their traditional economy and way of life and have occupied their traditional territory since time immemorial. At a minimum, the concept of self-determination should be held to be applicable to these people as it concerns the right of a people to their means of subsistence....

Before considering a communication on the merits, the Committee must ascertain whether it fulfils all conditions relating to its admissibility under the Optional Protocol.

With regard to the State party's contention that the author's communication pertaining to self-determination should be declared inadmissible because "the Committee's jurisdiction, as defined by the Optional Protocol, cannot be invoked by an individual when the alleged violation concerns a collective right," the Committee reaffirmed that the Covenant recognizes and protects in most resolute terms a people's right of self-determination and its right to dispose of its natural resources, as an essential condition for the effective guarantee and observance of individual human rights and for the promotion and strengthening of those rights. However, the Committee observed that the author, as an individual, could not claim under the Optional Protocol to be a victim of a violation of the right of self-determination enshrined in article 1 of the Covenant, which deals with rights conferred upon peoples, as such.

The Committee noted, however, that the facts as submitted might raise issues under other articles of the Covenant, including article 27....

On 22 July 1987, therefore, the Human Rights Committee decided that the communication was admissible in so far as it might raise issues under article 27 or other articles of the Covenant....

Summary of the submissions

At the outset, the author's claim, although set against a complex background, concerned basically the alleged denial of the right of self-determination and the right of the members of the Lubicon Lake Band to dispose freely of their natural wealth and resources.... It was claimed that the rapid destruction of the Band's economic base and aboriginal way of life had already caused irreparable injury. It was further claimed that the Government of Canada had deliberately used the domestic political and legal processes to thwart and delay all the Band's efforts to seek redress, so that the industrial development in the area, accompanied by the destruction of the environmental and economic base of the Band, would make it impossible for the Band to survive as a people. The author has stated that the Lubicon Lake Band is not seeking from the Committee a territorial rights decision, but only that the Committee assist it in attempting to convince the Government of Canada: (a) that the Band's existence is seriously threatened; and (b) that Canada is responsible for the current state of affairs.

From the outset, the State party has denied the allegations that the existence of the Lubicon Lake Band has been threatened and has maintained that continued resource development would not cause irreparable injury to the traditional way of life of the Band. It submitted that the Band's claim to certain lands in northern Alberta was part of a complex situation that involved a number of competing claims from several other native communities in the area, that effective redress in respect of the Band's claims was still available, both through the courts and through negotiations, that the Government had made an *ex gratia* payment to the Band of $C 1.5 million to cover legal costs and that, at any rate, article 1 of the Covenant, concerning the rights of people, could not be invoked under the Optional Protocol, which provides for the consideration of alleged violations of individual rights, but not collective rights conferred upon peoples.

This was the state of affairs when the Committee decided in July 1987 that the communication was admissible "in so far as it may raise issues under article 27 or other articles of the Covenant." In view of the seriousness of the author's allegations that the Lubicon Lake Band was at the verge of extinction, the Committee requested the State party, under rule 86 of the rules of procedure "to take interim measures of protection to avoid irreparable damage to [the author of the communication] and other members of the Lubicon Lake Band."

Since October 1987, the parties have made a number of submissions, refuting each other's statements as factually misleading or wrong....

The State party ... submits that serious and genuine efforts continued in early 1988 to engage representatives of the Lubicon Lake Band in negotiations in respect of the Band's claims. These efforts, which included an interim offer to set aside 25.4 square miles as reserve land for the Band, without prejudice to negotiations or any court actions, failed. According to the author, all but the 25.4 square miles of the Band's traditional lands had been leased out, in defiance of the Committee's request for interim measures of protection, in conjunction with a pulp mill to be constructed by the Daishowa Canada Company Ltd. near Peace River, Alberta, and that the Daishowa project frustrated any hopes of the continuation of some traditional activity by Band members.

Accepting its obligation to provide the Lubicon Lake Band with reserve land under Treaty 8, and after further unsuccessful discussions, the Federal Government, in May 1988, initiated legal proceedings against the Province of Alberta and the Lubicon Lake Band, in an effort to provide a common jurisdiction and thus to enable it to meet its lawful obligations to the Band under Treaty 8. In the author's opinion, however, this initiative was designated for the sole purpose of delaying indefinitely the resolution of the Lubicon land issues and, on 6 October 1988 (30 September, according to the State party), the Lubicon Lake Band asserted jurisdiction over its territory and declared that it had ceased to recognize the jurisdiction of the Canadian courts. The author further accused the State party of "practicing deceit in the media and dismissing advisors who recommend any resolution favourable to the Lubicon people."

Following an agreement between the provincial government of Alberta and the Lubicon Lake Band in November 1988 to set aside 95 square miles of land for a reserve, negotiations started between the federal Government and the Band on the modalities of the land transfer and related issues. According to the State party, consensus had been reached on the majority of issues, including Band membership, size of the reserve, community construction and delivery of programmes and services, but not on cash compensation, when the Band withdrew from the negotiations on 24 January 1989. The formal offer presented at that time by the federal Government amounted to approximately $C 45 million in benefits and programmes, in addition to the 95 square mile reserve.

The author, on the other hand, states that the above information from the State party is not only misleading but virtually entirely untrue and that there had been no serious attempt by the Government to reach a settlement. He describes the Government's offer as an exercise in public relations, "which committed the Federal Government to virtually nothing," and states that no agreement or consensus had been reached on any issue....

The State party rejects the allegation that it negotiated in bad faith or engaged in improper behaviour to the detriment of the interests of the Lubicon Lake Band. It concedes that the Lubicon Lake Band has suffered a historical inequity, but maintains that its formal offer would, if accepted, enable the Band to maintain its culture, control its way of life and achieve economic self-sufficiency and, thus, constitute an effective remedy. On the basis of a total of 500 Band members, the package worth $C 45 million would amount to almost $C 500,000 for each family of five. It states that a number of the Band's demands, including an indoor ice arena or a swimming pool, had been refused. The major remaining point of contention, the State party submits, is a request for $C 167 million in compensation for economic and other losses allegedly suffered. That claim, it submits, could be pursued in the courts, irrespective of the acceptance of the formal offer. It reiterates that its offer to the Band stands.

Further submissions from both parties have, *inter alia*, dealt with the impact of the Daishowa pulp mill on the traditional way of life of the Lubicon Lake Band. While the author states that the impact would be devastating, the State party maintains that it would have no serious adverse consequences, pointing out that the pulp mill, located about 80 kilometres away from the land set aside for the reserve, is not within the Band's claimed traditional territory and that the area to be cut annually, outside the proposed reserve, involves less than 1 per cent of the area specified in the forest management agreement.

The Human Rights Committee has considered the present communication in the light of the information made available by the parties, as provided for in articles 5, paragraph 1, of the Optional Protocol. In so doing, the Committee observes that the persistent disagreement between the parties as to what constitutes the factual setting for the dispute at issue has made the consideration of the claims on the merits most difficult....

Articles of the Covenant alleged to have been violated

The question has arisen of whether any claim under article 1 of the Covenant remains.... While all peoples have the right of self-determination and the right freely to determine their political status, pursue their economic, social and cultural development and dispose of their natural wealth and resources, as stipulated in article 1 of the Covenant, the question whether the Lubicon Lake Band constitutes a "people" is not an issue for the Committee to address under the Optional Protocol to the Covenant. The Optional Protocol provides a procedure under which individuals can claim that their individual rights have been violated. These rights are set out in part III of the Covenant, articles 6 to 27, inclusive. There is, however, no objection to a group of individuals, who claim to be similarly affected, collectively to submit a communication about alleged breaches of their rights.

Although initially couched in terms of alleged breaches of the provisions of article 1 of the Covenant, there is no doubt that many of the claims presented raise issues under article 27. The Committee recognizes that the rights protected by article 27, include the right of persons, in community with others, to engage in economic and social activities which are part of the culture of the community to which they belong....

Violations and the remedy offered

Historical inequities, to which the State party refers, and certain more recent developments threaten the way of life and culture of the Lubicon Lake Band, and constitute a violation of article 27 so long as they continue. The State party proposes to rectify the situation by a remedy that the Committee deems appropriate within the meaning of article 2 of the Covenant.

Questions and Discussion

1. *Deciphering the Committee's views.* Who won this case? What exactly are the rulings? What, if anything, is the State required to do? Even if the state party is not bound to any particular remedy, are there other potential benefits of winning a decision like this one from an international body?

2. *An "appropriate" remedy.* 10,000 square kilometers equals approximately 3,861 square miles. Does 95 square kilometers seem like a reasonable trade, even with the additional "benefits and programmes" worth $45 million? How much would those 3,765 square miles be worth today? Is it fair to offer a large amount of money to indigenous people for

their territory? What if the indigenous population is already integrated with the modern world? What if, as a result of integration, the indigenous population is living in extreme poverty?

3. *Economic self-sufficiency.* The government stated that its offer would allow the Lubicon Lake Band to achieve economic self-sufficiency. Should that be the main goal in the face of development pressure from the outside world?

4. *Related case.* See page 515 for a related case involving Daishowa pulp mill.

5. *Subsequent proceedings.* As of 2008, the disputes between the Lubicon Lake Band and the Canadian Government were continuing. In 2006 and 2007, both sides submitted "follow-up" submissions to the Human Rights Committee. Meanwhile, in May 2006 the U.N. Committee on Economic, Social and Cultural Rights issued a report recommending that Canada resume negotiations with the Lubicon Lake Band.

Länsman v. Finland (I)

U.N. Human Rights Committee
Communication No. 511/1992
U.N. Doc. CCPR/C/52/D/511/1992 (8 November 1994)

VIEWS UNDER ARTICLE 5, PARAGRAPH 4, OF THE OPTIONAL PROTOCOL

The authors of the communication are Ilmari Länsman and forty-seven other members of the Muotkatunturi Herdsmen's Committee and members of the Angeli local community. They claim to be the victims of a violation by Finland of article 27 of the International Covenant on Civil and Political Rights.

The facts as presented by the authors:

The authors are all reindeer breeders of Sami ethnic origin from the area of Angeli and Inari; they challenge the decision of the Central Forestry Board to pass a contract with a private company, Arktinen Kivi Oy (Arctic Stone Company) in 1989, which would allow the quarrying of stone in an area covering ten hectares on the flank of the mountain Etela-Riutusvaara. Under the terms of the initial contract, this activity would be authorized until 1993.

The members of the Muotkatunturi Herdsmen's Committee occupy an area ranging from the Norwegian border in the West, to Kaamanen in the East, comprising both sides on the road between Inari and Angeli, a territory traditionally owned by them. The area is officially administered by the Central Forestry Board. For reindeer herding purposes, special pens and fences, designed for example to direct the reindeers to particular pastures or locations, have been built around the village of Angeli....

The authors contend that the contract signed between the Arctic Stone Company and the Central Forestry Board would not only allow the company to extract stone but also to transport it right through the complex system of reindeer fences to the Angeli-Inari road....

The authors affirm that the village of Angeli is the only remaining area in Finland with a homogenous and solid Sami population. The quarrying and transport of anorthocite would disturb their reindeer herding activities and the complex system of reindeer fences determined by the natural environment....

The complaint:

The authors affirm that the quarrying of stone on the flank of the Etelä-Riutusvaara mountain and its transportation through their reindeer herding territory would violate their rights under article 27 of the Covenant, in particular their right to enjoy their own culture, which has traditionally been and remains essentially based on reindeer husbandry.

In support of their contention of a violation of article 27, the authors refer to the Views adopted by the Committee in the cases of Ivan Kitok (No. 197/1985) and *B. Ominayak and members of the Lubicon Lake Band v. Canada* (No. 167/1984), as well as to ILO Convention No.169 concerning the rights of indigenous and tribal people in independent countries....

Examination of the merits:

The Committee has examined the present communication in the light of all the information provided by the parties. The issue to be determined by the Committee is whether quarrying on the flank of Mt. Etelä-Riutusvaara, in the amount that has taken place until the present time or in the amount that would be permissible under the permit issued to the company which has expressed its intention to extract stone from the mountain (i.e. up to a total of 5,000 cubic metres), would violate the authors' rights under article 27 of the Covenant.

It is undisputed that the authors are members of a minority within the meaning of article 27 and as such have the right to enjoy their own culture; it is further undisputed that reindeer husbandry is an essential element of their culture. In this context, the Committee recalls that economic activities may come within the ambit of article 27, if they are an essential element of the culture of an ethnic community [Views on communication No. 197/1985 (*Kitok v. Sweden*), adopted on 27 July 1988, paragraph 9.2.].

The right to enjoy one's culture cannot be determined *in abstracto* but has to be placed in context. In this connection, the Committee observes that article 27 does not only protect traditional means of livelihood of national minorities, as indicated in the State party's submission. Therefore, that the authors may have adapted their methods of reindeer herding over the years and practice it with the help of modern technology does not prevent them from invoking article 27 of the Covenant....

A State may understandably wish to encourage development or allow economic activity by enterprises....

The question that therefore arises in this case is whether the impact of the quarrying on Mount Riutusvaara is so substantial that it does effectively deny to the authors the right to enjoy their cultural rights in that region....

Against this background, the Committee concludes that quarrying on the slopes of Mt. Riutusvaara, in the amount that has already taken place, does not constitute a denial of the authors' right, under article 27, to enjoy their own culture. It notes in particular that the interests of the Muotkatunturi Herdsmens' Committee and of the authors were considered during the proceedings leading to the delivery of the quarrying permit, that the authors were consulted during the proceedings, and that reindeer herding in the area does not appear to have been adversely affected by such quarrying as has occurred.

As far as future activities which may be approved by the authorities are concerned, the Committee further notes that the information available to it indicates that the State party's authorities have endeavoured to permit only quarrying which would minimize the impact on any reindeer herding activity in Southern Riutusvaara and on the environment;

the intention to minimize the effects of extraction of stone from the area on reindeer husbandry is reflected in the conditions laid down in the quarrying permit. Moreover, it has been agreed that such activities should be carried out primarily outside the period used for reindeer pasturing in the area. Nothing indicates that the change in herding methods by the Muotkatunturi Herdsmens' Committee could not be accommodated by the local forestry authorities and/or the company.

With regard to the authors' concerns about future activities, the Committee notes that economic activities must, in order to comply with article 27, be carried out in a way that the authors continue to benefit from reindeer husbandry. Furthermore, if mining activities in the Angeli area were to be approved on a large scale and significantly expanded by those companies to which exploitation permits have been issued, then this may constitute a violation of the authors' rights under article 27, in particular of their right to enjoy their own culture. The State party is under a duty to bear this in mind when either extending existing contracts or granting new ones.

The Human Rights Committee, acting under article 5, paragraph 4, of the Optional Protocol to the International Covenant on Civil and Political Rights, is of the view that the facts as found by the Committee do not reveal a breach of article 27 or any other provision of the Covenant.

Questions and Discussion

1. *Subsequent proceedings.* The Sami reindeer breeders continued to bring complaints to the U.N. Human Rights Committee in subsequent years. Each time, the Committee found no violation of Article 27. In *Länsman II*, the representatives of the same Herdsmen's Committee brought to the Human Rights Committee a complaint about government logging and road construction plans. They had raised the Article 27 claim in national courts but had lost in a 2–1 decision in the Rovaniemi Court of Appeal (*Rovaniemen hovioikeus*). The Supreme Court of Finland (*Korkein oikeus*) upheld that decision. In addition to Article 27, the Sami complaints to the Human Rights Committee invoked ILO Convention No. 169 on the rights of indigenous and tribal people in independent countries and the United Nations Draft Declaration on Indigenous Peoples. The Committee said it was "unable to conclude that the activities carried out as well as approved constitute a denial of the authors' right to enjoy their own culture." In particular, the Committee noted that the Muotkatunturi Herdsmen's Committee was consulted in the process of drawing up the logging plans and at the time did not react negatively to the plans for logging. It decided it could not conclude that the findings of the Court of Appeal, affirmed by the Supreme Court, misinterpreted or misapplied Article 27 of the Covenant, or that the impact of the logging plans would deny the herdsmen's rights under Article 27. The Committee said that if logging plans were to be approved on a scale larger than that already agreed to for future years, or the effects of logging already planned turned out to be more serious than expected, the complainants could return to the Committee. Considering also other large scale exploitations being planned and implemented in the area the Committee cautioned that the State party must bear in mind "that though different activities in themselves may not constitute a violation of this article, such activities, taken together, may erode the rights of Sami people to enjoy their own culture." *Views of the Human Rights Committee concerning Communication No. 671/1995*, U.N. Doc. CCPR/C/58/D/671/1995 (30 October 1996).

2. *The Sami lose a 2001 decision.* In *Anni Äärelä & Jouni Näkkäläjärvi v. Finland*, Communication 779/1997 (4 February 1997), U.N. Doc. No. CCPR/C/73/D/779/1997

(24 October 2001), the Committee again found that a logging plan did not violate the rights of the Sami herdsmen.

3. *The cumulative effect.* In *Länsman III,* the Committee took note of its earlier warning that more serious effects might constitute a violation of Article 27. It also restated that a violation of Article 27 might arise from the cumulative effects of several smaller activities. But it concluded that the effects of logging "have not been shown to be serious enough as to amount to a denial of the authors' right to enjoy their own culture in community with other members of their group under article 27 of the Covenant." Views of the Human Rights Committee concerning Communication No. 1023/2001, U.N. Doc. No. CCPR/C/83/D/1023/2001 (15 April 2005).

4. *The precautionary principle.* Can it be said that the Human Rights Committee observes the "precautionary principle" in making rulings under Article 27? (Under this principle, where information is uncertain but results could be significantly harmful, public bodies take action to avoid the risks of harm.) Some other principle? Where does it place the burden of proof? How heavy is that burden?

5. *National courts and deference.* Does *Länsman II* suggest that a State, by opening its national courts to Article 27 claims, can effectively insulate itself from losing in the U.N. Human Rights Committee? Is there anything wrong with that if it means that indigenous peoples have gained a new and potentially more effective avenue of redress at the national level?

B. Declaration on the Rights of Indigenous Peoples

In 2006 the United Nations' new Human Rights Council recommended to the U.N. General Assembly by a vote of 30 to 2 (Canada and Russia opposing, with 12 abstentions) that it adopt the Draft Declaration on the Rights of Indigenous Peoples that was first drafted in 1994. The Declaration was adopted in 2007.

Declaration on the Rights of Indigenous Peoples
G.A. Res. A/RES/61/295, U.N. Doc. A/61/L.67 (13 September 2007)

Article 3

Indigenous peoples have the right to self-determination. By virtue of that right they freely determine their political status and freely pursue their economic, social and cultural development.

Article 4

Indigenous peoples, in exercising their right to self-determination, have the right to autonomy or self-government in matters relating to their internal and local affairs, as well as ways and means for financing their autonomous functions.

Article 5

Indigenous peoples have the right to maintain and strengthen their distinct political, legal, economic, social and cultural institutions, while retaining their right to participate fully, if they so choose, in the political, economic, social and cultural life of the State.

Article 8

1. Indigenous peoples and individuals have the right not to be subjected to forced assimilation or destruction of their culture.

2. States shall provide effective mechanisms for prevention of, and redress for: ...

   (b) Any action which has the aim or effect of dispossessing them of their lands, territories or resources;

   (c) Any form of forced population transfer which has the aim or effect of violating or undermining any of their rights....

Article 10

Indigenous peoples shall not be forcibly removed from their lands or territories. No relocation shall take place without the free, prior and informed consent of the indigenous peoples concerned and after agreement on just and fair compensation and, where possible, with the option of return.

Article 12

1. Indigenous peoples have the right to manifest, practice, develop and teach their spiritual and religious traditions, customs and ceremonies; the right to maintain, protect, and have access in privacy to their religious and cultural sites....

Article 18

Indigenous peoples have the right to participate in decision-making in matters which would affect their rights, through representatives chosen by themselves in accordance with their own procedures, as well as to maintain and develop their own indigenous decision-making institutions.

Article 19

States shall consult and cooperate in good faith with the indigenous peoples concerned through their own representative institutions in order to obtain their free, prior and informed consent before adopting and implementing legislative or administrative measures that may affect them.

Article 20

1. Indigenous peoples have the right to maintain and develop their political, economic and social systems or institutions, to be secure in the enjoyment of their own means of subsistence and development, and to engage freely in all their traditional and other economic activities.

2. Indigenous peoples deprived of their means of subsistence and development are entitled to just and fair redress.

Article 24

1. Indigenous peoples have the right to their traditional medicines and to maintain their health practices, including the conservation of their vital medicinal plants, animals and minerals. Indigenous individuals also have the right to access, without any discrimination, to all social and health services....

Article 25

Indigenous peoples have the right to maintain and strengthen their distinctive spiritual relationship with their traditionally owned or otherwise occupied and used lands, territories, waters and coastal seas and other resources and to uphold their responsibilities to future generations in this regard.

Article 26

1. Indigenous peoples have the right to the lands, territories and resources which they have traditionally owned, occupied or otherwise used or acquired.

2. Indigenous peoples have the right to own, use, develop and control the lands, territories and resources that they possess by reason of traditional ownership or other traditional occupation or use, as well as those which they have otherwise acquired.

3. States shall give legal recognition and protection to these lands, territories and resources. Such recognition shall be conducted with due respect to the customs, traditions and land tenure systems of the indigenous peoples concerned.

Article 27

States shall establish and implement, in conjunction with indigenous peoples concerned, a fair, independent, impartial, open and transparent process, giving due recognition to indigenous peoples' laws, traditions, customs and land tenure systems, to recognize and adjudicate the rights of indigenous peoples pertaining to their lands, territories and resources, including those which were traditionally owned or otherwise occupied or used. Indigenous peoples shall have the right to participate in this process.

Article 28

1. Indigenous peoples have the right to redress, by means that can include restitution or, when this is not possible, just, fair and equitable compensation, for the lands, territories and resources which they have traditionally owned or otherwise occupied or used, and which have been confiscated, taken, occupied, used or damaged without their free, prior and informed consent.

2. Unless otherwise freely agreed upon by the peoples concerned, compensation shall take the form of lands, territories and resources equal in quality, size and legal status or of monetary compensation or other appropriate redress.

Article 29

1. Indigenous peoples have the right to the conservation and protection of the environment and the productive capacity of their lands or territories and resources. States shall establish and implement assistance programmes for indigenous peoples for such conservation and protection, without discrimination.

2. States shall take effective measures to ensure that no storage or disposal of hazardous materials shall take place in the lands or territories of indigenous peoples without their free, prior and informed consent.

Article 31

1. Indigenous peoples have the right to maintain, control, protect and develop their cultural heritage, traditional knowledge and traditional cultural expressions, as well as the manifestations of their sciences, technologies and cultures, including human and ge-

netic resources, seeds, medicines, knowledge of the properties of fauna and flora, oral traditions, literatures, designs, sports and traditional games and visual and performing arts....

Article 32

1. Indigenous peoples have the right to determine and develop priorities and strategies for the development or use of their lands or territories and other resources.

2. States shall consult and cooperate in good faith with the indigenous peoples concerned through their own representative institutions in order to obtain their free and informed consent prior to the approval of any project affecting their lands or territories and other resources, particularly in connection with the development, utilization or exploitation of mineral, water or other resources.

3. States shall provide effective mechanisms for just and fair redress for any such activities, and appropriate measures shall be taken to mitigate adverse environmental, economic, social, cultural or spiritual impact.

Questions and Discussion

1. *Indigenous use of the Declaration.* Consider how the Declaration might be used by indigenous peoples or individual members of indigenous groups to protect their environment, land, or resources. Although a Declaration is not legally binding as a matter of international law, would it have relevance in persuading a government body not to issue a permit for development that a group or individual opposes?

2. *Legal effect of the Declaration.* If the government issues a permit, can the Declaration be used in national courts? In an international human rights tribunal? In other ways?

3. *Compare.* If the Lubicon Lake Band brought their original case (page 149) under the Declaration on Indigenous Peoples, how might the outcome have differed? Is it more favorable to them than the Covenant on Civil and Political Rights? Is it less favorable because it does not have the status of a covenant?

C. ILO Convention No. 169 on Indigenous and Tribal Peoples

The International Labour Organization (ILO) was founded in 1919 and became the first specialized agency of the United Nations in 1946. Each year, the ILO hosts the International Labour Conference where Conventions can be adopted by a majority vote and opened for ratification by national governments. In 1957, the Conference adopted International Labour Organization Convention (No. 107) concerning the Protection and Integration of Indigenous and Other Tribal and Semi-Tribal Populations in Independent Countries, 328 U.N.T.S. 247. According to a leading expert,

> Convention No. 107 contains a fundamental flaw which has become apparent since 1957. It takes a patronizing attitude toward these population groups- for instance, referring to them as "less advanced" — and promotes eventual integration as the way to resolve the problems caused to states by their continued existence. It presumes that they will disappear as separate groups once they have the opportunity to participate fully in the national society, and it attempts to ease the transitional period.

Lee Swepston, *A New Step in the International Law on Indigenous And Tribal Peoples: ILO Convention No. 169 of 1989*, 15 Okla. City U. L. Rev. 677 (1990).

Recognizing these problems, in 1986 the ILO started negotiations on a revision of the Convention. Three years later, the International Labour Conference adopted Convention No. 169 Concerning Indigenous and Tribal Peoples in Independent Countries. *Id.* The negotiation process itself broke new ground procedurally, allowing indigenous peoples to express views regularly and to participate in formal and informal negotiations. Through this process, non-state actors (and peoples directly addressed by the treaty) were able, for the first time, to influence the outcome of the treaty text in a direct manner. Some NGOs, though, still felt they had inadequate representation.

As of 2008, ILO Convention No. 169 had been ratified by Argentina, Bolivia, Brazil, Colombia, Costa Rica, Denmark, Dominica, Ecuador, Fiji, Guatemala, Honduras, Mexico, Nepal, Netherlands, Norway, Paraguay, Peru, Spain, and Venezuela. Note that 12 of these countries are in Latin America, one is in the Caribbean, one is in Asia, one is in the Pacific, four are in Europe, and none is in Africa.

1. Text of Convention

Convention (No. 169) Concerning Indigenous and Tribal Peoples in Independent Countries

International Labour Organization, June 27, 1989
72 ILO Official Bull. 59 (1989); 28 I.L.M. 1382 (1989)

PART I. GENERAL POLICY

Article 1

1. This Convention applies to:

(a) Tribal peoples in independent countries whose social, cultural and economic conditions distinguish them from other sections of the national community, and whose status is regulated wholly or partially by their own customs or traditions or by special laws or regulations;

(b) Peoples in independent countries who are regarded as indigenous on account of their descent from the populations which inhabited the country, or a geographical region to which the country belongs, at the time of conquest or colonisation or the establishment of present State boundaries and who, irrespective of their legal status, retain some or all of their own social, economic, cultural and political institutions.

2. Self-identification as indigenous or tribal shall be regarded as a fundamental criterion for determining the groups to which the provisions of this Convention apply.

3. The use of the term "peoples" in this Convention shall not be construed as having any implications as regards the rights which may attach to the term under international law.

Article 2

1. Governments shall have the responsibility for developing, with the participation of the peoples concerned, coordinated and systematic action to protect the rights of these peoples and to guarantee respect for their integrity.

2. Such action shall include measures for:

(a) Ensuring that members of these peoples benefit on an equal footing from the rights and opportunities which national laws and regulations grant to other members of the population;

(b) Promoting the full realisation of the social, economic and cultural rights of these peoples with respect for their social and cultural identity, their customs and traditions and their institutions....

Article 4

1. Special measures shall be adopted as appropriate for safeguarding the persons, institutions, property, labour, cultures and environment of the peoples concerned.

2. Such special measures shall not be contrary to the freely-expressed wishes of the peoples concerned....

Article 6

1. In applying the provisions of this Convention, Governments shall:

(a) Consult the peoples concerned, through appropriate procedures and in particular through their representative institutions, whenever consideration is being given to legislative or administrative measures which may affect them directly;

(b) Establish means by which these peoples can freely participate, to at least the same extent as other sectors of the population, at all levels of decision-making in elective institutions and administrative and other bodies responsible for policies and programmes which concern them....

Article 7

1. The peoples concerned shall have the right to decide their own priorities for the process of development as it affects their lives, beliefs, institutions and spiritual well-being and the lands they occupy or otherwise use, and to exercise control, to the extent possible, over their own economic, social and cultural development. In addition, they shall participate in the formulation, implementation and evaluation of plans and programmes for national and regional development which may affect them directly....

3. Governments shall ensure that, whenever appropriate, studies are carried out, in co-operation with the peoples concerned, to assess the social, spiritual, cultural and environmental impact on them of planned development activities. The results of these studies shall be considered as fundamental criteria for the implementation of these activities.

4. Governments shall take measures, in co-operation with the peoples concerned, to protect and preserve the environment of the territories they inhabit....

Part II. Land

Article 13

1. In applying the provisions of this Part of the Convention governments shall respect the special importance for the cultures and spiritual values of the peoples concerned of their relationship with the lands or territories, or both as applicable, which they occupy or otherwise use, and in particular the collective aspects of this relationship.

2. The use of the term "lands" in Articles 15 and 16 shall include the concept of territories, which covers the total environment of the areas which the peoples concerned occupy or otherwise use.

Article 14

1. The rights of ownership and possession of the peoples concerned over the lands which they traditionally occupy shall be recognised. In addition, measures shall be taken in appropriate cases to safeguard the right of the peoples concerned to use lands not exclusively occupied by them, but to which they have traditionally had access for their subsistence and traditional activities. Particular attention shall be paid to the situation of nomadic peoples and shifting cultivators in this respect.

2. Governments shall take steps as necessary to identify the lands which the peoples concerned traditionally occupy, and to guarantee effective protection of their rights of ownership and possession.

3. Adequate procedures shall be established within the national legal system to resolve land claims by the peoples concerned.

Article 15

1. The rights of the peoples concerned to the natural resources pertaining to their lands shall be specially safeguarded. These rights include the right of these peoples to participate in the use, management and conservation of these resources.

2. In cases in which the State retains the ownership of mineral or sub-surface resources or rights to other resources pertaining to lands, governments shall establish or maintain procedures through which they shall consult these peoples, with a view to ascertaining whether and to what degree their interests would be prejudiced, before undertaking or permitting any programmes for the exploration or exploitation of such resources pertaining to their lands. The peoples concerned shall wherever possible participate in the benefits of such activities, and shall receive fair compensation for any damages which they may sustain as a result of such activities.

Article 16

1. Subject to the following paragraphs of this Article, the peoples concerned shall not be removed from the lands which they occupy.

2. Where the relocation of these peoples is considered necessary as an exceptional measure, such relocation shall take place only with their free and informed consent. Where their consent cannot be obtained, such relocation shall take place only following appropriate procedures established by national laws and regulations....

Questions and Discussion

1. *Article 6.* Article 6 has been called the "heart of the Convention." As new cases regarding this duty to consult indigenous and tribal peoples are decided, the scope of Article 6 becomes clearer. Not only must a State consult with indigenous people, but it must also create procedures that enable this consultation to be done in a meaningful way. As will be seen later in this chapter, page 168, the Constitutional Court of Colombia considered Article 6 in 2008, overturning national legislation for violating it, and in Ecuador, an ILO tripartite committee guided the State in forming measures that would meet the Article 6 requirements.

2. *Article 7.* Article 7 recognizes indigenous and tribal peoples' "right to decide" how they want to develop their natural resources, in conjunction with an environmental (and social, spiritual, and cultural) impact assessment performed by the State before any major project that might affect them. In addition, Article 7 requires States to ensure that their own structure allows indigenous and tribal peoples to "influence" any decision that affects these peoples.

3. *Land provisions.* As Lee Swepston has pointed out,

> The text provides for a legal regime for these peoples which may be separate from that applied to others in each country within existing structures, while allowing for development in the future. Some very fundamental positive rights are created, but above all procedural rights are laid down. These are intended to ensure that whenever an exception is made to the basic rights of continued ownership or possession (see below), it must be done openly and in such a way that conflicting claims and interests can be aired in public.

Lee Swepston, *A New Step in the International Law on Indigenous and Tribal Peoples: ILO Convention No. 169 of 1989*, 15 Okla. City U. L. Rev. 677 (1990).

4. For a complete exposition of Convention No. 169, see ILO, Lee Swepston and Manuela Tomei, *Indigenous and Tribal Peoples: A Guide to ILO Convention No. 169* (Geneva, July 1996).

5. *Heart of ILO No. 169.* ILO No. 169 stresses the State's duty to consult indigenous peoples in a way that thoroughly involves them in any decision to exploit natural resources on or under their land. Indigenous peoples, in turn, are invited to consider how to honor their own culture and traditions, within a framework of cooperating with the State in developing such resources. The State must maintain procedures that foster this participation in a way that conserves the resources and honors the indigenous people.

6. *ILO terminology.* The ILO uses both "indigenous" and "tribal" terminology because not all such peoples are the original inhabitants of the land, although they have generally inhabited their traditional territory for generations. The Governing Body sets up a "tripartite" committee to study claims brought before it. It is tripartite because the ILO must represent the interests of governments, workers, and employers.

7. *Definition of "consult."* How might the ILO further define the duty to consult indigenous peoples?

2. *International Remedies*

DEFENDING THE ENVIRONMENT: CIVIL SOCIETY STRATEGIES TO ENFORCE INTERNATIONAL ENVIRONMENTAL LAW (2006)

Linda A. Malone & Scott Pasternack

Like UNESCO, the International Labour Organization ("ILO") is another U.N. specialized agency with a potential dispute resolution process available to handle environmental human rights claims, albeit only for indigenous and tribal peoples at this time....

Whenever a state party to ILO No. 169 fails to adhere to these standards, then an industrial association of employers or workers on behalf of indigenous and tribal individuals and groups (but not those individuals or groups themselves) can pursue a two-part strategy against the state party. That two-part strategy is set forth in Articles 24 to 34 of the ILO Constitution and summarized below.

Although the number of ILO Members bound by ILO No. 169 is small, the list includes many countries that have permitted and/or will permit within their borders major development projects that advance the interests of multinational corporate and financial institutions at the expense of certain environmental human rights of indigenous and tribal peoples. Consequently, the two-step strategy to enforce ILO No. 169 obligations is an important accountability mechanism for such development. Moreover, because the strategy has not been used frequently, particularly in the case of ILO No. 169, the door is wide open to shape this area of international environmental law enforcement.

The first step involves submitting a representation of non-observance of ILO No. 169. An industrial association of employers or workers on behalf of indigenous and tribal individuals or groups (but not an individual or group itself) can present to the ILO's International Labour Office a representation that a state party "has failed to secure in any respect the effective observance within its jurisdiction of [ILO No. 169]...."

The International Labour Office provides the representation to the ILO Governing Body. After the ILO Governing Body declares the representation receivable as to form, an *ad hoc* committee appointed by the ILO Governing Body from among its members considers the substance of the representation. The *ad hoc* committee asks the government for comments and may also ask the filing organization for additional information. The *ad hoc* committee then reviews the materials and makes a recommendation to the ILO Governing Body.

Based on the recommendation, the ILO Governing Body decides whether the government's response is satisfactory. If the ILO Governing Body decides in favor of the government, the procedure is closed and the ILO Governing Body may publish the allegations and the government response. If the ILO Governing Body decides against the government, the ILO Governing Body may decide to pursue a complaint against the government and on behalf of the filing organization under Article 26 of the ILO Constitution as discussed below. In addition, the ILO Governing Body will still publish the allegations and the government response along with its own discussion of the case.

Thus, the representation stage can result in a statement of whether the government is complying with ILO No. 169. Moreover, the publication of the allegations, government response, and ILO Governing Body discussion, if any, alerts other ILO offices to potential concerns regarding ILO No. 169 compliance in a given country. Once alerted, those ILO offices are likely to monitor the situation as part of their future agenda.

The second step involves submitting a complaint of non-observance of ILO No. 169. Although neither an industrial association of employers or workers nor individuals or groups can submit a complaint, the ILO Governing Body can, if it decides that the government's response to a representation is not satisfactory. Moreover, any other ILO government and any delegate attending the International Labour Conference can submit a complaint. Thus, even if one government or delegate decides against submitting a representation or fails to do so adequately, other avenues exist for a filing organization to ask another government or International Labour Conference delegate to submit a complaint....

Just as with representations, the International Labour Office forwards materials to the ILO Governing Body which then forwards the complaint to the government for comments. The ILO Governing Body then establishes, at its discretion, a Commission of Inquiry.

The Commission of Inquiry can establish its own rules and procedures but usually follows established practices. Such practice includes requesting written submissions from both parties on the merits of the case. Such submissions are usually shared among the parties and opportunities for responses are usually provided. The Commission of Inquiry also can request information from other governments or NGOs, hold a hearing with parties and witnesses, and conduct on-site visits.

The Commission of Inquiry eventually produces a report in response to the complaint. That report includes recommendations and timetables to assure compliance with the Convention at issue (*i.e.*, ILO No. 169). The Director-General communicates the report to the ILO Governing Body and the concerned government(s), and then publishes it. Concerned governments have three months in which to decide to appeal the report to the International Court of Justice.

Similar to the outcome from the filing of representation, publication of the Commission of Inquiry recommendation will alert other ILO offices that likely will make the issue part of their future agenda. Moreover, if a government fails to comply with the Commission on Inquiry's recommendations within the specified time, or any decision from the International Court of Justice requiring compliance, then the ILO Governing Body may recommend certain actions to the entire ILO Conference and/or establish a subsequent Commission of Inquiry to verify compliance.

As for case studies, this two-party strategy discussed in this part does not appear to have been used yet to challenge a lack of compliance with ILO No. 169. Thus, although one can refer to the list of ILO cases, no specific case studies concern ILO No. 169.

The Ecuador Oil Consultation

In 1998, Ecuador signed a share agreement with Arco Oriente, Inc. (Arco), for oil exploitation on Block 24. Seventy percent of Block 24 is in the traditional territory of the Independent Federation of the Shuar People of Ecuador (FIPSE). In 2000, Arco signed over its Block 24 oil rights to Burlington Resources Ecuador Ltd. (Burlington Ecuador).

FIPSE decided not to allow any negotiations between any of its members and Arco, and stated that any attempt by Arco to engage in such activities would be "considered as a violation of the integrity of the Shuar people," under both the Constitution of Ecuador and ILO No. 169. In 1999, FIPSE filed an appeal for the protection of its constitutional rights in national court. The Court of First Instance ruled partially in favour of the FIPSE, ordering Arco to stay away from the FIPSE for the purpose of dialogue without FIPSE's authorization. Arco appealed to the Constitutional Court of Ecuador. Report of the Committee set up to examine the representation alleging non-observance by Ecuador of the Indigenous and Tribal Peoples Convention, 1989 (No. 169), made under article 24 of the ILO Constitution by the Confederación Ecuatoriana de Organizaciónes Sindicales Libres (CEOSL), ILOLEX 162000ECU169, GB.277/18/4 and GB.282/14/2 (2000).

Before the special ILO committee FIPSE alleged that "Arco tried to divide the local organizations and created fictitious committees to coordinate their activities and to denigrate indigenous organizations in the eyes of the public." The Shuar "were prevented from fully exercising their rights of possession over their ancestral territory, in violation of Articles 13(1) and 14(1)" of ILO No. 169.

CEOSL alleged (to the ILO committee) that Ecuador signed a document between Arco and some FIPSE members after the declaration not to allow such negotiations. CEOSL also alleged that Ecuador stopped the Shuar people from fully enjoying the guarantees of

Article 7 of ILO No. 169 by allowing such contacts "without proper consideration of the matter by the FIPSE assembly in accordance with its traditions." CEOSL also complained that Ecuador did not comply with Articles 2, 4(1), 5, 15, and 17 of ILO No. 169.

Ecuador replied that the Hydrocarbons Act, the share agreement, and Chapter 5 of the Constitution of Ecuador show the government's concern for the Shuar, but that the consultation requirements "would hinder … oil-related … processes, which are the responsibility of the government…." The Amazon region held "the greatest hydrocarbon potential, a resource that is part of the State patrimony," but it also held the greatest number of indigenous peoples. Ecuador pointed out that the Constitutional Court of Ecuador rejected an appeal for protection of constitutional rights related to this case. Decision No. 054-2000-TP.

The Committee observed that, although Ecuador was only responsible for its actions after adoption of ILO No. 169, certain situations created by the earlier actions continued, and the State would have to apply ILO No. 169 to remedy those circumstances….

> The Committee considers that the spirit of consultation and participation constitutes the cornerstone of Convention no. 169 on which all its provisions are based. Article 6(1) establishes the obligation for the States that ratify the Convention to consult the indigenous peoples on their territory….

The committee said that the duty to consult should be "considered in the light of the fundamental principle of participation" in Articles 7(1) and (3). This meant that the Shuar had the right to develop their own priorities according to their own beliefs and traditions, and this right included plans for natural resources. In addition, studies of the proposals should be carried out in consultation with the Shuar, so Articles 6 and 7 should be looked at in the light of the "general policy" in Article 2 (1) and (2)(b) of ILO No. 169.

The Committee agreed that Article 15(2) recognized the principle of national patrimony, but it also established "an obligation … to consult … prior to authorizing activities for the exploration and exploitation of the subsurface resources situated on indigenous territories…."

The committee said that the State must foster a "genuine dialogue … characterized by communication and understanding, mutual respect, good faith, and the sincere wish to reach a common accord," not just a "simple information meeting…." The State should involve the Shuar "as early as possible," and include them in preparing the "environmental studies," as well. Once the Convention "came into force" so did all of the State obligations outlined by the Committee. In addition, Articles 2(1), 2(2)(b), 6, 7, and 15(2) "impl[y] the obligation to develop a process … before taking measures that might affect [the Shuar] directly…."

The Committee also stressed that the "principle of representativity" is a vital component of the obligation of consultation. In light of Article 6(1)(c), the Committee stated that any "future" consultations regarding Block 24 "should take into account" the earlier declaration by FIPSE requiring Arco (now Burlington Ecuador) to get FIPSE's approval before consulting with any smaller associations under FIPSE's umbrella.

In closing, the Committee requested that Ecuador not only inform it of the "measures taken or envisaged" to ensure conformance with ILO No. 169, but also the progress "achieved in respect of consultations with the peoples situated in the zone of Block 24, including information on the participation of these peoples in the use, administration and conservation of said resources and in the profits from the oil-producing activities, as well as their perception of fair compensation for any damage caused by the exploration and exploitation of the zone…."

Questions and Discussion

1. *Legal persuasiveness for national laws.* Could arguments based on ILO No. 169 be persuasive in seeking national legislation?

2. *Legal persuasiveness in courts.* If an indigenous group is unable to go through the indirect procedures of the International Labour Organization, can you conceive some other ways that the group may vindicate the rights recognized by ILO No. 169? Could such arguments be used in another international court or tribunal? In a national court? Consider the next section.

3. National Remedies

Unconstitutionality of the General Forestry Act (Colombia)[a]
Constitutional Court of Colombia
2008

PRESS RELEASE No. 01

On January 23, 2008, during its plenary session, the Constitutional Court adopted, among other things, the following decision:

Case File D-6837 — Decision C-030/08
Magistrate Rapporteur: Dr. Rodrigo Escobar Gil

1. Denounced law

ACT 1021 of 2006 (April 20), "That officially issues the General Forestry Act."

2. Description of the legal problem

The Court should determine if Act 1021 of 2006, "That officially issues the General Forestry Act," is contrary to the constitutional ordinance, specifically, articles 1, 2, 3, 7, 9, 13, 93, and 330 of the Political Constitution, for issuing the Act having omitted the requirement to consult with indigenous and tribal communities, granted in article 6 of Convention 169 of the International Labour Organization (ILO).

3. Decision

To declare unconstitutional Act 1021 of 2006, "That officially issues the General Forestry Act."

4. Grounds for the decision

The Court upheld the jurisprudence regarding the recognition of ethnic and cultural diversity as a fundamental constitutional principle of Colombian nationality (articles 7 and 70 of the Political Constitution). The Court highlighted that this special protection is expressed in the obligation to implement consultation processes with indigenous and tribal communities for the adoption and execution of decisions that may affect them. This duty is the expression and advancement of Article 1 of the Constitution, which defines Colombia as a democratic, participatory and pluralistic State; article 2 [of the Political Constitution] which establishes the State's goal to facilitate the participation of everyone in decisions that affect them; article 7 of the Charter, that recognizes and pro-

---

a Press Release issued by the Colombian Constitutional Court translated by Meche Lu, ELAW, and Astrid Puentes, AIDA.

tects ethnic and cultural diversity; from [article] 40-2 that guarantees the right of all cit-izens to democratic participation; and article 70 that considers culture as a foundation of nationality.

According to this framework, the Court recalled that with regards to the indigenous and tribal communities, the right to consultation is one of the forms of democratic par-ticipation provided for in the Constitution, described in particular in articles 329 and 330 that provide for the participation of communities in the shaping of indigenous ter-ritorial entities and the exploitation of natural resources in their territories. This right is supported by ILO Convention 169, approved by Act 21 of 1991, that aims to assure the rights of indigenous peoples to their territory, and to the protection of their cultural, so-cial, and economic values, as a means to secure their subsistence as human groups. As ju-risprudence has repeatedly shown, the mentioned Convention is part of the constitutionality block [formed by international treaties that Colombia has ratified, which aim to protect human rights], and in its article 6 which provides that in applying the provisions of this Convention, the Governments shall "(a) Consult the concerned peoples [stakeholders], through appropriate procedures and in particular, through their representative institutions, whenever consideration is being given to legislative or administrative measures that may directly affect them."

In the case under examination, the Court concluded that: a) The General Forestry Act contains comprehensive regulation [of forestry] matters. b) Despite the fact that the law included provisions that preserved the autonomy of indigenous and Afro Colom-bian communities to use forestry resources in their territories, the truth is that the law established general policies, definitions, guidelines and criteria, which even if they were not applied directly to indigenous territories, could affect areas where communities are generally located and which consequently, could affect their lifestyle and the close re-lationship they maintain with the forest. c) To this extent, and as defined in Constitu-tional system and in particular, ILO Convention 169 that is part of the constitutionality block, these communities should have been consulted regarding the adoption of the law, in order to look for ideas regarding how to prevent the law from affecting them negatively, and even [to discuss] the content of the guidelines and criteria that could have a direct effect on tribal and indigenous territories or ways of life, even when they are applied generally. d) This consultation, which has special characteristics, was not com-plied with in this case, and cannot be substituted by a general participative process that the State complied with regarding the [Forest] bill. e) In order to have complied with the consultation requirement, it would have been necessary to inform the indigenous communities about the bill, illustrate its scope and how it could affect them, and give them opportunities to effectively state their opinions about the bill. [The State] did not comply with this process. For this reason the Court concluded that, given that the bill is about a matter that profoundly affects the worldview of these communities and their relationship with the earth, there is no other alternative than to declare this law unconstitutional.

RODRIGO ESCOBAR GIL

Presidente

Questions and Discussion

1. *ILO No. 169's influence on the constitutional order.* What place does ILO No. 169 have in the constitutional order of the legal system in Colombia?

2. *Forestry law procedure.* Are indigenous people entitled to procedural protections greater than those of other citizens in Colombia after this case? Since the victory was on a procedural matter, is it likely that the law on forestry would be changed substantively after this decision?

3. *Colombian law and other countries.* What would you expect the impact of this decision to be in other countries that have ratified ILO No. 169? What about countries that have not ratified it?

4. *Decision's effect on the chosen forum.* After this decision, would it make sense for indigenous groups to continue using the ILO's own complaint procedures, or would they be more likely to achieve success in national courts?

D. Convention on Biological Diversity

The Convention on Biological Diversity (CBD) is considered a second-generation, multilateral environmental agreement (MEA). Opened for signature at the U.N. Conference on Environment and Development (UNCED, Rio de Janeiro, June 3–14, 1992), the CBD is also known as the *Rio Treaty*. On its tenth anniversary, Kofi Annan stated, "[The CBD] is the key global instrument for the conservation and sustainable use of biological diversity, and for the fair and equitable sharing of benefits arising from the use of genetic resources. A landmark in international law, the Convention, together with its Cartagena Protocol on Biosafety, is an integral part of international efforts to achieve sustainable development, poverty alleviation and the Millennium Development Goals." *The Convention on Biological Diversity, from Conception to Implementation*, CBD News, Spec. Ed. (Secretariat of the Convention on Biological Diversity) 2004 at 3. By 2008, the CBD and its offspring had grown to involve worldwide participation as the most widely ratified international environmental treaty.

CONVENTION ON BIOLOGICAL DIVERSITY
June 5, 1992
1760 U.N.T.S. 143; 31 I.L.M. 818 (1992)

Article 8. In situ Conservation

Each Contracting Party shall, as far as possible and as appropriate: ...

(b) Develop, where necessary, guidelines for the selection, establishment and management of protected areas or areas where special measures need to be taken to conserve biological diversity....

(j) Subject to its national legislation, respect, preserve and maintain knowledge, invocations and practices of indigenous and local communities embodying traditional lifestyles relevant for the conservation and sustainable use of biological diversity and promote their wider application with the approval and involvement of the holders of such knowledge, innovations and practices and encourage the equitable sharing of the benefits arising from the utilization of such knowledge, innovations and practices....

(m) Cooperate in providing financial and other support for in-situ conservation....

Article 10. Sustainable Use of Components of Biological Diversity

Each Contracting Party shall, as far as possible and as appropriate: ...

(c) Protect and encourage customary use of biological resources in accordance with traditional cultural practices that are compatible with conservation or sustainable use requirements.

(d) Support local populations to develop and implement remedial action in degraded areas where biological diversity has been reduced; and

(e) Encourage cooperation between its governmental authorities and its private sector in developing methods for sustainable use of biological resources.

Questions and Discussion

1. *Enforcement.* The compliance mechanism under the Convention on Biological Diversity is available only to countries complaining about each other. Is this likely to provide an effective remedy for an individual or group claiming a violation of rights and of the terms of the Convention?

2. *Substance.* Does the Convention contain enforceable human rights or only express policy agreements among governments?

3. *Indigenous peoples walk out of CBD working group.* The second meeting of the Ad Hoc Open-ended Working Group on Protected Areas opened in Rome on February 11, 2008. In a statement dated February 11, IPCC, *Statement on UNEP/CBD/WG-PA/2/2*, Agenda item 3.1.1 and 3.1.2, the indigenous representatives related their concerns about their level of participation, and asked the Working Group to:

- Recognize our customary practices and legal system related to the sustainable use and conservation of biodiversity

- Recognize our rights to our territories, lands and resources and the rights of Free Prior Informed Consent

- Review and reform national protected areas policies and laws that contravene the goals and targets of program element 2.

- Train protected areas managers and personnel to participatory approaches and to recognize and respect our rights.

  ... The rush to expand protected areas networks without putting issues of equity and participation at its core can lead to an unjust and skewed implementation of the PoW [Programme of Work].

Two days later, representatives of the International Indigenous Forum on Biodiversity walked out of the meeting in protest, stating that they were being marginalized and not allowed to participate fully.

II. Regional Human Rights Instruments and Institutions

None of the three regional human rights treaties—the European Convention, the American Convention and the African Charter—contains an explicit provision for "indigenous" rights or "environmental" rights. However, members of indigenous communities have used other provisions successfully on behalf of both.

A. American Convention on Human Rights

Sovereignty, Self-Determination, and Environment-Based Cultures: The Emerging Voice of Indigenous Peoples in International Law
Peter McManus
23 Wis. Int'l L.J. 553 (2005)

On the regional level, the American Convention on Human Rights, echoing the international instruments being drafted in the late 1960s, set as its goal the wedding of the principles of human rights set forth in the American Declaration of the Rights and Duties of Man, the Universal Declaration of Human Rights, and the protections found in the domestic laws of the various American nations. Addressing its protections to all individuals, the American Convention was a pact among its signatory nations to adopt legislation and institute other means through which each nation's domestic laws could give effect to the Convention's list of individual rights and freedoms.

These rights included a litany of civil and political guarantees, including the right to recognition as a person under the law, the right to humane treatment, the right to live free from involuntary servitude, and the right to a fair trial. Rights that could encompass indigenous communities' environmental interests include those addressing honor and dignity, religion, thought and expression, association, property and residence. None of the provisions addressing rights that might include indigenous peoples' interest in historical territories and natural resources contemplate their potential applicability to such environmental interests....

American Convention on Human Rights
O.A.S.T.S. No. 36, 1144 U.N.T.S. 123, OEA/Ser.L.V/II.82 doc.6 rev.1 at 25 (1992)

Article 1
Obligation to Respect Rights

1. The States Parties to this Convention undertake to respect the rights and freedoms recognized herein and to ensure to all persons subject to their jurisdiction the free and full exercise of those rights and freedoms, without any discrimination....

Article 2
Domestic Legal Effects

Where the exercise of any of the rights or freedoms referred to in Article 1 is not already ensured by legislative or other provisions, the States Parties undertake to adopt, in accordance with their constitutional processes and the provisions of this Convention, such legislative or other measures as may be necessary to give effect to those rights or freedoms....

Article 4
Right to Life

1. Every person has the right to have his life respected. This right shall be protected by law and, in general, from the moment of conception....

Article 5
Right to Humane Treatment

1. Every person has the right to have his physical, mental, and moral integrity respected....

Article 21
Right to Property

1. Everyone has the right to the use and enjoyment of his property. The law may subordinate such use and enjoyment to the interest of society.

2. No one shall be deprived of his property except upon payment of just compensation, for reasons of public utility or social interest, and in the cases and according to the forms established by law....

Article 63

1. If the Court finds that there has been a violation of a right or freedom protected by this Convention, the Court shall rule that the injured party be ensured the enjoyment of his right or freedom that was violated. It shall also rule, if appropriate, that the consequences of the measure or situation that constituted the breach of such right or freedom be remedied and that fair compensation be paid to the injured party.

2. In cases of extreme gravity and urgency, and when necessary to avoid irreparable damage to persons, the Court shall adopt such provisional measures as it deems pertinent in matters it has under consideration. With respect to a case not yet submitted to the Court, it may act at the request of the Commission.

Questions and Discussion

1. *Ratifications.* Not all countries of the Americas have ratified the American Convention on Human Rights. Among those that have not are the United States of America and Canada.

2. *Indigenous environmental rights.* Professor McManus points out that no provision of the American Convention directly addresses the specific environmental concerns of indigenous peoples. Indeed, nothing in the convention addresses any environmental concerns at all. As Professor McManus characterizes it, the Convention instead contains "a litany of civil and political guarantees." Given that reality, would it nonetheless be possible for a creative lawyer to find the basis for an environmental right in Article 4? Could indigenous peoples find the basis for protection of their special interests in their culture and in their use of natural resources such as native forests and animals anywhere in Articles 5 or 21, even if they did not hold title to land? Does Article 21 depend on the concept of legal title? What is meant by "property"? Should that term be interpreted according to the European-derived legal concepts of those who drafted the Convention, or according to the concepts of those who might seek the Convention's protections? If an indigenous right to protect traditional lands were found in these articles, would Articles 1 and 2 be relevant to creating a remedy for a national legal system's failure to protect those rights? Would Article 63 be relevant to creating remedies?

3. *"Interest of society."* Article 21 says that the State may subordinate the right to the "use and enjoyment" of property to the "interest of society." Should a State consider how it will affect society that a large portion of its non-indigenous population might become disaffected and angry if the Convention is interpreted in favor of indigenous peoples?

The Mayagna Awas Tingni Community is an indigenous Mayagna, or Sumo, community of the Atlantic or Caribbean coast of Nicaragua. The Community has a population of approximately 630 individuals. Its principal village is on the Wawa River, in the municipality of Waspan, in the North Atlantic Autonomous Region. The Community's troubles began when the Ministry of the Environment and Natural Resources began considering the possibility of a logging concession on Community lands being granted to Sol del Caribe S.A. without it previously having been consulted.

The Inter-American Court of Human Rights, based in San Jose, Costa Rica, is charged with enforcing and interpreting the American Convention on Human Rights. Cases can be brought to it by either the Inter-American Commission on Human Rights or member states of the Convention. The Commission brought forward the following case against Nicaragua.

Mayagna (Sumo) Awas Tingni Community v. Nicaragua
Inter-American Court of Human Rights
Inter-Am. Ct. H.R. (Ser. C) No. 79 (31 August 2001)

Antônio A. Cançado Trindade, President; Máximo Pacheco-Gómez, Vice President; Hernán Salgado-Pesantes, Judge; Oliver Jackman, Alirio Abreu-Burelli, Sergio García-Ramírez, Carlos Vicente De Roux-Rengifo, Judges, and Alejandro Montiel Argüello, *ad hoc* Judge [dissenting]

[The Court established jurisdiction under Article 62(3). Nicaragua accepted the Court's contentious jurisdiction on February 12, 1991.

[Jaime Castillo Felipe, Syndic (representative) of the Community, filed a petition in his own name and on behalf of the Community, requesting precautionary measures to stop the State from granting an alleged logging concession to Sol del Caribe, S.A. (SOLCARSA). The Commission sent Report No. 27/98 to the State, granting Nicaragua 2 months to report on measures it had taken to comply with the Commission's recommendations.

[In the report, the Commission concluded that first, "by granting a concession to the company SOLCARSA" for logging and road building without the Community's consent, Nicaragua violated Article 21, and second, Nicaragua "did not guarantee an effective remedy to respond to the claims of the Community," in violation of Article 25. In addition, Articles 1 and 2 required the States "to take the necessary measures to give effect to the right contained in the Convention."]

VII
Proven Facts

After examining the documents, testimony, expert opinions, and the statements by the State and by the Commission, in the course of the instant proceedings, this Court finds that the following facts have been established:

a. the Awas Tingni Community is an indigenous community of the Mayagna or Sumo ethnic group, located in the Northern Atlantic Autonomous Region (RAAN) of the Atlantic Coast of Nicaragua; ...

e. the members of the Community subsist on the basis of family farming and communal agriculture, fruit gathering and medicinal plants, hunting and fishing. These activities, as well as the use and enjoyment of the land they inhabit, are carried out within a territorial space in accordance with a traditional collective form of organization;

f.   ... the State maintains that part of the lands claimed by the Awas Tingni Community belong to the State;

g.   the Community has no real property title deed to the lands it claims; ...

m. on February 27, 1997 the Constitutional Panel of the Supreme Court of Justice [of Nicaragua] declared the concession granted to SOLCARSA to be unconstitutional because it had not been approved by the plenary of the Regional Council of the [North Atlantic Autonomous Region, or RAAN]....

n.   on October 9, 1997, the Regional Council of the RAAN decided to: a) [approve] the logging concession in favor of the SOLCARSA corporation; ... and c) "[r]atify ... the Contract for Management and Use of the Forest, signed by the Minister of MARENA and ... SOLCARSA on March 13, 1996"; ...

IX

VIOLATION OF ARTICLE 21

RIGHT TO PRIVATE PROPERTY ...

Considerations of the Court

Article 21 of the American Convention recognizes the right to private [*sic*] property. In this regard, it establishes: a) that "[e]veryone has the right to the use and enjoyment of his property"; b) that such use and enjoyment can be subordinate, according to a legal mandate, to "social interest"; c) that a person may be deprived of his or her property for reasons of "public utility or social interest, and in the cases and according to the forms established by law"; and d) that when so deprived, a just compensation must be paid.

"Property" can be defined as those material things which can be possessed, as well as any right which may be part of a person's patrimony; that concept includes all movables and immovables, corporeal and incorporeal elements and any other intangible object capable of having value.

During the study and consideration of the preparatory work for the American Convention on Human Rights, the phrase "[e]veryone has the right to the use and enjoyment of private property, but the law may subordinate its use and enjoyment to public interest" was replaced by "[e]veryone has the right to the use and enjoyment of his property. The law may subordinate such use and enjoyment to the social interest." In other words, it was decided to refer to the "use and enjoyment of his property" instead of "private property."[57]

The terms of an international human rights treaty have an autonomous meaning, for which reason they cannot be made equivalent to the meaning given to them in domestic law. Furthermore, such human rights treaties are live instruments whose interpretation must adapt to the evolution of the times and, specifically, to current living conditions....

---

57. The right to private property was one of the most widely debated points within the Commission during the study and appraisal of the preparatory work for the American Convention on Human Rights. From the start, delegations expressed the existence of three ideological trends, i.e.: a trend to suppress from the draft text any reference to property rights; another trend to include the text in the Convention as submitted, and a third, compromise position which would strengthen the social function of property. Ultimately, the prevailing criterion was to include the right to property in the text of the Convention.

Through an evolutionary interpretation of international instruments for the protection of human rights, taking into account applicable norms of interpretation and pursuant to article 29(b) of the Convention—which precludes a restrictive interpretation of rights— it is the opinion of this Court that article 21 of the Convention protects the right to property in a sense which includes, among others, the rights of members of the indigenous communities within the framework of communal property, which is also recognized by the Constitution of Nicaragua....

Among indigenous peoples there is a communitarian tradition regarding a communal form of collective property of the land, in the sense that ownership of the land is not centered on an individual but rather on the group and its community. Indigenous groups, by the fact of their very existence, have the right to live freely in their own territory; the close ties of indigenous people with the land must be recognized and understood as the fundamental basis of their cultures, their spiritual life, their integrity, and their economic survival. For indigenous communities, relations to the land are not merely a matter of possession and production but a material and spiritual element which they must fully enjoy, even to preserve their cultural legacy and transmit it to future generations....

Indigenous peoples' customary law must be especially taken into account for the purpose of this analysis. As a result of customary practices, possession of the land should suffice for indigenous communities lacking real title to property of the land to obtain official recognition of that property, and for consequent registration....

Nicaragua recognizes communal property of indigenous peoples, but has not regulated the specific procedure to materialize that recognition, and therefore no such title deeds have been granted since 1990. Furthermore, in the instant case the State has not objected to the claim of the Awas Tingni Community to be declared owner, even though the extent of the area claimed is disputed.

It is the opinion of the Court that, pursuant to article 5 of the Constitution of Nicaragua, the members of the Awas Tingni Community have a communal property right to the lands they currently inhabit, without detriment to the rights of other indigenous communities. Nevertheless, the Court notes that the limits of the territory on which that property right exists have not been effectively delimited and demarcated by the State. This situation has created a climate of constant uncertainty among the members of the Awas Tingni Community, insofar as they do not know for certain how far their communal property extends geographically and, therefore, they do not know until where they can freely use and enjoy their respective property. Based on this understanding, the Court considers that the members of the Awas Tingni Community have the right that the State

a) carry out the delimitation, demarcation, and titling of the territory belonging to the Community; and

b) abstain from carrying out, until that delimitation, demarcation, and titling have been done, actions that might lead the agents of the State itself, or third parties acting with its acquiescence or its tolerance, to affect the existence, value, use or enjoyment of the property located in the geographical area where the members of the Community live and carry out their activities....

[T]he Court believes that, in light of article 21 of the Convention, the State has violated the right of the members of the Mayagna Awas Tingni Community to the use and enjoyment of their property, and that it has granted concessions to third parties to utilize the property and resources located in an area which could correspond, fully or in part, to the lands which must be delimited, demarcated, and titled....

XI
APPLICATION OF ARTICLE 63(1) ...

Considerations of the Court ...

[P]ursuant to article 2 of the American Convention on Human Rights, this Court considers that the State must adopt the legislative, administrative, and any other measures required to create an effective mechanism for delimitation, demarcation, and titling of the property of indigenous communities, in accordance with their customary law, values, customs and mores. Furthermore, as a consequence of the aforementioned violations of rights protected by the Convention in the instant case, the Court rules that the State must carry out the delimitation, demarcation, and titling of the corresponding lands of the members of the Awas Tingni Community, within a maximum term of 15 months, with full participation by the Community and taking into account its customary law, values, customs and mores. Until the delimitation, demarcation, and titling of the lands of the members of the Community have been carried out, Nicaragua must abstain from acts which might lead the agents of the State itself, or third parties acting with its acquiescence or its tolerance, to affect the existence, value, use or enjoyment of the property located in the geographic area where the members of the Awas Tingni Community live and carry out their activities.

The Court considers that due to the situation in which the members of the Awas Tingni Community find themselves due to lack of delimitation, demarcation, and titling of their communal property, the immaterial damage caused must also be repaired, by way of substitution, through a monetary compensation.... [T]he Court considers that the State must invest, as reparation for the immaterial damages, in the course of 12 months, the total sum of US$ 50,000 (fifty thousand United States dollars) in works or services of collective interest for the benefit of the Awas Tingni Community, by common agreement with the Community and under the supervision of the Inter-American Commission....

Joint Separate Opinion of Judges A.A. CANÇADO TRINDADE, M. PACHECO GÓMEZ and A. ABREU BURELLI

We, the undersigned Judges, ... feel obliged to add the brief reflections that follow, about one of its central aspects, namely, the *intertemporal dimension* of the communal form of property prevailing among the members of the indigenous communities....

As one of the members of the Community referred to pointed out in his testimony in the public hearing before the Court....

> Our grandparents lived in this hill, they then had had as their small animals ... the monkeys. The utensils of war of our ancestors, our grandparents, were the arrows. There they are stored.... We maintain our history, since our grandparents. That is why we have [it] as Sacred Hill.... Asangpas Muigeni is spirit of the hill, is of equal form to a human [being], but is a spirit [who] always lives under the hills....

As it can be inferred from the testimonies and expertises rendered in the aforementioned public hearing, the Community has a tradition contrary to the privatization and the commercialization and sale (or rent) of the natural resources (and their exploitation). The communal concept of the land—including as a spiritual place—and its natural resources form part of their customary law; their link with the territory, even if not written, integrates their day-to-day life, and the right to communal property itself has a cultural dimension. In sum, the habitat forms an integral part of their culture, transmitted from generation to generation....

Without the effective use and enjoyment of [their lands], they would be deprived of practicing, conserving and revitalizing their cultural habits, which give a meaning to their own existence, both individual and communitarian. The feeling which can be inferred is in the sense that, just as the land they occupy belongs to them, they in turn belong to their land.... Hence, moreover, the necessary prevalence that they attribute to the element of conservation over the simple exploitation of natural resources.... The concern with the element of conservation reflects a cultural manifestation of the integration of the human being with nature and the world wherein he lives. This integration, we believe, is projected into both space and time, as we relate ourselves, in space, with the natural system of which we are part and that we ought to treat with care, and, in time, with other generations (past and future), in respect of which we have obligations....

This communal conception, besides the values underlying it, has a cosmovision of its own, and an important intertemporal dimension, in bringing to the fore the bonds of human solidarity that link those who are alive with their dead and with the ones who are still to come.

[Judge Montiel Argüello dissented on the ground that an adequate procedure existed in Nicaragua for the Awas Tingni community to apply for land titles.]

Questions and Discussion

1. *The living, breathing law.* The Court states that human rights treaties are "live instruments." Should all law be treated as a live instrument? Is there anything in particular about human rights law that makes it more appropriate to be viewed as a live instrument? How about international law?

2. *Tribal community compared to Western fences.* How does the Court address the "social function of property"? How do differing views on the role of property in various societies affect the interpretation of international instruments? What problems are there when applying Western ideas of property to communal societies?

3. *Monetary compensation.* How appropriate is monetary compensation in environmental and human rights cases? How should damages be proven? Should damages have to be proven?

4. *Eminent domain.* Article 21 § 2 states, "No one shall be deprived of his property except upon payment of just compensation, for reasons of public utility or social interest, and in the cases and according to the forms established by law." Can this state power of eminent domain over lands belonging to indigenous groups be used for private development? What "social interests" should be considered in such a proceeding?

5. *Reach of the decision.* In *Awas Tingni*, what was the basis for the Court's expansion of the concept of "his property" beyond the formal holding of title to the more informal usage of land by indigenous people? Was this ruling based on the intent of the drafters of the American Convention, the policy views of the judges ("evolutionary interpretation"), the natural rights of indigenous peoples, the legislation of Nicaragua, the indigenous peoples' customary laws, or some combination? In a future case, if a nation does not have similar legislation or the indigenous peoples involved do not have similar customary laws, can the nation deal with land anyway that it chooses? In other words, which elements of the Court's decision on Article 21 are necessarily precedential for future cases involving other countries in the Americas?

6. *The definition of property.* The Court states that property can include "any other intangible object capable of having value." How could this be used in other cases involved in human rights and the environment? For instance, if a state party to the Convention pro-

vides a constitutional right to clean air or water, could that right be combined with this interpretation of property to constitute a violation of Article 21? Could floating or land-locked ice used by indigenous peoples in the Arctic for hunting seals and polar bears be considered "property" under this definition?

7. *Rights that travel through time.* How does the concurring opinion link the concepts of communal property, a spiritual dimension of such property, and the concept of intergenerational equity? Does the concept of intergenerational equity create enforceable "rights" to be held in the present by future generations? Is the recognition of such rights possible only under a regime of communal property and spiritual significance?

8. *Imposition of provisional measures.* In 2002, upon complaint by the Mayagna Community that Nicaragua was not carrying out the 2001 decision and that logging was continuing, the Inter-American Court found "the existence of a situation of extreme gravity and urgency regarding the property of the Mayagna Community." It issued an Order for "provisional measures," which in international human rights law is akin to an injunction. It ordered the State of Nicaragua to prevent third parties (such as the logging company) from causing irreparable damage until demarcation and titling indigenous lands is carried out, to allow the community to participate in the planning and implementation of demarcation, and to report every two months on progress to the Court. *Comunidad Mayagna (Sumo) Awas Tingni Case*, Order of the Court of September 6, 2002, Inter-Am. Ct. H.R., available at http://www.corteidh.or.cr/docs/medidas/mayagna_se_01_ing.pdf.

9. *Demarcation enables partial reparation.* In January 2003, the Nicaraguan National Assembly adopted new indigenous land demarcation laws. Maps documenting the community's demographics and traditional land tenure were completed in 2004. In 2007, according to the *Boletín Informativo El Caso Awas Tingni v. Nicaragua*, from the University of Arizona's Indigenous Peoples Law & Policy Program, the Northern Autonomous Regional Council of the North Atlantic (CRAAN) ratified a resolution of its Demarcation Commission for the first 20,000 hectares (about 50,000 acres) to be handed over to Awas Tingni by the government institution that is in charge of the actual delimitation, demarcation, and titling process. About 50,000 more hectares are also expected to be included.

10. *Lifting of provisional measures.* In 2007, a new panel of judges on the Court (with only one of the original judges still serving) ended the Court's "Provisional Measures regarding ... the Mayagna (Sumo) Awas Tingni Community," while stating that it would "continue monitoring." Order of the Inter-American Court of Human Rights, *Provisional Measures regarding Nicaragua Case of the Mayagna (Sumo) Awas Tingni Community*, Nov. 26, 2007, available at http://www.corteidh.or.cr/docs/medidas/mayagna_se_02_ing.pdf. The Court took this action despite claims by the Awas Tingi Community that Nicaragua had stalled on granting legal titles and that incursions on the property had continued, including one man selling "10,000 hectares ... to 20 mestizo families." They also claimed that the state was not preventing the illegal felling of trees nor punishing those who engaged in it. The Inter-American Commission similarly criticized the lack of action in the face of illegal tree-cutting and said that the "progress regarding the measures ordered has been tardy and insufficient." Despite this, the Court said:

> [N]ow that more than five years have elapsed since the adoption of the provisional measures, the Court has assessed the different State reports and the observations of the representatives and the Commission concerning the measures adopted to protect the ownership of the ancestral lands of the members of the

Awas Tigni Community, and observes that the information provided is closely related to compliance with the judgment of August 31, 2001.

Id. The Court ruled that monitoring would accomplish its goals, and it was unnecessary to maintain the provisional measures.

11. *The right to remain isolated.* Do remote, isolated tribes possess a human right not to be contacted by the outside world? Can they possess such a right if they do not know about, and have never been contacted by, the outside world? If they do, should that right be enforceable by governments or nongovernmental organizations? Should it be strong enough to prohibit people from entering the territory where they live, including both profit-making companies and religious or social missionaries? Should it be enforceable against a government that gives a permit for such activities? Survival International, a London-based organization, estimates that about 15 different isolated tribes exist in the Amazonian region of Peru. Survival International, *Isolated Indians in Peru* (2006). In 2007, the Inter-American Commission on Human Rights urged the Peruvian government to "adopt the necessary measures to guarantee the lives and personal integrity of members of the Mashco-Piro, Yora, and Amahuaca tribes living in voluntary isolation in the Madre de Dios department" of Peru. Peru's Ombudsman issued a report stating, "The government must not allow any organisation to explore for or exploit hydrocarbons if it endangers tribal peoples living in isolation, due to their particular vulnerability." http://www.survival-international.org/news/2365.

Many members of the N'djuka, from the South American country of Suriname, were massacred in the village of Moiwana in 1986 and lost their traditional territory. Although the massacre occurred before Suriname signed onto the Convention, the consequences of the massacre continued, placing governmental actions (or inactions) under the Court's jurisdiction.

The N'djuka believed they had to honor the remains of their dead and obtain justice for the manner of their families' deaths, or the spirits would remain displeased. Besides the spirits, the N'djuka feared more earthly reprisals if they were to return to Moiwana. An investigator, Inspector Gooding, was murdered as he began to uncover the secrets of the massacre, and Suriname never completed the investigation. In addition, many of the Moiwana community languished in cities, French Guiana, and a "temporary reception center."

In the following case, the Inter-American Court of Human Rights ruled that because Suriname had never restored what remains they could of the deceased N'djuka, had never completed an investigation and prosecution of those responsible for the massacre, and had put the N'djuka in fear of returning to their village, Suriname had, in effect, denied the N'djuka the right to their traditional territory.

Moiwana Community v. Suriname (I)

Inter-American Court of Human Rights
Inter-Am. Ct. H.R. (Ser. C) No. 124 (15 June 2005).

XI
VIOLATION OF ARTICLE 21
RIGHT TO PROPERTY ...

In the preceding chapter regarding Article 22 of the Convention, the Court held that the State's failure to carry out an effective [including the clarification of facts and punishment of the responsible parties] investigation into the events of November 29, 1986, ... has directly prevented the Moiwana community members from voluntarily returning to live in their traditional lands. Thus, Suriname has failed to both establish the conditions, as well as provide the means, that would allow the community members to live once again in safety and in peace in their ancestral territory; in consequence, Moiwana Village has been abandoned since the 1986 attack....

The relationship of an indigenous community with its land must be recognized and understood as the fundamental basis of its culture, spiritual life, integrity, and economic survival. For such peoples, their communal nexus with the ancestral territory is not merely a matter of possession and production, but rather consists in material and spiritual elements that must be fully integrated and enjoyed by the community, so that it may preserve its cultural legacy and pass it on to future generations....

[T]he Moiwana community members, a N'djuka tribal people, possess an "all-encompassing relationship" to their traditional lands, and their concept of ownership regarding that territory is not centered on the individual, but rather on the community as a whole. Thus, this Court's holding with regard to indigenous communities and their communal rights to property under Article 21 of the Convention must also apply to the tribal Moiwana community members: their traditional occupancy of Moiwana Village and its surrounding lands—which has been recognized and respected by neighboring N'djuka clans and indigenous communities over the years—should suffice to obtain State recognition of their ownership. The precise boundaries of that territory, however, may only be determined after due consultation with said neighboring communities....

The facts demonstrate, nevertheless, that they have been deprived of this right to the present day as a result of the events of November 1986 and the State's subsequent failure to investigate those occurrences adequately....

[T]he Court concludes that Suriname violated the right of the Moiwana community members to the communal use and enjoyment of their traditional property. In consequence, the Tribunal holds that the State violated Article 21 of the American Convention, in relation to Article 1(1) of that treaty, to the detriment of the Moiwana community members.

Unhappy with the Court decision above, Suriname filed a "Request for Interpretation" (Interpretation of the June 15, 2005 Judgment on the Preliminary Objections, Merits and Reparations), purportedly under Article 67 of the American Convention on Human Rights. The Court replied as follows.

Moiwana Community v. Suriname (II)

Inter-American Court of Human Rights
Inter-Am Ct. H.R. (Ser. C) No. 145 (8 February 2006)

V
ADMISSIBILITY ...

Article 67 of the Convention provides:

The judgment of the Court shall be final and not subject to appeal. In case of disagreement as the meaning or scope of the judgment, the Court shall interpret it at the request of any of the parties, provided the request is made within ninety days from the date of notification of the judgment.

Article 29(3) of the Rules of Procedure provides:

Judgments and orders of the Court may not be contested in any way....

Rather than expressing a lack of precision or clarity in the meaning or scope of the judgment, the State's arguments merely express its disagreement with certain aspects of that judgment, or with certain Rules or procedures of this Court. In fact, Suriname's request explicitly states its view that the faculty of requesting an interpretation gives "parties that disagree with the judgment the opportunity to petition your [...] Court." This view is not substantiated by the Convention, by the Court's Rules of Procedure, or by its case law....

In this regard, the Court deems pertinent to point out that, by recognizing the right of the Moiwana community members to the use and enjoyment of their traditional lands, the Court has not made any determination as to the appropriate boundaries of the territory in question. Rather, in order to render effective "the property rights of the members of the Moiwana community in relation to the traditional territories from which they were expelled," and having acknowledged the lack of "formal legal title," the Court has directed the State, as a measure of reparation, to "adopt such legislative, administrative and other measures as are necessary to ensure" those rights, after due consultation with the neighboring communities. If said rights are to be properly ensured, the measures to be taken must naturally include "the delimitation, demarcation and titling of said traditional territories," with the participation and informed consent of the victims as expressed through their representatives, the members of the other Cottica N'djuka villages and the neighboring indigenous communities. In this case, the Court has simply left the designation of the territorial boundaries in question to "an effective mechanism" of the State's design.

Separate Opinion of Judge A.A. Cançado Trindade

I have concurred with my vote to the adoption of the present Judgment of the Inter-American Court of Human Rights, regarding the request for interpretation of the Judgment on the case of *Moiwana Community versus Suriname*....

In the present Separate Opinion I am only referring to the question ... to which I attribute the most relevance: the delimitation, demarcation, titling and the return of land to the victims and their families, as a form of reparation....

I. Delimitation, Demarcation, Titling and the Return of Land as a Form of Reparation....

By means of delimitation, demarcation, titling, in the circumstances of the *cas d'espèce*, the effective protection (*effet utile*) of the rights guaranteed in Articles 21 and 22 of the American Convention is ensured. This latter is implicit under Article 33 (prohibition of *refoulement*) of the Convention on the Status of Refugees of 1951....

[In] *Community Mayagna Awas Tingni versus Nicaragua* (Judgment of 8/31/2001), the application ... claimed, for the first time in the history of the Tribunal, the lack of demarcation of the lands possessed by that Community, as well as the lack of an effective procedure in Nicaragua for the demarcation of those lands. The Court ordered ... the creation of "an effective mechanism for delimitation, demarcation and titling of the properties of the indigenous communities, in accordance with their customary laws, values, uses and customs." That Judgment forms part of the specialized juridical bibliography, and constitutes a landmark in the Court's jurisprudence regarding the question at issue. [Note: the edited version of *Awas Tingni* in this book omits the discussion of titling and Article 25 of the Convention.]

Subsequently, in the case of *Yakye Axa Indigenous Community versus Paraguay* (Judgment of 6/16/2005), ... [t]he Court ... recognized the linking of the "right to community property of the indigenous communities over their traditional territories and the natural resources linked to their culture" with the term [property] as contained in Article 21 of the Convention, and gave value to the guarantee of traditional expressions, customary law, the values and philosophy of those communities, and ordered the State to "identify the traditional territory of the members of the indigenous community of Yakye Axa and provide this free of charge."

Additionally, in the case of *Moiwana Community versus Suriname[I]*, ... the Court ordered that:

> [T]he State should adopt all the legislative and administrative measures and any others which are necessary to ensure the property rights of the members of the Moiwana Village in relation to the traditional territories from which they were expelled, and provide for the members' use and enjoyment of those territories. These measures shall include the creation of an effective mechanism for the delimitation, demarcation, and titling of said traditional territories....

I understand that the determination of the delimitation, demarcation, titling and return of the communal lands constitutes a legitimate and necessary form of non-pecuniary reparation ... in accordance with article 63(1) of the American Convention. It is not only a matter of *restitutio*, returning to the vulnerable *statu quo ante* of the victimized community, but also ensuring the *guarantee of non-repetition* of the harmful and especially grave events (the 1986 massacre).

II. THE GUARANTEE OF A VOLUNTARY AND SUSTAINABLE RETURN....

The delimitation, demarcation, and titling of the Community's lands [is] of fundamental importance, also to guarantee a *sustainable return*....

Since return—evidently voluntary—was not dealt with by the Convention on the [Status] of Refugees of 1951 nor by its Protocol of 1967, the specialized doctrine has given considerable attention to the question in the last few years, in order to address the new needs of protection of the human being. In Latin America, the issue has not passed unnoticed by the Declarations of Cartagena (1984), San José of Costa Rica (1994) and Mexico (2004), regarding refugees and displaced persons.... I am of the conviction that the Inter-American Court cannot remain indifferent or insensitive to it....

In the present case of the *Moiwana Community* the issue of the *return* ... brings to the forefront the issues of delimitation, demarcation and titling of the community's territories ordered by the Court.... The UNHCR has included it in ... Global Consultations on International Protection.... [P]articular concern was expressed [for] ... the sustainability of the return, which includes attention to, *inter alia*, aspects regarding land ownership....

III. THE NEED FOR RECONSTRUCTION AND PRESERVATION OF CULTURAL IDENTITY.

The Inter-American Court has recognized ... the relationship between the N'djuka community with their traditional territory as of "vital spiritual, cultural and material importance," even in preserving the "integrity and identity" of their culture. The Court has warned that "larger territorial land rights are vested in the entire people, according to N'djuka custom; community members consider such rights to exist in perpetuity and to be unalienable."

In my Separate Opinion.... I referred to the occurrence of a truly *spiritual damage* and, beyond damages to the *project of life*, I dared to elaborate conceptually on the *damages to the project of after-life*.

The Inter-American Court should, in my opinion, *say what the law is*, and not simply limit itself to resolving a matter in controversy.... [T]he Court should respond to a specific portion of Suriname's request ... and demonstrate—above all convince the State of—the imperious necessity to repair the *spiritual damages* suffered by the N'djukas ... and create conditions for a speedy reconstruction of their cultural tradition.

Accordingly, I find delimitation, demarcation, titling and the return of their traditional territories indeed essential.... Only then will their fundamental right to life *lato sensu* be rightfully protected, including their right to cultural identity.

The *universal juridical conscience*, which is, in my understanding, the *material* source of all Law, has evolved in such a manner that it recognizes this urgent need. It is illustrated in the significant triad of the Conventions of UNESCO, formed by the 1972 Convention concerning the Protection of the World Cultural and Natural Heritage [and two others]....

The 2003 UNESCO Convention [for the Safeguarding of the Intangible Cultural Heritage] seeks the safeguard of the *intangible cultural heritage* (for this it invokes the international instruments on human rights), and conceptualizes this latter as "the practices, representations, expressions, knowledge, skills ... that communities, groups, and in some cases individuals, recognize as part of their cultural heritage."

The recent 2005 UNESCO Convention [on the Protection and Promotion of the Diversity of Cultural Expressions] ... [stated] the idea of cultural diversity as a *common heritage of humanity*, explaining that "culture takes diverse forms across time and space" and this diversity is incorporated "in the uniqueness and plurality of the identities and cultural expressions of the peoples and societies making up humanity." The Convention added that cultural diversity can only be protected and promoted through the safeguard of human rights.

It is my understanding that the universal juridical conscience has evolved towards a clear recognition of the relevance of cultural diversity for the universality of human rights, and vice-versa. Additionally it has evolved toward the *humanization* of International Law, and the creation, at this beginning of the XXI century, of a new *jus gentium*, a new International Law for humankind.... [T]he aforementioned triad of UNESCO Conventions (of 1972, 2003, and 2005) are ... one of the ... manifestations of the human conscience to this effect.

IV. Conclusion....

The Court interprets and applies the American Convention, and not Suriname's regulations on *land rights*. If these internal regulations present obstacles to compliance with the reparation measures ordered by the Court, those obstacles should be removed, and national regulations relative to *land rights* should be harmonized with the American Convention, in a manner which provides reparations to all those victimized....

I hope, with this, to clarify the doubts respectfully presented to the Court by Suriname at the end of its written brief of 10/4/2005....

V. Epilogue: A Brief Metajuridical Reflection.

I would like to conclude this Separate Opinion with a brief reflection of a metajuridical character....

One cannot live in constant exile and displacement. Human beings share a spiritual need for roots. They cannot eternally float around a virtual world.... [M]embers of traditional communities attribute particular value on their land, which they consider belongs to them, and ... they "belong" to their lands....

On my part I cannot avoid the impression today that the "post-modernists" — enthusiastic, with their self-sufficient attitude, and with the frenzy of material "progress," — cannot even understand in a minimal form the world in which they live, their own environment. I have therefrom cultivated a respect for traditional cultures of those persecuted and forgotten by the world, — including the peoples of the Amazon forest....

The ancient, and unduly called "primitive" peoples, had a full awareness of their own vulnerability, and that was how their spirituality was developed, and their intimate co-existence with their own dead. On the other hand, the "post-modernists," ... upon freeing themselves from the cyclical time, integrated themselves into history, and ... became prisoners of their own unfounded belief in linear progression carried through with technological advances. They minimized the search for regeneration, attempted to avoid or to minimize human suffering through the search of material comfort (instead of accepting suffering, assuming it and intending to draw lessons from it), they stopped revering their dead, and cultivating their personal and collective memory.

It seems that they did not even learn from the tragedies of the atrocities of the contemporary world. They continue to be petrified before their electronic devices, obtaining a mass of information that they are not able to evaluate. It seems they have lost their memory, which is what liberates and saves one's identity. On the other hand, the present case of the N'djukas, ... rich in teachings, has salvaged the importance of the preservation of cultural expressions, as a form of communication of human beings with the same unsolvable mystery of the outside world, as well as cultivating the personal and collective memory, of a healthy co-existence of the living with their dead and of the imperative primacy of justice and respect of human relations, of the living *inter se*, and of them with their dead.

Questions and Discussion

1. *Traditional territory and return.* Why does Judge Cançado Trindade's separate opinion stress the importance of the delimitation, demarcation, and titling of the traditional indigenous territory? He argues that a return of indigenous territory would restore the N'djuka's very right to life, which in turn would help foster "justice and respect of human relations." Is there an implicit respect for the environment in this sentiment?

2. *Culture, progress, and memory.* Does the Judge's reference to post-modern people, "prisoners of their own unfounded belief in linear progression carried through with technological advances," contain an implicit challenge to the ability of non-indigenous judges or lawyers to develop an adequate jurisprudence of indigenous rights? Or are non-indigenous, post-modern persons, with their rationality and abandonment of myth and memory, more suited to do such work? Should legal teams who litigate in the Inter-American Court of Human Rights on behalf of indigenous peoples consist entirely of one type or the other?

———————

The Inter-American Court on Human Rights further defined the property rights of indigenous peoples in *Saramaka People v. Suriname*. Suriname sold logging and mining concessions on the Saramaka's traditional territory, without consulting this indigenous community. The Saramaka are, like the N'djuka, descendants of slaves who escaped into the forest.

Saramaka People v. Suriname
Inter-American Court of Human Rights
Inter-Am Ct. H.R. (Ser. C) No. 172 (28 November 2007)

VII
NON-COMPLIANCE WITH ARTICLE ... 21 (RIGHT TO PROPERTY) AND 25
(RIGHT TO JUDICIAL PROTECTION) OF THE AMERICAN CONVENTION ...

D. The right of the members of the Saramaka people to use and enjoy the natural resources that lie on and within their traditionally owned territory ...

In accordance with this Court's jurisprudence as stated in the *Yakye Axa* and *Sawhoya-maxa* cases, members of tribal and indigenous communities have the right to own the natural resources they have traditionally used within their territory for the same reasons that they have a right to own the land they have traditionally used and occupied for centuries. Without them, the very physical and cultural survival of such peoples is at stake. Hence the need to protect the lands and resources they have traditionally used to prevent their extinction as a people....

E. The State's grant of concessions for the exploration and extraction of natural resources found on and within Saramaka territory ...

E.2) Safeguards against restrictions on the right to property that deny the survival of the Saramaka people ...

Thus, in accordance with Article 1(1) of the Convention, in order to guarantee that restrictions to the property rights of the members of the Saramaka people by the issuance of concessions within their territory do not amount to a denial of their survival as a tribal people, the State must abide by the following three safeguards: First, the State must ensure the effective participation of the members of the Saramaka people, in conformity with their customs and traditions, regarding any development, investment, exploration or extraction plan (hereinafter "development or investment plan")[127] within Saramaka territory. Second, the State must guarantee that the Saramakas will receive a reasonable benefit from any such plan within their territory. Thirdly, the State must ensure that no concession will be issued within Saramaka territory unless and until independent and technically capable entities, with the State's supervision, perform a prior environmental and social impact assessment. These safeguards are intended to preserve, protect and guarantee the special relationship that the members of the Saramaka community have with their territory, which in turn ensures their survival as a tribal people....

Article 32 of the United Nations Declaration on the Rights of Indigenous Peoples, which was recently approved by the UN General Assembly with the support of the State of Suriname, states the following:

1. Indigenous peoples have the right to determine and develop priorities and strategies for the development or use of their lands or territories and other resources.

2. States shall consult and cooperate in good faith with the indigenous peoples concerned through their own representative institutions in order to obtain their free and informed consent prior to the approval of any project affecting their

---

127. By "development or investment plan" the Court means any proposed activity that may affect the integrity of the lands and natural resources within the territory of the Saramaka people, particularly any proposal to grant logging or mining concessions.

lands or territories and other resources, particularly in connection with the development, utilization or exploitation of mineral, water or other resources.

3. States shall provide effective mechanisms for just and fair redress for any such activities, and appropriate measures shall be taken to mitigate adverse environmental, economic, social, cultural or spiritual impact....

[T]he Court considers that the actual scope of the guarantees concerning consultation and sharing of the benefits of development or investment projects requires further clarification.

E.2.a) Right to consultation, and where applicable, a duty to obtain consent

First, the Court has stated that in ensuring the effective participation of members of the Saramaka people in development or investment plans within their territory, the State has a duty to actively consult with said community according to their customs and traditions. This duty requires the State to both accept and disseminate information, and entails constant communication between the parties. These consultations must be in good faith, through culturally appropriate procedures and with the objective of reaching an agreement. Furthermore, the Saramakas must be consulted, in accordance with their own traditions, at the early stages of a development or investment plan, not only when the need arises to obtain approval from the community, if such is the case. Early notice provides time for internal discussion within communities and for proper feedback to the State. The State must also ensure that members of the Saramaka people are aware of possible risks, including environmental and health risks, in order that the proposed development or investment plan is accepted knowingly and voluntarily. Finally, consultation should take account of the Saramaka people's traditional methods of decision-making.

Additionally, the Court considers that, regarding large-scale development or investment projects that would have a major impact within Saramaka territory, the State has a duty, not only to consult with the Saramakas, but also to obtain their free, prior, and informed consent, according to their customs and traditions. The Court considers that the difference between "consultation" and "consent" in this context requires further analysis.

In this sense, the U.N. Special Rapporteur on the situation of human rights and fundamental freedoms of indigenous people has similarly observed that:

> [w]herever [large-scale projects] occur in areas occupied by indigenous peoples it is likely that their communities will undergo profound social and economic changes that are frequently not well understood, much less foreseen, by the authorities in charge of promoting them. [...] The principal human rights effects of these projects for indigenous peoples relate to loss of traditional territories and land, eviction, migration and eventual resettlement, depletion of resources necessary for physical and cultural survival, destruction and pollution of the traditional environment, social and community disorganization, long-term negative health and nutritional impacts as well as, in some cases, harassment and violence.

Consequently, the U.N. Special Rapporteur determined that "[f]ree, prior and informed consent is essential for the [protection of] human rights of indigenous peoples in relation to major development projects." ...

[I]n addition to the consultation that is always required when planning development or investment projects within traditional Saramaka territory, the safeguard of effective participation that is necessary when dealing with major development or investment plans that may have a profound impact on the property rights of the members of the Saramaka people to a large part of their territory must be understood to additionally require the free, prior, and informed consent of the Saramakas, in accordance with their traditions and customs.

E.2.b) Benefit-sharing

The second safeguard the State must ensure when considering development or investment plans within Saramaka territory is that of reasonably sharing the benefits of the project with the Saramaka people....

The Court considers that the right to obtain compensation under Article 21(2) of the Convention extends not only to the total deprivation of property title by way of expropriation by the State, for example, but also to the deprivation of the regular use and enjoyment of such property. In the present context, the right to obtain "just compensation" pursuant to Article 21(2) of the Convention translates into a right of the members of the Saramaka people to reasonably share in the benefits made as a result of a restriction or deprivation of their right to the use and enjoyment of their traditional lands and of those natural resources necessary for their survival....

F. The fulfillment of the guarantees established under international law in relation to the concessions already granted by the State ...

[T]he Court concludes the following: first, that the members of the Saramaka people have a right to use and enjoy the natural resources that lie on and within their traditionally owned territory that are necessary for their survival; second, that the State may restrict said right by granting concessions for the exploration and extraction of natural resources found on and within Saramaka territory only if the State ensures the effective participation and benefit of the Saramaka people, performs or supervises prior environmental and social impact assessments, and implements adequate safeguards and mechanisms in order to ensure that these activities do not significantly affect the traditional Saramaka lands and natural resources; and finally, that the concessions already issued by the State did not comply with these safeguards. Thus, the Court considers that the State has violated Article 21 of the Convention, in conjunction with Article 1 of such instrument, to the detriment of the members of the Saramaka people.

Questions and Discussion

1. *Consent.* What were the three conditions attached to the definition of "consent" in the *Saramaka* decision? What new authority bolstered the Court's inclusion of these conditions?

2. *Effective participation.* Why did the Court add "effective" to "participation"?

3. Judge Cançado Trindade was not on the bench for the *Saramaka* decision. Would he approve?

B. African Charter on Human and Peoples' Rights

AFRICAN CHARTER ON HUMAN AND PEOPLES' RIGHTS
June 27, 1981
O.A.U. Doc. CAB/LEG/67/3 rev. 5; 21 I.L.M. 58 (1982)

Article 4

Human beings are inviolable. Every human being shall be entitled to respect for his life and the integrity of his person. No one may be arbitrarily deprived of this right.

Article 17 . . .

2. Every individual may freely, take part in the cultural life of his community.

3. The promotion and protection of morals and traditional values recognized by the community shall be the duty of the State. . . .

Article 21

1. All peoples shall freely dispose of their wealth and natural resources. This right shall be exercised in the exclusive interest of the people. In no case shall a people be deprived of it. . . .

5. States Parties to the present Charter shall undertake to eliminate all forms of foreign economic exploitation particularly that practised by international monopolies so as to enable their peoples to fully benefit from the advantages derived from their national resources.

Social and Economic Rights Action Center v. Nigeria
African Commission on Human and Peoples' Rights
Case No. ACHPR/Comm/A044/1, Decision Regarding Comm. No. 155/96 (2001)

[Excerpts from this case regarding Article 16 and 24 are presented in Chapter 2, at page 55.]

Article 21 provides

[See previous excerpts.]

The origin of this provision may be traced to colonialism, during which the human and material resources of Africa were largely exploited for the benefit of outside powers, creating tragedy for Africans themselves, depriving them of their birthright and alienating them from the land. The aftermath of colonial exploitation has left Africa's precious resources and people still vulnerable to foreign misappropriation. The drafters of the Charter obviously wanted to remind African governments of the continent's painful legacy and restore co-operative economic development to its traditional place at the heart of African Society.

Governments have a duty to protect their citizens, not only through appropriate legislation and effective enforcement but also by protecting them from damaging acts that may be perpetrated by private parties. This duty calls for positive action on part of governments in fulfilling their obligation under human rights instruments. The practice before other tribunals also enhances this requirement as is evidenced in the case *Velàsquez Rodríguez v. Honduras*. In this landmark judgment, the Inter-American Court of Human Rights held that when a State allows private persons or groups to act freely and with impunity to the detriment of the rights recognised, it would be in clear violation of its obligations to protect the human rights of its citizens. Similarly, this obligation of the State is further emphasised in the practice of the European Court of Human Rights, in *X and Y v. Netherlands*. In that case, the Court pronounced that there was an obligation on authorities to take steps to make sure that the enjoyment of the rights is not interfered with by any other private person.

The Commission notes that in the present case, despite its obligation to protect persons against interferences in the enjoyment of their rights, the Government of Nigeria facilitated the destruction of the Ogoniland. Contrary to its Charter obligations and despite such internationally established principles, the Nigerian Government has given the green light to private actors, and the oil Companies in particular, to devastatingly affect the well-being of the Ogonis. By any measure of standards, its practice falls short of the minimum conduct expected of governments, and therefore, is in violation of Article 21 of the African Charter....

The Complainants also allege that the Nigerian Government has violated Article 4 of the Charter which guarantees the inviolability of human beings and everyone's right to life and integrity of the person respected. Given the wide spread violations perpetrated by the Government of Nigeria and by private actors (be it following its clear blessing or not), the most fundamental of all human rights, the right to life has been violated.... The pollution and environmental degradation to a level humanly unacceptable has made ... living in the Ogoni land a nightmare. The survival of the Ogonis depended on their land and farms that were destroyed by the direct involvement of the Government. These and similar brutalities not only persecuted individuals in Ogoniland but also the whole of the Ogoni Community as a whole. They affected the life of the Ogoni Society as a whole. The Commission conducted a mission to Nigeria from the 7th–14th March 1997 and witnessed first hand the deplorable situation in Ogoni land including the environmental degradation.

The uniqueness of the African situation and the special qualities of the African Charter on Human and Peoples' Rights imposes upon the African Commission an important task. International law and human rights must be responsive to African circumstances. Clearly, collective rights, environmental rights, and economic and social rights are essential elements of human rights in Africa. The African Commission will apply any of the diverse rights contained in the African Charter. It welcomes this opportunity to make clear that there is no right in the African Charter that cannot be made effective. As indicated in the preceding paragraphs, however, the Nigerian Government did not live up to the minimum expectations of the African Charter.

Questions and Discussion

1. *Compare.* Compare the Nigeria case to the *Ominayak* (Lubicon Lake Band) and *Awas Tingni* cases. Which takes the most expansive readings of the treaties they interpret?

2. *Enforcement.* Which institution (committee, court, or commission) seems most likely to be obeyed? Which remedies seem most likely to be achieved? What are some methods one might use to enforce indigenous rights?

3. *Peoples.* Note the use of the terms "peoples" and "a people" in Article 21. Could Article 21 have been interpreted to only apply to Nigeria as a whole, rather than to the Ogoni people within Nigeria, so that as long as the government of Nigeria was benefiting from its arrangements with foreign oil companies, an argument could be made that Article 21 was not violated?

4. *Life and environment.* In what way did the Commission turn Article 4 from being a provision dealing exclusively with violence to being one dealing with environmental degradation? How did it then turn Article 4 from being a provision concerned with *individual* life to one applying to the Ogoni "community" and "society" as a whole? Could this interpretive technique be useful under other conventions, in other regions, on behalf of indigenous peoples?

5. *Uniqueness.* Sometimes human rights are said to be a Western concept, inapplicable to other societies. In what way did the Commission turn this argument on its head, arguing that the special nature of the African situation called for broader human rights protections rather than narrower ones?

6. *Article 17.* Could you make an argument that the State also violated Article 17?

C. European Convention on Human Rights

On the Fringes of Europe: Europe's Largely Forgotten Indigenous Peoples

Rainer Grote
31 Am. Indian L. Rev. 425 (2006–7)

I. Introduction

The concept of "indigenous peoples" or "indigenous minorities" is rarely used with regard to the original inhabitants of certain territories in Europe which, at a later stage in history, were invaded, either belligerently or peacefully, by groups of different ethnic origin whose descendants today form the politically, economically and culturally dominant majority population of the respective territories. The reason for this absence of the indigenous peoples from the European discussion is not hard to detect. The plight of indigenous peoples in many parts of the world, especially in the Americas, Australia and New Zealand, is the result of the conquest and colonization of overseas territories by Europeans and their descendants from the late fifteenth century onward, a process which in some cases continued until the late nineteenth century. A similar process of internal colonization took place in Europe a long time ago. . . .

Although problems could, and did, result from the redrawing of political boundaries which took place from time to time as a result of war and conquest, these problems were not viewed in terms of protecting an "indigenous" way of life of the conquered population against the pervasive influence of their new rulers, but rather were viewed as protecting the existence and certain rights of religious minorities and, since the nineteenth century increasingly, of national minorities. While colonial expansion still took place in modern Europe, it was largely limited to the far north and the far east of Europe, such as the border areas of Norway, Sweden and Finland and to eastern ranges of Russia and later the Soviet Union.

It is therefore highly uncommon to speak of "indigenous peoples" when referring to certain native populations living in the center, the west and the south of Europe, even if some of them might prima facie fit the description of indigenous peoples in International Labour Organization Convention 169 (ILO Convention No. 169). . . .

Since there is a widespread consensus today that the recognized principles and standards of minority protection do not adequately reflect the specific needs and concerns of indigenous peoples, this means that there is a lack of adequate rules and procedures with regard to the protection of indigenous peoples at the European level. . . .

II. Indigenous Peoples in Europe

When the term "indigenous peoples" is used in the current European debate, it is mainly restricted to the native populations living at the far ends of Europe: the Saami people, who live in the far north of Finland, Norway, Sweden and Russia; the Inuit living in Greenland; and the forty or so indigenous groups living in the Russian North and Siberia, which form part of the "Common List of Indigenous Small Peoples of Russia" approved by the government of the Russian Federation in March 2000. . . .

While Norway and Finland have acknowledged the status of the Saami people as indigenous peoples of their countries in their reports to international human rights bodies like the Committee on the Elimination of Racial Discrimination (CERD), Sweden continues to deal with these indigenous people under the heading of "national minorities." In Norway, the Saami have been granted a constitutional right to preserve their culture [as well as] special statutory property rights in the northernmost province of Finland. Similarly, "[t]he Russian Federation guarantees the rights of small indigenous peoples in accordance with the generally accepted principles and standards of international law and international treaties of the Russian Federation." [Konstitutsiia Rossiiskoi Federatsii [Konst. RF] [Constitution] art. 69 (Russ. Federation), available at http:// www.russian.embassy.org/RUSSIA/CONSTIT/chapter3.htm] ... However, each State continues to apply its own national laws to the indigenous peoples living within its boundaries, which are administered by its respective domestic court systems. This makes it difficult to find and to apply coherent solutions for those indigenous groups who live and reside in different national territories, like the Inuit, who have settled in the Arctic regions of Alaska, Canada and Greenland, or the Saami, whose places of settlement are divided among Norway, Sweden, Finland and Northern Russia.

III. Limited Relevance of Existing Regional Instruments with Regard to the Protection of Indigenous Rights

A. European Convention on Human Rights

The first instrument to which one would turn for the protection of indigenous rights is the European Convention on Human Rights.... However, the European Convention was conceived in the immediate post-war period, at a time when the protection of minority and group rights was not on the international human rights agenda and was even viewed by many as an insurmountable obstacle to any successful attempt of establishing an effective international human rights monitoring regime. It is, therefore, not surprising that the European Convention reflects the highly individualistic approach to fundamental rights protection of the "classic" liberal tradition: the rights granted by the Convention are those of the individual, and not those of any particular group to which the individual belongs.

An indirect reference to group affiliations is found in Article 14, which prohibits discrimination of individuals in the exercise of their Convention rights on grounds of "sex, race, colour, language, religion, political or other opinion, national or social origin, association with a national minority, property, birth or other status." This provision indirectly protects the individual's freedom to associate with religious, national or social groups; an individual's membership in these groups may not be used as a justification to deny his or her Convention rights. But this protection is purely "negative;" it protects the individual against state interference in the individual's Convention rights which are based on the individual's membership status in a group. By no means does it protect the existence or the rights of the group itself.

Although the Convention has been amended by a series of protocols which have extended the number and scope of the substantive rights protected by the Convention, this has not involved any change in its basic approach to fundamental rights protection which remains focused on the individual and has little, if any, regard for the rights of the group. Some individual rights may still be used to defend certain indigenous practices or institutions, like the freedom of religion, the freedom of assembly, or even the right to property. However, so far, the Convention's impact on the protection of indigenous Peoples' Rights has been very limited, more limited than that of Article 27 of the UN Covenant on Civil and Political Rights, which has been used, at least in some cases, by domestic courts in order to protect Saami economic and cultural rights. [See page 154.] There is, as yet, no ruling by the European Court of Human Rights on the scope of the Convention rights with regard to indigenous peoples.

III. National Jurisprudence and Legal Systems

A. Indigenous Property Rights under National Jurisprudence

Aurelio Cal v. Atty. Gen. of Belize

Supreme Court of Belize

Claim 121/2007 (18 October 2007)

Before The HONOURABLE ABDULAI CONTEH, Chief Justice.

The Claimants and the Nature of their case ...

All the claimants ... are members of Maya communities in Southern Belize.

[T]he people of Santa Cruz and Conejo Villages ... claim that the customary land rights of the Maya people of Belize, including the claimants, have been recognized and affirmed as property by the Inter-American Commission on Human Rights in the case of the *Maya Indigenous Communities of the Toledo District v. Belize*....

The claimants allege as well that the Government of Belize has consistently failed to recognize and protect their property rights in the lands they and their ancestors have traditionally used and occupied; and that this failure to accord the same legal recognition and protection to Maya customary property rights unlike that extended to other forms of property is discriminatory and a violation of sections 3 and 16 of the Belize Constitution....

Finally the claimants claim that the Maya people live, farm, hunt and fish; collect medicinal plants, construction materials and other forest resources; and engage in ceremonies and other activities on land within and around their communities; and that these practices have evolved over centuries from patterns of land use and occupancy of the Maya people. They claim that the property rights that arise from these customary practices are critical to their physical and cultural survival....

The Defendants and their Defence

The ... claims are ... against the Government of Belize....

Issues Agreed upon by the Parties

1. Whether there exists, in Southern Belize, Maya customary land tenure.

2. Whether the members of the villages of Conejo and Santa Cruz have interests in land based on Maya customary land tenure and, if so, the nature of such interests.

3. If the members of the villages of Conejo and Santa Cruz have any interests in lands based on Maya customary land tenure:

    a) Whether such interests constitute "property" that is protected by sections 3(d) and 17 of the Constitution.

    b) Whether any government acts and omissions violate the claimants' rights to property in sections 3(d) and 17 of the Belize Constitution.

    c) Whether any government acts and omissions violate the claimants' right to equality guaranteed by sections 3 and 16 of the Constitution.

d) Whether any government acts and omissions violate the claimants' rights to life, liberty, security of the person and the protection of the law guaranteed under sections 3(a) and 4 of the Constitution.

The Evidence ...

[O]n 3rd December 1996, The Toledo Maya Cultural Council (TMCC) and the Toledo Alcaldes Association filed a motion in this court for constitutional redress, very much akin in substance, to the present claim. But for some inexplicable reason that action was never fully heard or concluded....

Undaunted, and not getting a satisfactory response to their claims from the Courts in Belize, the Toledo Maya Cultural Council on behalf of the Maya Indigenous Communities of the Toledo District, launched on 7th August 1998, a Petition to the Inter-American Commission on Human Rights....

[B]oth the Supreme Court Action No. 510 of 1996 and the Petition to the Inter-American Commission on Human Rights were prompted by logging concessions and oil exploration licences the Government of Belize had granted in the mid-1990s over parts of Toledo District....

The Inter-American Commission on Human Rights delivered its Report No. 40/04 in case 12.053, on the merits, on 12th October 2004.

The defendants have, however, in the written submissions of their learned attorney, taken exception to this Report....

1. Is there in existence in Southern Belize, Maya customary land tenure?

The main thrust of the claimants' case is their contention that there is in existence in the Toledo District, in Southern Belize, Maya customary land tenure system ... and that this form of tenure is or should be a form of property cognizable at law, and like any other form of property, is deserving of the constitutional protection afforded by the Belize Constitution to property.

I am ... satisfied that on the evidence, the claimants have established that there is in existence in Southern Belize in the Toledo District, particularly in the villages of Santa Cruz and Conejo, Maya customary land tenure.

I am fortified in this conclusion by the finding of the Inter-American Commission on Human Rights ... when it stated at paragraph 127 of its Report:

> 127. Based upon the arguments and evidence before it, the Commission is satisfied that the Mopan and Ke'kchi Maya people have demonstrated a communal property right to the lands that they currently inhabit in the Toledo District. These rights have arisen from the longstanding use and occupancy of the territory by the Maya people, which the parties have agreed pre-dated European colonization, and have extended to the use of the land and its resources for purposes relating to the physical and cultural survival of the Maya communities....

Importantly also, I find from the evidence in this case, that the Government of Belize, had given its *imprimatur* and explicit recognition of the rights of the Maya people to lands and resources in southern Belize based on their long-standing use and occupancy. This significant development was arrived at on 12th October, 2000 in an Agreement between the Government of Belize and the Toledo Maya Cultural Council, the Toledo Alcaldes' Association, the Kekchi Council of Belize, the Toledo Maya Women's Council and the Association of Village Council Chairpersons....

Clause 6 of this Ten-Point Agreement, I find, is a clear and unequivocal governmental endorsement of the existence of the Maya people's rights to land and resources in southern Belize based on their long-standing use and occupancy. This, I find is a clear affirmation of the existence of Maya customary land tenure in southern Belize....

2. Whether the members of the villages of Conejo and Santa Cruz have interests in land based on Maya customary land tenure and, if so, the nature of such interests ...

From the totality of the evidence in this case, I am persuaded and satisfied that members of [the] Conejo [and Santa Cruz] Village[s] have interests in lands in that village based on Maya customary land tenure....

From the available evidence, it is manifest that there was and always had been a Maya presence in what is today Southern Belize....

The Nature of the Claimants' interests in land based on Maya Customary Land Tenure

I now turn to the subsidiary but equally important question articulated in the second issue agreed upon, namely, the nature of the claimants' interests in land based on Maya customary land tenure.

In my considered view, I think the position regarding the determination or interpretation of customary title or interests in land was helpfully and, I dare say, authoritatively adumbrated by the Privy Council in ... *Amodu Tijani [v. The Secretary, Southern Nigeria* (1921) 2 AC 399], when Viscount Haldane delivering the judgment of the Board stated:

> Their Lordships make the preliminary observation that in interpreting the native title to land, not only in Southern Nigeria, but other parts of the British Empire, much caution is essential. There is a tendency, operating at times unconsciously, to render that title conceptually in terms which are appropriate only to systems which have grown up under English law. But this tendency has to be held in check closely. As a rule, in the various systems of native jurisprudence throughout the Empire, there is no such full division between property and possession as English lawyers are familiar with. A very usual form of native title is that of a usufructuary right, which is a mere qualification of or burden on the radical or final title of the Sovereign where that exists.... In India, as in Southern Nigeria, there is yet another feature of the fundamental nature of the title to land which must be borne in mind. The title, such as it is, may not be that of the individual ... but may be that of a community.... To ascertain how far this latter development of right has progressed involves the study of the history of the particular community and its usages in each case....

> This statement of the law has been recognized judicially as the "the definitive position at common law" by the Court of Appeal in Malaysia in *Kerajaan Negeri Selangor v. Sagong Bin Tasi* [2005] 4 CLJ 169.... From the evidence, I am satisfied that the claimants have, by the Maya customary land tenure extant in the Toledo District, individual and communal rights to the lands in Conejo and Santa Cruz Villages. These rights, I find, are of a usufructuary nature. That is to say, the right to occupy the land, farm, hunt and fish thereon, and to take for their own use and benefit the fruits and resources thereof. The fact that, as disclosed by the evidence, the claimants can enjoy a communal title by Maya customary land tenure was recognized by the Privy Council in the *Amodu Tijani* case and the existence of such title in other jurisdictions.

I am therefore of the considered view, that on the evidence in this case, the communal title to lands in Conejo and Santa Cruz Villages in the Toledo District, inheres in the claimants in accordance with Maya customary land tenure. The nature of this title is communal, entitling the members of the community to occupy, use the lands for farming, hunting, fishing and utilizing the resources thereon as well as for other cultural and spiritual purposes, in accordance with Maya customary law and usage.

The core and nature of the Defence

[The defence] seemed to have pitched their tent against the claimants on the principal ground of British sovereignty over British Honduras....

Did change in or acquisition of territorial sovereignty extinguish pre-existing rights and interests in the land? ...

I have given deep and anxious consideration to this aspect of this case. I am, however, convinced and fortified by authorities that the ... mere acquisition or change of sovereignty did not in and of itself extinguish pre-existing title to or interests in the land....

From the evidence, it is manifest that throughout the unfolding drama regarding the territory, first, between Spain and later Guatemala on the one hand, and the British authorities on the other, the Maya people were all the while living on their land. There was some forced removal of some of the Maya people by Spanish authorities from some parts of the land; but the fact remains that they were never wholly removed so as to make the land *terra nullius* rendering it ownerless or unoccupied. The Maya, who are the indigenes of the land, remained with fluctuating numbers. And from the evidence, some of those whose ancestors had been removed came back to their ancestral lands....

I endorse with respect, the statement of principle on this point by Brennan J. in the High Court of Australia in *Mabo v. Queensland*, (No. 2) [(1992) 175 CLR 1, 57,] where he stated ... :

> The preferable rule ... is that a mere change in sovereignty does not extinguish native title to land ... ; the preferable rule equates the indigenous inhabitants of a settled colony with the inhabitants of a conquered colony in respect of their rights and interests in land and recognizes in the indigenous inhabitants of a settled colony the rights and interests recognized by the Privy Council in re Southern Rhodesia as surviving to the benefits of the residents of a conquered colony....

> I find as well that the introduction of grants of lands by the various Crown Lands Ordinances, culminating in the National Lands Act — Chapter 191 of the Laws of Belize, R.E. 2000, did not operate so as to extinguish the pre-existing Maya people's interests in and rights to their land....

Again, I adopt with respect, the statement in *Mabo* of Brennan J. in his analysis of extinguishment and indigenous title to land, when he stated, at para. 75: ...

> the exercise of a power to extinguish native title must reveal a clear and plain intention to do so, whether the action be taken by the Legislature or the Executive. This requirement, which flows from the seriousness of the consequences to indigenous inhabitants of extinguishing their traditional rights and interests in land, has been repeatedly emphasized by courts dealing with the extinguishing of the native title of Indian lands in North America....

I therefore conclude that the villagers of Conejo and Santa Cruz, as part of the indigenous Maya people of Toledo District, have interests in land based on Maya customary land tenure that still survive and are extant.

The Constitutional implications of the claimants' interests in land based on Maya customary land tenure

[The Court addressed the constitutional issues. First, the Court determined that the claimants' property interests in lands based on Maya customary land tenure constitute the kind of "property" protected by sections 3(d) and 17 of the Constitution.]

[As support for its conclusions, the Court cited the American Declaration on the Rights and Duties of Man, stating that communal property rights of the Mayan people are protectable under the Declaration. Moreover, the Court adopted the guidelines of the Privy Council that a generous interpretation should be given to constitutional provision protecting humans and their fundamental rights.

[Second, the Court concluded that the Government's acts and omissions violated the claimants' rights to property in sections 3(d) and 17 of the Constitution.

[Third, the Court determined that the Government's acts and omissions, in failing to provide legal protection to the Mayan customary land tenure, violated the claimants' guaranteed right to equality under sections 3 and 16 of the Constitution.

[Finally, the Court found that the Government's acts and omissions violated the claimants' right to life, liberty, security of the person, and the protection of the law guaranteed under sections 3(a) and 4 of the Constitution. [In addition to the four constitutional issues raised by the claimants, the Court next addressed the international law implications of the Government's actions.]

Treaty obligations

In contemporary international law, the right to property is regarded as including the rights of indigenous peoples to their traditional lands and natural resources. Belize is a party to several international treaties such as the International Covenant on Civil and Political Rights (ICCPR) 999 U.N.T.S. 171; the Convention on the Elimination of All Forms of Racial Discrimination (CERD), 660 U.N.T.S. 195; and The Charter of the Organization of American States (OAS) 119 U.N.T.S 3.; all of which have been interpreted as requiring states to respect the rights of indigenous peoples over their land and resources.

For example, in the case of Mayagna (Sumo) *Awas Tingni Community v. Nicaragua 79 Inter-Am.* Ct.H.R. (Ser C) (2001) that Court held that:

> Among indigenous peoples there is a communitarian tradition regarding a communal form of collective property of the land, in the sense that ownership of the land is not centered on an individual but rather on the group and its community. Indigenous groups, by the fact of their very existence, have the right to live freely in their own territory; the close ties of indigenous people with the land must be recognized and understood as the fundamental basis of their cultures, their spiritual life, their integrity, and their economic survival. For indigenous communities, relations to the land are not merely a matter of possession and production but a material and spiritual element which they must fully enjoy, even to preserve their cultural legacy and transmit it to future generations....

The United Nations Committee on the Elimination of All Forms of Racial Discrimination ... has confirmed that the failure of states to recognize and respect indigenous customary land tenure is a form of racial discrimination....

The Committee in a letter dated 9th March 2007 to the defendants through Belize's Ambassador to the United Nations stated that it "is preoccupied by reports regarding privatization and leasing of land without the prior consultation or consent of the Maya people, as well as the granting of concessions for oil development, logging and the production of hydro-electricity."

These considerations, engaging as they do Belize's international obligation towards indigenous peoples, therefore weighed heavily with me in this case in interpreting the fundamental human rights provisions of the Constitution.... I draw particular support and inspiration from the preamble of the Belize Constitution which requires policies of the state to "protect the identity, dignity and social and cultural values of Belizeans ... including Belize's indigenous peoples."

Belize's obligations under customary international law and general principles of international law

Treaty obligations aside, it is my considered view that both customary international law and general principles of international law would require that Belize respect the rights of its indigenous people to their lands and resources.... It is the position that both customary international law and the general principles of international law are separate and apart from treaty obligations, binding on States as well....

In *Mary and Carrie Dann v. United States*, Case 11.40, Report No. 75/02 of the Inter-American Commission of Human Rights dated 27th December 2002, a case concerning claims by members of the Western Shoshone indigenous people to lands in the State of Nevada, U.S.A., the Commission stated that the general international legal principles in the context of indigenous human rights include the following:

- the right to indigenous peoples to legal recognition of their varied and specific forms and modalities of their control, ownership, use and enjoyment of territories and property;

- the recognition of their property and ownership rights with respect to lands, territories and resources that they have historically occupied; and

- where property and user rights of indigenous peoples arise from rights existing prior to the creation of a state, recognition by that state of the permanent and inalienable title of indigenous peoples relative thereto and recognition that such title may only be changed by mutual consent between the state and respective indigenous peoples when they have full knowledge and appreciation of the nature or attributes of such property. This also implies the right to fair compensation in the event that such property and user rights are irrevocably lost....

Also, importantly in this regard is the recent Declaration on the Rights of Indigenous Peoples adopted by the General Assembly of the United Nations on 13 September 2007. Of course, unlike resolutions of the Security Council, General Assembly resolutions are not ordinarily binding on member states. But where these resolutions or Declarations contain principles of general international law, states are not expected to disregard them.

This Declaration—GA Res 61/295, was adopted by an overwhelming number of 143 states in favour with only four States against with eleven abstentions. It is of some signal importance, in my view, that Belize voted in favour of this Declaration. And I find its Article 26 of especial resonance and relevance in the context of this case, reflecting, as I think it does, the growing consensus and the general principles of international law on indigenous peoples and their lands and resources. Article 26 states:

Article 26

1. Indigenous peoples have the right to the lands, territories and resources which they have traditionally owned, occupied or otherwise used or acquired.

2. Indigenous peoples have the right to own, use, develop and control the lands, territories and resources that they possess by reason of traditional ownership or other traditional occupation or use, as well as those which they have otherwise acquired.

3. States shall give legal recognition and protection to these lands, territories and resources. Such recognition shall be conducted with due respect to the customs, traditions and land tenure systems of the indigenous peoples concerned.

I am therefore, of the view that this Declaration, embodying as it does, general principles of international law relating to indigenous peoples and their lands and resources, is of such force that the defendants, representing the Government of Belize, will not disregard it....

I conclude therefore, that the defendants are bound, in both domestic law in virtue of the Constitutional provisions that have been canvassed in this case, and international law, arising from Belize's obligation thereunder, to respect the rights to and interests of the claimants as members of the indigenous Maya community, to their lands and resources which are the subject of this case.

Conclusion ...

Accordingly, I order and grant as follows:

a) A declaration that the claimants Villages of Santa Cruz and Conejo and their members hold, respectively, collective and individual rights in the lands and resources that they have used and occupied according to Maya customary practices and that these rights constitute "property" within the meaning of sections 3(d) and 17 of the Belize Constitution.

b) A declaration that the Maya Villages of Santa Cruz and Conejo hold collective title to the lands their members have traditionally used and occupied within the boundaries established through Maya customary practices; and that this collective title includes the derivative individual rights and interests of Village members which are in accordance with and subject to Santa Cruz and Conejo and Maya customary law.

c) An order that the government determine, demarcate and provide official documentation of Santa Cruz's and Conejo's title and rights in accordance with Maya customary law and practices, without prejudice to the rights of neighboring Villages.

d) An order that the defendants cease and abstain from any acts that might lead the agents of the government itself, or third parties acting with its acquiescence or its tolerance, to affect the existence, value, use or enjoyment of the property located in the geographic area occupied and used by the Maya people of Santa Cruz and Conejo unless such acts are pursuant to their informed consent and in compliance with the safeguards of the Belize Constitution. This order include[s], but [is] not be limited to, directing the government to abstain from:

    i.   issuing any lease or grants to lands or resources under the National Lands Act or any other Act;

    ii. registering any such interest in land;

    iii. issuing any regulations concerning land or resources use; and

    iv. issuing any concessions for resource exploitation and harvesting, including concessions, permits or contracts authorizing logging, prospecting or exploration, mining or similar activity under the Forest Act, the Mines and Minerals Act, the Petroleum Act, or any other Act.

Questions and Discussion

1. *Weaving international law into national law.* If the various local organizations in the Maya community had not entered into the Agreement with the Government of Belize, would Chief Justice Conteh have been able to find "a clear and unequivocal governmental endorsement" of the Maya people's right to their land and their resources? The results of the community organizing around a common goal seems to support Judge Cançado Trindade's belief in the value of immersing oneself in community.

2. *Commonwealth common rulings.* What did Chief Justice Conteh use to tie the decisions from several seemingly disparate countries into precedent for the Court's finding that the Maya people "have interests in land based on Maya customary land tenure that still survive and are extant"?

3. *Indigenous title and common law.* In the common law countries (former British colonies, widely known now as the Commonwealth of Nations), indigenous human rights to land are not truly constitutional in nature, but in a sense might be considered "quasi-constitutional." That is, the courts recognize their existence as predating British occupation and as extinguishable only by clear legislative action. The Privy Council's 1921 decision in the *Amodu Tijani* case, cited in the Belize case and many others, is considered the definitive statement on this. The highest court of Malaysia explained this, in a recent decision rejecting the government's position that the leasing of an area to an oil company had extinguished what the court calls "native title":

> The learned State Attorney General vehemently contended that *Adong* and *Nor Anak Nyawai* should not be followed because they were decisions rooted upon the Australian case of *Mabo* (No. 2) [(1992) 175 CLR 1], an authority for the proposition that the common law of Australia which recognizes a form of "native titles" and the Canadian case of *Calder v. AG of British Columbia* which held that the "common law categorically recognized native rights over land."

> With respect, we are of the view that the proposition of law as enunciated in these two cases reflected the common law position with regard to native titles throughout the Commonwealth.

Superintendent Of Land & Surveys v. Madeli Salleh, [2007] 6 CLJ 509 (Federal Court of Malaysia). In *Superintendent Of Land & Surveys v. Nor Anak Nyawai*, [2005] 3 CLJ 555 (Court of Appeal of Malaysia). Despite the clear statement of the law, members of the Iban tribe lost their case against transfer of land to a pulp mill because they could not persuade the Court of Appeal that they had sufficient evidence to prove continuous occupation. On the other hand, in *Kerajaan Negeri Selangor v. Sagong Tasi*, [2005] 4 CLJ 169 (Court of Appeal of Malaysia), where indigenous land was taken for a highway, aboriginal people of the Temuan tribe, who had occupied the land in question for at least 210 years, won a court victory but received only monetary compensation for the trespass.

In *Delgamuukw v. British Columbia*, 1997 SCC 302 (CanLII); [1997] 3 S.C.R. 1010, Chief Justice Lamer of the Supreme Court of Canada held, "Aboriginal title encompasses an exclusive right to the use and occupation of land, i.e., to the exclusion of both non-aboriginals and members of other aboriginal nations." *Delgamuukw* constitutionalized indigenous peoples' land rights, and set standards for defining some of those rights. One of those rights was the duty to consult, which came to the fore in *Haida Nation v. British Columbia (Minister of Forests)*. As explained in the court's Headnote to the case:

> For more than 100 years, the Haida people have claimed title to all the lands of Haida Gwaii and the waters surrounding it, but that title has not yet been legally recognized. The Province of British Columbia issued a "Tree Farm License" (T.F.L. 39) to a large forestry firm in 1961, permitting it to harvest trees in an area of Haida Gwaii designated as Block 6. In 1981, 1995 and 2000, the Minister replaced T.F.L. 39, and in 1999, the Minister approved a transfer of T.F.L. 39 to Weyerhaeuser Co. The Haida challenged in court these replacements and the transfer, which were made without their consent and, since at least 1994, over their objections....

Haida Nation v. British Columbia (Minister of Forests) (Canada)

Supreme Court of Canada
[2004] 3 S.C.R. 511, 2004 SCC 73 ...

In *Delgamuukw*, the Court considered the duty to consult and accommodate in the context of established claims. Lamer C.J. wrote:

> The nature and scope of the duty of consultation will vary with the circumstances.... Some cases may even require the full consent of an aboriginal nation, particularly when provinces enact hunting and fishing regulations in relation to aboriginal lands.

Pending settlement, the Crown is bound by its honour to balance societal and Aboriginal interests in making decisions that may affect Aboriginal claims....

[The Haida] had expressed objections ... regarding the rate of logging of old-growth forests, methods of logging, and the environmental effects of logging....

T.F.L. 39 grants exclusive rights to Weyerhaeuser to harvest timber within an area constituting almost one quarter of the total land of Haida Gwaii....

Where the government has knowledge of an asserted Aboriginal right or title, it must consult the Aboriginal peoples on how exploitation of the land should proceed....

[T]he strength of the case for both the Haida title and the Haida right to harvest red cedar, coupled with the serious impact of incremental strategic accommodation to preserve the Haida interest pending resolution of their claims....

It follows, therefore, that the Province failed to meet it duty to engage in something significantly deeper than mere consultation. It failed to engage in any meaningful consultation at all....

Questions and Discussion

1. *The Haida right to log.* As mentioned at the beginning of this chapter, sometimes indigenous peoples' rights and environmentalists' wishes are not the same. The Haida people want the right to log what they consider to be their land, as do other indigenous peoples in British Columbia. Environmentalists continue to propose other possible revenue sources for the indigenous peoples, especially when endangered species are present. However, the revenue from old-growth wood is high, which is attractive to communities that may have previously struggled with poverty. Indigenous peoples normally demand more environmentally-sensitive logging methods than British Columbia does.

2. *Hunting and fishing regulations. Haida Nation* states that "full consent" might be required "when provinces enact hunting and fishing regulations" affecting aboriginal lands. If enacting regulations on these activities might require full consent, does it follow that granting concessions that will disrupt large areas where hunting and fishing occur (through resource extraction) might also require full consent? Consider the fishing rights of the Haida's indigenous neighbors.

B. U.S. Courts, Indian Treaties, and the Environment

1. The Right to Fish, and the Right to Insist on the Survival of Fish

Treaty with the Nisqualli, Puyallup, etc.
Dec., 26, 1854, Ratified Mar. 3, 1855, Proclaimed Apr. 10, 1855
10 Stat. 1132 (1855)

Article I

The said Tribes and bands of Indians hereby cede, relinquish, and convey to the United States, all their right title, and interest in and to the lands and country occupied by them....

Article III

The right of taking fish, at all usual and accustomed grounds and stations, is further secured to said Indians, in common with all citizens of the Territory ...

Questions and Discussion

1. *Environmental provisions?* Recall how the European Court of Human Rights turned the right to "private and family life" into a right protecting the environment. Is there anything in Article III of this treaty that might be used to protect the environment?

2. *Interpretations.* What are possible interpretations of the words "right of taking" and "in common"? Consider more than one possibility for each.

———————

In the 1855 Treaty with the Nisqualli, Puyallup, etc., known as the Treaty of Medicine Creek,[b] nine "tribes and bands of Indians" ceded all land "west of the Cascade Mountains and north of the Columbia River" to the United States. This pact is one of many treaties that Isaac Stevens, the first Governor and Superintendent of Indian Affairs of the Washington Territory, negotiated with the sovereign Indian tribes of the Pacific Northwest. In additional "Stevens Treaties," other Northwest tribes ceded land east of the Cascade Mountains and south of the Columbia River. The question whether the treaties merely guarantee the right of these indigenous people to catch what fish might swim by them, or also guarantee the right that the fish shall have environmental conditions conducive to their survival, is one of the great issues of human rights and the environment being played out today in a national court system.

In the 19th century, the United States wanted to reduce "friction" between the Indians and the non-Indians, so in return for the expanse of land ceded to the federal government,

———————

b. *See United States v. Washington (Phase II)*, 506 F. Supp. 187, 189–90, (W.D. Wash. 1980). Treaties with the intervenor tribes have identical or nearly identical Articles. *Id.* at 190, n. 2.

the United States carved out reservations of land the tribes would live on (often small), provided cash payments, and made various promises. In one such promise, the United States gave its word that it would always honor a birthright of these and other tribes of the Pacific Northwest, the right to fish. As arrangements made by sovereign nations, the Indian treaties have some similarities to international law.

The U.S. Supreme Court ruled long ago that the U.S. Government has a "trust responsibility" toward American Indians.[c] This responsibility has led the U.S. Government to represent and advocate for the interests of Indians in various ways, including the initiation of litigation on their behalf.

a. U.S. v. Washington, Phase I (Fair Share, 1970s)

In a history-making case brought by the U.S. Government on behalf of Northwest Indians against the State of Washington to enforce Indian fishing rights under the Stevens Treaties, U.S. District Judge George Boldt ruled in 1974 that the term "in common with all citizens of the Territory" (later, the States) reserved to the Indian tribes a right to approximately 50% of the salmon and steelhead in the rivers. *United States v. Washington (Phase I)*, 384 F. Supp. 312 (W.D. Wash. 1974).

Judge Boldt gathered extensive information concerning tribal life before the tribes entered into the treaties. Judge Boldt stated that "one common cultural characteristic among all of these Indians was the almost universal and generally paramount dependence upon the products of an aquatic economy, especially anadromous fish, to sustain the Indian way of life." Salmon were "vital to the Indian diet, played an important role in their religious life, and constituted a major element of their trade and economy. In order to depend on the fish, the Indians had to know the rhythms of the rivers, the ocean, and the fish. They had to know what tools would catch the most fish, and they had to know how to preserve the fish. Tribal members considered structures blocking fish passage, such as nets or temporary dams, to be communal, while individuals held specific locations along such weirs.

Religious ceremonies revolved around the salmon. "The first-salmon ceremony ... was essentially a religious rite to ensure the continued return of salmon. The symbolic acts, attitudes of respect and reverence, and concern for the salmon reflected a ritualistic conception of the interdependence and relatedness of all living things, which was a dominant feature of native Indian world view. Religious attitudes and rites insured that salmon were never wantonly wasted and that water pollution was not permitted during the salmon season."

The tribes gave salmon to each other during potlatches. Potlatches were (and are) communal feasts, usually marking milestones, such as birth, death, and marriage, but sometimes a big salmon catch was reason enough. Gifts and food were freely given, and for pre-treaty tribes, the gift of food was often salmon. This practice reinforced the strength

---

c. *See Cherokee Nation v. Georgia*, 5 Pet. 1, 17, 8 L.Ed. 25 (1831); *Worcester v. Georgia*, 6 Pet. 515, 557, 8 L.Ed. 483 (1832); *Choctaw Nation v. United States*, 119 U.S. 1, 27–28 (1886); *United States v. Sioux Nation of Indians*, 448 U.S. 371, 416–417 (1980); *United States v. Winans*, 198 U.S. 371, 380–81 (1905); *Sohappy v. Hodel*, 911 F.2d 1312, 1318–1319 (9th Cir. 1990) ("We will construe a treaty with the Indians as 'that unlettered people' understood it, and 'as justice and reason demand in all cases where power is exerted by the strong over those to whom they owe care and protection,' and counterpoise the inequality 'by the superior justice which looks only to the substance of the right without regard to technical rules.'").

of the communities, enhanced a family's or a tribe's status, and allowed for celebration or recognition.... In setting forth the above facts, Judge Boldt clearly noted the tribes' reverence for and reliance upon the salmon....

Judge Boldt reminded the parties that the Constitution protected treaty rights. He ruled that the State could not regulate the Tribes' fishing, except as necessary for conservation....

In a poetic quote from *Winans*, the Judge reminded the parties that not only did the United States guarantee the fishing rights; the Tribes already "possessed" those rights, rights of life-giving importance:

> The treaty-secured rights to resort to the usual and accustomed places to fish were a part of larger rights possessed by the treating Indians, upon the exercise of which there was not a shadow of impediment, and which were not much less necessary to their existence than the atmosphere they breathed.

In addition, the Tribes and non-treaty Indian fishers alike were entitled to 50% of the "harvestable number of fish that may be taken by all fishermen at usual and accustomed grounds and stations."

Judge Boldt was confident that reallocating the fish would not affect the amount of fish for conservation purposes:

> There is no reason to believe that a ruling which grants the Indians their full treaty rights will affect the necessary escapement of fish in the least. The only effect will be that some of the fish now taken by sportsmen and commercial fishermen must be shared with the treaty Indians, as our forefathers promised over a hundred years ago.

Id. at 346.

b. U.S. v. Washington, Phase II
(False Start at Conservation, 1980s)

In 1980, the U.S. District Court considered new arguments about the allocation of fish, as well as contentions that the State was allowing environmental degradation that threatened the viability of the salmon population. In *U.S. v. Washington, Phase II*, Judge William Orrick decided that the treaties include not only a right to catch a fixed portion of the available fish, but a right to protect the "fishery habitat" from "man-made despoliation." *U. S. v. Washington (Phase II)*, 506 F. Supp. 187, 203 (W.D. Wash. 1980). The judge's decision rested on several factors, including precedent, canons of construction, tribal concerns, the purpose of the treaty, and the Supremacy Clause of the U.S. Constitution.

Judge Orrick cited a long line of cases said to support the right to a healthy habitat for the salmon by recognizing the fishing clause as the overriding concern of the tribes, the "cornerstone of the treaties." In order to honor the right to fish, he said, the fish must exist. Judge Orrick noted that in an appeal of Judge Boldt's earlier decision (*U.S. v. Washington, Phase I*), the Supreme Court had declared, "The treaty assures the tribes something considerably more tangible than 'merely the chance ... occasionally to dip their nets into the territorial waters.'" *Id.*, quoting 443 U.S. at 679, 99 S.Ct. at 3071 (1979). Judge Orrick also noted that in *Confederated Tribes of the Umatilla Indian Reservation v. Alexander*, 440 F. Supp. 553 (D.Or. 1977), the court had stopped the construction of a dam that would prevent "all wild fish from swimming upstream.".

The Tribes and Governor Stevens believed that "the treaties entitled them to continue fishing in perpetuity and that the settlers would not qualify, restrict, or interfere with their right to take fish." *U. S. v. Washington*, 506 F. Supp. 187, 203 (W.D. Wash. 1980). Since treaties must be construed according to the beliefs at the time the treaty was signed, the non-Indians must not "qualify, restrict, or interfere" with the right to fish.

Judge Orrick wrote:

> In this case, there can be no doubt that one of the paramount purposes of the treaties in question was to reserve to the tribes the right to continue fishing as an economic and cultural way of life. It is equally beyond doubt that the existence of an environmentally-acceptable habitat is essential to the survival of the fish, without which the expressly-reserved right to take fish would be meaningless and valueless. Thus, it is necessary to recognize an implied environmental right in order to fulfill the purposes of the fishing clause.

Id. at 205.

On appeal, the Ninth Circuit ruled that Judge Orrick's decision was premature and made in the abstract. The court vacated the decision and said that the environmental issue would have to wait until a plaintiff brought a case asking for relief against a particular action. *U.S. v. Washington*, 759 F.2d 1353 (9th Cir. 1985).

In the years that followed, the number of salmon returning to streams in the Pacific Northwest plummeted dramatically.

The following article paints a picture of how things stood when the Tribes and the U.S. Government decided to return to the court with the more specific demand the Ninth Circuit said was necessary to any consideration of a potential environmental right.

Boldt Decision 'Very Much Alive' 30 Years Later
Lewis Kamb
Seattle Post-Intelligencer (February 12, 2004)

UPPER SKAGIT RESERVATION — When the decision came down three decades ago — the decision that would change everything — Scott Schuyler was a 10-year-old kid mesmerized by the glamour of it all: The skillful handling of skiff and gear. The bountiful harvests from the river named for his people. The fish and money trading hands on the river's banks — a culmination of a hard day's work and a hard-fought victory decades in the making.

"Back in the heyday after the Boldt Decision," Schuyler says now, "it was kind of glamorous. Seeing our fishers pull their boats in, buyers backing their trucks up to the bank and handing over a roll of bills."

Like Schuyler, a generation of tribal fishermen have since grown up under the landmark Boldt Decision — the federal court ruling handed down 30 years ago today that sent shock waves through this state and beyond. Hailed by some legal experts as the most significant ruling on Native treaty law in the past century, U.S. District Judge George Boldt's ruling held that the United States' mid-1850s treaties with Washington tribes provided that Indians always were entitled to half the salmon and steelhead harvest in their traditional fishing grounds off reservations.

Boldt ruled that Washington State virtually had no authority over tribal fishing; in fact, it was the tribes that ceded to non-Indian settlers the rights to fish — not the other way around. The decision also would instate tribes as "co-managers" with the state over Washington's salmon fisheries resources.

For sport and commercial fishermen, Boldt's ruling amounted to blasphemy—"special rights," they argued, that afforded a group making up less than 1 percent of Washington's population far too large a slice of the fisheries pie. But for tribes, whose members battled, demonstrated, got arrested and were jailed over more than two decades during what would become known as the "fish wars," Boldt's ruling was total victory. It had immediate economic and cultural benefits across reservations, restoring pride to struggling tribes that re-invested in fisheries and used money netted from catches to help build tribal governments and enhance reservation infrastructures. These benefits are what drew so many Native people back to their reservations—and what drew Schuyler's family back to the Upper Skagit.

But today, for young members of Schuyler's tribe based in the North Cascade foothills above Sedro-Woolley, the allure of salmon fishing isn't what it used to be. Marked by dwindling fish runs and a commercial market undercut in recent years by cheaper, farmed Atlantic salmon, the bounties and buyers are long gone.

"There's a handful of people still hanging on to the legacy," said Schuyler, now 40, with two children of his own.

"But now, the kids see grandpa drive 20, 30 miles to knock on doors, just to find someone to sell his catch to. Of course, they're not following in his footsteps like they once did—not into an industry with an outlook so dismal."

Since the peak of Washington's tribal fisheries in the mid-1980s, the Upper Skagit Tribe's salmon fleet has dwindled from 50 boats to fewer than 10, Schuyler says. A pound of even the lowest quality of his tribe's salmon that once could fetch 90 cents or more now garners maybe a dime—if it can be sold at all, he says. Thirty years after Boldt, the Upper Skagit's salmon fortunes are not unique: Overall, Puget Sound treaty tribes have experienced an 80 percent erosion in fishing fleets since the heyday of the '80s, according to the Northwest Indian Fisheries Commission. And tribal salmon catch figures today mirror those of the pre-Boldt era in the early 1970s—when the state still restricted tribal fishers from the bulk of Washington's catch.

For tribes, it's a reversal of fortune—caused by a declining market, environmental effects and other forces—that one Indian fisheries commission employee calls a "horrific irony" to the Boldt legacy. But Schuyler still plies the age-old practice of his people, pulling fish from the green waters of the Skagit. Only now, as natural resources manager for his tribe, he spends most days coordinating rather than catching—managing hatchery operations, habitat preservation, and other fishery conservation issues. He represents today's generation in tribal fisheries during an era focusing not on activism, quotas or economic empowerment, but on recovery, protection, and co-management of a fading cultural icon: Northwest salmon.

Thirty years later, there's no question that Western Washington tribes still hail the Boldt Decision. Nor is there doubt the 203-page decision remains a document of precedence that still reverberates loudly as a legal foundation for indigenous-rights cases in courtrooms near and far. But the tumult that surrounded the immediate pre- and post-Boldt era has quietly faded. It plays out not in the guts-and-glory stands of yesteryear, but rather, it's in the complexities of Endangered Species Act guidelines for threatened Puget Sound chinook.

It's in local, county and state wrangling over water rights and land use decisions. And, it's found in the sub-proceedings over habitat degradation issues and other parts of the milestone *U.S. v. Washington* case that have never fully been decided. Said Billy Frank Jr., the Nisqually Indian elder and activist who rose to prominence during the tumultuous fish wars: "It's not about fighting over fish or numbers anymore. That kind of fighting is done."

Although the pre and post-Boldt turmoil among tribes, the state, commercial and sport fishers has been well documented, the unique system of co-management over fisheries that came out of the case never has been much of a headline-grabber. It's not sexy, but the cooperative system between tribes and the state today guides everything from pre-season fish forecasts and seasonal catch limits to hatchery releases and cooperative restoration projects. But it took nearly a decade after Boldt to get to there. "In the early days after Boldt, we were more like accountants than fish biologists," said Rich Lincoln, a state Fish and Wildlife Department policy director who started with the agency about the time of the Boldt Decision. Because the ruling for the first time defined harvest quotas, state biologists initially concentrated on counting fish—something they really hadn't done well before, Lincoln said. Fish-tagging systems expanded, computer models developed, genetic programs engineered, and fish-count methodologies adopted—all in an effort to figure out how many salmon and steelhead were returning each season. Some say all the early emphasis on salmon counting impeded the shift toward preservation. Still, without it, Lincoln said, the state would never have been in a position to effectively manage for conservation—without really knowing the state of Northwest salmon.

"Before (Boldt), there was no ... management plan in this state—zero," added Frank, still as much a spitfire today, as chairman of the Northwest Indians Fisheries Commission, as he was as an activist during the fish wars. After the decision came, "everybody still was talking about the 50-50 (quota), just looking at the controversy," he said. "If we would've focused more on co-management in the beginning, we'd be way farther ahead today."

Effective co-management between treaty tribes and state developed slowly, through "years of friction," Lincoln said. Tribal and state fisheries officials had trouble deciding on the simplest of management strategies. And cases swamped a dispute resolution board. "Early cooperation wasn't a simple task," Lincoln said. "Suddenly, there were 20 different tribes to work with. No one really knew how to progress."

About a decade after the Boldt ruling—with establishment of the Puget Sound Salmon Management Act and the North of Falcon and Pacific Fisheries Management Council processes to determine salmon management roles and pre-season forecasts—common guidelines ultimately were found, effectively ushering in co-management. About the same time co-management began coming together, tribal fisheries peaked. Tribes had invested heavily in building up fleets, and catches soared to record levels. "In six or seven months, I could make enough money so I didn't have to work the rest of the year," said Glen Edwards, a Swinomish Indian gillnetter who now serves as a tribal senator. Unlike inner-river tribes such as the Upper Skagit, treaty tribes that traditionally fished in Puget Sound's salt water, like the Swinomish, could fetch higher prices for their fresher ocean catches." A guy could make $20,000 a night," Edwards said. "One night, I had 1,300 sockeye in my boat. That's at $3 or $4 per pound—in 1980s dollars."

Some commercial and sport fishermen argue tribal fishing in the '80s instigated the dramatic declines in fish runs seen in recent years. But former commercial fisherman Mark Cedergreen disagrees. The Boldt case indeed increased Indian salmon takes during a time when the fishery already was declining, says Cedergreen, now director of the Westport Charterboat Association. But at the same time, down cycles in ocean conditions, population growth, development and other environmental degradations contributed to dwindling runs, he said. "When someone says we'd be sailing off to Valhalla today if it weren't for tribal fishing," said Cedergreen, an active foe of the Boldt Decision, who later worked with tribes on salmon management issues, "it's at best ignorant and at worst disingenuous." Today, it's largely habitat preservation issues—not harvest numbers—that drive the Boldt saga forward.

"The debate on salmon management and catches that we pretty much litigated to death year after year has finally smoothed over," said Phil Katzen, an Indian law attorney who represented several tribes during the original case. "But the Boldt litigation is still very much alive today."

In his 1974 ruling, the issues involved in *U.S. v. Washington* were so complex, Boldt split the case into two pieces. Phase I—what's come to be known as the "Boldt Decision"—dealt with treaty interpretation and allocation: what the treaties tribes signed with Territorial Gov. Isaac Stevens in the 1850s really guaranteed them for fishing. The second phase, known as "Boldt II," dealt with environmental issues: What was the state's obligation to protect fish habitat, ensuring the tribes' rights to fish in perpetuity? Boldt left that issue to be taken up at a later date. It eventually was in 1980, when the 9th Circuit Court of Appeals ruled Washington had an obligation to take "reasonable steps" to protect fish habitat. But two years later, the court vacated its ruling, saying the case was based on theoretical arguments, rather than concrete ones.

Tribes had to find an actual case example to show how the state was destroying salmon habitat to pursue the issue. In 2001, tribes believed they did—filing a federal suit known as the "culvert case." It asserts that thousands of state culverts have been choking off salmon runs for years. So far, that case has been postponed from trial, as the state and tribes now negotiate the matter. While over the years, the Boldt Decision has expanded to just about every harvested fish species, salmon and steelhead remain at the heart of the issue.

Long before Boldt, the U.S. Supreme Court once observed that salmon "were not much less necessary to the existence of the Indians than the atmosphere they breathed." And even in these days of a depressed salmon market, tribes here still regard salmon in terms of their cultural identity. Although in recent years, shellfish harvests have eclipsed salmon as a more viable economic fishery, each treaty tribe continues to work toward recovery. "We're not through with this fishery," Frank said. "We have always fished salmon, and we always will."

For Schuyler's Upper Skagit Tribe, that means keeping tribal fisherman on the river however they can. These days, that means the Upper Skagit is buying its own tribal fishers' catch at a loss—subsidizing salmon fishing simply to "maintain our identity as a people," he said. At one time, a lone tribal fisherman here could make $30,000 or more in a season. Now the tribe's entire salmon fishery can take in half that in a year, Schuyler said.

As a kid, Schuyler tagged along at the heels of his mother, Doreen Maloney—a central figure in the post-Boldt days who helped treaty tribes set up fisheries enforcement courts to meet requirements of the landmark ruling. Years later, Schuyler would succeed his mom as the manager in charge of Upper Skagit fisheries. Now, his own kids tag at Schuyler's heels during his daily duties. "I see this as generational," Schuyler said. "Boldt gave us opportunities and responsibilities to help sustain the salmon fishery forever. I chose to follow into that. I just want to make sure that my kids will one day have that choice, too."

Questions and Discussion

1. *Disappearing salmon.* Besides local environmental degradation, what other pressures exist on salmon populations?

2. *4-Hs.* Professor William H. Rodgers stated that before 2000, it was popular to gather those pressures "under the heading of 4-H's ... Habitat, Hydroelectric, Hatchery, and Harvest." William H. Rodgers, Jr., ENVIRONMENTAL LAW IN INDIAN COUNTRY 797 (2005). Under the Endangered Species Act (ESA), "Three of these activities—habitat destruction, hydroelectric operations, and hatchery practices 'take' listed salmon but in a way that is "incidental" to otherwise lawful activity. These activities proceed, under supervision of law and with some constraint, but without serious restriction of the underlying activity.... The treaty fisheries are different.... [T]hese 'takes' are not incidental but direct." *Id.* This categorization meant that tribal entities could take fewer fish than nontribal interests. In 2000, the National Marine Fisheries Service (NMFS or NOAA for National Oceanic and Atmospheric Administration), enacted "a tribal 4(d) rule modifying Section 9 ..." of the Endangered Species Act (ESA), allowing the tribes to also "incidentally take" salmon. *Id.* at 798.

3. *Chemicals.* Two more hazards are peculiar to modern life: In the nineties, "Puget Sound's wild chinook salmon carr[ied] long-lived industrial chemicals at levels as high as those spotlighted by [a] landmark scientific report on farm-raised salmon.... In a few cases, the local fish were even more polluted." Robert McClure & Lisa Stiffler, *Sound's Salmon Carry High PCB Levels, But State Says Health Benefits of Eating the Fish Outweigh Risks*, Seattle P.I., Jan. 15, 2004, http://seattlepi.nwsource.com/local/156714_warning15.html. "PCBs still lie in the mud of Puget Sound, and scientists suspect the long-lived pollutant is also carried in the air from other countries where PCBs are unsafely disposed of or still being used." *Id.* Finally, "[b]eleaguered salmon populations are ... jeopardized by a new challenge, global warming, which is heating some rivers and streams to temperatures lethal to fish. The average temperature of British Columbia's Fraser River, for example, increased about 1.8 degrees F from 1953 to 1998, yielding a 50-percent mortality rate among the river's sockeye salmon. National Wildlife Federation (NWF) Newsletter, Ken Olsen, *Orcas on the Edge*, Oct/Nov 2006, vol. 44 no. 6, http://www.nwf.org/nationalwildlife/article.cfm?issueID=110&articleID=1385.

4. *Litigation choices.* With so many hazards facing the salmon today, could you choose one to litigate over? If so, what party would you sue? What remedy would you seek? How similar is this to the situation in which the Inuit people find themselves? See Chapter 12, page 557. Might the Northwest Tribes join the Inuit in litigation one day? Would the Court be more inclined to take notice with the addition of the Treaty of Medicine Creek tribes? What if tribes from Commonwealth Countries were to tie industrialized countries' actions to the immediate loss of their traditional territories?

5. *Cooperation in salmon management.* Consider the following:

> Each year, state and tribal representatives participate in two key public fish management processes. One is the Pacific Fishery Management Council (PFMC). This process sets annual fisheries in federal waters from three to 200 miles off the coasts of Washington, Oregon and California. State and tribal representatives sit on the PFMC and its technical committees....

> Parallel to the PFMC planning effort is the annual North of Falcon process which sets salmon fishing seasons for Indians and non-Indians in inland waters such as Puget Sound, Willapa Bay, Grays Harbor and state rivers. As with the PFMC, state and tribal fisheries experts participate in the North of Falcon process and sit on its technical committees. Those committees analyze technical information and use computer programs to set conservation goals for wild fish along with the state and tribal fisheries that focus on healthy runs of hatchery and wild salmon....

Washington Department of Fish and Wildlife, http://wdfw.wa.gov/factshts/comgrs.htm. Does it matter that Indian wildlife biologists are sitting at the table with wildlife biologists from the state government, rather than going to court? Which process is more likely to produce favorable results? Note that without the Boldt decision of 1974 there would be no table.

6. *Beyond allocation.* Is it enough to sit around the table and decide how many fish can be caught in an upcoming season? Is a right to allocation still an incomplete right? Consider the subsequent developments in the materials below.

2. The Tribes' Environmental Right: The "Culverts Case"

After the 1985 Ninth Circuit decision, requiring that a specific harm be identified before the courts could decide the environmental issue, the Tribes and the Federal Government did not return to litigation for 16 years. Then, on January 12, 2001, the Federal Government and the Tribes filed a Request for Determination in the U.S. District Court. *United States v. Washington,* Civil No. C70-9213, Subproceeding 01-01 (Phase II, Culverts). In 2006, after discovery proceedings, both they and the State of Washington submitted Motions for Summary Judgment. According to the Tribes' complaint, the State designed the culverts poorly. As a result, salmon could neither get upstream to lay eggs nor downstream to mature and continue the cycle. As a result, the Tribes, were "unable to sustain themselves by fishing." Negotiations broke down and the parties submitted the issue to the court for resolution. The decision came in 2007.

U.S. v. Washington (Phase II, Culverts)
Case No. CV 9213RSM, Subproceeding No. 01-01
Slip opinion, 2007 WL 2437166 (W.D. Wash. 2007)

ORDER ON CROSS-MOTIONS FOR SUMMARY JUDGMENT

RICARDO S. MARTINEZ, United States District Judge.

This matter was initiated by a Request for Determination ("Request") filed in 2001 by plaintiffs.... It is now before the Court for consideration of cross-motions for summary judgment filed by defendant State of Washington ("State") and by the plaintiff Tribes.... [M]ediation was unsuccessful, and the matter was ripe for issuance of a decision on the summary judgment motions....

For the reasons set forth below, the Court shall grant the Tribes' motion for partial summary judgment, and shall deny the summary judgment motion filed by the State of Washington.

BACKGROUND ...

The United States, in conjunction with the Tribes,[d] initiated this sub-proceeding in early 2001, seeking to compel the State of Washington to repair or replace any culverts that are impeding salmon migration to or from the spawning grounds. The Request for Determination, filed pursuant to the permanent injunction in this case, maintains that the State has a treaty-based duty to preserve fish runs so that the Tribes can earn a "moder-

---

d. The plaintiff tribes were these: Suquamish Indian Tribe, Jamestown S'Klallam, Lower Elwha Band of Klallam, Port Gamble Clallam, Nisqually Indian Tribe, Nooksack Tribe, Sauk-Suiattle Tribe, Skokomish Indian Tribe, Squaxin Island Tribe, Stillaguamish Tribe, Upper Skagit Tribe, Tulalip Tribe, Lummi Indian Nation, Quinault Indian Nation, Puyallup Tribe, Hoh Tribe, Confederated Bands and Tribes of the Yakama Indian Nation, Quileute Indian Tribe, Makah Nation, Swinomish Tribal Community, and Muckleshoot Indian Tribe.

ate living." The State's original Answer asserted cross- and counter-Requests for Determination, claiming injunctive and declaratory relief against the United States for placing
a disproportionate burden of meeting the treaty-based duty (if any) on the State. The
State also asserted that the United States has managed its own lands in such a way as to
create a nuisance that unfairly burdens the State.

In 2001, the United States moved to dismiss the counterclaims, contending that it has
not waived sovereign immunity with respect to these claims, and that the State lacks
standing to assert tribal rights derived from the Treaties.... [U]pon reconsideration the
motion to dismiss the counterclaims was granted. The Court found that it lacked jurisdiction over the State's counterclaims because sovereign immunity has not been waived.
A subsequent motion by the State for leave to file an amended Answer asserting counterclaims was denied. These cross-motions for summary judgment followed....

Discussion

This subproceeding arises from the language in Article III of the 1855 Treaty of Point
Elliot ("Stevens Treaties") in which the Tribes were promised that "[t]he right of taking
fish, at all usual and accustomed grounds and stations, is further secured to said Indians, in common with all citizens of the Territory...." The tribes ... state:

> In part due to the reduction of harvestable fish caused by ... actions of the State,
> the ability of the Tribes to achieve a moderate living from their Treaty fisheries has
> been impaired.

Request for Determination, Dkt. # 1, p. 1.

The Tribes requested mandatory relief "requiring Washington to identify and then to
open culverts under state roads and highways that obstruct fish passage, for fish runs returning to or passing through the usual and accustomed grounds and stations of the
plaintiff tribes."[2] Id....

The Tribes, in their Request, assert that between 1974, the year that this case was originally decided, and 1986, Tribal harvests of anadromous fish (salmon and steelhead) rose
dramatically, eventually reaching some 5 million fish. Then harvests declined, so that by
1999 harvests were back down to the 1974 levels. The Tribes contend that "[a] significant
reason for the decline of harvestable fish has been the destruction and modification of
habitat needed for their survival."

The Request addresses one specific type of habitat modification: the placement of culverts rather than bridges where roadways cross rivers and streams.... According to the Tribes,
culverts under State-owned or maintained roads block fish access to at least 249 linear miles
of stream, thus closing off more than 400,000 square meters of productive spawning habitat, and more than 1.5 million square meters of productive rearing habitat for juvenile fish....

The State argues that the Tribes have produced no evidence that the blocked culverts
"affirmatively diminish[] the number of fish available for harvest." The Tribes have, however, produced evidence of greatly diminished fish runs....

The issue then becomes a purely legal one: whether the Tribes' treaty-based right of taking fish imposes upon the State a duty to refrain from diminishing fish runs by con-

---

2. According to testimony and exhibits provided by the Tribes, culverts may become impassable
to fish either because they are blocked by silt or debris, or because they are "perched"—that is, the
outfall of the culvert is several feet or more above the level of the stream into which it flows. Salmon
migrating upstream to spawn are stopped by a perched culvert and cannot reach their spawning
grounds.

structing or maintaining culverts that block fish passage. The State asserts that this question has already been answered, and the Tribes' position rejected, by the Ninth Circuit Court of Appeals. However, that is not a correct characterization of the appellate court's prior rulings in this matter.

In 1976, after the Tribes won recognition of their treaty-based right to a fair and equitable share of harvestable fish in Phase I of this case, this Court turned to address environmental issues raised earlier. One of two questions addressed by the Court in Phase II was "whether the right of taking fish incorporates the right to have treaty fish protected from environmental degradation." *United States v. Washington*, 506 F.Supp. 187, 190 (1980). The district court held that "implicitly incorporated in the treaties' fishing clause is the right to have the fishery habitat protected from man-made despoliation." The Court then assigned to the State a burden "to demonstrate that any environmental degradation of the fish habitat proximately caused by the State's actions (including the authorization of third parties' activities) will not impair the tribes' ability to satisfy their moderate living needs."

The Ninth Circuit Court of Appeals reversed this portion of the district court's order, but not as conclusively as the State suggests.

> Let us repeat the essence of our interpretation of the treaty. Although we reject the environmental servitude created by the district court, we do not hold that the State of Washington and the Indians have no obligations to respect the other's rights in the resource Instead, ... we find on the environmental issue that the State and the Tribes must each take reasonable steps commensurate with the resources and abilities of each to preserve and enhance the fishery when their projects threaten then-existing levels.

United States v. Washington, 694 F.2d 1374, 1389 (9th Cir.1982).

Upon request for rehearing *en banc,* the three-judge panel's opinion was vacated. *United States v. Washington*, 759 F.2d 1353, 1354 (9th Cir.1985). A highly divided eleven-member court issued a *per curiam* decision vacating the district court's declaratory judgment on the environmental issue. The court's order did not contain broad and conclusive language necessary to reject the idea of a treaty-based duty in theory as well as in practice. Instead, the Court found that the declaratory judgment on environmental issues was imprecise and lacking in a sufficient factual basis.

> We choose to rest our decision in this case on the proposition that issuance of the declaratory judgment on the environmental issue is contrary to the exercise of sound judicial discretion. The legal standards that will govern the State's precise obligations and duties under the treaty with respect to the myriad State actions that may affect the environment of the treaty area will depend for their definition and articulation upon *concrete facts which underlie a dispute in a particular case.* Legal rules of general applicability are announced when their consequences are known and understood in the case before the court, not when the subject parties and the court giving judgment are left to guess at their meaning. It serves neither the needs of the parties, nor the jurisprudence of the court, nor the interests of the public for the judiciary to employ the declaratory judgment procedure to announce legal rules imprecise in definition and uncertain in dimension. Precise resolution, not general admonition, is the function of declaratory relief. These necessary predicates for a declaratory judgment have not been met with respect to the environmental issues in this case.

The State of Washington is bound by the treaty. If the State acts for the primary purpose or object of affecting or regulating the fish supply or catch in noncompliance with the treaty as interpreted by past decisions, it will be subject to immediate correction and remedial action by the courts. In other instances, *the measure of the State's obligation will depend for its precise legal formulation on all of the facts presented by a particular dispute.*

Id. at 1357 (emphasis added).

The appellate court's ruling, then, cannot be read as rejecting the concept of a treaty-based duty to avoid specific actions which impair the salmon runs. The court did not find fault with the district court's analysis on treaty-based obligations, but rather vacated the declaratory judgment as too broad, and lacking a factual basis at that time. The court's language, however, clearly presumes some obligation on the part of the State; not a broad "general admonition" as originally imposed by the district court, but a duty which could be defined by concrete facts presented in a particular dispute. This dispute, limited as it is to "only those culverts that block fish passage under State-owned roads," is capable of resolution through the declaratory relief requested by the tribes. The Tribes have presented sufficient facts, in the form of fish harvest data and numbers of blocked culverts, to meet the appellate court's stated requirements for issuance of a declaratory judgment. A narrowly-crafted declaratory judgment such as the one requested here does not raise the specter of a broad "environmental servitude" so feared by the State.

In moving for summary judgment, the State also asserts that "[n]o treaty language supports 'moderate living' as the measure of any servitude." Motion for Summary Judgment, p. 16. The State argues that the Tribes have proposed that the State has a duty to avoid impairing their ability to earn a "moderate living," but no tribal member can define the term "moderate living." The State further asserts that the term "moderate living" does not appear in the treaty, and that since the treaty is a contract, its provisions must be definite in order to be enforceable. According to the State, "the term is inherently ambiguous." Motion for Summary Judgment, p. 17.

The term "moderate living" was coined by the courts, not the parties. It is thus indeed not a part of the treaty "contract"; it is an interpretation that has been applied by the courts. In *State of Washington v. Washington State Commercial Passenger Fishing Vessel Association,* 443 U.S. 658 (1979), the Supreme Court stated,

> We also agree with the Government that an equitable measure of the common right should initially divide the harvestable portion of each run that passes through a "usual and accustomed" place into approximately equal treaty and nontreaty shares, and should then reduce the treaty share if tribal needs may be satisfied by a lesser amount....

> The division arrived at by the District Court is also consistent with our earlier decisions concerning Indian treaty rights to scarce natural resources. In those cases, after determining that at the time of the treaties the resource involved was necessary to the Indians' welfare, the Court typically ordered a trial judge or special master, in his discretion, to devise some apportionment that assured that the Indians' reasonable livelihood needs would be met. *Arizona v. California,* 373 U.S. at 600....

> Thus, [the district court] first concluded that at the time the treaties were signed, the Indians, who comprised three-fourths of the territorial population, depended heavily on anadromous fish as a source of food, commerce, and cultural cohesion. Indeed, it found that the non-Indian population depended on In-

dians to catch the fish that the former consumed. Only then did it determine that the Indians' present-day subsistence and commercial needs should be met, subject, or course, to the 50% ceiling....

As in *Arizona v. California* and its predecessor cases, the central principal here must be that Indian treaty rights to a natural resource that once was thoroughly and exclusively exploited by the Indians *secures so much as, but no more than, is necessary to provide the Indians with a livelihood—that is to say, a moderate living.*

Id. at 686 (citations omitted) (emphasis added).

The State's argument that the term "moderate living" is ambiguous and unenforceable in contract terms is thus without merit. It is neither a "missing term" in the contract, nor a meaningless provision; it is a measure created by the Court. To the extent that it needs definition, it would be for the Court, not the Tribes, to define it. No party has yet asked that the Court do so, and the Court finds it unnecessary at this time. The Tribes' showing that fish harvests have been substantially diminished, together with the logical inference that a significant portion of this diminishment is due to the blocked culverts which cut off access to spawning grounds and rearing areas, is sufficient to support a declaration regarding the culverts' impairment of treaty rights.

In finding a duty on the part of the State to refrain from blocking fish access to spawning grounds and rearing habitat, the Court has been guided by well-established principles of treaty construction. These were set forth as they applied to the treaties at issue here by the Supreme Court in *State of Washington v. Washington State Commercial Passenger Fishing Vessel Association.*

> [I]t is the intention of the parties, and not solely that of the superior side, that must control any attempt to interpret the treaties. When Indians are involved, this Court has long given special meaning to this rule. It has held that the United States, as the party with the presumptively superior negotiating skills and superior knowledge of the language in which the treaty is recorded, has a responsibility to avoid taking advantage of the other side."[T]he treaty must therefore be construed, not according to the technical meaning of its words to learned lawyers, but in the sense in which they would naturally be understood by the Indians." This rule, in fact, has thrice been explicitly relied on by the Court in broadly interpreting these very treaties in the Indians' favor.
>
> Governor Stevens and his associates were well aware of the "sense" in which the Indians were likely to view assurances regarding their fishing rights. During the negotiations, the vital importance of the fish to the Indians was repeatedly emphasized by both sides, and *the Governor's promises that the treaties would protect that source of food and commerce were crucial in obtaining the Indians' assent.* It is absolutely clear, as Governor Stevens himself said, that neither he nor the Indians intended that the latter "should be excluded from their ancient fisheries," and it is accordingly inconceivable that either party deliberately agreed to authorize future settlers to crowd the Indians out of any meaningful use of their accustomed places to fish. That each individual Indian would share an "equal opportunity" with thousands of newly arrived individual settlers is totally foreign to the spirit of the negotiations. Such a "right," along with the $207,500 paid the Indians, would hardly have been sufficient to compensate them for the millions of acres they ceded to the Territory. Moreover, in light of the far superior numbers, capital resources, and technology of the non-

Indians, the concept of the Indians' "equal *opportunity*" to take advantage of a scarce resource is likely in practice to mean that the Indians' "right of taking fish" will net them virtually no catch at all....

Id. at 675–677 [some emphasis added by District Court].

After rejecting the State's "equal opportunity" theory, the Court went on to discuss the meaning of "in common with" as used in the treaties.

> But we think greater importance should be given to the Indians' likely understanding of the other words in the treaties and especially the reference to the "right of *taking* fish"—a right that had no special meaning at common law but that must have had obvious significance to the tribes relinquishing a portion of their pre-existing rights to the United States in return for this promise. This language is particularly meaningful in the context of anadromous fisheries—which were not the focus of the common law—because of the relative predictability of the "harvest." In this context, it makes sense to say that a party has a right to "take"—rather than merely the "opportunity" to try to catch-some of the large quantities of fish that will almost certainly be available at a given time....
>
> This interpretation is confirmed by additional language in the treaties. The fishing clause speaks of "securing" certain fishing rights, a term the Court has previously interpreted as synonymous with "reserving" rights previously exercised. Because the Indians had always exercised the right to meet their subsistence and commercial needs by taking fish from treaty area waters, they would be unlikely to perceive a "reservation" of that right as merely the chance, shared with millions of other citizens, occasionally to dip their nets in to the territorial waters.

Id. at 678–680 (citations omitted; emphasis in italics in original).

It was thus the right to *take* fish, not just the right to fish that was secured by the treaties....

> [T]he Tribes were persuaded to cede huge tracts of land—described by the Supreme Court as "millions of acres"—by the promise that they would forever have access to this resource, which was thought to be inexhaustible. It was not deemed necessary to write any protection for the resource into the treaty because nothing in any of the parties' experience gave them reason to believe that would be necessary.

Declaration of Joseph Taylor III, Dkt. # 297, ¶ 7....

> [T]he representatives of the Tribes were personally assured during the negotiations that they could safely give up vast quantities of land and yet be certain that their right to take fish was secure. These assurances would only be meaningful if they carried the implied promise that neither the negotiators nor their successors would take actions that would significantly degrade the resource. Such resource-degrading activities as the building of stream-blocking culverts could not have been anticipated by the Tribes, who themselves had cultural practices that mitigated negative impacts of their fishing on the salmon stocks.

Declaration of Robert Thomas Boyd, Dkt. # 298, ¶ 6.

In light of these affirmative assurances given the Tribes as an inducement to sign the Treaties, together with the Tribes' understanding of the reach of those assurances, as set forth by the Supreme Court in the language quoted above, this Court finds that the Treaties do impose a duty upon the State to refrain from building or maintaining culverts in such a manner as to block the passage of fish upstream or down, to or from the Tribes' usual and accustomed fishing places. This is not a broad "environmental servitude" or the imposition of an affirmative duty to take all possible steps to protect fish runs as the State protests, but rather a narrow directive to refrain from impeding fish runs in one specific manner. The Tribes have presented sufficient facts regarding the number of blocked culverts to justify a declaratory judgment regarding the State's duty to refrain from such activity. This duty arises directly from the right of taking fish that was assured to the Tribes in the Treaties, and is necessary to fulfill the promises made to the Tribes regarding the extent of that right.

CONCLUSION

Accordingly, the State's motion for summary judgment is DENIED. The Tribes' cross-motion for partial summary judgment is GRANTED. The Court hereby declares that the right of taking fish, secured to the Tribes in the Stevens Treaties, imposes a duty upon the State to refrain from building or operating culverts under State-maintained roads that hinder fish passage and thereby diminish the number of fish that would otherwise be available for Tribal harvest. The Court further declares that the State of Washington currently owns and operates culverts that violate this duty.

Questions and Discussion

1. *Breadth of legal principle.* Development, whether in the form of a dam or a timber cut, may, at some point, block passage of the fish. Consider the following questions.

    a.   The fish cannot get past some dams because there are no fish ladders, or because they are inadequate. Will a judge rule that a dam, like a culvert, blocks passage of the fish, and order the dam removed?

    b.   The fish get past the dam, but lose their way in the slow-flowing reservoir. What ruling then regarding the continued existence of the dams and locks that provide navigation by ocean-going barges on the Columbia River for several hundred miles?

    c.   The fish swim past the dam and through the reservoir, but their eggs cannot survive in the silted streams caused by logging. What does the judge decide concerning whether the treaties restrict public or private logging?

    d.   The eggs hatch, the babies survive and are swimming back to the ocean. The fish get caught in the turbines of a major hydroelectric dam, providing electrical power to homes and businesses of the Pacific Northwest. What ruling?

2. *Defenses.* You are defending a group of timber companies. What will you cite in the *Culverts* decision or the previous Ninth Circuit decision to make your case that logging should be allowed, even though the silt is smothering the eggs?

3. *Culverts and fish wheels.* The Federal Government argued, on behalf of the Indians, that building a roadway whose culverts obstruct fish passage is the same as installing a fish wheel that obstructed fish passage, which the U.S. Supreme Court ruled to be invalid in *U.S. v. Winans.* The State answered that it is not the same, because to demand redesign of culverts would impose a "servitude" upon the land containing the road. How would a prohibition of fish-blocking culverts be different from a prohibition of fish-blocking fish wheels, in the view of the State? Is it that the inadequate culverts are upstream of the areas where Indians have traditionally fished (closer to the spawning areas), whereas

the fish wheels were downstream of those areas? Does that location make prohibiting them more of a "servitude" than in the case of the fish wheels?

4. *Right to a moderate living.* The State argued that the Indian treaty right does not necessarily include a right to a moderate living and that if environmental conditions no longer permit enough fish to survive to support a moderate living, the treaty right is essentially extinguished. In particular, the State notes that the States were told by the Supreme Court in *Fishing Vessel* that it could return to the court for adjustment in the "moderate living" standard for fish allocation if the 50% allocated proved to be more than the Indians needed. Does Judge Martinez' interpretation of that dictum by the Supreme Court suggest that the State could ask that a right to fish be extinguished on some other ground?

5. *International applicability.* The *Culverts Case* is based on specific treaty language and evolving interpretations of that language as applicable to environmental matters. In many countries indigenous peoples do not have treaties with the dominant government. Could the reasoning nonetheless be potentially applicable in other national legal systems? Under ILO Convention No. 169?

Chapter 6

Right to Information

Introduction

Various international legal instruments recognize a right to information, either explicitly or implicitly through interpretation. The Universal Declaration of Human Rights proclaims in Article 19 the right to freedom of opinion and expression. This right includes the "freedom to seek, receive and impart information and ideas through any media and regardless of frontiers." On a regional level, the European Convention for the Protection of Human Rights and Fundamental Freedoms provides in Article 10:

> Everyone has the right to freedom of expression. This right shall include freedom …
> to receive and impart information and ideas without interference by public authority and regardless of frontiers.

The American Convention on Human Rights in Article 13 contains an identical provision. The African Charter of Human and Peoples' Rights in Article 9 states:

1. Every individual shall have the right to receive information.
2. Every individual shall have the right to express and disseminate his opinions within the law.

Among the topics in this chapter is the question whether the "right to receive information" means that governments or private enterprises have a corresponding obligation to provide information? In other words, does a person have the right to receive information from any particular source, such as a government agency or company? Or does the phrase only mean that a person cannot be prohibited from having access to newspapers, radio and television, the Internet, or meetings with other people?

Several regional declarations have explicitly recognized a right of citizens to obtain, have access to, or acquire information.

> The states participating in the OSCE have confirmed the right of individuals, groups, and organizations to obtain, publish and distribute information on environmental issues. Conference on Security and Cooperation in Europe, Sofia Meeting on Protection of the Environment (October–November 1989), (CSCE/SEM.36, 2 November 1989). The Ministerial Declaration on Environmentally Sound and Sustainable Development in Asia and the Pacific (Bangkok, 16 October 1990), A/CONF.151/PC/38 para. 27, affirms "the right of individuals and non-governmental organizations to be informed of environmental problems relevant to them, to have the necessary access to information, and to participate in the formulation and implementation of decisions likely to affect their environment." The Arab De-

claration on Environment and Development and Future Perspectives of September 1991 speaks of the right of individuals and non-governmental organizations to acquire information about environmental issues relevant to them. Arab Declaration on Environment and Development and Future Perspectives, adopted by the Arab Ministerial Conference on Environment and Development (Cairo, September 1991), A/46/632, cited in U.N. Doc E/CN.4/Sub.2/1992/7, 20.

Dinah Shelton & Alexandre Kiss, JUDICIAL HANDBOOK ON ENVIRONMENTAL LAW (2005).

Several multilateral environmental agreements (MEAs) adopted after 1990 have included obligations of Parties to make information held by government accessible to members of the public.

> [T]he 1992 Paris Convention on the North-East Atlantic (Art. 9) ... requires the contracting parties to ensure that their competent authorities are required to make available relevant information to any natural or legal person, in response to any reasonable request, without the person having to prove an interest, without unreasonable charges and within two months of the request.
>
> The provisions of the Rotterdam Convention on the Prior Informed Consent Procedure for Certain Hazardous Chemicals and Pesticides in International Trade (Sept. 11, 1998) encourages parties to ensure that information on chemical and pesticide hazards is made available to the public. Art. 15(2) on implementation requires each state party to ensure, "to the extent practicable" that the public has appropriate access to information on chemical handling and accident management and on alternatives that are safer for human health or the environment than the chemicals listed in Annex III to the Convention.
>
> Other treaties require states parties to inform the public of specific environmental hazards. The IAEA Joint Convention on the Safety of Spent Fuel Management and on the Safety of Radioactive Waste Management recognizes the importance of informing the public on issues regarding the safety of spent fuel and radioactive waste management. Arts. 6 and 13, on siting of proposed facilities, require each state party to take the appropriate steps to ensure that procedures are established and implemented to make information available to members of the public on the safety of any proposed spent fuel management facility or radioactive waste management facility. Similarly, Art. 10(1) of the Convention on Persistent Organic Pollutants (Stockholm, May 22, 2001) specifies that each Party shall, within its capabilities, promote and facilitate provision to the public of all available information on persistent organic pollutants and ensure that the public has access to public information and that the information is kept up-to-date (Art.10 (1)(b) and (2)).

Id. In addition, the 1992 Convention on the Transboundary Effects of Industrial Accidents requires Parties to ensure that adequate information is given to the public in areas capable of being affected by an industrial accident arising out of a hazardous activity (Article 9.1). The 1992 United Nations Framework Convention on Climate Change requires state Parties to "promote and facilitate ... public access to information on climate change and its effects." Article 6(*a*)(ii).

One regional convention in particular has dealt with the matter at an almost statutory level of detail. The Convention on Access to Information, Public Participation in Decision-Making and Access to Justice in Environmental Matters, was signed on June 25, 1998, in the city of Aarhus, Denmark. It entered into force Oct. 30, 2001, covers most nations in Western and Eastern Europe, the Caucasus, and Central Asia, and is popularly known as the Aarhus Convention.

The right to information has existed much longer at the national level in some countries. The oldest national legislation guaranteeing freedom of information was enacted in Sweden over 200 years ago. "Public records laws" were first enacted in the United States in the 19th century. In recent years national legislation guaranteeing "access to information" or "freedom of information" has become common. In addition, some national courts have interpreted their constitutions to guarantee a right of access to information.

This chapter will discuss the right to information under both international and national law.

I. The Right to Request Information

There are two generally understood means of accessing governmental information, "passive" and "active." "Passive" access to information refers to a government body's allowable passivity until a member of the public exercises the right of access to information by making a request to the government. If an individual or organization wishes to view a particular piece of information, it must file a request. The right of "active" access to information involves a duty on the part of a government body to collect and disseminate information in an active manner. "Active" access to information will be discussed in Section II of this chapter.

A. Europe, Caucasus, Central Asia — International Rights

Convention on Access to Information, Public Participation in Decision-Making and Access to Justice in Environmental Matters (Aarhus Convention)
June 25, 1998
ECE/CEP/43, 2161 U.N.T.S. 447, 38 I.L.M 517 (1999)

Article 4
ACCESS TO ENVIRONMENTAL INFORMATION

1. Each Party shall ensure that, subject to the following paragraphs of this article, public authorities, in response to a request for environmental information, make such information available to the public, within the framework of national legislation, including, where requested and subject to subparagraph (b) below, copies of the actual documentation containing or comprising such information:

(a) Without an interest having to be stated;

(b) In the form requested unless:

(i) It is reasonable for the public authority to make it available in another form, in which case reasons shall be given for making it available in that form; or

(ii) The information is already publicly available in another form.

2. The environmental information referred to in paragraph 1 above shall be made available as soon as possible and at the latest within one month after the request has been submitted, unless the volume and the complexity of the information justify an extension of this period up to two months after the request. The applicant shall be informed of any extension and of the reasons justifying it.

3. A request for environmental information may be refused if:

(a) The public authority to which the request is addressed does not hold the environmental information requested;

(b) The request is manifestly unreasonable or formulated in too general a manner; or

(c) The request concerns material in the course of completion or concerns internal communications of public authorities where such an exemption is provided for in national law or customary practice, taking into account the public interest served by disclosure.

4. A request for environmental information may be refused if the disclosure would adversely affect:

(a) The confidentiality of the proceedings of public authorities, where such confidentiality is provided for under national law;

(b) International relations, national defence or public security;

(c) The course of justice, the ability of a person to receive a fair trial or the ability of a public authority to conduct an enquiry of a criminal or disciplinary nature;

(d) The confidentiality of commercial and industrial information, where such confidentiality is protected by law in order to protect a legitimate economic interest. Within this framework, information on emissions which is relevant for the protection of the environment shall be disclosed;

(e) Intellectual property rights;

(f) The confidentiality of personal data and/or files relating to a natural person where that person has not consented to the disclosure of the information to the public, where such confidentiality is provided for in national law;

(g) The interests of a third party which has supplied the information requested without that party being under or capable of being put under a legal obligation to do so, and where that party does not consent to the release of the material; or

(h) The environment to which the information relates, such as the breeding sites of rare species.

The aforementioned grounds for refusal shall be interpreted in a restrictive way, taking into account the public interest served by disclosure and taking into account whether the information requested relates to emissions into the environment.

5. Where a public authority does not hold the environmental information requested, this public authority shall, as promptly as possible, inform the applicant of the public authority to which it believes it is possible to apply for the information requested or transfer the request to that authority and inform the applicant accordingly.

6. Each Party shall ensure that, if information exempted from disclosure under paragraphs 3(c) and 4 above can be separated out without prejudice to the confidentiality of the information exempted, public authorities make available the remainder of the environmental information that has been requested.

7. A refusal of a request shall be in writing if the request was in writing or the applicant so requests. A refusal shall state the reasons for the refusal and give information on access to the review procedure provided for in accordance with article 9. The refusal shall be made as soon as possible and at the latest within one month, unless the complexity of the information justifies an extension of this period up to two months after the request. The applicant shall be informed of any extension and of the reasons justifying it.

8. Each Party may allow its public authorities to make a charge for supplying information, but such charge shall not exceed a reasonable amount.

Public authorities intending to make such a charge for supplying information shall make available to applicants a schedule of charges which may be levied, indicating the circumstances in which they may be levied or waived and when the supply of information is conditional on the advance payment of such a charge.

The Aarhus Convention: An Implementation Guide (2000)
Stephen Stec & Susan Casey-Lefkowitz, with Jerzy Jendroska
U.N. Doc. ECE/CEP/72

PILLAR I
ACCESS TO INFORMATION ...

Purpose of access-to-information pillar

Under the Convention, access to environmental information ensures that members of the public can understand what is happening in the environment around them. It also ensures that the public is able to participate in an informed manner.

What is access to information under the Convention?

The Convention governs access to "environmental information." Environmental Information is defined in article 2, paragraph 3, to include the state of the elements of the environment, factors that affect the environment, decision-making processes, and the state of human health and safety.

The access-to-information provisions of the Convention are found in article 4 on access to environmental information and article 5 on the collection and dissemination of environmental information. Article 4 sets out the general right of persons to gain access to existing information upon request, also known as "passive" access to information. Article 5 sets out the duties of the government to collect and disseminate information on its own initiative, also known as "active" access to information.

The preamble, article 1 on the objective and article 3 on general provisions support the provisions of articles 4 and 5, by establishing the right to information, guaranteeing that right and requiring Parties to take all necessary measures and to provide guidance to the public. Article 3, in particular, reminds Parties that the Convention's provisions, including those in articles 4 and 5, are minimum requirements and that Parties have the right to provide broader access to information for the public....

Article 4
Access to Environmental Information

Article 4 sets out a framework through which members of the public can gain access to environmental information from public authorities and, in some cases, from private parties. Once a member of the public has requested information, article 4 establishes criteria and procedures for providing or refusing to provide it. Under the Convention, all persons have the right of access to information.

The Convention starts out with a general rule of freedom of access to information. Parties are required to establish a system whereby a member of the public can request environmental information from a public authority and receive that information within a reasonable amount of time. This general rule is protected by safeguards concerning the timing of responses, the conditions for refusals, the documentation of the process in writing, and provision for review under article 9, paragraph 1.

Most of the provisions in article 4 are requirements that Parties and public authorities must meet. However, paragraphs 3 and 4 outline the circumstances when a Party *may* allow public authorities to refuse a request for information. Indeed, paragraphs 3 and 4 outline the *only* circumstances under which exceptions to the general rule apply. The Convention does not require Parties to adopt these optional provisions. In addition, even if the exceptions are adopted, under all of the following exceptions, Parties may allow the public authority under some circumstances to exercise discretion to provide the information requested. The conditions contained in article 4, paragraphs 3 and 4, simply outline circumstances under which public authorities may withhold the information if necessary to protect the relevant interests, limited in some cases by the public interest in disclosure....

Under the Convention, public authorities shall not impose any condition for supplying information that requires the applicant to state the reason he or she wants the information or how he or she intends to use it. Requests cannot be rejected because the applicant does not have an interest in the information. This follows the "any person" principle....

The interests set out in article 4, paragraph 4, are exceptions to the general rule that information must be provided upon request to members of the public. Parties are not required to incorporate these exceptions into their implementation of the Convention. For the exceptions Parties do accept, the Parties may provide criteria for the public authorities to apply within their discretion, or may categorically exclude certain information from disclosure.

In any case, public authorities must make a determination that disclosure will adversely affect any one of these interests....

In addition, as will be discussed later, either the Party or the public authority must take the public interest in disclosing the information into account, must consider whether the information relates to emissions, and must generally interpret the grounds for refusal laid out in article 4, paragraph 4, in a restrictive way....

Under the Convention, public authorities may choose not to disclose information that would adversely affect an intellectual property right. Intellectual property and intellectual property rights are protected under national and international law. The forms of intellectual property are copyright, patent and trade secret, plus rights for databases where applicable and with trade marks having some relevance as well. Generally, patents protect novel ideas or inventions, copyrights protect original expressions (art, literature, music, etc.), trade marks and geographical indications protect symbols and names used in commerce, and trade secrets protect proprietary business information of all kinds from improper acquisition and use. Intellectual property laws do not, as a general matter, protect "generic" ideas and concepts, principles of nature or scientific fact, or (except for geographical indications) ideas, names or expressions which are already in widespread public use. For patents, copyright and trade marks, protection is afforded to a specific individual person or corporate entity, is limited in duration, and has the primary goal of creating economic rewards for creators and inventors, through market transactions involving the intellectual property right or its subject matter....

The final clause of article 4, paragraph 4, instructs Parties and public authorities on how to interpret all of the exceptions to access to information under that paragraph....

Parties and public authorities must interpret the exceptions in a "restrictive way." For example, if an official refuses to release information by claiming one of the exceptions, he or she could be required to go through a process to ensure that the decision to use the exception is not arbitrary and that in each case the release of information would lead to actual harm to the relevant interest. The Convention contains two safeguards that help Parties understand what is meant by restrictive.

Under article 4, paragraph 4, Parties must take the public interest served by disclosure into account. As discussed in article 4, paragraph 3(c), "the public interest served by disclosure" is not clearly defined in the Convention. It is left for Parties to decide how and when the public interest will be taken into account, in conformity with the principles and objective of the Convention. The Guidelines on Public Participation in Environmental Decision-making (see Introduction) provide Parties with some guidance as to what could be meant by the reference to the public interest served by disclosure. Paragraph 6 of the Guidelines stipulates that the "aforementioned grounds for refusal are to be interpreted in a restrictive way with the public interest served by disclosure weighed against the interests of non-disclosure in each case." Most of the Signatories to the Aarhus Convention have endorsed the Sofia Guidelines, and the Guidelines are specifically mentioned in the preamble and the Resolution of the Signatories. In addition, national law provides some guidance for defining "public interest." ...

In a second safeguard, the Convention requires public authorities to take into account whether the information requested relates to emissions into the environment. As seen in the exception concerning commercial confidentiality (art. 4, para. 4(d)), the Convention places a high priority on releasing information on emissions.

Questions and Discussion

1. *National discretion.* According to Article 4, paragraph 1, of the Aarhus Convention, Parties "in response to a request for environmental information, [shall] make such information available to the public, within the framework of national legislation." Does this merely mean that national legislation should set out a framework for the process of answering information requests in accordance with the Convention, that national legislation may impose any limits the nation wishes, or that its national legislation may *limit* access to information only in accordance with the optional exceptions outlined in Article 4, paragraphs 3 and 4? The answer to this question can have significant implications for whether information rights among nations that are Parties to the Aarhus Convention are governed by a strict regional standard, a weak regional standard (essentially allowing a "margin of appreciation" or discretion), or none at all. The same question comes up repeatedly both under the Aarhus Convention and other international agreements.

2. *Summaries or raw documents.* Is a public authority obliged to provide only a summary of required documents or a copy of the original documents containing the required information? The Freedom of Information Act (FOIA) in the United States requires that "an agency shall provide the record in any form or format requested by the person if the record is readily reproducible by the agency in that form or format." 5 U.S.C. § 552(a)(3)(B).

3. *General or unreasonable requests.* Public authorities may refuse a request under the Aarhus Convention for information that is "manifestly unreasonable" or formulated in "too general a manner," according to Article 4, paragraph 3. What might this mean? The Con-

vention does not define those terms. If Parties choose to include such exceptions in national legislation, should they define "manifestly unreasonable" or "too general" to assist public authorities in determining where requests can be refused under these exceptions, or should it be left to the discretion of individual civil servants? If they create such exceptions but do not define them, should the courts review denials of information *de novo* or should they grant deference to civil servants? The Freedom of Information Act (FOIA) in the United States does not allow a request to be refused on the ground that it is manifestly unreasonable, but does allow search and copying fees to be charged to the requester in certain circumstances. FOIA also requires agencies to answer a request only if it "reasonably describes" the records being sought. 5 U.S.C. § 552(a)(3)(A)(i). Does this limitation allow refusal on the ground that a request is manifestly unreasonable, or does it refer to something else?

4. *National security.* The Convention allows Parties to refuse requests that would adversely affect "international relations, national defence or public security." Article 4, paragraph 4. Public authorities tend to decide on a case-by-case basis whether a request for information would harm these interests. Does this leave too much discretion to government decisionmakers, or is discretion essential? The same paragraph of the Convention provides that all the exemptions "shall be interpreted in a restrictive way, taking into account the public interest served by disclosure and taking into account whether the information requested relates to emissions into the environment." Is this an instruction to national legislatures, to individual civil servants, to judges, or to all of them? FOIA in the United States provides an exemption for matters that are "specifically authorized under criteria established by an Executive order to be kept secret in the interest of national defense or foreign policy and (B) are in fact properly classified pursuant to such Executive order." 5 U.S.C. § 552(b)(1)(A). Compare this to the Aarhus formulation. The final decision about all exemptions from the duty to release information is left to the courts in the United States:

> In such a case the court shall determine the matter de novo, and may examine the contents of such agency records in camera to determine whether such records or any part thereof shall be withheld under any of the exemptions set forth in subsection (b) of this section, and the burden is on the agency to sustain its action.

5 U.S.C. § 552(a)(4)(B).

5. *Business secrets.* A public authority under the Aarhus Convention may withhold information from the public on the basis of commercial confidentiality "in order to protect a legitimate economic interest." Article 4, paragraph 4(d). To do so, a Party must explicitly protect confidentiality of commercial or industrial information in its national law. What about information on pollutant emissions? Can it be kept confidential? The Convention states further, "Within this framework, information on emissions which is relevant for the protection of the environment shall be disclosed." *Id.* Who should determine relevancy?

Many countries have commercial, trade, and official secret exceptions, which limit information dissemination. This can be used to keep environmental information out of public hands. Some laws limit such exceptions, however. For example, section 114 of the Clean Air Act in the United States provides that information may be kept confidential if it would divulge a "trade secret" but conditions this as "other than emission data." 42 U.S.C. § 7414. Great battles have been fought in the U.S. courts on whether information showing harm to humans or the environment may be kept from the public on the ground that it is confidential commercial information. Are limitations based on commercial and trade secrets acceptable? What standards should be used when determining whether information should be withheld? Who should bear the burden of proof? The party advocating that the information should be disclosed to the public or the party claiming that the information should be withheld from the public?

6. *Public Interest Test.* How should the "public interest test" in Article 4, paragraph 3 be applied? FOIA in the United States does not have any similar override to its exemptions. On the other hand, the exemptions in the United States law are worded in quite a restrictive manner.

7. *Possession of information.* Article 4, paragraph 3(a), allows a public authority to refuse an information request if the authority does not hold requested information. Does the public authority have some other obligations in this situation?

8. *Which is the better law?* Compare the United States' FOIA to the Aarhus Convention. What are the benefits and drawbacks to each? Are there better answers than a case-by-case approach to enforcement?

Whether rights to information under the Aarhus Convention or similar international instruments are ultimately guaranteed depends on whether national courts insist that governments or others holding information release it to the public. Inability to get the information because of inadequate national legislation, unenlightened or reluctant civil servants, or unwilling national courts may not be the end of a story, however. In the case of the Aarhus Convention, an international body, akin to human rights bodies, considers claims that a Party is violating its obligations. The Aarhus Compliance Committee, as indicated in the following article, acts with independence. A case showing that independence follows the article.

The Aarhus Convention and Innovations in Compliance with Multilateral Environmental Agreements

Svitlana Kravchenko

18 Colo. J. Int'l Envtl. L. & Pol'y 1 (2007)

In just two years of considering cases, the Aarhus compliance mechanism has already dealt with several significant issues in each of the three areas that the Aarhus Convention covers: access to information, public participation, and access to justice. The Compliance Committee and Meeting of the Parties are interpreting the Aarhus Convention through their decisions and building a body of "case law."

III. COMPLIANCE MECHANISM OF THE AARHUS CONVENTION AND COMPARISONS TO OTHER MEAS

The compliance mechanism established under the Aarhus Convention is innovative in both structure and procedure. In terms of structure, NGOs have gained the right to nominate members of the independent body. In addition, the compliance body as a whole is composed of independent experts....

A. *Structure: NGO Nominations and Independent Experts*

1. *NGO Nominations*

Having members of the Committee nominated not only by Parties and Signatories— which is the general rule—but also by NGOs appears to be unique among environmental conventions and perhaps in international law. Nomination does not guarantee election, but in the author's experience, the Parties appear to be committed to taking the views of NGOs seriously in this process. Nomination by NGOs was one of the difficult issues upon which to reach a consensus during meetings of the Task Force on Compliance Mechanisms in 1999 and 2000 and subsequent negotiations in the Intergovernmental Working Group (IWG) on Compliance and Rules of Procedure in 2000 and 2001. In November 2001, the IWG had reported to the Working Group for the Preparation of the First Meeting of the Parties that unresolved compliance issues included "whether the proposed compliance committee should be made up of Parties to the Convention or of independent experts serving in a personal capacity, and if the latter, whether NGOs as well as Parties should be entitled to nominate the experts for election." At the second meeting of the Working Group for the First Meeting of Parties in Geneva in May 2002, the Chair recommended to resolve these outstanding issues by providing that "the compliance committee should comprise independent experts to be nominated by Parties, Signatories and NGOs and elected by the Parties...." After discussion during that May 2002 meeting, the Working Group "decided that the committee should comprise independent experts." The proposal from the Chair that NGOs should be able to nominate experts was accepted at the third meeting of the Working Group of the Parties in Pula, Croatia, in July 2002. This was the final preparatory meeting before the First Meeting of the Parties in Lucca, Italy. This was one of the features that drew the ire of the representative of the United States at the first Meeting of the Parties in Lucca, Italy, in October 2002. Despite such criticism, the compliance mechanism was adopted and two persons nominated by NGOs were elected to the committee. This unprecedented process can be seen as recognition that, for a Convention that has public participation as a core issue, it is a logical step for the public to nominate some of the experts who will play a role in encouraging compliance with the Convention.

2. Independent Experts

An equally important structural issue is the use of independent experts serving in their personal capacity rather than representatives of state Parties. The Parties to a convention or treaty, not independent experts, have usually been the ones who sit on any committee established to administer the treaty, including any "compliance" or "implementation" committee. The Aarhus Convention's Committee, however, is made up of eight persons, each serving in a "personal capacity" and the Committee is "composed of nationals of the Parties and Signatories to the Convention who shall be persons of high moral character and recognized competence in the fields to which the Convention relates, including persons having legal experience." The origin of this language can be traced to Article 28 of the International Covenant on Civil and Political Rights, signed in 1966, which established a United Nations Human Rights Committee of eighteen members elected to serve "in their personal capacity"; these members had to be "persons of high moral character and recognized competence in the field of human rights." Similar language can be found in the American Convention on Human Rights of 1969, establishing the Inter-American Commission on Human Rights, and numerous other human rights conventions.

Findings and Recommendations with Regard to Compliance by Kazakhstan

Communication ACCC/C/2004/01 by Green Salvation (Kazakhstan)
Aarhus Convention Compliance Committee, 18 February 2005
U.N. Doc. ECE/MP.PP/C.1/2005/2/Add.1 (11 March 2005)

INTRODUCTION

On 7 February 2004, the Kazakh non-governmental organization Green Salvation submitted a communication to the Committee alleging non-compliance by Kazakhstan with its obligations under article 4, paragraphs 1 and 7, article 6, paragraph 6, and article 9, paragraph 1, of the Aarhus Convention.

The communication concerned access to information related to the proposed draft act on the import and disposal of radioactive waste in Kazakhstan held by the National Atomic Company Kazatomprom. The communicant claims that its right to information was violated when a request to Kazatomprom for information purporting to substantiate a proposal to import and dispose of foreign radioactive waste was not answered. Subsequent appeal procedures in courts of various jurisdictions and instances failed, in the communicant's view, to meet the requirements of article 9, paragraph 1, of the Convention. According to the communication, the lawsuits were rejected first on grounds of jurisdiction and subsequently on procedural grounds as the courts did not acknowledge the right of a non-governmental organization to file a suit under article 9, paragraph 1, in its own name rather than as an authorized representative of its members....

The communication was forwarded to the Party concerned on 17 May 2004, following a preliminary determination as to its admissibility.

A response was received from the Party concerned on 27 October 2004, indicating, inter alia, that:

(a) The communicant did not fall under the definition of "the public concerned" within the meaning of article 2, paragraph 5, of the Convention for the type of decision-making process in question;

(b) As of the end of 2002, the information requested by the communicant from Kazatomprom did not relate to any ongoing decision-making procedure, as the matter was not under consideration by the Government;

(c) The National Atomic Company Kazatomprom did not fall under the definition of "public authority" within the meaning of article 2, paragraph 2, of the Convention.

The Party alleged that, as a consequence, the communication did not satisfy the formal requirements of admissibility for review of compliance under the Convention. However, it did welcome possible recommendations from the Compliance Committee, which could be used to improve both practice and legislation in Kazakhstan in the relevant field.

The Committee at its fourth meeting (MP.PP/C.1/2004/4, para. 18) determined on a preliminary basis that the communication was admissible, subject to review following any comments received from the Party concerned. Having reviewed the arguments put forward by the Party concerned in its response and having further consulted with both parties at its sixth meeting, the Committee confirms the admissibility of the communication, deeming the points raised by the Party concerned to be of substance rather than related to admissibility.

In accordance with paragraph 34 of the annex to decision I/7, the draft findings and recommendations were forwarded for comment to the Party concerned and to the communicant on 1 February 2005. Both were invited to provide comments, if any, by 14 February 2005. Comments were received from both the Parties concerned. The Committee, having reviewed the comments, took them into account in finalizing its findings and recommendations by amending the draft where the comments, in its opinion, affected the presentation of facts or its consideration, evaluation or conclusions.

I. SUMMARY OF FACTS

In 2001, the President of the National Atomic Company Kazatomprom, Mr. M. Jakishev, proposed for consideration by the Parliament a legislative amendment which would allow the import and disposal of foreign low- and medium-level radioactive waste in Kazakhstan.

Mr. Jakishev's statement in the press referred to a feasibility study justifying the proposed amendments.

On 11 November 2002, the Ecological Society Green Salvation requested Mr. Jakishev, in writing, to provide the calculations justifying his statement to the press.

Having received no response, the communicant challenged the refusal to provide the information requested, filing a lawsuit with one of the Almaty district courts on 4 February 2003.

Between 12 February 2003 and 23 May 2003, seven determinations were issued by judges of various courts in an attempt to determine the jurisdiction of the lawsuit. The case was heard on merit starting from 23 May 2003. At the hearing on 28 May 2003, a representative of the defendant (Kazatomprom) presented the court with a copy of the feasibility study of the disputed project. However, the case was dismissed on 13 June 2003 on procedural grounds for lack of standing. The decision stated, in particular, that, as an environmental non-governmental organization, the plaintiff could represent in court only the interests of its individual members and that it had failed to present a power of attorney from the individuals whose interest it represented.

The decision was unsuccessfully appealed to six instances, including three offices of the public prosecutor.

II. CONSIDERATION AND EVALUATION BY THE COMMITTEE ...

The Convention, as an international treaty ratified by Kazakhstan, has direct applicability in the Kazakh legal system. All the provisions of the Convention are directly applicable, including by the courts.

The communicant is a non-governmental organization working in the field of environmental protection and falls under the definition of "the public," as set out in article 2, paragraph 4, of the Convention.

The National Atomic Company Kazatomprom is a legal person performing administrative functions under national law, including activities in relation to the environment, and performing public functions under the control of a public authority. The company is also fully owned by the State. Due to these characteristics, it falls under the definition of a "public authority," as set out in article 2, paragraphs 2(b) and 2(c).

Information requested from Kazatomprom, in particular the feasibility study of the draft amendments, falls under the definition of article 2, paragraph 3(b), of the Convention.

It is, therefore, the opinion of the Committee that, as a public authority in the meaning of article 2, paragraphs 2(b) and 2(c), Kazatomprom was under an obligation to provide the environmental information requested by the communicant pursuant to article 4 and that failure to do so was not in conformity with that article.

The Committee has noted the information provided by the Party concerned that it is a general practice for an information request to include reasons for which such information is requested. Article 4, paragraph 1(a), of the Convention explicitly rules out making such justification a requirement. In this regard, the Committee notes with appreciation the Memo on Processing Public Requests for Environmental Information, prepared by the Ministry of the Environment of Kazakhstan and the Organization for Security and Co-operation in Europe (OSCE), issued in 2004. The Memo clearly states that a request for information does not need to be justified. In the Committee's opinion, practical implementation of the Memo would be important for changing the current practice and, furthermore, might bring about compliance with all the provisions of article 4.

The Convention, in its article 9, paragraph 1, requires the Parties to ensure that any procedure for appealing failure to access information is expeditious. However, as the time and number of determinations with regard to jurisdiction in this case demonstrate, there appears to be lack of regulations providing clear guidance to the judiciary as to the meaning of an expeditious procedure in cases related to access to information.

Finally, as events described above demonstrate, the requirement of article 9, paragraph 1, to ensure that any person (including a legal person, as set out in the definition of the public in article 2, paragraph 5, of the Convention) whose request for information under article 4 has not been dealt with in accordance with the provisions of that article has access to an expeditious review procedure, has not been properly transposed into the national legislation. Nor, it appears, was there any guidance issued to the judiciary with regard to the direct applicability of the Convention's provisions.

The Committee considers that the underlying reason for non-compliance with the requirements of articles 4 and 9, paragraph 1, as described in paragraphs 16 to 19 and 21 to 22 above, was a failure by the Party concerned to establish and maintain, pursuant to the obligation established in article 3, paragraph 1, a clear, transparent and consistent framework to implement these provisions of the Convention, e.g. by providing clear instructions on the status and obligations of bodies performing functions of public authorities, or regulating the issue of standing in cases on access to information in procedural legislation.

III. Conclusions

Having considered the above, the Committee adopts the findings and recommendations set out in the following paragraphs with a view to bringing them to the attention of the Meeting of the Parties.

A. Main findings with regard to non-compliance

The Committee finds that, by having failed to ensure that bodies performing public functions implement the provisions of article 4, paragraphs 1 and 2, of the Convention, Kazakhstan was not in compliance with that article.

The Committee also finds that the lengthy review procedure and denial of standing to the non-governmental organization in a lawsuit on access to environmental information was not in compliance with article 9, paragraph 1.

The Committee further finds that the lack of clear regulation and guidance with regard to the obligations of bodies performing public functions to provide information to the public and with regard to the implementation of article 9, paragraph 1, constitutes non-compliance with the obligations established in article 3, paragraph 1, of the Convention.

B. Recommendations

The Committee, pursuant to paragraph 35 of annex to decision I/7 and taking into account the cause and degree of non-compliance, recommends to the Meeting of the Parties to:

(a) Pursuant to paragraph 37(b) of the annex to decision I/7, request the Government of Kazakhstan to submit to the Compliance Committee, not later than the end of 2005, a strategy, including a time schedule, for transposing the Convention's provisions into national law and developing practical mechanisms and implementing legislation that would set out clear procedures for their implementation. The strategy might also include capacity-building activities, in particular for the judiciary and public officials, including persons having public responsibilities or functions, involved in environmental decision-making;

(b) Recommend the Government of Kazakhstan to provide officials of all the relevant public authorities on various levels of administration with training on the implementation of the Memo on Processing Public Requests for Environmental Information and to report to the Meeting of the Parties, through the Compliance Committee, no less than four months before the third meeting of the Parties on the measures taken to this end;

(c) Request the secretariat or, as appropriate, the Compliance Committee, and invite relevant international and regional organizations and financial institutions, to provide advice and assistance to Kazakhstan as necessary in the implementation of these measures.

Questions and Discussion

1. *What is a "public authority"?* In the *Green Salvation* case, the interpretation of the term "public authority" is an important issue as only public authority has an obligation to provide information upon request. Does the National Atomic Company Kazatomprom fall under the definition of "public authority" within the meaning of Article 2, paragraph 2, of the Convention?

2. *Standing for environmental NGOs.* When the communicant appealed the denial of information to the court, the case was dismissed on procedural grounds for lack of standing. The court stated that, as an environmental non-governmental organization, the plaintiff could only represent the interests of its individual members. What is wrong in this decision? What is the definition of the "public concerned" in Article 2, paragraph 5, of the Convention?

3. *Question of timing.* The *Green Salvation* case notes that, while the Aarhus Convention requires expeditious review procedures for denials of information requests, it does not provide guidance for the meaning of "expeditious." When might timing be critical for accessing environmental information? When applicants sue to enforce their right to information, they can spend years in the judicial and appeals process. What kind of procedures could a government implement to ensure that the public's right to access information is not made moot by prolonged appeals procedures?

4. *Subsequent developments.* After this case, the government of Kazakhstan, following recommendations of the Compliance Committee, developed a strategy and adopted a new Environmental Code and several regulations, including provisions on access to information. It also organized capacity-building activities, in particular for the judiciary and public officials. In March 2008, Green Salvation won a case on access of information in the Supreme Court of Kazakhstan. The Court recognized the plaintiff's right to information and obliged a public authority to give required information. The Supreme Court based its decision on domestic law and also directly applied the Aarhus Convention to the case.

B. Latin America — Statutory and International Rights

Latin American State Secrecy and Mexico's Transparency Law
Eric Heyer
38 George Washington International Law Review 437 © (2006)

I. Introduction

A fundamental building block of democratic societies is unhindered access to government-held information. Access to such information allows the public to critique government actions and make electoral and economic decisions accordingly, thereby underpinning the notion of a democratic government that derives its authority from the consent of the governed....

In approximately the last five years, Latin America has seen an unprecedented academic and public interest in governmental transparency and accountability result in the consideration of a number of national measures aimed at increasing public and media access to governmental information. Yet despite the widespread public interest in reducing corruption and increasing political accountability, most Latin American states still lack access-to-information regimes that are comprehensive in law, much less in practice. Nevertheless, some Latin American legislatures have very recently begun to undertake legal reforms aimed at increasing public accountability. One such country is Mexico, which in 2002 passed the Federal Transparency and Access to Government Information Law (Transparency Law).

Mexico's Transparency Law is notable in the Latin American context, both for its provisions and the processes surrounding its promulgation.... Mexico's Congress approved the Transparency Law following successful negotiations that incorporated input from non-governmental organizations, academics, and members of the press, granting the process surrounding the Law's promulgation a degree of public legitimacy seldom seen in many Latin American states. The Transparency Law is broad in scope and prescribes detailed procedures for answering access-to-information requests, establishing one of the first unified, comprehensive legal frameworks for access to official information in Latin America. Although further guarantees could still be incorporated into the Mexican Law, it goes a long way towards achieving compliance with international government accountability norms....

Mexico's Transparency Law should serve, in many respects, as a model transparency law for other Latin American states attempting to open governmental operations up to greater public scrutiny....

II. Discussion ...

A. Background: Transparency and Corruption in Latin America

Traditionally, the most common legal recourses for obtaining government-held information in Latin American countries have been the right to petition and *habeas data* actions. The utility of habeas data actions has historically been limited, however, because *habeas data* is generally considered to be an individualized and personal right available only to "interested parties," thereby making it ineffective for members of the press....

The tradition of secrecy surrounding state action in Latin American countries has historically played a significant role in the creation of a legal environment where the public perceives governmental corruption to be widespread....

[R]ecent survey data provide some insights into the perceived prevalence of corruption in Latin American governance. In a 2004 survey, Transparency International ranked countries on a global scale for its Corruption Perceptions Index. With the exceptions of

Chile and Uruguay, no country in Latin America ranked above a 5.0 on a 10-point scale; Paraguay, Guatemala, Bolivia, Venezuela, Honduras, and Argentina all received scores of 2.5 or below, putting them at or below the rankings of Eritrea, Vietnam, and Libya. According to Transparency International, scores below 3.0 indicate "rampant corruption." Further, corruption is also often perceived as an evil that hits close to home. In a similar 2003 poll, 64.6 percent of Costa Ricans surveyed reported that corruption affects their personal and family life.

Corruption also affects public perception of the legal systems in Latin American countries. In a February 2004 poll, 74 percent of respondents mentioned the judiciary as among the most corrupt institutions in Peru, topping even the police. In a 2001 Latinobarámetro poll, less than 30 percent of Latin Americans expressed "some" or "a lot" of confidence in their respective countries' judiciaries.... The Special Rapporteur received estimates that anywhere from 50 to 70 percent of all federal judges in Mexico were corrupt.

It is against this backdrop of public opinion on corruption that Latin American legislators must consider reform efforts to guarantee openness in governmental operations. Broader public understanding of daily governmental operations leads to greater consideration of individual and group interests in the outcomes of official decision-making, followed by closer scrutiny of questionable policies and more active societal participation in governance. The first step for Latin American legislators in creating this potentially virtuous cycle of public involvement is the establishment of a unified legal framework that rectifies the practical shortcomings of the *habeas data* action and the right to petition....

B. The International Legal Framework ...

For most Latin American countries, the international legal regime that has the most direct and concrete influence in promoting transparency is the Inter-American human rights regime under the American Convention on Human Rights. While national and international jurisprudence around the world has diverged to some extent in grounding the obligation to grant access to official information in the right to freedom of thought, the right to private and family life, and the right to freedom of expression, the Inter-American system firmly places the obligation within the last of these. Article 13 of the American Convention on Human Rights guarantees the right to freedom of expression and provides that, with limited exceptions, that right includes the right to "seek, receive and impart information of all kinds." ...

[T]he Declaration of Principles of Freedom of Expression (DPFE), which the Inter-American Commission on Human Rights adopted in 2000, focuses on the obligation to ensure access to governmental information.... Article 4 designates the right to access to official information as a fundamental right and presents one of the few acceptable constraints on the right:

> Access to information held by the state is a fundamental right of every individual. States have the obligation to guarantee the full exercise of this right. This principle allows only exceptional limitations that must be previously established by law in case of a real and imminent danger that threatens national security in democratic societies.... member states "are obliged to ... promote the adoption of any necessary legislative ... provisions to ensure [access to public information]." ...

C. Mexico's Transparency Law

   1. Background ...

Mexico's constitution, like that of many other Latin American countries, protects freedom of expression and the right to petition. Article VI provides that "[t]he expression of ideas shall not be subject to any judicial or administrative investigation, unless it offends good morals, infringes the rights of others, incites crime, or disturbs the public order. Freedom of information shall be guaranteed by the State." ...

Like their counterparts in many other Latin American countries, prior to the passage of the Transparency Law, Mexican citizens had no access to fundamental information.... Prior to the implementation of the Transparency Law, it was "almost impossible" to locate judicial decisions dealing with particular aspects of a given legal issue, as virtually no centralized public databases of decisions existed....

In the face of the pervasive culture of government secrecy perpetuated by the PRI, the unanimous passage of the Transparency Law in 2002 was the direct result of unified civil society efforts and the dedication of the Fox administration to reform initiatives.... The active advocacy of the media was also essential to the Law's passage, as the failure of media outlets to become actively involved in other Latin American countries had permitted other governments to withstand pressures to adopt freedom-of-information laws....

2. The Transparency Law's Provisions

a. General Overview

The scope of the Transparency Law is broad, as it covers all three branches of the federal government, as well as administrative tribunals and all autonomous bodies. Further, it defines information that should potentially be available to the public to include all records in any medium that official bodies generate, obtain, acquire, transform, or have on file, regardless of their source. The Law establishes a clear procedure for information requests, mandating the creation of an information liaison section in each executive branch government agency, as well as an information committee composed of a civil servant, the head of the liaison section, and the head of the internal oversight body. The committee is the ultimate body responsible within each agency for classifying and declassifying information.

The Transparency Law provides specific details requiring government agencies to publish information.... The judicial branch must also make rulings public, although individuals may object to the disclosure of their personal information. Similar rules apply to administrative decisions and draft bills....

Procedurally, any person or his or her representative may submit a request, and the Law specifies that in "no case shall the delivery of information be conditioned upon a motive or justification for its use, nor shall any demonstration of any [particular] interest be required." Notification of the decision on disclosure must occur within twenty working days, while the agency must provide the information sought within another ten days. The fees required may not exceed the cost of the materials used to reproduce the information, in addition to the cost of sending it to the petitioner.... In the event of a denial, the petitioner may appeal the decision, first to the administrative body described below, and, beyond that, to the courts.

b. Structural Safeguards ...

i. Autonomous Administrative Organ

Mexico's Transparency Law mandates creation of a new administrative organ called the Federal Institute for Access to Information (Instituto Federal de Acceso a la Información or IFAI), which performs a variety of functions stemming from its purpose of promoting public access to governmental information under the Transparency Law....

The IFAI's powers to ensure adherence to the letter of the Transparency Law in practice include the ability to request reports from each agency on information that has been classified and override such classifications, even in the absence of a case challenging the classification. The IFAI must also approve any decisions by administrative bodies to extend classification beyond the twelve-year limit. The IFAI also monitors agency performance and makes recommendations to specific entities to improve public access. Paramount in this regard are the body's powers to conduct on-site visits to other governmental agencies to determine compliance with its regulations and decisions. Most importantly, the IFAI acts as the administrative appellate body for access-to-information requests that are denied by the agency to which the petitioner presents the request.

A board of five commissioners heads the IFAI. This board decides individual petitions and reports on the Transparency Law's implementation through, among other means, an annual report to Congress detailing statistics on information requests and observed difficulties in the implementation of the Law. The Transparency Law contains provisions designed to guarantee the commissioners' political independence, barring from candidacy any recent holders of a variety of national political offices and directors of political parties or associations. The president names each commissioner, although the Senate may object to any nomination. Commissioners can only be removed for committing "serious or repeated violations of the provisions found in the Constitution and in this Law, when their actions or failures to act affect the Institute's prerogatives, or when they have been convicted of a felony." The law also seeks to establish the Institute's independence as a whole. The Transparency Law specifically states: "[f]or the purposes of its rulings, the Institute will not be subject to any authority, will make its decisions with full independence, and will be provided with the necessary human and material resources for carrying out its functions...."

c. Procedural Safeguards

In addition to the structural safeguards just described, the Mexican Transparency Law contains a number of procedural safeguards, all of which are intended to ensure maximum transparency in the face of less-than-sympathetic members of the judiciary or government officials. Among the most innovative are: (i) an explicit presumption favoring transparency; (ii) the unappealability of administrative decisions favoring disclosure; and (iii) strict time limits for negative responses to requests....

i. Explicit Presumption Favoring Transparency

Article 6 of the Mexican Transparency Law provides: "[i]n interpretations of this Law, the principle of publicity of information possessed by subjects compelled by the Law must be favored." This presumption not only seeks to limit judicial deviation from the principle of maximum transparency, but also serves as an important principle for regulations putting the Law into action....

ii. Unappealability of Decisions Favoring Disclosure

Article 59 provides: "[t]he Institute's rulings will be final for the agencies and entities. Private persons may challenge them before the Federation's Judicial Branch." By limiting opportunities for government entities to appeal IFAI rulings requiring disclosure of requested information, the Transparency Law minimizes any potential for politically motivated judicial decisions by judges that sometimes lack complete authoritativeness and independence from executive agencies.

iii. Strict Time Limits for Negative Responses

Article 53 of the Transparency Law provides that "[l]ack of response to a request for access within [20 days] will be understood as an acceptance of the request." This provision attempts to deal with concerns that significant delays in the disclosure of information may create disincentives for public inquiries. Indeed, very lengthy delays exist in certain sectors of the U.S. government, and so this provision seeks to ensure that such a situation is not re-created in Mexico. This provision also recognizes the time-sensitive nature of many information inquiries, particularly those presented by members of the press.

3. Implementation to Date ...

Though the Law has only been in effect for a short time, already a number of positive indications have arisen from its implementation.... Environmentalists have ... quickly taken advantage of the Law, as the Ministry of Environment and Natural Resources received over 1200 requests, and over 1500 requests were filed with the national oil company, PEMEX, and its various subsidiaries....

A. The Importance of a Regional Model

Consideration of the need for a distinctively Latin American transparency model will shed light on the role that the Mexican Law's safeguards can have in other Latin American countries.... [W]hen compared to the recent history of the Freedom of Information Act in the United States, Mexico's Transparency Law is better suited to serve as a legislative model for other Latin American regimes considering adoption of unified access to official information laws....

There are various reasons to conclude that the United States is currently disfavored among Latin American policymakers as a source for answers to the national security and other issues that the drafting of a comprehensive transparency law necessarily entails. Latin American commentators have observed that the perception persists in Latin American countries that notions of transparency in governmental operations belong to the culture of common-law legal systems and that such notions are incompatible with Latin American legal systems. The perceived subordination of some access-to-information guarantees to security concerns by anti-terrorism legislation since September 11th also makes the United States a less attractive source of inspiration for convincing reticent lawmakers of the need for comprehensive transparency laws....

For these reasons, the measures established by the Mexican Law will more likely win broad acceptance throughout Latin America than a model imported directly from the United States.

The Federal Institute for Access to Information & A Culture of Transparency — Follow Up Report
Benjamin Fernandez Bogado, Emilene Martinez-Morales,
Bethany Davis Noll, & Kyle Bell
December 2007
http://www.global.asc.upenn.edu/docs/FollowUp_Report_January_2008.pdf

II. Ifai Today ...

IFAI [Mexico's Instituto Federal de Acceso a la Información] and the obligated agencies have handled a remarkable number of requests since the passage of the law. Between June 2003 and June 2007, more than 218 thousand information requests were filed. In 2006, IFAI received 3533 appeals, a 33% increase over 2005. Since 2003, the agencies that have received the most requests have been the Mexican Institute of Social Security, the Secretary of Finance and Public Credit, the Secretary of Public Education, the Secretary of the Environment and Natural Resources, the Ministry of Public Administration, and the Attorney General of the Republic....

Awareness of the law remains low: while the number of those who know nothing about the law has dropped from 88% in 2003 to 51% in a 2006 poll, this is still far too high....

A. Constitutional Reform

On March 6, 2007, a constitutional reform initiative on the issue of transparency passed unanimously after less than three months of deliberation in Congress. The constitutional amendment was, by all accounts, the greatest accomplishment in the area of access to information in Mexico of 2007. It guarantees the public's right to information at all levels of government. It requires all state transparency laws to be standardized around certain basic principles within one year and gives the states two years to implement an electronic mechanism for simple anonymous submission of information requests....

The constitutional amendment changes the Sixth Article of the Constitution to reflect the right of free and unfettered access to government information (third clause), all of which, by nature, belongs to the public (first clause). Such information may only be withheld for reasons of public interest and for the length of time set by law (first clause). The fifth clause reads, "The obligated subjects must preserve their documents in up-to-date administrative archives and publish, through available electronic means, complete and current information about management indicators and usage of public resources." The amendment passed was published in the Official Reporter on July 20, 2007, after being ratified by all the states in one and a half months.

As we reported in 2006, the development of access to information has been uneven across the states. By mid-2007, all 31 states, as well as the Federal District, had passed transparency laws. But, the laws varied widely in effectiveness and in their basic principles....

In the 2006 study, we observed that for a deeply ingrained, robust culture of transparency to be established in Mexico, IFAI must involve state and municipal governments to promote transparency on the local level. We noted that the activities of the state and municipal governments are closer to the daily lives of average citizens, and thus the benefits of transparency can best be demonstrated at the local level through the disclosure of information held by those entities....

Questions and Discussion

1. *Mexico's transparency laws.* What are some of the strong features of Mexico's transparency laws? What are their weaknesses in comparison with the American Declaration or with the Aarhus Convention in Europe? What is special in the "explicit presumption favoring transparency" in Mexican Law? How is it different from the Aarhus Convention?

2. *Interest or motivation.* Who can submit a request for information in Mexico? Is it necessary to demonstrate an interest or motivation for submitting a request? What are special terms established by law for the government to provide information? Is information provided free of charge?

3. *Insulation from corruption.* In many countries, corruption within the courts and the government hinders the right to information. Is the establishment of independent agencies, insulated from outside influence, the answer to this problem of corruption? What are some other potential solutions?

Claude Reyes v. Chile

Inter-American Court Of Human Rights
Inter-Am. Ct. H.R. (ser. C) No. 151 (Sept. 19, 2006)

INTRODUCTION OF THE CASE

On July 8, 2005, in accordance with the provisions of Articles 50 and 61 of the American Convention, the Inter-American Commission on Human Rights (hereinafter "the Commission" or "the Inter-American Commission") lodged before the Court an application against the State of Chile (hereinafter "the State" or "Chile"). This application originated from petition No. 12,108, received by the Secretariat of the Commission on December 17, 1998.

The Commission submitted the application for the Court to declare that the State was responsible for the violation of the rights embodied in Articles 13 (Freedom of Thought and Expression) and 25 (Right to Judicial Protection) of the American Convention, in relation to the obligations established in Articles 1(1) (Obligation to Respect Rights) and 2 (Domestic Legal Effects) thereof, to the detriment of Marcel Claude Reyes, Sebastián Cox Urrejola and Arturo Longton Guerrero.

The facts described by the Commission in the application supposedly occurred between May and August 1998 and refer to the State's alleged refusal to provide Marcel Claude Reyes, Sebastián Cox Urrejola and Arturo Longton Guerrero with all the information they requested from the Foreign Investment Committee [FIC]on the forestry company Trillium and the Río Condor Project, a deforestation project to be executed in Chile's Region XII that "c[ould] be prejudicial to the environment and to the sustainable development of Chile."…

PROCEEDINGS BEFORE THE COMMISSION …

On March 7, 2005, pursuant to Article 50 of the Convention, the Commission adopted Report No. 31/05, in which it concluded that Chile had "violated the rights of Marcel Claude Reyes [and others] of access to public information and to judicial protection established in Articles 13 and 25 of the American Convention, respectively, in relation to Articles 1(1) and 2 of the Convention, by denying them access to information held by the Chilean Foreign Investment Committee and by not granting them access to Chilean justice to contest this refusal." …

PROCEEDINGS BEFORE THE COURT

On July 8, 2005, the Inter-American Commission submitted the application to the Court, attaching documentary evidence and offering testimonial and expert evidence.…

V

EVIDENCE

A) DOCUMENTARY EVIDENCE …

TESTIMONIES

a) Proposed by the Inter-American Commission on Human Rights …

2. Arturo Longton Guerrero, alleged victim

He has been a Member of Congress of the Republic of Chile for more than 16 years, and "during this time [has] been involved in various initiatives designed to safeguard fundamental human rights." "In 1997 [(*sic*)], as a concerned citizen, as well as in exercise of

[his] functions as a Deputy of the Republic of Chile, and worried about the possible indiscriminate felling of indigenous forests in the extreme south of Chile by a foreign company, ... together with ... Marcel Claude [Reyes, he] met with the Director of Foreign Investment in Chile to obtain information regarding the veracity of the affirmations of [the] company that was cutting down indigenous forests, requesting diverse elements of information about the foreign investor concerned ... and[,] in particular, about the background data that demonstrated his suitability and soundness." "This refusal of public information signified a violation of [his] human rights; it also affected and impaired [his] authority as a Deputy of the Republic and hindered [his] oversight responsibilities." ...

b) Proposed by the State ...

4. Liliana Guiditta Macchiavello Martini, lawyer of the Foreign Investment Committee....

At the time the petitioners in this case requested information from FIC, its Vice Presidency "considered that all information regarding third parties was of a confidential nature, if its disclosure could constitute a violation of the privacy of the owners of the information, irresponsibly endangering the results of the investors' activities in [Chile]." ...

Expert Opinions

a) Proposed by the alleged victims' representative

1. Tomás Vial Solar, lawyer

He was legal adviser to the Ministry-General Secretariat of the Presidency....

The new Article 8 of the Constitution introduced a constitutional principle of disclosure that applies to all State entities....

The constitutional provision indicates that acts, together with the decisions and procedures on which they are based, shall be public. The words "acts" and "procedures" should be understood in the broadest sense. Regarding the grounds for acts and decisions, all documents relating to any specific act of the State are public.... The new grounds established in Article 8 of the Constitution stipulate that secrecy or confidentiality can only be established when disclosure would affect due compliance with the functions of State entities, individual rights, national security and public interest....

3. Davor Harasic Yaksic, lawyer, President of the Chilean Chapter of Transparency International ...

He referred to the content of Chilean laws on access to State-held information. Act No. 19,653 of 1999 on Administrative Probity of the Body of the Administration, and the 2003 Administrative Procedure Act established the principles of transparency and disclosure as central elements of the proper exercise of public service. The 2005 constitutional reform elevated the principles of transparency and disclosure to constitutional rank and extended them to all the body of the State.

He mentioned what he considered are the obstacles and restrictions to access to public information in Chile. The law that formally incorporated the principle of disclosure into the Chilean legal system (the Administrative Probity Act) allowed the right of access to information to be restricted by providing that the grounds for refusing access could be established by legal or regulatory provisions. From 2001 to 2005, administrative practices were implemented that favored the confidentiality and secrecy of administrative acts, documents and background material. These practices were based on the Secrecy or Confidentiality Regulations created by Supreme Decree No. 26 of the Ministry–General Secretariat of the Presidency. The Regulations ... gave rise to the announcement of some one hundred decisions by [the] body of the Administration that transformed secrecy and confidentiality into "the general rule, impairing the principles of transparency and disclosure." Another obstacle was the limited and insufficient judicial protection arising from the special *amparo* (protection) remedy established in the Administrative Probity Act which, far from strengthening the principle of disclosure and access to information, has resulted in departmental heads choosing to "wait for a judicial decision," which also provides little protection to applicants.

b) Proposed by the State

    4. Claudio Francisco Castillo Castillo, lawyer

[T]he FIC Vice Presidency "was very careful not to provide this information to third parties." "The significant expansion of many of the country's productive sectors would not have been possible if FIC had not been prudent about how it managed the technical, financial and economic information relating to foreign investment projects...."

TESTIMONIES

a) Proposed by the Inter-American Commission

    1. Marcel Claude Reyes, alleged victim

He is an economist, and was a founder of the Terram Foundation as well as its Executive Director from 1997 to 2003. The basic aims of this organization were "to participate actively in public debates and in the production of sound, scientific information to support the social and civic efforts of the people of Chile in favor of sustainable development...."

Regarding his request for information from the Foreign Investment Committee in relation to the Río Cóndor project and the Trillium company, his intention had been to "play an active part ... in the debate and discussion on the Río Cóndor project ... from an economic perspective, in order to make a technical, financial and social evaluation of the project, and [to assess] the potential ... development of the region [and] of the country [as a result] of the project." The project had a "significant environmental impact" and gave rise to public debate.

Playing an active part "required a series of elements of information [from the Foreign Investment Committee], because the information held by the public entities involved in environmental matters and by the public itself was insufficient." A formal written request was made, asking, among other matters, for information on the suitability of the investor, his international experience and his compliance with the environmental, legal and fiscal laws and regulations. "As a result of [this] request, [they] received a note from the Executive Vice President of the Committee..., who invited [Arturo Longton and himself] to a meeting," during which he handed them "a sheet with the name of the investor, the name of his company [and] the amount of capital that he had asked to import into the country." Following the meeting, he received "a fax on the afternoon of that same day ... stating that ... the information on associated capital amounts had been omitted; however, this was not included in the fax." He stated that he had obtained partial information and had not received either an oral or written response concerning the missing information, or the reasons why he had not been given or would not be given this information.... Subsequently, after a "reasonable time" had elapsed and without knowing why the information had been refused, they resorted to the courts of law, filing a remedy of protection, which was rejected "because it was not pertinent"; an appeal for reconsideration of the judgment concerning the remedy for protection, which was rejected, and a complaint before the Supreme Court, which was also rejected.

Based on his experience in relation to environmental issues, he considers that "it is extremely difficult to have access to information." ... and that the State of Chile should end the practice of secrecy, which prevents its citizens from exercising their rights and is an obstacle to freedom of expression." ...

On December 24, 1991, the State of Chile signed a foreign investment contract with Cetec Engineering Company Inc. and Sentarn Enterprises Ltd. (foreign investors) and with Inversiones Cetec-Sel Chile Limitada (company receiving the capital). This contract was signed under Decree Law No. 600 (the Foreign Investment Statute) in order to invest in Chile a capital of U.S. $180,000,000.... This project "involve[d] the development of a comprehensive forestry complex, composed of a mechanized sawmill, a timber-processing plant, manufacture of boards and planks, a lumber chip recovery plant [and] an energy plant...." The project had a "significant environmental impact" and gave rise to public debate.

The Foreign Investment Committee approved the foreign investment application based on the examination of the background information provided by the investors.

An investment of approximately U.S. $33,729,540 was made under this investment contract....

The Río Cóndor Project was not executed; hence, Forestal Savia Limitada (formerly Forestal Trillium).... "receiver of the capital flows of the accredited foreign investor companies," did not implement the project.

VII
Violation of Article 13 of the American Convention Regarding to Articles 1(1) And 2 Thereof (Freedom of Thought and Expression)

The Commission's arguments

Regarding the alleged violation of Article 13 of the Convention, regarding Articles 1(1) and 2 thereof, the Commission indicated that:

(a) The disclosure of State-held information should play a very important role in a democratic society, because it enables civil society to control the actions of the Government to which it has entrusted the protection of its interests. "Article 13 of the Convention should be understood as a positive obligation on the part of the State to provide access to the information it holds"; ...

(b) There is a growing consensus that States have the positive obligation to provide the information they hold to their citizens. "The Commission has interpreted Article 13 to include a right of access to State-held information";

(c) "According to the broad terms of Article 13, the right of access to information should be governed by the 'principle of maximum disclosure.'" ...

(d) ... "The State of Chile has made a series of legislative modifications; however, ... these do not guarantee effective and broad access to public information." "The exceptions established by law ... grant an excessive degree of discretionality to the official who determines whether or not the information is disclosed"; ...

(g) The Foreign Investment Committee never provided a written response with regard to the missing information and has not shown how retaining the information in question was "necessary" to achieve one of the legitimate objectives established in Article 13 of the Convention....

(h) "The Chilean State did not guarantee the right of the [alleged] victims of access to information because a State entity refused access to information without proving that it was included in one of the legitimate exceptions to the general rule of disclosure established in Article 13. Also, ... the State did not have mechanisms to ensure the right of access to information effectively....

The Court's findings

Article 13 (Freedom of Thought and Expression) of the American Convention establishes, *inter alia*, that:

1. Everyone has the right to freedom of thought and expression. This right includes freedom to seek, receive, and impart information and ideas of all kinds, regardless of frontiers, either orally, in writing, in print, in the form of art, or through any other medium of one's choice....

Regarding domestic legal effects, Article 2 of the Convention establishes that:

Where the exercise of any of the rights or freedoms referred to in Article 1 is not already ensured by legislative or other provisions, the States Parties undertake to adopt, in accordance with their constitutional processes and the provisions of this Convention, such legislative or other measures as may be necessary to give effect to those rights or freedoms....

[The Court evaluated and weighed the evidence.]

XI
OPERATIVE PARAGRAPHS

Therefore,

THE COURT DECLARES,

Unanimously, that:

1. The State violated the right to freedom of thought and expression embodied in Article 13 of the American Convention on Human Rights, to the detriment of Marcel Claude Reyes ... in relation to the general obligations to respect and guarantee the rights and freedoms and to adopt provisions of domestic law established in Articles 1(1) and 2 thereof, in the terms of paragraphs 61 to 103 of this judgment.

By four votes to two, that:

2. The State violated the right to judicial guarantees embodied in Article 8 (1) of the American Convention on Human Rights, to the detriment of Marcel Claude Reyes and Arturo Longton Guerrero, with regard to the administrative authority's decision not to provide information, in relation to the general obligation to respect and guarantee the rights and freedoms established in Article 1(1) thereof, in the terms of paragraphs 114 to 123 of this judgment.

Unanimously, that:

3. The State violated the rights to judicial guarantees and judicial protection embodied in Articles 8(1) and 25 of the American Convention on Human Rights, to the detriment of Marcel Claude Reyes ... with regard to the judicial decision concerning the application for protection, in relation to the general obligation to respect and guarantee the rights and freedoms established in Article 1(1) thereof, in the terms of paragraphs 124 to 144 of this judgment.

AND DECIDES,

Unanimously, that: …

5. The State shall, through the corresponding entity and within six months, provide the information requested by the victims, if appropriate, or adopt a justified decision in this regard.…

7. The State shall adopt, within a reasonable time, the necessary measures to ensure the right of access to State-held information, pursuant to the general obligation to adopt provisions of domestic law established in Article 2 of the American Convention on Human Rights.…

8. The State shall, within a reasonable time, provide training to public entities, authorities, and agents responsible for responding to requests for access to State-held information on the laws and regulations governing this right.…

9. The State shall pay Marcel Claude Reyes … within one year, for costs and expenses, the amount established in … of this judgment.…

Questions and Discussion

1. *Suitability and soundness.* Is information about the foreign investor's "suitability and soundness" open to the public? What does "suitability and soundness" mean? Why should the public have the right to know not just whether a decision might significantly impact the environment but also the financial soundness of the foreign investor?

2. *Foreign investors.* Is information regarding the foreign investor "commercial" and therefore confidential? Do you agree with the FIC's argument that its disclosure constitutes a violation of the privacy of the owners of the information?

3. *Constitutional implications.* As noted, the new Article 8 of the Constitution introduced a constitutional principle of disclosure that applies to all State entities. In what way does this principle of disclosure apply to information provided by a foreign investor?

4. *Article 13.* Do all citizens of American countries that have ratified the American Convention on Human Rights now have a clear and enforceable human right to information, which cannot be excessively restricted by national governments or overly restrict legislation? (Note that the U.S. is not a party to the Convention.)

C. Asia — Constitutional and Statutory Rights

Forests Survey Inspection Request Case (Korea)
Constitutional Court of Republic of Korea
1 KCCR 176, 88Hun-Ma22 (September 4, 1989)[a]

CHO, KYU KWANG, Chief Justice

LEE, SEONG RYEOL, BYEON, JEONG SOO, KIM, JIN WOO, HAN, BYEONG CHAE, LEE, SI YOON, KIM, YANG KYOON, KIM, MOON HEE, Justices

A. Background of the Case

The complainant found that the land inherited from his father immediately after the Korean War became the state's property without his knowledge. In order to recover the

---

a. Translation by Su Jeong Suh, LL.M., University of Oregon.

title to the land, he repeatedly requested the respondent Supervisor of County of Inchon of the Kyong-ki Do (Province) for inspection and duplication of the old forests title records, private forests use surveys, land surveys, and land tax ledgers kept by the County. The respondent did not take any action on the land surveys and private forests use surveys. The complainant brought a constitutional complaint against this inaction for violating his right of property.

B. Summary of the Decision

Freedom of speech and press guaranteed by Article 21 of the Constitution envisages free expression and communication of ideas and opinions that require free formation of ideas as a precondition. Free formation of ideas is in turn made possible by guaranteeing access to sufficient information. Right to access, collection and processing of information, namely the right to know, is therefore covered by the freedom of expression. The core of the right to know is the people's right to know with respect to information held by the government, that is, the general right to request disclosure of information from the government (claim-right).

The right to know is given effect directly by the Constitution without any legislation implementing it. Therefore, if the complainant requested disclosure of information with legitimate interest in it, and the government failed to respond without any review, his freedom of speech and press, or freedom of expression of Article 21 or its component, the right to know, was abridged.

However, the right to know is not absolute, and can be reasonably restricted. The limit on the extent of restriction must be drawn by balancing the interest secured by the restriction and the infringement on the right to know. Generally, the right to know must be broadly protected to a person making the request with interest as long as it poses no threat to the public interest. Disclosure, at least to a person with a direct interest, is mandatory.

In this case, the requested estate records have not been classified as secret or confidential and their disclosure do not implicate invasion of another's privacy. There is no reason for insisting on non-disclosure of the requested documents themselves, or statutes or regulations. Therefore, the government's inaction on the complainant's request breached his right to know.

Article 21 of the Constitution guarantees freedom of speech and press, and it means free expression and communication of ideas and opinions. This is essential for an individual to maintain human dignity, to seek happiness, and to realize the sovereignty of the people, and it is one of the most important fundamental rights that the people have in a democratic nation. By the way, free expression and communication of ideas and opinions requires free formation of ideas as a precondition. Free formation of ideas is in turn made possible by guaranteeing access to sufficient information. The right to access to, collection, and processing of information, namely the right to know, is therefore covered by freedom of expression.

The right to know is closely connected with the openness of the national administration. Although the Constitution does not have an explicit provision about the openness of administration, the core of the right to know is the people's right to know with respect to the information held by the government, that is, the general right to request disclosure of information from the government (claim-right). This is a natural interpretation considering the preamble of the Constitution that declares the basic free and democratic order, Article 1 ((1) The Republic of Korea shall be a democratic republic. (2) The sovereignty of the Republic of Korea shall reside in the people, and all state authority shall emanate from the people) and Article 4 (The Republic of Korea shall seek unification and shall formulate and carry out a policy of peaceful unification based on the principles of freedom and democracy) of the Constitution. Although opinions may be divided about whether it is possible to implement the right to know without concrete legislation, in this case, it is not impossible to deal with the request by the complainant for inspection and duplication, despite the absence of legislation. Therefore, if the complainant requested disclosure of information with a legitimate interest in it, and the government failed to respond without any review of the request, his freedom of speech and press, or freedom of expression of Article 21 or its component, the right to know, was abridged.

However, the right to know is not absolute, and can be reasonably restricted. The limit on the extent of restriction must be drawn by balancing the interest secured by the restriction and the infringement of the right to know. Generally, the right to know must be broadly protected for a person making the request who has an interest, as long as it poses no threat to public interest. Disclosure, at least to a person with a direct interest, is mandatory.

In this case, the requested estate records have not been classified as secret or confidential and their disclosure does not involve invasion of another's privacy. There is no reason for insisting on non-disclosure of the requested documents themselves, nor are there statutes or regulations. Therefore, the government's inaction on the complainant's request breached his right to know.

Justice CHOE KWANG-RYOOL, dissenting

The complainant had a right to inspect and duplicate the above documents under Article 36(2) of the Governmental Records rules (Presidential decree no. 11547) and had not first exhausted the procedures for judicial review of administrative inaction available to him on that matter.

Article 68, paragraph 1of the Constitutional Court Act requires exhaustion of remedies that are available under other laws before filing a constitutional complaint. In this case, the majority opinion ruled that there was no provision of law that imposes an obligation on government to disclose official records, and the courts have held that internal factual actions of government or factual omissions of government are not objects of administrative litigation, so this case was an exceptional case that did not have to exhaust the procedures for judicial review. However, the complainant did have a right to inspect and duplicate the requested documents under Article 36(2) of the Governmental Records Rules (Presidential decree no. 11547), so the complainant can appeal for fulfillment of the request for inspection and duplication under the Administrative Appeals Act, and if the complainant fails in his appeal for fulfillment, the complainant can file a law suit for a determination of illegality of omission under the Administrative Litigation Act. Therefore, the complainant had not first exhausted the procedures for judicial review of administrative inaction available to him on that matter, and this case should be rejected under Article 68, paragraph 1, of the Constitutional Court Act.

Questions and Discussion

1. *Reaction to decision in Korea.* The website of the Korea Constitutional Court has this report of reactions to this important decision:

> Major newspapers generally praised the case for evincing the Court's commitment to active protection and promotion of people's rights until the draft of the Disclosure of Information Act was actually enacted. On September 5, 1989, the *Dong-A Ilbo*, signified the case as proposing a clear standard on the scope

and limit of disclosure that should be included in the Disclosure of Information Act, thereby precluding unconstitutional elements in advance. The *Hankyoreh Shinmun* on September 6, 1989, hailed it as the first case providing affirmative interpretation of the right to know as a claim-right and an important progress in light of the past laws related to press and publication.

Academic opinions were balanced. Some found the case rich in the justices' commitment to protection of basic rights but lacking in support of an established, constitutional theory. Others found it logically problematic in deriving from a liberty-right (freedom of speech and press) a much broader claim-right (right to know). Yet others praised it both for its revolutionary holding and excellent reasoning.

2. *Subsequent decision.* According to the Court's website: "The Court reconfirmed its position on the issue of the right to know in another case decided on May 13, 1991 (CC 90Hun-Ma133, the *Records Duplication Request Case*). In this case, the Chief of the Uijongbu Branch of the Seoul Prosecutor's Office refused to allow a former defendant in a criminal trial to inspect and duplicate the records of the concluded trial. The Court found it unconstitutional."

3. *Legislative response.* In the wake of a series of constitutional cases concerning the right to know, the National Assembly enacted the Act on Disclosure of Information by Public Agencies on December 31, 1996 (Act 5242, effective January 1, 1998), which specifically recognized the right to request disclosure of information.

4. *Constitutional interpretation in other countries.* "In a number of countries including India, Japan, … Pakistan, Israel, and France, the highest courts have found that there is a right of access to information found in the constitution, typically as an element of free expression or freedom of the press." David Banisar, *Freedom of Information Around the World 2006* 17, http://www.privacyinternational.org/foi/foisurvey2006.pdf. Furthermore:

> Some FOI laws have the level of a constitutional right in themselves; in Sweden, the Freedom of the Press Act is one of the four fundamental laws that make up the Swedish Constitution. Any changes to it require a longer procedure over two Parliaments. Some countries have given the information laws a higher legal status. In Canada, the courts have said that the Access to Information Act is "quasi Constitutional." In New Zealand, the Court of Appeals said in 1988 that "the permeating importance of the [Official Information] Act is such that it is entitled to be ranked as a constitutional measure."

Id.

5. *Explicit constitutional provisions.* While judicial interpretation is the source of the human right to information in some countries, in many more the right is explicitly written into the national constitution:

> Over 80 countries have adopted a constitutional provision giving citizens a right to access information. The number of constitutions with these provisions has increased substantially in the past ten years. Most newly written constitutions from countries in transition, especially in Central and Eastern Europe and Latin America, include a right of access. In addition, a number of countries with older constitutions including Finland and Norway have recently amended their constitutions to specifically include a right of access to information.
>
> Typically, the rights give any citizen or person the right to demand information from government bodies. The South African Constitution has one of the most expansive rights in the world. It goes even further and gives individuals

the right to demand information "that is held by another person and that is required for the exercise or protection of any rights." ... In Central Asia, a number of countries include a right of access to information relating to "their rights and interests."

Id.

6. *U.S. Constitution.* Article 21 of the Constitution of Korea states:

(1) All citizens enjoy the freedom of speech and the press, and of assembly and association....

(4) Neither speech nor the press may violate the honor or rights of other persons nor undermine public morals or social ethics....

The First Amendment to the U.S. Constitution prohibits the national government from "abridging the freedom of speech, or of the press; or the right of the people peaceably to assemble, and to petition the Government for a redress of grievances." The Fourteenth Amendment has been held to make these prohibitions applicable to state governments as well.

In *Richmond Newspapers, Inc. v. Virginia*, 448 U.S. 555 (1980), the U.S. Supreme Court ruled a state statute to be unconstitutional in authorizing a judge to close a criminal trial to the public and the press. Chief Justice Burger's plurality opinion was joined by two others. In an additional concurrence, Justice Stevens wrote:

Today..., for the first time, the Court unequivocally holds that an arbitrary interference with access to important information is an abridgment of the freedoms of speech and of the press protected by the First Amendment.

Id. at 583. Similarly, Justice Brennan, joined by Justice Marshall, wrote in concurring, "I believe that the First Amendment—of itself and as applied to the States through the Fourteenth Amendment—secures such a public right of access." *Id.* at 584. Justice Stewart agreed that the Constitution gives the press the right to attend criminal trials. Justice Blackmun, also concurring, referred to the plurality opinion as finding a right of the press to attend trials among "a veritable potpourri of [constitutional sources]—the Speech Clause of the First Amendment, the Press Clause, the Assembly Clause, the Ninth Amendment, and a cluster of penumbral guarantees recognized in past decisions," but said he would live with it. Justice Rehnquist, on the other hand, rejected all such constitutional arguments and accused the various opinions of the other justices of emulating the Lord Chancellor in the Gilbert and Sullivan operetta "Iolanthe," simply inventing a new constitutional right from whim. *Id.* at 604.

What is your view regarding interpretation of the U.S. Constitution in a manner similar to the interpretation of the Korean Constitution regarding freedom of information?

7. *Reaction to the Richmond Newspapers case.* Scholars reacted to the *Richmond Newspapers* case and the attempt to find a constitutional right of access to information in the United States Constitution with both scorn and praise. *See, e.g.,* David M. O'Brien, THE PUBLIC'S RIGHT TO KNOW: THE SUPREME COURT AND THE FIRST AMENDMENT (1981) (scorn) *and* Loren P. Beth, *The Public's Right to Know: The Supreme Court as Pandora?* 81 Mich. L. Rev. 880 (1983) (scorn) *with* Emerson, *The Affirmative Side of the First Amendment*, 15 Ga. L. Rev. 795 (1981) (praise). Some U.S. Courts of Appeals have explicitly extended *Richmond Newspapers* beyond criminal trials to include civil trials. *See, e.g., Brown & Williamson Tobacco Corp. v. F.T.C.*, 710 F.2d 1165 (6th Cir.1983). In the years since *Richmond Newspapers*, the U.S. Supreme Court has not gone further, just as the Korean Constitutional Court has apparently not dealt with the issue since 1991. In both countries, the right of access to information is pervasively guaranteed through legislation.

The Right to Information Act, 2005 (India)

The Gazette of India, Extraordinary, Part II-§ 1, June 21, 2005
http://righttoinformation.gov.in/RTIAct/RTI-Act.pdf

CHAPTER II
Right to information and obligations of public authorities

§ 3   Subject to the provisions of this Act, all citizens shall have the right to information.

§ 6   (1)   A person, who desires to obtain any information under this Act, shall make a request in writing or through electronic means ... to—

   (a)   the Central Public Information Officer or State Public Information Officer, as the case may be, of the concerned public authority; ...

specifying the particulars of the information sought by him or her:

Provided that where such request cannot be made in writing, the Central Public Information Officer or State Public Information Officer, as the case may be, shall render all reasonable assistance to the person making the request orally to reduce the same in writing.

   (2)   An applicant making request for information shall not be required to give any reason for requesting the information or any other personal details except those that may be necessary for contacting him.

§ 8   (1)   Notwithstanding anything contained in this Act, there shall be no obligation to give any citizen,—[various exemptions listed].

   (2)   Notwithstanding anything in the Official Secrets Act, 1923 nor any of the exemptions permissible in accordance with sub-section (1), a public authority may allow access to information, if public interest in disclosure outweighs the harm to the protected interests.

Questions and Discussion

1. Note that a person can make a request orally and need give no reason for requesting information. Note also that a public authority may disclose otherwise exempt information.

2. India's Access to Information Act, 2005, provides for the establishment of a Central Information Commission, which has the power to order the disclosure of information. See, e.g., *Satyapal v. CPIO, TCIL*, ICPB/A-1/CIC/2006 (Cent. Info. Comm.) (2006) (documents showing discussions leading to a decision, called "file notings," not necessarily exempt from disclosure). The Commission can also impose financial penalties on officials who wrongfully withhold information.

D. United States — Statutory Rights

Freedom of Information Around the World 2006

David Banisar
http://www.privacyinternational.org/foi/foisurvey2006.pdf

Following a long period of hearings and unsuccessful bills, the Freedom of Information Act (FOIA) was enacted in 1966 and went into effect in 1967. It has been substantially amended several times, most recently in 1996 by the Electronic Freedom of

Information Act. The law allows any person or organization, regardless of citizenship or country of origin, to ask for records held by federal government agencies. Agencies include executive and military departments, government corporations and other entities which perform government functions except for Congress, the courts or the President's immediate staff at the White House, including the National Security Council. Government agencies must respond in 20 working days.

There are nine categories of discretionary exemptions: national security, internal agency rules, information protected by other statutes, business information, inter and intra-agency memos, personal privacy, law enforcement records, financial institutions and oil wells data. There are around 140 different statutes that allow for withholding.

Appeals of denials or complaints about extensive delays can be made internally to the agency concerned. The federal courts can review de novo (without deference to agency decision) and overturn agency decisions. The courts have heard thousands of cases in the 40 years of the Act.

Management for FOIA is mostly decentralized. The US Justice Department (DOJ) provides some guidance and training for agencies and represents the agencies in most court cases.

The FOIA also requires that government agencies publish material relating to their structure and functions, rules, decisions, procedures, policies, and manuals. The 1996 E-FOIA amendments required that agencies create "electronic reading rooms" and make available electronically the information that must be published along with common documents requested. The DOJ has issued guidance that documents that have been requested three times be made available electronically in the Reading Room.

In 2004, there were over 4 million requests made to federal agencies under the FOIA and the Privacy Act, up from 3.2 million in 2003. However, a significant number of these requests were to bodies such as the Department of Veterans Affairs and the Social Security Administration by individuals seeking to obtain their own records and should have been treated as Privacy Act requests. Law enforcement and personal privacy are typically the most cited exemptions for withholding information.

The FOIA has been hampered by a lack of central oversight and long delays in processing requests. In some instances, information is released only after years or decades. The General Accounting Agency found in 2002 that "backlogs of pending requests government wide are substantial and growing, indicating that agencies are falling behind in processing requests." A review by Associated Press in 2006 found that nearly all executive departments had increasing delays ranging from three months to over four years, national security-related agencies were releasing less information and 30 percent of departments had not submitted their annual reports on time. The National Security Archive found that the oldest request on record was 17 years old. Some agencies had improved their backlogs since a 2003 review by the Archive but many of the oldest requests pointed out in the review had still not been resolved. The review also found that there was an increase in withholding from 2003 to 2005, many agencies did not have adequate tracking systems, and many lost requests.

The Bush Administration has engaged in a general policy of restricting access to information. In October 2001, Attorney General John Ashcroft issued a memo stating that the Justice Department would defend in court any federal agency that withheld information on justifiable grounds. Previously, the standard was that the presumption was for disclosure....

There are also laws in all fifty states on providing access to government records, some dating back to the 19th century. A number of states have information commissions or other review bodies which can issue opinions or review decisions.

Questions and Discussion

1. *Segregable portions.* As the article above notes, FOIA provides nine exceptions to the access to information. However, FOIA also mandates that the agency delete any "reasonably segregable portion." Remaining portions, not covered by an exemption, must be given to the requester. Further, the agency must disclose the fact that they removed portions and provide rationale for removal. 5 U.S.C. §552(b). This is an important aspect of FOIA because it prohibits an agency from withholding an entire document merely because one line, one page or one picture is exempt.

2. *Matter of interpretation.* Some U.S. Presidents and their Administrations have adopted a presumption of disclosure, while other Administrations have adopted the opposite presumption. After a particularly restrictive period, Congress adopted the Freedom of Information Act Amendments of 2007, Pub. L. 110-175. Among other things, the law now requires that if part of a document is withheld, the government agency must now specify the exemption that it claims to rely upon; that each agency have a high-level "Chief FOIA Officer"; and that attorney fees be paid to litigants if the agency decides to release information after a lawsuit is filed but without a court order.

3. *Review bodies.* In theory any violations of law can be sorted out in the courts, but how often are citizens likely to take such steps? Would it be better to have an independent organization handling FOIA requests, like Mexico has in its IFAI?

4. *Costs.* FOIA provides that requesters of information must pay for costs associated with acquiring the information. The fees include searching, reviewing, and duplicating costs and are usually charged at actual direct cost rates. Charging the requesters helps agencies recoup their costs, especially since a majority of the FOIA requests are made by commercial entities. However, individuals may request a fee waiver or reduced fees. Fee waivers are provided when disclosure is in the public interest because it: (a) is likely to contribute significantly to public understanding of the operations or activities of the government; and (b) is not primarily in the commercial interest of the requester.

II. The Right to Insist on Dissemination of Information

While "passive" access only requires the government to release certain information in response to a specific request, "active" provisions of information require the government to take an active role in the dissemination of information. It confers a duty upon the government to collect and distribute certain kinds of information on its own initiative, even if there is no request.

Guerra v. Italy

European Court of Human Rights
Reports of Judgments and Decisions 1998-I, 26 E.H.R.R. 357 (1998)
Judgment of 19 February 1998

[Other parts of this court decision are provided in Chapter 2, page 31.]

The Commission declared the case admissible only in relation to the complaint under Article 10. Before the Court, the applicants relied not only on Article 10, but also Article 2. In addition, they complained before the Court that their right to respect for family life under Article 8 of the Convention had been infringed, as a result of the authorities' failure to provide them with the relevant information....

PROCEEDINGS BEFORE THE COMMISSION

The applicants ... complained that the relevant authorities' failure to inform the public about the hazards and about the procedures to be followed in the event of a major accident ... infringed their right to freedom of information as guaranteed by Article 10....

JUDGMENT

I. Scope of the case ...

In its report of 25 June 1996 [the Commission] considered the case under Article 10 of the Convention and decided that that provision was applicable and had been breached since, at least during the period between the issue of D.P.R. 175/88 in May 1988 and the cessation of fertiliser production in 1994, the relevant authorities were under an obligation to take the necessary steps so that the applicants, who were living in a high-risk area, could "receive adequate information on issues concerning the protection of their environment." Eight members of the Commission expressed their disagreement in three dissenting opinions, two of which pointed to the possibility of a different approach to the case, on the basis that Article 8 of the Convention was applicable to the complaint declared admissible....

II. Alleged violation of Article 10 of the Convention

The applicants alleged that they were the victims of a violation of Article 10 of the Convention, which provides:

> 1. Everyone has the right to freedom of expression. This right shall include freedom to hold opinions and to receive and impart information and ideas without interference by public authority and regardless of frontiers....
>
> 2. The exercise of these freedoms, since it carries with it duties and responsibilities, may be subject to such formalities, conditions, restrictions or penalties as are prescribed by law and are necessary in a democratic society, in the interests of national security, territorial integrity or public safety, for the prevention of disorder or crime, for the protection of health or morals, for the protection of the reputation or rights of others, for preventing the disclosure of information received in confidence, or for maintaining the authority and impartiality of the judiciary.

The alleged breach resulted from the authorities' failure to take steps to ensure that the public were informed of the risks and of what was to be done in the event of an accident connected with the factory's operation....

B. Merits of the complaint ...

In the Government's submission, that provision merely guaranteed freedom to receive information without hindrance by States; it did not impose any positive obligation.... If a positive obligation to provide information existed, it would be "extremely difficult to implement" because of the need to determine how and when the information was to be disclosed, which authorities were responsible for disclosing it and who was to receive it.

Like the applicants, the Commission was of the Opinion that the provision of information to the public was now one of the essential means of protecting the well being and health of the population in situations in which the environment was at risk....

Article 10 imposed on States not just a duty to make available information to the public on environmental matters, a requirement with which Italian law already appeared to comply, ... but also a positive obligation to collect, process and disseminate such information, which by its nature could not otherwise come to the knowledge of the public. The protection afforded by Article 10 therefore had a preventive function with respect to potential violations of the Convention in the event of serious damage to the environment and Article 10 came into play even before any direct infringement of other fundamental rights, such as the right to life or to respect for private and family life, occurred.

The Court does not subscribe to that view. ...

The Court reiterates that freedom to receive information, referred to in paragraph 2 of Article 10 of the Convention, "basically prohibits a government from restricting a person from receiving information that others wish or may be willing to impart to him." That freedom cannot be construed as imposing on a State, in circumstances such as those of the present case, positive obligations to collect and disseminate information of its own motion.

In conclusion, Article 10 is not applicable in the instant case. ...

For these reasons, THE COURT ...

2. Holds by 18 votes to 2 that Article 10 of the Convention is not applicable in the instant case. ...

Concurring Opinion of Mrs. PALM, joined by Mr. R. BERNHARDT, Mr. RUSSO, Mr. MAC-DONALD, Mr. MAKARCZYK and Mr. VAN DIJK

I have voted with the majority in favour of holding that Article 10 of the Convention is not applicable in the present case. In doing so I have put strong emphasis on the factual situation at hand not excluding that under different circumstances the State may have a positive obligation to make available information to the public and to disseminate such information which by its nature could not otherwise come to the knowledge of the public. ...

Concurring Opinion of JUDGE JAMBREK

In their memorial the applicants also expressly complained of a violation of Article 2 of the Convention. The Court held that it was not necessary to consider the case under that Article given that it had found a violation of Article 8. I wish, nevertheless, to make some observations on the possible applicability of Article 2 in this case. ...

If information is withheld by a government about circumstances which foreseeably, and on substantial grounds, present a real risk of danger to health and physical integrity, then such a situation may also be protected by Article 2 of the Convention: "No one shall be deprived of his life intentionally."

Questions and Discussion

1. *Article 10.* Are the Court's reasons for not applying Article 10 of the Convention persuasive? The Court said that the freedom to receive information under Article 10 "basically prohibits a government from restricting a person from receiving information that others wish or may be willing to impart to him." That appears to be a rejection of the notion that government (or industry) might have any obligations for "active" providing of information. Can you construct an argument from the words of Article 10 that would contradict that limited view? For example, if a government has important health and safety information but some official or body does not transmit it to the public, can the person who refuses to offer the information be said to be engaged in "interference"? Are other arguments possible?

2. *Right to information—obligation of the government.* Information about the Chernobyl nuclear disaster in Ukraine in April 1986 was kept secret from the population of the country for several days after the explosion. The explosion caused radioactive contami-

nation of the environment and serious consequences for the health of people. The Council of Europe adopted Parliamentary Assembly Resolution 1087 on 26 April 1996 on the consequences of the Chernobyl disaster, referring not only to the risks associated with the production and use of nuclear energy in the civil sector but also to other matters. It states that "public access to clear and full information ... must be viewed as a basic human right." In a part of the opinion not excerpted above, the Court said the resolution "spoke merely of access, not a right, to information." Considering that the scope of the Chernobyl disaster resulted, in part, from the refusal of Soviet authorities to inform the public, is the Court's interpretation of the resolution's restrictive use of the word "access" as not involving a "right" rather difficult to justify? Does Article 5 of the Aarhus Convention provide a clearer obligation of the government to collect and disseminate environmental information?

Convention on Access to Information, Public Participation in Decision-Making and Access to Justice in Environmental Matters (Aarhus Convention)

June 25, 1998
ECE/CEP/43, 2161 U.N.T.S. 447, 38 I.L.M 517 (1999)

Article 5
COLLECTION AND DISSEMINATION OF ENVIRONMENTAL INFORMATION

1. Each Party shall ensure that:

(a) Public authorities possess and update environmental information which is relevant to their functions;

(b) Mandatory systems are established so that there is an adequate flow of information to public authorities about proposed and existing activities which may significantly affect the environment;

(c) In the event of any imminent threat to human health or the environment, whether caused by human activities or due to natural causes, all information which could enable the public to take measures to prevent or mitigate harm arising from the threat and is held by a public authority is disseminated immediately and without delay to members of the public who may be affected.

2. Each Party shall ensure that, within the framework of national legislation, the way in which public authorities make environmental information available to the public is transparent and that environmental information is effectively accessible, inter alia, by:

(a) Providing sufficient information to the public about the type and scope of environmental information held by the relevant public authorities, the basic terms and conditions under which such information is made available and accessible, and the process by which it can be obtained;

(b) Establishing and maintaining practical arrangements, such as:

(i)   Publicly accessible lists, registers or files;

(ii) Requiring officials to support the public in seeking access to information under this Convention; and

(iii) The identification of points of contact; and

(c) Providing access to the environmental information contained in lists, registers or files as referred to in subparagraph (b)(i) above free of charge.

3. Each Party shall ensure that environmental information progressively becomes available in electronic databases which are easily accessible to the public through public telecommunications networks. Information accessible in this form should include:

(a) Reports on the state of the environment, as referred to in paragraph 4 below;

(b) Texts of legislation on or relating to the environment;

(c) As appropriate, policies, plans and programs on or relating to the environment, and environmental agreements; and

(d) Other information, to the extent that the availability of such information in this form would facilitate the application of national law implementing this Convention, provided that such information is already available in electronic form.

4. Each Party shall, at regular intervals not exceeding three or four years, publish and disseminate a national report on the state of the environment, including information on the quality of the environment and information on pressures on the environment.

5. Each Party shall take measures within the framework of its legislation for the purpose of disseminating, inter alia:

(a) Legislation and policy documents such as documents on strategies, policies, programs and action plans relating to the environment, and progress reports on their implementation, prepared at various levels of government;

(b) International treaties, conventions and agreements on environmental issues; and

(c) Other significant international documents on environmental issues, as appropriate.

6. Each Party shall encourage operators whose activities have a significant impact on the environment to inform the public regularly of the environmental impact of their activities and products, where appropriate within the framework of voluntary eco-labelling or eco-auditing schemes or by other means....

9. Each Party shall take steps to establish progressively, taking into account international processes where appropriate, a coherent, nationwide system of pollution inventories or registers on a structured, computerized and publicly accessible database compiled through standardized reporting. Such a system may include inputs, releases and transfers of a specified range of substances and products, including water, energy and resource use, from a specified range of activities to environmental media and to on-site and offsite treatment and disposal sites.

10. Nothing in this article may prejudice the right of Parties to refuse to disclose certain environmental information in accordance with article 4, paragraphs 3 and 4.

The Aarhus Convention: An Implementation Guide (2000)
Stephen Stec & Susan Casey-Lefkowitz, with Jerzy Jendroska
U.N. Doc. ECE/CEP/72

Article 5

Collection and Dissemination of Information

Article 5 sets out the obligations of the Parties and public authorities to collect and disseminate environmental information. It covers a wide range of different types of information that Parties should actively provide to members of the public. Therefore, article 5 defines the types of information that fall under this active obligation for collection and dissemination. In general, it covers information such as emergency information, product information, pollutant release and transfer information, information about laws, policies and strategies. Some of its provisions require the Parties or public authorities to take certain specific steps for collection and dissemination. Other provisions give the Parties and public authorities some guidance as to the desired end result, but they leave the choice of process and implementation methods open....

Experience has shown that simply having a law or regulation giving the public access to information does not guarantee access in practice. Article 5, paragraph 2, requires Parties to make sure that when public authorities make environmental information available, they do so openly and ensure that the information is really accessible. Parties are required to do so "within the framework of national legislation." First, this means that Parties must have placed the obligations and mechanisms of article 5, paragraph 2, in their national legal framework. It also means that Parties can be flexible in implementing this provision within their own national legal frameworks. Article 5, paragraph 2, does require a minimum of several concrete mechanisms for ensuring transparency and effectively accessible information—all of which can be structured slightly differently depending on the system of national law.

Transparency means that the public can clearly follow the path of environmental information, understanding its origin, the criteria that govern its collection, holding and dissemination, and how it can be obtained. Article 5, paragraph 2, thus, builds on article 3, paragraph 1, requiring Parties to establish and maintain a clear and transparent framework to implement the Convention, and article 3, paragraph 2, requiring officials to assist the public in seeking access to information....

Paragraph 6 concerns the flow of information from an "operator" directly to the public. An "operator" can be a private enterprise or a governmental body that conducts activities with a significant impact on the environment. Paragraph 6 requires Parties to encourage these operators voluntarily to disseminate information about the environmental impact of their activities and products. This provision differs from paragraph 1, which requires the establishment of mandatory systems for operators to provide information to public authorities. Here, in the case of information flowing from an operator directly to the public, the Party need only provide incentives and other encouragement.

Questions and Discussion

1. *India and Aarhus.* Legislation in India imposes a clear duty on the government to provide information of all kinds:

> (2) It shall be a constant endeavour of every public authority to take steps in accordance with the requirements of clause (b) of sub-section (1) to provide as much information *suo motu* to the public at regular intervals through various means of communications, including internet, so that the public have minimum resort to the use of this Act to obtain information.

The Right To Information Act, 2005 (India), No. 22 of 2005, The Gazette of India, Extraordinary, Part II-§1, June 21, 2005, available at http://righttoinformation.gov.in/RTIAct/RTI-Act.pdf.

Compare the provision of the law of India with the details of the Aarhus Convention. Considering the activism of the Indian judiciary, is their statute sufficient for a litigant to demand as much detail as is mentioned in the Convention, or perhaps more?

2. *Definitions.* What does Article 5 of the Aarhus Convention mean when it mandates Parties to provide "sufficient" information and make it "effectively accessible"? What about "much information" in the Indian statute? Does having vague terms in a convention or statute expand or limit the public's ability to access information?

3. *Chernobyl and a constitutional right to information.* As a result of the public outcry in Ukraine about the secrecy surrounding the explosion at the Chernobyl nuclear plant (citizens were not told for 5 days, while school children took part in an open-air parade in Kyiv, the capital city), the government subsequently adopted, as one of the first laws of independent Ukraine, the Law on Information. It provides a "guaranteed right to information; transparency, accessibility, and freedom of information exchange; unbiased and authentic information; complete and accurate information...." According to this law all citizens, legal entities, and state bodies of Ukraine have the right to information—"envisaging the possibility of free receipt, use, distribution, and storage of any data as may be required for the implementation of their rights, freedoms, and lawful interests." Legislative, executive, and judiciary authorities as well as governmental officials are obliged to provide information. Denial of access to such information or its concealment may be appealed to a court. This law is one of the strictest in the world because violation "shall entail not only disciplinary, civil, and administrative liabilities, but also criminal prosecution."

The right to information was elevated to the highest level in the 1996 Constitution of Ukraine. Article 50 declares: "Everyone is guaranteed the right of free access to information about the environmental situation, the quality of food and consumer goods, and also the right to disseminate such information. No one shall make such information secret."

4. *Protocol on Pollutant Release and Transfer Register.* In accordance with paragraph 9 of the Article 5 of the Aarhus Convention, "a coherent, nationwide system of pollution inventories or registers on a structured, computerized and publicly accessible database" was required to be established. A separate Protocol on Pollutant Release and Transfer Register was signed during the Ministerial Conference, "Environment for Europe," in Kyiv in 2003. Its objective is "to enhance public access to information through the establishment of coherent, nationwide pollutant release and transfer registers (PRTRs)."

Chapter 7

Public Participation

Introduction

Public participation is the second "pillar" of environmental democracy and the second of the procedural environmental rights. (The other two are access to information, discussed in Chapter 6, and access to justice, discussed in Chapter 8.) Some officials believe that allowing robust public participation in government decisionmaking slows it down unacceptably and creates additional burdens. On the other hand, advocates of public participation argue that it makes the decisionmaking process transparent and holds public authorities accountable. They also contend that the public is more likely to support a decision made with public involvement.

Public participation may also lead to decisions that are better for the environment, protecting the rights of people not to have their health, communities, or natural areas degraded or destroyed. The public can bring expertise and knowledge to a decisionmaking process. Public experts may not only criticize mistakes or see negative sides of a plan or program, but also suggest good alternative solutions. They can introduce environmental and sustainability considerations into decisionmaking.

In this chapter, we examine the nature of public participation as a human right that aids in the protection of the environment. We discuss the principles underlying the right of public participation in decisions and actions with potential environmental consequences and consider some of the basic legal instruments elaborating the right. The chapter then considers in detail public participation rights in Europe, Caucasus, and Central Asia where a specific international convention gives them the strongest international grounding. Finally, we will look briefly at how they are implemented in other regions around the world, concluding with a brief look at United States law.

I. Public Participation as a Right

The Emerging International Law of Public Participation Affecting Global Mining, Energy and Resources Development
George (Rock) Pring & Susan Y. Noé
HUMAN RIGHTS IN NATURAL RESOURCE DEVELOPMENT
(D. Zillman, A. Lucas, & G. Pring, eds., 2002)

II. THE CONCEPTUAL AND HISTORICAL FRAMEWORK ...

A. The concept of public participation

"Public participation" is an all-encompassing label used to describe the various mechanisms that individuals or groups may use to communicate their views on a public issue. Public participation can take many forms, including voting; demonstrating, petitioning, lobbying, writing letters to the editors of newspapers and magazines, debating, campaigning, appearing and testifying at hearings, requesting access to government-held information, serving on citizen advisory panels, even bringing lawsuits....

C. Why public participation? Underlying rationales for public participation in environmental matters

The arguments in favour of public participation can be divided into two categories: (1) those that view public participation as an end in itself (the process-based goals perspective) and (2) those that view public participation as contributing to some further outcome (the substantive-based goals perspective). Both process-based and substantive-based goals perspectives offer valuable insights.

From the process-based perspective, public participation is desirable because it can serve the following ends:

- raise public awareness and educate the public;
- give the public an opportunity to express its concerns;
- foster a sense of empowerment in participants;
- strengthen local communities and other groups;
- reduce conflict among competing interests;
- facilitate governmental accountability;
- increase public acceptance of decisions reached; and
- contribute legitimacy to decisions.

From the substantive-based perspective, public participation is desirable because it can be the means that results in decisions that are:

- substantively "better";
- more equitable;
- more environmentally protective;
- more reflective of local needs; and
- more reflective of public values....

A common view is that public participation is actually necessary in order for any development-related decisions to be sustainable....

While public participation's benefits are assumed to be large, it is more difficult to measure actual results. For example, one recent study of environmental public participation in the United States was unable to confirm whether it actually produces "better" decisions. The key difficulty in validating public participation's contribution to decision-making is, of course, formulating a way to measure the quality of a decision. However, if "better" decisions are defined as those resulting in more demanding or stringent environmental policies, then there is some evidence that public participation does produce better decisions. One recent study of participation in international environmental agreements found that, in most cases studied, expanding participation resulted in more demanding environmental policies. This connection between increased public participation and more stringent environmental protections has been explained by one commentator as follows:

> A procedural or participatory approach promises environmental protection essentially by way of democracy and informed debate. The enthymeme [unstated premise] in this argument is that democratic decision-making will lead to environmentally friendly policies. The point remains to be demonstrated, but one argument in its favour is that in creating legal gateways for participation, it is possible to redress the unequal distribution of environmental costs and benefits. Thus marginalized groups who currently suffer the most deleterious effects of environmental degradation—including women, the dispossessed, and communities closely dependent upon natural resources for their livelihood—can be included in the social determination of environmental change. If the people who make the decisions are the same as those who pay for and live by the consequences of the decisions, then we go a long way toward protecting the environment.

One clearly positive benefit of public participation is that it does increase the amount and type of data upon which decisions may be based. For example, today many NGOs have scientific expertise that governmental authorities may lack, and indigenous people and local communities can be important sources of information not typically known by central government authorities, as acknowledged in various international environmental law instruments. The range of data available to decision-makers is also increased with public participation. For example, by involving the general public, it can bring out information about the subjective needs and interests of the participants—their environmental "concerns" as opposed to merely environmental "facts."

Evidence of the benefits of public participation can also be extrapolated from the negative outcomes of situations in which such participation did not take place. "By analyzing the results of non-participatory development projects around the world, comparative studies are providing increasing evidence of the importance of both building local participation and taking into account socio-cultural factors affecting project design, planning, and implementation." A 1995 World Resources Institute study of twenty-five projects sponsored by the World Bank which were lacking in local participation found that thirteen of such projects were prematurely discontinued by the local populations a few years after the Banks financial assistance ended. Lack of local participation appeared to be one of the main causes of the failure of the projects. A 1982 World Bank review of 164 projects found that where communities were not included in project planning "inaccurate assessments and information about local institutions were common." Additional evidence of the benefits of public participation comes from those situations in which lack of involvement of local populations has led them to reject or fiercely oppose projects.

But what are the counter-arguments? Although most of the focus today is on the positive benefits of public participation, there are some scholars (and of course some governments and development interests) who argue against it. For example, one legal scholar has identified the following criticisms that have been leveled against public participation in environmental decision-making:

- the public is emotional and ill-equipped to deal with technical matters;
- participation programmes demand large amounts of time and administrative resources;
- public participation can result in lowest-common-denominator decisions if an attempt is made to accommodate all interests;
- public participation hinders agency creativity in problem-solving;
- environmental decisions require the compilation of enormous amounts of data which can overwhelm lay participants;
- special interest groups promoting views that are opposed to public opinion on environmental matters are particularly powerful;
- public interest groups can create a "free-rider problem." reducing the amount of direct participation by individuals who choose to pay membership dues and allow organized groups to participate on their behalf;
- participants tend to be from upper socio-economic classes, leading to charges of elitism;
- public participation can lead to citizen frustration and increase distrust of the government, especially if participants do not achieve their goals.

Other commentators have argued that public participation can be merely an "empty ritual" used to maintain the status quo or a public relations "smokescreen." unless citizens have some degree of influence or power over decision-making.

On the whole, though, public participation today is viewed as a positive good—like all democratic values, not without its downsides which must be guarded against, but overall a value whose benefits vastly outweigh its disbenefits....

The Construction of Participatory Democracy in Central and Eastern Europe

John E. Bonine

HUMAN RIGHTS IN NATURAL RESOURCE DEVELOPMENT
(D. Zillman, A. Lucas, & G. Pring, eds., 2002)

Guns did not defeat communism in Eastern Europe. To a degree, environmentalism did so. Grassroots environmental groups made up a large part of the opposition movement in the final years of CEE [Central and Eastern Europe] communism, and provided leadership in the new democratic governments. The same groups quickly found themselves advocating that their new governments should listen not only on Election Day. Why did it happen this way? Why weren't the communist governments simply replaced with election-based governments and civil servants left to continue to work in the old ways, with new bosses? To some degree the answer must be that participation in bureaucratic decisions was simply the next logical development in democratic theory and practice, where societies had grown complex and governments remote. To some degree the answer must be that participation was on the agenda of important institutions at the time when new constitutions and laws were being created for the new democracies of CEE. To some degree, the answer must be that something dramatic and special happened as the walls came down.

It may be said that democracy in the world has passed through three phases: from direct to representative to participatory. In the original direct democracy of ancient Athens, those who were citizens could influence policies directly with their votes. This can still happen today in New England "town meetings" in the USA, or by the use of the initiative or referendum in various countries. But direct democracy does not work very well in organizing a complex society. ...

The increasing complexity of societies gave rise to representative democracy, in place of direct democracy. In its early days this form kept a reasonably strong link between citizens and policies. Those who were citizens (initially, of course, only men and only those of a higher social and economic class) elected their policy-makers on election day, but they could also communicate with them concerning policy in between elections. Representative democracy made some sense when most important policy decisions were made in legislative bodies, and at a time when implementation of decisions was reasonably straightforward. This election-based and representative version of democracy, including contact with legislative decision-makers, provided some reasonable amount of accountability to the people at the time and in the conditions then prevailing.

Today, however, we live in an age when a good deal of important governmental decision-making takes place primarily outside parliaments and legislatures. Thousands of civil servants with little direct accountability to the people work in hundreds of governmental bodies. These civil servants make crucial policy and implementation decisions, which are then approved often by unelected department heads. Endorsement of policies on election day has become increasingly theoretical, while communication with legislators can be seen as contacting the wrong people to affect policy-making."

To deal with these changes in the nature of governing, new approaches to the democracy of governance are being created in various countries. Since policymaking and implementation are often handled by the bureaucracy, the new kind of democracy includes a variety of techniques: inviting the public to submit written or oral comments during the creation of regulations by executive branch departments or government agencies; various methods of formal and informal public consultation; formal hearings; negotiations among government and various stakeholders; and other methods. Such participatory methods are used during the full spectrum of government action, from the highest and earliest levels (such as the preparation of government plans and policies, perhaps including drafting legislation), to the intermediate levels (drafting and later adoption of regulations), to the lower or final levels of implementation (actions on permits or licenses, enforcement, and the like).

International Norms for Public Participation

On the global level, principles of public participation were set out in Principle 10 of the Rio Declaration on Environment and Development and in Agenda 21 (1992). Principle 10 of the Rio Declaration declares that each individual "shall have" the opportunity to participate in decisionmaking processes, as well as declaring that countries "shall facilitate and encourage public awareness and participation." Rio Declaration, 31 I.L.M. at 878. The international community declared in Principle 10 of the Rio Declaration that "environmental issues are best handled with the participation of all concerned citizens" at the relevant level.

Several environmental treaties include public participation provisions. For example, the U.N. Framework Convention on Climate Change (1992), Article 6(a)(iii), requires Parties to "promote and facilitate ... public participation in addressing climate change and its effects and developing adequate responses." The United Nations Convention to Combat Desertification in Those Countries Experiencing Serious Drought and/or Desertification, Particularly in Africa (1994), requires decisions to be "taken with the participation of populations and local communities" Article 3(a). The Convention on Biological Diversity (1992) allows for public participation in environmental impact assessment procedures in Article 14.1. The Cartagena Protocol on Biosafety (2000) in Article 23 foresees providing information to the public, consulting with the public, and public participation in decisions concerning biosafety.

On the regional level in Europe, even before the Rio Conference on Environment and Development, the UNECE[a] Convention on Environmental Impact Assessment in a Transboundary Context (1991) (known as the Espoo Convention, for the city in Iran where the convention was signed) established environmental impact assessment of projects and activities that may have significant transboundary impacts on the environment. It has provisions on public participation in both countries of origin and affected countries. In a final decision on a proposed activity, Parties must take due account of the environmental impact assessment, including the outcome of consultations with the public.

The UNECE Convention on the Transboundary Effects of Industrial Accidents (1992), in Article 9, paragraph 2, requires a Party where an industrial accident might occur to give the public in affected areas "an opportunity to participate" regarding prevention and preparedness measures. Public participation provisions are included in the Protocol on Water and Health to the Convention on the Protection and Use of Transboundary Watercourses and International Lakes (1999), and the Protocol on Heavy Metals (1998) to the Convention on Long-Range Transboundary Air Pollution (1979).

The UNECE Convention on Access to Information, Public Participation in Decision-making and Access to Justice in Environmental Matters (1998) (known as the Aarhus Convention, for the city in Denmark where it was signed) contains the most comprehensive articulation of procedural rights among all regional initiatives. This may be due, in part, to how the convention was negotiated. For one of the first times in international law, members of the public (through the European ECO Forum, a coalition of environmental citizens' organizations) became intimately involved in negotiations, in the process of ratification, and in the implementation of the Aarhus Convention. (Both of the co-authors of this book have taken part and continue to do so.) NGOs had a seat at the table during negotiations and could raise their name card and ask to address the diplomats. The type and degree of involvement by nongovernmental organizations in the negotiations was a remarkable example of public participation, which helped shape the final document. The Aarhus Convention itself established clear, mandatory provisions on public participation in decisions on specific activities (Article 6), along with less detailed and more recommendatory provisions on public participation in plans, programs, and policies (Article 7) and in development of executive regulations and similar legal norms. (Article 8). The public participation provisions of the Aarhus Convention are discussed in detail in this chapter.

---

a. United Nations Economic Commission for Europe, a regional branch of the U.N. headquartered at the Palais des Nations in Geneva, Switzerland.

In North America, the North American Agreement on Environmental Cooperation (1993) (NAAEC, side agreement to the North American Free Trade Agreement (NAFTA) requires Parties to provide interested persons with a "reasonable opportunity" to comment on proposed "laws, regulations, procedures and administrative rulings of general application respecting any matter covered by this Agreement." Articles 4.1, 4.2. In East Africa, the 1998 Memorandum of Understanding between the Republic of Kenya and the United Republic of Tanzania and the Republic of Uganda for Cooperation on Environmental Management commits the three countries to provide for public participation environmental management and in environmental impact assessment.

Although beyond the scope of this book, public participation has also become an issue in the international legal system. With increasing frequency non-State actors are finding voice and influence within meetings of treaty Conferences of Parties, subsidiary bodies, and international commissions. *See* Jonas Ebbesson, *Public Participation*, in THE OXFORD HANDBOOK OF INTERNATIONAL ENVIRONMENTAL LAW 682–703 (D. Bodansky, J. Brunée, & E. Hey, eds., 2007). According to Professor Ebbesson, "Governments have lost the exclusive mandate, if they ever had it, to represent the public and to speak and act on behalf of public interests." He points out that some NGO activism occurred as early as the second half of the nineteenth century when NGOs pushed for a convention on protection of birds. At the World Summit on Sustainable Development in Johannesburg in 2002, 8,000 people represented various interests. Today, NGOs attend "almost every intergovernmental conference and meeting held within the framework of environmental agreements or intergovernmental organizations." *Id.* at 683.

As you study the materials in this chapter, ask yourself about the need for public participation in decisionmaking when a government is already elected by the people and is politically responsible to the people at the next election. What about the possibility that a narrow interest group could have influence on decisionmaking at the expense of the broader public? Or do narrow interest groups already have disproportionate influence through "private participation," so that officially open participation becomes a way to broaden the competition for influence?

II. Public Participation: Europe, Caucasus, Central Asia

From Europe to Central Asia, regional international agreements play an increasing role in environmental decisionmaking. This section discusses two of the major legal instruments. The legislation of individual countries as well as the legislation of the European Union, which provides an additional layer of legal obligations for its 27 members (and three more candidates), is beyond the scope of this book.

A. The Ladder of Public Participation

The right of public participation is easy to assert, but actual implementation requires a more fine-grained analysis. All legal norms on the subject make some distinctions regarding the type, details, and even amount of public participation that is considered appropriate, according to the type of government action that is being considered. This

variance in requirements has been called a "ladder" of public participation, with grada-
tions according to whether the government action involves a specific project, a program
of actions, an overall plan, a legal norm like an executive branch regulation, or a policy.
The following article provides some rationale for these distinctions.

The Aarhus Convention: An Implementation Guide (2000)
Stephen Stec & Susan Casey-Lefkowitz with Jerzy Jendroska
U.N. Doc. ECE/CEP/72

PILLAR II
PUBLIC PARTICIPATION IN DECISION-MAKING

Public participation in decision-making is the second "pillar" of the [Aarhus] Convention. Public participation cannot be effective without access to information, as provided under the first pillar, nor without the possibility of enforcement, through access to
justice under the third pillar.

In its ideal form, public participation involves the activity of members of the public in
partnership with public authorities to reach an optimal result in decision-making and policy-making.... The level of involvement of the public in a particular process depends on a
number of factors, including the expected outcome, its scope, who and how many will be
affected, whether the result settles matters on a national, region or local level, and so on. Many
speak of a "ladder" of participation, in which members of the public have the most power—
even approaching direct democratic decision-making—with respect to local matters with
no impact outside the community. As issues become more complex and involve more global
issues and affect larger numbers of people, the role of individual members of the public di-
minishes and the role of politicians and public authorities that must bear responsibility for
such decisions becomes greater. The involvement of the public can pass through various
stages as one climbs up the ladder—from direct decision-making to administrative status,
participation, consultation, to the right to be informed only. In addition, different persons
may have different status in connection with participation on a particular matter. Those
who are most affected by the outcome of the decision-making or policy-making should
have a greater chance to influence the outcome. This is behind the distinction between "public" and "public concerned" [in the words of Articles 6, 7, and 8]....

What is public participation under the Convention?

"Public participation" is not expressly defined in the Convention. The preamble, however, recites some of the values and considerations at the heart of public participation. The
most fundamental of these is the role of public participation in ensuring a mechanism for
the public to assert the right to live in an environment adequate to health and well-being,
and to fulfill its duty to protect the environment....

In the main text, the Convention shows how public participation should work in the
case of certain decision-making and policy-making processes. From this, it can be de-
duced that public participation should be timely, effective, adequate and formal, and
contain information, notification, dialogue, consideration, and response. The public participation provisions of the Convention are divided into three parts, according to the
kinds of governmental processes covered. Article 6 covers public participation in decisions on specific activities with a potential significant effect on the environment, for example decisions on the proposed siting, construction and operation of large facilities, or
on the licensing of products into the market place. Article 7 covers public participation
in the development of plans, programs and policies relating to the environment, which

include sectoral or land-use plans, environmental action plans, and environmental policies at all levels. Article 8 covers public participation in the preparation by public authorities of laws and regulations.

The Convention establishes firm obligations that Parties must meet in providing for timely, adequate and effective public participation. Among these are requirements concerning notification, timing, relevant information, commenting, response, and communication. The Convention also urges Parties to promote public participation through other mechanisms, such as encouraging project proponents to interact with the public at a preliminary stage. More precise obligations are established under article 6, in recognition that a high level of involvement of the public, adequately guaranteed by law, is appropriate in specific types of decision-making, reflecting the principle that those who are affected should have the right to influence the decision-making process.

Greater flexibility is offered to Parties in meeting the obligations of articles 7 and 8, especially with respect to policies and draft laws.

Article 3, furthermore, reminds Parties that the Convention's provisions, including the provisions in articles 6, 7 and 8, are minimum requirements and that Parties have the right to provide more extensive public participation in decision-making....

Question and Discussion

Varying participation. Is it more important to have public participation in decisions on specific projects or in the consideration of broad national policies, programs, and executive branch regulations? As you read the next sections, consider that question and the difference between the specificity with which the Aarhus Convention deals with participation in these different kinds of activities.

B. Participation for Specific Projects

Although, as noted at the beginning of this chapter, a number of international conventions, particularly in Europe, provide for public participation regarding specific projects, we will focus our attention on provisions of the Aarhus Convention. Article 6 provides detailed procedures and requirements for public participation in specific projects or activities. The language of the article is mandatory and legally binding. Later we will see the much less prescriptive approach that the Convention takes with regard to public participation when the government action involves formulation of plans, programs, policies, and regulations.

Convention on Access to Information,
Public Participation in Decision-Making and Access to Justice
in Environmental Matters (Aarhus Convention)
June 25, 1998
U.N. Doc. ECE/CEP/43, 2161 U.N.T.S. 447, 38 I.L.M 517 (1999)

Article 3
GENERAL PROVISIONS

1. Each Party shall take the necessary legislative, regulatory and other measures, including measures to achieve compatibility between the provisions implementing the information,

public participation and access-to-justice provisions in this Convention, as well as proper enforcement measures, to establish and maintain a clear, transparent and consistent framework to implement the provisions of this Convention....

Article 6
PUBLIC PARTICIPATION IN DECISIONS ON SPECIFIC ACTIVITIES

1. Each Party:

(a) Shall apply the provisions of this article with respect to decisions on whether to permit proposed activities listed in annex I;

(b) Shall, in accordance with its national law, also apply the provisions of this article to decisions on proposed activities not listed in annex I which may have a significant effect on the environment.... ; and

(c) May decide, on a case-by-case basis if so provided under national law, not to apply the provisions of this article to proposed activities serving national defence purposes, if that Party deems that such application would have an adverse effect on these purposes.

2. The public concerned shall be informed, either by public notice or individually as appropriate, early in an environmental decision-making procedure, and in an adequate, timely and effective manner, inter alia, of:

(a) The proposed activity and the application on which a decision will be taken;

(b) The nature of possible decisions or the draft decision;

(c) The public authority responsible for making the decision;

(d) The envisaged procedure, including, as and when this information can be provided:

   (i) The commencement of the procedure;

   (ii) The opportunities for the public to participate;

   (iii) The time and venue of any envisaged public hearing;

   (iv) An indication of the public authority from which relevant information can be obtained and where the relevant information has been deposited for examination by the public;

   (v) An indication of the relevant public authority or any other official body to which comments or questions can be submitted and of the time schedule for transmittal of comments or questions; and

   (vi) An indication of what environmental information relevant to the proposed activity is available; and

(e) The fact that the activity is subject to a national or transboundary environmental impact assessment procedure.

3. The public participation procedures shall include reasonable time-frames for the different phases, allowing sufficient time for informing the public in accordance with paragraph 2 above and for the public to prepare and participate effectively during the environmental decision-making.

4. Each Party shall provide for early public participation, when all options are open and effective public participation can take place.

5. Each Party should, where appropriate, encourage prospective applicants to identify the public concerned, to enter into discussions, and to provide information regarding the objectives of their application before applying for a permit.

6. Each Party shall require the competent public authorities to give the public concerned access for examination, upon request where so required under national law, free of charge and as soon as it becomes available, to all information relevant to the decision-making referred to in this article that is available at the time of the public participation procedure, without prejudice to the right of Parties to refuse to disclose certain information in accordance with article 4, paragraphs 3 and 4. The relevant information shall include at least, and without prejudice to the provisions of article 4:

(a) A description of the site and the physical and technical characteristics of the proposed activity, including an estimate of the expected residues and emissions;

(b) A description of the significant effects of the proposed activity on the environment;

(c) A description of the measures envisaged to prevent and/or reduce the effects, including emissions;

(d) A non-technical summary of the above;

(e) An outline of the main alternatives studied by the applicant; and

(f) In accordance with national legislation, the main reports and advice issued to the public authority at the time when the public concerned shall be informed in accordance with paragraph 2 above.

7. Procedures for public participation shall allow the public to submit, in writing or, as appropriate, at a public hearing or inquiry with the applicant, any comments, information, analyses or opinions that it considers relevant to the proposed activity.

8. Each Party shall ensure that in the decision due account is taken of the outcome of the public participation.

9. Each Party shall ensure that, when the decision has been taken by the public authority, the public is promptly informed of the decision in accordance with the appropriate procedures. Each Party shall make accessible to the public the text of the decision along with the reasons and considerations on which the decision is based....

11. Each Party shall, within the framework of its national law, apply, to the extent feasible and appropriate, provisions of this article to decisions on whether to permit the deliberate release of genetically modified organisms into the environment.

Questions and Discussion

1. *Public versus public concerned.* Who can participate in decisionmaking in environmental matters? What is the difference in Articles 6, 7, and 8, between the "public" and the "public concerned" for the purpose of the availability and type of public participation? (Article 7 and 8 are set out in this Chapter at page 276.) Note that in Article 6, paragraphs 2, 5, and 6, the "public concerned" must be notified and given access to information, but in paragraph 2(d)(ii) any member of the "public" may participate and in paragraphs 7 and 9 the "public" can submit comments and must be informed of the outcome of the decision. What is the reason for these differences? Do you agree with these distinctions?

2. *Early.* According to Article 6, paragraph 2, of the Aarhus Convention, "The public concerned shall be informed, either by public notice or individually as appropriate, early

in an environmental decision-making procedure." What does "early" mean? How early was notification provided in the Ukrainian case? Was it early enough?

3. *Notice and notification.* What is the difference between public notice and individual notification? What kind of information should public notice include? When is individual notice appropriate?

Jurisprudence of the Aarhus Compliance Committee

The following case (and several others in the book) represents jurisprudence of the Compliance Committee for the Aarhus Convention. The Committee was established in accordance with Article 15 as "a non-confrontational, non-judicial and consultative nature for reviewing compliance with the provisions of this Convention." The Compliance Committee is innovative in both structure and procedure. In terms of structure, NGOs have gained the right to nominate members of the independent body. In addition, the compliance body as a whole is composed of independent experts who do not answer to their own governments.

In terms of procedure, citizens and NGOs have gained the formal right to file complaints and to participate in preparation of national reports. The Aarhus Convention Compliance Committee has adopted a variety of transparent procedures. In some instances, these are unique; in others they are at the leading edge of changes that are occurring in international law.

The decisions of the Committee are in the form of Findings and Recommendations. "The Meeting of the Parties may, upon consideration of a report and any recommendations of the Committee, decide upon appropriate measures to bring about full compliance with the Convention." Decision I/7, Review of Compliance, adopted at the first meeting of the Parties held in Lucca, Italy, on 21–23 October 2002, ¶ 37, U.N. Doc. ECE/MP.PP/2/Add.8 (2 April 2004). In the period between the Meetings of the Parties the Compliance Committee has the power to "[p]rovide advice and facilitate assistance to individual Parties regarding the implementation of the Convention" in consultation with the Party concerned. Furthermore, if the Party agrees, the Committee may also make recommendations and request the Party to submit a strategy regarding the achievement of compliance and to report on the implementation of this strategy. *Id.* at ¶¶ 36, 37.

Findings and Recommendations with Regard to Compliance by Ukraine
Submission ACCC/S/2004/01 by Romania and Communication
ACCC/C/2004/03 by Ecopravo-Lviv (Ukraine)
Aarhus Convention Compliance Committee, 18 February 2005
U.N. Doc. ECE/MP.PP/C.1/2005/2/Add.3 (14 March 2005)

INTRODUCTION

On 5 May 2004, the Ukrainian non-governmental organization Ecopravo-Lviv [now known as Environment-People-Law, or EPL] submitted a communication to the Committee alleging non-compliance by Ukraine with its obligations under article 1 and article 6, paragraphs 2 to 4 and 6 to 9, of the Aarhus Convention.[b]

---

b. One of the co-authors of this textbook serves as President of EPL as well as Vice-Chair of the Aarhus Compliance Committee. As a consequence, she recused herself from participation in decisionmaking on this case.

The communication concerned a proposal to construct a navigation canal in the Danube Delta passing through an internationally recognized wetland. The communicant claimed that by failing to provide for proper public participation in a decision-making process on State "environmental *expertisa*" linked with the technical and economic evaluation of the proposed project and to provide access to documentation relevant to the process, the Party had failed to comply with its obligations under article 6 of the Convention. The communicant had sought redress in two instances of the domestic court system, winning in the first instance and losing in the appellate court. The full text of the communication is available at http://www.unece.org/env/pp/pubcom.htm.

The communicant submitted supplementary information on 1 December 2004, listing several additional facts of alleged non-compliance, in particular with regard to interpretation by the courts and the Ministry of Environment of the domestic requirements on public participation in the environmental impact assessment (EIA) process. A reference was also made to the findings of the special fact-finding mission led by the European Commission with regard to the project in question....

On 7 June 2004, the Government of Romania made a submission alleging failure by Ukraine to comply with the provisions of article 6, paragraph 2(e), of the Convention by failing, in the opinion of the submitting Party, to ensure that the public affected by the Bystre Canal project in the Danube Delta was informed early in the decision-making procedure that the project was subject to a national and transboundary environmental impact assessment procedure.

In a letter to the Committee dated 26 November 2004, the submitting Party provided further information.... In support of its position, it cited inter alia the failure of the Party concerned to involve various non-governmental organizations, including Ukrainian, Romanian and international ones that had expressed interest in or concern about the canal, in the decision-making on any of the phases of the project.

The representative of the Romanian Government further clarified during the discussion at the Committee's sixth meeting that the submission was also intended to address Ukraine's failure to comply with article 6 vis-à-vis its own citizens. He also stated that the Ukrainian Government had already been well aware of the concerns of the Romanian public with regard to the project prior to the final decision on the project's feasibility.

The communication was forwarded to the Government of Ukraine.... [It did not] provide information to or participate in the meeting of the Committee at which the matter was discussed....

The Committee discussed the communication at its sixth meeting (15–17 December 2004), with the participation of representatives of the Party making the submission [Romaine] and the communicant [EPL]....

I. SUMMARY OF FACTS

The matter concerns approval by the government of Ukraine of construction of the deep-water navigation canal in the Bystre arm in the Ukrainian part of the Danube river delta. The permitting process has been divided into three phases: feasibility study, approval of phase I and approval of phase II of the project. Each stage undergoes an approval process on the basis of a comprehensive State *expertisa* that includes environmental *expertisa* (an evaluation and, where appropriate, approval of the EIA by an authorized public authority). The Communication and the submission relate primarily to the decision-making on the project's feasibility study. However, both the communicant and the submitting Party maintain that subsequent decision-making on the phases of the project, while having certain formal improvements in the procedure, continuously failed to ensure effective participation as required by article 6 of the Convention.

The project in question potentially affects a nature conservation area of national and international importance and has clearly generated a great interest among both the Ukrainian and international civil society.

In its letters to the Ministry of Environment dated 30 April 2003 and 3 June 2003, the communicant expressed its interest in the decision-making process in question. The communicant has been in regular contact with the Ministry with regard to the issue of the canal construction since then.

The communicant lists several instances where it was refused access to documentation on the project either as a whole or in part. According to the report of the EU fact-finding mission, referred to in the supplementary information and the additional information provided by the submitting Party, several other organizations, including national, foreign and international organizations, both governmental and non-governmental, have been refused access to information of the types referred to in article 6, paragraph 6, of the Convention.

The Ministry of Environment, in its reply to a request for information from the communicant dated 18 June 2003, stated that materials developed in the course of an EIA were the property of the developer and therefore the Ministry was not in a position to provide access to such information. A similar response, as the report of the European Commission indicates, was given to subsequent requests for this documentation submitted by various organizations.

On 3 July 2003, the project investor published an environmental impact statement in the regional newspaper. No information with regard to the public participation procedure or other relevant information referred to in article 6, paragraph 2, of the Convention was provided.

The Ministry of Environment approved the conclusions of the State environmental *expertisa* on 10 July 2003, seven days following the first notification about the project.

On 7 August 2003, the Ministry of Environment sent a reply to the communicant's request for a copy of the conclusions of the State environmental *expertisa*, including a two-page summary of the conclusions and refusing to provide the whole document for technical reasons.

The Government of Ukraine notified the Government of Romania of the intended project in October 2003, following the conclusion of the decision-making procedure on the project's feasibility study.

Phase I of the project was approved in May 2004 and the construction works began immediately. Phase I of the project was concluded in August 2004....

On 13 October 2004, the Ministry of Environment in its written response to the second appeal filed by the communicant with the High Commercial Court of Ukraine stated that the assertion of the plaintiff that Ukrainian legislation provided for an obligation to ensure public participation in the state environmental *expertisa* was ungrounded. The court held that in accordance with Ukrainian legislation, the public authorities were not obliged to ensure public participation in decision-making with regard to EIA.

II. Consideration and Evaluation ...

The Convention, as an international treaty ratified by Ukraine, has direct applicability in the Ukrainian legal system. All the provisions of the Convention are directly applicable, including by the courts.

The decision-making process in question concerns construction of a deep-water navigation canal of a type that ... falls under article 6, paragraph 1 (a), of the Convention, triggering also the application of other provisions of that article.

The communicant is a non-governmental organization working in the field of environmental protection and falls under the definitions of the public and the public concerned as set out in article 2, paragraphs 4 and 5, of the Convention. Foreign or international non-governmental environmental organizations that have similarly expressed an interest in or concern about the procedure would generally fall under these definitions as well.

With regard to the facts included in paragraph 6 above, there is, in the opinion of the Committee, sufficient evidence that there were members of the public, both in Romania and in Ukraine, interested in or concerned about the project that had to be notified in accordance with article 6, paragraph 2, of the Convention.

Considering the nature of the project and the interest it has generated, notification in the nation-wide media as well as individual notification of organizations that explicitly expressed their interest in the matter would have been called for. The Party, therefore, failed to provide for proper notification and participation in the meaning of article 6 of civil society and specifically the organizations, whether foreign or international, that indicated their interest in the procedure....

The timeline ... failed to allow the public to study the information on the project and prepare and submit its comments. It also did not allow the public officials responsible for making the decision sufficient time to take any comments into account in a meaningful way, as required under article 6, paragraph 8.

In this regard, ... what seems to be a regular practice of short-cutting the decision-making procedure by providing parts of the EIA for evaluation and approval by the decision-making authority ... prior to any information being publicly available is of particular concern. Lack of clear domestic regulation of the time frames and procedures for commenting seem to be at the heart of this problem....

[P]ublic authorities should possess information relevant to [their] functions, including that on which they base their decisions, in accordance with article 5, paragraph 1, and should make it available to the public, subject to exemptions specified in article 4, paragraphs 3 and 4. The issue of ownership is not of relevance in this matter, as information is used in a decision-making by a public authority and should be provided to it for that purpose by the developer. The fact that such misinterpretation took place again points to a lack of clear regulatory requirements in the national legislation....

Lack of clarity or detail in domestic legislative provisions ... demonstrate[s], in the view of the Committee, that the Party concerned has not taken the necessary measures to establish and maintain a clear, transparent and consistent framework to implement the provisions of the Convention, as required by article 3, paragraph 1.

The Committee finds that by refusing to provide the text of the decision along with the reasons and considerations on which it is based and not indicating how the communicant could have access to it, the Party concerned did not comply with its obligations under the second part of article 6, paragraph 9, to make accessible to the public the text of the decision along with the reasons and considerations on which the decision is based....

III. CONCLUSIONS

Having considered the above, the Committee adopts the following findings and recommendations set out in the following paragraphs with a view to bringing them to the
attention of the Meeting of the Parties.

A. Main findings with regard to non-compliance

The Committee finds that, by failing to provide for public participation of the kind required by article 6 of the Convention, Ukraine was not in compliance with article 6, paragraph 1(a), and, in connection with this, article 6, paragraphs 2 to 8, and article 6,
paragraph 9 (second sentence)....

The Committee also finds that the lack of clarity with regard to public participation
requirements in EIA and environmental decision-making procedures for projects, such
as time frames and modalities of a public consultation process, requirements to take its
outcome into account, and obligations with regard to making available information in the
context of article 6, indicates the absence of a clear, transparent and consistent framework for the implementation of the Convention and constitutes non-compliance with
article 3, paragraph 1, of the Convention.

B. Recommendations

The Committee, taking into account the cause and degree of the non-compliance, and
noting with regret that no response to either the submission or the communication was
provided by the Party concerned pursuant to the requirements set out in the annex to
decision I/7, recommends to the Meeting of the Parties pursuant to paragraph 35 of the
annex to decision I/7 to:

(a) Request the Government of Ukraine to bring its legislation and practice into
    compliance with the provisions of the Convention and include information on
    the measures taken to that effect in its report to the next meeting of the Parties;

(b) Pursuant to paragraph 37(b) of the annex to decision I/7, request the Govern-
    ment of Ukraine to submit to the Compliance Committee, not later than the
    end of 2005, a strategy, including a time schedule, for transposing the Conven-
    tion's provisions into national law and developing practical mechanisms and im-
    plementing legislation that sets out clear procedures for their implementation.
    The strategy might also include capacity-building activities, in particular for the
    judiciary and public officials involved in environmental decision-making;

(c) Mandate the Working Group of the Parties to develop for consideration at the
    third meeting of the Parties guidance to assist Parties in identifying, notifying
    and involving the public concerned in decision-making on projects in border
    areas affecting the public in other countries but not requiring transboundary EIA
    under the Espoo Convention which includes procedures for public participation.

Questions and Discussion

1. *EIA and public participation.* The process of "environmental impact assessment"
(EIA) has become, in most countries, the primary opportunity for members of the public to exercise their right to participate in decisionmaking involving environmental matters. In Eastern Europe, Caucasus, and Central Asia an "environmental *expertisa*" is
prepared, which is linked to the EIA process. This case provides a look at both.

2. *Information ownership.* The Ministry of Environment of Ukraine, in its reply to a
request for information, stated that materials developed in the course of an environ-

mental impact assessment (EIA) were the property of the developer and therefore the Ministry was not in a position to provide access to such information. Can EIA documentation be the property of a developer? Does it fall under the provision of the Article 4, paragraph 4, of the Aarhus Convention, discussed in Chapter 6 at page 222?

3. *"Due account."* The Convention requires each Party to "ensure that in the decision due account is taken of the outcome of the public participation." What does "due account" mean? What does "outcome" mean in this context? The Ministry of Environment approved the conclusions of the State environmental *expertisa* just seven days following the first notification to the public about the project. Was it sufficient time to take the outcome of the public participation into account? What would be the implications of giving more time to the public to comment?

4. *Summary.* When the communicant requested the Ministry of Environment to send a copy of the conclusions of the environmental *expertisa*, the Ministry sent a two-page summary of the conclusions, refusing to provide a copy of the whole document. Does this comply with Article 6, paragraph 8, of the Convention? What are the advantages to the Ministry of Environment in only providing a summary? Disadvantages?

5. *Meeting of the Parties.* The Second Meeting of the Parties to the Aarhus Convention, held in Almaty, Kazakhstan, in June 2005, approved the Compliance Committee's recommendations. By 2008, Ukraine had failed to produce the requested strategy. In June 2008 the Third Meeting of the Parties in Riga, Latvia, issued a "caution" to Ukraine, to become effective if Ukraine did not produce an adequate strategy within six months.

C. Participation in Plans, Programs, Policies and Executive Regulations

Two international conventions in the region of Europe, Caucasus, and Central Asia provide for public participation when a government action involves formulation of plans, programs, policies, or regulations. We will look at both the Aarhus Convention's provisions and the provisions of the Protocol on Strategic Environmental Assessment.

1. Aarhus Convention

The language of Articles 7 and 8 of the Aarhus Convention is softer and more recommendatory than what Article 6 requires with regard to public participation in decisions on specific activities. Article 7 of the Aarhus Convention encourages public participation in the preparation of plans and programs relating to the environment. The language of Article 7 could even be characterized as merely advisory, especially on public participation in the preparation of policies: "*To the extent appropriate,* each party *shall endeavor* to provide opportunities for public participation in the preparation of policies relating to the environment."

As for executive regulations, in many parts of the world, formal rights for the public to comment on draft regulations are rare. Article 8 of the Aarhus Convention makes a significant advance in this regard. It provides: "Each party *shall strive* to promote effective public participation at an appropriate stage, and while options are open." Although the language is somewhat soft, it is perhaps stronger than that of Article 7. Rather than stating detailed requirements, Article 8 merely states that draft rules should be published and the public should be given an opportunity to comment on them.

In general, the States negotiating the Convention were not willing to go into as much detail regarding public participation in the fields of planning, programs, policies, and legal norms as they were under Article 6 for actions involving a specific project such as licensing or permitting.

Convention on Access to Information, Public Participation in Decision-Making and Access to Justice in Environmental Matters (Aarhus Convention)
June 25, 1998
U.N. Doc. ECE/CEP/43, 2161 U.N.T.S. 447, 38 I.L.M 517 (1999)

Article 7
PUBLIC PARTICIPATION CONCERNING PLANS, PROGRAMMES AND POLICIES RELATING TO THE ENVIRONMENT

Each Party shall make appropriate practical and/or other provisions for the public to participate during the preparation of plans and programmes relating to the environment, within a transparent and fair framework, having provided the necessary information to the public. Within this framework, article 6, paragraphs 3, 4 and 8, shall be applied. The public which may participate shall be identified by the relevant public authority, taking into account the objectives of this Convention. To the extent appropriate, each Party shall endeavour to provide opportunities for public participation in the preparation of policies relating to the environment.

Article 8
PUBLIC PARTICIPATION DURING THE PREPARATION OF EXECUTIVE REGULATIONS AND/OR GENERALLY APPLICABLE LEGALLY BINDING NORMATIVE INSTRUMENTS

Each Party shall strive to promote effective public participation at an appropriate stage, and while options are still open, during the preparation by public authorities of executive regulations and other generally applicable legally binding rules that may have a significant effect on the environment. To this end, the following steps should be taken:

(a) Time-frames sufficient for effective participation should be fixed;

(b) Draft rules should be published or otherwise made publicly available; and

(c) The public should be given the opportunity to comment, directly or through representative consultative bodies.

The result of the public participation shall be taken into account as far as possible.

The Aarhus Convention: An Implementation Guide (2000)
Stephen Stec & Susan Casey Lefkowitz, with Jerzy Jendroska
U.N. Doc. ECE/CEP/72

Article 7

Article 7 covers public participation with respect to plans, programs and policies. The obligations of authorities and the rights of the public are somewhat less clearly defined than in article 6, although several of the provisions of article 6 are incorporated by reference, at least with respect to plans and programs. Article 7 allows Parties more flexibility in finding appropriate solutions for public participation in this category of decision-making.

Article 7 distinguishes between plans and programs on the one hand and policies on the other. As far as plans and programs are concerned, it incorporates certain provisions of article 6 relating to the time-frames and the effectiveness of opportunities for public participation, as well as the obligation to ensure that public participation is actually taken into account. There is also an express reference to the objectives of the Convention. With respect to policies there is no express incorporation of the provisions of article 6.

Providing for implementation provisions

The Convention emphasizes that Parties shall, at a minimum, make practical provisions for public participation in such plans and programs. This is consistent with its overall goal that opportunities for public participation should be real and effective....

Article 8

The Convention recognizes that, in addition to the rights to take part in basic decisions affecting their lives, members of the public also have a role to play in the development of laws and normative acts. The applicability of the Convention to lawmaking was thoroughly discussed during the negotiations. This is reflected in the preambular provision that recognizes "the desirability of transparency in all branches of government" and invites "legislative bodies to implement the principles of this Convention in their proceedings." But governments were reluctant to negotiate specific requirements for parliaments, considering this a prerogative of the legislative branch.

Nevertheless, the Convention addresses the role of the executive branch of government in law-making, and specifically provides that the public shall be involved. Public participation in the making of law is thus an important aspect of the overall scope of the Convention. This area of activity is covered by a comparatively soft obligation to use best efforts, and uses indicative rather than mandatory wording for the steps to be taken. Nonetheless, article 8 should be interpreted as obliging the Parties to take concrete measures in order to fulfill the objectives of the Convention....

The term "rules" is here used in its broadest sense, and may include decrees, regulations, ordinances, instructions, normative orders, norms and rules. It also includes the participation of the public authorities in the legislative process, up until the time that drafts prepared by the executive branch are passed to the legislature. Article 8 establishes public participation in the preparation of such rules as a goal of the Convention, and sets forth certain requirements that Parties should meet in reaching it.

———————

The next case concerns the alleged lack of public participation opportunities in both the planning process for an industrial park and the project approval process for a thermal electric power station in Albania, on the Adriatic Sea. Pay close attention to the differences between approving a site for a *future* industrial park and approving a *construction site* for a thermal electric station. Consider the line between the concepts of "planning" versus "projects" (or "specific activities"), and the applicability of the differing requirements of Articles 6 and 7 of Aarhus regarding the two. In addition, take note of the claims regarding public participation, in light of the evidence submitted and the Committee's close examination of it.

Findings and Recommendations with Regard to Compliance by Albania

Communication ACCC/C/2005/12 by the Alliance for the
Protection of the Vlora Gulf (Albania)
Aarhus Convention Compliance Committee, 15 June 2007
U.N. Doc. ECE/MP.PP/C.1/2007/4/Add.1 (31 July 2007)

I. BACKGROUND ...

A. General issues

On 27 April 2005, the Albanian non-governmental organization (NGO) Alliance for the Protection of the Vlora Gulf ... submitted a communication to the Committee alleging violation by Albania of its obligations under article 3, paragraph 2; article 6, paragraph 2; and article 7 of the Aarhus Convention.

The communication alleged that the Party concerned [Albania] had failed to notify the public properly and in a timely manner or to consult the public concerned in the decision-making on planning of an industrial park comprising of, inter alia, oil and gas pipelines, installations for the storage of petroleum, three thermal power plants and a refinery near the lagoon of Narta, on a site of 560 ha [hectares] inside the Protected National Park. The communicant also alleged that the Party failed to make appropriate provision for public participation in accordance with article 7 of the Convention. The full text of the communication is available at http://www.unece.org/env/pp/pubcom.htm....

The Party concerned responded on 25 November 2005, disputing the claim of non-compliance. It stated, inter alia, that:

(a) The government had not made a decision on the development of the proposed industrial park as a whole;

(b) A decision-making process for the establishment of a thermal electric power station (TES) was under way, but no decision on an environmental permit had been taken; ...

(e) The public had had the possibility to participate in the decision-making process for the TES, as three public meetings had been organized at different stages of the process (feasibility study, scoping and environmental impact assessment), with participation of local citizens and NGOs; ...

On 12 June 2006, the Party concerned provided the Committee with the text of three decisions of the Council of Territorial Adjustment of the Republic of Albania, all dated 19 February 2003. Decision No. 8 approved the use of the territory for the development of an industrial and energy park; Decision No. 9 approved the construction site for a coastal terminal for the storage of oil and oil by-products and associated port infrastructure in Vlora; and Decision No. 20 approved the construction site of the TES in Vlora. The Party concerned also sent the Committee a chronology of the participation of the public in the decision-making process for the TES, stating that the procedures had been in accordance with national and international law....

[O]n 21 October 2006, the Party concerned answered some of the outstanding questions. However, it failed to answer a number of other questions, including on public notification and participation procedures in the decision-making process for the industrial energy park....

On 1 December 2006, the Party concerned ... failed to answer a crucial question about the notification of the public and public participation in decision-making on the industrial park....

B. Involvement of international financial institutions ...

The World Bank office in Tirana [stated] in a letter dated 2 August 2006 ... that it was not and had never been involved in the development of the industrial park project, but that it had consistently advised the Government of Albania that the development of any facility planned for such a park should be subject to an appropriate environmental assessment. Regarding the TES in Vlora, the World Bank, EBRD [European Bank for Reconstruction and Development] and the European Investment Bank (EIB) had agreed to finance the project and consultants funded by the United States Trade and Development Agency (USTDA) had selected the location based on a detailed siting study, taking into consideration environmental issues. According to the above letter, the siting study had been followed by preparation of a full environmental assessment, during which several scoping sessions and public consultations had been organized, and public input had been taken into account....

The communicant sent a letter to the Committee on 30 September 2006 commenting on the response by the World Bank. The letter stated that ... public presentations of the project had only addressed the impact and emissions from a 100 MW power station, thus failing to take into account the future cumulative environmental impact of these projects....

The communicant furthermore stated that there was no evidence that intellectuals and NGOs of Vlora had participated in the meeting on 31 October 2002 [concerning proposed construction of the TES]. Besides, this meeting had taken place after the approval of the Siting Study and Feasibility Study. The communicant argued that at that stage there had been a lack of publication of information....

II. Summary of the Facts, Evidence and Issues ...

1. Industrial and Energy Park

On 19 February 2003, the Council of Territorial Adjustment of the Republic of Albania approved through Decision No. 8 the site of an industrial and energy park immediately to the north of the city of Vlora...." Decision No. 8 furthermore deemed that the Ministry of Industry and Energy "should coordinate work" with various Ministries and other bodies "to include within this perimeter [of the industrial and energy park] the projects of the above mentioned institutions, according to the designation "Industrial and Energy Park." It stated also that various Ministries "must carry out this decision" and "This decision comes to force immediately."

The Party concerned informed the Committee that the decision had been subject to an EIA procedure; however, the EIA was not detailed, because it was considered that the separate components of the proposed park would each carry their own more demanding EIA requirements.

The Committee has not been provided with any evidence of public participation, including notification or public announcement, in the process leading up to Decision No 8.

In October 2005, following a change of government the Prime Minister established an ad hoc commission to consider the economic and environmental aspects of Vlora industrial and energy park project. Three meetings were held with stakeholders, two in Tirana (22 and 29 October 2005) and one in Vlora (11 November 2005). The communicant has not contested that these meetings took place and that they enabled the concerned stakeholders to participate, and it has confirmed that its representatives did indeed participate in them. Its objections relate rather to the perception that there was a lack of willingness to from the proponents of the project, including the Government, to "listen and to take into consideration the opinion and the will of the people," thereby reducing the decision-making process to "a mere rubber stamp."...

2. Thermal electric power station

On 19 February 2003, the Council of Territorial Adjustment approved Decision No. 20 on the construction site of the TES in Vlora. Through this Decision, signed and stamped by Mr. Fatos Nano, Chairman of the Council, who was the Prime Minister at the time, the Council "Decided: to approve the construction site with a surface of 14 hectares for the facility of the new Port of Vlora, within the industrial Energy Park ... according to the attached layout." It stated also that the Council of the District of Vlora and the Ministry of Energy and industry should carry out this decision" and "This decision comes to force immediately."

The Party concerned informed the Committee that in order to address the problem with electricity supply in Albania, the Ministry for Industry and Energy and KESH [Korporata Elektroenergjetike Shqiptare] began to study the technical and financial viability of installing new base load thermal generation facilities in Albania. KESH asked for funding from EBRD, the World Bank and EIB.

The USTDA awarded a grant to the Government of Albania to assist in the development of the new thermal generation facility. The Albanian Ministry of Industry and Energy hired international consultants Montgomery Watson Harza (MWH) to select the best site and technology, to conduct a feasibility study, and to conduct an environmental impact assessment (EIA) of the proposed facility.

Site selection was undertaken during the period April–September 2002. A draft Siting Report was completed on 6 June 2002 recommending Vlora as the best site.... On 21 June 2002, the Ministry of Energy and KESH approved the recommendation. MWH then conducted a detailed feasibility study to evaluate the technical requirements and the financial, environmental, and social viability of the proposed generation facility with an installed capacity range of 90 to 130 MW at the selected site. On 21 October 2002, the feasibility study was completed and "introduced in Vlora."

On 31 October 2002, the Ministry of Energy and Industry convened a public meeting in Vlora to introduce the project and begin the public consultation process....

As regards the participation of the public..., varying degrees of information are available to the Committee:

    (a) The introductory meeting on 31 October 2002 which addressed the proposed construction of the TES in Vlora was attended by various representatives of national and local authorities as well as, according to the Party concerned, intellectuals and NGOs of Vlora.... The Committee repeatedly requested the Party concerned to provide specific information concerning the process of notification for the meeting (for residents, NGOs and other stakeholders) and a list of participants. In the course of nearly two years ... the Party concerned failed to provide any such information. On 18 May 2007, the Party concerned belatedly provided a report and list of participants of the meeting which took place in October 2002.... No information with regard to the notification procedure has been provided.

    (b) The meeting on 2 April 2003 to review the scope of the EIA was attended by more than 100 people, 40 of whom signed an attendance sheet a copy of which was made available to the Committee. The communicant commented that "there was not a single NGO represented or any important environmental activist in this meeting" and that public opinion was not taken into account in the decision.... The Party concerned ... did not provide the Committee with any details of who was invited to participate, or more generally of the steps taken to notify the public concerned.

(c) The meeting on 3 September 2003 to review the draft EIA was attended by some 35 people, a list of whom was included in the EIA study. Of these, five appear to have been technical experts, 15 represented various public authorities, five represented various local enterprises, the affiliation of six was not indicated, and four appear to have been associations, including three environmental organizations. Again, information requested from the Party concerned regarding the process of notification of the public concerned has not been forthcoming....

(f) A document entitled "Summary of Environmental Impacts Associated with the Vlore Thermal Power Station." prepared for the purposes of meeting the requirements of EBRD's public disclosure and consultation procedure, states that "The public was well engaged in a dialogue concerning the project early on in the EIA process. Public announcements were thorough, transparent and well distributed."...

The EIA study was finalized on 6 October 2003. On 18 October 2003, KESH issued a press release launching a public discussion on the evaluation of the EIA. It invited all interested parties to participate in an open consultation process and provided information on where the relevant documents could be obtained.

On 10 February 2004 KESH issued a further press release along similar lines.... Specifically, the EIA materials would be available for a 120-day period from 9 February 2004 to 7 June 2004 for public review and comment, in a number of public locations, including in Vlora, in accordance with EBRD's public consultation and disclosure procedure. Announcements containing this information were also placed in various newspapers....

III. CONSIDERATION AND EVALUATION BY THE COMMITTEE ...

B. Legal basis ...

[T]he case concerns a number of different issues and proposed activities: the energy and industrial park, the TES, the oil storage facility, the oil and gas pipelines, among others. Each of these issues and proposed activities has its own decision-making processes, and to a certain extent they relate to different provisions of the Convention....

The Committee decided to concentrate primarily on the issue of public participation with regard to the making of three decisions by the Council of Territorial Adjustment of the Republic of Albania, all made on 19 February 2003, namely Decision No. 8 (approving the site of the proposed industrial and energy park) and Decision No. 20 (approving the construction site of the proposed TES)....

The Committee will first have to consider whether the relevant decisions amount to decisions on specific activities under article 6 of the Convention, or decisions on plans under article 7.... Also as previously observed by the Committee, ... the Convention does not establish a precise boundary between article 6-type decisions and article 7-type decisions. [The Committee decided that some decisions in the project area were project-level decisions, under article 6, while others were more in the nature of planning, under article 7.] ...

[T]he public participation requirements for decision-making on an activity covered by article 7 are a subset of the public participation requirements for decision-making on an activity covered by article 6. Regardless of whether the decisions are considered to fall under article 6 or article 7, the requirements of paragraphs 3, 4 and 8 of article 6 apply....

The Committee is aware that at least one of the two decisions that it has chosen to focus on would need to be followed by further decisions on whether to grant environmental, construction and operating permits (and possibly other types of permit) before the activities in question could legitimately commence. However, public participation must take place at an early stage of the environmental decision-making process under the Aarhus Convention. Therefore it is important to consider whether public participation has been provided for at a sufficiently early stage of the environmental decision-making processes in these cases.

C. Substantive issues

1. Industrial and Energy Park

The Party concerned has informed the Committee that there was "no complex decision taken on the development of industrial park as a whole." It has emphasized that Decision No. 8 of the Council of Territorial Adjustment of the Republic of Albania "On the Approval of the Industrial and Energy Park-Vlore." which approved the development of "The Industrial and Energy Park-Vlore," was just a location (siting) decision. However, this does not detract from its importance, both in paving the way for more specific decisions on future projects and in preventing other potentially conflicting uses of the land. Several Ministries were instructed to carry out this decision. The decision came into force immediately. It is clear to the Committee that this was a decision by a public authority that a particular piece of land should be used for particular purpose, even if further decisions would be needed before any of the planned activities could go ahead.

No evidence of any notification of the public concerned, or indeed of any opportunities for public participation being provided during the process leading up to this decision, has been presented to the Committee by the Party concerned, despite repeated requests.... The Committee is therefore convinced that the decision was made without effective notification of the public concerned, which ruled out any possibility for the public to prepare and participate effectively during the decision-making process....

[E]ven if public participation opportunities were to be provided subsequently with respect to decisions on specific activities within the industrial and energy park, the requirement that the public be given the opportunity to participate at an early stage when all options are open was not met in this case.... Thus the Party concerned failed to implement the requirements set out in paragraphs 3, 4 and 8 of article 6, and consequently was in breach of article 7....

2. Thermal electric power station ...

[T]he decision-making process relating to the proposed TES involved some elements of public participation, e.g. public notifications, public meetings, availability of EIA documentation and so on. However, as regards Decision No. 20, dated 19 February 2003, which establishes the site of the TES, the only element of public participation in this phase of the process appears to have been the public meeting that took place in Vlora on 28 or 31 October 2002.... As mentioned above, the Party concerned asserted that among those who participated in the meeting were "intellectuals and NGOs of Vlora." This assertion has been strongly disputed by the communicant. Unfortunately, despite repeated requests by the Committee, the Party concerned had failed to provide specific information on these points up until May 2007. Indeed, even the actual date on which the meeting took place could not be clearly established.

Having received the report, minutes and the list of participants of the October 2002 meeting, the Committee, prompted by a correspondence received from the communicant, examined them in comparison with the minutes and the list of participants of the meeting [3] September 2003. In this regard the Committee notes that out of 16 questions put forward by the participants of the first meeting and 18 questions raised at the second meeting, 12 are exactly the same. Of these nine received practically verbatim identical replies. Introductions to the meetings and some of the general interventions made by the public officials are also identical. Furthermore, the Committee notes that the lists of participants of the two meetings differ only in the four additional public officials who attended the first meeting. The results of this comparative analysis raise serious concerns regarding the extent to which the report of the meeting can be relied upon as an accurate record of the proceedings as well as regarding the genuine nature of the questions and concerns raised, recorded and subsequently taken into account in the decision-making process. The unclear circumstances around the meeting in October 2002, and the failure of the Party concerned to provide anything to substantiate the claim that the meeting was duly announced and open for public participation, as well as the concerns about the quality of the meeting records leads the Committee to conclude that the Party concerned failed to comply with the requirements for public participation set out in paragraphs 3, 4 and 8 of article 6 of the Convention....

[T]he Committee wishes to make clear that once a decision to permit a proposed activity in a certain location has already been taken without public involvement, providing for such involvement in the other decision-making stages that will follow can under no circumstances be considered as meeting the requirement under article 6, paragraph 4, to provide "early public participation when all options are open." This is the case even if a full environmental impact assessment is going to be carried out. Providing for public participation only at that stage would effectively reduce the public's input to commenting on how the environmental impact of the installation could be mitigated but would preclude the public from having any input on the decision on whether the installation should be there in the first place, as that decision would have already been taken.

The two meetings that took place on 2 April 2003 and 3 September 2003, respectively, obviously occurred after the adoption of Decision No. 20, and therefore cannot be considered as events contributing to the involvement of the public in that decision. Thus, they do not mitigate the failure of the Party concerned to comply with the Convention in the process leading to Decision No. 20 of 19 February 2003.

Even so, the Committee wishes to make a short comment on these meetings as well, since they also give rise to concern. No information has been provided by the Party concerned to demonstrate that the meetings in April and September 2003 were publicly announced, so as to make it possible also for members of the public opposing the project to actively take part in the decision-making. Nor has the Party concerned been able to give any reasonable explanation as to why the rather strong local opposition to the project, indicated by the 14,000 people calling for a referendum, was not heard or represented properly at any of these meetings. This gives raise to concerns that the invitation process also at this stage was selective and insufficient. The only public notification, in the form of newspaper advertisements, that was presented to the Committee related to meetings that took place later in 2004. Thus the Committee notes that, despite some subsequent efforts to improve the means for public participation, there were several shortcomings also in the decision-making process after February 2003....

IV. CONCLUSIONS

Having considered the above, the Committee adopts the findings and recommendations set out in the following paragraphs.

A. Main findings with regard to non-compliance

With respect to the proposed industrial and energy park, the Committee finds that the decision by the Council of Territorial Adjustment of the Republic of Albania to allocate territory for the Industrial and Energy Park of Vlora (Decision No. 8 of 19 February 2003) falls within the scope of article 7 and is therefore subject to the requirements of article 6, paragraphs 3, 4 and 8. The Party concerned has failed to implement those requirements in the relevant decision-making process and thus was not in compliance with article 7.

With respect to the proposed thermal electric power plant, the Committee finds that the decision by the Council of Territorial Adjustment of the Republic of Albania on the siting of the TES near Vlora (Decision No. 20 of 19 February 2003) is subject to the requirements of article 6, paragraphs 3, 4 and 8. Although some efforts were made to provide for public participation, these largely took place after the crucial decision on siting and were subject to some qualitative deficiencies, leading the Committee to find that the Party concerned failed to comply fully with the requirements in question....

B. Recommendations ...

The Committee recommends that the Party concerned take the necessary legislative, regulatory, administrative and other measures to ensure that:

(a) A clear, transparent and consistent framework to implement the provisions of the Convention in Albanian legislation is established, including a clearer and more effective scheme of responsibility within the governmental administration;

(b) Practical and/or other provisions for the public to participate during the preparation of plans and programmes relating to the environment are in place not only during preparation of individual projects, including through development of detailed procedures and practical measures to implement article 25 of the EIA Law of Albania;

(c) The public which may participate is identified;

(d) Notification of the public is made at an early stage for projects and plans, when options are open, not when decisions are already made;

(e) Notification of the entire public which may participate, including non-governmental organizations opposed to the project, is provided, and notifications are announced by appropriate means and in an effective manner so as to ensure that the various categories of the public which may participate are reached, and records kept of such notifications;

(f) The locations where the draft EIA can be inspected by the public before public meetings are publicized at a sufficiently early stage, giving members of the public time and opportunities to present their comments; public opinions are heard and taken into account by the public authority making the decision....

Questions and Discussion

1. *The industrial park: project, plan, or neither?* Is the siting decision for a future Industrial Energy Park a project, plan, or neither? What is the difference between Articles

6 and 7 of the Aarhus Convention in general and in application to the Albania case? See pages 268 and 276. Which requirements of Article 6 apply to a decision that falls under Article 7? Does the Convention establish a precise boundary between Article 6-type decisions and Article 7-type decisions?

2. *Early stage.* Did public participation on the industrial park planning take place at an early stage, when all options were open? Compare the communicant's and the Party's arguments on that issue. Why does the Committee decide that later public participation cannot make up for the lack of earlier participation? If you are a lawyer operating in a country covered by the Aarhus Convention, how might you use this decision in a national court to interpret either the Convention or a national law purporting to implement the Convention?

3. *TES: Pro forma public participation.* In what ways did the Committee decide that the construction of the thermal electric power plant (TES) by the Albanian government constituted a violation of Article 6 of the Aarhus Convention? The government organized three public meetings during the EIA process and claimed that it invited NGOs and the public. It stated, "The public was well engaged in a dialogue concerning the project early on in the EIA process. Public announcements were thorough, transparent and well distributed." What did the Committee do to investigate the veracity of this claim? What documentation did the committee find lacking? If you are a lawyer working for a government body or developer, what advice will you give after this case? If you are a lawyer contacted by an NGO and asked to challenge a project on the ground of inadequate public participation, what kind of investigations will you launch, after reading this case?

4. *Exhaustion of domestic remedies.* Is exhaustion of domestic remedies required for admissibility to the Aarhus Convention Compliance Committee? Did the communicant try to use domestic remedies before applying to the Compliance Committee? The communicant organized a referendum in opposition to the projects and collected for that purpose 14,000 signatures, as required by the law. Can this be considered as a domestic remedy under the Aarhus Convention?

2. *Strategic Environmental Assessment*

The idea to develop a protocol (an additional international agreement) to flesh out Articles 7 and 8 of the Aarhus Convention and make requirements more certain was the subject of much discussion soon after the Convention was adopted. However, instead of preparing a protocol to the Aarhus Convention, governments decided to prepare a Protocol on Strategic Environmental Assessment (SEA) under the Convention on Environmental Impact Assessment in a Transboundary Context (1991) (Espoo Convention). During negotiations some strong provisions of the original draft were weakened. Furthermore, rather than addressing public participation generally, they do so only as part of the process of environmental assessment.

The SEA Protocol is thus a separate international treaty, primarily involving the assessment of the impact of *plans* and *programs* that are likely to have significant environmental, including health, effects (primarily, but not limited to, transboundary impacts). "To the extent appropriate" the Protocol may apply to *policies* and *legislation* (including laws and executive regulations). The SEA Protocol calls for application of environmental assessment at an early stage of decisionmaking. Article 8 of the Protocol requires each Party to ensure early, timely and effective public participation in SEA of plans and programs. The Protocol was signed in 2003 in Kyiv by 36 countries of Europe. As of early 2008, seven of the 16 ratifications needed for it to enter into force had been deposited with the United Nations.

Protocol on Strategic Environmental Assessment to the Convention on Environmental Impact Assessment in a Transboundary Context
May 23, 2003
U.N. Doc. MP.EIA/2003/1 (2003)

Article 4
FIELD OF APPLICATION CONCERNING PLANS AND PROGRAMMES

1. Each Party shall ensure that a strategic environmental assessment is carried out for plans and programmes referred to in paragraphs 2, 3 and 4 which are likely to have significant environmental, including health, effects.

2. A strategic environmental assessment shall be carried out for plans and programmes which are prepared for agriculture, forestry, fisheries, energy, industry including mining, transport, regional development, waste management, water management, telecommunications, tourism, town and country planning or land use, and which set the framework for future development consent for projects listed in annex I and any other project listed in annex II that requires an environmental impact assessment under national legislation. [Both annexes contain long and detailed lists of specific types of development projects such as pipelines, oil refineries, and other projects.]

[Paragraphs 3 and 4 provide for assessment of additional plans and programs only where a Party "so determines" after a screening process.]

Article 8
PUBLIC PARTICIPATION

1. Each Party shall ensure early, timely and effective opportunities for public participation, when all options are open, in the strategic environmental assessment of plans and programmes.

2. Each Party, using electronic media or other appropriate means, shall ensure the timely public availability of the draft plan or programme and the environmental report.

3. Each Party shall ensure that the public concerned, including relevant non-governmental organizations, is identified for the purposes of paragraphs 1 and 4.

4. Each Party shall ensure that the public referred to in paragraph 3 has the opportunity to express its opinion on the draft plan or programme and the environmental report within a reasonable time frame.

5. Each Party shall ensure that the detailed arrangements for informing the public and consulting the public concerned are determined and made publicly available....

Article 13
POLICIES AND LEGISLATION

1. Each Party shall endeavour to ensure that environmental, including health, concerns are considered and integrated to the extent appropriate in the preparation of its proposals for policies and legislation that are likely to have significant effects on the environment, including health.

2. In applying paragraph 1, each Party shall consider the appropriate principles and elements of this Protocol.

3. Each Party shall determine, where appropriate, the practical arrangements for the consideration and integration of environmental, including health, concerns in accordance with paragraph 1, taking into account the need for transparency in decision-making....

Questions and Discussion

1. *Who should be allowed to participate?* Article 8 of the SEA Protocol, like various public participation provisions of the Aarhus Convention, states that the "public concerned" should be allowed to participate, not the entire "public." Is Article 8 more restrictive than Article 7 of the Aarhus Convention in this regard? Does this Protocol provide appropriate involvement for NGOs? What do you think about the following arguments for giving the entire public a voice in decisionmaking processes in environmental matters?

> Another normative justification for the incorporation of all stakeholders in environmental governance, both international and national, is grounded in prevailing democratic tenets. It is not, however, just confined to the notion that governing must be done with the consent of the governed, in the sense of participatory rights in the electoral process. Rather, and especially in the environmental context, emphasis is placed on entitlements such as the rights of access to information, environmental impact assessment, participation in decision-making on environmental issues, legal redress and effective remedies in case of environmental damage. The underlying idea is that democratic decision-making will lead to environmentally friendly policies. Creating legal gateways for participation would arguably also equalise the distribution of environmental costs and benefits, allowing marginalized groups (e.g., women, the dispossessed, and communities closely dependent upon natural resources for their livelihood) to be included in the social determination of environmental change.

Roda Mushkat, *The Principle of Public Participation: An Asia-Pacific Perspective,* in INTERNATIONAL LAW AND SUSTAINABLE DEVELOPMENT — PRINCIPLES AND PRACTICE 607, 609–10 (N. Schrijver & F. Weiss, eds., 2004).

2. *Detailed arrangements.* Does Article 8 of the SEA Protocol provide more details regarding the procedures for public participation than Article 7 of the Aarhus Convention, or less?

III. Public Participation in Other Regions

A. Latin America

The Inter-American Strategy for the Promotion of Public Participation in Decision-Making for Sustainable Development (2000) (ISP) is a nonbinding framework but has the potential to foster better public access to information, participation, and justice in the region.

Environmental Public Participation in the Americas

Jorge Caillaux, Manuel Ruiz, & Isabel Lapeña

THE NEW "PUBLIC": GLOBALIZATION OF PUBLIC PARTICIPATION

(C. Bruch, ed., 2002)

I. LEGAL AND CONSTITUTIONAL PROVISIONS IN THE COUNTRIES OF THE REGION

In contrast to the dictatorial and authoritarian regimes that ruled Latin America during the 1970s and part of the 1980s, from 1990 onwards, there have been significant political changes throughout the region. Democratic rule has emerged in many countries, and weak democracies have been strengthened. The frequent change of regimes in the region has led to constitutional reforms, and the new constitutions have incorporated modern concepts of governance and human rights. From 1972 to 1999, new constitutions have been elaborated in 16 countries in the region. All of them have sought to provide answers to new social demands, including environmental protection. This phenomenon has been termed the "Greening of Constitutions in Latin America." ...

A growing number of constitutions include provisions on environmental public participation. Colombia's 1991 Constitution—considered to be an environmentally oriented constitution with more than sixty environmental provisions—expressly includes a chapter on "Collective Rights and the Environment." For example, Article 79 recognizes that "every person has the right to enjoy a healthy environment. Law will guarantee community participation in the decisions that could affect it." Society's participation is, on the other hand, considered a state duty in Article 127 of the 1999 Venezuelan Constitution. The 1998 Ecuador Constitution establishes in Article 88 that every governmental decision that could affect the environment should first take into account the communities' views and, in this regard, society should be previously informed about proposed decisions. Furthermore, Ecuador's Constitution requires laws to guarantee the communities' right to participate.

Pursuant to these constitutional provisions, extensive laws and regulations have been elaborated by national environmental laws or codes, particularly those that create a national environmental framework. The holistic and systemic view of the environment that followed new environmental legislation must coexist, however, with previous but still prevailing sectoral regulation of water, forests, minerals, and other specific environmental aspects. This sectoral legislation has progressively started to adapt to environmental requirements.

However, this sectoral tradition has meant that public participation is regulated independently in the various sectors, and thus the elaboration of sound environmental procedures with respect to access to information, public participation, and justice has not been uniform. The immediate consequence has been legislative and institutional dispersion, inconsistency, practical gaps in the environmental and public participation guarantees, and limited coordination among authorities to respond to such fragmentation.

Prior to the adoption of the Inter-American Strategy for the Promotion of Public Participation in Decision-Making for Sustainable Development (ISP) in 2000 by the OAS, most laws and regulations included some formulation of a right to participate in decisionmaking processes, but less than half really included participation provisions per se. Bolivia and Chile appear to be the countries with the most laws including participation provisions, while Argentina, Ecuador, and Mexico remain the countries with the fewest participation provisions.

Among the legislatively mandated public participation provisions, priority is given to the right of the public to have access to decisionmaking, followed by access to justice and access to information. Although it seems to be a good sign that more emphasis is placed on processes of participation in decisionmaking—where a diverse range of mechanisms can be included to engage citizens directly in choices about environmental protection—the notable lack of laws ensuring access to information, however, significantly limits participation in matters of collective interest and, in particular, environmental matters. When translated into practice, these limited provisions for environmental information represent a failure or limitation in the participation framework, as information is a critical component of a citizen's effective right to participate in decisionmaking and to exercise his right to access to justice.

II. The Inter-American Strategy for the Promotion of Public Participation in Decision-Making for Sustainable Development

A. Background ...

Over two years, the OAS collaborated with a broad array of government and civil society representatives throughout the hemisphere, national focal points, and a project advisory committee to develop an Inter-American Strategy for the Promotion of Public Participation in Decision-Making for Sustainable Development (ISP). In April 2000, the OAS Inter-American Council for Integral Development approved the ISP.

The process leading up to the ISP was the first time that public participation experiences in so many different American countries were analyzed and the best practices in the region summarized. From these summaries, a comprehensive approach to public participation was developed from a regional perspective. It was also the first time that the importance of the interaction between governments and civil society was so prominently highlighted as a critical component for sustainable development and was translated into an international strategy through policy recommendations and concrete guidelines for action. These guidelines establish a reference for future institutional design and legal frameworks in the countries of the region.

The ISP is based on the understanding that public participation supports, rather than impedes, sustainable development. This premise rejects the idea that sustainable development requires a proactive, centralist environmental policy. Rather, promoting broad participation and the implicit extensive notions of democracy are considered beneficial to the sustainable management of natural resources.

The ISP blurs the boundaries between the national and international contexts. The ISP responds to the increased concern of international law with issues that once were considered to be essential attributes of states sovereignty—public participation in governmental decisionmaking, transparency and secrecy, domestic legal procedures, and public administration, among others. The same flexibility becomes apparent when treating the dichotomy between private and public interests. The ISP defines not only the role that the state should play but also the position of private persons and their responsibilities in participating in sustainable development in their own countries. However, the ISP only addresses states when establishing policy recommendations. It does not oversee the mutual responsibility of governments and civil society when implementing the other lines of action set forth in the ISP.

Public participation is defined as "all interaction between government and civil society, and includes the process by which government and civil society open dialogue, establish partnerships, share information, and otherwise interact to design, implement, and evaluate development policies, projects and programs." Therefore, public participation policies are understood not only from the side of public institutions, for example by providing information or institutional mechanisms to allow participation. From the civil society perspective, public participation also means creating public responsibilities and awareness, so that real public participation in decisionmaking becomes feasible through necessary interaction....

[I]t is mainly the concept of legitimization that serves as a theoretical foundation for public participation in the ISP document. Public participation promotes legitimacy and, as a consequence, acceptance of decisions related to the environment. Moreover, the ISP states that public participation introduces a broad range of ideas that motivate the development of alternative solutions, enhances the knowledge of decisionmakers, reduces the potential for serious conflict, increases the likelihood of improved and lasting solutions, strengthens the fulfillment of public standards and policies, provides opportunities for cooperation, builds trust among the participants, and leads to the creation of long-term collaborative relationships....

In contrast with the 1998 Aarhus Convention, which was recently ratified by European and Central Asian countries and has become a landmark for public participation, the ISP was born as a voluntary instrument. The text of the ISP focuses on the description of general provisions and objectives that could offer guidance to the countries in the region, rather than establishing specific and binding norms with compulsory timeframes. Therefore, it creates a framework of principles and recommendations for action that can guide state policies and civil society towards increased and more effective interaction. The document identifies common principles, presents a set of objectives, makes recommendations for achieving public participation, and urges the different states to adopt the participation measures contained in its recommendations. It leaves the parties to determine, according to each country's background and culture, the means by which the objectives can be attained.

Although the ISP developed from a regional initiative, it does not address how to promote public involvement at a regional level. It does not create regional procedures for participation or regional compliance mechanisms that could resolve regional environmental problems, such as transboundary conflicts. It also does not propose regional platforms in which participation initiatives and barriers could be addressed or environmental information shared at an international context. The ISP applies to the OAS member states, and it is from this point of view that policy recommendations are made....

D. ACCESS TO DECISIONMAKING ...

2. ISP Recommendations

The ISP proposes different lines of action that focus primarily on involving the public in decisionmaking through legislative, regulatory, and institutional reforms. For example, the ISP explicitly recommends that "legislative and administrative bodies should ensure public access throughout the process of formulating and implementing policies, laws and regulations, including the approval of development proposals, projects and budgets, the granting of permits, the process of assessing environmental impacts, and the establishment of specific environmental performance standards. Thus, public participation in decisions relating to projects as well as broader programs, policies, regulations, and laws is advanced.

For effective participation to occur, the legal standing "to participate in development decision-making and implementation should be granted to all who are interested or affected by the decisions, regardless of their race, ethnicity, culture or gender." While the ISP does impose some limit on who may have a right to participate (they should have some personal interest in the outcome of the decision), the ISP notably does not require any special interest. Moreover, the ISP mandates nondiscrimination in public participation, so that those persons and communities that traditionally have been marginalized — including women and vulnerable groups such as indigenous populations, youth, and disadvantaged racial and ethnic minorities, including disadvantaged populations of African descent — have an equal claim and opportunity to participate in decisions that could affect them. The ISP also highlights the need to facilitate local and grassroots participation through the development of community organizations....

In regards to incorporating participatory practices into the approval process for developing projects, the ISP recommends that governments and private institutions create management tools that can be used throughout the project cycle, in order to provide a flexible, dynamic, and two-way consultative process. Specifically, the ISP recommends roundtables, public hearings, workshops, and technical meetings be convened during the evaluation of social and environmental impact assessments. In addition, decisionmakers have a final obligation to incorporate or respond to public comments they received during the process.

In contrast to the Aarhus Convention, the ISP does not give any guidance for activities that may have a significant effect on the environment. The ISP also does not specifically refer to the importance of early public participation in different processes when there still exists an opportunity to choose among different development alternatives and, therefore, public participation can be most effective.

3. Advances in the Region toward Access to Decisionmaking

Some Latin American constitutions recognize a citizen's right to participate in decisionmaking which affects the citizen's quality of life. For example, Ecuador's Constitution introduces criteria in Article 83 for community participation in environmental control. It guarantees that indigenous communities have a collective right to be consulted on nonrenewable resources exploitation, conservation of renewable natural resources located on their lands, and the preservation of their biodiversity management practices. Furthermore, Article 88 also requires the government to take into account communities, their right to be informed, and their participation in any governmental decision that may affect the environment.

Many national laws, particularly general, framework environmental laws, establish procedures for involving the public in governmental decisionmaking processes. For example, Colombia's General Environmental National System Law guarantees every person's right to intervene in administrative processes related to the concession of permits and licenses that could affect the environment; the obligation to hold public hearings in such processes; and the publication of final decisions, which includes notification to all citizens who would have previously demanded the information. Similar requirements have also been introduced when administrative and legal reforms may affect the environment. For example, Article 63 of the 1996 Constitution of the Province of Buenos Aires Constitution mandates public hearings on legislative proposals related to urban planning, siting commercial or industrial facilities, or modifications in the use or status of public domain resources.

In addition, according to the inventory conducted by the OAS during the process of elaborating the ISP, the majority of environmental laws in the region include some form of participation in decisions regarding specific projects through environmental impact assessments (EIA) processes. Citizens are more likely to have a right to participate under EIA laws than they do under other areas of environmental laws, such as water quality laws. For example, this has been the case in the energy and mining sector policies in Peru, where the Ministry of Energy and Mines issued a 1996 Decree requiring public hearings as part of the approval process for EIAs.

As a practical matter, it is often difficult for legal proposals of public participation to develop into anything beyond a merely *pro forma* requirement. For example, it is a common feature for consultation processes to be developed ex-post, once the development decision has been made and just before its final approval, instead of being articulated ex-ante, at the beginning of the assessment of the project when all options are open and public participation can be most effective. Even where the public participates early in the process, practice often shows that government authorities are do not know how, or are unwilling, to take into account the input from the public participation. The lack of adequate capacity and organization at the grassroots level frequently impedes effective public participation in the development of policies and projects. To ensure grassroots representation, Bolivia's Public Participation Law promotes and gives legal personality to indigenous and farming committees constituted as Organizaciones Territoriales de Base....

Interesting initiatives have also emerged in the effort to develop new forms of participation and new platforms to embrace public and private interests in sustainable development issues. One example can be found in the Regional Environmental Commissions (CARs) in Peru, which are formed by representatives of local government agencies, members of different sectors of the national government, the private business sector, NGOs, and academic institutions to coordinate local institutional actions and elaborate an Environmental Action Plan for the Regions. Similar initiatives have also been adopted in formal governmental decisionmaking processes by involving representatives from social and environmental NGOs, so that complex environmental problems can be studied from a broad, pluralistic perspective....

III. The ISP's Potential ...

[T]he importance of the ISP resides in its consolidation as a regional initiative to create a policy framework, to direct countries' efforts towards the formulation of public participation policies that ensure citizen participation, and to steer the implementation of such policies at the national level. The ISP represents a new instrument in which agreed principles of public participation are explicitly stated as a turning point in the policies of the region, as well as the future direction for governance. Hence, it is the state parties to whom the ISP is first addressed.

Some of the provisions of the ISP have already been implemented through environmental legislation and institutions introduced in some countries. However, this development has not been uniform in the region. On the contrary, there are evident differences. The advances mentioned in this chapter are generally found in only the countries that have been specifically identified, and do not necessarily apply generally to the region. Moreover, those countries in which participatory mechanisms have been introduced through laws need more consolidated structures to guarantee their implementation. At both the national and regional levels, the ISP proposals are significant for introducing a participatory culture and recommendations for better practices....

In the region, many legal mechanisms adopted to promote public participation in environmental decisionmaking have been expressed in general frameworks or in instruments that have a voluntary character. In this context, however, there are often situations in which governments do not take the general frameworks into account and, therefore, implementation is limited. It is essential that general provisions adopted in environmental laws are adequately developed through regulatory mechanisms that allow real implementation. This is also true at the regional level. The ISP seeks to overcome this general lack of concrete actions, mechanisms, and institutions, through well-defined participatory proposals.

Questions and Discussion

1. *Voluntarism.* Are there both advantages and disadvantages of a voluntary framework at the international level, as compared to the binding nature of the Aarhus Convention? Are there differences in culture between Latin America and the Aarhus region that might make one more appropriate than the other in the region involved?

2. *Mandatory treaty.* Can you see ways that the ISP could be made stronger, even if its voluntary nature were retained? Would you recommend that a regional treaty be negotiated for the Americas, as happened with the Aarhus Convention? Or should Latin American countries simply accede to (ratify) the Aarhus Convention? What are the arguments for and against that?

3. *Reducing conflict.* How does the ISP "reduce the potential for serious conflict?"

4. *"Standing" to participate.* A prerequisite for participation suggested under the ISP is that the individual must have some personal interest in the outcome of the decision. Is this requirement inclusive or exclusive? Can you suggest ways to modify such restrictions? Would broadened participation be more appropriate or less appropriate in Latin America than in countries that allow anyone to participate?

5. *Early participation.* In contrast to the Aarhus Convention, the ISP does not suggest early public participation, which could mean that concerned citizens might get involved too late in the planning process to make significant changes. Is this "gap" covered by any other provisions or suggestions in the ISP?

B. Africa

African Initiatives for Public Participation in Environmental Management
Collins Odote & Maurice O. Makoloo
THE NEW "PUBLIC": GLOBALIZATION OF PUBLIC PARTICIPATION
(C. Bruch, ed., 2002)

Historically in Africa, public participation was central to natural resource management. In traditional African societies, governance was consultative and participatory. This traditional governance included mechanisms for citizen involvement and participation in decisions within the community. The advent of colonialism, with its attendant negative impacts, dealt a severe blow to African concepts and practices of public participation in governance.

Current developments globally make public participation very important in Africa. First, African governments increasingly tend to discourage direct government involvement in economic activities and instead support and encourage private investment to boost economic growth. This approach combined with the state's limited ability to monitor the environmental impacts of private activities make it imperative for citizens to play a greater role in environmental management. The importance of citizen involvement is compounded by the fact that most citizens in Africa are not only poor and live in rural areas but are also principally reliant on the continent's natural resources.

The second factor making public participation an imperative in Africa is the colonial legacy. Despite the independence of most states for over four decades, their laws and institutions are still a relic of the colonial past. These laws and institutions still inhibit transparency, participation, and accountability, especially in environment matters where the importance of natural resources make them a source of power.

II. AFRICA-WIDE INITIATIVES

Several of the African charters, declarations, and organizations include provisions encouraging or mandating public access to information, participation, and justice. These instruments could provide a basis for the development of a set of African environmental government principles, including provisions for public access to information, public participation, and access to justice. These principles could be either binding or persuasive.

A. AFRICAN CHARTER ON HUMAN AND PEOPLES' RIGHTS ...

[T]he Charter at Article 24 provides that "all peoples' shall have the right to a general satisfactory environment favourable to their development." The charter therefore contains provisions that can be used and expanded upon to guarantee good environmental governance and public participation within the continent. The institutional mechanism established by the Charter to protect human rights is the African Commission on Human and Peoples' Rights. Compared to other regional human rights treaties, notably those for the European and American regions, the African Charter's protective regime is remiss in several respects. First, until 1998, the African human rights system did not have a human rights court. It was only in 1998 that the Assembly of Heads of States signed a protocol to the Charter that established an African Court on Human and People's Rights. Second, the Commission has dealt with very few cases and its interventions are usually after the event. The success of the African Charter on Human and Peoples' Rights in promoting environmental governance and public participation has been limited. It needs to be strengthened, and one critical measure would be through a specific regional instrument on procedural rights.... The end result is that despite having provisions that encourage public involvement, the Charter's mechanisms are weak.

In July 1996, the OAU summit passed a Declaration, "Africa: Preparing for the 21st Century," which addressed good governance within the continent.... This declaration clearly identified the importance of good governance and thus provides a fertile ground for advancing public participation.... The greatest hindrance to public participation and good governance within the context of the OAU was the emphasis placed on the principle of non-interference in internal affairs of states. At Article 3(2) of the Charter, the member states clearly stipulated that one of the principles that would guide them in achieving the objects and goals of OAU was that of non-interference in the internal affairs of states. Unfortunately, the over-reliance on this principle led to the failure and eventual collapse of the OAU, as it was never able to promote good governance within the continent. Its weakness led to efforts to replace it with a more effective successor, the African Union (AU). The African Union has sought to depart from its predecessor in several aspects. Principally, the AU was modeled along the lines of the European Union and places good governance at the root of its obligations. The Constitutive Act of the AU, however, still contains the principle of non-interference in the internal affairs of its members as one of its objectives.

C. THE AFRICAN MINISTERIAL CONFERENCE ON THE ENVIRONMENT (AMCEN) ...

At the recently concluded AMCEN 9th meeting in Kampala, Uganda a declaration on "The Environment for Development" (Kampala Declaration) was approved, which noted the importance of environmental governance within the continent. In its preamble at paragraph 10, the Kampala Declaration recognized that "success in achieving global sustainable development will ultimately depend upon development and implementation of sound and cost-effective national response policies and measures; good environmental governance, effective participation by civil society and collection and exchange of quality data and information on the environment for use by national decision-makers." This clause in the preamble of the Declaration identifies environmental governance generally and public participation and access to information specifically as essential for sustainable development....

The environmental governance sub-theme offers an opportunity for NEPAD [the New Partnership for Africa's Development, a regional development initiative overseen by African heads of state] to fully develop principles and rules for public participation. Such rules could take the form of a regional strategy (such as the Inter-American Strategy for the Promotion of Public Participation in Decision-Making for Sustainable Development), a document on good practices (ASEM), or a binding convention (such as the Aarhus Convention). Whatever form it takes, the rules or principles should clearly expand on the three pillars of access to environmental information, public participation, and access to justice. Already NEPAD has proposed a process of enforcing standards within African countries through an African Peer Review Mechanism.... Good governance is at the core of NEPAD's implementation strategy ... [to] influence public decisions. The identification of governance as one of the critical aspects of the environment initiative provides an opportunity for African countries to secure the three pillars of environmental governance — access to information, public participation, and access to justice — and thus achieve the NEPAD agenda, which is based on partnership.... The third meeting of the steering committee of the environmental component of NEPAD held in Dakar, Senegal, from June 12–14, 2002, adopted the framework of an action plan for the environment initiative of NEPAD. Although the action plan is only a framework, uses terms such as "may" and "should," and lacks time-specific targets, it does identify the importance of environmental governance and procedural rights.

One of the objectives of the action plan is to enhance effective participation of African major groups and their important contribution to inform intergovernmental decisionmaking and improve the institutional framework for regional environmental governance. This regional framework could include the establishment of institutions through an agreement to ensure access to information, participation, and justice. Despite its noble intentions, NEPAD has so far failed to fully involve non-state actors and citizens in its conceptualization and implementation, with the consequence that it risks being seen as a sole initiative of heads of states. This runs counter to the spirit of partnership championed in the document and that is so essential for the success of the effort. Despite this weakness, NEPAD offers an opportunity for Africa and Africa's people to advance environmental governance within the continent....

F. THE AFRICA CONVENTION ON THE CONSERVATION OF NATURE AND NATURAL RESOURCES IN AFRICA

The Africa Convention on the Conservation of Nature and Natural Resources in Africa, popularly known as the Algiers Convention, was adopted on September 15, 1968 in Algiers, Algeria by the heads of state and government of (the then) independent African states.... Perhaps due to lapse of time as well as recent developments in environmental management and especially the influence of the Rio Conference, the Convention has been marked for several amendments. One such proposed amendment is the introduction of a new article on procedural rights. If adopted, the proposed new Article 16 would provide: The parties shall adopt legislative and regulatory measures necessary to ensure timely and appropriate (a) dissemination of environmental information; (b) access of the public to environmental information; (c) participation of the public in decisionmaking with a potentially significant environmental impact; and (d) access to justice in matters related to the protection of the environment and natural resources. The adoption of this amendment, together with other suggested amendments would truly herald a significant step forward in the journey of environmental governance.

II. Sub-Regional Initiatives in Africa

A. East African Memorandum of Understanding (MOU) ...

The most explicit provisions dealing with public involvement within the context of East Africa are in a Memorandum of Understanding (MOU) among the three East African countries for cooperation in environmental management. The MOU clearly recognizes and gives prominence to the importance of public access to environmental information, public participation, and access to the courts. Article 7 of the MOU sets forth the commitment of the partner states to guarantee public participation generally. This Article guarantees the "full involvement of (the) People in the sustainable use and management of environment and natural resources." Public participation is further secured by Article 16 (2)(a), which states that partner states agree "to promote public awareness programmes and access to information as well as measures aimed at enhancing public participation on environmental management and issues." Public participation is also included in the context of environmental impact assessment (EIA) where the states agree to ensure public participation at all stages of the process, and again in the context of forest management, where it encourages partnerships with local people.... The legal authority of the MOU is weaker than a formally binding legal convention or protocol. Indeed, in its provisions it contemplates the development of a protocol in the area of environment and natural resource management. It does, however, offer a strong basis for developing a sub-regional instrument on environmental governance encompassing the three pillars of access to information, public participation, and access to justice.

B. The Southern Africa Development Community (SADC)

The Southern Africa Development Co-ordination Conference (SADCC) was formed in Lusaka, Zambia, on April 1, 1980, following the adoption of the Lusaka Declaration by nine founding member states. Twelve years later on August 17, 1992 in Windhoek, Namibia, the Declaration and Treaty establishing the Southern Africa Development Community (SADC), replaced the Coordination Conference. The SADC Treaty is a legally binding and all-encompassing framework by which countries of the region must coordinate, harmonize, and rationalize their policies and strategies for sustainable development.... SADC has developed a number of binding protocols on natural resources for its 12 members to adopt, including one on shared watercourses and one on mining. These protocols contain, to varying degrees, environmental governance principles.... Together, these provisions are concerned with the collection of a wide range of information, making that information publicly available, and promoting public participation in the management of international watercourses in southern Africa.

In October 1999, the environmental ministers of the SADC region agreed to establish a binding environmental protocol, and the efforts to develop the protocol remain ongoing. This protocol could build upon national experiences in the sub-region as well as international initiatives to promote public involvement. Specifically, it could recognize that this protocol could incorporate procedural aspects of environmental management—such as public participation and access to justice—that are essential to implementing substantive environmental norms and standards.

IV. CONCLUSION ...

The initiatives underway within the African continent point to the importance of environmental governance for the continent's success in sustainable development. Owing, however, to the scattered nature of provisions on environmental governance in several instruments and declarations and also the legal status of some of the instruments, time should be ripe for these efforts and initiatives to coalesce into one legally binding instrument on environmental governance. This could be done through a collective effort among AMCEN, AU, and the environment initiative of NEPAD. Such an instrument would elevate environmental governance to its rightful place and clearly expound on the three pillars of environmental information access, access to justice, and public participation in a manner that is sensitive to African conditions and peculiarities.

Earthlife Africa (Cape Town) v. Dept. of Envt'l Affairs & Tourism & Eskom Holdings (South Africa)

High Court of South Africa (Cape of Good Hope Prov. Div.)
Case No 7653/03
(26 January 2005)

GRIESEL J:

Introduction

The second respondent (Eskom) wishes to construct a demonstration model 110 MegaWatt class pebble bed modular reactor (PBMR) at the site of its Koeberg Nuclear Power Station near Cape Town. On 25 June 2003, the first respondent, the Director-General of the Department of Environmental Affairs and Tourism (the DG), granted Eskom the requisite authorisation in terms of § 22(3) of the Environment Conservation Act 73 of 1989 (ECA), subject to certain conditions which are not material for present purposes. This application is brought by the applicant to review and set aside that decision by the DG.

The applicant is Earthlife Africa (Cape Town), a non-governmental, non-profit, voluntary association of environmental and social activists in Cape Town. Its professed aims are to campaign against perceived "environmental injustices" in the Cape Town area and to participate in environmental decision-making processes with a view to promoting and lobbying for good governance and informed decision-making....

Applicable Legislation ...

[A]n applicant for authorisation is required in terms of [the EIA law] to appoint an independent consultant to comply with the regulations on its behalf; ... one of the responsibilities of an applicant for authorisation ... is "to ensure that all interested parties ... are given the opportunity to participate in all the relevant procedures contemplated in these regulations."

Factual Background ...

In an application, dated 26 June 2000, Eskom applied to the DG for the necessary authorisation in terms of § 22 of ECA for "the construction, commissioning, operation/maintenance and decommissioning" of a PBMR.... The consultants duly undertook an environmental impact assessment, accompanied by an extensive process of public participation....

Review Grounds ...

The applicant, while conceding that it did participate in the public process that led up to the submission of the final EIR, maintained nevertheless that the hearing afforded to it was flawed or deficient in the following respects: ...

(b) The applicant was not afforded an opportunity of making submissions on the consultants' *final* EIR, but was confined to submissions on the *draft* EIR; and

(c) The applicant was confined to making submissions to Eskom's consultants, and *not* to the DG himself, who was the decisionmaker....

Submissions on Draft EIR ...

The respondents' approach implies that full public participation in the process was required, but only up to submission of the final EIR. Thereafter, according to their argument, public participation is only revived to the limited extent that interested parties have a right of appeal to the Minister against the decision.

I find this approach to be fundamentally unsound. The regulations provide for full public participation in "all the relevant procedures contemplated in these regulations." The respondents seek to limit such participation to the "investigation phase" of the process (as contemplated by regs 5, 6, and 7). After submission of the EIR, however, the "adjudicative phase" of the process commences, involving the DG's consideration and evaluation, not only of the EIR, but also—more broadly—of all other facts and circumstances that may be relevant to his decision. There is nothing in the Act (ECA) or the regulations that expressly excludes public participation or application of the audi rule during this "second stage" of the process. In line with settled authority, therefore, it follows that procedural fairness demands application of the audi rule also at this stage.

A further reason why I find the respondents' approach to be unsound, is because it overlooks the fact that, on the DG's own version (though not Eskom's), the final EIR was "substantially different" from the draft EIR. The final EIR made material changes and incorporated substantially more documentation than the draft EIR. The question for decision can therefore be narrowed down to an enquiry whether it was procedurally fair to take administrative action based on "substantially different" new matter on which interested parties have not had an opportunity to comment....

In the present case, where the draft EIR was substantially overtaken by the final EIR, it is clear to my mind that *new facts* had indeed been placed before the decisionmaker on behalf of Eskom. In these circumstances, I am of the view that the applicant, as an interested party, was entitled, as part of its right to procedural fairness, to a reasonable opportunity to make representations to the DG on the new aspects not previously addressed in its submissions in relation to the draft EIR....

I do not think that it would be placing an undue burden on the department if it were required to consider further submissions from interested parties regarding the contents of the final EIR, especially in view of the fact that the department went to the trouble of making the report widely available to interested parties....

Representations to the DG ...

The applicant's [other] complaint was that the DG, who was the decisionmaker in this case, did not afford it a hearing at all....

I am satisfied that the present case is an appropriate one where the DG would be entitled to rely on the assistance and expert advice of others in coming to his decision. Nevertheless, it is an essential requirement that, before making his or her decision, the decisionmaker should be fully informed of the submissions made on behalf of interested parties and he or she should properly consider them. As pointed out by the Privy Council in *Jeffs v. New Zealand Dairy Production and Marketing Board,* [[1966] 3 All ER 863 (PC) at 870G-H], in some circumstances it may suffice for the decisionmaker to have before it and to consider "an accurate summary of the relevant evidence and submissions if the summary adequately discloses the evidence and submissions to the (decisionmaker)." What is required, as a minimum, is that the summary will contain "a fair synopsis of all the points raised by the parties so that the repository of the power can consider them in order to come to a decision."

This is *not* what happened in this case. The applicant's submissions to Eskom's consultants on their draft EIR were incorporated in an annexure to the final EIR. But the DG did not read those submissions or even a summary thereof. The DG does say that he read the executive summary of the final EIR and that he "considered" the report of the panel of experts. But it is clear from the report itself that it is a brief and rather perfunctory one that does not even mention the applicant's submissions. Thus, as a fact, the DG took his decision without any regard to the applicant's submissions and indeed without knowing what they were.

Conclusion ...

I would accordingly regard it as just and equitable, in setting aside the DG's decision, to issue directions to provide for the reconsideration by the DG of the matter after the applicant — and other interested parties — have been afforded an opportunity to address further written submissions to the DG on the final EIR as well as any other relevant considerations that may affect the decision.

Davis J: I agree.

Moosa J: I agree.

Questions and Discussion

1. *Continents.* Compare the provisions for public participation in the Americas, Europe, and Africa. Would you recommend changes? Are there cultural reasons to treat public participation as having a different value on one continent or another, or are the human rights issues the same?

2. *Interference.* What are the implications of the African Union's objective of not interfering in the internal affairs of its members? How will this affect people's rights? Are there benefits to this policy? Which is more important: the objective of non-interference or the promotion of public participation?

3. *Sub-regional efforts.* Compare the sub-regional and Africa-wide actions in terms of public participation. For Africa, does it appear to be more effective to initiate change on a large scale or small scale?

4. *Commenting to contractors or decisionmakers.* In the *Earthlife Africa* case, are you satisfied that the result of the remand could make a difference in the actual decisionmaking? If not, is it worthwhile filing cases like this? Are there other benefits of such litigation?

5. *Treaties, memoranda, laws, and regulations.* Note that the right of public participation may be implemented at various levels. Are some levels more important for human rights doctrine than others? Are some more likely than others to have an actual effect on making participation possible?

C. Asia and Pacific

The Principle of Public Participation: An Asia-Pacific Perspective
Roda Mushkat
INTERNATIONAL LAW AND SUSTAINABLE DEVELOPMENT — PRINCIPLES AND PRACTICE
(N. Schrijver & F. Weiss, eds., 2004)

There is little doubt that, at the rhetorical and "soft law" level, the principle of "public participation" is firmly endorsed in the Asia-Pacific region....

Yet, at the implementation level, efforts to democratise environmental decision-making in the Asia-Pacific region have been on the whole somewhat limited. Governmental transparency and accountability to the public are not always practiced.... Impermeability to citizen input occasionally results in development and investment decisions that generally demonstrate little concern for social factors.

The "right to access to information" — which underpins effective and meaningful public participation — has been given little formal recognition in the region, although some exceptions do exist. By the same token, the people's right to be informed, even if acknowledged, might be severely curtailed, permitting the public to obtain only information that government officials are prepared to provide. Yet, attempts are being made in [countries including China, Hong Kong, Japan, and South Korea] to disclose general environmental data, including release of indicators pertaining to water or air quality....

On the positive side, some scope for public participation has been afforded under EIA systems that form part of the regulatory infrastructure of many countries in the region. Relevant provisions, nonetheless, generally fail to clearly define the public's role in the process. Nor are procedures provided for rigorous public scrutiny of judicial review.

Active involvement of the public is further hampered by the lack of public interest laws. However, "creative" judges in certain jurisdictions in the region may have paved the way for increased public interest litigation and for more extensive recourse to courts to challenge government (and businesses). Indeed, the region boasts some exceptional illustrations of liberalisation of the *locus standi* rules, as well as procedural and remedial flexibility....

Perhaps the most encouraging development with respect to public involvement has been the increased activity of NGOs in the region and improvement of linkages between these organisations and governmental institutions.... Yet, notwithstanding their proliferation and enhanced networks — as well as their more vocal, aggressive, and, constructive engagement with governments — NGOs in the region face structural and functional limitations, restricting their capacity to challenge governmental monopolies on environmental decision-making....

Promoting and Strengthening Public Participation in China's Environmental Impact Assessment Process: Comparing China's EIA Law and U.S. NEPA
Jesse L. Moorman & Zhang Ge
8 Vt. J. Envtl. L. 281 (2007)

Chinese citizens experienced unprecedented change with respect to their legal right to participate in decisions affecting the environment when, in 2003, the National People's Congress of the People's Republic of China enacted the Environmental Impact Assessment Law of the People's Republic of China (EIA Law) Although environmental impact assessment (EIA) had existed in China at least conceptually since 1973, prior to 2003, the public had been effectively absent from the process. The enactment of the EIA Law marked a watershed moment for public participation in China, as public involvement became a required component of the environmental decision-making process.

The extent of public involvement in China's EIA process is unclear, however. In November 2005 the State Environmental Protection Administration of China (SEPA) issued a set of draft measures for comment in an effort to clarify and strengthen the role of public participation provided under the EIA Law. Subsequently, on February 22, 2006, SEPA released provisional guidelines (SEPA Guidelines) after reviewing comments received on the Draft Regulations. Thus, it is clear that the process is still in a state of flux, and that SEPA may further revise the rules....

III. Public Participation in China under the EIA Law ...

B. 2003 Environmental Impact Assessment Law

The 2003 Environmental Impact Assessment Law builds on the existing EIA framework in two significant ways. First, it expands the EIA mandate to encompass government plans, as well as construction projects. Second, and more important for our purposes, the EIA Law makes public participation a required component of the process.

Prior to 2003, EIA in China was singularly project-based, applying only to individual construction projects. But the EIA Law adds a Strategic Environmental Assessment (plan-based) overlay to the existing EIA process, whereby government plans for land use and regional development, as well as plans for industry, agriculture, energy, transportation, urban development, tourism, and natural resource development must now undergo EIA. In principle, environmental impact assessment can be undertaken for an individual project such as a hydroelectric dam, an athletic stadium, airport, or assembly plant (project-based EIA) or for plans, programs, and policies, which is commonly referred to as Strategic Environmental Assessment (SEA). China's recent embrace of SEA is an attempt to more effectively address problems of pollution and resource scarcity by attacking them at their sources....

C. Public Participation under the EIA Law

In broad and ambiguous terms, the EIA Law sets forth a novel policy in Chinese EIA, which is to encourage the public to participate in the EIA process in appropriate ways. Two significant provisions of the EIA Law, applicable to plans and projects, respectively, give teeth to this new policy by requiring some form of public participation in the preparation of an EIR [environmental impact report, prepared by developer for project] before it is submitted for approval.

The form of public participation is broadly delineated; the only requirement being that some opportunity is to be made available prior to the completion of a draft EIR. Responsible entities are given the option of holding a hearing or adopting other forms of soliciting public opinion on the EIR. For plan-based EIRs, this requirement appears to be conditioned on whether or not the environmental impacts of the proposed plan involve environmental rights and interests of the public. There is no indication of how or when such rights and interests are implicated. On the other hand, the participation requirement for project-based EIRs is only limited in conditions where secrecy is required by State stipulations....

Similar to NEPA, the text of the EIA Law makes only limited references to the scope of public participation in the EIA process. Although the participation requirement is only broadly defined, the EIA Law makes clear the fact that public participation is to play some role in the draft EIR stage of both plan- and project-based EIA. Yet in the context of an institutional system that is currently experiencing huge reform, there are gaps between law and practice. In an effort to address this, the provisions for public participation in the EIA Law are in the process of being supplemented.

IV. Recent Measures to Define the Public's Role in China's EIA Law

Recently promulgated SEPA Guidelines are an effort to fill in the gap between the law and practice concerning public participation in Chinese EIA. The Guidelines, which became effective March 18, 2006, clarify the process for soliciting public opinion during the drafting of EIRs for all plans and projects that require them. The new Guidelines reaffirm the broad public participation mandates established by the EIA Law, and explain the rights and obligations of both developers and the public in detail....

B. The Timing and Form of Public Disclosure and Public Involvement

The SEPA Guidelines require public disclosure of EIA information at the outset of an EIA investigation and prior to the designated time for public participation. In general, developers, agencies, or the organizations that have been commissioned to conduct EIA investigations ... are encouraged to solicit the views of the public prior to submitting EIA documents to the environmental agency for approval.

Within 15 days from commencing an EIA investigation, a responsible entity must make public the details of the project or plan that is subject to EIA. Among other things, this initial disclosure must identify the initiating developer or agency, as well as the organization that has been hired to conduct the EIA investigation, and the major items and methods of soliciting public suggestions and opinions. Thereafter, once the responsible entity has finalized a draft EIA document, it must publish notice of the availability of EIA information and solicit suggestions and opinions about the EIA document from the public prior to submitting it for approval.

The Guidelines suggest several ways in which a responsible entity might solicit public comments on EIA documents, including: questionnaires, expert consultations, workshops, debates, and hearings. Discretion rests with the responsible entity to choose the form and time of public participation, which they must then include in the notice of EIA availability, along with a summary of the possible environmental impacts of the project or plan, and the major issues about which they wish to receive public input. This notice must be made available at least ten business days prior to the time set for public participation. Notice may be published in newspapers, on websites, or by posting abridged versions of the EIA documents in public places.

The Guidelines envision the involvement of a broad spectrum of individuals and organizations in the EIA process. Responsible entities are encouraged to seek representation from residents, experts, and social organizations, when soliciting comments on EIA documents. When the time for public comment has passed, the responsible entity is then required to clearly explain why certain opinions were accepted and others were rejected and include these explanations with the draft EIA document when it is filed for approval. Finally, if any member of the public feels that the responsible entity has not clearly explained its decision to reject an opinion, they may send their comments directly to the environmental agency in charge of approving the EIA. It is not clear exactly what the agency is required to do in response to public complaints of non-compliance.

Questions and Discussion

1. *Future of participation rights.* Why do you think that public participation has remained "soft law" in the Asia Pacific region as Roda Mushkat indicates? In late 2007 the

Council of Jurists of the Asia Pacific Forum of National Human Rights Institutions recommended that the right to a healthy environment by protected by human rights law in Forum states. The jurists said that an effective right to the environment would include a range of participatory rights, such as the right of people to access information, to participate in decision-making and to seek remedies if they suffer harm as a result of a degraded environment. See http://www.asiapacificforum.net/news/jurists-call-for-right-to-environment.html.

2. *Law and practice.* What is necessary to fill the gap between public participation provisions in the new EIA Law and Guidelines and actual practice in China? What is the role of civil society? What about public interest lawyers?

3. *Encouragement.* The developer or agency responsible for conducting an EIA in China is "encouraged to solicit the views of the public prior to submitting EIA documents to the environmental agency for approval." Is it enough to "encourage" the developer (agency) or should it be mandatory? Is public participation required at an early stage? Is it sufficient to make a developer responsible for conducting an EIA? Compare those provisions with what is required under the National Environmental Policy Act in the United States.

4. *Access to justice.* In case of non-compliance, what agency can enforce China's EIA law? Can the public go to the court?

Note on Thailand's 1997 Constitution

A remarkable example of a right to public participation in environmental decision-making in Asia had been the Constitution of the Kingdom of Thailand (1997), "providing for public participation in the governance and inspecting the exercise of State power … having particular regard to public opinions…." It was called the "People's Constitution" because of public participation in the drafting process. The Constitution gave the right to traditional communities to "participate in the management, maintenance, preservation and exploitation of natural resources and the environment in a balanced fashion and persistently as provided by law." (Section 46) It also provided:

> The right of a person to give to the State and communities participation in the preservation and exploitation of natural resources and biological diversity and in the protection, promotion and preservation of the quality of the environment … shall be protected, as provided by law. Section 56.

In the same section of the Constitution, public participation in environmental impact assessments was established by providing:

> Any project or activity which may seriously affect the quality of the environment shall not be permitted, unless its impacts on the quality of the environment have been studied and evaluated and opinions of an independent organisation, consisting of representatives from private environmental organisations and from higher education institutions providing studies in the environmental field, have been obtained prior to the operation of such project or activity, as provided by law.

It guaranteed public participation by providing access to justice:

> [T]he right of a person to sue a State agency, State enterprise, local government organisation or other State authority to perform the duties as provided by law under paragraph one and paragraph two shall be protected.

Section 59 also provided the right

> to receive information, explanation and reason from a State agency, State enterprise or local government organisation before permission is given for the operation of any project or activity which may affect the quality of the environment, health and sanitary conditions, the quality of life or any other material interest concerning him or her or a local community and shall have the right to express his or her opinions on such matters in accordance with the public hearing procedure, as provided by law.

Questions and Discussion

1. *Thailand and Aarhus.* In what ways were the standards of public participation in the Constitution of Thailand (1997) the same as, or different from, those in the Aarhus Convention? Compare the Aarhus Convention's requirement for public participation in the "early stage" with the provisions in Section 59 of the 1997 Constitution of the Thailand.

2. *Abolition.* On September 19, 2006, this Constitution was abolished, as a result of a military *coup d'etat* by the leader of the "Council for Democratic Reform."

Policy Responses — Asia and Pacific
United Nations Environment Programme
UNEP GEO — 2000 GLOBAL ENVIRONMENTAL OUTLOOK (R. Clark, ed., 1999)
http://www.unep.org/geo2000/ov-e.pdf

NGOs have emerged as major partners in development and conservation activities, performing a multitude of roles including environmental education and awareness-raising among the public. NGOs have helped design and implement environment policies, programmes and action plans, and set out specifications for EIAs. They also play crucial advocacy roles through their environmental campaigns.

For example, in Sri Lanka NGOs have been active in preventing logging of the Singharaja Forest, setting up a Tiger-top lodge in Udawala National Park, stopping the construction of a thermal plant at Trincomalee, and questioning the blind implementation of the National Forestry Master Plan. In India, thousands of NGOs have helped raise awareness of environment-development issues and mobilized people to take action. Although not an NGO, the Narmada Bachao Andolan movement has brought together scattered voices of protest against the damming of the river Narmada and has raised awareness in India and among the international community.... In the Pacific, local community and NGO inputs come mainly through programmes to build community awareness and expand environmental education. Some NGOs find trade opportunities which provide a return for local people wishing to manage resources such as timber on a sustainable basis. Others have linked with international NGOs to build ecotourism opportunities in partnership with landowners.

NGOs, while retaining their individual identity, have also collaborated effectively with national and local governments on a wide range of issues. In the Philippines, a consortium of 17 environmental NGOs (NGOs for Protected Areas, Inc.) received a US$27 million grant to implement a seven-year Comprehensive Priority Protected Areas Programme. The programme is a major component of the World Bank-GEF Sectoral Adjustment Loan initiative being managed by the Department of Environment and Natural Resources.

The Mongolian Government cooperates closely with NGOs, for example with the Mongolian Association for the Conservation of Nature and Environment, which coordinates the voluntary activities of local communities and individuals to protect nature and wildlife, and with the Green Movement which promotes public environmental education in support of traditional protection methods.

NGO networks are springing up throughout the region. Among the most prominent are the Asian NGO Coalition for Agrarian Reform and Rural Development and the Asia Pacific People's Environment Network. Networks also exist at national level. For example, the Korean Federation Environmental Movement in the Republic of Korea provides an umbrella organization for nearly 200 NGOs engaged in environment-related issues.

Many countries have encouraged public participation in environmental management, through local government and community-based groups. For example, in Thailand, Article 7 of the Environment Act of 1992 delegates the work on environmental management to provincial and local authorities, and encourages people's participation through environmental NGOs. Article 56 of the Thailand Constitution (1997) recognizes the rights of people to participate in the protection of natural resources and environment. In the Philippines, small fishing communities are given the right to manage their fishery resources and community-based forest resource management has helped protect and conserve forest resources. Similarly, many coastal community groups in Thailand protect mangroves and seagrass. Amongst SPREP members, a variant of the NEAP process — known as the NEMS (National Environmental Management Strategy) — was developed prior to the 1992 Earth Summit. The strength of this process was to involve all national stakeholders in a debate about environmental priorities and key actions, and then to present a national consensus to external counterparts, especially in the donor community.

Community participation is required by law under New Zealand's Resource Management Act. When developing their ten-year policies and plans, regional and district councils are required to consult widely with community stakeholders and interest groups, including the indigenous Maori people. The main constraints on citizen participation are the time and costs involved but motivation levels are reportedly high.

The Chinese government has long been aware that public participation is an essential prerequisite for successful environmental protection and management ... The 'Law on the Protection of Women's Interest and Rights of the People's Republic of China', the Committee in charge of the Work of Women and Children established under the State Council in 1993, and the 'Development Program of Chinese Women' issued by the State Council in 1995 all aim to protect Chinese women's rights and ensure their participation in national management and environmental decision-making. Women are now playing more and more important roles....

Many of these initiatives depend on voluntary action. Such actions have played a particularly important role in Japan where local communities, citizens' groups and government together take the initiative to negotiate with major polluters. Several Japanese companies have now taken voluntary actions on pollution control which include stricter standards than the national ones. In addition, the Japan Federation of Economic Organizations (Keidanren) adopted a Global Environmental Charter in 1991 which includes a provision that companies should carry out environmental impact assessments of their activities, use and develop low pollution technologies, and participate in local conservation programmes (OECD 1994).

Questions and Discussion

NGOs or the public? Is participation by NGOs more useful than participation by individuals? More useful to whom? Is this more appropriate in Asia than elsewhere? Why or why not?

D. United States

1. Participation for Specific Projects: EISs and EAs

In the United States, the rights of the public to participate in decisionmaking on development projects takes place primarily at the state or local level. Many states have laws requiring assessment of environmental impacts of both private and public projects. Those requiring a federal permit or license must, in addition, undergo a review of their environmental impacts under the National Environmental Policy Act (NEPA). This law, the first of its kind in the world but emulated in some form or another in nearly every country in the past four decades, requires federal agencies to incorporate environmental values into their decisionmaking processes. The regulations implementing it contain extensive details on the kinds of public participation that are required.

National Environmental Policy Act of 1969
Pub. L. No. 91-190, Jan. 1, 1970, 83 Stat. 852, as amended,
42 U.S.C. 4331-4370f

Sec. 101 [42 USC § 4331]

(a) The Congress, recognizing the profound impact of man's activity on the interrelations of all components of the natural environment, ... declares that it is the continuing policy of the Federal Government ... to use all practicable means and measures ... to create and maintain conditions under which man and nature can exist in productive harmony, and fulfill the social, economic, and other requirements of present and future generations of Americans.

(b) In order to carry out the policy set forth in this Act, it is the continuing responsibility of the Federal Government to use all practicable means, consistent with other essential considerations of national policy, to improve and coordinate Federal plans, functions, programs, and resources to the end that the Nation may—

1. fulfill the responsibilities of each generation as trustee of the environment for succeeding generations;

2. assure for all Americans safe, healthful, productive, and aesthetically and culturally pleasing surroundings;

3. attain the widest range of beneficial uses of the environment without degradation, risk to health or safety, or other undesirable and unintended consequences;

4. preserve important historic, cultural, and natural aspects of our national heritage, and maintain, wherever possible, an environment which supports diversity, and variety of individual choice;

5. achieve a balance between population and resource use which will permit high standards of living and a wide sharing of life's amenities; and

6. enhance the quality of renewable resources and approach the maximum attainable recycling of depletable resources.

(c) The Congress recognizes that each person should enjoy a healthful environment and that each person has a responsibility to contribute to the preservation and enhancement of the environment.

Sec. 102 [42 USC § 4332]

The Congress authorizes and directs that, to the fullest extent possible:

(1) the policies, regulations, and public laws of the United States shall be interpreted and administered in accordance with the policies set forth in this Act, and

(2) all agencies of the Federal Government shall— …

    (c) include in every recommendation or report on proposals for legislation and other major Federal actions significantly affecting the quality of the human environment, a detailed statement by the responsible official on—

        (i) the environmental impact of the proposed action,

        (ii) any adverse environmental effects which cannot be avoided should the proposal be implemented,

        (iii) alternatives to the proposed action,

        (iv) the relationship between local short-term uses of man's environment and the maintenance and enhancement of long-term productivity, and

        (v) any irreversible and irretrievable commitments of resources which would be involved in the proposed action should it be implemented.…

Regulations for Implementing NEPA
Council on Environmental Quality
40 C.F.R. 1500 et seq.

§ 1500.2 Policy.

Federal agencies shall to the fullest extent possible: …

(d) Encourage and facilitate public involvement in decisions which affect the quality of the human environment.

§ 1503.1 Inviting comments.

(a) After preparing a draft environmental impact statement and before preparing a final environmental impact statement the agency shall: …

4. Request comments from the public, affirmatively soliciting comments from those persons or organizations who may be interested or affected.

§ 1503.4 Response to comments.

(a) An agency preparing a final environmental impact statement shall assess and consider comments both individually and collectively, and shall respond by one or more of the means listed below, stating its response in the final statement. Possible responses are to:

1. Modify alternatives including the proposed action.

2. Develop and evaluate alternatives not previously given serious consideration by the agency.

3. Supplement, improve, or modify its analyses.

4. Make factual corrections.

5. Explain why the comments do not warrant further agency response, citing the sources, authorities, or reasons which support the agency's position and, if appropriate, indicate those circumstances which would trigger agency reappraisal or further response.

(b) All substantive comments received on the draft statement (or summaries thereof where the response has been exceptionally voluminous), should be attached to the final statement whether or not the comment is thought to merit individual discussion by the agency in the text of the statement....

§ 1506.6 Public involvement.

Agencies shall:

(a) Make diligent efforts to involve the public in preparing and implementing their NEPA procedures.

(b) Provide public notice of NEPA-related hearings, public meetings, and the availability of environmental documents so as to inform those persons and agencies who may be interested or affected.

§ 1508.10 Environmental document.

"Environmental document" includes the documents specified in Sec. 1508.9 (environmental assessment), Sec. 1508.11 (environmental impact statement), Sec. 1508.13 (finding of no significant impact), and Sec. 1508.22 (notice of intent).

Questions and Discussion

1. *NEPA's purposes.* Congress enacted NEPA in 1969, and President Nixon signed it on January 1, 1970, declaring it "the first act of the environmental decade." The twin purposes of NEPA are better informed decisions and citizen involvement. NEPA applies to a variety of federal actions, including construction projects, funding of private actions, development of federally owned land, and federal permitting decisions for non-federal activities. The environmental effects that must be considered include impacts on natural resources and effects on social, cultural, and economic resources.

2. *NEPA implementation.* Section 101 of NEPA declares environmental protection to be national policy and requires each agency to achieve a list of objectives. It also states that each person "should" enjoy a healthful environment. Section 102 expresses no such lofty sentiments. Instead, it requires circulation of a "detailed statement" on environmental impacts of any proposed project. The "detailed statement" became known as an "environmental impact statement," or EIS. Which of these two sections of the law would you imagine has had more impact on the actions of government departments?

3. From its inception, NEPA has been shaped by the courts. In *Calvert Cliffs' Coordinating Committee v. U. S. Atomic Energy Commission*, 449 F.2d 1109, 1111 (D.C. Cir. 1971), the Court of Appeals stated that the courts' duty "is to see that important legislative purposes, heralded in the halls of Congress, are not lost or misdirected in the vast hallways of the federal bureaucracy." The courts have carried out that duty by insisting on public participation in the EIS process. After nearly a decade of such cases, the President's Council on Environmental Quality under President Jimmy Carter promulgated binding regulations, excerpted above, laying out requirements for EISs in detail.

4. *Public comments on EISs.* 40 C.F.R. § 1503.1, excerpted above, makes it clear that the agency must invite the participation of people and groups that may be affected by or are interested in the decision making when preparing an EIS. When the time for public comment has ended, the agency must analyze the comments from the draft and prepare a final EIS. As shown in the excerpts above, any significant comments made by groups or individuals must be answered—by changes made to the EIS, by the creation of alternative measures in the proposed action, or by an explanation why changes are not being made. 40 C.F.R. § 1503.4(a).

5. *Public comments when no EIS is prepared.* The number of formal environmental impact statements prepared by federal agencies has fallen dramatically over the years since NEPA's enactment—from over 2,000 per year in 1973 to barely 500 annually from 1984 to the present. http://www.epa.gov/oecaerth/resources/publications/nepa/number eis_1973_2006.pdf. Instead of preparing full EIS, agencies have resorted to preparing much simpler "environmental assessments," or EAs. The number of EAs annually is approximately 50,000. *See, e.g.,* Council on Envtl. Quality, ENVIRONMENTAL QUALITY: 25TH ANNIVERSARY REPORT 51 (1994–1995). If the EA concludes that there are no significant environmental impacts (sometimes the project is modified in order to reach such a conclusion), a short "finding of no significant impact" (FONSI) is prepared instead of an EIS. (In addition, agencies increasingly adopt what is called a "categorical exclusion," stating that entire areas of government actions will not have impacts.) *See generally* 40 C.F.R. § 1508.9.

Is public participation required at the crucial stage of preparation of an EA? Take a look at the CEQ regulations, above. What happens if you combine §§ 1506.6 and 1508.10? Must government agencies circulate all EAs in draft form before they are finalized, and accept comments? Compare *Anderson v. Evans,* 314 F.3d 475 487(9th Cir.2004) (yes, dictum), with *Bering Strait Citizens for Responsible Resource Development v. U.S. Army Corps of Engineers,* 511 F.3d 1011 (9th Cir. 2008) (not always, but *petition for rehearing en banc pending*). What happens when an EA acts as the functional equivalent of an EIS? See *Save Our Ecosystems v. Clark,* 747 F.2d 1240, 1247 (9th Cir. 1984) (public comment opportunity required). For more discussion, see Joseph M. Feller, *Public Participation under NEPA,* in NEPA LITIGATION GUIDE (K. Sheldon & M. Squillace, eds., 1999); George Cameron Coggins and Robert L. Glicksman, *NEPA,* in 2 PUB. NAT. RESOURCES L. § 17:6 (2d ed., 2008).

6. *Judicial review.* If a member of the public is concerned that a Federal agency's actions have violated NEPA, that person or group can seek judicial review in a federal court under the Administrative Procedure Act (APA). Under 5 U.S.C. § 706, reviewing courts "shall compel agency action unlawfully withheld or unreasonably delayed; and hold unlawful and set aside agency action, findings and conclusions" that are found to be, among other things: arbitrary, capricious, an abuse of discretion, contrary to constitutional right, and without observance of procedure required by law. 5 U.S.C. § 706.

7. *Comparisons.* Which elements of NEPA do you recognize from environmental policies in other parts of the world?

2. *Executive Regulations and Public Participation Rights*

Environmental impact statements are required for policies and regulations, but other laws also speak to public participation on such matters in both the federal government of the United States and in all state governments. This formal involvement of the public in policy-making is far more developed than in most countries of the world. For federal agencies, prior notice and an opportunity for comment by any member of the public is mandated by the Administrative Procedure Act, 5 U.S.C. § 553.

Administrative Procedure Act

60 Stat. 237 (1946), 5 U.S.C. 553

5 U.S.C. §553 Rule making ...

    (b) General notice of proposed rule making shall be published in the Federal Register.... The notice shall include—

        (1) a statement of the time, place, and nature of public rule making proceedings;

        (2) reference to the legal authority under which the rule is proposed; and

        (3) either the terms or substance of the proposed rule or a description of the subjects and issues involved....

    (c) After notice required by this section, the agency shall give interested persons an opportunity to participate in the rule making through submission of written data, views, or arguments with or without opportunity for oral presentation. After consideration of the relevant matter presented, the agency shall incorporate in the rules adopted a concise general statement of their basis and purpose....

Questions and Discussion

APA and Aarhus. Compare the requirements of section 553 of the Administrative Procedure Act to Article 8 of the Aarhus Convention. Does one require more widespread notification than the other when executive regulations are at issue? Does one restrict participation more than the other? Is one or the other more specific regarding the form that public participation should take? Which one more clearly states that the views expressed by the public shall be considered in making a final decision?

Chapter 8

Access to Justice: Compliance, Enforcement, and Remedies

Introduction

Although making human rights claims is a useful step in national or international policy discussions, most people would consider ability actually to enforce the claim in a court or tribunal to be an essential test of a right's existence. This chapter will discuss enforcement of environmental rights. Of the numerous matters that could be covered, this chapter focuses on particular types of enforcement and on two common issues that arise: who can bring claims to judicial or quasi-judicial bodies (standing to sue) and financial barriers to attaining justice (equal access to justice).

Some tribunals that are clearly judicial exist at the international level for protection of human rights. The primary examples are the International Criminal Court, the individual war tribunals (such as those for the former Yugoslavia and Rwanda), and the three regional human rights courts (European, Inter-American, and African). Others we may term "quasi-judicial," such as the compliance mechanisms and committees of some international environmental conventions.

The most familiar setting for vindication of rights is, of course, in national or local courts. Thus most of this chapter's focus is on access to justice in national or local courts to gain redress for violations of national law.

I. Regional Courts and Tribunals

Among the regional human rights systems, only in the European Court of Human Rights can individuals or nongovernmental organizations (NGOs) petition the Court directly. In the other two regional courts—the Inter-American Court of Human Rights and the African Court on Human and Peoples' Rights—there is no direct "standing" for individuals and NGOs. Instead, the Inter-American Commission on Human Rights and the African Commission on Human and Peoples' Rights serve as filters. The Commission communicates with the State Party upon receiving individual complaints and makes recommendations. If the problem is not solved, only the Commission can present the case to the Court. In 1999, Protocol 11 to the European Convention on Human Rights abolished the European Commission on Human Rights as a mandatory first stage. All three regional Courts do, however, require exhaustion of domestic remedies as a precondition for application. This precondition can be waived if the complainant proves that domestic remedies are not available.

We do not further study the question of access to justice in international courts and tribunals in this textbook.

II. Committees and Mechanisms

A. U.N. Human Rights Committee

Among the institutions before which individuals have standing to file complaints is the United Nations Human Rights Committee, some of whose cases are found in chapter 5. Here is a brief explanation of the right of individuals to have access to this committee.

Introduction to the Human Rights Committee
Office of the High Commissioner for Human Rights
http://www.unhchr.ch/html/menu2/6/a/introhrc.htm

The International Covenant on Civil and Political Rights and its first Optional Protocol allowing individuals to submit complaints to the Human Rights Committee were adopted by the General Assembly on 16 December 1966 and entered into force on 23 March 1976....

The Human Rights Committee was established to monitor the implementation of the Covenant and the Protocols to the Covenant in the territory of States parties....

Each session of the Committee is preceded by two simultaneous pre-sessional working groups established under rules 62 and 89 of its rules of procedure. The working group established under rule 89 is entrusted with the task of making recommendations to the Committee regarding communications received under the Optional Protocol.

———————

The committee keeps busy with "communications" or complaints filed by a large number of individuals, as indicated in this report:

> As of early June 2004, 1,295 such complaints had been registered by the Committee, of which 362 had been declared inadmissible under the criteria described in articles 3 and 5 of the Protocol and 452 considered on the merits of the case. Of those, violations of the Covenant were found in 349 cases; 178 were withdrawn, and 305 were pending. Further updates on these figures may be obtained at: http://www.unhchr.ch/html/menu2/8/stat2.htm. Typically, it may take several years for a complaint to proceed from initial submission through the series of exchanges between the parties to a final decision by the Committee. In certain circumstances, a final resolution may be achieved much more quickly.

Office of the High Commissioner for Human Rights, *Fact Sheet No. 15/Rev. 1, Civil and Political Rights: The Human Rights Committee,* available at http://www.ohchr.org/Documents/Publications/FactSheet7Rev.1en.pdf. Procedures for bringing a complaint are laid out in *Fact Sheet No. 7/Rev. 1, Complaints Procedure,* available at http://www.ohchr.org/Documents/Publications/FactSheet7Rev.1en.pdf.

B. Compliance Committees

The Aarhus Convention and Innovations in Compliance with Multilateral Environmental Agreements

Svitlana Kravchenko
18 Colo. J. Int'l Envtl. L. & Pol'y 1 (2007)

In one remarkable international convention, individual citizens and their organizations have acquired formal tools for pushing nations toward compliance with the international commitments they have made. The Aarhus Convention is the first multinational environmental treaty or convention that focuses exclusively on obligations of nations to their citizens and nongovernmental organizations (NGOs). At the First Meeting of the Parties in October 2002, the Parties adopted a truly innovative mechanism to assess how well the parties comply with the convention to help enforce these obligations. This mechanism goes beyond the steps taken under other international environmental conventions and suggests the need for a new look at compliance mechanisms.

At the time of its adoption, the United States government sharply criticized the Aarhus Convention's compliance mechanism for its "variety of unusual procedural roles that may be performed by non-State, non-Party actors, including the nomination of members of the [Compliance] Committee and the ability to trigger certain communication requirements by Parties under these provisions."[6] The United States declared further that "the United States will not recognize this regime as precedent." When the United States, which was not a signatory, made these comments at the First Meeting of the Parties under the Aarhus Convention in 2002, several delegations including the spokesman for the European Union responded with vigor from the floor in defense of the proposed compliance mechanism. The Parties immediately proceeded to adopt the compliance mechanism by acclamation....

III. Compliance Mechanism of the Aarhus Convention and Comparisons to Other MEAs

The compliance mechanism established under the Aarhus Convention is innovative in both structure and procedure. In terms of structure, NGOs have gained the right to nominate members of the independent body. In addition, the compliance body as a whole is composed of independent experts. In terms of procedure, citizens and NGOs have gained the formal right to file complaints and to participate in preparation of national reports. The Aarhus Convention Compliance Committee (the Committee) has adopted a variety of transparent procedures. In some instances, these are unique; in others they are at the leading edge of changes that are occurring in international law.

B. Public Participation: Communications from the Public

1. The Aarhus Approach

An important and rather unusual feature of the Aarhus Convention is that the Compliance Committee accepts not only the submissions of Parties and referrals from the Secretariat about non-compliance with the Convention (which are the only sources of information for other conventions) but also communications from the public. Article 15 of the Convention provides:

---

6. Statement by the Delegation of the United States with Respect to the Establishment of the Compliance Mechanism, Annex to *Report of the First Meeting of the Parties* at 19, U.N. Doc. ECE/MP.PP/2.

> The Meeting of the Parties shall establish, on a consensus basis, optional arrangements of a non-confrontational, non-judicial, and consultative nature for reviewing compliance with the provisions of this Convention. These arrangements shall allow for appropriate public involvement and may include the option of considering communications from members of the public on matters related to this Convention.

In most MEAs [multilateral environmental agreements], the triggers of the compliance procedure can be submissions by one Party against another Party, by the Secretariat, or by a Party in respect to itself (self-reporting), but only the third is common; Party-to-Party submissions are rare and unusual. In some instances, self-reporting can even insulate a Party from sanctions, at least for some period. For example, under the Non-Compliance Procedure of the Montreal Protocol if a developing country with low per capita consumption of ozone-depleting chemicals self-reports by notifying the Secretariat that, having taken all practicable steps, it is unable to implement any or all of the control measures, the formal non-compliance procedure should not be invoked against this Party until the Meeting of the Parties considers the matter....

[T]here were extensive discussions as well as opposition from some governments on the issue of acceptance of communications from the public, with several countries expressing strong objections. Finally, at the last Working Group meeting held before the First Meeting of the Parties the idea of public complaints was accepted....

As a result, the compliance mechanism provides that communications about a Party for whom the Convention has entered into force "may be brought before the Committee by one or more members of the public concerning that Party's compliance with the Convention." [Decision I/7, Review of Compliance, Addendum to Report of the First Meeting of the Parties, U.N. Doc. ECE/MP.PP/2/Add.8 (2 April 2004)] ... The Committee can refuse to consider a communication that it considers to be an "abuse of the right to make such communications" or "manifestly unreasonable." The Committee is to consider whether domestic remedies were available and were used, but there is no requirement for an absolute exhaustion of domestic remedies." ...

This openness to public participation by civil society has already produced remarkable results in the functioning of the Committee. Eighteen cases have been initiated by communications from NGOs.... The idea of accepting communications from the public has a strong history in human rights instruments. For example, the European Convention on Human Rights guarantees the right of "any person, non-governmental organization or group of individuals claiming to be the victim" of a violation of rights to submit a "petition" to the European Court of Human Rights. Similarly, the First Optional Protocol to the International Covenant on Civil and Political Rights states that "individuals who claim that any of their rights enumerated in the Covenant have been violated ... may submit a written communication to the Committee for consideration."

  2. Other Conventions ...

Attempts for civil society to play a role in reporting noncompliance under the Basel Convention have failed. The Conference of the Parties of the Basel Convention, "after arduous negotiations on submission of information to the [Compliance] Committee by entities other than the Parties and the Secretariat," rejected the idea. In June 2000, Denmark submitted a paper to the Legal Working Group under the Basel Convention asserting that "civil society, NGOs, and other organisations" should be able to trigger the compliance mechanism, "probably through the secretariat that could act like some sort of filter." Australia, on the other hand, argued in a competing paper that NGOs should not have the right to trigger the compliance mechanism. The majority of delegations agreed with Australia. The only involvement of civil society that they allowed was that "a Party may also consider and use relevant and appropriate information provided by civil society on compliance difficulties."

An effort to allow NGOs to trigger the non-compliance procedure under the Montreal Protocol failed in a working group of legal experts in 1991. The Implementation Committee of the Montreal Protocol only accepts information concerning compliance with the Protocol from NGOs if it is forwarded by the Secretariat. As one scholar has observed, "This kind of information may be regarded as compensation for the fact that NGOs are not entitled to trigger the procedure."

Similarly, neither the Kyoto Protocol compliance regime nor the Cartagena Protocol on Biosafety compliance procedure allows members of the public to trigger the procedure. If change is to occur outside the Aarhus Convention context, it might seem logical that it would take place under the Espoo EIA Convention, which has strong public participation provisions. However, its Implementation Committee also does not yet accept direct communications from the public. In mid-2003, after the Canadian delegate presented a paper suggesting the option, the Implementation Committee decided "to propose that this matter should not be addressed at this stage...." Despite this lack of direct access to the Implementation Committee, the compliance procedure does provide:

> Where the Committee becomes aware of possible non-compliance by a Party with its obligations, it may request the Party concerned to furnish necessary information about the matter. Any reply and information in support shall be provided to the Committee within three months or such longer period as the circumstances of a particular case may require. The Committee shall consider the matter as soon as possible in the light of any reply that the Party may provide.

Could this provide an alternative means for the public to bring matters to the Committee? A Ukrainian NGO unsuccessfully tried to use this method to bring information about non-compliance to the attention of the Committee through the Secretariat. In its fourth meeting in October 2003, the Implementation Committee received from the Secretariat the NGO's information about alleged non-compliance by the government of Ukraine in proposed construction of a deep navigation canal in the Danube Delta that could have transboundary effects on Romania. The Delta includes a bilateral Romanian-Ukrainian biosphere reserve, a UNESCO World Heritage site, and a Ramsar Site of wetlands of international importance. In response, the Implementation Committee asked the Secretariat to require the NGO to send additional information to prove that the construction had significant transboundary effect and fell under Annex I, a list of projects with such effects. The Secretariat received this information from the NGO and transferred it to the Implementation Committee.

However, at its fifth meeting in December 2003, the Implementation Committee decided not to consider the information. By a majority vote, the Committee took the position that it was not within its current mandate to consider unsolicited information from NGOs and the public relating to non-compliance. A minority strongly disagreed, interpreting the mandate to mean that "there were no restrictions on how the Committee became aware of a case of possible non-compliance, preferring to examine the information further." ...

Questions and Discussion

1. *MEAs and human rights conventions.* What features make the Aarhus Convention compliance mechanism relatively unique? Its unique features are discussed further in Veit

Koester, *Review of Compliance under the Aarhus Convention: a Rather Unique Compliance Mechanism*, 2 J. Eur. Envtl. & Plan. L. 31 (2005). What reasons could there be for keeping the compliance mechanisms under other multilateral environmental agreements (MEAs) closed to access by individuals or non-governmental organizations (NGOs)? Some regional human rights systems allow individuals and NGOs to trigger their procedures (e.g., the European Court of Human Rights, the Inter-American Commission on Human Rights, but not the Inter-American Court of Human Rights). Is it more logical to expect that compliance mechanisms for human rights conventions, as compared to those for environmental agreements, would be open to public complaints? Is that a reasonable distinction or not?

2. *National versus international remedies.* Is access to justice in national courts not sufficient to resolve environmental or human rights complaints? Why would countries agree to some international mechanism?

3. *Exhaustion requirements.* Could access to international mechanisms lead to misuse or a flood of litigation? Do the procedures for the Aarhus Compliance Committee require it to be used only as a last resort, after a person or NGO has tried to use domestic remedies and found them to be unavailable? Is there an absolute exhaustion requirement? If not, why not? Should regional human rights courts have a requirement for exhaustion of domestic judicial remedies before they may be approached?

4. *Water and Health Protocol.* Recently the Parties to the London Protocol on Water and Health to the 1992 Convention on the Protection and Use of Transboundary Watercourses and International Lakes, U.N. Doc. MP.WAT/2000/1, EUR/ICP/EHCO 020205/8Fin (17 June 1999), created a compliance mechanism that allows the public to bring non-compliance to the attention of a compliance committee. Decision on review of compliance, Addendum to Report of the Meeting of the Parties, U.N. Doc. ECE/MP.WH/2/Add.3 (3 July 2007). As with the Aarhus Convention mechanism, members of the public may file complaints ("communications") with the compliance committee. This mechanism is based on provisions of the compliance regime under the Aarhus Convention.

5. *Aarhus Convention.* The Aarhus compliance procedure can be found in Decision I/7, Review of Compliance, Addendum to Report of the First Meeting of the Parties, U.N. Doc. ECE/MP.PP/2/Add.8 (2 April 2004). Chapters 6, 7, and 8 of this book have included various Findings and Recommendations from the Aarhus Compliance Committee.

III. National Courts

A. Standing to Sue

1. Standing in Various Jurisdictions

The worldwide move toward citizen enforcement of environmental laws and obligations is one of the most striking aspects of the field. Any lawyer can have difficulty in conceiving of basic legal concepts outside the framework of her own legal system. For example, law students in the United States are taught that standing-to-sue is mostly a matter of constitutional law. They are taught that standing consists mostly of examining whether three "constitutional minima" are met (injury-in-fact, causation, and redressability), with some "prudential" criteria such as meeting a "zone of interests" test possibly arising from time to time. In almost no other countries, however, does standing have any "constitutional" requirements at all. Several U.S. states also do not use any constitutional test. This part of the chapter will focus on alternative views on standing to sue, in which policies regarding standing are either a matter of constitutional right (instead of constitutional limitation) or are considered to be wholly within the power of the legislature to define.

Oposa v. Factoran (Philippines)

Supreme Court of Philippines
G.R. No. 101083, 224 SCRA 792 (July 30, 1993),
33 I.L.M. 173 (1994)

[Other parts of this case are excerpted in Chapter 3 at page 79.]

DAVIDE, JR., J:

In a broader sense, this petition bears upon the right of Filipinos to a balanced and healthful ecology which the petitioners dramatically associate with the twin concepts of "inter-generational responsibility" and "inter-generational justice." Specifically, it touches on the issue of whether the said petitioners have a cause of action to "prevent the misappropriation or impairment" of Philippine rainforests and "arrest the unabated hemorrhage of the country's vital life-support systems and continued rape of Mother Earth."

The controversy has its genesis in Civil Case No. 90-777 which was filed before Branch 66 (Makati, Metro Manila) of the Regional Trial Court (RTC), National Capital Judicial Region. The principal plaintiffs therein, now the principal petitioners, are all minors duly represented and joined by their respective parents.... The complaint was instituted as a taxpayers' class suit and alleges that the plaintiffs "are all citizens of the Republic of the Philippines, taxpayers, and entitled to the full benefit, use and enjoyment of the natural resource treasure that is the country's virgin tropical rainforests." The same was filed for themselves and others who are equally concerned about the preservation of said resource but are "so numerous that it is impracticable to bring them all before the Court." The minors further asseverate that they "represent their generation as well as generations yet unborn." Consequently, it is prayed for that judgment be rendered: ...

> ordering defendant, his agents, representatives, and other persons acting in his behalf to—
>
> (1) Cancel all existing timber license agreements in the country;
>
> (2) Cease and desist from receiving, accepting, processing, renewing or approving new timber license agreements.

and granting the plaintiffs ... "such other reliefs just and equitable under the premises."

The complaint starts off with the general averments that the Philippine archipelago of 7,100 islands has a land area of thirty million (30,000,000) hectares and is endowed with rich, lush and verdant rainforests in which varied, rare and unique species of flora and fauna may be found; these rainforests contain a genetic, biological and chemical pool which is irreplaceable; they are also the habitat of indigenous Philippine cultures which have existed, endured and flourished since time immemorial; scientific evidence reveals that in order to maintain a balanced and healthful ecology, the country's land area should be utilized on the basis of a ratio of fifty-four per cent (54%) for forest cover and forty-six per cent (46%) for agricultural, residential, industrial, commercial, and other uses; the distortion and disturbance of this balance as a consequence of deforestation have resulted in a host of environmental tragedies, such as (a) water shortages..., (c) massive erosion and the consequential loss of soil fertility and agricultural productivity, ... (d) the endangering and extinction of the country's unique, rare, and varied flora and fauna, (e) the disturbance and dislocation of cultural communities, including the disappearance of the Filipino's indigenous cultures, ... and (k) the reduction of the earth's capacity to process carbon dioxide gases which has led to perplexing and catastrophic climatic changes such as the phenomenon of global warming, otherwise known as the "greenhouse effect." ...

As their cause of action, they specifically allege that:

CAUSE OF ACTION ...

8. Twenty-five (25) years ago, the Philippines had some sixteen (16) million hectares of rainforests constituting roughly 53% of the country's land mass.

9. Satellite images taken in 1987 reveal that there remained no more than 1.2 million hectares of said rainforests or four per cent (4.0%) of the country's land area.

10. More recent surveys reveal that a mere 850,000 hectares of virgin old-growth rainforests are left, barely 2.8% of the entire land mass of the Philippine archipelago and about 3.0 million hectares of immature and uneconomical secondary growth forests....

12. At the present rate of deforestation, i.e. about 200,000 hectares per annum or 25 hectares per hour—nighttime, Saturdays, Sundays, and holidays included—the Philippines will be bereft of forest resources after the end of this ensuing decade, if not earlier....

14. The continued allowance by defendant of TLA holders to cut and deforest the remaining forest stands will work great damage and irreparable injury to plaintiffs—especially plaintiff minors and their successors—who may never see, use, benefit from and enjoy this rare and unique natural resource treasure.

This act of defendant constitutes a misappropriation and/or impairment of the natural resource property he holds in trust for the benefit of plaintiff minors and succeeding generations.

15. Plaintiffs have a clear and constitutional right to a balanced and healthful ecology and are entitled to protection by the State in its capacity as the parens patriae....

18. The continued failure and refusal by defendant to cancel the TLA's is an act violative of the rights of plaintiffs, especially plaintiff minors who may be left with a country that is desertified (sic), bare, barren, and devoid of the wonderful flora, fauna and indigenous cultures which the Philippines has been abundantly blessed with....

20. Furthermore, defendant's continued refusal to cancel the aforementioned TLA's is contradictory to the Constitutional policy of the State to ...

    d.   "protect and advance the right of the people to a balanced and healthful ecology in accord with the rhythm and harmony of nature." (Section 16, Article II, id.)

21. Finally, defendant's act is contrary to the highest law of humankind—the natural law—and violative of plaintiffs' right to self-preservation and perpetuation....

On 22 June 1990, the original defendant, Secretary Factoran, Jr., filed a Motion to Dismiss the complaint based on two (2) grounds, namely: (1) the plaintiffs have no cause of action against him and (2) the issue raised by the plaintiffs is a political question which properly pertains to the legislative or executive branches of Government....

On 18 July 1991, respondent Judge issued an order granting the aforementioned motion to dismiss....

Plaintiffs thus filed the instant special civil action for certiorari under Rule 65 of the Revised Rules of Court and ask this Court to rescind and set aside the dismissal order on the ground that the respondent Judge gravely abused his discretion in dismissing the action. Again, the parents of the plaintiffs-minors not only represent their children, but have also joined the latter in this case....

Petitioners contend that the complaint clearly and unmistakably states a cause of action as it contains sufficient allegations concerning their right to a sound environment based on Articles 19, 20 and 21 of the Civil Code (Human Relations), Section 4 of Executive Order (E.O.) No. 192 creating the DENR, Section 3 of Presidential Decree (P.D.) No. 1151 (Philippine Environmental Policy), Section 16, Article II of the 1987 Constitution recognizing the right of the people to a balanced and healthful ecology, the concept of generational genocide in Criminal Law and the concept of man's inalienable right to self-preservation and self-perpetuation embodied in natural law. Petitioners likewise rely on the respondent's correlative obligation, per Section 4 of E.O. No. 192, the safeguard the people's right to a healthful environment....

On the other hand, the respondents aver that the petitioners failed to allege in their complaint a specific legal right violated by the respondent Secretary for which any relief is provided by law. They see nothing in the complaint but vague and nebulous allegations concerning an "environmental right" which supposedly entitles the petitioners to the "protection by the state in its capacity as parens patriae." Such allegations, according to them, do not reveal a valid cause of action. They then reiterate the theory that the question of whether logging should be permitted in the country is a political question which should be properly addressed to the executive or legislative branches of Government. They therefore assert that the petitioners' recourse is not to file an action in court, but to lobby before Congress for the passage of a bill that would ban logging totally....

Before going any further, we must first focus on some procedural matters.... We hereby rule that the said civil case is indeed a class suit. The subject matter of the complaint is of common and general interest not just to several, but to all citizens of the Philippines. Consequently, since the parties are so numerous, it becomes impracticable, if not totally impossible, to bring all of them before the court. We likewise declare that the plaintiffs therein are numerous and representative enough to ensure the full protection of all concerned interests....

This case, however, has a special and novel element. Petitioners minors assert that they represent their generation as well as generations yet unborn. We find no difficulty in ruling that they can, for themselves, for others of their generation and for the succeeding generations, file a class suit. Their personality to sue in behalf of the succeeding generations can only be based on the concept of intergenerational responsibility insofar as the right to a balanced and healthful ecology is concerned. Such a right, as hereinafter expounded, considers the "rhythm and harmony of nature." Nature means the created world in its entirety....

Needless to say, every generation has a responsibility to the next to preserve that rhythm and harmony for the full enjoyment of a balanced and healthful ecology. Put a little differently, the minors' assertion of their right to a sound environment constitutes, at the same time, the performance of their obligation to ensure the protection of that right for the generations to come.

The locus standi of the petitioners having thus been addressed, We shall now proceed to the merits of the petition....

We do not hesitate to find for the petitioners and rule against the respondent Judge's challenged order for having been issued with grave abuse of discretion amounting to lack of jurisdiction....

The complaint focuses on one specific fundamental legal right—the right to a balanced and healthful ecology which, for the first time in our nation's constitutional history, is solemnly incorporated in the fundamental law. Section 16, Article II of the 1987 Constitution explicitly provides:

> Sec. 16. The State shall protect and advance the right of the people to a balanced and healthful ecology in accord with the rhythm and harmony of nature.

This right unites with the right to health which is provided for in the preceding section of the same article:

> Sec. 15. The State shall protect and promote the right to health of the people and instill health consciousness among them.

While the right to a balanced and healthful ecology is to be found under the Declaration of Principles and State Policies and not under the Bill of Rights, it does not follow that it is less important than any of the civil and political rights enumerated in the latter. Such a right belongs to a different category of rights altogether for it concerns nothing less than self-preservation and self-perpetuation—aptly and fittingly stressed by the petitioners—the advancement of which may even be said to predate all governments and constitutions.

As a matter of fact, these basic rights need not even be written in the Constitution for they are assumed to exist from the inception of humankind. If they are now explicitly mentioned in the fundamental charter, it is because of the well-founded fear of its framers that unless the rights to a balanced and healthful ecology and to health are mandated as state policies by the Constitution itself, thereby highlighting their continuing importance and imposing upon the state a solemn obligation to preserve the first and protect and advance the second, the day would not be too far when all else would be lost not only for the present generation, but also for those to come—generations which stand to inherit nothing but parched earth incapable of sustaining life.

The right to a balanced and healthful ecology carries with it the correlative duty to refrain from impairing the environment....

A denial or violation of that right by the other who has the correlative duty or obligation to respect or protect the same gives rise to a cause of action. Petitioners maintain that the granting of the TLAs, which they claim was done with grave abuse of discretion, violated their right to a balanced and healthful ecology; hence, the full protection thereof requires that no further TLAs should be renewed or granted....

The foregoing considered, Civil Case No. 90-777 cannot be said to raise a political question. Policy formulation or determination by the executive or legislative branches of Government is not squarely put in issue. What is principally involved is the enforcement of a right vis-a-vis policies already formulated and expressed in legislation....

WHEREFORE, being impressed with merit, the instant Petition is hereby GRANTED, and the challenged Order of respondent Judge of 18 July 1991 dismissing Civil Case No. 90-777 is hereby set aside....

[FELICIANO, J., issued a separate opinion concurring in the result.]

Questions and Discussion

1. *The concept of standing.* Standing to sue, or *locus standi* in Latin, has many different names. It is called "title or interest to sue" in Scotland," legal capacity to litigate" in Greece, *Verbandsklagerecht* in Germany, and increasingly a "right of access to justice" in the European Community. The term "access to justice," however, is normally seen as being broader than "standing," including also issues of costs, injunction bonds, and practical accessibility. In some countries, the existence of a "cause of action" in a person is understood to be the same as legal standing, while in others lawyers will insist that they are quite separate concepts.

2. *Reasons for standing requirements.* Why should the judicial system be available only to some persons and not others? If your answer is that the courts should not be overburdened, is restricting the types of persons who may seek relief the best way to avoid that? Are other means possible? What about letting anyone sue, but throwing out cases on the basis that they are frivolous or unimportant, and perhaps imposing sanctions on those who bring such cases? Should companies that might suffer financial harm have a greater right to call the courts' attention to illegal actions of the government than citizens whose harm is non-financial?

3. *Open standing in public interest appeals.* The idea of allowing judicial review of government action at the behest of any member of the public, rather requiring that a litigant have a special stake in the matter, is very old. One of the oldest terms for this concept of open standing, dating back some 2,000 years, is the Latin term, *actio popularis* (people's legal action). In Brazil this is called an *ação populare*. In Spanish-speaking Latin America such suits are often called *acciones populares,* an almost literal translation of the Roman law term. See, for example, German Sarmiento Palacio, LAS ACCIONES POPULARES EN EL DERECHO PRIVADO COLOMBIANO (2006). The term *acciones difusas* is also used to characterize the idea, based on the notion that the interests involved are diffuse—shared in common by many persons. *Jus tertii* (third party rights) is a term used more in international law than in domestic systems. The British and early U.S. practice spoke as well of "informers' actions." "Citizens suit" is a newer phrasing, particularly in the U.S. under certain environmental statutes, although that term is also used to refer to lawsuits authorized to be filed against private parties, as explained below.

4. *Future generations.* Should future generations have standing to sue? The plaintiffs in *Oposa* brought a class action suit to "prevent the misappropriation or impairment" of the Philippine rainforests on behalf of current and future generations unborn. The court found that continued deforestation violated the rights of the minor Oposa children, who "may be left with a country that is desertified, bare, barren, and devoid of the wonderful flora and fauna and indigenous cultures which the Philippines has been blessed with." Further, the court found that the plaintiffs could represent themselves, other generations, and succeeding generations in a class suit because environmental health should be equitably available to the present as well as future generations. Compare this to the Chilean case, *Comunidad de Chañaral v. Codeco División el Saldor*, mentioned in Chapter 3 at page 70. A similar case brought by children in Costa Rica also resulted in legal standing.

Carlos Roberto García Chacón, Sala Constitucional de la Corte Suprema de Justicia, Decision 3705/93 of 30.6.1993.

Is the court actually granting standing to future generations, or to the lawyer who brings the case (in this case, the plaintiffs' father, a famous environmental lawyer)? Does this open the judicial system to manipulation to achieve ends that should be achieved instead in legislative bodies? Or is granting standing for future generations simply a means of removing barriers on access to justice that previous generations of judges erected to deal with the problems of a previous era? Do the plaintiffs (or their lawyers) in this case seek political ends or ordinary judicial review of agency action alleged to violate constitutional or statutory commands?

5. *Persuasive authority.* Can *Oposa* or other cases about future generations be used as precedent or persuasive authorities in other countries? At least one state within the United States has included protection of future generations in its state constitution. Pennsylvania's Constitution states, "Pennsylvania's public natural resources are the common property of all the people, including generations yet to come." Standing to sue under state law is not bound by the precedents of the U.S. Supreme Court, as shown in the *Kellas* case, below at page 332. Could the cited constitutional provision be used in environmental cases to overcome limitations on standing that may otherwise exist in Pennsylvania jurisprudence?

6. *"Generalized grievances."* An oft-cited U.S. case on standing states that "a plaintiff raising only generalized grievances about government-claiming only his and every citizen's interest ... and seeking relief that no more directly and tangibly benefits him from than it does the public at large ..." does not have a sufficient interest to establish standing. *Lujan v. Defenders of Wildlife* 504 U.S. 555, 573–74 (1992). *Lujan* will be discussed in various places in this chapter. Compare its reasoning to the *Oposa* case from the Philippines. Consider what harm the *Lujan* court is trying to avoid by limiting access to individuals suing the government based on the existence of many similarly situated people. More recently, the U.S. Supreme Court in *Massachusetts v. E.P.A.,* __ U.S. __. 127 S. Ct. 1438 (2007), endorsed standing for the Government of Massachusetts to represent the interests of its citizens in challenging E.P.A. on legal issues involving global warming. Is that approach closer to *Lujan* or *Oposa*?

M. C. Mehta v. Union of India

Supreme Court of India
WP 12739/1985 (1986.12.20) 01/01/1987
AIR 1987 SC 1086

BHAGWATI, C.J.

This writ petition under Article 32 of the Constitution has come before us on a reference made by a Bench of three Judges. The reference was made because certain questions of seminal importance and high constitutional significance were raised in the course of arguments when the writ petition was originally heard.... [W]hile the writ petition was pending there was escape of oleum gas from one of the units of Shriram on 4th and 6th December 1985 and applications were filed by the Delhi Legal Aid & Advice Board and the Delhi Bar Association for award of compensation to the persons who had suffered harm on account of escape of oleum gas. These applications for compensation raised a number of issues of great constitutional importance....

Mr. Diwan, learned counsel appearing on behalf of Shriram raised a preliminary objection.... These applications for compensation are for enforcement of the fundamental right to life enshrined to Art. 21 of the Constitution and while dealing with such applications, we cannot adopt a hypertechnical approach which would defeat the ends of justice.... [T]here is no reason why these applications for compensation which have been made for enforcement of the fundamental right of the persons affected by the oleum gas leak under Art. 21 should not be entertained. The Court while dealing with an application for enforcement of a fundamental right must look at the substance and not the form....

Thus it was in *S.P. Gupta v. Union of India* that this Court held that

> where a legal wrong or a legal injury is caused to a person or to a determinate class of persons by reasons of violation of any constitutional or legal provision or without authority of law or any such legal wrong or legal injury or illegal burden is threatened, and any such person or determinate class of persons is by reason of poverty or disability or socially or economically disadvantaged position unable to approach the Court for relief, any member of the public or social action group can maintain an application for an appropriate direction, order or writ in the High Court under Art. 226 and in case of breach of any fundamental right of such person or class of person, in this Court under Art. 32 seeking judicial redress for the legal wrong or injury caused to such person or determinate class of persons.

This Court also held in *S.P. Gupta's case* that procedure being merely a hand-maiden of justice it should not stand in the way of access to justice to the weaker sections of Indian humanity and therefore where the poor and the disadvantaged are concerned who are barely eking out a miserable existence with their sweat and toil and who are victims of an exploited society without any access to justice, this Court will not insist on a regular writ petition and even a letter addressed by a public spirited individual or a social action group acting *pro bono publico* would suffice to ignite the jurisdiction of this Court. We wholly endorse this statement of the law in regard to the broadening of *locus standi* and what has come to be known as epistolary jurisdiction....

[T]his Court has a Public Interest Litigation Cell to which all letters addressed to the Court or to the individual justices are forwarded and the staff attached to this Cell examines the letters and it is only after scrutiny by the staff members attached to this Cell that the letters are placed before the Chief Justice and under his direction, they are listed before the Court....

Questions and Discussion

1. *Standing and rights.* Note the India Supreme Court's observation that its precedents have established that "any member of the public or social action group" can bring a case "in case of breach of any fundamental right" of a disadvantaged person in society. Does this suggest that locating an environmental human right as "fundamental" is an important step in broadening standing to sue?

2. *"Epistolary jurisdiction."* Note that "even a letter addressed by a public spirited individual or a social action group acting *pro bono publico* would suffice to ignite the jurisdiction of this Court" and that the Supreme Court of India has established a "Public Interest Litigation Cell" to process such letters. Is such a dramatic alteration in normal court procedures feasible in other countries? Is there something about India that makes it appropriate only on the sub-continent?

3. *South Asia.* The courts in South Asia have been particularly active in public interest litigation, as a result of low barriers to standing, following the lead of the Supreme Court of

India. A thorough study of the most important cases can be found in Jona Razzaque, PUB-
LIC INTEREST ENVIRONMENTAL LITIGATION IN INDIA, PAKISTAN, AND BANGLADESH (2004).
A list of hundreds of such cases can be found at http://www.elaw.org/assets/word/JDESA-
Content.doc. Summaries of all of those, plus the full text of many of the cases can be found
at http://www.elaw.org/resources/regional.asp?region=Asia.

Truth About Motorways v.
Macquarie Infrastructure Management (Australia)
High Court of Australia
(2000) 200 CLR 591

GLEESON CJ, GAUDRON, MCHUGH, GUMMOW, KIRBY, HAYNE and CALLINAN JJ

GLEESON CJ and MCHUGH J.

The primary issue for determination is whether the Parliament, in legislating with respect to a subject matter specified in § 51 of the Constitution, (in this case, corporations
of the kind referred to in § 51(xx)), may provide for the judicial enforcement of the law
at the suit of any person....

At first sight, a provision that a law concerning the conduct of corporations may be enforced by a court at the suit of any person appears to be within the power given by § 51(xx).
That power, however, is subject to the Constitution. It is argued that the enactment of such
a law is inconsistent with Ch III of the Constitution, and with the arrangements made by
Ch III for the exercise of the judicial power of the Commonwealth....

The alleged misleading and deceptive conduct related to the publication of a prospec-
tus inviting the public to subscribe for units in an investment trust. The investment concerned the construction of a toll road. The applicant complains that information given
concerning the volume of traffic on the road was misleading.

The applicant claims no special interest in the subject matter of the dispute. It has not
suffered any loss or damage by reason of the respondent's conduct. It invokes the jurisdiction conferred on the Federal Court by §§ 80 and 163A simply in its capacity as a (corporate) person.

The respondent challenges the applicant's standing to bring the proceedings, and has
raised a number of questions which have been made the subject of a Case Stated for this Court.

The first question asks whether §§ 80 and 163A of the Act are invalid, insofar as they
purport to confer standing on the applicant to bring the present proceedings....

It has been established for more than 20 years that § 80 means what it says. In *Phelps
v. Western Mining Corporation* the Full Court of the Federal Court rejected an argument
that the words "any other person" in § 80 should be read down as meaning that only persons who are affected by a contravention of Pt V could seek relief under § 80....

The relevant provisions of Ch III of the Constitution ... are as follows. Section 76 (ii)
empowers the Parliament to make laws conferring original jurisdiction on the High Court
in any matter arising under any laws made by the Parliament. Section 77 enables the same
jurisdiction to be conferred on another federal court.... The essence of the respondent's
argument is that in a case such as the present, there is no "matter," and the purported
conferment of jurisdiction is therefore invalid. The reason why there is no matter, it is submitted, is that there is no justiciable controversy. That, in turn, is said to follow from the
absence of any direct or special interest of the applicant in the subject matter of the proceedings....

Reliance was placed upon authorities concerning art. III of the United States Constitution and the power of Congress to confer standing in citizen suits. The constitutional context in which those cases were decided is materially different from the Australian context. In particular, the references in art. III to "cases" and "controversies," as opposed to "matters," and the somewhat different role of the Executive, means that the United States learning is not of assistance in the resolution of the Australian problem....

GAUDRON J. . . .

In *Gouriet v. Union of Post Office Workers*, Lord Wilberforce described the general rule that only the Attorney-General or a person who has been granted the Attorney-General's fiat may bring proceedings with respect to a public wrong as "constitutional" in nature, explaining "[t]hat it is the exclusive right of the Attorney-General to represent the public interest." In that regard, his Lordship referred to the observation of Lord Westbury LC in *Stockport District Waterworks Company v. Mayor of Manchester* that "the constitution of [Great Britain] ha[d] wisely intrusted the privilege [of representing the public interest] with a public officer, and has not allowed it to be usurped by a private individual."

It is clear from what was said in *Gouriet* that the general rule that only the Attorney-General may institute proceedings for a public wrong derives not from any constitutional limitation as to the role or jurisdiction of courts, but from the constitutional role of the Attorney-General. . . .

Once it is appreciated that the "constitutional" nature of the rule that only the Attorney-General may bring proceedings with respect to a public wrong derives from the status of the Attorney-General in British law, it follows that there is no equivalent constitutional basis for that rule in this country. . . . Thus in this country, the general rule that only the Attorney-General may bring proceedings with respect to a public wrong is simply a rule of the common law. . . .

[T]here is no reason why it cannot be abrogated by the Parliament so as to allow any person to represent the public interest. . . .

Chapter III of the Constitution: "Judicial power" and "matter"

It is convenient to note, at once, that although Ch III of the Constitution has significant similarities with art. III of the Constitution of the United States of America, there are, as this Court has often noted, significant differences. In particular, the latter is concerned with "Cases" and "Controversies," whereas Ch III selects "matters" as the subject-matter of federal jurisdiction. And "matters" is a word of such generality that it necessarily takes its content from the categories of matter which fall within federal jurisdiction and from the concept of "judicial power." There is, thus, no reason why the position in this country should equate precisely with that reached in the United States of America. . . .

GUMMOW J. . . .

This attack is mounted on the ground that there is no "justiciable controversy" and no "matter" to be determined. . . . There is no such requirement for enforcement of a law as a matter arising under § 76(ii) of the Constitution. . . .

United States authorities

At the time § 80 was first enacted, there was significant United States authority which would indicate that such a provision was valid. As long ago as 1943, when giving the decision of the Court of Appeals for the Second Circuit in *Associated Industries v. Ickes*, Judge Frank had said: . . .

Instead of designating the Attorney General, or some other public officer, to bring such proceedings, Congress can constitutionally enact a statute conferring on any non-official person, or on a designated group of non-official persons, authority to bring a suit to prevent action by an officer in violation of his statutory powers; for then, in like manner, there is an actual controversy, and there is nothing constitutionally prohibiting Congress from empowering any person, official or not, to institute a proceeding involving such a controversy, even if the sole purpose is to vindicate the public interest. Such persons, so authorized, are, so to speak, private Attorney Generals.

However, the respondent placed particular reliance upon more recent United States decisions. They are *Lujan, Secretary of the Interior v. Defenders of Wildlife, Bennett v. Spear* and *Steel Co. v. Citizens for a Better Environment*. The cases appear to suggest that there is a "core requirement" with respect to all matters of federal jurisdiction under art. III of the United States Constitution. This will deny standing to such a "stranger," even where Congress has expressly authorised "citizen suits" to enforce certain laws of the United States in federal courts....

In *Lujan, Secretary of the Interior v. Defenders of Wildlife*, Scalia J, delivering the opinion of the Court on this point, supported the decision that the plaintiffs lacked standing on the grounds that the engagement of the courts in the way stipulated by Congress to vindicate the public interest, in the observance by the executive branch of the Constitution of laws made by Congress, would exceed the constitutional role of the third branch of government.... More recently, in his dissenting judgment in *Federal Election Commission v. Akins*, Scalia J explained his position as being that the judicial branch of government was "designed not to protect the public at large but to protect individual rights" and that the "primary responsibility" of compelling "Executive compliance with the law" was given by the United States Constitution to the President....

The reasoning in the recent United States decisions respecting statute-based "citizen suits" has been both criticised[128] and praised[129] by commentators. Moreover, the case law is not static. The debate may be expected to continue in the light of the 1998 decision of the Supreme Court in *Federal Election Commission v. Akins*. Breyer J, delivering the opinion of the Court, considered the requirement for standing of an "injury in fact." His Honour held that this "injury" was established by the inability of a group of electors to obtain information respecting donors to an organisation which lobbied elected officials and disseminated information about candidates for public office.... The effect of the holding in *Akins* appears to be "that Congress by statute can create rights that would not otherwise exist and the alleged violation of those rights is sufficient for standing, even under a broad citizen suit provision and even where the injury is widely shared in society." ...

Upon the merits of the continuing debate in the United States this Court cannot enter. It is sufficient to say that, in the context of the Australian Constitution and for the reasons given above, the recent United States decisions do not supply the support which the respondent sought to derive from them in demonstrating that §§ 80 and 163A cannot be supported by § 76(iii) of the Constitution.

---

128. Sunstein, "What's Standing after *Lujan*? Of Citizen Suits, Injuries, and Article III," (1992) 91 *Michigan Law Review* 163; Nichol, "Justice Scalia, Standing, and Public Law Litigation," (1993) 42 *Duke Law Journal* 1141.

129. Breger, "Defending *Defenders*: Remarks on Nichol and Pierce," (1993) 42 *Duke Law Journal* 1202.

Conclusions ...

[I]t is unnecessary for there to be a "matter" that there be imposed upon the respondent any obligation or "duty" not to contravene any of those Parts of the Act stipulated in §§ 80 and 163A by injuring or threatening to injure the personal, economic or other individual interests or "rights" of that "person" who actually sues for contravention of the Act....

It is not the case that the only members of the class who may institute and prosecute proceedings under §§ 80 and 163A are those who complain of such an injury....

Kirby J.

The meaning of the word "matter" in Ch III of the Constitution, is elusive. These proceedings require examination of the extent to which the concept imports a particular requirement about standing to sue. The doctrine of standing is itself "a house of many rooms." This Court should not accept the attempt to use the constitutional notion of "matter" to erode significantly the legislative powers of the Federal Parliament and to import a serious and unnecessary inflexibility into the Constitution....

United States authorities are inapplicable

Because of the parallels between Ch III of the Australian Constitution and art. III of the United States Constitution, it is certainly appropriate to consider developments in the United States concerning the latter. However, for a number of reasons I am not persuaded that the United States decisions require this Court to adopt a conclusion contrary to that which the foregoing analysis of the law applicable in Australia would otherwise suggest....

I agree in the orders proposed by Gleeson CJ and McHugh J.

Hayne J....

The respondent's contention, that there is no "matter" arising under a law made by the Parliament ... should be rejected....

Callinan J....

I point out at this stage that § 80 itself evinces a clear legislative intention that neither the Minister, the Commission nor any other person should in all cases have an exclusive right of enforcement, or the same rights or obligations in making claims for relief pursuant to the section....

There is no case in this Court in which any argument as far reaching as that advanced by the respondent has been upheld....

So far as the cases in the United States are concerned, it is sufficient for present purposes to point out that the word "matter" was chosen as the appropriate expression for Ch III of the Australian Constitution as opposed to either "case" or "controversy" (the United States' choices) because "matter" was an expression which was thought to have, and indeed is clearly capable of having a wider meaning than the words chosen in that country....

Access to Justice in Environmental Law: An Australian Perspective

Hon Justice Peter McClellan
Chief Judge at Common Law, Supreme Court of New South Wales
Commonwealth Law Conference, London (2005)

Although democracy has an ancient tradition it is only in recent generations that western societies have allowed most of their citizens to participate in the processes of the State.

It is salutary to remember that for many years women were not to be trusted with the vote and in some countries property or wealth were an essential qualification to be able to participate in an election. Although laws are made for the welfare and protection of all of the citizens of the State, special rules have been constructed by the courts which exclude most people from bringing proceedings to enforce them. Various justifications have been offered. The fear of the intermeddler opening the "floodgates" and clogging the business of the courts and frustrating the ambitions of the executive government has meant that a member of the public could not, without the Attorney-General's fiat, bring proceedings to restrain a breach of a public law. This paper considers the manner in which the ability of a citizen to bring proceedings to enforce a public law in Australia has been confined by the courts and, in New South Wales, at least in relation to environmental laws, expanded by the legislature....

Standing at common law ...

[L]ocus standi was for many years defined by the well-known decision in *Boyce v. Paddington Borough Council* [(1903) 1 Ch 109] [U.K.]. The effect was that there were few, if any, proceedings initiated by individuals or corporations without the Attorney-General's fiat ... [I]n *Boyce* the plaintiff was troubled by the erection of a hoarding which would obstruct the access of light to the plaintiff's windows and brought proceedings to restrain the Council from proceeding with the project.... In words which for many years defined a plaintiff's right to obtain relief Buckley J said:

> A plaintiff can sue without joining the Attorney-General in two cases: first, where the interference with the public right is such as that some private right of his is at the same time interfered with (eg, where an obstruction is so placed in a highway that the owner of premises abutting upon the highway is specially affected by reason that the obstruction interferes with his private right to access from and to his premises to and from the highway); and, secondly, where no private right is interfered with, but the plaintiff, in respect of his public right, suffers special damage peculiar to himself from the interference with the public right. [Ibid at 114]....

The *Boyce* test contained two limbs. The first limb recognised the right in an individual to enforce his or her private rights even if in the process a public right is vindicated. The second limb — the requirement for "special damage" — ultimately proved troublesome and, both in England and Australia, has undergone significant modification....

In *Australian Conservation Foundation* [(1981) 146 CLR 493] the second limb in *Boyce* was reformulated and the concept of "special interest" was substituted for "special damage." The case concerned a challenge by the Australian Conservation Foundation, a body with the fundamental objective of protecting the environment, to the validity of decisions by the Minister to establish a resort and tourist area at Yeppoon near Rockhampton in Queensland.... The Australian Conservation Foundation sought declarations that there had been a failure to comply with the requirements of the Act.

It was held by the majority (Murphy J dissented) that the Australian Conservation Foundation did not have standing. The Australian Conservation Foundation argued, inter alia, that it had standing under the second limb of *Boyce* because it had a well-known concern for the Australian environment evidenced in its previous activities....

Although the Australian Conservation Foundation failed, Gibbs J found the *Boyce* formulation of "special damage" inappropriate for contemporary problems. His Honour said:

Although the general rule is clear, the formulation of the exceptions to it which Buckley J made in *Boyce v. Paddington Borough Council* is not altogether satisfactory. Indeed the words which he used are apt to be misleading. His reference to 'special damage' cannot be limited to actual pecuniary loss, and the words 'peculiar to himself' do not mean that the plaintiff, and no one else, must have suffered damage. However, the expression 'special damage peculiar to himself' in my opinion should be regarded as equivalent in meaning to 'having a special interest in the subject matter of the action.' [(1981) 146 CLR 493, 527].

Gibbs J indicated that before there could be the relevant interest it must be more than intellectual or emotional, but, need not be pecuniary....

In *Onus*, two plaintiffs, Lorraine Sandra Onus and Christina Isabel Frankland, who claimed to be the descendants of the Gournditch-jmara aboriginal people, sought relief to restrain Alcoa from undertaking a mining project which it was said would be likely to damage aboriginal relics on their people's traditional lands. [*Onus v. Alcoa of Australia Ltd* (1981) 149 CLR 27]. The High Court distinguished *Australian Conservation Foundation* and, because of the cultural and spiritual significance of the relics for the Gournditch-jmara community, held that the plaintiffs had the relevant special interest to entitle them to sue....

In *Bateman's Bay Local Aboriginal Land Council [v. The Aboriginal Community Benefit Fund* [(1998) 194 CLR 247]], the New South Wales Supreme Court held that the plaintiffs did not have standing to sue to control the way in which the Land Council, a body created by statute to assist aboriginal people, proposed to conduct a funeral benefit fund. It was not a case concerned with the environment. The question raised for consideration by the High Court was the criterion for standing in a case where a plaintiff seeks an injunction to prevent possible economic loss as a consequence of ultra vires activities by a statutory body using or enjoying recourse to public monies. In the joint judgment of Gaudron, Gummow, and Kirby JJ the evolution of the standing rules in the absence of the Attorney-General was considered. The early view had its clearest statement in *Evan v. Avon Corporation* [(1860) 29 Beav 144 [54 ER 581]] where Sir John Romilly said that:

> there is a public trust for the town and inhabitants, and a suit to enforce such a trust ought to be by information by the Attorney-General, and not by a private individual" [Ibid at 152 [at 585]].

More than a century later this statement was strongly condemned by the joint judgment. Their Honours said of it:

> Such a state of affairs can have little to recommend it.... This, it has been said, "is a matter which should be determined by known rules of law, and not by the undisclosed practice of a minister of the Crown" (see Wade and Forsyth, ADMINISTRATIVE LAW, 7th ed. (1994), p 607).... The evolution of the *Boyce* doctrine of 'sufficient special interest' represents an attempt to alleviate that state of affairs whilst keeping at bay 'the phantom busy body or ghostly intermeddler' (Craig, Administrative Law, 3rd ed (1994), p 484). The result is an unsatisfactory weighting of the scales in favour of defendant public bodies. Not only must the plaintiff show the abuse or threatened abuse of public administration which attracts equitable intervention, but the plaintiff must also show some special interest in the subject matter of the action in which it is sought to restrain that abuse [*Bateman's Bay Local Aboriginal Land Council v. The Aboriginal Community Benefit Fund* (1998) 194 CLR 247, 260–261]....

Although McHugh J joined in the unanimous decision of the court, he was careful to mark out the limits on the capacity of a citizen to seek relief to enforce a public law. Identifying that the basic purpose of the civil courts is "to protect individual rights" his Honour said that it was "not part of their function to enforce the public law of the community or to oversee the enforcement of the civil or criminal law, except as an incident in the course of protecting the rights of individuals whose rights have been, are being, or may be interfered with by reason of a breach of law." ... [Ibid at 276].

His Honour confirmed the conventional philosophical basis for confining standing seemingly putting himself at odds with Brennan, Gaudron, and Gummow JJ. McHugh J said:

> The enforcement of the public law of a community is part of the political process; it is one of the chief responsibilities of the executive government. In most cases, it is for the executive government and not for the civil courts acting at the behest of disinterested private individuals to enforce the law. There are sometimes very good reasons why the public interest of a society is best served by not attempting to enforce a particular law. To enforce a law at a particular time or in particular circumstances may result in the undermining of the authority of the executive government or the courts of justice. In extreme cases, to enforce it may lead to civil unrest and bloodshed. [Ibid at 276–277.]

There may be good reasons why any person in a community should not have a right to bring a criminal prosecution, or, at least, the state should have the right to terminate such a prosecution. However, with respect, it is difficult to understand how it can be legitimately argued that any citizen should not have the right to bring proceedings to enforce a public law. If, as Justice McHugh argues, the particular law is no longer relevant or appropriate, having regard to contemporary problems, the legislature may repeal it, or, a court in the exercise of its discretion, may decline to enforce it. To adopt the position that a citizen cannot approach a court to ask that a member of the executive or a government agency should obey the law, which the Parliament has provided in the interests of the general community may itself carry significant dangers for the stability of the community....

The position of the Australian Law Reform Commission

In a report published in 1996 the Australian Law Reform Commission reviewed the question of standing in relation to proceedings to enforce a public law. [Australian Law Reform Commission, Report No 78, *Beyond the Door-Keeper: Standing to Sue for Public Remedies*, AGPS, Canberra, 1996] Its recommendation was that the complex restrictions which existed to deny standing should be removed in favour of open standing. It further recommended that any person should be able to commence proceedings having a public element subject to only two matters. The first and obvious matter was if the relevant legislation provides otherwise. The second consideration was that the litigation would unreasonably interfere with the ability of a person having a private interest in the issue to deal with it as he or she wishes....

The recommendation of the Law Reform Commission has not been adopted by the Australian Government.

The review and recommendations of the Law Reform Commission were made after the New South Wales Parliament had legislated to provide open standing to enforce environmental law within that State. Although the Commonwealth Government has responsibility for some areas of environmental law the control upon the use of land in both the urban and rural environment rests with State Governments. Accordingly, by providing open standing, the New South Wales Parliament provided a mechanism which facilitated proceedings by any person, including the misguided intermeddler and the major commercial competitor.

The legislative framework in NSW

The New South Wales *Environmental Planning and Assessment Act* provides the legislative structure for the control of planning and development in New South Wales....

Proceedings to enforce the Act and the provisions of any planning instrument are litigated exclusively in the Land and Environment Court [§71 Land and Environment Court Act 1979]. Standing is provided to any person by §123 of the *Environmental Planning & Assessment Act.*

(1) Any person may bring proceedings in the Court for an order to remedy or restrain a breach of this Act, whether or not any right of that person has been or may be infringed by or as a consequence of that breach.

(2) Proceedings under this section may be brought by a person ... or a body corporate or unincorporated (with the consent of its committee or other controlling or governing body), having like or common interests in those proceedings....

Section 123 is complemented by §124 of the Act. That section is in the following terms:

(1) Where the Court is satisfied that a breach of this Act has been committed or that a breach of this Act will, unless restrained by order of the Court, be committed, it may make such order as it thinks fit to remedy or restrain the breach....

Conclusion

It is apparent that the open standing provided by §123 modifies the common law to provide that any person can bring proceedings to enforce the *Environmental Planning & Assessment Act,* whether or not they have any particular interest in the activities which are allegedly being carried out contrary to its provisions. Although the common law in Australia, with significant cautionary words from some members of the High Court, has been moving towards a liberalisation of standing to enforce public laws, the New South Wales Parliament has removed any impediment in relation to many environmental laws.

So far as it is possible, the analysis undertaken of various cases over the 25 years since the Act commenced operation does not suggest that a "flood of cases" has come to the court which could not have been brought but for the provisions of §123. There are some cases where standing may have been an arguable issue and some where it may have been denied, but many cases and probably most cases would fall within the common law principles defined by the Australian High Court as they have more recently been applied....

It is apparent from the many cases in relation to the exploitation of natural resources, particularly forestry, that the opportunity for a plaintiff to bring proceedings without having to establish standing has meant that it has been possible to use the plaintiff's, sometimes limited, resources to debate matters relating to the operation of the relevant planning laws rather than debating issues of standing. Many of these cases have significantly enhanced the quality of environmental decision-making within New South Wales....

Any fears that open standing will encourage proceedings which have the potential to destabilise orderly government have been unfounded. Although the government has felt it necessary to legislate in a very few cases, there has been no suggestion that the open standing provisions have led to litigation which adversely impacts upon the well-being of the whole community. The contrary is undoubtedly true. In relation to some of the projects about which there has been litigation, in particular the forestry matters, members of the public have gathered and, at times, engaged in civil disobedience, including the physical obstruction of bulldozers and other heavy equipment. On a number of occasions persons lives have been at risk. Because it has been possible to access the court and litigate the lawfulness of these projects the possibility of injury to members of the public, or damage to plant and equipment has been alleviated and in almost every case avoided. Far from damaging the "body politic" open standing, to the extent that it has facilitated proceedings to enforce environmental laws, has proved beneficial. . . .

Questions and Discussion

1. Compare the views expressed by McHugh J, as quoted above in the *Bateman's Bay* case, with those of then-Professor Antonin Scalia, writing in 1983:

> [T]he ability [of the executive branch] to lose or misdirect laws [through non-enforcement and non-compliance] can be said to be one of the prime engines of social change.

Antonin Scalia, *The Doctrine of. Standing as an Essential Element of the Separation of Powers*, 17 Suffolk U.L. Rev. 881, 897 (1983). Supreme Court Justice Scalia subsequently wrote in his majority opinion in *Lujan v. Defenders of Wildlife*, 504 U.S. 555, 577 (1992):

> To permit Congress to convert the undifferentiated public interest in executive officers' compliance with the law into an "individual right" vindicable in the courts is to permit Congress to transfer from the President to the courts the Chief Executive's most important constitutional duty, to "take Care that the Laws be faithfully executed," Art. II, §3.

Do McHugh and Scalia have it right? Or do Gaudron, Gummow and Kirby JJ, cited in this court's reference to *Bateman's Bay* have the better view?

2. *Effects of open standing.* Notice that, in Justice McClellan's opinion, open standing in New South Wales on environmental matters has not had led to a "flood of cases." Do you think there are unique circumstances in this jurisdiction making this the case or might this evidence be relevant to other jurisdictions? Might other factors make frivolous cases unlikely if standing rules are relaxed? Australian High Court Judge Murray Wilcox expressed this opinion in a famous case broadening standing:

> The idol and whimsical plaintiff, a dilettante who litigates for a laugh, is a spectre which haunts the legal literature, not the court room. Litigation — in the public interest and for no personal advantage, especially against a wealthy opponent and under a cost regime requiring the losing party to pay the costs incurred by the victor — has some similarity to marriage as described in the Book of Common Prayer: it is not by any to be enterprised nor taken in hand, unadvisedly, lightly or wantonly.

Ogle v. Strickland, (1987) 14 FCR 474.

Kellas v. Department of Corrections (USA)
341 Or. 471, 145 P.3d 139 (2006)

The legislature's policy choice regarding standing in ORS 183.400(1) is unambiguous. The legislature intends by the statute to authorize any person to invoke the judicial power of the court to test the validity of every administrative rule under existing statutory and constitutional law and, thus, to advance the objective that all agency rulemaking shall remain within applicable procedural and substantive legal bounds. So understood, petitioner satisfies the standing requirement that ORS 183.400(1) identifies. The remaining question is whether some other source of law—in this case, the Oregon Constitution—imposes any additional requirement or limitation regarding a party's standing to challenge an administrative rule....

We are aware of no qualification on the legislature's authority in the Oregon Constitution that would restrict the legislature from authorizing any member of the public to initiate litigation concerning the validity of administrative rules....

The plenary lawmaking authority of the Oregon legislature stands in marked contrast to the limitations that pertain to lawmaking by the United States Congress. For example, in authorizing litigation in the courts of the United States, Congress must respect the limitation in Article III, section 2, of the United States Constitution, which provides that the judicial power of the United States extends to the resolution of "cases" or "controversies." That clause has given rise to an extensive body of federal law regarding the justiciability of disputes in federal court.

The Oregon Constitution contains no "cases" or "controversies" provision. Moreover, the United States Supreme Court has determined that "the constraints of Article III do not apply to state courts...." For that reason, we cannot import federal law regarding justiciability into our analysis of the Oregon Constitution and rely on it to fabricate constitutional barriers to litigation with no support in either the text or history of Oregon's charter of government. As former Justice Linde of this court has explained:

> In sum, rejecting premature or advisory litigation is good policy, but rigid tests of 'justiciability' breed evasions and legal fictions. It is prudent to keep judicial intervention within statutory or established equitable and common law remedies. It is not prudent to link a decision declining adjudication to non-textual, self-created constitutional barriers, and thereby to foreclose lawmakers from facilitating impartial, reasoned resolutions of legal disputes that affect people's public, rather than self-seeking, interests.

Hans A. Linde, *The State and the Federal Courts in Governance: Vive La Différence!,* 46 Wm. & Mary L. Rev. 1273, 1287–88 (2005)....

> Here, the question is whether the legislature has the authority to empower any citizen to act as a private attorney general to enforce public rights.... [T]he Oregon Constitution does not limit the legislature's power to deputize its citizens to challenge government action in the public interest....

> This court's cases ... consistently have held that the legislature can recognize the right of any citizen to initiate a judicial action to enforce matters of public interest.

Questions and Discussion

1. *Lack of "case or controversy" language.* Oregon's lack of a "case or controversy" clause provided the Oregon legislature the room necessary to pass ORS 183.400(1). Does your own jurisdiction have a similar constitution, lacking such language? If so, do the courts in your jurisdiction allow the legislature to adopt open standing provisions?

2. *What are "controversies"?* Even if your jurisdiction's constitution has "case or controversy" language, is it certain that its precedents restrict "controversies" to only those in which there is a *judicially* cognizable injury?

The Public's Right to Enforce Environmental Law
John E. Bonine
HANDBOOK ON ACCESS TO JUSTICE (S. Stec, ed., 2001)

[A.] National legislation for expanded enforcement/standing

Several broad legislative models are used with respect to standing ... *actio popularis;* NGO standing; sufficient interest standing; and legal rights standing.

[1] Actio popularis

Some countries use a model in which legislation declares that "any person" can sue the government when it breaks the law—an *actio popularis*. This is fully consistent with article 9 of the Aarhus Convention, even though it is not required by the Convention.

The Netherlands may well have the least restrictive legislative criteria in Europe for accessing the courts. Furthermore, the Netherlands links administrative standing and judicial standing by allowing "anyone" to participate in the consultation process with a public authority and then granting anyone who has lodged objections at the consultation stage the right to ask a court for judicial review of the decision. Additionally, the Netherlands also extends standing to NGOs in civil lawsuits much like Italy, Switzerland, or many German *Lander*....

The question of standing for judicial review requires consultation of both the General Administrative Law Act and the Environmental Protection Act. [Professor] Betlem explained this as follows:

> The combined effect of these two Acts entitles those who have lodged objections in the consultation stage of the decision making process to apply for judicial review of the decision. Because "anyone" has the right to make reservations in the preparatory phase of the licensing process, a two stage *actio popularis* accordingly applies. In technical legal terms, in the main it [is] so-called "interested persons" who have *locus standi*, including public authorities and non-governmental organisations.

A well-known court case in the Netherlands also recognised NGO standing. In the *Reinwater* case, the highest Dutch court gave environmental organisations standing to sue where (1) the stated purpose of an organisation has been affected, (2) the interests in the lawsuit lend themselves to grouping, and (3) the interests served by the litigation are protected by civil law.

As a final note, environmental NGOs in the Netherlands are allowed to appear in the administrative court (but not the civil court) without being represented by a lawyer. Thus, in practice, many cases in the administrative courts are argued by economists, scientists and engineers.

[2] Legislated NGO standing for recognised NGOs

The second model can be loosely termed *NGO standing*. Under this model, several countries grant a special right to NGOs to file lawsuits without showing that they are personally interested or in some way affected by a decision. Legislation either specifies the characteristics of NGOs that are given standing, or it provides that a state authority will create and maintain a list of NGOs that are automatically granted standing and permitted to take claims of illegal acts by government to the courts.

According to a 1992 study, Switzerland was the first European country to legislate a right of action (or standing to sue) for environmental NGOs. In Switzerland, article 12 of the Federal Nature and Heritage Conservation Act of 1966 allows appeals against administrative decisions to the Supreme Court, for nationwide nature associations. The same can be found in article 55 of the Environmental Protection Act of 1983 for nationwide nature NGOs, provided they were founded at least ten years before the lawsuit and are officially recognised by the federal government. A third law, the Trails and Footpaths Act of 1987, also uses this accreditation procedure.

In Italy, articles 13(1) and 18(5) of Law no. 349 of 1986 grant environmental associations the right to sue in administrative courts if they have been recognised for this purpose in a ministerial decree.

[3] Sufficient interest: Flexible subjective requirements for standing

A third model, *sufficient interest standing,* grants legal standing to those who are "affected" (sometimes "interests" have to be affected). This may be granted either in general terms for all persons, or as a part of granting legislated NGO standing,....

What exactly is the "interest" of an NGO organised to serve a broader public interest, and not the narrow interest of its "owners?" Article 3.4 of the Aarhus Convention answers that, unless there is national legislation imposing special requirements, interest is simply the fact that an NGO is devoted to environmental protection.

In Belgium, legislation requires that a person have an "interest." The courts have generally interpreted the legislation to require that a natural or legal person must show a personal and direct interest in order to have access to any courts. [One case] confronted the question in 1981 of determining whether an NGO's definition of its "interest" in its own statute (charter, or legal registration) could be used in deciding whether it can sue to enforce environmental laws. The Council of State (which hears administrative cases) decided that protection of the environment was a public interest and that an environmental group only needs to represent a point of view that concurs with that of a group interested in the environment.

The Council of State's broadened approach to standing was not followed in the civil courts. In the same year..., the Supreme Court ruled (and has since reaffirmed on numerous occasions) in a civil case involving the same issue and plaintiff that a purpose in an NGO's "statute" *cannot* be considered a personal and direct interest for the purposes of the *civil* courts.

A second method of gaining access to the Council of State to challenge administrative acts is for an NGO to show that its "statutory purpose" is affected by the decision that it is challenging. The question of NGOs satisfying the "personal and direct interest" requirement before the Council of State has continuously arisen in several cases. In [a third case], the Council of State ruled that NGO purposes such as promoting nature conservation and protecting wildlife are only "general" interests and not "personal" ones for the purposes of gaining access to justice; that an interest in nature reserves is not a personal interest if the act being challenged does not directly impact on one of the reserves being operated by the NGO; and that an interest in protecting birds is not sufficient to challenge a decision that will harm frogs.

This question was also fermenting in the Belgian legal system because of legislation adopted in 1993 that sought to broaden access to the courts by NGOs, using a "special procedure." One commentator notes that Belgium's Right of Action Relating to the Protection of the Environment Act of 1993 "recognizes a restricted right in associations: they must be registered as environmental protection associations for at least three years, can challenge specific elements in environmental statutes, and may request either injunctive relief or imposition of preventive measures." ...

In some instances, where legislation recognises broadened standing in environmental cases, the public authority claims that the matter is not environmental, and the broadened standing test therefore does not apply. This was the situation in … the *Balaton Highway Case* [in Hungary]. The Somogy Nature Conservation Organisation was denied standing in cases opposing permits for a new road that would cut through a forest. The courts, including ultimately the Supreme Court, ruled that, even though environmental NGOs have standing without doubt in "environmental" cases, a case related to the construction of a highway is not an "environmental" case. The court apparently ruled that a matter has to be explicitly classified as "environmental" by the Act on Environmental Protection, such as EIA and environmental audit cases.

[4] Legal rights or individual interests: restrictive subjective requirements for standing

Countries using the fourth and oldest model, *legal rights or legal interests standing,* grant legal standing only to those with economic interests, or similar very specific interests, to protect. A variety of terms is used, such as a requirement for a "direct and personal" interest, the "violation of a right," or a "legal interest." It is important to note that a person with an economic interest will usually be admitted into the court under the fourth model, while those with an interest in *non*-economic values or enforcement of the rule of law will often not be able to sue.

The legislation in some jurisdictions appears to restrict standing more explicitly on its face, granting standing only for those with a "direct and individual" or "direct and personal" interest. Interpretations of these terms can vary dramatically, however, as can be seen when comparing decisions of the European Court of Justice and the Council of State of Greece.…

The European Court of Justice refused to take a broad view of standing in environmental matters in the 1998 case *Stichting Greenpeace Council v. European Commission.* Several individuals and NGOs brought suit in the European court of first instance, contesting the legality of EC funding for two fossil fuel-fired power plants being built by Spain in the Canary Islands. The court denied standing. On appeal, the European Court of Justice also denied standing. The relevant provision of the Treaty Establishing the European Community is article 230(4):

> Any natural or legal person may, under the same conditions, institute proceedings against a decision addressed to that person or against a decision which, although in the form of a regulation or a decision addressed to another person, is of direct and individual concern to the former.

The court of first instance said that the individual plaintiffs (including local residents, farmers and fishermen) would not suffer from the decision in any way other than that of other residents of the Canary Islands, and therefore the matter could not be of "direct and individual concern." Furthermore, Greenpeace, as an NGO, could not have standing since it did not simply represent individuals who would have standing, nor did it have some special, individualised interest of its own. Furthermore, participating in prior proceedings was not enough to give Greenpeace a special, individualised interest. The European Court of Justice upheld the lower court. For individuals, it said:

> [T]he specific situation of the applicant was not taken into consideration in the adoption of the act, which concerns him in a general and abstract fashion and in fact, like any other person in the same situation, the applicant is not individually concerned by the act.

As for Greenpeace, its arguments for general public interest standing and about the vacuum in enforcement of EU laws created by restrictive interpretations of article 230 fell on deaf ears. So did its argument that the right to be informed and consulted in an EIA procedure gives it a right to go to court.

In Greece administrative acts can be challenged in front of the Council of State, which is the supreme administrative court in the country. The situation can be compared to that in Belgium, as discussed above. According to a professor of public law and environmental law at the University of Athens, "[t]he jurisprudence of this court, on environmental matters, has been very rich and very innovative, since 1977." The Council of State's jurisdiction over environmental law is based on the fact that article 24 of the Constitution of 1975 makes the protection of the environment an obligation of the state. At the beginning of the 1990s, the Fifth Section, a separate section of the Council of State was created for environmental disputes. The court has annulled illegal administrative acts, suspended the execution of harmful administrative acts, and formulated fundamental environmental principles that have strongly influenced environmental legislation.

Locus standi in front of the Council of State to annul an administrative act is available to both natural and legal persons (organisations and businesses), but only if they prove "a personal, direct and present legal interest." But this "legal interest" has been interpreted by the Council of State to be broader in environmental disputes than in other matters. If a natural person has "any kind of a territorial relation with the area" of environmental damage, the person can have standing. This allows an interest that need not be strictly personal, may be only indirect, and can even be merely potential rather than already in existence. This is based on article 24 of the Constitution which, by creating a *duty* on the state is considered to create a collective and "supra-individual" right.

Traditional legal doctrine in Germany has disfavoured allowing the public to go to court to require the state to abide by the law. As one writer has put it, "German standing doctrine is built on deeply-engrained principles against the general legality view of access to court and the right of citizen groups to challenge administrative action." On the other hand, many of the *Lander*, or states, have been notably more progressive and open toward granting standing to sue, particularly for established environmental NGOs....

Some countries with seemingly restrictive "legal interest" tests have found a way to liberalise standing through interpretation. For example, environmental protection associations have had some success in gaining standing in Norway even though it uses a "legal interest" test. As long ago as the *Alta* case in Norway in 1979, Norges Naturvernforbundet (Norwegian Society for the Preservation of Nature) successfully achieved legal standing. The Norwegian Supreme Court stated:

> It has been accepted under the circumstances that a plaintiff may have a legal interest in bringing an action even though the decision has no direct influence on his own legal position. Depending on the circumstances, also an interest organization may have the required legal interest even though the decision in the matter is of no direct consequences to the organization's or the members' rights. The need for judicial control of the public administration may be the decisive factor here.

According to one scholar, "[t]he grounds in the *Alta* case for accepting the organization's legal interest were the allegations concerning nature conservation interests."

[B.] Judicial interpretations and expanded standing

Legislative changes are not the only means for broadening or narrowing categories of those who can enforce environmental or other laws. The judicial system in many countries has something important to say about standing—whether it is the interpretation of statutes (discussed above), the explicit common law reasoning of England, Wales and Northern Ireland, or the use of constitutional interpretation as a tool.

[1] Common law expansion of standing

A series of decisions made it clear how broad the right of legal standing is in England, at least in environmental cases. The environmental group Greenpeace was granted standing in the *Thorp Nuclear Case* to challenge a proposed licence for a nuclear power plant. The High Court said that Greenpeace was a "responsible and respected body with a genuine concern for the environment" and that the granting of standing to pursue the litigation would save the court's time. Greenpeace would efficiently and effectively represent the interests of 2,500 of its supporters living in the area of the proposed nuclear plant. This may be seen as a kind of "representational standing," or perhaps "third-party standing," in lieu of others who would have had ordinary standing. Judge Otton said:

> I reject the argument that Greenpeace is a "mere" or "meddlesome busybody" ...
> I regard the applicants as eminently respectable and responsible and their genuine interest in the issues raised is sufficient for them to be granted *locus standi*.

Ex parte Richard Dixon continued the liberalisation and the exposition of the viewpoints that public law is about duties, not rights. Justice Sedley wrote:

> Public law is not at base about rights, even though abuses of power may and often do invade private rights; it is about wrongs — that is to say, misuses of public power; and the courts have always been alive to the fact that a person or organisation with no particular stake in the issue or the outcome may, without in any sense being a mere meddler, wish and be well placed to call the attention of the court to an apparent misuse of public power.

[2] Constitutional interpretations expanding standing

The constitutions of a growing number of countries form the basis for increased access to justice through judicial interpretation. Sometimes constitutions are explicit in their *locus standi* provisions, while others have been used by judges to broaden standing.

In Europe, some courts have found that the constitutional rights to a safe environment embody implied rights of access to justice. As the emerging democracies of [Eastern Europe] rewrote their constitutions in the early 1990s in the wake of the fall of Communism, they included two significant types of provisions that are not to be found in the older constitutions of the U.S. or Western European countries.

The first was the right to a safe or healthy environment, while the second proclaimed rights of access to information, public participation and access to the courts....

At least two constitutional courts in [Eastern Europe] have interpreted the right to a safe environment thus far. The Constitutional Court of Slovenia has stated that the right to a healthy environment guarantees at least the right of access to the courts — an abolition of restrictions on standing to sue in environmental matters. The Constitutional Court of Hungary has gone even further.

Section 162 of the Constitution of Slovenia provides that "[a]ny person who can show a proper legal interest, as determined by statute" may bring a case before the Constitutional Court. As recently as 1993, the Constitutional Court explicitly rejected the idea of an *actio popularis* that could allow any person to bring a case based upon an interest in upholding the rule of law. In a typical case the Court said:

> A general interest in ensuring constitutionality and legality and implementing the principles of the Rule of Law is insufficient to fulfill the constitutionally defined

condition for lodging an initiative, since such a wide interpretation of legal interest could be invoked by anyone in any case, whereby the limiting meaning of the second paragraph of Article 162 of the Constitution would be lost. The legal interest of the initiator himself must thus be demonstrated, not just a general social interest in ensuring constitutionality and legality." Without *actio popularis,* however, another legal basis had to be found for environmental matters to come to the Constitutional Court. The question became, then, whether a statute, explicitly or implicitly, has provided a person with a "legal interest.

The Constitutional Court of Slovenia granted standing in a case brought by the Association of Ecologists of Slovenia, a national NGO and 25 individuals.

The NGO achieved standing in large part because the Environmental Protection Act, which came into effect in 1993, provided that the protection of the environment is the responsibility of, inter alia, professional and other NGOs committed to environmental protection. The court therefore concluded that the NGO could bring lawsuits based on its stated purposes. Individuals were also granted standing to sue. The Constitutional Court recognised the legal interest of an individual in such a matter for the first time, on the basis that article 72 of the Constitution contains the right to a healthy environment in which to live. The Court ruled that a person's interest is not limited only to the environment close to the place where he or she lives. Essentially, a right that on its face is substantive was converted by the Court into a procedural right giving access to the judicial process....

The Hungarian Constitution contains a "right to a safe environment" that is similar to that of Slovenia. It is asserted that this right can be used to obtain access to the courts in Hungary....

In fact, in the *Protected Forest Case*, the Constitutional Court of Hungary held that articles 18 and 70/D of the Constitution demand a high level of environmental protection, that citizens can enforce this right, and that the court can overturn a law as unconstitutional if it concludes that it has contravened this right....

Questions and Discussion

1. *NGO standing.* Legislatively granted NGO standing allows particular NGOs standing to sue over environmental concerns. If you are an ordinary citizen of a country that allows NGO standing, is this fair to citizens who are not part of an approved NGO?

Under the specific interest model, does the European Court's logic in *Stichting Greenpeace Council* make sense? Why was Greenpeace's standing denied? Is giving court access only to individuals who are specially affected, as opposed to the general population when it is affected, a good or bad thing? Is there any similarity between the *Stichting Greenpeace Council* decision and previously discussed decisions made by the U.S. Supreme Court?

2. *Court-created restrictions and liberalizations.* The England High Court's decision in the *Thorp Nuclear Case* granted Greenpeace standing because of its "genuine concern for the environment." Compare that to the *Stichting Greenpeace Council* decision above. In the *Thorp* case, the court acknowledged that Greenpeace could "efficiently and effectively" represent all those that would have *normally* had standing in the case. Is judicial efficiency a reason to liberalize standing requirements? (Is judicial inefficiency a reason to restrict standing?)

3. *Leaving it to the legislature.* By far the most common approach to standing to sue in countries other than the United States is to leave the matter to the legislature. Are there

advantages for the rule of law in favor of such an approach? Advantages in terms of democratic choice? Are there potential harms to leaving standing to the legislature? Generally, statutes are easier to change than constitutions. Thus, is legislatively granted standing easier to take away than constitutionally granted standing? Is it easier to grant? Does any of that matter?

4. *Constitutional standing.* While the courts of the United States stand alone in the world in asserting a power to strike down Congressional grants of standing on the basis of asserted constitutional requirements, the courts of several countries have done the opposite: strike down statutory *restrictions* on standing, by interpreting their constitutions as granting broad or unlimited standing. A few constitutions, such as that of Portugal, are clear on their face in recognizing an *actio popularis.* In other countries, such as Chile, the courts have interpreted a constitutional right to a healthy or safe environment as preventing the legislature from restricting standing. See *Comité de Desarrollo de Putre y COD-EFF v. Ministro de Obras Publicas (Recurso de Protección)*, Arica, Corte Suprema, Dec. 19, 1985, Rol. 824. There, in the "Lago Chungará" case, a group of Chilean attorneys was granted standing in a suit filed to protect a high lake in the Andes. The attorneys themselves had never visited the lake. Furthermore, the legislation of Chile restricted standing. However, the court decided that the constitutional guarantee to "every citizen" of a safe environment meant that any citizen in the nation must be allowed to bring court cases in defense of the environment. See Rafael Asenjo, *Innovative Environmental Litigation in Chile: The Case of Chañaral*, 2 Geo. Int'l Envtl. L. Rev. 99 (1989). A suit by a farmer was also successful, the court saying that he had standing in part because the Chilean Constitution's protections for the environment were for the benefit of future generations. See Chapter 3, page 70. Compare this to the *Oposa* case, at the beginning of this chapter, page 317.

5. *"Standing" to sue private parties.* The use of the term "standing" in the United States has been restricted in the past 100 years primarily to lawsuits challenging government action. The similar concept for lawsuits challenging private actions, such as for personal injury or for statutory damages, has instead generally been given the name "cause of action" or "private right of action." Where suits are authorized to be brought by any person against private parties for enforcement of environmental laws since 1970, they have been called "citizen suits." *See, e.g.,* Clean Air Act § 304, 42 U.S.C. § 7604. The idea was first advocated by Professor Joseph Sax, who drafted a law, which was introduced in the Michigan Legislature by Representative Thomas Anderson on April 1, 1969, as Enrolled House Bill No. 3055, Public Act No. 127 of 1970. Joseph L. Sax, DEFENDING THE ENVIRONMENT: A STRATEGY FOR CITIZEN ACTION 247–52 (1970). In July 2007, a conservative 4–3 majority of the Supreme Court of Michigan ruled that under the Michigan Constitution the legislature was powerless to allow open standing. *Michigan Citizens for Water Conservation v. Nestle Waters North America*, 479 Mich. 280, 737 N.W.2d 447 (2007).

6. *Separation of powers.* In the case of legislated NGO standing, is it harmful for the legislature to decide that an individual citizen is permitted to sue government agencies for alleged violations of law without demonstrating a unique interest or injury? Only in the United States have the courts assumed the power to prohibit the national legislature from making such authorizations. What conflicting interests might judges in the United States have that motivate them to control the issue of standing?

2. New International Law on National Standing

The third pillar of the Aarhus Convention on access to justice guarantees implementation of the two previous pillars. Article 9 provides a review procedure by an independent and impartial body established by law. Paragraph 1 provides for review of decisions made under Article 4, involving access to environmental information. Paragraph 2 provides a review procedure related to public participation issues under Article 6 and other relevant provisions of the Convention. Paragraph 3 provides review procedures for acts and omissions of private persons or public authorities concerning national law relating to the environment. Paragraph 4 establishes minimum standards applicable to access to justice procedures: adequate and effective remedies, fairness, timeliness and expenses. Paragraph 5 deals with removal of financial and other barriers to access to justice.

Convention on Access to Information, Public Participation in Decision-Making and Access to Justice in Environmental Matters (Aarhus Convention)
June 25, 1998
U.N. Doc. ECE/CEP/43, 2161 U.N.T.S. 447, 38 I.L.M. 517 (1999)

Article 9
ACCESS TO JUSTICE

1. Each Party shall, within the framework of its national legislation, ensure that any person who considers that his or her request for information under article 4 has been ignored, wrongfully refused, whether in part or in full, inadequately answered, or otherwise not dealt with in accordance with the provisions of that article, has access to a review procedure before a court of law or another independent and impartial body established by law.

In the circumstances where a Party provides for such a review by a court of law, it shall ensure that such a person also has access to an expeditious procedure established by law that is free of charge or inexpensive for reconsideration by a public authority or review by an independent and impartial body other than a court of law.

Final decisions under this paragraph 1 shall be binding on the public authority holding the information. Reasons shall be stated in writing, at least where access to information is refused under this paragraph.

2. Each Party shall, within the framework of its national legislation, ensure that members of the public concerned

(a) Having a sufficient interest or, alternatively,

(b) Maintaining impairment of a right, where the administrative procedural law of a Party requires this as a precondition,

have access to a review procedure before a court of law and/or another independent and impartial body established by law, to challenge the substantive and procedural legality of any decision, act or omission subject to the provisions of article 6 and, where so provided for under national law and without prejudice to paragraph 3 below, of other relevant provisions of this Convention.

What constitutes a sufficient interest and impairment of a right shall be determined in accordance with the requirements of national law and consistently with the objective of giving the public concerned wide access to justice within the scope of this Convention. To this end, the interest of any non-governmental organization meeting the requirements referred to in article 2, paragraph 5, shall be deemed sufficient for the purpose of subparagraph (a) above. Such organizations shall also be deemed to have rights capable of being impaired for the purpose of subparagraph (b) above.

The provisions of this paragraph 2 shall not exclude the possibility of a preliminary review procedure before an administrative authority and shall not affect the requirement of exhaustion of administrative review procedures prior to recourse to judicial review procedures, where such a requirement exists under national law.

3. In addition and without prejudice to the review procedures referred to in paragraphs 1 and 2 above, each Party shall ensure that, where they meet the criteria, if any, laid down in its national law, members of the public have access to administrative or judicial procedures to challenge acts and omissions by private persons and public authorities which contravene provisions of its national law relating to the environment.

4. In addition and without prejudice to paragraph 1 above, the procedures referred to in paragraphs 1, 2 and 3 above shall provide adequate and effective remedies, including injunctive relief as appropriate, and be fair, equitable, timely and not prohibitively expensive. Decisions under this article shall be given or recorded in writing. Decisions of courts, and whenever possible of other bodies, shall be publicly accessible.

5. In order to further the effectiveness of the provisions of this article, each Party shall ensure that information is provided to the public on access to administrative and judicial review procedures and shall consider the establishment of appropriate assistance mechanisms to remove or reduce financial and other barriers to access to justice.

Questions and Discussion

1. *Access to information and public participation.* Article 9, paragraph 1 (also known as Article 9.1), requires that countries that are Parties to the Aarhus Convention must allow any person whose request for information is refused to seek judicial (or equivalent) review. Article 9.2 provides for seeking judicial or equivalent review for issues involving public participation, but is much more complex. The complexities have been explained as follows:

> *Who can ask for a review?— The issue of standing*

> The Convention sets out—as a minimum—that members of the "public concerned" have standing to pursue review in public participation cases. The public concerned is defined in article 2, paragraph 5, as "the public affected or likely to be affected by, or having an interest in, the environmental decision making."...

> Under article 9, paragraph 2, the public concerned must have a "sufficient interest" in the matter under review or maintain an impairment of a right. These two obligations in article 9, paragraph 2 (*a*) and (*b*), are two ways of trying to reach the same result, given the differing legal systems to be accommodated among the Parties....

> Under paragraph 2 (*a*), the Convention raises the question of which members of the public concerned have a sufficient interest. With respect to NGOs meeting the definition of "public concerned," the Convention answers this question itself. The Convention states clearly that NGOs meeting the requirements of article 2, paragraph 5, automatically have "sufficient interest." However, for other persons, including individuals, the Convention allows sufficiency of interest to be determined in accordance with the requirements of national law and consistently with the objective of giving the public concerned wide access to justice.

> In this case the term "in accordance with the requirements of national law" indicates that Parties will most likely find different ways of determining "suffi-

cient interest," depending on constraints that may exist in their national administrative or environmental laws. However, the added requirement that "sufficient interest" should be determined "consistently with the objective of giving the public concerned wide access to justice within the scope of this Convention" indicates that Parties should interpret the application of their national law requirements within the light of the general obligations of the Convention as found in articles 1, 3 and 9.

Paragraph 2 (*b*) was devised for those countries with legal systems that require a person's rights to be impaired before he or she can gain standing.... However, Parties must provide, at a minimum, that NGOs have rights that can be impaired. Meeting the Convention's objective of giving the public concerned wide access to justice ... will require a significant shift of thinking in those countries where NGOs have previously lacked standing in cases because they were held not to have maintained impairment of a right.

Stephen Stec and Susan Casey-Lefkowitz, THE AARHUS CONVENTION: AN IMPLEMENTATION GUIDE 129 (2000).

2. *Review of administrative decisions and suing private defendants.* Article 9.3 involves the question of standing to sue and citizen enforcement against both administrative agencies (public authorities) and private defendants. Consider the next case.

Findings and Recommendations with Regard to Compliance by Belgium

Findings and Recommendations
Communication ACCC/C/2005/11 by
Bond Beter Leefmilieu Vlaanderen VZW (Belgium)
Aarhus Convention Compliance Committee, 16 June 2006
U.N. Doc. ECE/MP.PP/C.1/2006/4/Add.2 (28 July 2006)

INTRODUCTION

On 3 January 2005, the Belgian non-governmental organization Bond Beter Leefmilieu Vlaanderen VZW (BBL; hereinafter the communicant) submitted a communication to the Committee alleging non-compliance by Belgium with its obligations under article 2, paragraph 5, article 3, paragraph 1, and article 9, paragraphs 1 to 4, of the Aarhus Convention.

The communication concerns access to justice for environmental organizations in Belgium. The communicant claims that Belgian legislation and case law do not comply with the "third pillar" of the Convention, namely with the provisions requiring access to justice in environmental matters. More specifically, the concept of "interest" as a criterion for standing before the Belgian judicature is too narrowly interpreted—for example, by the Council of State in cases concerning construction permits and planning decisions. This constitutes a barrier to wide access to justice for environmental organizations....

During the discussion at the ninth meeting, the Communicant ... argued that the case concerned the general issue of standing for environmental organizations, as reflected in the cases referred to. The Party concerned pointed out that it also understood the communication as addressing the legal issue as a whole rather than focusing on individual cases....

I. SUMMARY OF FACTS

The matter concerns access to justice for environmental organizations, as evidenced by legislation and court practice up to the point of the entry into force of the Convention for Belgium. Due to the federal structure of Belgium, the implementation of the Convention involves federal law as well as the laws of the three regions (Flanders, Wallonia and Brussels Capital Region). Environmental and planning laws are part of the regions' competence, and so is the administrative structure for managing these laws…. Legislation concerning standing, access to courts and judicial review as well as the structure of the court system is federal. The criteria for standing are set out in different laws.…

Most important for the present case is the extent to which environmental organizations have access to the Council of State in order to challenge various administrative decisions. When trying a case, the Council of State restricts itself to either set aside the disputed act partially or in its entirety, or to confirm it…. [A]n environmental organization needs to show "either a violation or an interest" in order to have access to the Council of State at all.

The Council of State has taken a less strict position than the Supreme Court in deciding on how to interpret the criterion of "interest." The jurisprudence of the Council of State is set out e.g. in the two most recent cases referred to by the Communicant. As pointed out, both cases were initiated before, but finally decided after the date the Convention entered into force for Belgium. In the first case, Judgment 133.834 of 13 July 2004, environmental organizations asked the Council of State to annul a decision by the Walloon Government concerning an area plan … providing for a landfill. In the second case, Judgment 135.408 of 24 September 2004, environmental organizations asked the Council of State to annul a town planning permit … granted by the Mayor and Deputy Mayors … of the municipality of Grez-Doiceau for certain residential constructions. In both cases, the requests by the environmental organizations were turned down for lack of standing.

It follows from these and other cases that environmental organizations can act before the Council of State if they satisfy the conditions that apply to all natural and legal persons, i.e. to be able to show a direct, personal and legitimate interest as well as a "required quality." This required quality is proven by an organization when it acts in accordance with its statutory goals and these goals do not coincide with the protection of a general interest or a personal interest of its members. Two criteria must be fulfilled in order to appreciate the general character of the organization's statutory goal, a social and a geographical criterion. The case is not admissible if the objective of the organization is so broadly defined that it is not distinct from a general interest. As to the geographical criterion, an act cannot be challenged by an organization if the act refers to a well-defined territory and the activities of the organization are not territorially limited or cover a large geographical area, unless the organization also has a specifically defined social objective. Moreover, an organization whose objective expands to a large territory may only challenge an administrative act if the act affects the entire or a great part of the territory envisaged by the organization's statutes.…

The Communicant and the Party concerned have made references to several judgments by the Council of State to prove their case. The Communicant lists cases where environmental organizations have been denied access to the Council of State, and Belgium in its reply refers to cases where the Council of State admitted standing for environmental organizations.

The Communicant alleges that despite the less strict attitude taken by the Council of State compared with the Supreme Court, even the interpretation by the former is too narrow to comply with article 9 of the Convention. In particular, environmental organizations are denied access to the Council of State when the claim is not brought by a local organization. Because of this various claims by organizations have been declared inadmissible. Also the different jurisprudence of the Supreme Court and Council of State (and the Court of Arbitration) as such complicates predictability. For this reason, the Communicant alleges that Belgium is also not in compliance with the requirement of article 3, paragraph 1, of the Convention, that each Party take the necessary measures to establish and maintain a clear, transparent and consistent framework to implement the provisions of the Convention.

In its reply, the Party concerned argues that the Communicant gives an imbalanced image of Belgian law by its selective citation. According to the Party concerned, the Council of State has often accepted the personal interest or damage of local environmental organizations, and annulled and suspended many decisions concerning hunting and bird protection. The Party concerned also considers the allegation of the Communicant, that the different approaches of the courts are inadequate to provide access to justice for environmental organizations, to be simplistic. The reason why the courts consider the notion of "interest" differently is because the different environmental laws concern different kinds of interests.

II. Consideration and Evaluation by the Committee

Belgium ratified the Convention on 21 January 2003. The Convention entered into force for Belgium on 21 April 2003.

The Communicant has referred to eleven cases decided by various courts in order show that Belgium fails to comply with the Convention.... [T]he Committee notes that none of the cases referred to by the Communicant to prove that Belgium currently fails to comply with the Convention, was initiated after its entry into force for Belgium. Two cases were finally dismissed by the court after the entry into force of the Convention for Belgium, but even these cases had been initiated before a public authority before the entry into force of the Convention.

In both decisions made after the entry into force for Belgium the Council of State actually refers to the Convention. In one of the cases (Judgment 133.834 of 13 July 2004), it explicitly considers that the Convention had not yet entered into force at the date of the requests for the annulment. For this reason, the Committee cannot exclude the possibility that had the Convention entered into force for Belgium; it would also have been considered by the Council of State so as to alter its previous jurisprudence. In the view of the Committee, these cases therefore cannot be used to show that Belgian law, i.e. its court practice, remains the same as before the entry into force and that Belgium is still not complying with the Convention (cf. article 28 of the Vienna Convention on the Law of Treaties).

Nevertheless, the view of the Communicant is based on well-established court practice and a new court practice has not yet been revealed. It is therefore pertinent to consider and evaluate the established practice of the Council of State in the light of the principles on access to justice in the Convention. In this way, the findings of the Committee reveal its views on Belgian law, if the court practice is not altered. For the given reasons, however, even if the Committee will find that the court practice reflected in the given cases is not consistent with the Convention, this will not lead to the conclusion that Belgium is in a state of non-compliance with the Convention.

Nine of the eleven cases referred to are decisions by the Council of State, and almost all of them concern planning decisions.... The Committee therefore limits its findings and evaluation to whether Belgian law, up to the point of entry into force of the Convention, would have provided access to justice for challenging decisions concerning town planning permits and area plans in accordance with the Convention....

The Convention obliges the Parties to ensure access to justice for three generic categories of acts and omissions by public authorities. Leaving aside decisions concerning access to information, the distinction is made between, on the one hand, acts and omissions related to permits for specific activities by a public authority for which public participation is required under article 6 (article 9, paragraph 2) and, on the other hand, all other acts and omissions by private persons and public authorities which contravene national law relating to the environment (article 9, paragraph 3) . It is apparent that the rationales of paragraph 2 and paragraph 3 of article 9 of the Convention are not identical.

Article 9, paragraph 2, applies to decisions with respect to permits for specific activities where public participation is required under article 6. For these cases, the Convention obliges the Parties to ensure standing for environmental organizations. Environmental organizations, meeting the requirements referred to in article 2, paragraph 5, are deemed to have a sufficient interest to be granted access to a review procedure before a court and/or another independent and impartial body established by law. Although what constitutes a sufficient interest and impairment of a right shall be determined in accordance with national law, it must be decided "with the objective of giving the public concerned wide access to justice" within the scope of the Convention.

Article 9, paragraph 3, is applicable to all acts and omissions by private persons and public authorities contravening national law relating to the environment. For all these acts and omissions, each Party must ensure that members of the public "where they meet the criteria, if any, laid down in its national law" have access to administrative or judicial procedures to challenge the acts and omissions concerned. Contrary to paragraph 2 of article 9, however, paragraph 3 does not refer to "members of the public concerned," but to "members of the public."

When determining how to categorize a decision under the Convention, its label in the domestic law of a Party is not decisive. Rather, whether the decision should be challengeable under article 9, paragraph 2 or 3, is determined by the legal functions and effects of a decision, i.e. on whether it amounts to a permit to actually carry out the activity....

Based on the information received from the Party concerned and the Communicant, the Committee understands that decisions concerning area plans do not have such legal functions or effects as to qualify as decisions on whether to permit a specific activity. Therefore, article 9, paragraph 3, is the correct provision to review Belgian law on access to justice with respect to area plans, as provided for in Walloon legislation.

The situation is more complicated with respect to the legal functions and effects of town planning permits as defined by Walloon law.... [I]t is not possible for the Committee to generally conclude whether Belgian law on access to justice for these cases should be assessed in light of article 9, paragraph 2 or 3. Therefore, the Committee will assess the case under both provisions.

In the view of the Committee, the criteria that have been applied by the Council of State with respect to the right of environmental organizations to challenge Walloon town planning permits would not comply with article 9, paragraph 2. As stated, in these cases environmental organizations are deemed to have a sufficient interest to be granted access to a review procedure before a court or an independent and impartial body established by law. Although what constitutes a sufficient interest and impairment of a right shall be determined in accordance with national law, it must be decided "with the objective of giving the public concerned wide access to justice" within the scope of the Convention. As shown by the cases submitted by the Communicant with respect to town planning permits this is not reflected in the jurisprudence of the Council of State. Thus, if the jurisprudence is maintained, Belgium would fail to comply with the article 9, paragraph 2, of the Convention.

To the extent that a town planning permit should not be considered a permit for a specific activity as provided for in article 6 of the Convention, the decision is still an act by a public authority. As such it may contravene provisions of national law relating to the environment. Thus, Belgium is obliged to ensure that in these cases members of the public have access to administrative or judicial procedures to challenge the acts concerned, as set out in article 9, paragraph 3. This provision is intended to provide members of the public with access to adequate remedies against acts and omissions which contravene environmental laws, and with the means to have existing environmental laws enforced and made effective. When assessing the Belgian criteria for access to justice for environmental organizations in the light of article 9, paragraph 3, the provision should be read in conjunction with articles 1 to 3 of the Convention, and in the light of the purpose reflected in the preamble, that "effective judicial mechanisms should be accessible to the public, including organizations, so that its legitimate interests are protected and the law is enforced."

While referring to "the criteria, if any, laid down in national law," the Convention neither defines these criteria nor sets out the criteria to be avoided. Rather, the Convention is intended to allow a great deal of flexibility in defining which environmental organizations have access to justice. On the one hand, the Parties are not obliged to establish a system of popular action ("actio popularis") in their national laws with the effect that anyone can challenge any decision, act or omission relating to the environment. On other the hand, the Parties may not take the clause "where they meet the criteria, if any, laid down in its national law" as an excuse for introducing or maintaining so strict criteria that they effectively bar all or almost all environmental organizations from challenging act or omissions that contravene national law relating to the environment.

Accordingly, the phrase "the criteria, if any, laid down in national law" indicates a self-restraint on the parties not to set too strict criteria. Access to such procedures should thus be the presumption, not the exception. One way for the Parties to avoid a popular action ("actio popularis") in these cases, is to employ some sort of criteria (e.g. of being affected or of having an interest) to be met by members of the public in order to be able to challenge a decision. However, this presupposes that such criteria do not bar effective remedies for members of the public....

When evaluating whether a Party complies with article 9, paragraph 3, the Committee pays attention to the general picture, namely to what extent national law effectively has such blocking consequences for environmental organizations, or if there are remedies available for them to actually challenge the act or omission in question.... This evaluation is not limited to the wordings in legislation, but also includes jurisprudence of the Council of State itself.

Up to the point of entry into force of the Convention for Belgium, the general criteria for standing of environmental organizations before the Council of State have not differed from those of natural persons. According to this practice, to be able to challenge a town planning permit or a plan before the Council of State, an environmental organization must thus claim *a direct, personal, and legitimate interest*. It must also prove that, when acting in accordance with its *statutory goals*, the goals do not coincide with the protection of a general interest or a personal interest of its members. Hence, federations of environmental organizations have generally not been able to meet this criterion, since their interest is not seen as distinct from the interests of its members. Moreover, according to this practice, two criteria must be fulfilled in order to appreciate the general character of the organization's statutory goal, a social and a geographical criterion. The case is not admissible if the objective of the organization is so broadly defined that it is not distinct from a general interest. As to the *geographical criterion*, an act cannot be challenged by an organization if the act refers to a well-defined territory and the activities of organization are not territorially limited or cover a large geographical area, unless the organization also has a specifically defined social objective. Furthermore, an organization whose objective expands to a large territory may only challenge an administrative act if the act affects the entire or a great part of the territory envisaged by the organization's statutes.

The Convention does not explicitly refer to federations of environmental organizations. If, in the jurisdiction of a Party, standing is not granted to such federations, it is possible that, to the extent that member organizations of the federation are able to effectively challenge the act or omission in question, this may suffice for complying with article 9, paragraph 3. If, on the other hand, due to the criteria of a direct and subjective interest for the person, no member of the public may be in a position to challenge such acts or omissions, this is too strict to provide for access to justice in accordance with the Convention. This is also the case if, for the same reasons, no environmental organization is able to meet the criteria set by the Council of State.

The Convention does not prevent a Party from applying general criteria of the sort found in Belgian legislation. However, even though the wordings of the relevant Belgian laws do not as such imply a lack of compliance, the jurisprudence of the Belgian courts, as reflected in the cases submitted by the Communicant, implies a too restrictive access to justice for environmental organizations. In its response, the Party concerned contends that the Communicant "presents an unbalanced image by its "strategic use" of jurisprudence," and that "the difficulties that the BBL experiences by the Communicant to bring an action in court are not representative for environmental NGOs in general." In the view of the Committee, however, the cases referred to show that the criteria applied by the Council of State so far seem to effectively bar most, if not all, environmental organizations from challenging town planning permits and area plans that they consider to contravene national law relating to the environment, as under article 9, paragraph 3. Accordingly, in these cases, too, the jurisprudence of the Council of State appears too strict. Thus, if maintained by the Council of State, Belgium would fail to provide for access to justice as set out in article 9, paragraph 3, of the Convention. By failing to provide for effective remedies with respect to town planning permits and decisions on area plans, Belgium would then also fail to comply with article 9, paragraph 4.

In this context, the Committee notes that the Party concerned, in its reply, makes two points that concern a State's internal law and constitutional structure in relation to its obligation under international law to observe and comply with a treaty.... First, the Party concerned holds that the federal structure of the Belgian State sometimes complicates the implementation of the Convention. Second, it argues that the separation of powers between the legislative, executive, and judicial branches of government, as a fundamental part of the Belgian State, should be taken into account. The Committee therefore wishes to stress that its review of the Parties' compliance with the Convention is an exercise governed by international law. As a matter of general international law of treaties, codified by article 27 of the 1969 Vienna Convention on the Law of Treaties, a State may not invoke its internal law as justification for failure to perform a treaty. This includes internal divisions of powers between the federal government and the regions as well as between the legislative, executive, and judicial branches of government. Accordingly, the internal division of powers is no excuse for not complying with international law.

An independent judiciary must operate within the boundaries of law, but in international law the judicial branch is also perceived as a part of the state. In this regard, within the given powers, all branches of government should make an effort to bring about compliance with an international agreement. Should legislation be the primary means for bringing about compliance, the legislature would have to consider amending or adopting new laws to that extent. In parallel, however, the judiciary might have to carefully analyse its standards in the context of a Party's international obligation, and apply them accordingly.

The Committee also recalls that according to article 3, paragraph 1, the Parties shall take the necessary legislative, regulatory, and other measures to establish and maintain a clear, transparent and consistent framework to implement the provisions of the Convention. This too reveals that the independence of the judiciary, which is indeed presumed and supported by the Convention, cannot be taken as an excuse by a Party for not taking the necessary measures....

III. Conclusions

Having considered the above, the Committee adopts the findings and recommendations set out in the following paragraphs.

A. *Main findings with regard to non-compliance*

Since all the court decisions submitted by the Communicant refer to cases initiated before the entry into force of the Convention for Belgium, they cannot be used to show that the practice has not been altered by the very entry into force of the Convention. Therefore, the Committee is not convinced that Belgium fails to comply with the Convention. However, as evidenced by the consideration and evaluation of the Committee, if the jurisprudence of the Council of State is not altered, Belgium will fail to comply with article 9, paragraphs 2 to 4, of the Convention by effectively blocking most, if not all, environmental organizations from access to justice with respect to town planning permits and area plans....

The Committee appreciates the statement in the reply from Belgium to the effect that it continues to make efforts and is open to improvements on its implementation of the Convention.

B. *Recommendations*

While the Committee is not convinced that the Party concerned fails to comply with the Convention, it considers that a new direction of the jurisprudence of the Council of State should be established; and notes that no legislative measures have yet been taken to alter the jurisprudence of the Council of State. It also notes that the Party concerned agrees that the Committee take the measure referred to in paragraph 37 (b) of the annex to decision I/7.

Therefore, the Committee, pursuant to paragraph 36 (b) of the annex to decision I/7, recommends the Party concerned to: (a) Undertake practical and legislative measures to overcome the previous shortcomings reflected in the jurisprudence of the Council of State in providing environmental organizations with access to justice in cases concerning town planning permits as well as in cases concerning area plans; and (b) Promote awareness of the Convention, and in particular the provisions concerning access to justice, among the Belgian judiciary.

Questions and Discussion

1. *The Council of State's jurisprudence.* Would the criteria of a "direct, subjective and legitimate interest" and "geographical criterion"—set by the Council of State of Belgium in its jurisprudence before the Aarhus Convention entered into force for Belgium—be sufficient to comply with the Aarhus Convention?

2. *Standing under Aarhus.* Note the special standing that the Aarhus Convention requires its ratifying nations to give to environmental NGOs. What is the difference between standing to sue for NGOs under Article 9.2 and NGO standing under 9.3 of the Aarhus Convention? What is the purpose for the distinction? Under either section, is it necessary to have a "sufficient interest" or to be individually affected? How does all this compare to the doctrine of standing to sue in U.S. federal courts? With the trends in Australian jurisprudence?

3. *An organization's goals.* In reviewing the current state of Belgian law, the Committee describes a two-pronged test that NGOs must meet to establish standing before the Council of State. Is the distinction between a "general interest" and "personal interest" judicially manageable? Under this system, is it necessary to live in the affected area to establish standing? Would an NGO with a Post Office box in a given jurisdiction meet the geographic requirement? Could an umbrella NGO located in the capital of the county defend the interests of affected local people in a court far away from the headquarters of the organization? From the NGO's standpoint, is it an advantage in terms of standing to have a limited membership, or many members? If the issue before the Council of State was multidisciplinary in nature, might a given NGO be limited to briefing the Council of State solely on the issues related to their statutory goals (e.g. environmental degradation issues but not social relocation inequities).

4. *Sufficient interest.* What is a "sufficient interest"? According to the Convention "a sufficient interest and impairment of a right shall be determined in accordance with national law and consistently with the objective of giving the concerned public concerned wide access to justice." What are the implications, in terms of interpreting the convention, of the convention giving deference to national law, then limiting this deference with a broadly worded modifier? To what extent can nations limit NGO standing under Aarhus? Can national law completely limit the availability of courts to those whose "rights" are impaired?

5. *The Committee's non-decision.* Did the Compliance Committee find Belgium in compliance or non-compliance with Articles 9.2 and 9.3 of the Convention? Or something in between? Is the Committee sidestepping a difficult issue, or showing a salutary self-restraint?

6. *Advice from the Committee.* The Committee states that "if the jurisprudence of the Council of State is not altered, Belgium will fail to comply with article 9, paragraphs 2 to 4, of the Convention." Is there a risk for an international compliance committee to give this kind of advice to national judges? Is there a greater risk if it *fails* to give such advice? Are there reasons that some courts (such as federal courts in the U.S.) purport to refrain from offering explicit advisory opinions like this? Is it really any different if courts include *obiter dicta* in their opinions? Is the Aarhus Compliance Committee in a different position that a court?

7. *Actio popularis.* What is "actio popularis"? Are countries obliged by the Aarhus Convention to include this doctrine in their national laws? To some extent?

Summary Report on the Inventory of EU Member States' Measures on Access to Justice in Environmental Matters

Esther Pozo Vera, Nathy-Rass Masson, & Ludwig Krämer
Milieu-Environmental Law and Policy, for European Union DG Environment
(Study Contract No 07-010401/2006/450607/MAR/A1)
(September 2007)

1. Introduction

  1.1. Background ...

Article 9 of the Aarhus Convention deals with the so-called third pillar of access to justice and it is by far the most challenging aspect in the implementation of the Aarhus Convention. The third provision (Article 9(3) of the Convention) requires the Parties to grant access to justice in cases of actions and omissions by private persons and public authorities which contravene national law relating to the environment....

A decision recently issued by the Compliance Committee of the Aarhus Convention [*Findings and Recommendations with Regard to Compliance by Belgium*, above at page 343] provided a first interpretation of Article 9(3) and related provisions of the Aarhus Convention. The Committee differentiated between Article 9(2) of the Convention, which refers to "members of the public concerned," and Article 9(3), which refers to "members of the public." The Committee considered that the provision should be interpreted as including environmental organisations, and entitling members of the public to "adequate remedies against acts and omissions which contravene environmental laws." The Committee completed the analysis of Article 9(3) by interpreting the expression "the criteria, if any, laid down in national law." The Compliance Committee, while reiterating that the Convention does not require to "establish a system of popular action in their national laws," indicated that "the Parties may not take the clause ... as an excuse for introducing or maintaining so strict criteria that they effectively bar all or almost all environmental organizations from challenging acts or omissions that contravene national law relating to the environment."

The EU [European Union] Member States belong to different traditions with some of them granting a broad access to justice (including *actio popularis*) and others having a more limited approach. The differences among Member States may have impacts in the overall implementation of the third pillar of the Convention within the EU....

2.2. Legal standing

  2.2.1. General overview

The issue of legal standing is essential for access to justice. The criteria for standing are very different from Member State to Member State. In general, individuals need to show the impairment of a right (*e.g.*, property, health, procedural rights) or that they have a sufficient interest (*e.g.*, geographic vicinity) to be granted standing. In some cases, NGOs meeting certain criteria are considered "privileged applicants" and do not have to show an interest to challenge acts or omissions before administrative boards or courts. In other cases, associations and organisations (including NGOs) have to show the impairment of a right or an interest, as any other individual, the interpretations given by courts to the concept of "interest" differing from one Member State to another.

Despite these differences, it is possible to group Member States depending on the main criterion established by law or used by the courts to recognise *locus standi*.

- *Actio popularis*

Some countries provide for an *actio popularis*. This is the case in Portugal, which is probably the country with the widest accessibility to administrative and judicial remedies. The Portuguese Constitution recognises an *actio popularis* in judicial procedures for the protection of diffuse interests including public health, consumers' rights, quality of life, preservation of the environment and cultural heritage and so on. This right does not differentiate between national and foreign individuals or organisations. *Actio popularis* is also recognised in administrative procedures but only to challenge administrative decisions on plans, location and execution of works, and public investment. In the remaining cases, persons (legal or individual) challenging decisions using the administrative route will have to show an interest, which can be collective or diffuse.

However, Portugal is not the only example of *actio popularis*. In the UK, Ireland and Latvia, the broad interpretation given by the courts to the concept of "interest" has led to *de facto* recognition of an *actio popularis*. In Spain, *actio popularis* exists for land use planning, coastal waters, national parks and criminal law. In Estonia, *actio popularis* exists for land use planning. In Slovenia, for civil law suits, the Environmental Protection Law also grants broad access to civil courts to citizens acting as individuals or through societies, associations and organisations.

- *Impairment of a right and sufficient interest*

In most countries, those challenging an action or omission of the administration in breach of environmental legislation have to show an interest. Alongside the traditional interpretation of the concept of "interest" as individual, direct, actual and legitimate, some Member States have broadened the scope of the concept to *cover diffuse and collective interests*, thus granting legal standing to organisations or groups representing and defending those interests. In other cases, the interpretation of the concept of "interest" is similar to the *concept of the public concerned* mentioned in the Aarhus Convention.

(a) Strict interpretation

The countries where a strict interpretation of the concept of "interest" applies are Austria, Belgium, Germany and Malta (and Slovenia). In Germany and Austria the claimant has to show that he or she is "directly concerned," meaning that a "subjective right" has been affected by the decision. The interpretation is very strict in practice and, in Austria, for example, with the exception of waste management and IPPC facilities, members of the public can do little more than encourage the administration to change a decision.

In Belgium, the jurisprudence of the Supreme Court and the Council of State have reduced the scope of the concept of concerned person, making it difficult for NGOs to have access to justice. Neighbours and individuals, however, will more easily be granted standing. Only NGOs whose aim is environmental protection in a specific, geographically circumscribed area in which the effects of the challenged act are likely to be localised or NGOs specialised in a very specific aspect of environmental protection have any chance of meeting the criteria for standing. If the statutory purposes of the NGO are too general in their wording, they will not have legal standing....

In Malta, individuals will normally have access to court (because they can show the impairment of a right or be individually concerned due to geographical links and so on). The main problem for NGOs and citizens' organisations is that one of the criteria for legal standing is to have legal personality. NGOs do not have legal personality in Malta and thus have no legal standing....

Finally, some countries (The Netherlands and Poland) are limiting access to justice by excluding the right to appeal certain decisions. In the Netherlands, there is a so-called "negative list," *i.e.*, a list of decisions against which no appeal is available. This prohibition is an additional hurdle, i.e., even parties having a legal interest may be denied access to the appeal procedure. In Poland, decisions on building and emission permits can only be contested by the addressees, excluding any other appellant.

(b) Broad interpretation of interest: diffuse/collective interest, geographic connection, the objectives of the association

Countries where the concept of "interest" has been broadened to recognise "collective" and "diffuse" interests are the Netherlands, Lithuania, Italy and Spain. In some cases, the specific collective interest (in this case, protection of the environment or related) has to be spelled out in the statutes of the organisation. However, this is not a condition *sine qua non* in the Netherlands, Spain or Italy, which allow *ad-hoc* citizens' associations or platforms to have legal standing.

In Italy, associations not meeting specific criteria for standing (privileged associations) will have to show an interest, the defence of a *collective interest or diffuse interest* being enough. Geographic proximity will be one of the elements proving that the association or individual has an interest in a specific case. The same rule applies in Spain for those cases where *actio popularis* does not apply or where an NGO does not meet the requirements to be granted "privileged" access to justice. In the Netherlands, judicial remedies are possible provided the association shows it protects the interest of the members, including the environmental interest....

In Lithuania, the problem derives from the lack of uniform interpretation by the courts of the concept of "interest"; in some cases this is broad, in others strict, which creates a situation of legal uncertainty.

In many cases a geographical criterion will also be needed to have standing or to be considered "individually concerned." This criterion allows neighbours and municipalities to be granted standing in almost all countries (with the exception of cases where no appeal is possible or appeal is limited to the addressees of a decision). The geographical criterion will also play a significant role in the recognition of NGOs standing in some countries, *alone or combined with the existence of a collective/diffuse interest* (*e.g.*, Greece, Cyprus, France and Hungary)....

In France, individuals will have to show a direct, personal and legitimate interest. The geographical criterion will be important to establish "interest" in a particular case, allowing for neighbours and municipalities to have standing. In the case of associations, with the exception of the specific regime established for "recognised NGOs" (see below), declared associations will have *locus standi* provided they represent a collective interest and there is a geographical connection with a particular case....

Finally, in some countries, the way the objectives and purposes of an association have been laid down in the statutes will be essential to be granted standing. In these cases, there must be a connection between the law governing the contested decision and the field of activities of the specific association (*e.g.*, Denmark). In Denmark, NGOs will have standing in court provided there is a connection between the law governing the dispute (*e.g.*, waste management act) and the specific objectives indicated by the NGO in its statutes (*e.g.*, waste production prevention).

- *Standing based on procedural rights*

A significant group of countries is formed by those Member States where legal standing is based on participation or the existence of a right to participate in the decision making process. The broader the situations where public participation is possible, the broader the possibilities are for standing....

In Finland, Germany and Poland, NGOs will have to meet certain criteria to be able to participate in the administrative decision making process, which will afterwards give them the right to challenge the decision. In Finland, NGOs have to be registered, must promote health and environmental protection and have a geographical connection with the area in which the decision will produce its effects. In Germany, NGOs have to have carried out a prior registration by filing an application, must have as their main purpose nature protection, should be active in more than one Land, must have existed for at least 3 years and must have open membership.

In Poland, however, NGOs have easier access to participation in the decision making process in EIA and IPPC cases, and more difficult access in other environmental cases. The criteria in Poland are to act in the field of environmental protection and to have a geographical link. However, these are only a formal (not actual) requirement, i.e., it is sufficient if the NGO states in its statutes that it can be active in the territory of the entire country (the majority of NGOs have such a provision in their statutes).

In Austria, registered NGOs will have access to justice but only for procedures concerning waste facilities. NGOs can be registered if they have existed for at least 3 years, its purpose is to protect the environment and has a non-profit status.

- *Countries with a system granting "privileged" status to environmental NGOs*

In addition, some Member States have acknowledged the specificity of environmental claims carried out by NGOs and have widely recognised their legal standing to challenge action/omissions by the administration, either in general or only for certain claims. This approach is similar to the "qualified entities" recognised in the proposal for a Directive on access to justice.

In Greece, France, Italy and Spain NGOs meeting the criteria laid down by the law will have legal standing to challenge actions and omissions by the administration without having to show an interest. In general some years of existence (3 or 5) are required as well as protection of the environment as the main purpose laid down in their statutes. In some cases democratic rules are also required. However, criteria vary from country to country....

In Luxembourg, recognised associations in the area of environment have special legal standing for procedures on classified facilities, air pollution, water protection, nature protection and waste management, *inter alia*.

In Sweden, NGOs with three years of activities in Sweden, aiming at the protection of the environment, open to the public and democratic and with 2000 members have privileged status to contest decisions on permits, approvals and exceptions. However, most of the decisions that can be appealed under Chapter 16 sec.13 of the Environmental Code are permit-related actions and omissions, therefore falling under Article 9(2) of the Aarhus Convention. As a consequence, in practice, NGOs have only limited possibilities to contest supervisory actions and omissions by the administration falling under Article 9(3) of the Aarhus Convention. Only certain exceptions and approvals (*e.g.*, chemicals-related decisions) can be contested. From August 1, [2007,] NGOs meeting the criteria mentioned above will be able to contest supervisory decisions (including omissions or zero decisions) but only in contaminated land cases. This is a consequence of the transposition in Swedish law of the Environmental Liability Directive (which is outside of the scope of this study)....

In Slovenia, NGOs have privileged legal standing in administrative cases only for nature conservation cases. NGOs have also broad access to civil courts if they are acting in the interest of nature conservation or in the public interest of environmental protection....

Finally, Portugal has provided for specific rules on standing for administrative review of plans, locations, execution of works and public investments.

2.2.2. Conclusions

Legal standing seems to be a significant obstacle for individuals and associations to challenge actions/omissions by the administration in Austria, Belgium, Germany and Malta, although in Malta the situation is expected to change soon. Access to justice is limited to very specific cases in Germany and Finland (especially for members of the public).

Sometimes limits to access to justice stem from attempts by the administration to limit the cases where participation in the decision-making process is required or by limiting the concept of "participant." This is the case in the Czech Republic, Hungary and Slovakia. In these countries, the administration has tried to limit actions by members of the public by restricting public participation in cases where previously this participation was required.

In other cases, problems with respect to standing derive from the strict conditions that organisations have to meet to be considered "privileged applicants," *i.e.*, "NGOs acting in public interest." This problem has been reported in Sweden and Slovenia, in the latter case only for administrative remedies, judicial remedies remaining accessible.

Finally, in some countries, specific acts have been exempted from any challenge. This is the case in the Netherlands, where "negative lists" of acts that cannot be contested have been created (*e.g.* decisions on the Schipol airport). Similarly in Poland, certain decisions on building and emissions permits can only be contested by the addressees, excluding any other appellant.

Questions and Discussion

1. *Compliance Committee challenges.* With its Member States having such a diverse set of standing requirements, what are potential challenges facing the European Union? Could complaints be pursued successfully before the European Court of Human Rights under any theory? Before the Aarhus Convention Compliance Committee for violations of Article 9?

2. *Public participation equals standing?* Some of the countries listed above grant standing to only those persons who participated in the administrative decision making process. Why should standing be limited to only those who became involved early in the process? Recall the discussions in Chapter 7 about restrictions on who *can* participate in the administrative processes. Conversely, if a person *does* gain access to the administrative process, that fact in some countries can ensure legal standing in court. In the United States, jurisprudence sometimes requires public participation and specific comments as a precondition to raising issues later in court. However, commenting on proposed agency decisions does not ensure legal standing in federal court (although it does in some state courts). Should the U.S. consider restricting public access to the decision making process,

but ensuring standing to those who participate? On the other hand, should public comment opportunities be open to everyone even if they lack standing later to challenge a decision in court? What are the arguments on various sides of these questions?

B. Financial Barriers to Access to Justice

Access to Justice in Environmental Matters (2003)

Nicolas de Sadeleer, Gerhard Roller, & Miriam Dross[a]
E.U. Doc. ENV.A.3/ETU/2002/0030 (2003)

1 Introduction

1.1 Background to the study

Public participation and access to justice in environmental matters have been on the agenda of the European Community for a number of years now. The EC signed the UN-ECE Aarhus Convention in 1998.... The Convention obliges the Contracting Parties to implement information, participation and litigation rights for individuals and environmental associations.... [T]he [European] Commission ordered a study to assess recent developments and the current situation concerning access to justice in environmental matters in selected member states. These member states are Belgium, Denmark, France, Germany, Italy, Netherlands, Portugal and the UK....

2 Main empirical findings on access to justice ...

2.1 Overall number of cases ...

[T]he actual number of environmental association law-suits is ... revealing when put in perspective against the overall number of court proceedings in a given country. For example, in Germany the number of actions brought by environmental NGOs before the administrative courts, which are the only venue possible for a public interest action in Germany, represents only 0.0148% of all the cases the administrative courts decided between 1996 and 2001. This result can be seen also in the figures for Belgium. While the Belgian Council of State decided around 30,000 cases between 1996 and 2001, only 101 related to environmental matters brought by NGOs.

But even in countries which provide as a matter of law for a very broad access to the courts in environmental matters, the actual number of cases brought by NGOs is limited....

As a general proposition, it may confidently be said that the introduction of or expansion of the possibilities for environmental associations to bring or participate in such court proceedings will not automatically result in the courts being overloaded, a point so often asserted....

4 Conditions for access to justice

4.5 Costs

An important factor for environmental associations when considering whether to bring an action is the question of the expenses it might face at the end of the proceeding. Among the costs, one can make a distinction between:

- court fees
- expert and witnesses fees

---

a. Report Commissioned by the European Commission, ENV.A.3/ETU/2002/0030.

- fees of party's own lawyer
- winning's party lawyer's fees if the petitioner is losing the case (e.g. Denmark, Germany, United Kingdom, the Netherlands in civil cases).

Only the Portuguese and the Danish legislation exempts NGOs from court fees (in Portugal in the proceedings where they take part as plaintiff or assistant to the prosecution; in Denmark before the appeal boards). In the UK, it is possible that the courts will make no order as to costs against an environmental NGO if they consider the action to be in the public interest.

Generally, the court fees do not pose a major problem because they are rather modest or at least affordable in all countries. It is especially the fees for lawyers and experts, where needed, and the "loser pays principle" that have a decisive impact on the costs of a claim. For example in the UK, having to pay the costs of the other side in the event of losing the case was called the single most effective barrier to access to justice in environmental cases. Sometimes lawyers or experts are working pro bono for environmental NGOs (Portugal and the UK) but this is not the rule....

Thus, in practice the costs are one of the main obstacle for NGOs to sue polluters or to seek redress. If the procedure is too expensive or entails the risk for the NGOs to pay the costs for the counter party in case of a loss, the NGO will seek other means to solve the problem. For instance, the fact that there are only few civil actions brought by Dutch NGOs is due to the considerable risk to compensate the winning party. In Germany and the UK, bringing public interests actions has also involved a high risk of costs for NGOs....

Shortage of funds may explain that very few actions have been brought in some member states to the courts even though the conditions for standing are rather flexible....

6 Policy recommendations ...

(13) Costs for public interest law suits have to be reduced

One finding of this study is that costs can represent a major hurdle for environmental associations wishing to bring public interest actions. This is especially the case in countries where the losing party has, in principle, to bear the costs of the winning party, as the perception of NGOs can well be that the risks in bringing a law-suit are too high.

It may be said that it is open to question why NGOs should have to bear costs in public interest actions as in these proceedings they represent interests of the general public as opposed to private interests.

A new directive [from the European Union] should provide that NGOs do not have to bear the fees of the other side if the action is lost. It may be noted that the minimum requirement of Art. 9(4) of the Aarhus Convention that forbids "prohibitively expensive" procedures has a particular resonance for environmental associations which rely on donations and membership fees to finance law-suits.

Removing Barriers and Providing Incentives for Citizen Enforcement of Environmental Laws

John E. Bonine
4th IUCN Acad. Envt'l L. Colloquium, New York
(16–20 October 2006)

In country after country around the world, a common complaint is heard: "We have environmental laws, but they are not really enforced." Among the reasons are the power and influence wielded by business enterprises, which discourage public authorities from enforcing or applying laws that restrict or guide the activities of private companies and government officials. The most important problem is not legal standing-to-sue, but the lack of funding for citizens' enforcers. Added to this lack are the risks that citizens will have to pay industry lawyers or even governments if they bring an enforcement or judicial review case and lose. These problems are almost never acknowledged by governments that purport to be concerned with improving access to justice. But they ultimately block such improvements from having significant effect....

A potential litigant who simply wants environmental laws to be applied or enforced will normally not benefit financially through the litigation, yet litigating a case to protect the environment can be prohibitively expensive, even if a person or NGO does not have the risk of paying the lawyers on the *other* side of the case. (In countries with the "loser pays" policy, the person or nongovernmental organization thinking about filing a lawsuit to enforce the law must also evaluate the possibility of losing and being responsible for the attorney fees of the winning side.)

I. Low Numbers of Citizen Enforcers

The most successful examples of citizen and NGO enforcement are in the United States, where about 250 environmental lawyers have funding to bring litigation to the courts on behalf of citizens or nongovernmental groups. Another 250 environmental lawyers have regular, funded employment for the purpose of advancing environmental concerns but do not litigate. An additional 250 are "private public interest lawyers" working for environmental causes on a regular basis while practicing private law in small firms that do not represent major economic interests. (*See* John E. Bonine, *The New Private Public Interest Bar,* 1 J. of Envir. L. & Litig. 1 (1986).) The number of lawyers in large firms willing to litigate on behalf of environmental groups as "*pro bono*" work is minuscule. Many corporate clients of such firms do not tolerate their lawyers volunteering to do such work, so it is rare. The number of public interest environmental lawyers is dwarfed by the country's 20,000 to 30,000 environmental lawyers who are working for businesses. Those business environmental lawyers also dwarf the number of lawyers working for governments at all levels. Possibly 1,500 environmental lawyers work for the U.S. Government in various departments and agencies and perhaps another 500 work in State or local government bodies. A recent study for the European Commission by law professors and experts concluded that "even in countries which provide as a matter of law for a very broad access to the courts in environmental matters, the actual number of cases brought by NGOs is limited." Latin America has a similar imbalance. In a region of 460 million people, only about 20–25 environmental lawyers receive funding on a regular basis in nongovernmental organizations in Latin America and the Caribbean to enforce environmental laws for citizens in the courts.

II. Funding for NGO Lawyers and Experts

Relying on private lawyers or law professors to donate their time for litigation is hardly a stable or predictable model for helping the public enforce environmental laws on a continuing basis. The only options, therefore, are funding by the government or by private, philanthropic foundations.

A. Government funding

Legal aid for environmental cases exists in a few places. In Australia, most state governments support "Environmental Defenders Offices" (EDOs). The lawyers in these offices are expected to represent the interests of the diffuse public in environmental matters. They bring cases against state bodies and private enterprises for violations of environmental laws. In England, lawyers can apply to government-funded Legal Aid schemes when their clients are in poverty, although this is neither simple nor financially very rewarding. Change may eventually come elsewhere. Forty-one countries in Europe, the Caucasus, and Central Asia, have committed themselves under the Aarhus Public Participation Convention to "consider the establishment of appropriate assistance mechanisms to remove or reduce financial and other barriers to access to justice." Article 9, paragraph 5. The Parties also agree to make court procedures "free of charge or inexpensive." Article 9, paragraph 1.

B. Philanthropic foundation funding

In the United States private, philanthropic foundations provide financial support for some NGO law firms to litigate on behalf of the environment. In most of the world, however, such sources of support appear to be rare or non-existent. In fact, it appears that almost every NGO law firm in Latin America has to rely on grants from philanthropic foundations in the U.S.A. As for Western Europe, it is hard to find any such philanthropic support at all.

Litigators who work for NGOs to enforce environmental laws have to find ways to be efficient with the limited resources that they have. One method that they have adopted is the creation of the Environmental Law Alliance Worldwide (E-LAW). *See* www.elaw.org. This network of public interest litigators [co-founded by one co-author and including the other co-author of this textbook] consists of colleagues who are personally committed to helping each other across national borders. Working quietly in the background, the network enables NGO litigators to share legal and scientific expertise with one another. NGO litigators in 70 countries can consult with 300 other lawyers and some scientists on all continents.

III. Why Doesn't the "Loser Pays" Policy Help Citizens?

Some may speculate that individuals, NGOs, or lawyers interested in enforcing the environmental laws could finance lawsuits through the "loser-pays" policy that applies in one form or another throughout much of Latin America, Europe, Asia, and Africa[b] (although not in the United States). Instead of being a help, however, the policy is a significant barrier to access to justice when it is applied as a routine matter. It discourages potential middle-class plaintiffs more than others, because they have something to lose personally but no equivalent personal benefit to gain from winning a lawsuit whose purpose is not for economic compensation but to demand compliance with the law. As for the supposed positive side, even the lawyers for the environmental plaintiffs cannot count on an award of their fees at the end of a successful case if the award is discretionary with the court. On the other hand, in many countries the "loser pays" policy does not apply in administrative law cases. In Spain, a losing litigant in the administrative court of first instance has no obligation to pay the fees of the government attorneys on the winning side, except in cases of bad faith or *temeridad*.

IV. The "American Rule" and "Modified American Rule"

A. The "American Rule"—half an answer

Both the federal courts in the United States of America and the courts of every State except for Alaska follow a completely different policy from the "loser pays" policy that is

---

b. A few of the countries that follow the policy include Argentina, Australia, Austria, Brazil, Canada, Chile, Colombia, Costa Rica, Denmark, Dominican Republic, France, Germany, Greece, Hungary, India, Italy, Iran, Kenya, Luxembourg, Malaysia, Mexico, the Netherlands, New Zealand, Poland (in civil courts), Portugal, Romania, Sweden, Switzerland, Turkey, and Yemen.

prevalent in much of the world. Under the so-called "American Rule" losing individuals, NGOs, and businesses are ordinarily *not* obligated to pay the costs of the attorneys on the winning side. This solves half of the problem.

B. The "modified American Rule"—the rest of the answer

While not having to pay the other side's attorney fees allows far more public interest environmental litigation in the United States than in other countries—by reducing the risks—it still leaves the problem that citizens or groups have in paying lawyers to represent them. To some degree this has been solved by a kind of "modified American rule." A great deal of legislation has modified the normal American rule, particularly in environmental, social justice, health, and civil rights laws. These laws provide what can be termed "one-way attorney fees"—government authorities must pay the attorney fees of individual persons, nongovernmental organizations, or small businesses that defeat the government in court. At the same time, the government is not normally given authority to collect fees from others, even if the government wins the lawsuit. Notable examples of federal "fee-shifting" statutes include all the major environmental statutes (starting with the Clean Air Act in 1970), the Freedom of Information Act as amended in 1974, and the Civil Rights Attorney Fees Award Act of 1976.

This trend eventually culminated in the Equal Access to Justice Act of 1980, Public Law 96-481; 94 Stat. 2325 *et seq.*, 28 U.S.C. 2412 (d), which applies to litigation between the government and a private person or corporation (or NGO) in all fields, including both successful suits against a government body and suits where the government sues a private person in an enforcement action but loses. In both types of cases the federal courts can award attorney fees to the non-government party.

The "American Rule" removes one of the largest negative risks and economic barriers to access to justice, while the "modified American Rule" provides a positive incentive to citizen enforcement of environmental laws. With such legal policies government authorities will be more likely to obey the law because they know that their transgressions are more likely to be caught by the courts.

V. Constitutions, Human Rights, and International Law

While the issues have been discussed above as policy issues, to be decided by legislatures or courts as a matter of public policy, financial barriers to access to justice may present constitutional issues in some countries. They also may present issues under various international human rights and multilateral environmental treaties and conventions. As to the constitutional dimension, these are among the questions that deserve further investigation: Are high court fees for suing the government or a private party potentially an unconstitutional restriction on access to the courts under various national constitutions? Are state policies that require a private citizen or NGO that loses a case to pay the attorney fees of the winner a violation of any constitutional right of access to justice under various national constitutions? Can a constitutional right to have a lawyer provided for free in environmental or other social justice cases be argued under any national constitutions?

Questions and Discussion

1. *A perfect system.* Does the "loser pays" system have advantages over the traditional American rule of each party bearing its own costs? Assuming that a given court gets the correct outcome most of the time, which system makes more sense? Is getting the "correct" outcome the only relevant value?

2. *Law enforcement.* Are citizen suits an important supplement to agency environmental law enforcement efforts? Would societies be better off allocating resources toward strengthening agency enforcement? How much of this depends on the cost of litigation and the strength of access and information laws?

3. *Judicial review of agency decisions.* If citizens lack the resources to challenge agency decisions in court, does that mean that all agency law-breaking will go unchallenged? Or does it mean that challenges will continue to come from one side of environmental issues but not from the other? If so, does that have the potential to distort agency decision-making? Are public officials likely to make decisions in part on the basis of whether they expect their agency to be sued? Are citizen groups the only ones that face financial barriers in gaining access to justice? What about small businesses and individuals? Is there any particular reason for the title of the Equal Access to Justice Act? Note that this statute, along with other "one-way" attorney fee award statutes (in which someone suing the government may have fees awarded, but the government may almost never obtain them against the citizen, organization, or business) has become a major basis for the growth of public interest litigation in the United States.

Access to Justice as a Guarantee of Economic, Social, and Cultural Rights

Inter-American Commission on Human Rights
O.A.S. Doc. OEA/Ser.L/V/II.129, Doc. 4 (7 September 2007)

II. THE RIGHT OF ACCESS TO JUSTICE AND THE OBLIGATION TO REMOVE ECONOMIC OBSTACLES TO ENSURE SOCIAL RIGHTS ...

One aspect that affects the extent of the right of access to justice has to do with economic or financial obstacles in access to the courts and with the scope of the positive obligation of the State to remove those obstacles in order to ensure an effective right to a hearing by a tribunal....

A. The Obligation to Provide Free Legal Counsel

It was in Advisory Opinion OC-11/90 [that] the Inter-American Court of Human Rights ... first specifically addressed the need to remove obstacles in access to justice that might originate from a person's economic status. On that occasion, the IACHR submitted a request for an advisory opinion to the Court in which it inquired, inter alia, if the rule of exhaustion of domestic legal remedies applied to an indigent, who, because of economic circumstances, was unable to avail himself of the legal remedies within a country....

In this framework, the Inter-American Court confirmed the prohibition of discrimination against persons by reason of their economic status and found that "... [i]f a person who is seeking the protection of the law in order to assert rights which the American Convention guarantees finds that his economic status (in this case, his indigence) prevents him from so doing because he cannot afford ... the necessary legal counsel..., that person is being discriminated against by reason of his economic status and, hence, is not receiving equal protection before the law." ...

IV. DUE PROCESS OF LAW IN JUDICIAL PROCEEDINGS CONCERNING SOCIAL RIGHTS ...

B. Elements that Comprise Due Process of Law in Judicial Proceedings

1. The Principle of Equality of Arms

In a proceeding, the unequal economic or social status of the litigants frequently has the effect of rendering the possibility of defense unequal at trial. Procedural inequality can also arise in social-rights litigation with the State, like an unwelcome reminder of the traditional positions in administrative law under which the State usually enjoys advantages vis-à-vis those under its administration. Accordingly, the principle of equality of arms should be recognized as one of the integral elements of the guarantee of a fair trial.

In an action involving social rights, safeguarding this principle is, without question, an important aspect of any defense strategy. The [Inter-American System] has identified the principle of equality of arms as an integral part of due process of law and has begun to outline standards with a view to its observance and assurance.

In this connection, in Advisory Opinion OC-16/99, *The Right to Information on Consular Assistance in the Framework of the Guarantees of the Due Process of Law*, the Inter-American Court makes its position clear on the principle under discussion here:

> In the opinion of this Court, for "the due process of law" a defendant must be able to exercise his rights and defend his interests effectively and in full procedural equality with other defendants. It is important to recall that the judicial process is a means to ensure, insofar as possible, an equitable resolution of a difference. The body of procedures, of diverse character and generally grouped under the heading of the due process, is all calculated to serve that end.... To accomplish its objectives, the judicial process must recognize and correct any real disadvantages that those brought before the bar might have, thus observing the principle of equality before the law and the courts and the corollary principle prohibiting discrimination.

Having recognized the significance of this principle, the Court posits that the presence of real disadvantages necessitates that the State adopt countervailing measures that help to reduce or eliminate the obstacles and deficiencies that impair or diminish an effective defense of one's interests. The foregoing is based on the fact that, absent those countervailing measures, widely recognized in various stages of the proceeding, "one could hardly say that those who have the disadvantages enjoy a true opportunity for justice and the benefit of the due process of law equal to those who do not have those disadvantages." ...

Questions and Discussion

1. *Equality of arms.* To what extent should "equality of arms" be required? Should the standard differ in civil cases as compared to criminal cases? Do you accept the notion that where equality of arms is not achieved, due process guarantees have been breached? In the United States, the U.S. Supreme Court long ago interpreted the guarantee of due process to require the state to provide free legal counsel in felony cases, *Gideon v. Wainwright*, 372 U.S. 335 (1963), but has not extended that concept to civil cases. Under the American Convention on Human Rights, does a guarantee of "due process" apply not only in criminal cases, but also in civil cases brought by a party against the government?

2. *Who bears the burden?* Is it the state's responsibility to cure any of these inequalities? To provide state-funded legal aid? Is this a practical solution for environmental cases? Consider the workload of most U.S. public defenders and legal aid offices. In Britain legal aid is theoretically available for environmental cases, but practitioners there contend that obtaining it is difficult and not at all ensured even when economically justified by a client's situation.

3. *An Australian solution.* In Australia, the governments of most of the Australian states provide some public funding for environmental cases by supporting independent Environmental Defenders Offices that are available to take cases on behalf of citizens. Is spend-

ing public funds on such offices a realistic solution in most countries? Are their advantages to having a specialized environmental legal aid office that develops expertise over the years?

4. *Legal aid in civil suits in Europe.* In *Steel & Morris v. United Kingdom,* No. 68416/01, ECHR 2005-II, E.H.R.R. 22 (2005), excerpted in chapter 11 at page 528, the European Court of Human Rights held that failure to provide funding to civil litigants defending themselves against defamation suits violated Article 6 of the European Convention on Human rights. Read the excerpts there regarding legal aid and equality of arms before reading the following analysis.

Steel & Morris v. United Kingdom: Legal Aid in the European Court of Human Rights
Shirley Shipman
25 Civ. Just. Q. 5 (2006)

Introduction

English law has long recognised the centrality of the right of access to court in relation to civil justice. The role of the court is important in safeguarding and enforcing the legal rights of individuals and regulating their dealings with others.... A significant barrier to access in the English civil justice system is the cost of litigation.... Legal aid is not available at all for certain civil proceedings, including defamation actions. The lack of provision in relation to defamation proceedings has been challenged on a number of occasions.... On each occasion the challenge has been unsuccessful. But finally, in the judgment of *Steel & Morris v. United Kingdom,* the court ruled in the applicants' favour. Miss Steel and Mr. Morris, defendants in the McDonald's Restaurants Ltd libel case, were deprived of a fair hearing in breach of Art.6 (1) of the ECHR. The denial of legal aid contributed to an unacceptable inequality of arms with McDonald's and deprived them of the opportunity to present their case effectively.

The decision of the court in the *Steel* case in relation to Art.6 (1) is to be applauded. The applicants faced significantly complex proceedings due to the sheer scale of the case (it was the longest trial in English history).... Whilst they were "articulate and resourceful" the sheer volume of material, together with the magnitude of proceedings, led to the conclusion that without sustained and competent legal assistance they were unable to present an effective defence and that there was a substantial disadvantage (inequality of arms) vis-à-vis McDonald's....

[T]he court found also that the lack of procedural fairness and equality of arms gave rise to a violation of the applicants' right to freedom of expression under Art.10 of the ECHR. This will be explored briefly prior to the main discussion.

Article 10

The applicants argued that the burden of proof, which required them to prove the veracity of the allegedly defamatory statements on the balance of probabilities, was incompatible with Art.10 of the ECHR. The court disagreed.... According to the court, the balance was to be struck between the "public interest in open debate about business practices" and the "competing interest in protecting the commercial success and viability of companies," both for the good of stakeholders and the wider economic good. In this case that balance had tilted unfairly in McDonald's favour, not due to the burden of proof or to the corporate size of the claimant, but rather because, due to the lack of legal aid provision, the United Kingdom had failed to ensure procedural fairness and equality....

Article 6(1)

Whilst lack of legal aid provision for civil cases is not itself an infringement of Art.6(1) (contracting states are not required under the express provisions to provide state-funded legal assistance in civil proceedings), it appears that refusal to fund publicly civil litigation may lead to a violation of Art.6(1) in three situations. First, if the applicant has been unable consequently to pursue a case in the courts, this may constitute a breach of the right of access to a court. Secondly, applicants may conduct their own case but the court may find that there is a denial of the opportunity to present an effective case. Thirdly, the lack of provision may lead to an inequality of arms, such that there is a substantial disadvantage vis-à-vis the adversary. The focus here will be on the second and third of these possibilities.

1. Effective defence

The Strasbourg jurisprudence makes it clear that where an applicant has been denied access to a court (the first situation) such denial may be justified where the restriction on access does not impair the very essence of the right of access to a court, serves a legitimate aim and the means used to achieve that objective is proportionate (the Ashingdane test). To this end, the court has repeatedly stated that the right of access is not absolute and may be subject to restrictions....

2. Equality of arms

A state's refusal to grant legal aid may lead also to a violation of Art.6(1) where there is an inequality of arms, such that the applicants have not had a reasonable opportunity to present their case under conditions that do not place them at a substantial disadvantage vis-à-vis the adversary. Ensuring equality of arms between the parties cannot be considered an aspect of the right to access a court but is rather an important element of a fair hearing.... Determination of an inequality of arms is a matter of degree. The test is whether or not the applicant suffered a substantial disadvantage compared to his adversary; if so, the hearing was unfair and there is no cause for assessing the justifiability, or otherwise, of the state refusal. Unfortunately, the court failed to make this clear in the *Steel* case: rather it appeared to elide its discussion of whether the applicants had been afforded an opportunity to present an effective defence with the equality of arms point....

The issue of equality is determined by an assessment of whether the parties are equally equipped to conduct the proceedings to the extent that there is no "substantial disadvantage," and of whether procedural rules are applied even-handedly.... The court took no opportunity to provide guidance as to what constitutes "substantial disadvantage" vis-à-vis the opponent such that the state should provide legal aid. This is a matter of degree and, whilst it might be considered a clear issue in the *Steel* case, in other situations it may be less certain.

3. Legal aid and justifiable restrictions ...

The court has recognised that legal aid systems cannot function unless there is a means of selecting the cases that should qualify for legal aid. Since the requirement under Art.6(1) is to ensure a fair hearing in the determination of an individual's legal civil rights and obligations, and not to provide a fair hearing for the resolution of each and every ... dispute of its citizens, this point is clearly a concession to the available public resources. Without a means of discriminating between cases the state would be committed to providing legal aid on demand. The court has recognised that the right of access to court is not absolute and must be subject to restrictions according to the needs and resources of the community.... The following brief comments refer to three of the limitations imposed on the distribution of legal aid funding accepted by Strasbourg as proportionate in pursuing the legitimate aim of ensuring that public funds are used appropriately.

First, the Commission accepted that it is reasonable to impose conditions on the availability of legal aid involving the financial situation of the litigant. If the accepted legitimate reason for limiting legal aid provision is to minimise the drain on public resources, it is certainly arguable that legal aid provision should be targeted where it is financially necessary....

Secondly, it has been held also that it is reasonable to take into account the prospects of success of litigation should the case be brought to court. Again, it must be ensured that an appropriate assessment of the prospects of the case takes place.... The key here is the issue of arbitrariness. Arbitrariness is determined on the facts and circumstances particular to the case before the court and provided that the decision on the facts of the case is not arbitrary, the refusal to grant legal aid will be considered justifiable....

The future

The court decision in the *Steel* case poses problems for the UK Government. It would appear that it is no longer possible to exclude entirely defamation proceedings from legal aid provision. However, there have been changes in the provision of civil litigation funding since Miss Steel and Mr. Morris fought their case in the national courts. First, under the Access to Justice Act 1999, s.6(8)(b) ("AJA 1999"), the Lord Chancellor is able to authorise the provision of legal aid for those proceedings generally excluded from legal aid provision.... [T]he benchmark will be those cases where the Strasbourg Court has indicated that the right of access to court has effectively been denied due to lack of public funding.... [T]he issue as to when the court will find that there has been a violation of Art.6(1) due to the refusal of legal aid is not straightforward....

Whilst much of the parliamentary debate surrounding the issue of whether or not to exclude legal aid from such proceedings centred round the potential for vexatious litigation, there were also those who were concerned about the cost of funding such litigation. Moreover, the government has in recent years been curtailing its public funding of litigation....

The decision in *Steel*, in line with the seminal judgment in the *Airey* case, ignores the economic consequences for the government. This is to be applauded: if the Art.6(1) right is to be of worth then the contracting states must ensure that litigants are able to present an effective case in a fair hearing, irrespective of cost....

Questions and Discussion

1. *Irrespective of cost.* The last line of the passage above suggests that access to justice, at least in terms of equality of arms, should be considered "irrespective of cost." Is this a feasible solution for most governments? Consider the amount of money spent by U.S. states on prosecuting criminals as opposed to the amounts spent defending those who are accused. Further consider that such expenditures are tied to criminal prosecutions, whereas many U.S. Constitutional rights are protected only through civil proceedings.

2. *Weighing justice.* If funding is provided, but cost is taken into account, how do those in control of the funds determine where financial support should be lent to equalize arms? Would it be based on the likelihood of success of a given suit, financial need, overall public benefit, political considerations, or other criteria?

3. *Access to justice generally.* Considering the discussion of standing above, what presents a greater challenge to access to justice: gaining the right to sue (standing) or gaining the means to sue (equality of arms)?

Chapter 9

Corporate Accountability

Introduction

Two different kinds of questions need to be asked about violations of human rights by corporate actors. The first is what norms of applicable law may exist. The second is what institutions or remedies may exist. These questions have both international and national dimensions. Regarding norms, a corporation may be subject to international norms for protection of human rights as well as national legal norms, including those of tort law. As for remedies, they could be available in international institutions, but for the most part they exist, if at all, in the courts and jurisprudence of national legal systems. In addition to substantive norms, requirements of transparency, disclosure, and evaluation can affect corporate behavior. This chapter will look at each of these possibilities. In addition to potential legal remedies, the chapter will discuss some examples of self-regulation through voluntary codes of conduct and disclosure, along with the possibility that international lending and trade institutions might "enforce" human rights obligations on corporations.

I. International Standards, Liability, and Aspirations

International human rights norms are not necessarily applicable only to governmental bodies. Some of them clearly apply to individuals and even "legal persons" (corporations). In this first part of the chapter we will consider guidelines and voluntary efforts involving human rights and the environment.

A. From Soft Law to Norms?

Challenge of Imposing Human Rights Norms on Corporate Actors
Olivier de Schutter
Transnational Corporations and Human Rights
(O. de Schutter ed., 2006)

The debate on the question of the human rights responsibilities of companies is hardly new.... A draft Code of Conduct on Transnational Corporations was even being prepared up to 1992 within the U.N. Commission on Transnational Corporations.... The U.N. Draft Code of Conduct provided, inter alia, that "Transnational corporations shall respect human rights and fundamental freedoms in the countries in which they operate...." The Draft Code failed to be adopted, however, because of major disagreements between industrialized and developing countries, in particular on the reference to international law and on the inclusion in the Code of standards of treatment for TNCs: while the industrialized countries were in favor of a Code protecting TNCs from discriminatory treatment or other behavior of host States which would be in violation of certain minimum standards, the developing States primarily sought to ensure that TNCs would be better regulated, and in particular would be prohibited from interfering either with political independence of the investment-receiving States or with their nationally defined economic objectives....

[T]he OECD adopted, on 21 June 1976, the Guidelines for Multinational Enterprises. These Guidelines have been revised on a number of occasions since their initial adoption, and most recently in 2000, when the supervisory mechanism was revitalized and when a general obligation on multinational enterprises to "respect the human rights of those affected by their activities consistent with the host government's international obligations and commitments" was stipulated. Although they are addressed only to the 30 member States of the OECD and the handful of non-member countries who have chosen to adhere to them, the Guidelines still constitute the most widely used instrument defining the obligations of multinational enterprises.[7] ... [B]y seeking to minimize the risk of conflicting requirements being imposed on multinational enterprises, the Guidelines were seen as a means to encourage the opening up of foreign economies to foreign direct investment. They sought to ensure that all States parties would contribute, by the setting of national contact points and their cooperation with the OECD Investment Committee, to ensuring a certain level of control on the activities of multinational enterprises incorporated under their jurisdiction, even if this supervision remains purely voluntary and may not lead to the imposition of sanctions.

Almost simultaneously, the ILO [International Labour Organization] adopted the Tripartite Declaration of Principles concerning Multinational Enterprises and Social Policy.... Apart from specific references to fundamental workers' rights as guaranteed under conventions and recommendations adopted within the ILO ... the Tripartite Declaration contains a general provision relating to the obligation to respect human rights.

Although of high moral significance because of its adoption by consensus by the ILO Governing Body at which governments, employers and workers are represented, the Tripartite Declaration remains, as such, a non-binding instrument....

Neither the 1976 OECD Guidelines for Multinational Enterprises nor the 1977 ILO Tripartite Declaration of Principles ... may be described as effective instruments imposing human rights obligations on transnational enterprises. These instruments impose on States certain obligations of a procedural nature: States must set up national contact points (NCPs) under the OECD Guidelines in order to promote the Guidelines and to receive "specific instances," or complaints by interested parties in cases of non-compliance by companies; they must report on a quadrennial basis under the ILO Tripartite Declaration on the implementation of the principles listed therein. However, both these instruments are explicitly presented as non-binding instruments, with respect to the multinational enterprises whose practices they ultimately seek to address.... [N]o sanc-

---

7. ... As most multinational enterprises are domiciled in industrialized countries that are members of the OECD, the Guidelines are practically of almost universal applicability to transnational business enterprises.

tions may be imposed on multinational enterprises which either refuse to cooperate with the NCP, or are found to be in violation of the Guidelines. Under the OECD Guidelines, the only incentive for companies to comply resides in the adverse publicity they will be subjected to if they refuse to cooperate in identifying a solution to the "specific instance" presented to an NCP. Such an incentive is even absent from the procedures for the supervision and interpretation of the ILO Tripartite Declaration.

Questions and Discussion

1. *Voluntary codes.* Many governments do not enforce human rights obligations against corporations, deferring to soft law and voluntary codes of conduct and guidelines. Is it possible that soft law instruments can actually play a significant role in controlling the behavior of corporate actors, even without government enforcement? Or are they likely to be primarily a public relations exercise?

2. *Voluntary compliance.* Professor de Schutter seems to be quite skeptical about the efficacy of such codes and guidelines. After the following materials, we shall return to that question.

————————

The United Nations Global Compact styles itself "the world's largest voluntary corporate responsibility initiative."

U.N. Global Compact
http://www.unglobalcompact.org/AboutTheGC/index.html

Human Rights

Principle 1: Businesses should support and respect the protection of internationally proclaimed human rights; and

Principle 2: make sure that they are not complicit in human rights abuses....

Environment

Principle 7: Businesses should support a precautionary approach to environmental challenges;

Principle 8: undertake initiatives to promote greater environmental responsibility; and

Principle 9: encourage the development and diffusion of environmentally friendly technologies.

————————

The Organization for Economic Co-operation and Development (OECD) first promulgated Guidelines for multinational corporations in 1976, with the most recent revision taking place in 2000. Among the significant additions were provisions relating to human rights and changes regarding behavior toward the environment. The following excerpts focus primarily on the human rights and environmental provisions of the Guidelines.

OECD Guidelines For Multinational Enterprises
Organisation for Economic Co-operation and Development (OECD) (Revision 2000)
www.oecd.org/daf/investment/guidelines

I. Concepts and Principles

The Guidelines are recommendations jointly addressed by governments to multinational enterprises. They provide principles and standards of good practice consistent with applicable laws. Observance of the Guidelines by enterprises is voluntary and not legally enforceable....

II. General Policies

Enterprises should take fully into account established policies in the countries in which they operate, and consider the views of other stakeholders. In this regard, enterprises should:

1. Contribute to economic, social and environmental progress with a view to achieving sustainable development.

2. Respect the human rights of those affected by their activities consistent with the host government's international obligations and commitments....

V. Environment

Enterprises should, within the framework of laws, regulations and administrative practices in the countries in which they operate, and in consideration of relevant international agreements, principles, objectives, and standards, take due account of the need to protect the environment, public health and safety, and generally to conduct their activities in a manner contributing to the wider goal of sustainable development. In particular, enterprises should:

1. Establish and maintain a system of environmental management appropriate to the enterprise, including:

   a) Collection and evaluation of adequate and timely information regarding the environmental, health, and safety impacts of their activities.

   b) Establishment of measurable objectives and, where appropriate, targets for improved environmental performance ... ; and

   c) Regular monitoring and verification of progress toward environmental, health, and safety objectives or targets.

2. Taking into account concerns about cost, business confidentiality, and the protection of intellectual property rights:

   a) Provide the public and employees with adequate and timely information on the potential environment, health and safety impacts of the activities of the enterprise ... ; and

   b) Engage in adequate and timely communication and consultation with the communities directly affected....

3. Assess and address in decision-making, the foreseeable environmental, health, and safety-related impacts associated with the processes, goods and services of the enterprise over their full life cycle. Where these proposed activities may have significant environmental, health, or safety impacts, and where they are subject to a decision of a competent authority, prepare an appropriate environmental impact assessment.

4. Consistent with the scientific and technical understanding of the risks, where there are threats of serious damage to the environment, taking also into account human health and safety, not use the lack of full scientific certainty as a reason for postponing cost-effective measures to prevent or minimise such damage.

5. Maintain contingency plans for preventing, mitigating, and controlling serious environmental and health damage from their operations, including accidents and emergencies; and mechanisms for immediate reporting to the competent authorities....

ILO Tripartite Declaration of Principles Concerning Multinational Enterprises and Social Policy

Adopted by the Governing Body of the ILO at its 204th Session
(November 1977), and revised at the 279th Session (November 2000)
Official Bulletin, Vol. LXXXIII, 2000, Series A, No. 3

7. This Declaration sets out principles in the fields of employment, training, conditions of work and life and industrial relations which governments, employers' and workers' organizations and multinational enterprises are recommended to observe on a voluntary basis....

GENERAL POLICIES

8. All the parties concerned by this Declaration should respect the sovereign rights of States, obey the national laws and regulations, give due consideration to local practices and respect relevant international standards. They should respect the Universal Declaration of Human Rights and the corresponding International Covenants adopted by the General Assembly of the United Nations as well as the Constitution of the International Labour Organization and its principles according to which freedom of expression and association are essential to sustained progress....

CONDITIONS OF WORK AND LIFE ...

38. Multinational enterprises should maintain the highest standards of safety and health, in conformity with national requirements, bearing in mind their relevant experience within the enterprise as a whole, including any knowledge of special hazards....

Questions and Discussion

1. *Global Compact.* The website of the U.N. Global compact stresses:

> The Global Compact is not a regulatory instrument — it does not "police," enforce or measure the behavior or actions of companies. Rather, the Global Compact relies on public accountability, transparency and the enlightened self-interest of companies, labour and civil society to initiate and share substantive action in pursuing the principles upon which the Global Compact is based.

Are transparency, accountability, and enlightened self-interest a sufficient basis for expecting environmental and other human rights to be respected by corporations?

2. *Voluntary nature of the OECD Guidelines.* The OECD Guidelines explicitly state that observance of the Guidelines is voluntary and not legally enforceable. The Directorate for Financial, Fiscal, and Enterprise Affairs has published "Procedural Guidance," which provides that complaints may be made to "national contact points" (not to an international body). OECD Doc. DAFFE/IME/WPG(2000)15/FINAL. Is reliance on "national contact points" to review complaints likely to be successful?

3. *Voluntary ILO Tripartite Declaration.* The ILO Tripartite Declaration is also voluntary. Organizations of workers, but not members of the public or their non-governmental organizations, can ask for an "interpretation" of the Declaration from the ILO's Committee on Multinational Enterprises, according to procedures adopted by the Gov-

erning Body of the International Labour Office at its 232nd Session (Geneva, March 1986). *Official Bulletin* (Geneva, ILO), 1986, Vol. LXIX, Series A, No. 3, pp. 196–197. Such an interpretation is forwarded to the parties concerned and published in the Official Bulletin of the International Labour Office.

4. *Beyond voluntarism?* Does the voluntary nature of these declarations and guidelines mean that they have no value? Or, do they get ethical corporations to think? What about other corporations? Could they be used in lobbying campaigns by reformers? In lawsuits?

5. *Broad language: good, bad, sufficient?* The language of these documents encompasses a great many activities of multinational enterprises. Is it broad enough? Can you think of any categories of activities that may have been omitted? Does the nature of the language provide sufficient protection, or does it give multinational enterprises too much discretion?

(Draft) Norms on the Responsibilities of Transnational Corporations and Other Business Enterprises with Regard to Human Rights
U.N. Working Group on the Working Methods and Activities of Transnational Corporations
U.N. Doc. E/CN.4/Sub.2/2003/12 (2003)

A. General obligations

1. States have the primary responsibility to promote, secure the fulfilment of, respect, ensure respect of and protect human rights recognized in international as well as national law, including ensuring that transnational corporations and other business enterprises respect human rights. Within their respective spheres of activity and influence, transnational corporations and other business enterprises have the obligation to promote, secure the fulfilment of, respect, ensure respect of and protect human rights recognized in international as well as national law, including the rights and interests of indigenous peoples and other vulnerable groups....

E. Respect for national sovereignty and human rights

10. Transnational corporations and other business enterprises shall recognize and respect applicable norms of international law, national laws and regulations, as well as administrative practices, the rule of law, the public interest, development objectives, social, economic and cultural policies including transparency, accountability and prohibition of corruption, and authority of the countries in which the enterprises operate.

11.... Transnational corporations and other business enterprises shall refrain from any activity which supports, solicits, or encourages States or any other entities to abuse human rights. They shall further seek to ensure that the goods and services they provide will not be used to abuse human rights.

12. Transnational corporations and other business enterprises shall respect economic, social and cultural rights as well as civil and political rights and contribute to their realization, in particular the rights to development, adequate food and drinking water, the highest attainable standard of physical and mental health, adequate housing, privacy, education, freedom of thought, conscience, and religion and freedom of opinion and expression, and shall refrain from actions which obstruct or impede the realization of those rights....

G. Obligations with regard to environmental protection

14. Transnational corporations and other business enterprises shall carry out their activities in accordance with national laws, regulations, administrative practices and policies relating to the preservation of the environment of the countries in which they operate, as well as in accordance with relevant international agreements, principles, objectives, responsibilities and standards with regard to the environment as well as human rights, public health and safety, bioethics and the precautionary principle, and shall generally conduct their activities in a manner contributing to the wider goal of sustainable development.

H. General provisions of implementation

15. As an initial step towards implementing these Norms, each transnational corporation or other business enterprise shall adopt, disseminate and implement internal rules of operation in compliance with the Norms. Further, they shall periodically report on and take other measures fully to implement the Norms and to provide at least for the prompt implementation of the protections set forth in the Norms. Each transnational corporation or other business enterprise shall apply and incorporate these Norms in their contracts or other arrangements and dealings with contractors, subcontractors, suppliers, licensees, distributors, or natural or other legal persons that enter into any agreement with the transnational corporation or business enterprise in order to ensure respect for and implementation of the Norms.

16. Transnational corporations and other business enterprises shall be subject to periodic monitoring and verification by United Nations, other international and national mechanisms already in existence or yet to be created, regarding application of the Norms. This monitoring shall be transparent and independent and take into account input from stakeholders (including non-governmental organizations) and as a result of complaints of violations of these Norms. Further, transnational corporations and other business enterprises shall conduct periodic evaluations concerning the impact of their own activities on human rights under these Norms.

17. States should establish and reinforce the necessary legal and administrative framework for ensuring that the Norms and other relevant national and international laws are implemented by transnational corporations and other business enterprises.

18. Transnational corporations and other business enterprises shall provide prompt, effective and adequate reparation to those persons, entities and communities that have been adversely affected by failures to comply with these Norms through, inter alia, reparations, restitution, compensation and rehabilitation for any damage done or property taken. In connection with determining damages, in regard to criminal sanctions, and in all other respects, these Norms shall be applied by national courts and/or international tribunals, pursuant to national and international law.

Questions and Discussion

1. *Generality or specificity in drafting.* Paragraph 14 refers generally to international agreements, principles, and the like. Is such a broad statement sufficient to guide transnational corporations and enforcement authorities, or is a greater degree of specificity required? Should the drafters have opted to refer to specific agreements, at least as examples? Or would examples have acted to limit imagination and progressive thinking? How much debate would have been consumed in deciding whether particular examples should be included or not? Consider that much of the world, including many in the European Union, refers to the "precautionary principle," with the international law implications

that the word "principle" carries, while others insist that there is only at most a "precautionary approach." One author who has expressed reservations about a general precautionary principle is Professor Cass Sunstein in Laws of Fear: Beyond the Precautionary Principle (2005).

2. *Failure to adopt.* The draft Norms have not been adopted. They were proposed to the full United Nations Commission on Human Rights (recently reorganized as the Human Rights Council), but they were not accepted. To understand how they were set aside, see Olivier de Schutter, *Challenge of Imposing Human Rights Norms on Corporate Actors,* in Transnational Corporations and Human Rights (O. de Schutter ed., 2006).

B. Analysis

Mapping International Standards of Responsibility and Accountability for Corporate Acts

John Ruggie

U.N. Doc. A/HRC/4/35 (19 February 2007)[a]

Introduction

There is no magic in the marketplace. Markets function efficiently and sustainably only when certain institutional parameters are in place. The preconditions for success are generally assumed to include the protection of property rights; the enforceability of contracts; competition; and the smooth flow of information. But a key requisite is often overlooked: curtailing individual and social harms imposed by markets. History demonstrates that without adequate institutional underpinnings, markets will fail to deliver their full benefits and may even become socially unsustainable....

I. State Duty to Protect ...

[O]f those States responding [to a survey by the Special Representative], very few report having policies, programmes or tools designed specifically to deal with corporate human rights challenges. A larger number say they rely on the framework of corporate responsibility initiatives, including such soft law instruments as the Organization for Economic Cooperation and Development (OECD) Guidelines for Multinational Enterprises, or voluntary initiatives like the United Nations Global Compact. Very few explicitly consider human rights criteria in their export credit and investment promotion policies or in bilateral trade and investment treaties, points at which government policies and global business operations most closely intersect....

III. Corporate Responsibility for Other Human Rights Violations under International Law ...

The Universal Declaration of Human Rights occupies a unique place in the international normative order. Its preamble proclaims that "every individual and every organ of society ... shall strive by teaching and education to promote respect for these rights and freedoms and by progressive measures, national and international, to secure their universal and effective recognition and observance." In Louis Henkin's famous words: "Every indi-

---

a. Report of the Special Representative of the Secretary-General on the Issue of Human Rights and Transnational Corporations and Other Business Enterprises. Full title: *Business and human rights: mapping international standards of responsibility and accountability for corporate acts,* Implementation of General Assembly Resolution 60/251 of 15 March 2006 entitled "Human Rights Council."

vidual includes juridical persons. Every individual and every organ of society excludes no one, no company, no market, no cyberspace. The Universal Declaration applies to them all." ... But that does not equate to legally binding effect.

Many provisions of the Universal Declaration of Human Rights have entered customary international law. While there is some debate, it is generally agreed that they currently apply only to States (and sometimes individuals) and do not include its preamble. Most of its provisions have also been incorporated in the Covenants and other United Nations human rights treaties. Do these instruments establish direct legal responsibilities for corporations? Several of them include preambular, and therefore non-binding, recognition that individuals have duties to others. But the operational paragraphs do not address the issue explicitly....

[T]he treaties [Covenants] do not address direct corporate legal responsibilities explicitly, while the commentaries of the treaty bodies on the subject are ambiguous....

On purely logical grounds, a stronger argument could be made for direct corporate responsibilities under the ILO [International Labour Organization] core conventions.... But logic alone does not make law, and the legal responsibilities of corporations under the ILO conventions remain indirect.

At the regional level there is greater diversity. The African Charter on Human and Peoples' Rights is unusual because it imposes direct duties on individuals, but opinions vary on their effect and whether they apply to groups, including corporations. Expert commentary suggests that the Inter-American Court of Human Rights may have moved away from the traditional view when it recognized that non-discrimination "gives rise to effects with regard to third parties," including in private employment relationships, "under which the employer must respect the human rights of his workers." The Inter-American Commission on Human Rights has limited itself to condemning non-State actor abuses. The European Court of Human Rights has generally adopted the traditional view....

In conclusion, it does not seem that the international human rights instruments discussed here currently impose direct legal responsibilities on corporations. Even so, corporations are under growing scrutiny by the international human rights mechanisms. And while States have been unwilling to adopt binding international human rights standards for corporations, together with business and civil society they have drawn on some of these instruments in establishing soft law standards and initiatives. It seems likely, therefore, that these instruments will play a key role in any future development of defining corporate responsibility for human rights.

IV. Soft Law Mechanisms

Soft law is "soft" in the sense that it does not by itself create legally binding obligations. It derives its normative force through recognition of social expectations by States and other key actors. States may turn to soft law for several reasons: to chart possible future directions for, and fill gaps in, the international legal order when they are not yet able or willing to take firmer measures; where they conclude that legally binding mechanisms are not the best tool to address a particular issue; or in some instances to avoid having more binding measures gain political momentum....

A prominent example of the normative role of soft law is the ILO Tripartite Declaration of Principles Concerning Multinational Enterprises and Social Policy, endorsed not only by States but also by global employers' and workers' organizations. It proclaims that all parties, including multinational enterprises, "should respect the Universal Declaration of Human Rights and the corresponding international Covenants."

The OECD Guidelines perform a similar role. They acknowledge that the capacity and willingness of States to implement their international human rights obligations vary. Accordingly, they recommend that firms "respect the human rights of those affected by their activities consistent with the host Government's obligations and commitments"— the commentary expressly indicating that these include the host State's international commitments.

Both instruments are widely referenced by Governments and businesses and may, in due course, crystallize into harder forms. Thus, soft law's normative role remains essential to elaborating and further developing standards of corporate responsibility.

Several intergovernmental initiatives have recently focused not only on promulgating standards for companies, but also on ways to enhance accountability for compliance. For example, due to civil society demands, anyone can now bring a complaint against a multinational firm, operating within the sphere of the OECD Guidelines, to the attention of a National Contact Point (NCP)—a non-judicial review procedure. Some NCPs have also become more transparent about the details of complaints and conclusions, permitting greater social tracking of corporate conduct, although the overall performance of NCPs remains highly uneven. And the OECD Investment Committee has expanded its oversight of NCPs, providing another opportunity to review their treatment of complaints.

For its part, the International Finance Corporation (IFC) now has performance standards that companies are required to meet in return for IFC investment funds. They include several human rights elements. Depending on the project, IFC may require impact assessments that include human rights elements and community consultation. Client compliance is subject to review by an ombudsman, who may hear complaints from anyone adversely affected by the social or environmental consequences of an IFC-funded project. [See Chapter 10, page 475, in this textbook.] The IFC standards also have accountability spillover effects, as they are tracked by banks adhering to the Equator Principles, which account for some two thirds of global commercial project lending.

Beyond the intergovernmental system, a new multi-stakeholder form of soft law initiatives is emerging. Most prominent among them are the Voluntary Principles on Security and Human Rights (Voluntary Principles), promoting corporate human rights risk assessments and training of security providers in the extractive sector; the Kimberley Process Certification Scheme (Kimberley) to stem the flow of conflict diamonds; and the Extractive Industries Transparency Initiative (EITI), establishing a degree of revenue transparency in the taxes, royalties and fees companies pay to host Governments.

Driven by social pressure, these initiatives seek to close regulatory gaps that contribute to human rights abuses. But they do so in specific operational contexts, not in any overarching manner....

These initiatives may be seen as still largely experimental expressions of an emerging practice of voluntary global administrative rulemaking and implementation, which exist in a number of areas where the intergovernmental system has not kept pace with rapid changes in social expectations....

The credibility of their governance structures, in turn, is said to hinge on three factors: participation, transparency, and ongoing status reviews. Thus, regarding participation, civil society and industry members collaborated with States to develop the standards for, and now participate in, the governance of the Voluntary Principles, EITI and Kimberley....

A second measure of effectiveness is whether they serve as examples for others. Indeed, the relative ease with which they can be established, in contrast with treaty-based instruments, together with their perceived potential, have directly inspired parallel efforts in related fields, including rules regarding private security forces and also for businesses beyond the extractive sector.

One final feature of recent innovations in soft law arrangements—both the intergovernmental and multi-stakeholder variety—should be noted. As they strengthen their accountability mechanisms, they also begin to blur the lines between the strictly voluntary and mandatory spheres for participants. Once in, exiting can be costly. No company has to accept IFC financing or loans from Equator banks but if they do, certain performance criteria are required for continued funding. Countries are free to join the EITI or not, but if they do then extractive companies are required to issue public reports of their payments to Governments. Suspension or expulsion from Kimberley has a direct economic impact on countries and companies. Voluntary Principles language—and in some cases the actual text—has been incorporated into legal agreements between Governments and companies. And once the Voluntary Principles adopt participation criteria, non-compliance similarly could lead to expulsion.

V. Self-Regulation

In addition to legal standards, hard or soft, the mandate of the Special Representative includes evolving social expectations regarding responsible corporate citizenship, including human rights. One key indicator consists of the policies and practices that business itself adopts voluntarily, triggered by its assessment of human rights-related risks and opportunities, often under pressure from civil society and local communities....

However, mapping the entire universe of business enterprises is impossible. More than 77,000 transnational corporations currently span the globe, with roughly 770,000 subsidiaries and millions of suppliers. Those numbers are dwarfed by local firms, and an even bigger informal sector in developing countries.

Therefore, the Special Representative conducted studies of a subset of business entities to determine how they perceive corporate responsibility and accountability regarding human rights. One was a questionnaire survey of the *Fortune* Global 500 firms (FG500), which are under social scrutiny as the world's largest companies. The second ("business recognition study") consisted of three parts: actual policies, rather than questionnaire responses, of a broader cross-section of firms from all regions (including developing countries) screened as likely to have policies that include human rights; eight collective initiatives that include human rights standards, like the Fair Labor Association (FLA) or the International Council on Metals and Mining (ICMM); and the human rights criteria employed by five socially responsible investment funds (SRI funds).

Such a mapping could barely have been done five years ago because few corporate human rights policies existed. Uptake has been especially rapid among large global firms, a group still predominantly domiciled in Europe, North America and Japan. Newer entrants from other regions lag behind, although it is unclear whether this lag reflects a fundamental difference or merely timing. Numerous firms in the business recognition study only recently joined initiatives like the Global Compact and are only beginning to develop human rights policies....

All FG500 respondents, irrespective of region or sector, included non-discrimination as a core corporate responsibility, at minimum meaning recruitment and promotion based on merit. Workplace health and safety standards were cited almost as frequently. More than three quarters recognized freedom of association and the right to collective bargaining, the prohibition against child and forced labour, and the right to privacy. European firms were more likely than their United States counterparts to recognize the rights to life, liberty, and security of person; health; and an adequate standard of living....

Companies referenced international instruments in formulating their policies. Among the FG500, ILO declarations and conventions topped the list, followed by the Universal Declaration of Human Rights. United Nations human rights treaties were mentioned infrequently. The Global Compact was cited by just over 50 per cent, the OECD Guidelines by just under 50 per cent. More than 80 per cent also said they worked with external stakeholders on their human rights policies. NGOs topped that list, followed by industry associations....

The broader cross-section of companies paralleled the FG500 in recognizing labour standards. But their recognition of other rights was consistently lower: the highest, at 16 percent, was the right to security of the person, encompassing both the right to life and the freedom from cruel and unusual punishment. For areas covered by social, economic, and cultural rights these companies tended to emphasize their philanthropic contributions.

Firms in both samples participated in one of the eight collective initiatives. The recognition of rights by these initiatives closely reflected industry sectors: for example, those in manufacturing focused more on labour rights, whereas the extractive initiatives emphasized community relations and indigenous rights. Moreover, they drew on international standards: the FLA and Social Accountability 8000 meet or exceed most core ILO rights, while Equator banks track the IFC's performance standards. The SRI indices mirrored the overall high recognition of labour rights, and several exhibited a particular concern for rights related to indigenous peoples, as well as the right to a family life.

How do these companies and other business entities respond to social expectations regarding accountability? Most FG500 firms said they had internal reporting systems to monitor their human rights performance. Three quarters indicated that they also reported externally, but of those fewer than half utilized a third-party medium like the Global Reporting Initiative (GRI). Some form of supply chain monitoring was relatively common. But only one third said they routinely included human rights criteria within their social/environmental impact assessments....

In short, leading business players recognize human rights and adopt means to ensure basic accountability. Yet even among the leaders, certain weaknesses of voluntarism are evident. Companies do not necessarily recognize those rights on which they may have the greatest impact. And while the rights they do recognize typically draw on international instruments, the language is rarely identical. Some interpretations are so elastic that the standards lose meaning, making it difficult for the company itself, let alone the public, to assess performance against commitments....

Where self-regulation remains most challenged, however, is in its accountability provisions....

The number of firms reporting their social, environmental and human rights profiles, called "sustainability reporting," has risen exponentially. But quality has not matched quantity. Far fewer companies report systematically on how their core business strategies and operations impact on these sustainability issues. Instead, anecdotal descriptions of isolated projects and philanthropic activity often prevail.... The GRI provides standardized protocols to improve the quality and comparability of company reporting, but fewer than 200 firms report in accordance with GRI guidelines, another 700 partially do so, while others claim to use them informally.

Assurance helps people to know whether companies actually do what they say. A growing proportion of sustainability reports (circa 40 per cent) include some form of audit statement, typically provided by large accounting firms or smaller consultancies....

Supply chain assurance faces the greatest credibility challenges. Global brands and retailers, among others, have developed supplier codes to compensate for weak or unenforced standards in some countries, because global social expectations require them to demonstrate adherence to minimum standards. However, without independent external assurance of some sort these systems lack credibility, especially for companies with questionable performance records. Standards for supply chain auditing are highly variable. Among the most trusted are the brand certification and SA8000 factory certification systems of the Fair Labor Association (FLA), both of which involve multi-stakeholder governance structures....

For several reasons, the initiatives described in this section have not reached all types of companies. First, because many of the tools were developed for large national and transnational firms, they are not directly suitable for small- and medium-sized enterprises. Existing tools need to be adapted or new ones developed. Second, as noted, large developing country firms are just beginning to be drawn into this arena. Third, a more serious omission may be major state-owned enterprises based in some emerging economies: with few exceptions, they have not yet voluntarily associated themselves with such initiatives, nor is it well understood when the rules of State attribution apply to their human rights performance. Finally, as is true of all voluntary—and many statutory initiatives—determined laggards find ways to avoid scrutiny. This problem is not unique to human rights, nor is it unprecedented in history. But once a tipping point is reached, societies somehow manage to mitigate if not eliminate the problem. The trick is getting to the tipping point....

Questions and Discussion

1. *Draft norms.* The 2007 Report of the Special Representative of the Secretary-General, Professor John Ruggie, was prepared in response to a resolution of the United Nations Commission on Human Rights (now Human Rights Council), after it could not agree on adoption of the draft Norms on the Responsibilities of Transnational Corporations and other Business Enterprises with Regard to Human Rights (2003).

2. *Options for Accountability.* If the United Nations' Special Representative is correct that neither declarations nor the core U.N. and ILO treaties impose direct legal responsibilities on corporations, what options might be considered for those who seek to impose accountability on corporations for environmental and human rights violations? Are there other international law theories that might be used? Will national legal remedies do the job? If so, what kinds of national remedies are possible and under the laws of what nations? Do voluntary guidelines have a role to play?

3. *Soft Law.* Does it seem likely that the soft law instruments mentioned in the Special Representative's Report would lead to hard laws, either in international treaties, international customary law, or national legislation? Or are these instruments more likely to keep discussions of hard laws off the table?

4. *Self-regulation.* Is self-regulation the best available option? What about self-monitoring? Self-accountability?

5. *Weaknesses of Voluntarism.* In order to meet social expectations for corporate actions, firms will often publicize isolated projects and philanthropic activity but neglect to

report on the totality of their activities. Is it enough that corporations are at least doing some good voluntarily? Does this have the potential of deflecting critical attention to other activities of the corporation?

II. Litigating in National Courts for Harms Abroad

A. Corporate Liability for Crimes Abroad

Mapping International Standards of Responsibility and Accountability for Corporate Acts
John Ruggie
U.N. Doc. A/HRC/4/35 (19 February 2007)[b]

II. Corporate Responsibility and Accountability for International Crimes

Individuals have long been subject to direct responsibility for the international crimes of piracy and slavery, although in the absence of international accountability mechanisms they could be held liable only by national legal systems. The International Military Tribunals established after the Second World War confirmed that individuals bear responsibility for crimes against peace, war crimes, and crimes against humanity, and also imposed accountability on those within their jurisdiction, including corporate officers. With the entry into force of the Rome Statute of the International Criminal Court (ICC) in 2002, a permanent forum now exists in which individuals can be held directly accountable for genocide, crimes against humanity, and war crimes if States parties fail to act.

Long-standing doctrinal arguments over whether corporations could be "subjects" of international law, which impeded conceptual thinking on this issue and the attribution of direct legal responsibility to corporations, are yielding to new realities. Corporations are increasingly recognized as "participants" at the international level, with the capacity to bear some rights and duties under international law. As noted, they have certain rights under bilateral investment treaties; they are also subject to duties under several civil liability conventions dealing with environmental pollution. Although this has no direct bearing on corporate responsibility for international crimes, it makes it more difficult to maintain that corporations should be entirely exempt from responsibility in other areas of international law.

The ICC preparatory committee and the Rome conference on the establishment of the ICC debated a proposal that would have given the ICC jurisdiction over legal persons (other than States), but differences in national approaches prevented its adoption. Nevertheless, just as the absence of an international accountability mechanism did not preclude individual responsibility for international crimes in the past, it does not preclude the emergence of corporate responsibility today....

[N]ational courts interpreting corporate liability for international crimes have drawn on principles of individual responsibility, as the United States Court of Appeals for the Ninth Circuit did in its *Unocal* ruling.[19]

---

b. See full title information on page 374.
19. *Doe v. Unocal*, 395 F.3d 932 (9th Cir.2002). The case settled and the decision was vacated. [See page 393 of this textbook.]

At the same time, the number of jurisdictions in which charges for international crimes can be brought against corporations is increasing, as countries ratify the ICC Statute and incorporate its definitions into domestic law. Where national legal systems already provide for criminal punishment of companies the international standards for individuals may be extended, thereby, to corporate entities....

Domestic incorporation may also have an extraterritorial dimension. Several countries provide for extraterritorial jurisdiction with respect to international crimes committed by or against their nationals; and a few rely on "universal jurisdiction" to extend their laws, regardless of nationality links. Again, if they also permit criminal punishment of firms, those extraterritorial provisions could be extended to corporations.

Apart from national incorporation of international standards, a number of legal systems are evolving independently towards greater recognition of corporate criminal liability for violations of domestic law. Most common law countries have such provisions, at least for economic and some violent crimes. Many European civil law countries have moved beyond purely administrative regulation to adopt some form of criminal responsibility for corporations.

In this fluid setting, simple laws of probability alone suggest that corporations will be subject to increased liability for international crimes in the future. They may face either criminal or civil liability depending on whether international standards are incorporated into a State's criminal code or as a civil cause of action (as under the United States Alien Tort Claims Act, or ATCA).... In short, the risk environment for companies is expanding slowly but steadily, as are remedial options for victims.

Adding to the uncertainty for corporations, significant national variations remain in modes of attributing corporate liability. Given the difficulty of establishing a corporate "mind and will" in criminal cases, a number of jurisdictions have adopted a "corporate culture" approach. In Australia, where a firm's culture has been deemed expressly or tacitly to permit the commission of an offence by an employee, the firm may be held liable. In the United States, federal sentencing guidelines take corporate culture into account in assessing monetary penalties.[25] ...

Few legitimate firms may ever directly commit acts that amount to international crimes. But there is greater risk of their facing allegations of "complicity" in such crimes. For example, of the more than 40 ATCA cases brought against companies in the United States (now the largest body of domestic jurisprudence regarding corporate responsibility for international crimes), most have concerned alleged complicity where the actual perpetrators were public or private security forces, other government agents, or armed factions in civil conflicts.[27]

Corporate complicity is an umbrella term for a range of ways in which companies may be liable for their participation in criminal or civil wrongs. With nuanced differences, most national legal systems appear to recognize complicity as a concept. The international tribunals have developed a fairly clear standard for individual criminal aiding and abetting liability: knowingly providing practical assistance, encouragement or moral sup-

---

25. The 2005 Federal Sentencing Guidelines permit judicial consideration of whether a corporation has an "organizational culture that encourages ethical conduct and a commitment to compliance with the law" § 8B2.1(a).

27. The Supreme Court's only decision under ATCA, *Sosa v. Alvarez-Machain* 542 U.S. 692 (2004), does not preclude such liability for corporations, and the weight of current U.S. judicial opinion appears to support it, although there is disagreement among lower courts over its content and, in some cases, its existence. [See pages 388 to 391 of this textbook, including questions.]

port that has a substantial effect on the commission of the crime. Where national courts adopt this standard it is likely that its application to corporations would closely track its application to individuals, although the element of "moral support" may pose specific challenges.

"Moral support" can establish individual liability under international law, and the tribunals have extended it to include silent presence coupled with authority. But a company trying in good faith to avoid involvement in human rights abuses might have difficulty knowing what counts as moral support for legal purposes. Mere presence in a country and paying taxes are unlikely to create liability. But deriving indirect economic benefit from the wrongful conduct of others may do so, depending on such facts as the closeness of the company's association with those actors. Greater clarity currently does not exist. However, it is established that even where a corporation does not intend for the crime to occur, and regrets its commission, it will not be absolved of liability if it knew, or should have known, that it was providing assistance, and that the assistance would contribute to the commission of a crime.

Questions and Discussion

1. *Criminal versus civil liability.* How important is it for the regulation of corporate behavior that corporations be made subject to criminal law—domestic or international? Is such liability likely to lead to a company paying greater attention to legal norms than would result from civil liability alone? Is the legal advice given to a corporation likely to attract more attention on the part of corporate officers if criminal liability is in the picture?

2. *Standards of proof.* Does the high standard of proof generally required for criminal liability make it less likely that criminal sanctions will be applied than civil sanctions?

B. Corporate Liability for Torts Abroad

1. Enforcing the Law of Nations in U.S. Courts

Transnational Public Law Litigation
Harold Hongju Koh
100 Yale L.J. 2347 (1991)

Several years ago, I called attention to the burgeoning of "transnational public law litigation": suits brought in United States courts by individual and governmental litigants challenging violations of international law. As recent examples of this phenomenon, I included international human rights suits brought by aliens against foreign and United States governments and officials under the Alien Tort Statute, as well as actions by foreign governments against individual, American government, and corporate defendants.

Like its domestic counterpart..., transnational public law litigation seeks to vindicate public rights and values through judicial remedies. In both settings, parties bring "public actions," asking courts to declare and explicate public norms, often with the goal of provoking institutional reform.... [T]ransnational public law litigants have sought redress, deterrence, and reform of national governmental policies through clarification of rules of international conduct....

Private individuals, government officials, and nations sue one another directly, and are sued directly, in a variety of judicial fora, most prominently, domestic courts. In these fora, these actors invoke claims of right based not solely on domestic or international law, but rather, on a body of "transnational" law that blends the two. Moreover, contrary to "dualist" views of international jurisprudence, which see international law as binding only upon nations in their relations with one another, individual plaintiffs engaged in this mode of litigation usually claim rights arising directly from this body of transnational law.

As in traditional domestic litigation, transnational public lawsuits focus retrospectively upon achieving compensation and redress for individual victims. But as in traditional international law litigation, the transnational public law plaintiff pursues a prospective aim as well: to provoke judicial articulation of a *norm* of transnational law, with an eye toward using that declaration to promote a political settlement in which both governmental and nongovernmental entities will participate. Thus, although transnational public law plaintiffs routinely request retrospective damages or even prospective injunctive relief, their broader strategic goals are often served by a declaratory or default judgment announcing that a transnational norm has been violated....

I. The Evolution of Transnational Public Law Litigation

A. *The Law of Nations in American Courts ...*

As England became the preeminent global power, the law of nations was domesticated first into English common law, then applied to the American colonies, and subsequently incorporated into United States law. With American independence, the law of nations became part of the common law of the United States. The Continental Congress resolved to send a diplomatic letter stating that the United States would cause "the law of nations to be most strictly observed." The Federalist Papers made extensive mention of the law of nations' role in United States courts. In Article I of the Constitution, the Framers expressly gave Congress the power to define and punish "Piracies ... committed on the high Seas, and Offences against the Law of Nations." Moreover, Article III extended the judicial power of the United States not simply to cases arising under the Constitution and laws of the United States, but also to cases arising under treaties, and a large class of international cases—those affecting Ambassadors, public Ministers and consuls, admiralty and maritime cases, and cases involving foreign parties.

The Framers never expected such cases and controversies to be decided solely under domestic law. As Professor White has recounted, "[t]he Framers' Constitution anticipated that international disputes would regularly come before the United States courts, and that the decisions in those cases could rest on principles of international law, without any necessary reference to the common law or to constitutional doctrines." All three branches quickly recognized the applicability of the law of nations in American courts. Executive officials such as Thomas Jefferson heralded the law of nations as "an integral part ... of the laws of the land." Congress immediately enacted as part of the First Judiciary Act the Alien Tort Statute, which gave the district courts jurisdiction "of all causes where an alien sues for a tort only in violation of the law of nations or a treaty of the United States." Shortly thereafter, Congress passed statutes criminalizing piracy and assaults upon ambassadors. American courts regularly decided cases under the law of nations, particularly those involving piracies and prize jurisdiction (captures of enemy ships as prizes of war), and applied and clarified international law principles in cases concerning offenses against the law of nations, acquisition and control of territory, boundary disputes, questions of nationality, foreign sovereign immunity, and principles of war and neutrality....

[T]hroughout the early nineteenth century, American courts regularly construed and applied the unwritten law of nations as part of the "general common law," particularly to resolve commercial disputes, without regard to whether it should be characterized as federal or state....

> [I]n 1895, Justice Gray ... proclaim[ed] in *Hilton v. Guyot* [159 U.S. 113 (1895).] that:
>
>> International law, in its widest and most comprehensive sense—including not only questions of right between nations, governed by what has been appropriately called the law of nations; but also questions arising under what is usually called private international law, or the conflict of laws, and concerning the rights of persons within the territory and dominion of one nation, by reason of acts, private or public, done within the dominions of another nation—is part of our law, and must be ascertained and administered by the courts of justice, as often as such questions are presented in litigation between man and man, duly submitted to their determination.

Although conceding that treaties or statutes provided American courts with "[t]he most certain guide ... for the decision of such questions," when "there is no written law upon the subject," Justice Gray repeated, "the duty still rests upon the judicial tribunals of ascertaining and declaring what the law is, whenever it becomes necessary to do so, in order to determine the rights of parties to suits regularly brought before them." ...

Marbury's command [is] that "[i]t is emphatically the province and duty of the judicial department to say what the law is." ... [A]bsent a contrary statute, "the Court is bound by the law of nations which is a part of the law of the land." That same year [Marshall] announced that "[t]he law of nations is the great source from which we derive those rules, respecting belligerent and neutral rights, which are recognized by all civilized and commercial states."

As the twentieth century opened, Justice Gray repeated almost verbatim [Marshall's] words ... in a famous prize case, *The Paquete Habana,* [175 U.S. 677, 700 (1900)]. But over the first half of this century, the scope of the law of nations applied in American courts substantially narrowed. By overruling *Swift* in 1938, *Erie R.R. Co. v. Tompkins,* 304 U.S. 64 (1938), interred the general common law, raising fears that the law of nations might be subordinated into state, not federal, law. The laws merchant and maritime were assimilated into domestic law and the public/private distinction seized prominence, as conflict of laws was "privatized" and treated as a body of primarily domestic legal principles governing disputes with foreign interests or persons. As the century proceeded, the courts increasingly invoked three concerns to mitigate their duty to declare the law of nations: *comity, separation of powers,* and *judicial incompetence....*

Separation of powers and judicial incompetence, the second and third leitmotifs of the Court's new international jurisprudence, surfaced as the Court began increasingly to defer to claimed presidential authority and expertise in foreign affairs.

B. *Modern Transnational Public Law Litigation*

Modern transnational public law litigation began with the 1946 war crimes trials at Nuremburg and Tokyo, which redefined the permissible party structures, claims, and fora of international litigation.

The Allied victory in World War II triggered a remarkable change in the global legal order. The Allies self-consciously sought to transform international law from an interstitial, state-to-state system of narrow, informal customary rules based upon mutual respect and abstention—"do-no-harm" rules of neutrality and diplomatic immunity, for example—into an ambitious affirmative construct. The United Nations and the Bretton Woods systems heralded a postwar legal order based on institutionalism and constitutionalism: international institutions governed by multilateral treaties organizing cooperative assaults on all manner of global problems.

Tokyo and Nuremburg pierced the veil of state sovereignty and dispelled the myth that international law is for states only, re-declaring that individuals are subjects, not just objects, of international law. Thereafter, private citizens, government officials, nongovernmental organizations and multinational enterprises could all be rightsholders and responsible actors under international law, and hence, proper plaintiffs and defendants in transnational actions.... Tokyo and Nuremberg galvanized the international human rights movement: the drive for global human rights standards that has provided transnational public law litigation with its authoritative texts.

[A]fter Nuremburg, several factors converged to shift transnational public law litigation out of international settings and into American courts. Ambitious proposals to create an international criminal court surfaced repeatedly, but to this day have never materialized. [Note: Since Prof. Koh's article was written, the ICC has begun operation. See page 380.] Evolving dispute-settlement regimes chose to grant nonstate parties only limited direct access to international tribunals. Over time, the International Court of Justice failed to provide a meaningful forum for resolving international disputes, much less for enunciating international human rights norms or curbing national misconduct. Thus, after Nuremburg, global confidence in international adjudication steadily declined.

At about the same time, the American civil rights movement pressed international human rights norms into service in its war against racial discrimination. [In the late 1940s and early 1950s] American civil liberties groups filed suits in both state and federal courts, citing the human rights provisions of the United Nations Charter and the Universal Declaration of Human Rights to challenge racial discrimination in education, transportation, employment, housing, and land ownership.

These early cases created widespread concern that our new global treaty commitments, coupled with the Supremacy Clause, might undermine state sovereignty and domestic autonomy.[75] In response, the courts fashioned two doctrines that frustrated this initial wave of suits. Numerous state and federal courts first invoked the doctrine of "nonself-executing treaties" to prevent individuals from directly enforcing the new positive law. By its terms, the Supremacy Clause makes treaties the supreme law of the land. It nowhere distinguishes between so-called self-executing treaties (which become part of domestic law immediately upon ratification) and nonself-executing treaties (which must be implemented by statute to acquire domestic legal effect). Nor did the Framers ever hint at such a distinction.

Chief Justice Marshall first drew that line in *Foster & Elam v. Neilson*, [27 U.S. (2 Pet.) 253 (1829)].... Marshall clearly intended nonself-executing treaties to be the exception, not the rule. Nevertheless, post-Nuremburg courts revitalized and expanded the doctrine to hold a series of human rights treaties nonself-executing.... [C]ourts have fragmented

---

75. These concerns spurred the unsuccessful drive to adopt the Bricker Amendment, which would have overruled *Missouri v. Holland,* 252 U.S. 416 (1920). *See generally* D. Tananbaum, THE BRICKER AMENDMENT CONTROVERSY: A TEST OF EISENHOWER'S POLITICAL LEADERSHIP (1988). *Holland* held that a statute implementing a migratory bird treaty could regulate matters apparently reserved to the states, notwithstanding the Tenth Amendment. Thus, under *Holland,* Congress would have had the authority to implement the Genocide Convention (had the United States ratified it) by enacting sweeping civil rights legislation. Fear of this result helped delay United States' ratification of the Genocide Convention for thirty-eight years; meanwhile, Congress ultimately enacted broad civil rights legislation anyway, invoking the commerce clause and section 5 of the Fourteenth Amendment.

the nonself-executing treaty doctrine into a series of preliminary obstacles that litigants must now overcome to enforce treaties through the courts.

The second judicial barrier to transnational public law litigation solidified in 1964, when the Court recast the Act of State doctrine into its modern form in *Banco Nacional de Cuba v. Sabbatino*[, 376 U.S. 398 (1964)]. An odd coalition of the judicial restraint and anticolonialist elements on the Court formed an eight-Justice majority that voted not simply to defer to a Cuban expropriatory decree, but also to *enforce* it against an expropriated company's American owners. Although *Sabbatino* was technically a commercial case, replete with vertical elements, the Court declined even to apply international law to review the validity of the act of a recognized foreign sovereign fully executed within its own territory. By so saying, the Court went far beyond the comity rationale that had guided its previous Act of State decisions, now emphasizing separation of powers and judicial incompetence as the main reasons why American courts should not adjudicate cases under international law.

By explicitly linking the Act of State Doctrine to separation of powers, *Sabbatino* implied that determinations regarding the legality of foreign state acts are quasi-political questions, whose decision is appropriately confided in the Executive Branch or Congress, not the courts. Moreover, the Court concluded that courts have limited competence to find the law in international cases, a conclusion belied both by Justice White's powerful dissent and extensive judicial precedents. *Sabbatino* especially urged abstention in customary international law cases where no clear consensus exists on the content of the rule in question. Together with the self-executing treaty doctrine, *Sabbatino* thus cast a profound chill upon the willingness of United States domestic courts to interpret or articulate norms of international law—both customary and treaty-based—in both private and public cases....

The courts soon read *Sabbatino,* together with earlier precedents regarding judicial deference to executive discretion in foreign affairs and political question notions imported from the domestic electoral context, as a general directive to stay out of foreign affairs adjudication. This chill stimulated a period of American judicial withdrawal from the arena of public international norm-enunciation that lasted for more than a decade....

As the 1970's closed, however, two complementary trends engendered a new generation of transnational public law cases in United States judicial fora. The first was the by now well-chronicled rise of *domestic* public law litigation: a growing acceptance by litigants of United States courts as instruments of social change....

This growing faith in the capacity of the courts to engage in domestic public law litigation coincided with a second trend: the explosion of *transnational commercial* litigation in United States courts....

The resurgence of transnational private law litigation forced reevaluation of the comity, separation-of-powers, and incompetence rationales for judicial abstention in transnational public law cases. The persistent question arose, "if contracts, why not torture?" If American courts could subject the commercial conduct of foreign sovereigns to legal scrutiny without offending comity, why should comity immunize that same sovereign from judicial examination of its egregious public conduct? These precedents also cast doubt upon *Sabbatino*'s separation-of-powers conclusion that the lawfulness of foreign governmental acts is a quasi-political question, which courts may not constitutionally decide. If a court could hold a foreign sovereign defendant in violation of a commercial contract without usurping the executive function, why couldn't it hold the same defendant in violation of a human rights treaty, or a clearly defined *jus cogens* norm against torture? ... The growing codification and hence, accessibility of customary international law rules—through statutes, unratified treaties, and scholarly treatises—belied the claim that such rules were hopelessly beyond a domestic court's law-finding capacities....

In 1980, these trends came together in the Second Circuit's landmark decision in *Filartiga v. Pena-Irala*, 630 F.2d 876, 884, n. 15 (2d Cir. 1980). *Filartiga* held that the Alien Tort Statute conferred district court jurisdiction over a suit by Paraguayans versus a Paraguayan official who had tortured their relative to death in Paraguay, while acting under color of governmental authority. On remand, the federal district court awarded judgment of nearly $ 10.4 million, comprising compensatory damages based on Paraguayan law and punitive damages based on United States cases and international law....

[T]he core issue in the case was quintessentially legal: whether the victims had a right to be free from torture that was actionable in federal court. Resolution of that question required standard legal determinations—judicial construction of the Alien Tort Statute and human rights treaties—and a conclusion that the customary international law norm against torture was definable, obligatory, and universal....

Since *Filartiga,* transnational public law litigation has followed two tracks: cases brought by individual plaintiffs and those brought by nation-states.... International tort suits have generated the greatest activity in United States courts. *Filartiga* provided the paradigm for a series of Alien Tort Statute suits by alien plaintiffs against foreign officials acting under color of governmental authority, claiming violations of the plaintiffs' internationally recognized human rights.... These small successes encouraged Alien Tort Statute plaintiffs to expand the class of defendants beyond foreign government officials to a second group, foreign governments....

The most novel development in transnational public law litigation has been its expansion beyond individual to state plaintiffs. The litigation brought by the Government of India against Union Carbide in United States and Indian courts in the wake of the Bhopal tragedy provides the most dramatic example. Following an environmental disaster, the importing state sued a private multinational entity in domestic, rather than international, court, making complex claims based on transnational law. India sued as *parens patriae* for its citizens, claiming to seek judicial reparations for their injuries, but its apparent motive in turning to American courts was not so much to win enforceable relief, as to obtain a judicial declaration of Union Carbide's strict liability for the disaster. Although India hoped to use such a declaration to provoke a political settlement that would potentially bind Union Carbide, India, the United States, as well as the private Indian plaintiffs, that ambition was not realized....

Transnational public law litigation thus constitutes a novel and expanding effort by both state and individual plaintiffs to fuse international legal rights with domestic judicial remedies. Transnational litigation, which originated in the context of private commercial suits against foreign governments, has now migrated into the realm of public human rights suits against the United States and foreign governments and officials. State-initiated litigation, once restricted to international tribunals, has also migrated into American courts, reflecting failing faith in international adjudication as a process for obtaining meaningful remedies....

Whether transnational public law litigation in United States courts will flourish or fail remains to be seen....

III. Domestic Courts and the New International Legal Process ...

In international cases [a] dialogue proceeds not just between courts and litigants, or between courts and the political branches, but also between American courts and other law-declaring institutions of the international system....

[C]learly, transnational public law litigation itself—a judicial phenomenon with venerable roots—is entering a new era, in which the possibilities for dialogue among American and international tribunals are greater than at any time in modern memory. In this uncertain future, the normative possibilities for transnational public law litigation can only expand. . . .

Sosa v. Alvarez-Machain
542 U.S. 692 (2004)

Justice SOUTER delivered the opinion of the Court.

I . . .

In 1985, an agent of the Drug Enforcement Administration (DEA), Enrique Camarena-Salazar, was captured on assignment in Mexico and taken to a house in Guadalajara, where he was tortured over the course of a 2-day interrogation, then murdered. . . . DEA officials in the United States came to believe that respondent Humberto Alvarez-Machain (Alvarez), a Mexican physician, was present at the house and acted to prolong the agent's life in order to extend the interrogation and torture.

In 1990, a federal grand jury indicted Alvarez for the torture and murder of Camarena-Salazar, and the United States District Court for the Central District of California issued a warrant for his arrest. . . . [T]he DEA approved a plan to hire Mexican nationals to seize Alvarez and bring him to the United States for trial. As so planned, a group of Mexicans, including petitioner Jose Francisco Sosa, abducted Alvarez from his house, held him overnight in a motel, and brought him by private plane to El Paso, Texas, where he was arrested by federal officers. . . .

[Alvarez's] case was tried in 1992, and ended at the close of the Government's case, when the District Court granted Alvarez's motion for a judgment of acquittal.

In 1993, after returning to Mexico, Alvarez began the civil action before us here. He sued Sosa [and several others] . . . under the ATS [Alien Tort Statute] for a violation of the law of nations. . . . The [ATS] provides in its entirety that "[t]he district courts shall have original jurisdiction of any civil action by an alien for a tort only, committed in violation of the law of nations or a treaty of the United States." [28 U.S.C.] § 1350.

The District Court . . . awarded summary judgment and $25,000 in damages to Alvarez on the ATS claim. A three-judge panel of the Ninth Circuit then affirmed the ATS judgment. . . .

A divided en banc court came to the same conclusion. . . . As for the ATS claim, the court called on its own precedent, "that [the ATS] not only provides federal courts with subject matter jurisdiction, but also creates a cause of action for an alleged violation of the law of nations." . . . The Circuit then relied upon what it called the "clear and universally recognized norm prohibiting arbitrary arrest and detention" . . . to support the conclusion that Alvarez's arrest amounted to a tort in violation of international law. . . .

III . . .

[Sosa] argues (as does the United States supporting him) that there is no relief under the ATS because the statute does no more than vest federal courts with jurisdiction, neither creating nor authorizing the courts to recognize any particular right of action without further congressional action. Although we agree the statute is in terms only jurisdictional, we think that at the time of enactment the jurisdiction enabled federal courts to hear claims in a very limited category defined by the law of nations and recognized at common law. We do not believe, however, that the limited, implicit sanction to entertain the handful of international law *cum* common law claims understood in 1789 should be taken as authority to recognize the right of action asserted by Alvarez here....

[The "very limited category" Justice Souter mentioned consisted of those few international law violations recognized in 1789 that, despite their international character, had a potential for personal liability. The Court concluded that the ATS is best read as a grant of jurisdiction over this narrow field of international causes of action.

[By way of example, the Court identified three such offenses, as listed by William Blackstone in his *Commentaries* of 1769. These offenses were the violation of safe conducts, the infringement of the rights of ambassadors, and piracy. Blackstone, 4 Commentaries on the Laws of England 68 (1769).]

IV

We think it is correct, then, to assume that the First Congress understood that the district courts would recognize private causes of action for certain torts in violation of the law of nations, though we have found no basis to suspect Congress had any examples in mind beyond those torts corresponding to Blackstone's three primary offenses.... We assume, too, that no development in the two centuries from the enactment of § 1350 to the birth of the modern line of cases beginning with *Filartiga v. Pena-Irala*, 630 F.2d 876 (2d Cir. 1980), has categorically precluded federal courts from recognizing a claim under the law of nations as an element of common law.... Still, there are good reasons for a restrained conception of the discretion a federal court should exercise in considering a new cause of action of this kind. Accordingly, we think courts should require any claim based on the present-day law of nations to rest on a norm of international character accepted by the civilized world and defined with a specificity comparable to the features of the 18th-century paradigms we have recognized. This requirement is fatal to Alvarez's claim.

A

A series of reasons argue for judicial caution when considering the kinds of individual claims that might implement the jurisdiction conferred by the early statute. First, the prevailing conception of the common law has changed since 1789 in a way that counsels restraint in judicially applying internationally generated norms. When § 1350 was enacted, the accepted conception was of the common law as "a transcendental body of law outside of any particular State but obligatory within it unless and until changed by statute." *Black and White Taxicab & Transfer Co. v. Brown and Yellow Taxicab & Transfer Co.*, 276 U.S. 518 (1928) (Holmes, J., dissenting). Now, however, in most cases where a court is asked to state or formulate a common law principle in a new context, there is a general understanding that the law is not so much found or discovered as it is either made or created....

Second, along with, and in part driven by, that conceptual development in understanding common law has come an equally significant rethinking of the role of the federal courts in making it. *Erie R. Co. v. Tompkins*, 304 U.S. 64 (1938), was the watershed in which we denied the existence of any federal "general" common law ... [T]he general practice has been to look for legislative guidance before exercising innovative authority over substantive law. It would be remarkable to take a more aggressive role in exercising a jurisdiction that remained largely in shadow for much of the prior two centuries.

Third, this Court has recently and repeatedly said that a decision to create a private right of action is one better left to legislative judgment in the great majority of cases.... [T]he possible collateral consequences of making international rules privately actionable argue for judicial caution.

Fourth, the subject of those collateral consequences is itself a reason for a high bar to new private causes of action for violating international law, for the potential implications for the foreign relations of the United States of recognizing such causes should make courts particularly wary of impinging on the discretion of the Legislative and Executive Branches in managing foreign affairs.... Since many attempts by federal courts to craft remedies for the violation of new norms of international law would raise risks of adverse foreign policy consequences, they should be undertaken, if at all, with great caution....

The fifth reason is particularly important in light of the first four. We have no congressional mandate to seek out and define new and debatable violations of the law of nations, and modern indications of congressional understanding of the judicial role in the field have not affirmatively encouraged greater judicial creativity....

C

We must still, however, derive a standard or set of standards for assessing the particular claim Alvarez raises, and for this action it suffices to look to the historical antecedents. Whatever the ultimate criteria for accepting a cause of action subject to jurisdiction under § 1350, we are persuaded that federal courts should not recognize private claims under federal common law for violations of any international law norm with less definite content and acceptance among civilized nations than the historical paradigms familiar when § 1350 was enacted. See, e.g., *United States v. Smith*, 5 Wheat. 153, 163–180, n. 8 (1820) (illustrating the specificity with which the law of nations defined piracy)....

Thus, Alvarez's detention claim must be gauged against the current state of international law, looking to those sources we have long, albeit cautiously, recognized.

> [W]here there is no treaty, and no controlling executive or legislative act or judicial decision, resort must be had to the customs and usages of civilized nations; and, as evidence of these, to the works of jurists and commentators, who by years of labor, research and experience, have made themselves peculiarly well acquainted with the subjects of which they treat. Such works are resorted to by judicial tribunals, not for the speculations of their authors concerning what the law ought to be, but for trustworthy evidence of what the law really is.

The Paquete Habana, [175 U.S. 677, 700 (1900)].

To begin with, Alvarez cites two well-known international agreements that, despite their moral authority, have little utility under the standard set out in this opinion. He says that his abduction by Sosa was an "arbitrary arrest" within the meaning of the Universal Declaration of Human Rights (Declaration).... And he traces the rule against arbitrary arrest not only to the Declaration, but also to article nine of the International Covenant on Civil and Political Rights (Covenant), Dec. 16, 1966, 999 U.N.T.S. 171..., to which the United States is a party, and to various other conventions to which it is not. But the Declaration does not of its own force impose obligations as a matter of international law.... And, although the Covenant does bind the United States as a matter of international law, the United States ratified the Covenant on the express understanding that it was not self-executing and so did not itself create obligations enforceable in the federal courts.... Accordingly, Alvarez cannot say that the Declaration and Covenant themselves establish the relevant and applicable rule of international law. He instead attempts to show that prohibition of arbitrary arrest has attained the status of binding customary international law....

Alvarez ... invokes a general prohibition of "arbitrary" detention defined as officially sanctioned action exceeding positive authorization to detain under the domestic law of some government, regardless of the circumstances. Whether or not this is an accurate reading of the Covenant, Alvarez cites little authority that a rule so broad has the status of a binding customary norm today.[27] ...

Whatever may be said for the broad principle Alvarez advances, in the present, imperfect world, it expresses an aspiration that exceeds any binding customary rule having the specificity we require.[29] Creating a private cause of action to further that aspiration would go beyond any residual common law discretion we think it appropriate to exercise.... It is enough to hold that a single illegal detention of less than a day, followed by the transfer of custody to lawful authorities and a prompt arraignment, violates no norm of customary international law so well defined as to support the creation of a federal remedy.

The judgment of the Court of Appeals is

Reversed.

[Concurrences omitted.]

Questions and Discussion

1. *Federal common law.* Justice Scalia did not join part IV of the Court's opinion. He believed that applying customary international law according to the Court's schema required the creation of general federal common law, a practice the court had abolished in *Erie.* 542 U.S. at 746. The Court responded that "*Erie* did not in terms bar any judicial recognition of new substantive rules, no matter what the circumstances...." *Id.* at 729. The Court further noted that "[f]or two centuries we have affirmed that the domestic law of the United States recognizes the law of nations." *Id.*

2. *Acceptance and specificity.* At the beginning of part IV, the Court says that a claim based on the law of nations must rest on an international norm that is both "accepted by the civilized world" and "defined with a specificity" comparable to those from the 18th century that the Court references. In part IV-C, the Court cites a 17-page footnote from an 1820 case for this specificity. The sources cited in the footnote are in English, French, Spanish, and primarily Latin. Are there any environmental rights that can be said to have similarly widespread acceptance and specific definition?

3. *Legislative guidance.* The Court mentions in part IV-A the advantages in general of waiting for "legislative guidance," deferring to "legislative judgment," and the benefits of a "congressional mandate." Nevertheless, the Court declines Justice Scalia's invitation to hold that only definite legislation can provide the basis for a claim under the Alien Tort

---

27. Specifically, he relies on a survey of national constitutions [and two other arguments].... None of these suffice. The [constitutional] survey does show that many nations recognize a norm against arbitrary detention, but that consensus is at a high level of generality.

29. It is not that violations of a rule logically foreclose the existence of that rule as international law. Cf. *Filartiga v. Pena-Irala,* 630 F.2d 876, 884, n. 15 (C.A.2 1980) ("The fact that the prohibition of torture is often honored in the breach does not diminish its binding effect as a norm of international law"). Nevertheless, that a rule as stated is as far from full realization as the one Alvarez urges is evidence against its status as binding law; and an even clearer point against the creation by judges of a private cause of action to enforce the aspiration behind the rule claimed.

Statute (ATS) (also known as the Alien Tort Claims Act, or ATCA). Is the great body of U.S. environmental legislation a sufficient basis, in conjunction with similar legislation elsewhere in the world, for the courts to move forward and declare various environmental rights as sufficient for ATS claims? Consider the Court's discussion of a similar point in footnotes 27 and 29.

4. *Foreign policy consequences.* The Court also mentions in part IV-A the potential adverse foreign policy consequences if the federal courts were to craft remedies for the violation of new norms of international law. Would this caution apply more to some environmental rights claims than to others? What about claims based on procedural rights? Rights asserted to be violated by emissions of greenhouse gases by either transnational or localized industries causing global warming?

5. *Corporations as defendants under the ATS.* To date, no court above the trial level has expressly held that corporations may be defendants under the ATS. But such an express holding does not seem to be necessary. Several ATS claims against corporate defendants have withstood scrutiny at the trial and appellate levels without the corporate defendant's capacity being questioned or even mentioned.

In *Presbyterian Church of Sudan v. Talisman Energy, Inc.*, the U.S. District Court for the Southern District of New York used that fact as an affirmative basis for holding that corporations may be sued under the ATS.

> Historically, states, and to a lesser extent individuals, have been held liable under international law. However, … substantial international and United States precedent indicates that corporations may also be held liable under international law, at least for gross human rights violations. Extensive Second Circuit precedent further indicates that actions under the ATCA against corporate defendants for such substantial violations of international law, including *jus cogens* violations, are the norm rather than the exception.
>
> Such a result should hardly be surprising. A private corporation is a juridical person and has no *per se* immunity under U.S. domestic or international law.… Given that private individuals are liable for violations of international law in certain circumstances, there is no logical reason why corporations should not be held liable, at least in cases of *jus cogens* violations. Indeed, while *Talisman* disputes the fact that corporations are capable of violating the law of nations, it provides no logical argument supporting its claim. As noted at length *supra*, substantial U.S. and international precedent indicates that corporations may be responsible, in certain cases, for violations of international law. In this case, where plaintiffs allege *jus cogens* violations, corporate liability may follow. Consequently, the Court denies *Talisman*'s motion to dismiss for lack of subject matter jurisdiction on this basis.

Presbyterian Church of Sudan v. Talisman Energy, Inc., 244 F. Supp. 2d 289, 318–319 (S.D.N.Y. 2003).

The *Presbyterian Church* litigation carried on; meanwhile, the Supreme Court decided *Sosa* in 2004. Talisman then tried using *Sosa* to support a motion for judgment on the pleadings. Talisman argued that there was no international-law norm of corporate liability that could meet the *Sosa* standard of clarity and acceptance, and therefore the district court's 2003 reasoning was no longer a valid justification for letting the case proceed. 374 F. Supp. 2d 331, 334–335 (S.D.N.Y. 2005). The district court rejected that argument, noting that since *Sosa* the Second Circuit had continued to allow cases against corporate defendants to go forward, and that *Sosa* "explicitly contemplates the existence of corporate liability under customary international law." *Id.* at 335 (citing *Sosa*, 542 U.S. at 732 n. 20). At the time of publication, the case continued in the district court.

6. A thoughtful overview of the field is provided in William A. Fletcher, *International Human Rights in American Courts*, 93 Va. L. Rev. 653 (2007). The author is a judge on the U.S. Court of Appeals for the Ninth Circuit.

7. *Complicity.* One of the issues that may arise in an Alien Tort Claims Act case against a corporation is whether acts by state bodies (such as the military) can be attributed to a corporation working with a state body. This is known as "complicity." The following case illustrates the way in which corporations may be held liable for acts by state bodies.

Doe I v. Unocal
395 F.3d 932 (9th Cir. 2002), *dismissed after settlement*, 403 F.3d 708 (9th Cir. 2005)c

PREGERSON, Circuit Judge.

This case involves human rights violations that allegedly occurred in Myanmar, formerly known as Burma. Villagers from the Tenasserim region in Myanmar allege that the Defendants directly or indirectly subjected the villagers to forced labor, murder, rape, and torture when the Defendants constructed a gas pipeline through the Tenasserim region. The villagers base their claims [inter alia] on the Alien Tort Claims Act, 28 U.S.C. § 1350....

The District Court, through dismissal and summary judgment, resolved all of Plaintiffs' federal claims in favor of the Defendants. For the following reasons, we reverse in part and affirm in part the District Court's rulings.

I. FACTUAL AND PROCEDURAL BACKGROUND ...

In 1988, a new military government, Defendant-Appellee State Law and Order Restoration Council ("the Myanmar Military"), took control [of Burma] and renamed the country Myanmar. The Myanmar Military established a state owned company, Defendant-Appellee Myanmar Oil and Gas Enterprise ("Myanmar Oil"), to produce and sell the nation's oil and gas resources.

In 1992, Myanmar Oil licensed the French oil company Total S.A. ("Total") to produce, transport, and sell natural gas from deposits in the Yadana Field off the coast of Myanmar ("the Project")....

Also in 1992, Defendant-Appellant Unocal Corporation and its wholly owned subsidiary Defendant-Appellant Union Oil Company of California, collectively referred to below as "Unocal," acquired a 28% interest in the Project from Total....

It is undisputed that the Myanmar Military provided security and other services for the Project, and that Unocal knew about this....

There is also evidence sufficient to raise a genuine issue of material fact whether the Project hired the Myanmar Military, through Myanmar Oil, to provide these services,

---

c. After this Court of Appeals opinion, the parties negotiated a settlement. As a condition of that settlement, the parties jointly moved the Court of Appeals to dismiss the appeal, which it did *en banc*, 403 F.3d 708 (9th Cir. 2005). The plaintiff-appellants also agreed to move to vacate the District Court opinion, a motion that was also granted. *Id.* Regardless of this dismissal, corporate counsel are likely to continue to pay great attention to the 2002 panel discussion as it is the most thorough extant judicial discussion of corporate liability for certain actions in infrastructure projects abroad.

and whether Unocal knew about this.... Furthermore, there is evidence sufficient to raise a genuine issue of material fact whether the Project directed the Myanmar Military in these activities, at least to a degree, and whether Unocal was involved in this....

Plaintiffs allege that the Myanmar Military forced them, under threat of violence, to work on and serve as porters for the Project....

Plaintiffs also allege in furtherance of the forced labor program just described, the Myanmar Military subjected them to acts of murder, rape, and torture. For instance, Jane Doe I testified that after her husband, John Doe I, attempted to escape the forced labor program, he was shot at by soldiers, and in retaliation for his attempted escape, that she and her baby were thrown into a fire, resulting in injuries to her and the death of the child.... Plaintiffs finally allege that Unocal's conduct gives rise to liability for these abuses.

[E]ven before Unocal invested in the Project, Unocal was made aware—by its own consultants and by its partners in the Project of this record and that the Myanmar Military might also employ forced labor and commit other human rights violations in connection with the Project.... And after Unocal invested in the Project, Unocal was made aware—by its own consultants and employees, its partners in the Project, and human rights organizations—of allegations that the Myanmar Military was actually committing such violations in connection with the Project....

[The case on appeal is a consolidation of two similar lawsuits ("Roe I" and "Doe I") filed in the fall of 1996 by two separate groups of Tenasserim villagers alleging, among other claims, violations of international law within ATCA jurisdiction.]

On August 31, 2000, the District Court granted Unocal's consolidated motions for summary judgment on all of Plaintiffs' remaining federal claims in both actions. The District Court granted Unocal's motion for summary judgment on the ATCA claims based on murder, rape, and torture because Plaintiffs could not show that Unocal engaged in state action and that Unocal controlled the Myanmar Military....

[Both Doe and Roe plaintiffs] appeal the District Court's grant of summary judgment in favor of Unocal on their ATCA claims against Unocal....

II. ANALYSIS

A. Liability Under the Alien Tort Claims Act.

1. Introduction ...

[A] threshold question in any ATCA case against a private party, such as Unocal, is whether the alleged tort requires the private party to engage in state action for ATCA liability to attach, and if so, whether the private party in fact engaged in state action.... The Second Circuit first noted [in *Kadic v. Karadzic*, 70 F.3d 232 (2d Cir. 1995)] that genocide and war crimes—like slave trading—do not require state action for ATCA liability to attach. The Second Circuit went on to state that although "acts of rape, torture, and summary execution," like most crimes, "are proscribed by international law only when committed by state officials or under color of law" to the extent that they were committed in isolation, these crimes "are actionable under the Alien Tort [Claims] Act, without regard to state action, to the extent that they were committed *in pursuit of genocide or war crimes*." (emphasis added).... We agree with this view and apply it below to Plaintiffs' various ATCA claims.

2. Forced Labor

Our case law strongly supports the conclusion that forced labor is a modern variant of slavery. Accordingly, forced labor, like traditional variants of slave trading, is among the "handful of crimes ... to which the law of nations attributes individual liability," such that state action is not required....

Plaintiffs argue that Unocal aided and abetted the Myanmar Military in subjecting them to forced labor. We hold that the standard for aiding and abetting under the ATCA is, as discussed below, knowing practical assistance or encouragement that has a substantial effect on the perpetration of the crime. We further hold that a reasonable factfinder could find that Unocal's conduct met this standard....

District Courts are increasingly turning to the decisions by international criminal tribunals for instructions regarding the standards of international human rights law under our civil ATCA.... We agree with this approach. We find recent decisions by the International Criminal Tribunal for the former Yugoslavia [in *Prosecutor v. Furundzija*, IT-95-17/1 T (Dec. 10, 1998), reprinted in 38 I.L.M. 317 (1999)] and the International Criminal Tribunal for Rwanda especially helpful for ascertaining the current standard for aiding and abetting under international law as it pertains to the ATCA....

The *Furundzija* standard for aiding and abetting liability under international criminal law can be summarized as knowing practical assistance, encouragement, or moral support which has a substantial effect on the perpetration of the crime....

[W]e do not need to decide whether it would have been enough if Unocal had only given moral support to the Myanmar Military. Accordingly, we may impose aiding and abetting liability for knowing practical assistance or encouragement which has a substantial effect on the perpetration of the crime, leaving the question whether such liability should also be imposed for moral support which has the required substantial effect to another day.

First, a reasonable factfinder could conclude that Unocal's alleged conduct met the *actus reus* requirement of aiding and abetting as we define it today, i.e., practical assistance or encouragement which has a substantial effect on the perpetration of the crime of, in the present case, forced labor.

Unocal's weak protestations notwithstanding, there is little doubt that the record contains substantial evidence creating a material question of fact as to whether forced labor was used in connection with the construction of the pipeline....

The evidence also supports the conclusion that Unocal gave practical assistance to the Myanmar Military in subjecting Plaintiffs to forced labor.... The practical assistance took the form of hiring the Myanmar Military to provide security and build infrastructure along the pipeline route in exchange for money or food. The practical assistance also took the form of using photos, surveys, and maps in daily meetings to show the Myanmar Military where to provide security and build infrastructure....

Second, a reasonable factfinder could also conclude that Unocal's conduct met the *mens rea* requirement of aiding and abetting.... Unocal knew or should reasonably have known that its conduct—including the payments and the instructions where to provide security and build infrastructure—would assist or encourage the Myanmar Military to subject Plaintiffs to forced labor.

Viewing the evidence in the light most favorable to Plaintiffs, we conclude that there are genuine issues of material fact whether Unocal's conduct met the *actus reus* and *mens rea* requirements for liability under the ATCA for aiding and abetting forced labor. Accordingly, we reverse the District Court's grant of Unocal's motion for summary judgment on Plaintiffs' forced labor claims under the ATCA.

3. Murder, Rape, and Torture

Plaintiffs further allege that the Myanmar military murdered, raped or tortured a number of the plaintiffs.... According to Plaintiffs' deposition testimony, all of the acts of murder, rape, and torture alleged by Plaintiffs occurred in furtherance of the forced labor program. As discussed above..., forced labor is a modern variant of slavery and does therefore never require state action to give rise to liability under the ATCA. Thus, under *Kadic*, state action is also not required for the acts of murder, rape, and torture which allegedly occurred in furtherance of the forced labor program....

The same reasons that convinced us earlier that Unocal may be liable under this standard for aiding and abetting the Myanmar Military in subjecting Plaintiffs to forced labor also convince us now that Unocal may likewise be liable under this standard for aiding and abetting the Myanmar Military in subjecting Plaintiffs to murder and rape. We conclude, however, that as a matter of law, Unocal is not similarly liable for torture in this case.

Initially we observe that the evidence in the record creates a genuine question of material fact as to whether Myanmar soldiers engaged in acts of murder and rape involving Plaintiffs.... The record does not, however, contain sufficient evidence to establish a claim of torture (other than by means of rape) involving Plaintiffs. Although a number of witnesses described acts of extreme physical abuse that might give rise to a claim of torture, the allegations all involved victims other than Plaintiffs....

[W]e reverse the District Court's grant of Unocal's motion for summary judgment on Plaintiffs' murder and rape claims under the ATCA. By contrast, the record does not contain sufficient evidence to support Plaintiffs' claims of torture. We therefore affirm the District Court's grant of Unocal's motion for summary judgment on Plaintiffs' torture claims....

C. Plaintiffs' claims against Unocal are not barred by the Act of State Doctrine.

Unocal also argues that Plaintiffs' claims against it are barred by the "act of state" doctrine.... In the present case, an act of state issue arises because the court must decide that the conduct by the Myanmar Military violated international law in order to hold Unocal liable for aiding and abetting that conduct....

In *Banco Nacional de Cuba v. Sabbatino*, 376 U.S. 398 (1964), the Supreme Court developed a three-factor balancing test to determine whether the act of state doctrine should apply:

> [1] [T]he greater the degree of codification or consensus concerning a particular area of international law, the more appropriate it is for the judiciary to render decisions regarding it.... [2] [T]he less important the implications of an issue are for our foreign relations, the weaker the justification for exclusivity in the political branches. [3] The balance of relevant considerations may also be shifted if the government which perpetrated the challenged act of state is no longer in existence....

We have added a fourth factor to this test: [4] "[W]e must [also] consider ... whether the foreign state was acting in the public interest." [*Liu v. Republic of China*, 892 F.2d 1419, 1432 (9th Cir.1989).] With the exception of the third factor, all of these factors weigh against application of the act of state doctrine in this case....

Because the four factor balancing test weighs against applying the act of state doctrine, we find that Plaintiffs' claims are not barred by this doctrine....

III. Conclusion

For the foregoing reasons, we REVERSE the District Court's grant of summary judgment in favor of Unocal on Plaintiffs' ATCA claims for forced labor, murder, and rape.

We however AFFIRM the District Court's grant of summary judgment in favor of Unocal on Plaintiffs' ATCA claims for torture.... We REMAND the case to the District Court for further proceedings consistent with this opinion.

Questions and Discussion

1. *Private actions.* Trace the steps by which the Ninth Circuit concluded that, in the building of the pipeline in Myanmar-Burma, it might be possible to prove at trial that Unocal was liable for aiding and abetting forced labor, rape, and murder but not torture. First, how does the court conclude that private actions involving forced labor violate the modern law of nations? Second, how does the court conclude that, while private actions of rape and murder do not by themselves violate the modern law of nations, they might do so in this case? Third, how does aider-and-abettor liability then attach?

In the case *Khulumani v. Barclay Nat. Bank Ltd.*, 504 F.3d 254 (2d Cir. 2007), the Second Circuit by a 2–1 vote agreed that aiding and abetting a crime against the law of nations gives rise to a claim under ATCA. The two judges in the majority relied on different approaches—one saying that the federal common law allowed such liability (Judge Hall, 504 F.2d at 284) and the other saying that international customary law did so (Judge Katzmann, 504 F.2d at 264). The defendants petitioned for certiorari to the Supreme Court. Four Justices recused themselves, so the Court lacked the six needed for a quorum. This left the decision as affirmed. 128 S.Ct. 2424 (2008).

For further discussion of aider-and-abettor liability, *see* Daniel Diskin, *Note: The Historical and Modern Foundations for Aiding and Abetting Liability under the Alien Tort Statute*, 47 Ariz. L. Rev. 805 (2005).

2. *Foreign policy and the "act of state" doctrine.* In conjunction with *Doe v. Unocal*'s discussion of the "act of state" doctrine, recall Dean Koh's observations on that doctrine. Several cases have been filed, or proceeded, after *Doe I v. Unocal*, including one in the District of Columbia involving acts of the Indonesian military in protecting and securing Exxon Mobil Corporation's liquid natural gas extraction pipeline and liquification facility against attack by Achenese rebels in Aceh State, Indonesia. The suit alleges that the company was complicit in acts of murder, rape, enslavement, and torture by the military. The district court disallowed the ATCA claims but allowed state tort claims to proceed. *Doe I v. Exxon Mobil Corp.*, 393 F. Supp. 2d 20 (D.D.Cir. 2005) rejected the defendants' arguments that the suit would interfere with U.S. foreign policy and relations with other nations. *Id.* at 28–29.

The D.C. Circuit rejected an interlocutory appeal of the district court's refusal to dismiss. 473 F.3d 345 (D.C.Cir. 2007), petition for certiorari to the Supreme Court denied, __ S.Ct. __, 2008 WL 2404105 (Mem). Judge Kavanaugh dissented, stating:

> This lawsuit could potentially disrupt the on-going and extensive United States efforts to secure Indonesia's cooperation in the fight against international terrorist activity. Indonesia is the fourth largest state in the world, with a population of some 210 million. It is also the largest Muslim nation, and serves as a focal point for U.S. initiatives in the ongoing war against Al Qaida and other dangerous terrorist organizations. U.S. counter-terrorism initiatives could be imperiled in numerous ways if Indonesia and its officials curtailed cooperation in response to perceived disrespect for its sovereign interests.

473 F.3d at 358. Should the fight against international terrorist activity, which President Bush characterized as likely to continue for decades, require dismissal of any tort suits, whether under ATCA or state law, against corporations operating in Muslim nations based on actions taken in complicity with abusive but cooperating militaries?

3. *Interested parties: the National Association of Manufacturers.* The National Association of Manufacturers argued in an *amicus* brief in *Doe I v. Unocal* that subjecting companies to ATCA causes harm to companies in the U.S. "Because it is only companies within the jurisdictional reach of U.S. courts that may be sued under the ATP, foreign companies with no U.S. presence enjoy a competitive advantage—they may do business abroad free from the risk of reputation-injuring and financially threatening ATP actions."

4. *State action.* The court explained that "a threshold question in any ATCA case against a private party, such as Unocal, is whether the alleged tort requires the private party to engage in state action for ATCA liability to attach, and if so, whether the private party in fact engaged in state action." Note how, for some acts such as murder, the plaintiffs must first prove state involvement but must then prove that the state involvement is not such as to insulate the private company from punishment.

5. *Environmental abuses.* A large number of student-authored law review notes, comments, and articles have argued that environmental abuses could form the basis for ATCA liability. *See, e.g.*, Mini Kaur. *Note: Global Warming Litigation under the Alien Tort Claims Act: What Sosa v. Alvarez Machain and its Progeny Mean for Indigenous Arctic Communities*, 13 Wash. & Lee J. Civil Rts. & Soc. Just. 155 (2006); Consider the material in the next subsection on this question.

2. Do Environmental Abuses Violate the "Law of Nations"?

In *Sosa v. Alvarez-Machain*, discussed on page 388, the Supreme Court held:

> We think it is correct, then, to assume that the First Congress [in 1789] understood that the district courts would recognize private causes of action for certain torts in violation of the law of nations, though we have found no basis to suspect Congress had any examples in mind beyond those torts corresponding to Blackstone's three primary offenses: violation of safe conducts, infringement of the rights of ambassadors, and piracy.... [W]e think courts should require any claim based on the present-day law of nations to rest on a norm of international character accepted by the civilized world and defined with a specificity comparable to the features of the 18th-century paradigms we have recognized.

Can environmental abuses be said to violate the Supreme Court's requirement that a norm be "of international character accepted by the civilized world" and "defined with a specificity comparable to the features of the 18th-century paradigms"? Consider the following materials.

Litigating Environmental Abuses under the Alien Tort Claims Act: A Practical Assessment

Richard L. Herz
40 Va. J. Int'l L. 545 (2000)

This Article demonstrates that some victims of environmental abuses like those committed by Texaco and Freeport may have strong cases for redress in U.S. courts under the Alien Tort Claims Act (ATCA). ATCA opens federal courts to civil suits by aliens for torts committed in violation of customary international law, even when the case involves acts perpetrated in another country by a non-U.S. citizen. Recently, courts have recognized that under certain circumstances, ATCA permits suits against TNCs for human rights abuses associated with their projects. Given this development, the time is ripe to determine whether ATCA can provide redress to victims of TNCs' massive environmental degradation. The waters are untested....

The stakes in such suits are enormous. For the plaintiffs, an ATCA action might represent the only means even theoretically available to prevent or receive some compensation for the loss of their livelihoods, cultures, health and even lives. Conversely, because corporations ... cause such extensive harm, the costs of a judgment involving damages, remediation and/or the future operation of a project in an environmentally responsible manner would be high. More generally, these suits challenge the impunity with which TNCs have heretofore destroyed the environments of unwilling communities. Indeed, the very existence of ATCA suits may cause at least some TNCs to reevaluate the way they do business abroad in order to avoid potential liability.

Although customary international law as applied through ATCA is sufficiently broad to permit some suits for environmental harms, plaintiffs face many obstacles....

[P]laintiffs' best chance of success rests in presenting claims that are narrowly crafted and based on compelling facts....

Beanal v. Freeport-McMoran
197 F.3d 161 (5th Cir. 1999)

CARL E. STEWART, Circuit Judge:

Tom Beanal ("Beanal") brought suit against the defendants in federal district court for alleged violations of international law. The district court dismissed Beanal's claims pursuant to Fed.R.Civ.Proc. 12(b)(6). After a careful review of Beanal's pleadings, we affirm the district court.

Factual & Procedural History

This case involves alleged violations of international law committed by domestic corporations conducting mining activities abroad in the Pacific Rim. Freeport-McMoran, Inc., and Freeport-McMoran Copper & Gold, Inc., ("Freeport"), are Delaware corporations with headquarters in New Orleans, Louisiana. Freeport operates the "Grasberg Mine," an open pit copper, gold, and silver mine situated in the Jayawijaya Mountain in Irian Jaya, Indonesia. The mine encompasses approximately 26,400 square kilometers. Beanal is a resident of Tamika, Irian Jaya within the Republic of Indonesia (the "Republic"). He is also the leader of the Amungme Tribal Council of Lambaga Adat Suki Amungme (the "Amungme"). In August 1996, Beanal filed a complaint against Freeport in federal district court in the Eastern District of Louisiana for alleged violations of international law. Beanal invoked jurisdiction under ... the Alien Tort Statute, 28 U.S.C. § 1350, ... In his First Amended Complaint, he alleged that Freeport engaged in environmental abuses, human rights violations, and cultural genocide. Specifically, he alleged that Freeport mining operations had caused harm and injury to the Amungme's environment and habitat. He further alleged that Freeport engaged in cultural genocide by destroying the Amungme's habitat and religious symbols, thus forcing the Amungme to relocate.... Freeport moved to dismiss Beanal's claims under Fed.R.Civ.Proc.12(b)(6).... Pursuant to Rule 12(e), the district court instructed Beanal to amend his complaint to state more specifically his claims of genocide and individual human rights violations.... In March 1998, the district court granted Freeport's motion to strike Beanal's Third Amended Complaint and dismissed his claims with prejudice. Beanal now appeals the district court's rulings below....

Discussion ...

A. Alien Tort Statute ...

Beanal does not claim that Freeport violated a United States treaty. Thus, the issue before us is whether Beanal states claims upon which relief can be granted for violations under the "law of nations," i.e., international law....

Beanal's allegations under the ATS can be divided into three categories: (1) individual human rights violations; (2) environmental torts; and (3) genocide and cultural genocide. ...

2. Environmental Torts and Abuses ...

Beanal argues that Freeport through its mining activities engaged in environmental abuses which violated international law. In his Third Amended Complaint, Beanal alleges the following:

> FREEPORT, in connection with its Grasberg operations, deposits approximately 100,000 tons of tailings per day in the Aghwagaon, Otomona and Akjwa Rivers. Said tailings have diverted the natural flow of the rivers and have rendered the natural waterways of the plaintiff unusable for traditional uses including bathing and drinking. Furthermore, upon information and belief, the heavy metal content of the tailings have and/or will affect the body tissue of the aquatic life in said rivers. Additionally, tailings have blocked the main flow of the Ajkwa River causing overflow of the tailings into lowland rain forest vegetation destroying the same.

> FREEPORT in connection with its Grasberg operations has diverted the aforesaid rivers greatly increasing the likelihood of future flooding in Timika, the home of the plaintiff, TOM BEANAL.

> FREEPORT, in connection with its Grasberg mining operations has caused or will cause through the course of its operations 3 billion tons of "overburden" to be dumped into the upper Wanagon and Carstensz creating the likely risk of massive landslides directly injurious to the plaintiff. Furthermore, said "overburden" creates acid rock damage which has created acid streams and rendering the Lake Wanagon an "acid lake" extremely high in copper concentrations, ...

However, Freeport argues that Beanal's allegations of environmental torts are not cognizable under the "law of nations" because Beanal fails to show that Freeport's mining activities violate any universally accepted environmental standards or norms. Furthermore, Freeport argues that it would be improper for a United States tribunal to evaluate another county's environmental practices and policies....

Beanal and the *amici* refer the court to several sources of international environmental law to show that the alleged environmental abuses caused by Freeport's mining activities are cognizable under international law. Chiefly among these are the PRINCIPLES OF INTERNATIONAL ENVIRONMENTAL LAW I: FRAMEWORKS, STANDARDS AND IMPLEMENTATION 183-18 (Phillip Sands ed,. 1995) ("Sands"),[5] and the *Rio Declaration on Environment and Development,* June 13, 1992, U.N. Doc. A/CONF. 151/5 rev.1 (1992) (the "Rio Declaration")....

---

5. Sands features three environmental law principles: (1) the Polluter Pays Principle; (2) the Precautionary Principle; and (3) the Proximity Principle.

Beanal fails to show that these treaties and agreements enjoy universal acceptance in the international community. The sources of international law cited by Beanal and the *amici* merely refer to a general sense of environmental responsibility and state abstract rights and liberties devoid of articulable or discernable standards and regulations to identify practices that constitute international environmental abuses or torts. Although the United States has articulable standards embodied in federal statutory law to address environmental violations domestically, see The National Environmental Policy Act (42 U.S.C. § 4321 et seq.) and The Endangered Species Act (16 U.S.C. § 1532), nonetheless, federal courts should exercise extreme caution when adjudicating environmental claims under international law to insure that environmental policies of the United States do not displace environmental policies of other governments. Furthermore, the argument to abstain from interfering in a sovereign's environmental practices carries persuasive force especially when the alleged environmental torts and abuses occur within the sovereign's borders and do not affect neighboring countries.[6] Therefore, the district court did not err when it concluded that Beanal failed to show in his pleadings that Freeport's mining activities constitute environmental torts or abuses under international law....

Flores v. Southern Peru Copper
414 F.3d 233 (2d Cir. 2003)

José A. Cabranes, *Circuit Judge*:

The question presented is whether plaintiffs' claims are actionable under the Alien Tort Claims Act ("ATCA"), 28 U.S.C. § 1350.

Plaintiffs in this case are residents of Ilo, Peru, and the representatives of deceased Ilo residents. They brought personal injury claims under the ATCA against Southern Peru Copper Corporation ("SPCC"), a United States company, alleging that pollution from SPCC's copper mining, refining, and smelting operations in and around Ilo caused plaintiffs' or their decedents' severe lung disease.... Plaintiffs claimed that defendant's conduct violates the "law of nations"—commonly referred to as "international law" or, when limited to non-treaty law, as "customary international law." In particular, they asserted that defendant infringed upon their customary international law "right to life," "right to health," and right to "sustainable development."

The United States District Court for the Southern District of New York (Charles S. Haight, Jr., *Judge*), held that plaintiffs ... had not alleged a violation of customary international law—*i.e.*, that they had not "demonstrated that high levels of environmental pollution within a nation's borders, causing harm to human life, health, and development, violate well-established, universally recognized norms of international law." *Flores v. Southern Peru Copper Corp.*, 253 F. Supp. 2d 510, 525 (S.D.N.Y. 2002) (internal quotation marks omitted)....

---

6. Although Beanal cites the Rio Declaration to support his claims of environmental torts and abuses under international law, nonetheless, the express language of the declaration appears to cut against Beanal's claims. Principle 2 on the first page of the Rio Declaration asserts that states have the "sovereign right to exploit their own resources pursuant to their own environmental and developmental policies," but also have "the responsibility to ensure that activities within their jurisdiction or control do not cause damage to the environment or other States or areas beyond the limits of national jurisdiction." Beanal does not allege in his pleadings that Freeport's mining activities in Indonesia have affected environmental conditions in other countries.

Discussion . . .

II. The Alien Tort Claims Act . . .

  B. The "Law of Nations"

    1. Definition of "Law of Nations," or "Customary International Law," for Purposes of the ATCA

The ATCA permits an alien to assert a cause of action in tort for violations of a treaty of the United States and for violations of "the law of nations," which, as used in this statute, refers to the body of law known as customary international law. The determination of what offenses violate customary international law, however, is no simple task. . . . [T]he body of customary international law [has] a "soft, indeterminate character" . . . that [makes it] subject to creative interpretation. . . . Accordingly, in determining what offenses violate customary international law, courts must proceed with extraordinary care and restraint.

In short, customary international law is composed only of those rules that States universally abide by, or accede to, out of a sense of legal obligation and mutual concern. . . .

    2. Sources and Evidence of Customary International Law . . .

In *United States v. Yousef*, we explained why the usage and practice of States—as opposed to judicial decisions or the works of scholars—constitute the primary sources of customary international law. In that case, we looked to the Statute of the International Court of Justice ("ICJ Statute")—to which the United States and all members of the United Nations are parties—as a guide for determining the proper sources of international law. . . .

Article 38 [of the ICJ Statute] embodies the understanding of States as to what sources offer competent proof of the content of customary international law. It establishes that the proper *primary* evidence consists only of those "conventions" (that is, treaties) that set forth "rules expressly recognized by the contesting states," *id.* at 1(a) (emphasis added), "international custom" insofar as it provides "evidence of a general practice *accepted as law*," *id.* at 1(b) (emphasis added), and "the general principles of *law* recognized by civilized nations," *id.* at 1(c) (emphasis added). It also establishes that acceptable *secondary* (or "subsidiary") sources summarizing customary international law include "judicial decisions," and the works of "the most highly qualified publicists," as that term would have been understood at the time of the Statute's drafting. . . .

Notably absent from Article 38's enumeration of the sources of international law are conventions that set forth broad principles without setting forth specific rules. . . . Such a regime makes sense because, as a practical matter, it is impossible for courts to discern or apply in any rigorous, systematic, or legal manner international pronouncements that promote amorphous, general principles. *See Beanal v. Freeport-McMoran, Inc.*, 197 F.3d 161, 167 (5th Cir. 1999) (concluding that customary international law cannot be established by reference to "abstract rights and liberties devoid of articulable or discernable standards and regulations"). Moreover, as noted above, customs or practices based on social and moral norms, rather than international legal obligation, are not appropriate sources of customary international law because they do not evidence any intention on the part of States, much less the community of States, to be legally bound. . . .

III. Plaintiffs Have Failed to Allege a Violation of Customary International Law

Having established the proper framework for analyzing ATCA claims, we must now decide whether plaintiffs have alleged a violation of customary international law.

A. The Rights to Life and Health Are Insufficiently Definite to Constitute Rules of Customary International Law

As an initial matter, we hold that the asserted "right to life" and "right to health" are insufficiently definite to constitute rules of customary international law....

Far from being "clear and unambiguous," the statements relied on by plaintiffs to define the rights to life and health are vague and amorphous. For example, the statements that plaintiffs rely on to define the rights to life and health include the following:

> Everyone has the right to a standard of living adequate for the health and well-being of himself and of his family....

Universal Declaration of Human Rights, Art. 25, G.A. Res. 217A(III), U.N. GAOR, 3d Sess., U.N. Doc. A/810, at 71 (1948).

> The States Parties to the present Covenant recognize the right of everyone to the enjoyment of the highest attainable standard of physical and mental health.

International Covenant on Economic, Social and Cultural Rights, Art. 12, *opened for signature* Dec. 19, 1966, 993 U.N.T.S. 3, 6 I.L.M. 360.

> Human beings are ... entitled to a healthy and productive life in harmony with nature.

Rio Declaration on Environment and Development ("Rio Declaration"), United Nations Conference on Environment and Development, Rio de Janeiro, Brazil, June 13, 1992, Principle 1, 31 I.L.M. 874 .

These principles are boundless and indeterminate. They express virtuous goals understandably expressed at a level of abstraction needed to secure the adherence of States that disagree on many of the particulars regarding how actually to achieve them. But in the words of a sister circuit, they "state abstract rights and liberties devoid of articulable or discernable standards and regulations." *Beanal,* 197 F.3d at 167....

For the foregoing reasons, plaintiffs have failed to establish the existence of a customary international law "right to life" or "right to health."

B. Plaintiffs Have Not Submitted Evidence Sufficient to Establish that Customary International Law Prohibits Intranational Pollution

Although customary international law does not protect a right to life or right to health, plaintiffs' complaint may be construed to assert a claim under a more narrowly-defined customary international law rule against *intranational* pollution. However, the voluminous documents and the affidavits of international law scholars submitted by plaintiffs fail to demonstrate the existence of any such norm of customary international law.

1. Treaties, Conventions, and Covenants ...

Treaties, which sometimes are entitled "conventions" or "covenants," are proper evidence of customary international law because, and insofar as, they create *legal obligations* akin to contractual obligations on the States parties to them. Like contracts, these instruments are legally binding only on States that become parties to them by consenting to be bound. Under general principles of treaty law, a State's *signing* of a treaty serves only to "authenticate" its text; it "does not establish [the signatory's] consent to be bound." A State only becomes bound by—that is, becomes a party to—a treaty when it ratifies the treaty.[32]

---

32. The United States becomes a "party" to a treaty—that is, becomes contractually bound to obey its terms—only when, upon concurrence of "two thirds of the Senators present," U.S. Const. art. II, § 2, cl. 2 the President ratifies the treaty.

Accordingly, only States that have ratified a treaty are legally obligated to uphold the principles embodied in that treaty, and the treaty only evidences the customs and practices of those States....

[A] treaty will only constitute *sufficient proof* of a norm of customary international law if an overwhelming majority of States have ratified the treaty, *and* those States uniformly and consistently act in accordance with its principles. The evidentiary weight to be afforded to a given treaty varies greatly depending on (i) how many, and which, States have ratified the treaty, and (ii) the degree to which those States actually implement and abide by the principles set forth in the treaty....

The only treaty relied on by plaintiffs that the United States has ratified is the non-self-executing International Covenant on Civil and Political Rights ("ICCPR"), *opened for signature* Dec. 19, 1966, 999 U.N.T.S. 171, 6 I.L.M. 368. In addition to the United States, 148 nations have ratified the ICCPR. Plaintiffs rely on Article 6(1) of the ICCPR, which states that "every human being has the inherent right to life" that "shall be protected by law," and that "no one shall be arbitrarily deprived of his life." As noted above, the "right to life" is insufficiently definite to give rise to a rule of customary international law. Because no other provision of the ICCPR so much as suggests an international law norm prohibiting intranational pollution, the ICCPR does not provide a basis for plaintiffs' claim that defendant has violated a rule of customary international law.

Similarly, the American Convention on Human Rights ("American Convention") does not assist plaintiffs because, while it notes the broad and indefinite "right to life," it does not refer to the more specific question of environmental pollution, let alone set parameters of acceptable or unacceptable limits. Moreover, the United States has declined to ratify the American Convention for more than three decades, indicating that this document has not even been universally embraced by all of the prominent States within the region in which it purports to apply.

Plaintiffs also rely on the unratified International Covenant on Economic, Social and Cultural Rights ("ICESCR"). This instrument arguably refers to the topic of pollution in article 12, which "recognizes the right of everyone to the enjoyment of the highest attainable standard of physical and mental health," and instructs the States parties to take the steps necessary for "the improvement of all aspects of environmental and industrial hygiene," *id.* art. 12(2)(b). Although article 12(2)(b) instructs States to take steps to abate environmental pollution within their borders, it does not mandate particular measures or specify what levels of pollution are acceptable. Instead, it is vague and aspirational, and there is no evidence that the States parties have taken significant uniform steps to put it into practice. Finally, even if this provision were sufficient to create a rule of customary international law, the rule would apply only to state actors because the provision addresses only "the steps to be taken *by the States Parties*," ICESCR art. 12(2) (emphasis added), and does not profess to govern the conduct of private actors such as defendant SPCC.

The last treaty on which plaintiffs principally rely is the United Nations Convention on the Rights of the Child, which has not been ratified by the United States. Plaintiffs rely on two sections of the Convention in support of their claims. First, they cite Article 24, section 1, of the Convention, which "recognizes the right of the child to the enjoyment of the highest attainable standard of health." This provision does not address the issue of intranational pollution. Moreover, it is extremely vague, clearly aspirational in nature, and does not even purport to reflect the actual customs and practices of States. Plaintiffs also cite Article 24, section 2(c) of the Convention, which instructs States to "take appropriate measures ... to combat disease and malnutrition ... through ... the provision of adequate nutritious foods and clean drinking water, taking into consideration the dangers and risks of environmental pollution." While Article 24 of the Convention expressly addresses environmental pollution, it does not attempt to set its parameters or regulate it, let alone to proscribe it.... Moreover, as with Article 12 of the ICESCR, this provision only addresses concerns as to which "appropriate measures" are to be taken *by States themselves*, and does not profess to govern the conduct of private parties such as defendant SPCC.

For the foregoing reasons, the treaties, conventions or covenants relied on by plaintiffs do not support the existence of a customary international law rule against intranational pollution.

2. Non-Binding General Assembly Declarations

Plaintiffs rely on several resolutions of the United Nations General Assembly in support of their assertion that defendant's conduct violated a rule of customary international law.[36] These documents are not proper sources of customary international law because they are merely aspirational and were never intended to be binding on member States of the United Nations.

The General Assembly has been described aptly as "the world's most important political discussion forum," but it is not a law-making body. General Assembly resolutions and declarations do not have the power to bind member States because the member States specifically denied the General Assembly that power after extensively considering the issue [prior to and during the founding of the United Nations]....

Because General Assembly documents are at best merely advisory, they do not, on their own and without proof of uniform state practice ... evidence an intent by member States to be legally bound by their principles, and thus cannot give rise to rules of customary international law.

Our position is consistent with the recognition in *Filartiga* that the right to be free from torture embodied in the Universal Declaration of Human Rights has attained the status of customary international law. *Filartiga* cited the Universal Declaration for the proposition that torture is universally condemned, reasoning that "a [United Nations] declaration may *by custom* become recognized as [a] rule[]" of customary international law. The Court explained that non-binding United Nations documents such as the Universal Declaration "create[] an expectation of adherence," but they evidence customary international law only "insofar as the expectation is *gradually justified by State practice*."

> In considering the Universal Declaration's prohibition against torture, the *Filartiga* Court cited extensive evidence that States, in their domestic and international practices, repudiate official torture....

In the instant case, the General Assembly documents relied on by plaintiffs do not describe the actual customs and practices of States. Accordingly, they cannot support plaintiffs' claims.

3. Other Multinational Declarations of Principle ...

Apart from the General Assembly documents addressed above, plaintiffs principally rely on two multinational declarations in support of their claims. First, they draw our attention to the American Declaration of the Rights and Duties of Man, promulgated by the Organization of American States ("OAS"). As one of our sister Circuits has correctly observed, the American Declaration "is an aspirational document which ... did not on its

---

36. General Assembly documents cited by plaintiffs in their briefs include the Universal Declaration of Human Rights, arts. 3 (right to life), 25 (right to health), and the World Charter for Nature.

own create any enforceable obligations on the part of any of the OAS member nations." *Garza v. Lappin*, 253 F.3d 918, 925 (7th Cir. 2001).

Plaintiffs also rely on Principle 1 of the Rio Declaration, which sets forth broad, aspirational principles regarding environmental protection and sustainable development. The Rio Declaration includes no language indicating that the States joining in the Declaration intended to be legally bound by it.

Because neither of these declarations created enforceable legal obligations, they do not provide reliable evidence of customary international law.

4. Decisions of Multinational Tribunals

Plaintiffs also rely on judicial decisions of international tribunals in support of their claims. In particular, they rely on decisions of the International Court of Justice, and on the European Court of Human Rights, a regional institution. But neither of these tribunals is empowered to create binding norms of customary international law....

Accordingly, the international tribunal decisions cited by plaintiffs are not primary sources of customary international law. And while these decisions may constitute subsidiary or secondary sources insofar as they restate and apply the European Convention, nothing in that regional convention addresses pollution, let alone intranational pollution.

5. Expert Affidavits Submitted by Plaintiffs

Plaintiffs submitted to the District Court several affidavits by international law scholars in support of their argument that strictly *intranational* pollution violates customary international law. After careful consideration, the District Court declined to afford evidentiary weight to these affidavits....

In its seminal decision in *Paquete Habana*, the Supreme Court designated "the works of jurists [*i.e.*, scholars] and commentators" as a possible source of customary international law. However, the Court expressly stated that such works "are resorted to by judicial tribunals, *not for the speculations of their authors concerning what the law ought to be, but for trustworthy evidence of what the law really is.*" *Id.* (emphasis added), *quoted in Filartiga*, 630 F.2d at 881....

Similarly, Article 38 of the ICJ Statute does *not* recognize the writings of scholars as primary or independent sources of customary international law. Section 1(d) of Article 38 provides in pertinent part that courts may consult "the teachings of the most highly qualified publicists [*i.e.*, scholars or "jurists"] of the various nations, *as subsidiary means for the determination of rules of law.*" ICJ Statute, June 26, 1945, art. 38(1)(d) (emphasis added)....

The Supreme Court and the drafters of Article 38 recognized the value of the role traditionally played by scholars in identifying and recording the practices of States and thereby revealing the development of customary international law rules. But neither *Paquete Habana* nor Article 38 recognizes as a source of customary international law the policy-driven or theoretical work of advocates that comprises a substantial amount of contemporary international law scholarship. Nor do these authorities permit us to consider personal viewpoints expressed in the affidavits of international law scholars....

Conclusion

For the reasons stated above, we affirm the judgment of the District Court dismissing plaintiffs' complaint for lack of jurisdiction and failure to state a claim under the ATCA.

Questions and Discussion

1. *Abstract rights versus standards.* How "articulable" a standard can be found in the National Environmental Policy Act (NEPA), which the *Beanal* court appears to cite as an example of a law that would be specific enough if it were on the international level? Consider the language from NEPA in Chapter 7 at page 306.

2. *Forum non conveniens.* The Second Circuit in *Flores* did not rule on the issue of *forum non conveniens.* That issue is discussed below at pages 410 to 415, including the *Aguinda v. Texaco* case.

3. *Herbicides and the law of nations.* A U.S. District Court rejected a suit by Vietnamese nationals against chemical companies that manufactured ingredients for Agent Orange, a mixture of the pesticides 2, 4-D and 2, 4, 5-T. Agent Orange was sprayed by the U.S. military during the Vietnam War to defoliate areas thought to be used by the enemy. Agent Orange contained dioxin, which was blamed for birth defects and other adverse health effects. *In re Agent Orange Product Liability Litigation*, 373 F. Supp. 2d 7 (E.D.N.Y. 2005). Despite various arguments for liability by the plaintiffs, the court ruled that there was no "international convention or instrument that solely and specifically addresses environmental law relevant to the legality of herbicide use during war up to 1975." *Id.* at 127.

4. *Common law reasoning.* The *Flores* decision quotes from the *Beanal* decision to the effect that customary international law cannot be established by reference to "abstract rights and liberties devoid of articulable or discernable standards and regulations." Isn't that what common law tort liability does in U.S. states and other common law nations? Is there an important reason why U.S. decisions regarding the content of customary international law should not be established by the same process of decisionmaking?

Sarei v. Rio Tinto

221 F. Supp. 2d 1116 (C.D. Cal. 2002)
Affirmed in part, vacated in part, and reversed in part, 487 F.3d 1193
(9th Cir. 2007) Rehearing *en banc* pending, 499 F.3d 923 (Aug. 20, 2007)

[Plaintiffs were residents of the island of Bougainville, Papua New Guinea. Defendant Rio Tinto, with the cooperation of the Papua New Guinea government ("PNG"), built and operated one of the world's largest open-pit copper mines in the middle of Bougainville. Among factual allegations that framed an epic array of human rights and environmental abuses, plaintiffs alleged that Rio Tinto's mining operation severely polluted the island's Kawerong-Jaba river system and Empress Augusta Bay with mine tailings. This pollution rendered the water unsafe for drinking and bathing and also killed off crops and fish, diminishing the Bougainvillians' native food supply.

[Plaintiffs brought a claim under the ATCA, citing the United Nations Convention on the Law of the Sea ("UNCLOS") as evidence of a customary international law norm against marine pollution.]

UNCLOS — an international treaty that prohibits certain acts of pollution in the marine environment — has been ratified by 166 nations, including PNG. The United States has not ratified the treaty. Plaintiffs assert that Rio Tinto's operation of the mine violated two treaty provisions: (1) one requiring that "states take 'all measures ... that are necessary to prevent, reduce and control pollution of the marine environment' that involves 'hazards to human health, living resources and marine life through the introduction of substances into the marine environment;'" and (2) another mandating that states "adopt laws and regulations to prevent, reduce, and control pollution of the marine environment caused by land-based sources."

Although the United States has not ratified UNCLOS, it has signed the treaty. Moreover, the document has been ratified by 166 nations and thus appears to represent the law of nations.... The Convention has been signed by the President, but it has not yet been ratified by the Senate. Consequently, we refer to UNCLOS only to the extent that it incorporates customary international law, though we also note that the United States 'is obliged to refrain from acts that would defeat the object and purpose of the agreement,'"...

Because UNCLOS reflects customary international law, plaintiffs may base an ATCA claim upon it. Defendants argue that the court should nevertheless dismiss the claim because UNCLOS does not cover the activities alleged.... Citing plaintiffs' allegation that waste from the mine extends "several kilometers" into Empress Bay, defendants contend that UNCLOS governs only pollution of the "open sea," i.e., international waters beyond the twelve mile limit of sovereign territorial jurisdiction. Additionally, defendants assert, UNCLOS requires the exhaustion of national remedies, and provides that disputes arising under it will be adjudicated by an international tribunal in Hamburg, Germany.

It is true that plaintiffs allege that "[t]ailing accumulated at the mouth of the river, creating an artificial cape covering 1000 hectares and stretching several kilometers into the Empress Augusta Bay." The complaint contains several additional allegations regarding pollution of the Bay, however, and specifically alleges that Rio Tinto polluted the Pacific Ocean....

Given these allegations, and the lack of any proof at this stage of the proceedings regarding the extent of the pollution in Empress Augusta Bay and/or the Pacific Ocean, the court concludes that plaintiffs have adequately stated a claim for violation of the customary international law reflected in UNCLOS.... For these reasons, the court denies defendants' motion to dismiss plaintiffs' claim based on the violation of international law as reflected in UNCLOS.

[The district court, however, dismissed the UNCLOS claim on prudential grounds after concluding that it presented a nonjusticiable political question.]

Subsequent history. The Ninth Circuit waited until after *Sosa* to review, 456 F.3d 1069, then withdrew that review and reheard, as shown next. On rehearing, the Court of Appeals found by a 2–1 vote (including in the majority one District Judge sitting by appointment) that the U.S. State Department's "Statement of Interest," which had been the basis for the political question dismissal by the District Court, was not controlling on the political question issue. The Court of Appeals panel vacated the district court's dismissal of the UNCLOS claim and returned it to the District Court for reconsideration. Circuit Judge Bybee dissented on the ground that remedies had not been exhausted.

Sarei v. Rio Tinto

487 F.3d 1193 (9th Cir. 2007)

FISHER, Circuit Judge:

This appeal presents questions of justiciability and exhaustion in the context of the Alien Tort Claims Act, 28 U.S.C. § 1350 ("ATCA"). Plaintiffs are current or former residents of Bougainville, Papua New Guinea ("PNG"), who allege that they or their family members were the victims of numerous violations of international law as a result of defendant mining corporation Rio Tinto, PLC's ("Rio Tinto") Bougainville mining operations and the 10-year civil conflict that followed an uprising at the Rio Tinto mine. The plaintiffs appeal the district court's dismissal of their lawsuit seeking redress under the ATCA, which provides that "[t]he district courts shall have original jurisdiction of any civil action by an alien for a tort only, committed in violation of the law of nations or a treaty of the United States." 28 U.S.C. § 1350.

Although several different doctrines of justiciability are at issue here—the political question doctrine, the act of state doctrine and the doctrine of international comity— all in effect provide different ways of asking one central question: are United States courts the appropriate forum for resolving the plaintiffs' claims? The answer to this question turns in part on the weight to be given to a statement of interest submitted by the United States Department of State ("State Department") asserting that continuation of the lawsuit "would risk a potentially serious adverse impact … on the conduct of [United States] foreign relations." Rio Tinto's cross-appeal also argues that the ATCA requires exhaustion of local remedies—yet another way of questioning whether there is a different and more appropriate forum to develop and try these claims.

We conclude that most of the plaintiffs' claims may be tried in the United States. We hold that the district court erred in dismissing all of the plaintiffs' claims as presenting nonjusticiable political questions, and in dismissing the plaintiffs' racial discrimination claim under the act of state doctrine. We also vacate for reconsideration the district court's dismissal of the plaintiffs' United Nations Convention on the Law of the Sea ("UNCLOS") claim under the act of state doctrine, and its dismissal of the racial discrimination and UNCLOS claims under the international comity doctrine. Although Rio Tinto and *amicus curiae* have asserted several plausible rationales in support of an exhaustion requirement, we affirm the district court's conclusion that no such requirement presently exists, and leave it to Congress or the Supreme Court to alter the status quo if warranted.

Questions and Discussion

1. *Rehearing en banc.* After the 2–1 split decision of 2007, the Court of Appeals granted a petition for rehearing *en banc*. At the time of textbook publication, the question whether the Convention on the Law of the Sea can be used for claims under the Alien Tort Claims Act had not yet been resolved in the Ninth Circuit.

2. *Indirection.* Even if environmental claims cannot be brought directly, can litigants achieve some of their goals by attacking destructive environmental projects indirectly, by bringing traditional human rights claims, such as slavery, rape, etc.? Or will these only result in some compensation for the litigants, as in the settlement that occurred after *Doe v. Unocal*, without any impact on the project itself?

3. *Creativity.* Do you believe that the Second and Ninth Circuits are unjustifiably cautious in their views of whether some environmental claims can be brought under customary international law? Is it appropriate to conclude that there are not sufficient norms for corporate behavior abroad that justify courts in the U.S. becoming involved? Should courts be similarly reluctant to expand common law tort actions? Availability of remedies for global warming pollution?

4. *Prudence.* Regardless of your answer to the previous question on the law, should courts refuse litigation of this type on grounds of prudence? Is that appropriate where Congress has provided jurisdiction and allowed a cause of action? Should Congress have the last word when such litigation might interfere with U.S. foreign policy? Should all lit-

igation that involves the behavior of U.S. corporations abroad be considered a threat to the conduct of U.S. foreign policy?

C. The Issue of *Forum non Conveniens*

Among the first attempts by foreign nationals to sue for environmental injuries was the Bhopal case in the 1980s. A gas plant owned by Union Carbide Co., an American corporation, in the city of Bhopal, India, had an explosion. A deadly cloud of methyl isocyanate gas spread throughout the city, killing hundreds. When residents of Bhopal sued Union Carbide in New York, the case was dismissed on the ground that New York was an inconvenient place for such a lawsuit—*forum non conveniens. See, e.g., In Re Union Carbide Corp. Gas Plant Disaster at Bhopal*, 634 F.Supp. 842 (S.D.N.Y. 1986); 809 F.2d 195 (2d Cir. 1987).

Many other cases have met the same fate. For example, residents of the Amazon in Ecuador sued the Texaco Corporation for damages to their environment due to oil drilling and production. The following article summarizes the legal maneuverings in U.S. courts.

Transnational Operations, Bi-National Injustice— Chevrontexaco and Indigenous Huaorani and Kichwa in the Amazon Rainforest in Ecuador
Judith Kimerling
31 Am. Indian L. Rev. 445 (2006)

I. Introduction

In 1993, a class action lawsuit was filed against Texaco in federal court in New York on behalf of indigenous and settler residents of Ecuador's oil fields who have been harmed by pollution from the company's operations. In 2002, the case, *Aguinda v. Texaco, Inc.*, was dismissed on the ground of forum non conveniens, in favor of litigation in Ecuador. The court denied the plaintiffs a day in court in Texaco's homeland, ruling that the lawsuit belongs in Ecuador because it has "everything to do with Ecuador and nothing to do with the United States." The dismissal was conditioned on Texaco's agreement to submit to jurisdiction of Ecuador's courts and was affirmed by the Second Circuit Court of Appeals....

II. Background: Governments and Policy in Ecuador

Texaco's discovery of commercially valuable oil sparked an oil rush, and petroleum quickly came to dominate Ecuador's economy....

When the oil rush began, Ecuadorian institutions had very little presence or influence in the Amazon region. The discovery of black gold made the conquest of Amazonia a national imperative. It also provided infrastructure to penetrate remote, previously inaccessible areas, and monies to support the military and bureaucracy. Ecuador launched a policy of national integration to incorporate the Amazon into the national economy and assimilate its native peoples into the dominant national culture. Successive governments have viewed the Amazon as a frontier to be conquered, a source of wealth for the State, and an escape valve for land distribution pressures in the highland and coastal regions....

In the environmental arena, Ecuador's Law of Hydrocarbons has included boilerplate environmental directives since at least 1971. Early provisions required oil field operators to "adopt necessary measures to protect the flora, fauna and other natural resources" and to prevent contamination of water, air, and soil. Similarly, Texaco's production contract with Ecuador, negotiated after the discovery of commercially valuable reserves and signed in 1973, required Texaco "to adopt suitable measures to protect flora, fauna, and other natural resources and to prevent contamination of water, air and soil under the control of pertinent organs of the state." In theory, those and other, comparable requirements in generally applicable laws offer mechanisms for regulation of significant sources of oil field pollution. In practice, however, Texaco and other oil companies have ignored the laws, and successive governments have failed to implement and enforce them.

When Texaco began its operations, there was little public awareness or political interest in environmental issues....

In the environmental law vacuum, Texaco set its own environmental standards and policed itself. As Petroecuador's "professor," Texaco also set standards for that company's operations. Texaco's standards and practices, however, did not include environmental protection or monitoring. The company did not instruct its Ecuadorian personnel about environmental matters....

Thus, Ecuador's petroleum policy in the 1970s and 1980s revolved around economic and national development issues and did not include a serious environmental component. The evidence in the historical record, however, does not suggest that environmental neglect was a conscious and informed policy choice by Ecuador at that time. Unlike Texaco, which had, or should have had, knowledge about both the hazards of oil field pollution and the technology that could be used to reduce it, such as reinjecting rather than discharging oil field brine (a high-volume waste, also known as "produced water"), the Ecuadorians were inexperienced and apparently unaware of the environmental trade-offs in the oil patch. In the triumphalist welcome to Texaco's discovery of commercially valuable oil and the struggle over whether petroleum policy should accommodate foreign companies or be nationalistic, environmental protection was eclipsed altogether.

Indeed, when environmental officials in Ecuador's Ministry of Energy and Mines (MEM) were confronted in 1990 with a study (subsequently published as AMAZON CRUDE) by an environmental lawyer from the United States (the author) that documented shocking pollution and other impacts from operations by Texaco and other companies, the officials professed ignorance. Texaco was their "professor," they explained; the company taught them how to produce oil but did not teach them environmental protection....

In the wake of AMAZON CRUDE, environmental protection has become an important policy issue in Ecuador. Since the early 1990s, both government officials and oil companies must at least appear to be "green." It remains to be seen, however, whether those changes in consciousness and discourse will lead to environmentally significant changes in the field....

III. Texaco's Operations and the Affected Peoples

Oil exploration and production is an industrial activity. Among other impacts, it generates large quantities of wastes with toxic constituents and presents ongoing risks of spills. The consortium led by Texaco extracted nearly 1.5 billion barrels of Amazon crude over a period of twenty-eight years (1964–1992).... They also generated more than 3.2 million gallons of toxic wastewater (produced water) every day, virtually all of which was dumped into the environment via unlined, open-air earthen waste pits, without treatment or monitoring—a practice that has been generally banned in the United States by federal law since 1979....

In addition to routine, willful discharges and emissions, Texaco spilled nearly twice as much oil as the Exxon Valdez from the main pipeline alone, mostly in the Amazon basin.... Texaco's response in Ecuador was limited to shutting off the flow of petroleum into the damaged portion of the pipeline and allowing the oil already in the line to spill into the environment before making the necessary repairs. No cleanup activities were undertaken, and no assistance or compensation was provided to affected communities....

IV. *Aguinda v. Texaco*

Texaco's production contract expired in 1992, and in November 1993, a class action lawsuit was filed against Texaco, Inc. in federal court in New York, on behalf of indigenous and colonist residents who have been harmed by pollution from the company's Ecuador operations. The suit, *Aguinda v. Texaco, Inc.*, was filed by U.S.-based attorneys after they read about the AMAZON CRUDE study. The case was a toxic tort action, based on common law claims of negligence, public and private nuisance, trespass, civil conspiracy, and medical monitoring. It also included an international law claim under the Alien Tort Claims Act, based on alleged (unspecified) violations of the law of nations, and a claim for equitable relief "to remedy the contamination and spoilation of their properties, water supplies and environment." ...

In response to the lawsuit, Texaco denied any wrongdoing and vigorously fought the legal action. In submissions to the court and in the media, Texaco alleged that the operations had complied with Ecuadorian law and then-prevailing industry practices. Moreover, the company argued, it had not operated in Ecuador since 1990, and any legal claims should be pursued there instead of in the United States. In court, Texaco also denied parent company control over the operations, which, as noted above, were carried out by a wholly-owned subsidiary, Texaco Petroleum Company, in a consortium, initially with Gulf and subsequently with Petroecuador....

Outside court, Texaco and Ecuador moved quickly to negotiate issues raised by the lawsuit, in what ABC News Nightline later called an "exit agreement." They signed a series of agreements in 1994–1995 ("Remediation Contract"). Under the accord, Texaco agreed to implement limited environmental remediation work; make payments to Ecuador for socio-economic compensation projects; and negotiate contributions to public works with municipal governments of four boom towns that sprang up around the company's operations and, in the wake of *Aguinda v. Texaco*, sued Texaco Petroleum in Ecuador. In exchange, the government and Petroecuador agreed to release and liberate Texaco Petroleum and Texaco (and their subsidiaries and successors) from all claims, obligations, and liability to the Ecuadorian State and national oil company "related to contamination" from the operations....

In court, after nine years of litigation, Texaco's efforts to dismiss the case were successful, and the *Aguinda* plaintiffs were essentially told to go home and sue in Ecuador. The case was dismissed on the ground of forum non conveniens, a doctrine that allows a court to dismiss a case that could be tried in a different court, in the interest of justice or for the convenience of the parties....

In *Aguinda*, the district court ruled that Ecuador's courts provide an alternative forum and that the balance of private and public interest factors "tips overwhelmingly in favor of dismissal." Despite the fact that Texaco's headquarters was just a few miles from the courthouse where the case was filed, the judge concluded that the case has "everything to do with Ecuador and nothing to do with the United States."

Some of the facts used by the court to support its legal analysis are uncontested. For example, there were no allegations of injury in the United States; Texaco built and operated the facilities; and after operations began, Ecuador acquired majority ownership of the assets and continued to operate them after Texaco Petroleum's contract expired. Other facts, however, are in dispute. One area that is especially germane relates to control of the operations. While not determinative, in and of itself, of the legal questions, the factual issue of where decisions were made about the technology and practices that caused the pollution, and who made them, was a material element of the analysis of both private and public interest factors and clearly colored the decision to dismiss.

The proposition, advocated by Texaco and accepted by the court, that Ecuadorians controlled the relevant decisions, that no one from Texaco or anyone else operating out of the United States made any material decisions or was involved in designing, directing, guiding, or assisting the activities that caused the pollution, and that environmental practices were heavily regulated by Ecuador, is a recurring theme. The court also distinguished Texaco from Texaco Petroleum, the subsidiary that operated in Ecuador.... The *Aguinda* court's determination that an adequate alternative forum exists was also colored by questionable factual assumptions, including erroneous and unsupported findings of fact about the history of litigation in Ecuador's courts. Specifically, the court found that several plaintiffs had already recovered judgments against Texaco Petroleum and Petroecuador in Ecuadorian courts for claims arising out of the facts alleged by the *Aguinda* plaintiffs, a finding that is clearly erroneous. A related finding, that Ecuadorian oil field workers had won personal injury lawsuits against Texaco Petroleum based on claims of alleged negligence, is not supported by evidence in the *Aguinda* litigation record and is contradicted by the historical record....

Despite a multitude of submissions by Texaco, including ample, but vague, allegations about the litigation record in Ecuador, a gaping hole remained: no final judgment by a court of law in favor of a plaintiff against an oil company based on environmental injuries, or against Texaco (or Texaco Petroleum) in any lawsuit, was submitted by the defendant. The only judgment in the record in favor of a plaintiff—an action by a municipality against Petroecuador and its insurer for damages caused by an oil spill from a former Texaco facility—was vacated on appeal by Ecuador's Supreme Court, which also assessed costs for the defendants' attorneys against the judges who ruled for the plaintiff in the unprecedented environmental action. As a general matter, the notion implicit in the court's analysis, that environmental lawsuits against ChevronTexaco and Petroecuador in Ecuador could somehow be insulated from the social and political context in which they operate and enjoy immunity from systemic deficiencies in the legal and judicial systems, is implausible. Both the historical record and the *Aguinda* litigation record make it clear that the road to effective judicial reform—and the rule of law—in Ecuador will be long and difficult. In the oil frontier in Amazonia, law and politics continue to be characterized by gross inequities that favor oil company interests at the expense of indigenous peoples, campesinos, and the environment.

The *Aguinda* plaintiffs appealed to the Second Circuit Court of Appeals. However, because forum non conveniens involves the exercise of discretion by the trial court, appellate courts have limited powers of review. In this case, the Second Circuit found no abuse of discretion. In a footnote, the appellate court also rejected the plaintiffs' argument that the district court judge, Jed Rakoff, should have recused himself. The plaintiffs had asked the judge to disqualify himself from further proceedings in *Aguinda* after they learned that he attended "an all expense paid resort trip and 'seminar'" at a ranch in Montana sponsored by The Foundation for Research on Economics & the Environment (FREE). FREE is "funded partially by Defendant Texaco, Inc," and Texaco's former Chairman of the Board, Alfred DeCrane, was "one of the principal speakers at the 'seminar.'" In another footnote, the Second Circuit declined to rule on whether the Alien Tort Claims Act encompasses the environmental claims in *Aguinda*, or whether it expresses a strong U.S. policy interest in providing a forum for litigation. Even if those legal arguments were accepted, said the note, the private and public interest factors would nonetheless require the appellate court to uphold the judgment of the district court.

In its review of the district court judgment, the Second Circuit did not repeat all of the detailed factual rulings discussed above, but it quoted Judge Rakoff's general finding that *Aguinda* "has everything to do with Ecuador and nothing to do with the United States," and apparently relied on at least some of the more specific findings to reject the plaintiffs' appeal....

VII. Conclusion and Recommendations ...

The *Aguinda v. Texaco* lawsuit created an unprecedented opportunity for corporate accountability and environmental justice. The allegations in the complaint echoed long-standing grievances in the oil patch. The idea of equality before the law and the international spotlight held by the litigation emboldened affected populations and catalyzed many people to action....

The application of the forum non conveniens doctrine to dismiss the case represents an abdication of responsibility by the federal judiciary and sends a troubling message: that U.S. laws and institutions create and protect multinational corporations, but generally do not regulate their operations and decline to act when they harm people and the environment abroad....

In this case, the harmful operations were transnational in nature, and two national legal systems have had jurisdiction over myriad claims. One state, Ecuador, embraces the discourse of international law and has even written much of it into the highest law of the land, the constitution, but its political institutions, including the courts, are so notoriously corrupt and dysfunctional that there is a staggering gap between those legal ideals and social and political realities. The other state, the United States, has a rich but uneven judicial history of applying international law and adjudicating international disputes, and appears to be more open to adjudicating commercial litigation and to protecting the legal rights and interests of U.S. corporations than to hearing tort litigation by foreign residents who need remedies for injuries that those companies cause.

Although litigation by foreign plaintiffs in U.S. courts based on development activities that are carried out in a foreign country, in partnership with the government of that county, raises difficult legal, political, and practical issues, there is a significant public interest and moral obligation in the United States to remedy injuries in other countries that result from the activities of U.S. corporations.... Until governments develop effective regulation of transnational corporations and credible, effective fora to adjudicate grievances and remedy the injuries they cause, U.S. courts should not use the forum non conveniens doctrine to deny foreign plaintiffs who have real grievances against U.S.-based corporations a day in court....

––––––––––

After the district court in *Aguinda* first dismissed the suit on the ground of *forum non conveniens* in 1996, the U.S. Court of Appeals for the Second Circuit reversed, holding that the district court had not assessed the ability of the Ecuadorian courts to handle the litigation. *Jota v. Texaco*, 157 F.3d 153 (2d Cir. 1998). On remand, the district court ruled that Ecuador was an adequate, alternative forum and again dismissed on the ground of *forum non conveniens*. *Aguinda v. Texaco*, 142 F. Supp. 2d 534 (S.D.N.Y. 2001). The following appeal resulted.

Aguinda v. Texaco
303 F.3d 470 (2d Cir. 2002)

LEVAL, *Circuit Judge*:

These are consolidated appeals from judgments of the United States District Court for the Southern District of New York (Jed S. Rakoff, *Judge*) dismissing two putative class actions for *forum non conveniens*. Plaintiffs are residents of the Oriente region of Ecuador and an adjoining area in Peru. Defendant is Texaco, Inc. ("Texaco"), a United States-based oil company, which, at the pertinent time, was headquartered in New York. The complaints allege environmental and personal injuries arising out of Texaco's oil exploration and extraction operations in the Oriente region between 1964 and 1992.

We modify the judgments in one respect explained below, but otherwise affirm the dismissal of the actions by reason of *forum non conveniens*.

Background

We briefly summarize the background as follows.

A. Texaco's Oil Operations in Ecuador

In 1964, Texaco Petroleum Company ("TexPet"), a fourth-level subsidiary of the defendant Texaco, began oil exploration and drilling in the Oriente region of eastern Ecuador. In 1965 TexPet started operating a petroleum concession for a consortium (the "Consortium") owned in equal shares by TexPet and Gulf Oil Corporation. In 1974 the government of the Republic of Ecuador ("Republic" or "Ecuador"), through its state-owned oil agency known as PetroEcuador, obtained a 25 percent share in the Consortium. Within two years, PetroEcuador acquired Gulf Oil's interest and became the majority stakeholder in the Consortium. Through 1989 TexPet operated a Trans-Ecuadorian oil pipeline, at which time PetroEcuador took over that function. TexPet operated the Consortium's drilling activities until July 1990, when PetroEcuador took over that responsibility as well. In June 1992, TexPet relinquished all its interests in the Consortium, leaving it owned entirely by PetroEcuador....

Discussion

Plaintiffs contend that the district court abused its discretion in determining that Ecuador was an adequate alternative forum and that the balance of private and public interest factors tilted in favor of dismissal. Finding no abuse of discretion, we affirm with modification.

After determining the degree of deference owed to a plaintiff's choice of forum, a district court engages in a two-step inquiry. First, the court must consider whether an adequate alternative forum exists. If so, it must "then balance a series of factors involving the private interests of the parties in maintaining the litigation in the competing fora and any public interests at stake." [*Wiwa v. Royal Dutch Petroleum*, 226 F.3d 88, 100.] The defendant seeking dismissal bears the burden as to both questions. *Wiwa*, 226 F.3d at 100. After assuming a strong presumption of validity for plaintiffs' choice of forum, the district court found that the presumption was overcome by the balance of public and private interest factors.

A. Does an Adequate Alternative Forum Exist?

Ordinarily, the requirement of an adequate alternative forum "will be satisfied when the defendant is "amenable to process" in the other jurisdiction. In rare circumstances, however, where the remedy offered by the other forum is clearly unsatisfactory, the other forum may not be an adequate alternative...." *Piper Aircraft Co. v. Reyno*, 454 U.S. 235, 255 n. 22, (1981); ...

Plaintiffs contend first that Ecuador does not offer an alternative forum because Law 55 precludes them from proceeding in Ecuadorian courts. Law 55 provides, "Should the lawsuit be filed outside Ecuadorian territory, this will definitely terminate national competency as well as any jurisdiction of Ecuadorian judges over the matter." Plaintiffs argue that Law 55 deprives Ecuadorian courts of competency to assert jurisdiction because both suits were first filed in the United States. They contend that dismissal for *forum non conveniens* would leave them without a forum in which to proceed. We agree with the district court's skepticism as to the law's retroactivity, as well as its application to cases dismissed for *forum non conveniens*.... We need not determine the scope of Law 55, as the district court qualified its dismissal specifying that, in the event the cases were dismissed in Ecuador under Law 55 and this result were affirmed by Ecuador's highest court, it would be open to reconsider the question.

We find no merit in plaintiffs' further argument that Ecuadorian courts are unreceptive to tort claims. The record shows that several plaintiffs have recovered judgments against TexPet and PetroEcuador for claims arising out of the very facts here alleged....

[Plaintiffs object] that Ecuadorian courts do not recognize class actions. On the other hand, Ecuador permits litigants with similar causes of action arising out of the same facts to join together in a single lawsuit. While the need for thousands of individual plaintiffs to authorize the action in their names is more burdensome than having them represented by a representative in a class action, it is not so burdensome as to deprive the plaintiffs of an effective alternative forum.

Plaintiffs point further to several respects in which Ecuadorian procedure is less efficient than U.S. procedure. While Ecuador's judicial procedures may be less streamlined than ours, that does not make Ecuador's procedures ineffective or render Ecuador inadequate as an alternative forum.

Plaintiffs contend that Ecuadorian courts are subject to corrupt influences and are incapable of acting impartially. After ordering supplemental briefing on this question, Judge Rakoff made detailed findings.... We cannot say that these findings were an abuse of discretion....

B. Balancing Private and Public Interest Factors

Having demonstrated the availability of an adequate alternative forum, Texaco must next establish that the balance of private and public interest factors "tilts strongly in favor of trial in the foreign forum." *Wiwa*, 226 F.3d at 100.

1. Private Interest Factors

Private interests include "the relative ease of access to sources of proof; availability of compulsory process for attendance of unwilling, and the cost of obtaining attendance of willing, witnesses; possibility of view of the premises, if view would be appropriate to the action; and all other practical problems that make trial of a case easy, expeditious and inexpensive." *Gulf Oil Corp. v. Gilbert*, 330 U.S. 501, 508. We find no abuse of discretion in the district court's conclusion that these interests "weigh heavily" in favor of an Ecuadorian forum. The relative ease of access to sources of proof favors proceeding in Ecuador. All plaintiffs, as well as members of their putative classes, live in Ecuador or Peru. Plaintiffs sustained their injuries in Ecuador and Peru, and their relevant medical and property records are located there. Also located in Ecuador are the records of decisions taken by the Consortium, along with evidence of Texaco's defenses implicating the roles of PetroEcuador and the Republic. By contrast, plaintiffs have failed to establish that the parent Texaco made decisions regarding oil operations in Ecuador or that evidence of any such decisions is located in the U.S.

If these cases proceeded to trial, it would be onerous for a New York court to manage the translation difficulties arising from cases with 55,000 putative class members of different indigenous groups speaking various dialects. In addition, it would be far more feasible for an Ecuadorian court to view the polluted areas in question than for a New York court to do so. . . .

To the extent that evidence exists within the U.S., plaintiffs' concerns are partially addressed by Texaco's stipulation to allow use of the discovery already obtained. Furthermore, Texaco's counsel agreed at oral argument that Texaco would not oppose further discovery in Ecuador that would otherwise be available in the U.S. . . .

2. Public Interest Factors . . .

We conclude that the district court was within its discretion in dismissing the actions on the basis of *forum non conveniens.*

Conclusion

The district court's judgment dismissing for *forum non conveniens* is AFFIRMED, subject to the modification that the judgment be conditioned on Texaco's agreement to waive defenses based on statutes of limitation for limitation periods expiring between the institution of these actions and a date one year subsequent to the final judgment of dismissal.

Questions and Discussion

1. *Burdens.* The court said that it would be onerous for a New York court to manage translation difficulties in cases involving different indigenous groups. Would that be easier for an Ecuadorian court?

2. *Presumptions.* Compare the apparent presumption in the decision that cases will be transferred to the seemingly opposite presumption in the following case from Britain.

3. *Proof.* Re-examine the court's assumption about the "relative ease of access to sources of proof" in Ecuador after reading pages 427 to 428, below.

4. *Language.* Does the court's concern about languages and dialects suggest that it might not certify a class action brought by immigrants to the U.S. speaking various dialects?

Englebert Ngcobo v. Thor Chemicals (United Kingdom)
High Court of Justice, Queen's Bench Division (in Chambers)
No. 1994 N 1212 (11 April 1995)
Transcribed from Shorthand Notes[d]

JUDGMENT
(As Approved)

MR. JAMES STEWART, Q.C., (Sitting as a Deputy Judge of the High Court)

THE JUDGE: By their summons dated the 19th January 1995 the three Defendants to this action, Thor Chemicals Holdings Limited, Thor Chemicals (UK) Ltd. and Desmond John Cowley, seek a stay of these proceedings on the ground that England is not an ap-

---

d. Available in Charles Okidi, ed., COMPENDIUM OF JUDICIAL DECISIONS ON MATTERS RELATED TO ENVIRONMENT: NATIONAL DECISIONS, Vol. 1 (December 1998).

propriate forum for the trial of this action, and South Africa is clearly or distinctly a more appropriate forum....

The factual background to this claim is as follows. Englebert Ngcobo, Albert Dlamini and Peter Zibonele Cele were all temporary workers at the Cato Ridge plant of Thor Chemicals, South Africa (Proprietary) Ltd. in Natal, South Africa. This company is a wholly owned subsidiary of the first Defendant. The third Defendant is and was at all material times the chairman of the South African company, the chairman and managing director of the first Defendant and a director of the second Defendant. The second Defendant was a wholly owned subsidiary of the first Defendant. The Plaintiffs allege that this company was responsible for the Group's Margate operation.

The South African plant, inter alia, manufactured and reprocessed mercury compounds. Mr. Ngcobo worked there from April 1991 until the 24th January 1992; Mr. Dlamini from October 1991 until a date in March 1992 and Mr. Cele from August 1991 until the 31st January 1992.

There is no dispute that all three in the course of their employment were exposed to hazardous and unsafe quantities of mercury, mercury vapour and/or mercury compounds. This caused Mr. Ngcobo to be ill on the 22nd February 1992; he was hospitalized on the 26th February 1992; he remained in hospital until his death on the 11th February 1995. He was then 55 years of age. His widow now sues on behalf of his dependents and his estate as the first Plaintiff. The second Plaintiff, who is now 27 years of age, became ill in early April 1992; he was hospitalized on the 16th April 1992 and continues to suffer from a major disability. Mr. Cele became ill in early February 1992; he was hospitalized on the 3rd March 1992 and died on the 1st July 1993 at the age of 22. His mother now sues on behalf of his dependents and his estate as third Plaintiff.

None of these Plaintiffs could have sued the employer, Thor South Africa (Proprietary) Ltd. in South Africa by reason of the provisions of Section 7 of the (South African) Workmen's Compensation Act 1941. This prohibits actions by an employee against his employer for injuries sustained at work....

Notwithstanding the prohibition under Section 7, Section 8 of the same Act expressly permits a workman to sue a third party tortfeasor such as these Defendants in South Africa in respect of injuries sustained at work.... However, as the Plaintiffs' case is that negligence by all three Defendants in England as well as South Africa caused the exposure to mercury, they have brought their claims in England against all three Defendants whose domiciliary forum is England.

The Plaintiffs' Claim.

The Plaintiffs in their re-amended Statement of Claim make the following allegations:

1. That the first and second Plaintiffs had a mercury processing plant in Margate, England, which was set up by the third Defendant together with a plant foreman/production manager called Bill Smith, both of whom were servants of the first and second Defendants.

2. Between 1981 and 1987 inspectors from the Health and Safety Executive in England reported high levels of mercury in the air and in the urine of the workforce in the Margate plant.

3. In about 1987, the mercury processing operation at Margate was closed down, having been moved in two stages in 1985 and 1987 to the South African subsidiary at Cato Ridge.

4. That all three Defendants were responsible for the research, design, set-up and commissioning of the South African plant and that Bill Smith was sent out to South Africa by the Defendants to assist in the setting up process and in the supervision of plant workers, including Messrs. Ngcobo, Dlamini and Cele.

5. That all the Defendants and Mr. Smith were well aware of the potential hazards to health and safety by exposure to high levels of mercury.

6. That it was Mr. Smith's job to ensure that the workers were aware of these hazards....

7. That the negligence of all three Defendants has caused the exposure of the three temporary workers to hazardous levels of mercury....

In summary, therefore, the Plaintiffs allege that the Defendants' liability arises out of research and development in England, the export of unsafe plant and processes from England to South Africa and the commissioning in South Africa of processes, plant and practices which to their knowledge were hazardous. This caused, it is said, the workmen to be subjected to severe chronic exposure to hazardous levels of mercury and mercuric compounds over a substantial period of time, which in turn caused personal injury and loss. The defence I am told will be that the Cato Ridge plant was sabotaged causing a sudden explosion in the absence of negligence by anyone, but certainly not on the part of these Defendants.

Relevant Law as to Forum Conveniens.

The leading case on *forum [non] conveniens* is *Spiliada Maritime Corporation v. Cansulex Ltd.* (1987) 1 AC 460. The relevant principles are enunciated in the speech of Lord Goff and I summarise them as follows:

(a) The basic principle is that a stay will only be granted on the ground of *forum non conveniens* where the court is satisfied that there is some other available forum having competent jurisdiction in which the case may be tried more suitably in the interests of all the parties and in the interests of justice....

(d) In determining whether there exists some other forum which is clearly more appropriate, the court will first look to see what factors there are which point in the direction of another forum. The natural forum is that with which the action has the most "real and substantial connection." Connecting factors will include: (i) factors of convenience, expense and expense such as availability of witnesses; (ii) the law governing the relevant transaction; (iii) where the parties reside or carry on business.

(e) If the court concludes at that stage that there is no other available forum which *prima facie* is clearly more appropriate for the trial of the action it will ordinarily refuse a stay.

(f) If, however, the court concludes at that stage that there is some other available forum which *prima facie* is clearly more appropriate for the trial of the action, it will ordinarily grant a stay unless there are circumstances by reason of which justice requires that a stay should nevertheless not be granted.

In this inquiry the court should consider all the circumstances of the case, including circumstances which go beyond those taken into account when considering connecting factors with other jurisdictions. One such factor can be the fact that if established objectively by cogent evidence the Plaintiff will not obtain justice in the foreign jurisdiction....

(g) As to the extent to which a legitimate personal or juridical advantage may be relevant, the mere fact that the Plaintiff has such an advantage in proceedings in England cannot be decisive; the fundamental principle is where the case may be tried suitably for the interests of all the parties and for the ends of justice.

Thus damages on a higher scale, a more appropriate procedure of discovery, a power to award interest as a general rule in England should not deter a court from granting a stay simply because the Plaintiff will be deprived of such an advantage, provided that the court is satisfied that substantial justice will be done in the appropriate available forum.

....

It is pointed out that the trend of modern conventions is to sue a defendant in his domiciliary forum....

It will be seen that the central issue here is whether or not there was a chronic long-term exposure or an acute exposure, as the Defendants submit, arising out of sabotage.

Conclusion

The conclusion which I have reached is that the Defendants have failed to satisfy me that this case would be tried more suitably in the interests of all the parties and the ends of justice in South Africa and that South Africa is clearly or more distinctly the more appropriate forum. The Plaintiffs have, in my judgment, formidable evidence to demonstrate a nexus between negligence in England and the damage which occurred in South Africa. I accept Mr. Stewart's submission that at the end of the day the toxicologists will play a major role in this case upon liability and that South Africa is not a clearly more appropriate forum for their evidence than England. If I granted a stay, the Plaintiffs may have difficulty in mounting their case in South Africa insofar as it relates to negligence in England, and there is a grave danger that justice would not be done....

I have been specifically asked by counsel to indicate whether, had I ruled in favour of the Defendants and ordered a stay, I would nevertheless have ruled that justice requires that a stay should not be granted, in particular on the basis that the Plaintiffs have legal aid here which, in all probability, would not be available in South Africa.... It is pointed out by Mr. Hawkesworth in accordance with the *ratio* in the *Abidin Daver* (1984) AC 398 that in exercising its discretion it is not normally appropriate for the court to compare the quality of justice obtainable in a foreign court which adopts a different procedural system with that obtainable in a similar case and conducted in an English court....

In Dicey & Moins 12th edition chapter 12, page 395, it is pointed out that there may be cases where there is a risk that justice will not be obtained in a foreign court for ideological or political reasons, or because of the inexperience or inefficiency of the judiciary or excessive delay in the conduct of the business of the court, or the unavailability of appropriate remedies....

Even if it were right that these Plaintiffs would not obtain legal aid in South Africa, I cannot see that Lord Goff [in the *Spiliada* case] ever envisaged that a plaintiff's impecuniosity would of itself constitute a basis for refusing a stay.... There is, in my judgment, nothing inherent in the system in South Africa which prevents these Plaintiffs obtaining justice. The mere fact that higher damages may be awarded here would not deter me from granting a stay and there is no sufficient evidence before me that substantial justice would not be done in South Africa. However, for the reasons already given, the Defendants have failed to discharge the burden upon them and accordingly this application for a stay is refused....

Questions and Discussion

1. *South African system and justice.* If there is "nothing inherent in the system in South Africa which prevents these Plaintiffs obtaining justice," why did this court refuse to transfer the case ("stay" the case in the U.K.)?

2. *Spiliada two-stage test.* The *Spiliada* case laid down a two-stage test for the doctrine of forum non conveniens in English courts. What are the differences between the "most 'real and substantial connection'" stage and the "interests of justice" stage? Is there a difference between the U.K. approach to forum non conveniens and the doctrine in U.S. federal courts providing that a defendant must show both that an adequate alternate forum exists and that the balance of public and private interests favors shifting the suit to the alternate forum? If so, what additional factor appears to sway the U.K. courts? If not, is there some other reason that U.S. courts would be more hostile to entertaining suits against U.S. corporations for damages suffered abroad? What should be the correct approach for a society in considering forum non conveniens arguments made by a defendant?

3. *Connecting factors.* In the first stage, what connecting factors did the *Spiliada* case say should be used in determining whether there exists some other forum, and how did Judge James Stewart use them in the *Ngcobo v. Thor* case?

4. *Factors to be considered.* What factors will be considered in the second-stage inquiry and which ones did the court say would not be proper to consider? Why should the court ignore the quality of justice likely to be dispensed under a different procedural system, as the court near the end says it would have done if it had not otherwise refused the stay? Why should it ignore the lack of legal aid in another country and the poverty of the clients? What are the potential consequences if corporations can relocate their polluting businesses to foreign countries, secure in the knowledge that injured people there would have much less chance of winning compensation than in the country of corporate origin?

5. *Causation.* On what allegations did the plaintiffs base the causal relationship between negligence in England and the damage which occurred in South Africa? If it could be shown that the subsidiary company in South Africa was itself negligent, would this break the chain of causation and the court decision be different? Can corporations shield themselves from the forum non conveniens rules of British courts by ensuring that all decisions are made by their foreign subsidiaries? Is pre-trial discovery by a plaintiff's lawyer important in uncovering evidence that this has not been done successfully?

D. Ordinary Tort Liability in an Age of *Forum non Conveniens*

1. Litigating Multinational Liability in the Country of Damage

Jungle Law

William Langewiesche

Originally published in Vanity Fair (May 2007)

In a forsaken little town in the Ecuadorean Amazon, an overgrown oil camp called Lago Agrio, the giant Chevron Corporation has been maneuvered into a makeshift courtroom and is being sued to answer for conditions in 1,700 square miles of rain forest said by environmentalists to be one of the world's most contaminated industrial sites. The pollution consists of huge quantities of crude oil and associated wastes, mixed in with the toxic compounds used for drilling operations—a noxious soup that for decades was dumped into leaky pits, or directly into the Amazonian watershed.... Chevron is represented by high-priced firms of experienced lawyers in Quito and Washington, D.C., whose collective fees run to millions of dollars annually. Its antagonists are 30,000 Amazonian settlers and indigenous people, who call themselves Los Afectados—the Affected Ones. These plaintiffs are represented by a low-budget but serious team of North American and Ecuadorean attorneys....

As for the plaintiffs, under Ecuadorean law they are not suing individually, and personally may never see a dime. They have sued to seek compensation for past damages and to force Chevron to clean up the residual mess that continues, they believe, to taint the soil and water today. It is unclear how a cleanup would proceed and to what extent it could succeed, but over decades the cost might run to $6 billion or more—making this potentially the largest environmental lawsuit ever to be fought....

This is not, however, a U.S.-style legal drama. The Lago Agrio court follows Ecuadorean procedures, which minimize oral arguments and rely heavily on submitted documents to get at the truth. So far the proceedings have generated close to 200,000 pages. There is no jury to sway. There is a single presiding judge, drawn from a pool of three on a rotating basis for a two-year term of unusual pressure....

Pablo Fajardo, aged 34, ... was born into extreme poverty and toiled for years as a manual laborer in the forest and oil fields, yet managed by force of intellect to complete his secondary education in night school, and through a correspondence course to earn a degree in law. He became a lawyer only three years ago, in 2004, yet has assumed the lead in the suit against Chevron in this, his very first trial. Chevron is represented by lawyers from Ecuador's ruling class, an oligarchy whose women fondly sing "Y Viva España" at Quito garden parties. They may have assumed that they could run Fajardo over. No one makes that assumption now....

Pacing has become a major point of contention in the trial. At the core is the sheer size of the ... operation. During its stay in the region, the company drilled approximately 325 productive wells and built 18 associated crude-oil-processing facilities—creating a total of more than 340 locations where wastes were stored or released into the watershed. After the start of the trial, in 2003, the court invited each side to choose from among these locations the sites where it wanted its own "judicial inspections" to be performed. Each judicial inspection would involve a visit to the site by the presiding judge along with the opposing attorneys and their technical teams. Once on the scene the judge would tour around, hear arguments on relevant law and history..., and order the opposing sides to take field samples to ascertain the degree of contamination. Altogether 122 sites were listed, the great majority on demand of the plaintiffs. Chevron requested 36. The judicial inspections turned out to be expensive and cumbersome affairs—episodes of political theater as much as of science, involving elaborate preparation, crowds of participants and protesters, police, bodyguards, soldiers, fleets of vehicles, shade tents, catered food, and plenty of grandstanding for television cameras. Predictably, a sampling war broke out, with the plaintiffs claiming to find extreme levels of contamination, Chevron claiming to find little, and each side impugning the science of the other. After four years, by early 2007, only 45 judicial inspections had been done. Believing that the process could continue another 10 years, that the findings of each side were proving to be duplicative, and that sufficient evidence had been presented to proceed to the final phase of the trial, Fajardo in 2006 withdrew the request for 64 of the judicial inspections originally sought by the plaintiffs.... Chevron, for its part, insists that delay is not its object. The plaintiffs' lawyers are persuaded that it is. [One of plaintiff's North American lawyers] once explained to me the cold logic of delay. Take $6 billion as a figure, he said. Simply by sticking the money into a savings account Chevron could make $300 million for every year it doesn't pay. That sum multiplied by the four years of the trial so far would amount to $1.2 billion, which is far more than, say, $50 million spent on legal fees, even if Chevron now loses the case....

To connect [the oil wells] to the market, [Chevron's predecessor Texaco] also built a major pipeline, mostly aboveground, from a Pacific port in Esmeraldas, across the Andes at 13,000 feet, and down into the jungle to Lago Agrio, a distance of 312 miles....

Over the 17 years that Texaco operated this conduit to the sea, until 1989, the pipeline suffered 27 major breaks and spilled nearly 17 million gallons of oil, much of which was not cleaned up. The volume of the spills has been widely reported. For comparison, the grounding of the Exxon Valdez spilled 11 million gallons. More to the point, over the first quarter century of its life, from 1977 through 2002, the 800-mile Alaskan pipeline spilled only 1,675,000 gallons—almost all of which was cleaned up. Fajardo is convinced that the industry knew how to handle itself better than Texaco handled itself in the Amazon. At the core of his argument in court is an assertion—vigorously disputed by Chevron—that contamination that exists today results from choices Texaco made to maximize its profits by setting up an operation in disregard of the environmental standards that it maintained at the same time in the United States....

As always, the oil emerged from wells mixed with undesirable water and natural gas. This mixture was piped to local separation stations, where it flowed into a series of tanks in which, specialists estimate, more than 95 percent of the desirable crude was extracted. The extracted crude was pumped off to the Trans-Ecuadorean pipeline for the trip across the Andes. The mixture that remained behind consisted of natural gas, residual crude, and a large volume of "produced water," which, depending on the wells, was variably laced with heavy metals, salts, and carcinogenic petroleum compounds in solution....

Over the 20 years of its operation Texaco poured at least 12 billion gallons of this juice into the Amazon. Fajardo says he first realized that perhaps there was a problem when he was about 14....

"After we formed the human-rights group, in 1991, I started to visit more communities, and I saw all the damage, how the poor suffered—that they had no clean water, that their animals were dying, that a lot of people were sick. Over the next few years I became more and more convinced that it is everyone's duty to fight for this cause, to have a better environment." ...

In 1995, Fajardo was elected president of his neighborhood—the poorest in Shushufindi—and he began to attend town meetings.... On weekends he and about a dozen other leaders took correspondence courses from a Quito university on the environment and human rights....

In the spring of 1997, his daughter was born, and she was healthy and bright. A few months later the Catholic priests, who had been observing him for years, found resources to provide him a law school scholarship. It was for books and tuition only, for a six-year correspondence course, but eight of Pablo's friends got together and made a commitment of their own to help sustain him for the period involved. Determination drove him through the next six years. Every day he woke at 3:30 in the morning, had a quick bite, studied law books until 8:00, rushed to the human-rights office, worked on cases there until midday, rushed to the Shushufindi radio station, went on the air from noon until 1:00 to read the news (which he had to prepare), rushed back to the office, worked there until closing time, took an hour to come up with a lesson plan for the class he had to teach, went to the night school and taught, got home around 11:00 to sleep for a few hours, and did it all over again the next day. In other words, he thrived.

Meanwhile, [a case had been filed] in U.S. federal court in New York ... [and it] was dragging on. The plaintiffs' attorneys had opted for a U.S. court because there are more due-process protections, including a jury—an option not provided in Ecuador—and they knew that the Ecuadorean courts were historically weak and corrupt. Before the case could go to a jury trial, however, Texaco's attorneys diverted it into an esoteric argument over the U.S. court's jurisdiction. That argument would last nine years, during which time the first U.S. judge died, Chevron acquired Texaco, and in faraway Shushufindi, Fajardo nearly finished law school....

In May 2001, the federal court ruled in Texaco's favor and dismissed the lawsuit. The plaintiffs declared that they would appeal.... [O]n October 9, 2001, Chevron swallowed Texaco whole....

The following summer a U.S. Court of Appeals upheld the earlier decision on jurisdiction in favor of Texaco and threw the plaintiffs' case out of the United States. But there was a catch, and it was an important one. As part of the decision, the U.S. judge required Chevron to accept the jurisdiction of the Ecuadorean courts and to agree to pay any judgment that might be imposed. [See *Aguinda v. Texaco* at page 415.] Effectively the U.S. judge had reached out and reinforced the Ecuadorean courts, if only for this one case. There was reason to believe that the plaintiffs' attorneys had exhausted their resources, and that after 10 years of struggle they would come to their senses and quit. They did not.... Fajardo was closely involved from the start.... His salary was low by any standard, but he did not accept a contingency deal, in part because such an arrangement is highly unusual in Ecuador and would not be understood by his friends. In January 2004 he graduated and became a licensed lawyer.... In January 2004 the human-rights office was burglarized and trashed, and Fajardo lost valuable papers, including his law school thesis, which had taken him six months to research and write, and which, had he been able to deliver it, would have earned him the exalted title of Doctor.... Instead, in the courtroom of Lago Agrio he is referred to as mere advocate, a smaller man, Abogado Fajardo.

A few months later, his best friend was killed. He was a taxi driver and one of the eight men who had helped Fajardo financially, to get through law school.... Sunday, August 8, 2004, he spent as usual in Shushufindi, working at the human-rights office. That night he stayed quietly at home with his family. In the morning he rose early and caught the six-o'clock bus for Lago Agrio and the office of the Front. When he got there, about two hours later, he received a phone call informing him that his beloved brother had been murdered....

For six months he stayed off the streets and moved whenever possible by taxi. At work he tried never to be alone. He carried a gun. Every time he said good-bye to someone, he thought that it might be for the last time. Ultimately, though, he learned to live with the risk. He became fatalistic. He thought, Whatever God wants. Gradually he emerged onto the streets. For a while the pressure eased. The shock of his brother's death did not leave him, but he carried on as before.

He was deeply involved in the trial. In June 2005, he assumed the lead for the plaintiffs.... The legal team appealed to international commissions on human rights, including of the United Nations, and the commissions responded with pro forma requests that the Ecuadorean government provide protection.

The government? Which part of it? In the summer of 2006, a case was opened in the office of the public prosecutor in Shushufindi, charging Fajardo himself with terrorism and sabotage. Others were charged at the same time. Fajardo was said to be their mastermind. Arrest warrants had still not been issued several months later, when we met, but the threat was hanging over Fajardo's head. He seemed just to mix it in with all the other threats....

Were Chevron to settle out of court, it could probably get away for a lot less than the $6 billion the plaintiffs are seeking. And the truth is that Chevron could afford the bill, which would be spent over a decade or more. In 2005, a single year, Chevron posted earnings of $193.6 billion and cleared $14.1 billion in profit. The first figure is more than six times the entire gross domestic product of Ecuador. But Chevron shows no sign of giving up.

Fajardo said, "One of the problems with modern society is that it places more importance on things that have a price than on things that have a value. Breathing clean air, for instance, or having clean water in the rivers, or having legal rights — these are things that don't have a price but have a huge value. Oil does have a price, but its value is much less." ...

William Langewiesche is Vanity Fair's international correspondent.

2. Anti-Forum non Conveniens *Legislation*

Litigation by Nicaraguan banana workers in Texas against U.S. companies for use of the pesticide DBCP, which causes sterility in males, was dismissed in 1995 on the ground of *forum non conveniens. Delgado v. Shell Oil Co.*, 890 F. Supp. 1324 (S.D. Tex. 1995). In 2007, ten Nicaraguan banana workers won a verdict of $5.8 million in California against the Dole Food Company on the same grounds. (See page 442.) The following material provides a case study of what happened in the intervening 12 years and what may happen in future disputes.

Forum Non Conveniens Checkmated? —
The Emergence of Retaliatory Legislation
Winston Anderson
10 J. Transnat'l L. & Pol'y 183 (2001)

While *Delgado* undoubtedly represents another victory for the beneficiaries of forum non conveniens, the case may very well turn out to be the high water mark of the influence and effectiveness of the doctrine. States whose citizens have been affected by what one Texas Supreme Court Justice in an earlier DBCP case referred to as "connivance to avoid corporate accountability," have been stung into taking retaliatory legislative action....

II. Legislative Alternatives

In the wake of Justice Lake's dismissal of the DBCP litigation, states in the developing world had to consider how to respond in the best interests of their citizens and residents.... The view of many developing countries was that the nexus between the United States and the tortious conduct of the defendants was so great that the cases should be returned for trial in the United States.

Adoption of overly anti-forum non conveniens legislation, which would extinguish national jurisdiction once the plaintiff had elected to file suit in America so that an American judge would not be able to find the foreign courts open to the plaintiff, was actively deliberated by legislatures in Africa and Latin America. Indeed, the Environmental Committee of the Latin American Parliament, PARLATINO, introduced a resolution to the Parliament which recommended that all Latin American and Caribbean countries adopt this type of legislation.

The extinguishing of jurisdiction in national courts was not considered feasible in the Commonwealth Caribbean. Apart from the issue of the constitutional right of access, there was also the consideration that legislative abolition of jurisdiction may not have resulted in the intended objective of retention of jurisdiction by the American court. The legislation eventually adopted was designed to obtain the best of both worlds; it made provision for local trial but also enabled the local court to utilize the rules of evidence, liability, and award damages available to foreign courts....

IV. Conclusion

The 1997 Transnational Causes of Action Act of Dominica represents a significant Caribbean contribution to the jurisprudence of private international law. It does not contain all the protections sought by the local plaintiffs in transnational actions, and it has been criticized for being excessively focussed on the need to remedy defects in one particular type of case. Given the rather specialized area with which it deals, it is not expected that the Act will be used in everyday litigation. Further, the drafting of its provisions leaves large and important areas of discretion in the hands of local judges.

Nonetheless, the legislative effort of the Dominican House of Assembly and of the President of Dominica deserves the highest commendation. The Act is clearly a landmark development in "checkmating" the pernicious effects of forum non conveniens....

Dominica has sent a clear and meaningful message to the international community in general and to other developing states in particular. That message is best articulated in the words of the Chief Justice of the Indian Supreme Court spoken in the context of upholding the constitutionality of broadly equivalent legislation enacted to protect the interests of victims of the Bhopal Plant Gas Leak Disaster against an American multinational corporation. The Chief Justice said:

> [W]hen citizens of a country are victims of a tragedy because of the negligence of a multi-national corporation, a peculiar situation arises which calls for suitable effective machinery to articulate and effectuate the grievance and demands of the victims, for which the conventional adversary system could be totally inadequate. The state in discharge of its sovereign obligation must come forward.

Forum Non Conveniens, Latin America and Blocking Statutes
Henry Saint Dahl
35 U. Miami Inter-Am. L. Rev. 21 (2003)

I. Blocking Statutes

In 1997 and 1998, some foreign jurisdictions enacted specific laws to block the effects of FNC....

II. Reasons for the Blocking Statutes ...

B) Loss of Evidence when Case is Transferred to Latin America ...

To shed more light on what has motivated these laws, we should now consider some evidentiary aspects. Anybody familiar with U.S. and Latin American evidentiary systems knows proof in the U.S. carries more weight and is much easier to obtain than in Latin

American systems. The blocking statutes do not mention the law of evidence as a specific reason to oppose FNC. Still, this issue lurks heavily in the background and it must be explained to obtain a fair picture of why these laws were conceived.

Latin American evidentiary systems know of testimonial proof, public and private documents, confession, opinions by experts, judicial inspections and presumptions. At first blush, the system is not so different from its U.S. counterpart. However, a closer inspection reveals that Latin American rules are structurally weak and very restrictive. Generally speaking, it would not be an exaggeration to estimate that if a case were transferred to a Latin American jurisdiction, the evidence obtainable would be at least 80% weaker than if the case remained in the U.S. That is so for the following reasons:

1. No depositions. Depositions in the American sense—attorneys examining witnesses outside the presence of the court—are unheard of in Latin America.

2. No discovery. Latin American systems do not engage in discovery. The principle of immediacy ("principio de inmediatez") forces all evidence to go through the court. Evidence produced outside the presence of the judge is invalid.

3. Restrictions on witnesses. Witnesses in the Latin American systems are restricted in two ways. First, they are limited in number. This restriction becomes more severe when considering that depositions do not exist and only live testimony is possible. Secondly, and more important still, is the exclusion of people who, under the U.S. system, would be deemed crucial witnesses. This includes: the parties themselves, their spouses, their close family members, their friends and enemies, their trusted employees, or anyone having a direct or an indirect interest in the outcome of the case. Practically speaking most, if not all, witnesses normally proposed in U.S. litigation would be excluded in the Latin American system.

One of the most striking restrictions is the exclusion of trusted employees (empleado de confianza). This is particularly damaging for the purposes of obtaining evidence against a corporation. Practically any employee in middle or upper management would classify as an "empleado de confianza". These are exactly the people who would be in a position to know facts crucial to the case and who, in U.S. litigation, would be prime targets for depositions and live testimony. This exclusion virtually assures a protection akin to "attorney-client privilege" to a party's medium and senior management.

4. Limitation on experts. In many Latin American countries, the parties lack the power to freely appoint the experts they wish. In some instances, experts are limited in their number. In others, only the court may appoint experts. In Argentina, for instance, the rule is to have only one expert, appointed by the court. Exceptionally, the court may appoint three experts.

5. Feeble power to compel document production. The possibility to request documents does not exist. Typically, the requesting party should describe the content of the specific document requested, saying who signed it, when, etc. A document of an unknown origin cannot be requested.

Furthermore, broad categories of documents are considered "private" and as such the court cannot force their production. In Costa Rica, for instance, art. 24 of the Constitution protects "the right of privacy, freedom and secrecy of communications." The Law for Searching, Seizing and Evaluating Private Documents and Interfering with Communications, of 8/1/94, authorizes judicial inspection of private documents only when it is absolutely necessary in a criminal case. Private documents are broadly defined as:

> letters, correspondence sent by fax, telex, telemetric or other means, videos, cassette tapes, magnetic tapes, records or disks, diskettes, writings, books, briefs, records

or registrations, blueprints, drawings, paintings, X-rays, photographs, and any other form of recording information of a private nature, used with a representative or declarative intent to illustrate or prove something.

As a result, many documents that would be discoverable in the U.S. can be kept out of Costa Rican and other Latin American courts.

6. Evidence in the U.S. is wasted. Federal Rule of Evidence 1782 allows the American court to cooperate with its foreign counterpart seeking evidence in the U.S. The same can be said of other mechanisms, such as the Hague Convention on the Taking of Evidence Abroad in Civil or Commercial Matters. Some U.S. courts mistakenly believe that such international rules allow Latin American courts a free rein to obtain documents or depose witnesses in the U.S. This is a naïve assumption that seldom works. In practice, the witnesses would most likely be protected by Latin American rules about privilege and the documents would not be discoverable according to Latin American law. The Latin American court, of course, would not be able to request U.S. judicial assistance in a way that breaches that requesting State's standards, even if such evidence were unrestricted in the U.S.

C) Impracticality

... There are also significant practical obstacles created by FNC when applied to a Latin American context. Some of these obstacles, which typically burden the plaintiff, are as follows:

1. International service of process. Latin American codes of civil procedure were enacted at a time when international relations were a rarity. Accordingly, international service of process is regulated in a very cumbersome way. International service of process normally requires several layers of Latin American bureaucracy: the Supreme Court of the issuing country, the Ministry of Foreign Relations, and that country's Consulate to finally effect the actual service on the U.S. defendant. This procedure can easily take one year. It can also be very expensive. Latin American consulates have very large jurisdictions in the U.S. If a defendant in a Costa Rican lawsuit had to be served in Hawaii, for instance, the Costa Rican Consulate in Los Angeles would have to perform service of process. The plaintiff would then have to pay for the Consul's airfare to Hawaii and back, a hotel in Hawaii for two days and the rental of a car for the same period.

This problem is considerably lessened between countries that, like the US, have signed the Inter-American Convention on Letters Rogatory, which facilitates international service of process.

2. Filing fees. Some Latin American countries require a filing fee that is proportional to the amount claimed. For instance, in Argentina, the rule is that any action claiming a sum of money requires a filing fee equal to three percent (3%) of the amount claimed.

3. English rule. Generally, Latin American jurisdictions apply the English rule, which makes plaintiffs liable for defendant's fees in case the action is defeated. This usually produces a chilling effect in litigation principally operating as a deterrent on parties that are economically weak.

4. Atomization of the case. When several plaintiffs are nationals of several different countries, it seems impractical to apply FNC and send them to re-file similar lawsuits in their respective countries when a single lawsuit in the U.S. could resolve the entire case.

Even concerning a single foreign country, a case can require several lawsuits when plaintiffs suffered damages in different jurisdictions. This is because internal rules will assign venue to different courts.

5. Congested dockets and other delays. Any attorney who has practiced in both systems knows that Latin American courts are much more congested than their American counterparts. Among other reasons, this is because cases settle less frequently and the judge must preside over all the evidence. Furthermore, the codes of civil procedure are truly ancient and inefficient and it is not unprecedented that strikes of judicial employees can close the courts for weeks, or even moths, at a time.

6. Impossibility to implead third parties. In some Latin American systems it is impossible to implead third parties. If A sues B, and B believes that C is to blame, then B has to file an independent lawsuit against C. That second lawsuit probably has to wait until B is defeated by A, for B's action against C to accrue. This, for instance, is the situation in Costa Rica.

7. Difficulty in finding legal counsel. The stated reasons of lack of jurisdiction, loss of evidence and an array of practical problems make the case very uncertain. After a FNC dismissal, the case becomes so difficult in Latin America that it becomes practically impossible to find local attorneys who would take it on a contingency fee basis. The uncertainty, cost and additional time presented by the issue of enforcing the decision in the USA—without considering all the other associated problems—is enough to dissuade most foreign attorneys from taking the case on a contingency basis.

Where There's a Will, There's a Way:
The Cause for a Cure and Remedial Prescriptions for
Forum Non Conveniens as Applied in Latin American
Plaintiffs' Actions against U.S. Multinationals

E.E. Daschbach
13 L. & Bus. Rev. Am. 11 (2007)

2. Big Bonds and Even Bigger Judgments: Nicaragua's Blow to Forum Non Conveniens in Nicaragua

Latin American legislative efforts aside, other more aggressive mechanisms implemented by at least one Latin American country are enjoying a measure of success. Indeed, Nicaragua garnered much press for its 2002 judgment ordering defendants Shell Oil Company, Dole Food Company, and Dow Chemical to pay $489 million to over 400 banana workers for damages allegedly caused by exposure to the pesticide DBCP. Importantly, plaintiffs brought their suit in Nicaragua before bringing suit in the United States. And, presiding over the matter, the Nicaraguan court set a bond of $100,000 per claimant to be paid by defendants, ultimately levying the $489 million in damages against the absentee defendants.

In one commentator's opinion, the judgment "landed a crushing blow to the doctrine of forum non conveniens." The theory has both strategic and pragmatic bases. First, "[w]ith a large judgment against the defendant corporations awaiting them in Nicaragua, it is now the corporations and not the plaintiffs who are the parties decrying the inadequacies of the foreign forum." As such, it might be argued that in light of their arguments on this score, defendants would be estopped from later arguing in a U.S. court that Nicaragua is the more convenient forum for plaintiffs' claims against them.

Regardless, and most remarkable of all, is that it appears defendants have been truly cornered. As the theory goes:

With the advance notice of a hostile judgment in Nicaragua, the defendants have no choice but to enlist the U.S. legal system for relief.... By obtaining a judgment against the corporations at the outset, the plaintiffs have preemptively attacked the defense of forum non conveniens.... Now, seeking a dismissal by the defendants [in a U.S. action] means facing an unreceptive foreign forum that has already rendered a most unfriendly judgment and large award in plaintiffs' favor. The defendants have no alternative left but the U.S. courts, the exact place the plaintiffs had been trying to reach for countless years.

See Paul Santoyo, Comment, *Bananas of Wrath: How Nicaragua May Have Dealt Forum Non Conveniens a Fatal Blow Removing the Doctrine as an Obstacle to Achieving Corporate Accountability*, 27 Hous. J. Int'l L. 703, 732 (2005)

From a very broad-based policy perspective, Nicaragua's tactic may not be the most appealing remedial prescription. It does little, for example, to address the actual shortcomings in the forum non conveniens analysis or to improve on any inadequacies in Nicaraguan courts. And in the increasingly globalized market, where more multinational corporations will find their way into the still-developing areas of Latin America, both a revamping of U.S. forum non conveniens analysis and judicial reform efforts in Latin America will no doubt prove to be central to protecting Latin American plaintiffs. There is also some question as to the viability of the Nicaraguan judgment insofar as defendants have contested the Nicaraguan court's jurisdiction over them.

All that being said, as far as interim measures go, there is no contest; Nicaragua's was a good one.

———

Nicaragua's *Special Law for the Conduct of Lawsuits Filed by Persons Affected by the Use of Pesticides Manufactured with a DBCP Base*, known also as Law No. 364, specifically addresses lawsuits against U.S. companies for DBCP-related harm caused in Nicaragua. Law No. 364 makes Nicaragua a less desirable forum for defendants. The law sets a minimum award for actual damages at $100,000 (US) per successful plaintiff (Article 3). To guarantee payment, defendants must post a bond of $100,000 per plaintiff within ninety days of being served notice (Article 4). If they do not post the bond, they must submit unconditionally to U.S. court jurisdiction and expressly waive assertion of *forum non conveniens* there (Article 7). Manufacturer defendants and defendants other than plaintiffs' employers must additionally post a 300 million cordoba (roughly $16 million US) bond to guarantee payment of any judgment against them (Article 8). The law also sets minimum amounts for pain and suffering compensation (Article 11).

Law No. 364 of Nicaragua[e]

Special Law to Process Lawsuits Filed by People Affected by the
Use of Pesticides Manufactured with DBCP
National Assembly of the Republic of Nicaragua

Art. 1. The purpose of the present Law is to determine and to facilitate the prosecution of lawsuits for damages filed by people whose physical, psychological or pathological health has bee adversely affected by the use and application of the DBCP pesticide....

———

e. English translation provided in Henry Saint Dahl, *Forum Non Conveniens, Latin America and Blocking Statutes*, 35 Univ. of Miami Inter-Am. L. Rev. 21, 50 (2003–2004).

Art. 2. The enterprises who manufacture the products mentioned in Article 1 of the present law as well as the enterprises who import, distribute, market and apply such products in Nicaragua, who although having had full knowledge of the effects caused by those pesticides on humans, such as: sterility and injury to the kidneys, liver and spleen, reasons due to which their use was banned in the United States of North America, could be civil and criminally liable, according to our legal system....

Art. 3. Enterprises sued in the United States of America which have opted to have the lawsuits transferred to Nicaraguan courts and are presently being sued before our national courts ... shall be bound to indemnify with a minimum mount equivalent to one hundred thousand American dollars, or its equivalent in cordobas at the official exchange rate applicable at the time such indemnity is paid, depending on the gravity of the case, to each affected person who has filed a claim before our courts provided that one can show that his health has been physically or psychologically affected.

Art. 4. The defending enterprises shall deposit, to guarantee payment of the judgment, within (90) ninety days of the respective lawsuits having been filed before the Courts of the Republic, the amount of one hundred thousand dollars ... as a procedural condition for participation in the lawsuit....

Art. 5. The posting of a bond mentioned in Article 4 of this Law shall be made to cover the costs of the lawsuit before the national courts, besides, it shall be held as part of the future indemnity received by people affected by any physical, psychological or pathological deformation caused by sterility, cancer and other diseases and physical and moral damages proven to be a consequence of the use and application of the DBCP pesticide....

Art. 6. This law declares that the civil liability and criminal sanctions imposed on people who were public servants at the time when the imports were authorized and who authorized their use and application, as well as the manufacturing, importing, distributing, marketing and applying enterprises, shall never be time-barred if the commission of the illegal act were proven, in conformity with the criminal code in force.

Art. 7. Enterprises that, within (90) ninety days of being notified of the present Law by the plaintiff and the claim having been served through the pertinent means, have not posted the bond established by Article 4 of the same Law, shall submit unconditionally to the jurisdiction of the Courts of the United States of North America for the final decision of the case in question, expressly waiving the exception of "Forum Non Conveniens" raised before those Courts....

Art. 8. Within ninety (90) days after having been served with the claims filed before the Courts of the Republic, each one of the manufacturers of these products, as well as the other defendants that have not settled with the workers must post the additional amount of C$ 300,000,000.00 (Three hundred million Cordobas) in a special account, in a bank of their choice, to guarantee payment of the eventual indemnity to the workers and other costs of the lawsuit.

Art. 9. The affected people who ... have been rendered sterile, shall enjoy from the benefit and the irrebuttable presumption that such sterility was caused by said pesticides....

Art. 11. The following table of minimum indemnities, which shall be paid joint and severally by the defendants, is established.

People Affected	Indemnities
a) Azoospermia	US $ 100,000.00
b) Severe oligospermia	US $ 50,000.00
c) Other injuries	US $ 25,000.00

Art. 12. In all cases brought before national courts, at the request of the interested party, the plaintiff, the Court shall apply, in matters of indemnity and the corresponding related sanction according to law, the evidentiary means, the parameters and relevant amounts of the pertinent foreign law, duly accredited in the lawsuit according to Nicaraguan law....

Art. 13. In case those affected by the use of the pesticide mentioned in Article 1 of this Law, lack the economic means to obtain professional legal assistance to enforce their rights in a lawsuit, the State of the Republic of Nicaragua shall be bound to guarantee such professional legal assistance in defense of their rights, both in national and in foreign courts....

Art. 14. The appeals against decisions by the District Court, issued pursuant to the present rules, shall be for review purposes only and shall not prevent the payments or the posting of bonds ordered by this Law.

Art. 15. This law is declared to embody public policy and to be of social and of national interest. The present Law shall also be applicable to judicial proceedings already started at the time it became effective.

Issued in the City of Managua, in the Session Room of the National Assembly, on October 5, 2000.

Oscar Moncada Reyes, President of the National Assembly, by Law.

Pedro Joaquin Rios Castellon, Secretary of the National Assembly.

Accordingly: Let it be held as Law of the Republic, Let it be Published and Let it be Enforced. Managua, November 23, 2000. Arnoldo Aleman Lacayo, President of the Republic of Nicaragua.

Consultation on Law 364[f] (Nicaragua)

Supreme Court of Justice of Nicaragua
Managua, October 16, 2003

On September 10, 2002, the then President of the Supreme Court of Justice, Doctor Ivan Escobar Fornos, received an Opinion issued by the Attorney General, Doctor Francisco Fiallos Navarro, related to Law 364 "Special Law to Process Lawsuits Filed by People Affected by the Use of Pesticides Manufactured on the Basis of DBCP," published on January 17, 2001, in *La Gaceta*, Official Newspaper, No. 12, the date when it became effective.

In essence, the Attorney General of the Republic, issued an opinion at that time stating that said Law: 1.—Violates the Code of Civil Procedure concerning appeals, evidence, precautionary measures, civil and criminal liability, and the domicile rules, stressing the issue of the bond requested from defendants. 2.—That it violates the Principle of Equality and the Principle of Retroactivity of the Law, as well as the "Convention between the Government of the Republic of Nicaragua and the Government of the United States of America Concerning the XXX and Reciprocal Protection of Investments," and the Pact of San Jose. At the end he states:

> Accordingly, if the purported Law 364 violates the Nicaraguan legal structure
> and contradicts the Political Constitution in any of its points, it must be considered

f. English translation provided in Henry Saint Dahl, *Forum Non Conveniens, Latin America and Blocking Statutes*, 35 Univ. of Miami Inter-American Law Review 21, 53–57 (2003–2004).

unconstitutional," — the Attorney General requests that the opinion be sent to all the Civil Judges in the country, with jurisdiction over this type of lawsuit, for better illustration in their respective judicial decisions.

Afterwards, the Attorney General changed his position as it can be seen in his statements and in those of the Nicaraguan Government in EXHIBITS V, VIII, IX, X, XIII and, particularly, XVIII and XX.

Although the Supreme Court of Justice acknowledged the constitutionality of Law 364 in two Communiqués of 13 and 20 of November 2002, attached, and the declarations of Justices Francisco Rosales Arguello and Rafael Solis Cerda conveyed the Supreme Court's respect for Law 364 (EXHIBIT XIX), the undersigned Justices of the Supreme Court of the Republic of Nicaragua, are willing to offer the following considerations concerning the Opinion issued by the then Attorney General of the Republic, Doctor Francisco Fiallos Navarro, taking into account that we cannot decide in this case through a jurisdictional avenue since Law 364 establishes only two phases by contemplating only an appeal and also because no Constitutional Challenge was presented against Law 364 at the relevant time.

I. Concerning form:

First: The powers granted to the Attorney General of the Republic by law 411, "Organic Law of the Attorney General's Office of the Republic" do not include declaring the constitutionality or otherwise of any law, decree, regulation or resolution, or to interpret the same; these powers are exclusively reserved to the Supreme Court of Justice and to the Honorable National Assembly, according to the constitutional mandate in articles 164, paragraph 4, and 138 paragraph 2, both of the Political Constitution, respectively. To the contrary, according to the case in question, the Attorney General's Office has the power to "Intervene in the defense of the environment with the purpose of guaranteeing a healthy and ecologically balanced environment" (Art. 2, paragraph 5 of Law 411).

Second: Legal Opinions by the Republic's Attorney General's Office are only binding for the Executive Power. They have no mandatory power at all outside that sphere....

Third: Our Law of Amparo, presently in force, indicates the requirements and formalities necessary for an Unconstitutionality Challenge, which are mandatory. One of these is the term or deadline for filing, which is sixty days (Law of Amparo, art. 10). The applicable term has obviously expired over two years ago since Law 364 became effective in January 2001. It will soon be three years old. Further, only physical persons, not juridical persons, have standing to file a Challenge for Unconstitutionality. The Republic's Attorney General's Office shall be a party when the Challenge for Unconstitutionality is decided. Once the challenge is filed, the Attorney General's Office is notified, and should express its view within six days. This is not what has happened here.

Consequently, the opinion for unconstitutionality issued by the Attorney General at the time is not binding for the Judiciary System of the Nicaraguan Republic, just as the same Attorney General admitted later through the media.

II. Concerning substance:

First: By enacting Law 364, "SPECIAL LAW TO PROCESS LAWSUITS FILED BY PEOPLE AFFECTED BY THE USE OF PESTICIDES MANUFACTURED ON THE BASIS OF DBCP" the National Assembly has only instituted a special and agile procedure to guarantee the Principle of Effective Judicial Protection or, according to Anglo-Saxon law, of Due Legal Process (due process of law), embodied in article 33 of the Political Constitution, which establishes that:

> Nobody can be subject to arbitrary detention or arrest, or be deprived of freedom, except for reasons established in the law as determined in a legal procedure.;

as well as the Principle of Effective Judicial Protection sustained in article 34 of the Political Constitution, which establishes that:

> Any party in a case has the right to the following minimum guarantees, on a basis of equality: 1) To be tried without delay by a court with jurisdiction established by law. Special courts cannot be created. Nobody can be taken away from a judge with jurisdiction, nor taken to a jurisdiction of exception; 4) To have one's participation and defense guaranteed from the beginning of the case and to have adequate time and means to defend oneself; 8) To have judgment issued within the legal terms in each phase of the case; 9) To have access to a higher court, for the case to be reviewed when one has been condemned for any crime;

and more specifically, in article 52 of the Political Constitution, which literally states:

> Citizens have the right to make petitions, to report irregularities and to make constructive criticism, individually or collectively, to the Powers of the State, or any authority; to obtain a quick answer and to have the result communicated within the time determined by the law.

Second: Everybody knows that the people affected by pesticides based on DBCP are rural workers who were employed in banana plantations, without sufficient economic means to sue a transnational corporation. Such circumstances motivated the urgent enactment of Law 364, to make it possible for those affected to obtain Effective Judicial Protection. Not just to file a lawsuit, but to obtain judgment in a reasonable time and to promote healthy conditions. But also to allow such judgment to become effective, guaranteed and enforced as soon as possible, without subjecting the workers to a slow, ordinary proceeding which would only contribute to an economic hemorrhage which plaintiffs cannot afford.

Third: Law 364 has resorted to a variation of the Principle of Equality, that of Positive Discrimination. That is to say, the one that, in the face of a real inequality offers advantages, incentives or more favorable treatment in a premeditated way to marginalized social groups, in this case the rural workers affected by DBCP. This particularity of the Principle of Equality is grounded in the country's social reality, reflected in Art. 48, paragraph two of the Political Constitution, which acknowledges real inequality when pointing out that:

> The State is obligated to eliminate the obstacles that prevent in fact equality among Nicaraguans and their effective participation in the country's political, economic and social life.

In the present case, this Positive Discrimination is reflected in Law 364, where article 4 states:

> The defending enterprises shall deposit, to guarantee payment of the judgment, within (90) ninety days of the respective lawsuits having been filed before the Courts of the Republic, the amount of one hundred thousand dollars…, as a procedural condition for participation in the lawsuit.…

Article 5 determines that said deposit shall be to cover the cost of the lawsuit in national courts; besides it shall be considered as part of future compensation that the affected people may receive for any physical, psychological or pathological deformity, for sterility, cancer and any other physical or moral infirmity and damages that are proven to be consequence of the use and application of the DBCP pesticide.

These rules have not violated the Principle of Equality which, in procedural terms consists of the legislator's duty to treat the same those who are in the same circumstances, and differently those who are in different circumstances. In the present case it is obvious that the defending enterprises, transnational corporations, are not in equal circumstances as plaintiffs, who are rural workers without economic means. Accordingly, the deposit requested to the defending enterprises if they submit to Nicaraguan jurisdiction, does not breach the Principle of Equality. It must not be analyzed under that angle but rather as a precautionary measure aimed at guaranteeing the outcome of the case. It is evident that the purpose of Law 364 is not to control an ordinary proceeding but rather the damage caused to human beings by the forbidden use of a toxic substance such as DBCP. This Law aims at protecting human life, enshrined in articles 23 and 36 of the Political Constitution. Concerning the defendant's constitutional guarantees, Law 364 respects Due Process, or due process of law, beginning by offering the choice of jurisdiction more convenient to such defendant (Nicaraguan or American), the right to be heard, to offer evidence and the right to appeal, due to which the Principle of Equality is not breached....

It is known that civil lawsuits, among others, can last a long time. This, in fact, may lead to the loss of plaintiffs' rights. Plaintiff may obtain a writ of execution. However, there is the danger that it cannot be enforced because defendant has taken steps that limit, or even prevent, the exercise of such right, for instance, by watering down his assets. Consequently, an accelerated procedure must be made available which gives the creditor some provisional assurances that the final judgment obtained is not useless. Judicial Protection would not be effective if, when judgment is rendered, it becomes difficult or practically impossible to enforce it. The delay in proceedings could give rise that when judgment is rendered, it lacks any meaning....

Fourth: Law 364 responds to the need to regulate situations created with the application of banned pesticides, extended in time, and its consequent damage to people who lived in banana plantations and surrounding areas.... In keeping with the Principle of Validity, all law is enacted because the previous one is considered deficient or because social interest so demands it. Therefore, its applicability must not be delayed. But ... there are individual interests too which must be respected and guaranteed by law, since such guarantee is one of its essential functions. There must be a limit and, that furthermost point is found in the respect for acquired rights, except concerning laws that further rights inherent to humans as such, like the law abolishing slavery. Merlín was right in saying that those rules that "revitalizing a law written in the Eternal Code of nature, they erase with one stroke the omnipotence of actions that were secretly carried in violation of the most sacred rights of men"; it could then be said that, on occasion, it is reasonable that in certain cases the legislator may direct the effects of the law to the past, to prevent impunity for acts committed before the law was created. Now, a law is retroactive when it destroys or restricts an Acquired Right under a previous law. But it is not if it throws out a legal faculty or a simple expectation. Concerning Law 364 and its implementing regulations, it is absurd to think, from any natural, human, ethical, moral, religious, political, juridical, etc. point of view, that a physical or a juridical person may have the expectation, faculties, and much less Acquired Rights that stem from injuring, causing damage, harming, ignoring life, health and the physical, psychic and moral integrity of any human being....

Consequently, Law 364, "Special Law to Process Lawsuits Filed by People Affected by the Use of Pesticides Manufactured on the Basis of DBCP," published on January 17, 2001, in *La Gaceta*, Oficial Newspaper, No. 12, the date when it became effective, enjoys full substantive and formal validity according to our Political Constitution. It doesn't violate any article of the Political Constitution and cannot be challenged as retroactive.

Managua, October 16, 2003. (Signatures follow).

2007 National Trade Estimate Report on Foreign Trade Barriers
Office of the U.S. Trade Representative
2 April 2007

Foreword

The 2007 National Trade Estimate Report on Foreign Trade Barriers (NTE) is the twenty-second in an annual series that surveys significant foreign barriers to U.S. exports.

In accordance with section 181 of the Trade Act of 1974 (the 1974 Trade Act), as amended, ... the Office of the U.S. Trade Representative is required to submit to the President, the Senate Finance Committee, and appropriate committees in the House of Representatives, an annual report on significant foreign trade barriers.

The statute requires an inventory of the most important foreign barriers affecting U.S. exports of goods and services, foreign direct investment by U.S. persons, and protection of intellectual property rights. Such an inventory facilitates negotiations aimed at reducing or eliminating these barriers....

Nicaragua—Other Barriers—Law 364

U.S. multinational firms and the U.S. Chamber of Commerce have expressed concern regarding Nicaraguan Law 364, enacted in October 2000 and published in January 2001. Law 364 retroactively imposes liabilities on foreign companies that manufactured or used the chemical pesticide DBCP in Nicaragua. DBCP was banned in the United States after the Environmental Protection Agency cancelled its certificate for use (with exceptions) in 1979. U.S. multinationals have expressed concern that the law and its application under Nicaragua's judicial system lack due process, transparency and fundamental fairness. In particular, the law allows for retroactive application of no-fault liability related to a specific product, waiver of the statute of limitations, irrefutable presumption of causality, truncated judicial proceedings, imposition of a $100,000 non-refundable bond per defendant as a condition for firms to put up a defense in court, escrow requirements of approximately $20 million earmarked for payment of awards and minimum liabilities as liquidated damages (ranging from $25,000 to $100,000.) In January 2006, the National Assembly placed an embargo on the trademark rights of an American multinational because of its involvement in the production of this pesticide. Some plaintiffs seek to lay claim to U.S. company assets in other countries. The U.S. Government has been working with the affected companies and the Nicaraguan government to facilitate resolution of this issue.

Questions and Discussion

1. *Fairness.* Are the provisions of Law 364 fair? To companies that invest in Nicaragua? To workers in Nicaragua? To Nicaraguan society? Is it fair to force companies to defend themselves in their home countries? Is it fair to force injured people to litigate only in their home countries?

2. *Investment.* Will foreign corporations be reluctant to operate in Nicaragua in the future because of the risk of such retroactive laws applying to any severe damage that they might cause? Will they be willing to operate in Nicaragua if they are liable under U.S. tort law and unable to reduce that exposure significantly through a *forum non conveniens* motion? Is everything that makes corporations concerned about their responsibilities or liabilities in a country's legal system a "trade barrier"?

3. *Attorney General.* Why would the Attorney General of Nicaragua issue a legal opinion 21 months after Law 364 became effective, stating that the law violated various constitutional principles? Do you suppose that he was acting on his own initiative? Considering that Nicaraguan law provides for a constitutional challenge to a new law for only 60 days after it became effective and no challenge was filed, does it appear that companies affected by the law failed to receive good legal advice at the time?

4. *Positive discrimination.* Is Nicaragua's constitutional "Principle of Positive Discrimination" appropriate to its social and economic situation? Would it be appropriate in the United States in some situations?

5. *Retroactivity.* Is the Court's determination on retroactivity and expectations a reasonable one? To what degree is it based on natural law?

3. *The U.S. DBCP Litigation*

Dow v. Calderon
422 F.3d 827 (9th Cir. 2005)

BERZON, Circuit Judge:

The Dow Chemical Company, Shell Oil Company, and Shell Chemical Company ("the Companies") sued more than a thousand Nicaraguan citizens ("the Nicaraguans") in federal district court in California. The Companies seek a declaration that (1) they are not liable for any injuries to the Nicaraguans caused by dibromochloropropane, a toxic pesticide commonly known as "DBCP"; and (2) any judgments of Nicaraguan courts to the contrary are not enforceable in this country. The question before us is whether the Nicaraguans consented to personal jurisdiction by either (1) choosing to file suit in Nicaragua under a Nicaraguan law that requires American companies to deposit a specified sum or submit unconditionally to the jurisdiction of U.S. courts; or (2) defending on the merits a declaratory judgment action brought by a different company in the same federal district court concerning the same set of underlying Nicaraguan judgments. The district court rejected both of these contentions. Agreeing with the district court, we hold that the Nicaraguan defendants did not consent to personal jurisdiction in this action.

After 23 years of trying, Central American banana plantation workers rendered sterile by DBCP finally achieved a verdict in a U.S. courtroom in 2007. The trial is likely to be the first of several. The fact that a trial occurred in the U.S. was directly attributable to Nicaragua's Law No. 364, discussed above. Unwilling to undergo the conditions imposed by Law No. 364, the Dole Company and Dow Chemical Company chose to take their chances before a jury in California state court. The following document shows the causes of action that were pleaded.

Tellez v. Dole

Los Angeles Superior Court
2004 WL 5468592 (Filed, L.A. County Super. Ct. 2004)

	)	No. BC312852
Jose Adolfo TELLEZ;	)	
Carlos Enrique Diaz Artiaga;	)	First Amended Complaint for
Felix Amado Garcia Avendano;	)	Compensatory Damages and
Carlos Miguel Blanco, et al.	)	Other Relief Re: (1) Strict
v.	)	Liability; (2) Negligence; and (3)
Dole Food Co., Inc., et al.	)	Fraudulent Concealment

Plaintiffs allege:

I. Capacity of the Parties

Plaintiffs

1. Plaintiffs were exposed to 1, 2 Dibromo-3-Chloropropane (DBCP), a pesticide designed, developed, and manufactured in the United States, and distributed from the United States, while plaintiffs were working on banana plantations operated by United States defendants in Nicaragua. This exposure caused plaintiffs to suffer significant injuries, including but not limited to, azoospermia (sterility), oligospermia (abnormally low sperm counts), and other reproductive injuries.

2. In Nicaragua, under the control and direction of the United States defendants, DBCP was commonly applied by mixing it with sprinkler irrigation water or by injecting it into the ground....

4. Plaintiffs worked on banana plantations [from as early as 1964 to as late as 1990]. During this time plaintiffs were exposed to DBCP through a variety of routes, including but not limited to dermal exposure, inhalation of DBCP from ambient air, and ingestion of DBCP from contaminated drinking water....

6. As a consequence of exposure to DBCP plaintiffs have suffered serious and permanent injuries, including, but not limited to, total and irreversible sterility or infertility.... Due to the imperceptibility of the injury, the fact that it can only be perceived and diagnosed through costly medical testing and laboratory analysis, the absence or shortage of medical care available to plaintiffs in Nicaragua, and plaintiffs' economic standing which prevents them from affording and obtaining medical care, Plaintiffs did not discover, and, with the exercise of reasonable diligence, could not have discovered their injuries and their causes of action sooner than they did. In addition, defendants fraudulently and actively concealed information [from plaintiffs regarding the harm to which they had been exposed]....

[Defendants] ...

[The complaint splits the defendants into two groups. The "manufacturer defendants" are The Dow Chemical Company ("Dow") and Amvac Chemical Corporation ("Amvac"). The "fruit company defendants" are Dole Food Company, Inc., ("Dole"), Dole Fresh Fruit Company, Standard Fruit Company ("Standard Fruit") and Standard Fruit and Steamship Company.] ...

II. General Factual Allegations ...

18. DBCP was used, among other things, in pesticide products to control nematodes (microscopic worms that infest the roots of plants). DBCP was commonly used for this purpose in fruit orchards, including banana plantations, around the world. DBCP is a

volatile organic chemical and is remarkably persistent in the subsurface environment, remaining in soil or groundwater for decades after its use.

19. The manufacturer defendants manufactured and sold DBCP and designed, developed, formulated, manufactured, controlled, distributed, patented, licensed, and sold pesticides containing DBCP, in the United States. Decisions about.... DBCP were made by manufacturer defendants in the United States.

20. The fruit company defendants purchased DBCP in the United States and re-sold and distributed DBCP from the United States to their subsidiaries and affiliates in various countries around the world, including Nicaragua. Decisions about the purchase, resale, distribution, use, handling, and control of DBCP were made in the United States by fruit company defendants, and decisions about application of DBCP were made in the United States and Nicaragua.

21. DBCP is extremely toxic. Even at extremely low levels (one part per million or less), exposure causes azoospermia (sterility), oligospermia (abnormally low sperm counts), and other reproductive injuries. DBCP is the most potent testicular toxin known to science....

26. Defendants, and each of them, knew, or reasonably should have known at all relevant times, that DBCP (1) is a toxic substance which poses a substantial risk of harm to human health, (2) ... causes sterility and other significant physical harm, (3) is persistent in the environment, (4) poses a substantial risk of contaminating groundwater and drinking water supplies, and (5) was defective in design and manufacture.

27. Defendant Dole Food Company, Inc. has alleged under oath, in a complaint recently filed in federal court styled *Dole Food Company Inc. v. Walter Antonio Gutierrez et al.*..., that:

> Civil trials in Nicaragua under [a] special DBCP law deprive American defendants a fair opportunity to defend themselves and virtually ensure a judgment in favor of Nicaraguan [plaintiffs]. After the fraudulent and groundless judgments are obtained, they are brought to the United States with the goal of enforcing them against American companies.

28. This complaint does not seek to enforce any judgments obtained in Nicaragua. Rather, this complaint is being filed in the United States, in state court, in Dole Food Company Inc.'s home state, the state in which Dole Food Company, Inc., decided to undertake the actions which are the subject of this complaint....

First Cause Of Action

[Strict Liability] ...

36. When sold and/or re-sold by defendants, pesticides containing DBCP are defective products because, among other things:

(a) DBCP causes infertility ... and [other] extensive harm to human health, even when used in a foreseeable and intended manner.

(b) The benefits of using DBCP in pesticides, if any, are greatly outweighed by the associated costs and negative impacts imposed on society, consumers, workers, and the environment. It is impossible to apply DBCP in a manner that controls pests but does not create an unacceptable exposure and corresponding risk to human health.

(c) DBCP and pesticides containing DBCP, when used in a reasonably foreseeable manner, do not and did not perform as safely as an ordinary consumer would have expected, because they are persistent and contaminate drinking water and caused serious injuries, including ... harm to reproductive organs....

39. DBCP, and pesticides containing DBCP, were used in the manner in which they were foreseeably intended to be used, and as a direct and proximate result of the defects previously described, and defendants' acts and omissions alleged above, plaintiffs were exposed to harmful levels of DBCP and have been rendered sterile, and/or infertile. Plaintiffs have sustained a loss of opportunity to have and enjoy children and grandchildren, disruption in marital relations, loss of self-esteem, loss of family lineage, distress, mental anguish and suffering. Physically, plaintiffs have sustained testicular atrophy, damage to sperm producing cells, and the seminiferous tubules, genetic damage, and damage to other tissues throughout the body.... Plaintiffs have incurred and will continue to incur medical and other expenses due to their exposure to DBCP....

Exemplary Damages Allegations

41. Defendants The Dow Chemical Company, Amvac Chemical Corporation, Dole Food Company, Inc., Dole Fresh Fruit Company, Standard Fruit Company, and Standard Fruit and Steamship Company ... knew that it was substantially certain that their alleged acts and omissions described above would cause serious injury, including reproductive injury. Said defendants committed each of the above-described acts and omissions knowingly, willfully, and with oppression, fraud, and/or malice, and with conscious disregard of the health and safety of others in at least the following respects:

(a) As early as 1958, scientists employed by Dow noted marked testicular effects in laboratory animals exposed to DBCP even at the lowest levels of exposure.... Despite this knowledge, Dow decided not to conduct further toxicological studies on DBCP at lower exposure levels, not to monitor the reproductive health of DBCP-exposed workers, and instead began selling and marketing DBCP for use on crops around the world in the 1950s without disclosing the known reproductive toxicity of DBCP....

(c) In 1977, 35 of 114 workers manufacturing DBCP at Occidental's Lathrop, California plant were found to be sterile. Shortly thereafter, the State of California banned the use of DBCP. The EPA provisionally banned the use of DBCP for most purposes in the United States in 1977, and made the ban permanent in 1979....

(d) The EPA did not, however, ban the export of DBCP, and Dow still had large stocks to sell. When Dow informed the fruit company defendants that it planned to halt sales and wait for EPA test results, Dole complained that "[y]our halt on shipping our outstanding orders is viewed as a breach of contract. Your advice on what Dow will do in seeing these commitments met will be appreciated." Dow finally relented to the fruit company defendants' demand for the sale of DBCP only after the fruit company defendants agreed to indemnify Dow against claims for personal injuries resulting from DBCP use.

(e) Dow sent to the fruit company defendants a revised manual on DBCP safety procedures, providing a number of detailed recommendations about ways of minimizing exposure to DBCP. However, Dole rejected a number of Dow's recommendations, including Dow's recommendation that field applicators use respirators. Even after receiving further recommendations and instructions from Dow and Shell, the fruit company defendants still did not provide adequate safety information, personal protective clothing or equipment to their workers in Nicaragua and elsewhere.

(f) Said defendants knew DBCP products would contaminate groundwater, water supplies, and/or the ambient air where plaintiffs worked. Nonetheless, these defendants continued to manufacture, distribute, supply and/or apply these toxic substances, or to cause their subsidiaries and affiliates to do so.

(g) Said defendants knew that DBCP products caused adverse effects on male fertility and other serious harm. Nonetheless, these defendants actively suppressed and concealed information regarding the hazards of DBCP products from regulators, or caused their subsidiaries or affiliates to do so.

42. This conduct by the said defendants is reprehensible, despicable, and intended to promote sales of DBCP products and profits in conscious disregard of the known risks of injury to human health and property.... Therefore, plaintiffs request an award of exemplary damages in an amount to punish these defendants....

Second Cause Of Action

[Negligence] ...

44. Defendants had a duty to use due care ... and to cause their subsidiaries or affiliates to do so.

45. The manufacturer defendants so negligently, carelessly, and/or recklessly designed, developed, ... promoted, distributed, handled, supplied, sold, used and disposed of DBCP, that they breached their duties to plaintiffs and other foreseeable users, and thereby directly and proximately caused plaintiffs' injuries as alleged in this complaint.

46. The fruit company defendants so negligently, carelessly and/or recklessly purchased, used, applied, [etc.] DBCP ... that they breached their duties to plaintiffs and other foreseeable users, and thereby directly and proximately caused plaintiffs' injuries as alleged in this complaint....

49. The defendants identified above as liable for exemplary damages knew that it was substantially certain that their acts and omissions and negligent breaches of duty described above would harm human health as alleged in this complaint, yet they committed each of the above-described acts and omissions with reckless disregard for the health and safety of others, including plaintiffs.

50. This conduct is reprehensible, despicable, and was performed to promote sales of DBCP and profits in reckless disregard of the known risks of injury to human health and property. Plaintiffs therefore request an award of exemplary damages in an amount sufficient to punish and deter said defendants.

Third Cause Of Action

[Fraudulent Concealment] ...

52. Defendants ... concealed and actively suppressed material facts from plaintiffs which were within defendants' knowledge....

54. Defendants intentionally concealed and suppressed these material facts from plaintiffs so that plaintiffs would work in the banana plantations, so that defendants could continue to sell and purchase DBCP and profit from the continued use of DBCP, all at the risk and detriment to plaintiffs' health and well-being....

56. The concealment and suppression of these facts directly and proximately caused plaintiffs to be exposed to harmful levels of DBCP and to be rendered sterile and/or infertile....

57. The defendants identified above as liable for exemplary damages knew that it was substantially certain that their concealments and suppressions of facts as described above would harm human health as alleged in this complaint....

58.... Plaintiffs therefore request an award of exemplary damages in an amount sufficient to punish and deter said defendants.

————

The *Tellez* case was the first time that U.S. corporations were taken to trial in the U.S. over DBCP-related harm occurring outside the U.S. Defendant Amvac Chemical Corp. settled with plaintiffs in April 2007. The remaining defendants, Dole and Dow, proceeded to trial in cases brought by twelve of the original plaintiffs. The jury returned verdicts in November 2007, awarding compensatory damages to six of the twelve plaintiffs; exemplary (punitive) damages were awarded to five.

$2.5 Million in Punitive Damages Awarded to Banana Workers
Noaki Schwartz, Associated Press
Thursday, November 15, 2007

A jury Thursday found that the American food giant Dole should pay $2.5 million in punitive damages to five workers who claimed they were made sterile by use of a pesticide on Nicaraguan banana plantations in the 1970s.

Last week, the Superior Court jury awarded $3.3 million in actual damages to six workers, most of it to be paid by California-based Dole and the remainder by Dow Chemical Co. of Michigan. The jury's finding that Dole acted maliciously in harming five of the six allowed punitive damages to be considered for the five....

Twelve workers originally filed suit, but the jury determined that only six had been substantially harmed by the pesticide. The six won actual damage awards ranging from $311,200 to $834,000.

The case marked the first time a U.S. jury heard a lawsuit involving sterility and DBCP. Legal experts said the case raised the issue of whether multinational companies should be held accountable in the country where they are based or the countries where they employ workers.

Dow was not liable for punitive damages because the judge granted the company's petition to apply Michigan law to the amount and types of damages earlier in the trial. Michael L. Brem, one of the attorneys for the Midland, Mich.-based company said this would prevent punitive damages and cap any compensatory damages at $394,200 per plaintiff....

Superior Court Judge Victoria Chaney noted after the punitive damages were read that the case was only the first in a series before her involving thousands of agricultural workers.

Chaney, saying it had been the "bellwether case," urged the jurors to discuss their reasoning with the trial attorneys.

The other cases involve workers in Ecuador, Nicaragua, Costa Rica, Guatemala, Honduras and Panama who claim they were left sterile after being exposed to the pesticide. Other growers and manufacturers are named as defendants in those cases.

Questions and Discussion

1. *The effect of Law No. 364.* The Nicaraguan law referred to in paragraph 27 of the *Tellez* complaint is the *Special Law for the Conduct of Lawsuits Filed by Persons Affected by*

the Use of Pesticides Manufactured with a DBCP Base, known also as Law No. 364, shown above at page 430. Law No. 364 specifically addresses lawsuits against U.S. companies for DBCP-related harm caused in Nicaragua. It makes Nicaragua a substantially less desirable forum for defendants than the United States. To summarize, the law sets a minimum award for actual damages at $100,000 (U.S. dollars) per successful plaintiff (Article 3). To guarantee payment, defendants must post a bond of $100,000 per plaintiff within ninety days of being served notice (Article 4). If they do not post the bond, they must submit unconditionally to U.S. court jurisdiction and expressly waive assertion of *forum non conveniens* there (Article 7). Manufacturer defendants and defendants other than plaintiffs' employers must additionally post a 300 million cordoba (roughly $16 million US) bond to guarantee payment of any judgment against them (Article 8). The law also sets minimum amounts for pain and suffering compensation (Article 11).

2. *The future of home-country litigation.* Does the result in the *Tellez* case suggest that citizens in countries like Ecuador, Papua New Guinea, and Indonesia, among others, would benefit from the adoption of similar legislation by their countries? Are they likely to have the political power to obtain such legislation? Was the situation in Nicaragua unique and not likely to be replicated elsewhere? Or does it provide an answer for some of the limitations seen in other remedies in this chapter?

3. *Punitive damage award canceled.* In 2008, the trial judge in *Tellez v. Dole* rejected the jur's punitive damages award, thereby cutting the jury award in half. Her decision was on appeal at the time of this book's publication.

Chapter 10

Human Rights and International Financial Institutions

Introduction

Numerous human rights criticisms have been lodged against development projects that have international financing. In response, the various multilateral development banks (MDBs) have developed procedures for filing complaints with internal review bodies.

This chapter will focus on primarily on the World Bank Group and its Inspection Panel, along with the International Finance Corporation and its ombudsman. Although this chapter's focus is primarily on the World Bank Group and its subsidiaries, keep in mind that other MDBs face many of the same challenges in terms of preventing their projects from violating environmental rights.

I. Multilateral Development Banks

A. History of MDBs

The term multilateral development banks (MDBs) generally refers to five multinational institutions, including the World Bank Group, The African Development Bank, The Asian Development Bank, The European Bank for Reconstruction and Development, and the Inter-American Development Bank. Each bank's membership is made up of borrowing developing countries and developed donor countries, which provide financial support as well as economic and social policy advice to developing countries. MDBs provide financial assistance in the form of long-term loans with varying interest rates and occasional grants. For further information, see World Bank, *Multilateral Development Banks*, http://go.worldbank.org/F3REECOMB1.

The impetus for the World Bank's formation came in 1944 at the Bretton Wood Conference in New Hampshire. The conference, which aimed generally to stabilize international financial order after World War II (WWII), also gave rise to the Bretton Woods system of international monetary management. By January of 1945, 28 countries were members of the World Bank, including countries from Europe, North and South America, Asia, and the Middle East. The bank now consists of 185 member countries. See generally Devesh Kapur, John P. Lewis, & Richard Webb, THE WORLD BANK: ITS FIRST HALF CENTURY, Vol.

1, at 57–84 (1997); Benjamin Cohen, *Bretton Woods System*, in ROUTLEDGE ENCYCLOPEDIA OF INTERNATIONAL POLITICAL ECONOMY (2002); World Bank, *The World Bank Group Historical Chronology* (2005), http://siteresources.worldbank.org/EXTARCHIVES/Resources/WB_Historical_Chronology_1944_2005.pdf.

As Professors Kapur, Lewis, and Webb explain, the Bank's first loan, given to France in 1947, illustrates that the Bank's original focus was on rebuilding Europe after WWII. Other WWII reconstruction project loans went to the Netherlands, Luxembourg, and Denmark. The bank's emphasis as a reconstruction bank largely ended in 1947, after making just four reconstruction loans. In 1947, the Marshall Plan began providing huge sums for reconstruction purposes and the World Bank's focus shifted to project-based lending.

Though the bank's founders aimed to make it an "instrumentality of sovereign governments and not private financial interests," the unequal bargaining power of the various countries led to some structural inequities within the bank. For instance, the United States, which provided the most funding for the bank at its inception, gained several advantages. Under the Bank charter, it was permitted to establish the Bank's headquarters in Washington, D.C., and by convention, it also nominates a U.S. national as the bank's president. See Catherine Gwin, U.S. RELATIONS WITH THE WORLD BANK 1945–92, at 4 (1994).

Originally synonymous with the International Bank for Reconstruction and Development (IBRD), the name World Bank also now refers to the International Development Association (IDA). A broader term, World Bank Group, includes the aforementioned, as well as the International Financial Corporation (IFC), the Multilateral Investment Guarantee Association (MIGA) and the International Centre for Settlement of Investment Disputes (ICSID).

Each World Bank-related group is governed by similar but separate Articles of Agreement, which stipulate their governing principles and general policy. See World Bank, *About Us: Articles of Agreement*, http://go.worldbank.org/BAEZH92NH0. Akin to administrative rules, the Bank also has an Operational Manual, which contains sections on management, environmental assessment, and disclosure procedures.

In recent years, MDBs have declared respect for both procedural and substantive human rights and mandated environmental impact assessment in their policies. While critics recognize some progress compared to the past, many continue to voice strong dissatisfaction with the Banks' lending practices.

B. Critiques of MDBs

For Richer or for Poorer: Assessing the Criticisms Directed at the Multilateral Development Banks

John W. Head
52 U. Kan. L. Rev. 241 (2004)

As a starting point, we should recognize the diversity that exists between the various MDBs [multilateral development banks]. There are, after all, six principal institutions at issue: the International Bank for Reconstruction and Development ("IBRD"), chartered at the Bretton Woods conference in 1944; the International Development Association ("IDA"), chartered in 1960 to reflect the growing needs of less economically developed countries; the three regional development banks that were chartered in the late 1950s and 1960s—the Inter-American Development Bank ("IADB"), the African Development Bank ("AfDB"), and the Asian Development Bank ("AsDB")—and the most recent regional development bank to be created, the European Bank for Reconstruction and Development ("EBRD"), which was chartered at the close of the Cold War. The first two of these—the IBRD and the IDA—operate for most purposes as a single institution and are referred to jointly as the World Bank....

[D]espite their diversity, [MDBs] all share the same fundamental precepts and structures that are most important for purposes of evaluating the criticisms currently leveled against them. For example, all of the MDBs have economic development as their motivating aim. To this end, they provide loans (and some grants) to finance economic development projects such as roads, irrigation systems, port facilities, power plants, rural health facilities, teacher training, fertilizer production, agricultural credit, and institutional strengthening....

All of the MDBs operate under charters that take the form of multilateral treaties obligating their member states to pay for certain portions of subscribed capital and to observe certain privileges and immunities of the institutions and their staff members....

The MDBs may be viewed as being "generational" in character, with three generations now having run their course, or nearly so. The first generation is represented by the IBRD, born in the closing days of World War II with the reconstruction of Europe as its main priority. The fact that the U.S. Government soon took over the bulk of that task under the Marshall Plan prompted the IBRD to focus its attention more on the "D" in IBRD—that is, economic development in its non-European member countries.

A second generation began around 1960. With the rapid emergence of many new states following the massive decolonization of the 1940s and 1950s, the IBRD found itself unable to provide as much useful assistance as was needed in those new states because IBRD loans carried market-based interest rates. In 1960, the IDA was established as a companion to the IBRD—yielding the double institution we now call the World Bank—to provide a mechanism for making much cheaper money ("soft loans") available to the less developed countries ("LDCs"), by relying on contributions from rich member countries to finance projects similar to those that the IBRD had already been funding. At about the same time (between the late 1950s and mid-1960s), the IADB, the AfDB, and the AsDB were formed as regional sources of development financing to supplement the resources available through the World Bank. All three of these regional development banks sooner or later developed the same authority to make "soft loans" that the IDA makes. Hence these four institutions—the IDA, the IADB, the AfDB, and the AsDB—represent the second generation in the evolution of the MDBs, in which their role and scope were expanded in order to cater better to the needs of LDCs.

The EBRD represents a third generation in the evolution of MDBs. Formed in 1990, about four decades after the IDA and the earliest of the regional MDBs, the EBRD introduced several novel features into the operations of MDBs. Instead of prohibiting any consideration of political factors, as the charters of the earlier MDBs do, the charter of the EBRD expressly adopts a political mandate requiring the institution to take concrete steps to assist the countries of its operations—originally a handful of Eastern and Central European states newly released from the Soviet sphere of influence and now a couple of dozen states reaching from Central Europe across to Central Asia—in making their transition from Communist political control to an embrace of "the principles of multiparty democracy [and] pluralism...." The EBRD charter also in-cluded two other types of mandate absent from the charters of the earlier MDBs. Its economic mandate requires the EBRD "to foster the transition toward open market-ori-ented economies" in its countries of operation. Its environmental mandate requires the EBRD to "promote in the full range of its activities environmentally sound and sus-tainable development." ...

The establishment of the EBRD was a blatant manifestation of a trend that had al-ready begun in the other MDBs. It was a trend toward using the MDBs as instruments of global policy guidance or influence—or what I would call global policy regulation. This trend is exemplified by the gradual expansion of MDB operations into ... policy-based lending ... ; so extensive has this expansion been that today it is common to find these institutions requiring their borrowing member countries to accept and adhere to pre-scribed policies on environmental protection, indigenous peoples, involuntary resettle-ment, governance, corruption, public participation, the role of women in development, and poverty reduction.

Indeed, given the breadth and depth of such policy requirements, I believe the MDBs should be regarded as having been transformed from financial institutions into regula-tory agencies—that is, into agencies involved in global policy "regulation." They still carry out development banking functions, of course, but those banking functions have increasingly become instruments for achieving regulatory aims.... I believe this evolu-tion of MDBs into instruments of global policy regulation is a principal reason they have attracted so much attention in recent years. Many of the criticisms summarized below in Part II and evaluated in Part III have taken on a high profile in the popular press and public sentiment because the character of MDBs has changed so dramatically. I consider it important that we view the current cacophony of criticism against this his-torical backdrop.

II. A Menu of Criticisms—Substantive, Procedural, and Constitutional ...

A. Substantive Criticisms ...

2. Criticism #2—Environmental degradation

This criticism claims that some MDB-financed projects have devastating effects on the environment. For example, the MDBs favor large dams, road-building projects, and a general addiction to fossil fuels. The MDBs permit and promote environmentally de-structive projects because the MDBs simply disregard the environmental effects of the projects at both the design and the implementation phase. Why is this the case? Partly be-cause the MDBs are controlled by anti-environment influences, including corporate in-terests..., and partly because the MDB staff and management are out of step with modern views of sustainable development....

3. Criticism #3—Human rights shortcomings

According to this criticism, the MDBs typically give no regard to human rights of var-ious types, including the right to education and the rights of indigenous people, and they act independently of any accepted human rights norms and institutions. MDB projects and policies often set the pricing of health, education, and water services out of the reach of ordinary people. Moreover, MDBs support, at least tacitly, the notion of cultural ex-ceptionalism by which universal human rights norms are ignored by some countries. In addition, the MDBs are ineffective at addressing corruption in government, thus disre-garding the human right to effective governance.... Indeed, the MDBs fuel corruption by virtue of the huge financial flows that they control and disburse to government officials.

B. Procedural and Institutional Criticisms ...

3. Criticism #7 — Disregard for citizens' groups and NGOs

This criticism runs as follows: at the same time that they give undue influence to corporations..., the MDBs give too little attention to non-government organizations ("NGOs") and citizens' groups whose aim is to protect the public interest at large — sometimes referred to as "civil society" organizations. The contribution that such groups can make in the development process is ignored, and this in turn prompts some of these groups to take drastic, sometimes violent, actions that pit them against the MDBs as enemies. This needless antagonism represents both (i) a squandering by the MDBs of the opportunity to benefit from the NGOs' enthusiasm and expertise and (ii) a disregard by the MDBs of the recent moves within the United Nations to encourage the involvement of public interest (civil society) organizations.

4. Criticism #14 — Unaccountability and democracy deficit

According to this criticism, the MDBs lack legitimacy in today's world because they lack, as a structural or constitutional matter, any meaningful form of accountability. This criticism takes several forms, of which four are most important. First, the MDBs make no accommodation for citizen involvement. That is, not only do the MDBs operate on the basis of secrecy..., which prevents individuals or groups from knowing how they operate, what they have done, and what they plan to do; but the MDBs provide no mechanism for influence by members or representatives of civil society. In a world in which the importance of participatory rights is broadly accepted — for example, in human rights treaties that have been ratified by over three-quarters of all countries — such unaccountability is anachronistic and unacceptable.

Second, the general unaccountability of the MDBs is exacerbated by the specific form of governance that applies to them: weighted voting. Under the weighted voting system, as noted earlier, a country's voting power is generally proportional to that country's subscription to the MDB's capital. From their inception, the MDBs have had capital structures in which a handful of countries (including most markedly the United States) has controlled the bulk of the subscribed capital. Hence, that handful of countries controls a preponderance of the votes. For example, the G-7 countries — none of which borrows from the MDBs, of course — control about forty-three percent of the votes in the World Bank and about forty-one percent of the votes in the AsDB, and the voting power exceeds fifty percent if (as often happens) the G-7 countries are joined by a few other European countries in decision-making. This is one reason why the lack of symmetry in the making and enforcing of MDB policies (see Criticism #8) is regarded as so venal: a handful of mainly Western countries can effectively impose economic and financial policies on most of the world's other countries, without having to hew to those policies themselves.

Third, another constitutional peculiarity of the MDBs contributes further to their unaccountability: the MDBs are not subject to any outside judicial review. In particular, the MDB charters vest in the MDBs themselves the sole authority to determine whether they are acting in compliance with their own charters. Naturally, any such determination is itself made via the weighted voting system. Although steps have been taken recently by some MDBs to establish "inspection panels" to assess whether the institution has followed its own rules, these steps (so the criticism runs) have been inadequate to overcome this structural deficiency.

Fourth, as if the structural deficiencies were not enough, the MDBs exhibit yet another form or cause of unaccountability: many of their member states' governments, particularly in the poorer countries, are themselves undemocratic in character....

III. Assessing the Criticisms — Which Are Valid and Which Are Not?

A. Criticisms I Largely Dismiss ...

5. Criticism #7 — Disregard for citizens' groups and NGOs

I doubt there are many NGOs that have made a reasonable effort to convey their opinions to MDBs in the past five years and found it difficult to do so. Some of the MDBs have established liaison offices within their headquarters for the express purpose of welcoming and discussing NGOs' opinions and involvement in the MDBs' work.

The AsDB reports that nearly two-thirds of the public-sector projects approved for AsDB financing in 2000 involved NGOs in some significant way — as, for example, by relying on microfinance NGOs to assist flood victims in Bangladesh and by working with NGOs to develop low-cost solutions to sanitation problems in Papua New Guinea. Regular forums, workshops, and other meetings are conducted by MDBs with NGOs, and officials of NGOs regularly work in the MDBs under secondment arrangements. In these and other ways, much has been done to involve NGOs and "civil society" in MDB work. Protestors marching outside the World Bank headquarters during a joint annual meeting of the World Bank and the IMF are unlikely to get invited to lunch that day with a World Bank official, but under less confrontational circumstances such meetings can occur. In short, I am not persuaded by complaints that the views and representatives of NGOs are systematically disregarded or excluded now by the MDBs.

However, it is important to recognize the relation between Criticism #7 — disregard for citizens' groups and NGOs — and Criticism #14 — unaccountability and the democracy deficit. As explained below, I endorse the latter of these criticisms and suggest that several steps be taken to respond to it. One of those steps would aim to provide still easier and more direct mechanisms for input by all persons or groups interested in the MDBs' operations....

B. Criticisms I Generally Endorse

1. Criticism #2 — Environmental degradation

Some of this criticism is out of date. For example, those critics who complain about MDB involvement in big hydroelectric dams apparently do not realize that the MDBs are now largely out of the dam-building business. Those critics who claim that the MDBs regularly disregard effects of the projects they design either are engaging in intentional misinformation or are ignorant of the enormous change that has taken place over the past two decades in the mindset, the policies, and the structures of the MDBs to incorporate environmental considerations into the operations of those institutions. The World Bank recruited its first environmental advisor in 1969. By 1990, it had a total of fifty-four high-level staff members, assisted by over twenty consultants, working in its Environment Department and regional Environmental Divisions, and it had adopted an Operational Directive on Environmental Assessment in order "to ensure that development options are environmentally sound and sustainable and that any environmental consequences are recognized early in the project cycle and taken into account in project design." As of 1998 it had over five times that many environmental specialists (over three hundred) and had committed close to twelve billion dollars for scores of primarily environmental projects. Today, the World Bank's commitment to environmental matters is reflected in the fact that it has a vice presidency for Environmentally Sustainable Development, has implemented numerous operational policies on environmental and related issues, and has taken a lead role in creating new funding mechanisms to support sustainable development. Similar steps have been taken at the AsDB and at the IADB and the AfDB. In the case of the EBRD, as noted above, a specific mandate was included in the charter, requiring that institution "to promote in the full range of its activities environmentally sound and sustainable development." As a consequence of these changes, the MDBs all have procedures for conducting environmental impact assessment on any proposed projects that could have any significant effect in this regard, and most of the reports of these assessments are publicly available.

However, more should be done. A study undertaken for the AsDB about four years ago concluded that although that institution did a relatively good job of incorporating environmental considerations into its design and selection of projects for AsDB financing, these efforts often did not get carried through adequately to the project implementation stage. That is, the best laid plans for avoiding or mitigating environmental damage often went awry in the process of actually building a road or carrying out some other project work. This should be remedied.

More fundamentally, however, I believe that environmental considerations should be placed at the heart of MDB operations as a legal and policy matter. The year 2002 marked the 30th anniversary of the Stockholm Conference on the Human Environment. Just as in 1972, the world remains divided on some key issues of environmental protection, although now the fault lines appear more over the issue of who should pay for environmental protection than over the question of whether a national government has an obligation to protect its environment....

2. Criticism #3 — Human rights shortcomings ...

Although it is absurd to suggest that the MDBs give no regard to human rights in their operations — they do, after all, require various types of assessments during project design and selection (i) to guard against any interference with the rights of indigenous people, (ii) to enhance the role of women, and (iii) to assess the impact of proposed projects on the social fabric of the communities that the project would directly affect — the MDBs could and should take further steps in this regard. A linkage between the MDB charters and the key human rights treaties is one such step....

Why should the MDBs take on additional responsibility in the area of human rights, as well as in the area of environmental protection? Because (i) these are responsibilities that need to be taken on by some institution or other, and (ii) the MDBs have the resources and the leverage to do so effectively. I assume that the first of these points is fairly well accepted; an international consensus seems to have developed that effective action is needed at the international level to protect human rights and the environment. As for the second of these points, I believe that the prime movers in defining the terms under which economic development (broadly defined) will take place — and indeed in defining a wide range of standards by which national governments will provide services and leadership to their populations — in the coming years are the global economic institutions: the WTO, the IMF, the World Bank, and the regional development banks. Unlike the global and regional regimes established to focus exclusively on human rights protection or on environmental protection, these global economic institutions have the kind of influence that seems to matter most in today's world: economic influence. This being the case, I believe the response to Criticisms #2 and #3 — environmental degradation and human rights shortcomings — should not be (i) to shut down the MDBs so that they cannot cause any more injury to the environment or to human rights, or (ii) to restrict the mission of the MDBs in a way that excludes environmental and human rights considerations, leaving such considerations to other institutions, but instead (iii) to create formal and legal linkages between the MDBs and broadly accepted treaty norms on environmental protections and human rights and the entities specifically responsible for working in those areas....

3. Criticism #5—Lack of transparency and access

As with Criticisms #2 and #3, Criticism #5 (at least as I have summarized it in Part II, above) contains some chaff along with the wheat. For example, those who complain that the MDBs operate entirely behind a veil of secrecy are simply wrong. In the past few years, these institutions have adopted and implemented document disclosure policies that make vastly more information available about the MDBs now than even a decade ago. For example, detailed reports issued by the AsDB president to the AsDB Board of Directors regarding loan proposals—enumerating the specific conditionalities accepted by a borrower—would have been almost impossible to obtain a few years ago without inside access to the AsDB. Now they can be ordered from the AsDB's website.

However, more should be done to facilitate public understanding of how the MDBs operate, what they have done, and what they plan to do. In this respect, the same types of "open meetings" principles adopted in many countries for the conduct of public business should be adopted within the MDBs. Records of meetings of the MDBs' governing boards should, as a general rule, be made publicly available, with exceptions and safeguards as necessary to guard against disclosure of information that is legitimately confidential.

7. Criticism #14—Unaccountability and democracy deficit

In my view, this is one of the most important and persuasive criticisms. As I described it above in Part II of this Article, this criticism has several elements: (i) the MDBs provide little accommodation for citizen involvement in MDB decision-making; (ii) the weighted voting system places control of the MDBs in the hands of a very few countries, leaving most people in borrowing member countries with virtually no influence over the actions taken by the MDBs' governing boards; (iii) the operations of MDBs are not subject to any outside judicial review; and (iv) the member states' governments themselves are in many cases undemocratic in character.

Questions and Discussion

1. *Making environment a priority.* The Article states that "environmental considerations should be placed at the heart of MDB operations as a legal and policy matter." Given the context in which MDBs were founded, as well as their historical goals of traditional development, do you believe MDBs can make environmental concerns a priority through self-governance? If not, what governmental mechanisms could be used for this task? Is there an effective way for developed countries to ensure their investment dollars are not used by MDB's to harm human rights and environmental resources abroad?

2. *MDBs as policy makers.* As the scope and lending goals of MDBs have broadened, their role as global policy makers has become undeniable. From a human rights perspective, is this positive thing? In what way are MDB board members held accountable? To what extent are they democratically elected? Concerning Bank policy, is the current weighted voting system, based on contributions, favorable to a one country one vote system?

3. *MDBs and treaty enforcement.* One of the greatest challenges in addressing human rights and environmental concerns in an international context is the dearth of enforce-

able law. The typical treaty ratification process in the United States, for example, involves a series of carefully selected reservations, understandings, and declarations drafted by lawyers to ensure that the treaty will effect virtually no change on domestic law. Do you agree, as the article suggests, that MDBs are a logical and effective means of enforcing these treaty norms? What problems can you foresee with such a system?

C. Information and Participation Rights in MDB Projects

Democratizing Multilateral Development Banks

Nathalie Bernasconi-Osterwalder & David Hunter

THE NEW "PUBLIC": THE GLOBALIZATION OF PUBLIC PARTICIPATION
(C. Bruch, ed., 2002)

Traditionally, only nation-states have had the right to participate in the creation and implementation of international law. This model led to non-transparent international negotiations and institutions managed behind closed doors. However, in the past decades, civil society and some governments have begun to demand more transparency and [wider] participation in international affairs. As a consequence, a number of intergovernmental organizations—including various bodies of the United Nations (U.N.), international financial institutions, and trade regimes—have gradually moved toward more open and participatory governance....

I. Rio Declaration Principle 10: Acknowledging the Importance of Public Involvement ...

International institutions, however, have made little room for direct citizen involvement and, thus, their decisions increasingly lack legitimacy. Reflecting these concerns, Agenda 21, a detailed action plan for realizing the Rio Declaration's goals, provides that the "United Nations system, *including international finance and development agencies,* and all intergovernmental organizations and forums," should enhance or establish procedures to draw upon the expertise and views of civil society and to provide access to information.

II. Public Access to Information and Participation in the Decisionmaking Processes of Multilateral Development Banks ...

A. Access to Information

In the past decade, the public's access to information in MDBs has improved significantly, in large part due to strong external pressure....

Each of the MDBs has adopted formal, written policies setting out clear standards for the release of information, particularly information relating to project design and preparation....

While all policies set out a presumption in favor of disclosure, in practice there is no such presumption. In part this is because the disclosure policies all identify lists of specific documents that are to be disclosed. As a result, MDB staff tend to presume that documents not on the list may not [be] meant [to] be disclosed. The presumption in favor of disclosure also runs counter to a deep-seated culture of secrecy at the Bank, in which staff are used to designing their projects in consultation with only a relatively small group of members of the borrowing country's finance ministry.

1. Availability of Documents

The disclosure policies specify which categories of information are, and which are not, available to the general public or to interested individuals and groups. The types of information that are listed as available to the public are subject to explicit confidentiality and sensitivity exceptions. Private sector financing, such as by the IFC, for example, is generally (but not always) subject to more restrictive information disclosure than public sector lending.... To varying degrees amongst the different MDBs, the availability of documents—under pressure of civil society—is gradually increasing. However, among the wide range of documents now available from certain MDBs, most are released only after the project commitments have been made, that is, generally after approval of the Boards of Directors. This calls into question the timeliness of the access to information. All of the disclosure policies examined here, including the World Bank's most recent policy, generally provides access to final documents, rather than documents in draft form. This denies the public access to information in time for meaningful participation in bank decisions, including project design and policymaking.

For transparency to be effective, denials of access to information should only be possible on the basis of a list of clearly defined exceptions. All of the MDBs' policies examined here include a list of well-defined types of information that are not publicly available. However, in addition to the list of exceptions to disclosure, the policies also set out less clearly defined derogations.... Because these grounds are not well defined, they are subject to the discretion of the relevant MDB staff. If broadly defined exceptions ... are not interpreted very narrowly, they could render the disclosure requirements useless.

Perhaps most disturbingly, the IFC excludes from disclosure all confidential business information, which is defined to be any information provided by the business and labeled confidential. Incredibly, businesses are able to exempt any information from disclosure by citing confidentiality reasons without any independent assessment whether the information should in fact be classified as confidential. This exemption has been used to keep critical information about the IFC's operations out of the public's hands....

2. Board Meetings

The meetings of the Boards of Directors of the MDBs examined here are closed to the public and to journalists. Moreover, neither transcripts of these meetings nor minutes are disclosed....

3. Effectiveness of Access to Information

Under the disclosure policies examined here, access to information is available to any individual, public interest organization, or business group, with no necessary demonstration of interest in the information and regardless of nationality or the reasons for the request. However, the policies lack the precision of procedures and timeframes for responding to requests for information.

In addition, none of the policies require that refusals to provide information be in writing nor that they state the reasons for the refusal. In addition, insufficient attention has been paid by MDBs to the importance of the language in which documents are available....

B. Participation and Consultation

In the past fifteen years, MDBs have begun to acknowledge the importance of engaging civil society in the development process and in policy dialogues as an essential precondition for effective poverty alleviation and sustainable development. The recognition that local participation enhances development effectiveness is reflected in a host of the MDBs' internal documents, ranging from internal policies and guidelines to resource books and handbooks. However, none of the MDBs have adopted an overarching mandatory policy on participation. Public consultation is only assured in those projects that are covered by standards in other policies—i.e., in projects that significantly affect the environment, involuntarily resettle people, or affect the interests of indigenous peoples. Thus, consultation practices have generally developed ad hoc, designed at the discretion of the staff in response to the specific demands being made by outside critics. As a consequence, public participation processes have been inconsistent and their success has varied accordingly....

2. Environmental Assessment and Consultation

While MDBs lack general mandatory standards or processes of consultation, they do have several specific operational policies and guidelines that include provisions requiring stakeholder participation in the design and implementation of development policies and plans. Such operational policies or guidelines include, among others, environmental assessment policies, indigenous peoples policies, and resettlement policies.

Environmental Assessment policies provide the most detailed framework for public consultation. MDBs usually distinguish between at least three types of projects based on the scale of impact on the environment. Each category is subjected to different requirements. The category of projects likely to have the most severe environmental impact (usually referred to as "Category A" or "Category 1" projects) requires full environmental impact assessments. For these projects, the consultation processes for the preparation of environmental impact assessments are outlined in a reasonably detailed manner across the various MDB environmental policies and guidelines. However, the language used tends to be discretionary in many instances....

Additionally, some environmental policies and procedures do not appear to give sufficient guidance with respect to the process of consultation. For example, the [Inter-American Development Bank's] procedures provide only that "[t]he Bank *expects* borrowers to consult affected communities and other local parties" and that the Bank "requires that borrowers: (i) employ *reasonable* consultation procedures to elicit the informed opinion of concerned local groups, and take their views into account during project preparation and implementation, especially during the scoping and draft phases of an impact assessment."

The second category of projects (usually referred to as Category B), which comprises projects likely to have detrimental environmental impacts that can be minimized, do not require a full impact assessment. None of the MDB documents require public consultation regarding these projects.

Analysis of the various environmental policies and guidelines indicate that many MDBs do not provide sufficient minimum substantive standards for effective public consultation....

Another issue is the timing of the release of information. For Category A projects, the environmental impact assessment is generally released 120 days before Board consideration for public sector projects and 60 days before Board consideration for private sector projects. For Category B projects, the document is generally released 60 days before Board consideration for public sector projects and only 30 days for private sector projects. Thus, in some cases, the public has only 30 days to review the assessment and prepare comments. Consultation requirements for private sector projects have become almost worthless.

3. Internal MDB Policies and Procedures

In the past five years, the IFC and the World Bank have regularly consulted the public during the adoption or revision of policies. It is now routine that draft policies or strategies are released on an MDB's website with a specific amount of time provided for public comment. This form of "notice and comment" rulemaking is frequently complemented by public meetings held either in the Bank's headquarters or, in some cases, in regional offices. Although the timelines and processes for these consultations are ad hoc and, thus, not subject to any set standards, there is, nonetheless, developing a consistent practice of open and participatory rulemaking.

The primary shortcomings of current approaches are that deadlines for submitting comments are often too short and that MDB staff almost never provide meaningful responses to the comments....

Questions and Discussion

1. *Private or public model?* Normally access to information and public participation are associated with governmental, not private, activities. Neither a commercial bank nor a private corporation would normally open its documents to the public or ask for public comment before making investment or management decisions. When a multilateral development bank is involved in providing funding or guaranteeing private investments should access to information and public participation follow the model of governments or the model of private enterprises?

2. *Right to request information.* Who should have the right to request documents from, or participate in the decisions of, an MDB—the persons who are directly affected by a project, any citizen in the country where the project is taking place, expert nongovernmental organizations from abroad, or any person in the world?

3. *Draft documents.* Unlike the World Bank's access to information policy, the U.S. Freedom of Information Act does not limit citizens' access to "final documents," but refers only to "agency records." 5 U.S.C. § 552(a)(3)(A). As a result, even facts in draft form may require disclosure. What policy considerations favor or disfavor allowing the public to access incomplete reports?

4. *Applicability of national laws.* To what extent should a MDB be subject to the information laws of a country in which it operates? Where a particular government appoints board members and provides substantial funding to an MDB, has the bank essentially become a government agency? As defined in the U.S. Freedom of Information Act all agencies are subject to relatively liberal disclosure requirements. The definition of agency includes "the executive department, military department, Government corporation[s], Government controlled corporation[s] or other establishment[s] in the executive branch of the Government ... or any independent regulatory agency." 5 U.S.C. § 552(f)(1). Is the World Bank a U.S. agency under this definition? Consider the definition of agency in 5 U.S.C. § 551, which includes "each authority of the government of the United States." Would U.S. representatives to the World Bank be subject to the F.O.I.A. under this definition of agency? Given that the U.S. has provided approximately one-third of the World Bank's funding and has appointed all eleven World Bank presidents, should it be?

II. The World Bank Inspection Panel

A. Overview

Democratizing Multilateral Development Banks
Nathalie Bernasconi-Osterwalder & David Hunter
THE NEW "PUBLIC": THE GLOBALIZATION OF PUBLIC PARTICIPATION
(C. Bruch, ed., 2002)

C. Access to Justice and the Accountability Mechanisms

After the environmental and social policy frameworks were adopted at the various development banks, concerns began to arise regarding whether and how these policies would be enforced. The MDBs enjoy immunity under international law and are not subject to the jurisdiction of national courts. Additionally, there was no mechanism in international law where citizens could press their concerns relating to the activities of MDBs. In this respect, the MDBs were "lawless" institutions with no accountability either to affected communities or to the member countries that had established the environmental and social policies. At the same time, a number of controversial cases (most notably the Narmada dam in India) highlighted major policy violations and led civil society to call for international fact-finders into the impacts of MDB-financed projects.

The World Bank was the first international organization of any kind to provide a mechanism for citizens to bring claims regarding policy violations without going through their respective national governments. The World Bank's Inspection Panel was created in 1993. It covered projects financed by the IBRD and the IDA and was followed in subsequent years by accountability mechanisms at several other MDBs.

1. World Bank Inspection Panel

The World Bank Inspection Panel was created ... "for the purpose of providing people directly and adversely affected by a Bank-financed project with an independent forum through which they can request the Bank to act in accordance with its own policies and procedures...."

The World Bank's Inspection Panel is comprised of three permanent members, each of whom serves for five years. Panel members are nominated by the President and approved by the Board. To ensure the independence of the Panel, Panel members cannot have served the Bank in any capacity for the two years preceding their selection to the Panel. More importantly, Panel members are forbidden from ever working at the Bank again. The Panel also has a permanent Secretariat with five staff.

The Panel receives and investigates claims from project-affected people alleging that they have been harmed by the Bank's violations of its policies and procedures. Any affected group of more than one person residing in the borrower's territory can file a claim to the Inspection Panel. Claims must be in writing but can be in any language.... A majority of the requests have cited violations of the World Bank's environmental assessment, indigenous peoples, and involuntary resettlement policies. Also frequently cited are the World Bank's policies on information disclosure and project supervision. A number of claims have involved the failure to screen the projects correctly under the environmental assessment or indigenous peoples policy (which then has implications for consultation requirements), as well as the failure to extend the rights of consultation to all of the project-affected people who should be consulted according to the norms within the policy....

Some general conclusions can be drawn from the Panel's history thus far. The Panel is widely respected as credible and independent by civil society organizations around the world. The Panel has also clearly strengthened the Board's ability to review staff compliance with World Bank policies, and placed a greater emphasis on consistency in applying the safeguard policies internally. On the other hand, the Panel's lack of authority to provide recommendations for resolving the problems of affected people and to monitor the implementation of remedial actions adopted in light of Panel claims has meant that Panel decisions have not necessarily benefited project affected people on the ground. The Panel's mandate to "inspect" the performance of the Bank has also created strong dissent among staff and some developing country members, creating a polarized atmosphere around Inspection Panel claims. The Panel is also marginalized within the World Bank, with its findings and policy interpretations largely ignored by staff as soon as a specific case is over.

Questions and Discussion

1. *Independence.* Does it appear that the Inspection Panel needs more independence from the World Bank or less? The Inspection Panel has various links to the Bank. The Panel's offices are in the Bank's Headquarters. Panel members are assisted by the secretariat selected by the Panel itself with the exception of the Executive Secretary, who is chosen by the President of the World Bank. The Panel's budget is distinct from that of the Bank's but the Bank nevertheless provides the resources. The article mentions a "polarized atmosphere" on the staff regarding Inspection Panel claims and says the Panel's "findings and policy interpretations [are] largely ignored by staff as soon as a specific case is over." How would you design a structure that made it more likely that the Panel would influence the Bank's culture and future decisions, rather than just criticizing them without long-lasting impact?

2. *Judicial or supervisory?* What is the legal status of the Inspection Panel? Is it a judicial body or a supervisory control body? Mariarita Circi has the following comments:

> There are two elements in favor of the first classification. Firstly, the intervention of the Panel is invited by private parties who hold an interest or a right which is deemed to have been damaged by the action of an international organization, in violation of its own legal rules and procedures. The Panel, therefore, has the task of assessing the causal nexus between the injury and the violation of the legal rules with which the Bank should have complied.

> On the other hand, the Panel is not a third body with respect to the parties involved, since it is an emanation of one of them, and before this forum a hearing procedure takes place, which has not yet evolved into a full-fledged trial.

> Furthermore, the Panel's mandate is not one of granting protection to damaged private interest but only to assess the damage in a report to be sent to the Board of the Bank: the decision of the Panel is not a judgment that can be subject to appeal, but it is simply a recommendation for the Board which can choose to act or not act as it deems fit.

> Besides, the role of the Panel was made clear in the 1999 review of the Establishing Resolution which explained that its members, during the inspection, must remain as faithful as possible to the role of the body to which they belong, being that of "a fact-finding body on behalf of the Board." The Panel would then be a supervisory body, auxiliary to the Board.

Mariarita Circi, *The World Bank Inspection Panel: Is It Really Effective?* 6 Global Jurist Advance 9 (2006).

3. *Accessibility* . Is the Inspection Panel really accessible? One hurdle for parties requesting an Inspection Panel investigation is approval of the World Bank's Board of Executive directors. Statistics demonstrate the level of accessibility of the Inspection Panel's services over the first 11 years of its existence.

> ... [F]rom September 1993 to December 2005 thirty-seven requests were presented for thirty-one projects.... Of the total thirty-seven requests..., five—two in the first five years and three in the second six—were [not deemed to be admissible] because not deemed actionable or coherent with the Panel's mandate.
>
> ... [T]he Panel asked for inspection for eighteen of which the Board approved fourteen. Therefore, the Board approved inspection in about 43% of the cases recorded, while the Panel had requested authorization for inspection in about 56% of the cases.

Mariarita Circi, *The World Bank Inspection Panel: Is It Really Effective?* 6 Global Jurist Advance 9 (2006).

4. *Effect of recommendations.* Are the Inspection Panel's recommendations mandatory? Do its recommendations make a difference in reality? Does the Panel provide effective redress and remedy? Does it have oversight authority over the implementation of remedial measures? Consider these questions in the next section.

B. Recourse and Remedies

The World Bank and Human Rights:
The Need for Greater Accountability
Dana L. Clark
15 Harv. Hum. Rts. J. 205 (2002)

After decades of lending that promoted a paradigm of economic growth but paid scant attention to the environmental and social costs of Bank projects, the public has insisted that public funds not be used for projects that harm the environment or externalize development costs to the poorest members of society. In response to pressure from civil society and donor governments, the World Bank has adopted a set of binding policies governing a broad array of its activities, including mitigation of the social and environmental impacts of Bank lending.

The development of the social and environmental policy framework at the World Bank was an important step in moving the institution toward a rights-based approach to development, greater accountability, and the goal of sustainable development. On paper, the Bank's policies are considered to be among the most comprehensive in the world. The policies require Bank staff and borrowers to consult with and provide information to local communities; carefully assess and minimize the risks (economic, social, and environmental) associated with projects; avoid displacement of people and ensure that displaced persons improve or at least restore their standard of living; and respect the rights and vulnerabilities of indigenous peoples....

While the shift in the discourse at the Bank has been significant, there is a gap between the rhetoric and the implementation of the policy framework. The unfortunate reality is that these "safeguard" policies are often violated, and people whose rights are harmed have only limited access to recourse and remedy....

V. The Inspection Panel: Recourse but Often No Redress ...

The Inspection Panel process allows two or more local people to request an independent investigation into the Bank's role in a project. To be eligible for review, the claim must focus on the actions or omissions of the Bank (not the borrower) and allege that those actions have caused — or are threatening to cause — material harm in violation of the Bank's policies and procedures. The jurisdiction of the Panel is defined by the Bank's policy framework: the Panel evaluates the extent to which a project is in compliance with Bank policies, and the harm, if any, suffered by the claimants as a result of policy violations. The Panel is intended to be a forum of last resort, and local people must first exhaust other remedies by raising their concerns with the Bank prior to filing a claim. Management is given an opportunity to respond in writing to allegations made in the claim, and the Panel evaluates the merits of both submissions.

Once it has conducted an investigation — which may include field visits, interviews with Bank staff, and review of relevant files — the Panel prepares a report and recommendations for the Bank's Board of Executive Directors, detailing its findings. Management then has six weeks to develop a response plan, outlining its own recommendations for bringing the project into compliance with Bank policies. According to both the Board Resolution and Panel Procedures, the Board is then required to review the Panel report and Management's response plan (often called "action plans"), and determine what remedial steps, if any, the Bank must take to rectify the problems identified by the Panel.

Herein lies the weak link in the process: the Inspection Panel does not have oversight authority over the implementation of those remedial measures; nor is it able to provide the Board with an assessment of whether Management's proposed remedial measures would satisfy the concerns of the claimants and/or bring the project into compliance with Bank policy. The lack of independent oversight has meant that remedial action plans do not always lead to satisfactory remedies or action....

While denying oversight authority to the Panel, the Board failed to create an alternative mechanism for determining the success of Management's action plans in bringing projects into compliance with Bank policies.

Although each claim to the Panel has its own fact scenario, the Board generally requests that Management submit periodic progress reports on the action plans. However, the Board is overwhelmed with information and quickly loses focus on past cases. It does not have a standing committee to track the implementation of action plans or to evaluate the effectiveness of remedial measures in Inspection Panel cases. Attention to action plans is therefore minimal. There is rarely any critical discussion of Management's progress reports, and the Board largely accepts Management's word on the status of a project without independently verifying the facts on the ground or surveying the opinions of claimants. Accordingly, there is little threat of Board interference with Management's course of action. As a result, there are many "lost cases" — cases where the Inspection Panel finds violations of Bank policies resulting in harm to claimants, but where no effective remedy is provided.

The lack of a system of redress is the key weakness in the Inspection Panel process and in the institutional architecture of the Bank. Achieving real change on the ground in particular projects has proven to be quite difficult.

VII. The Need for Effective Remedies ...

The World Bank's lack of capacity and commitment could be addressed through the creation of a problem-solving unit that is responsible for remedying the social and environmental policy violations identified by the Inspection Panel and helping to ensure that displaced and aggrieved communities are adequately compensated and assisted to improve their standards of living. This problem-solving unit could be known as the "Development Effectiveness Remedy Team" (DERT). The DERT would be tasked with solving problems, promoting compliance, and providing technical and financial assistance to borrowers and Bank staff to help accomplish the social and environmental policy objectives.

In order to be effective and credible, certain steps would have to be taken to ensure the independence of the DERT from Bank Management. For instance, the DERT would report directly to the Board of Executive Directors. The DERT would operate in a transparent manner, with its findings and reports made available to the public, including periodic progress reports on projects under review. To ensure that the DERT itself has the capacity to effectively handle multi-faceted issues and communicate with affected communities, there must be community representatives on the DERT, including those who have directly experienced development-induced displacement. In addition, there must be established mechanisms for dialogue between affected communities and the DERT, so that local people can present and document their grievances and suggest remedial measures.

The DERT would have an explicit mandate to work with the Inspection Panel and the Board of Executive Directors in providing oversight and technical assistance to efforts to bring into compliance projects that have been the subject of Inspection Panel investigations. It would supervise the implementation of Management's action plans in Inspection Panel cases, working and consulting with the claimants and the affected community. In addition, the DERT's mandate should include addressing the legacy of failed World Bank-financed resettlement projects and, in consultation with the affected communities, structuring remedial measures to meet their development priorities and bring the projects into compliance with Bank policy.

Questions and Discussion

1. *Procedures.* What are the eligibility requirements? Is it necessary to exhaust domestic remedies before complaining to the Inspection Panel? What is the procedure for handling an inspection request? Does the procedure provide for public participation? At what stage? Are only affected persons allowed to participate, or could any member of the public or NGO do so?

2. *Self-regulation.* The article focuses on enforcement of inspection panel recommendations by creation of "Development Effectiveness Remedy Teams" (DERTs) internal auditing groups within the MDB's. Is self-regulation of MDBs a realistic expectation? Given that MDBs are essentially conglomerations of multiple sovereign governments working together, are the layers of bureaucracy in creating DERTs justifiable? Could World Bank member governments collaborate on compliance with recommendations on individual projects more efficiently?

C. The Chad-Cameroon Pipeline

Although the Chad-Cameroon Pipeline has now been built and is in operation, bringing oil from several oil fields in the African nation of Chad overland through Europe for shipment to the world's economies, the involvement of the World Bank and the complaints brought before its Inspection Panel present a case worth studying.

Rhetoric and Reality: Human Rights and the World Bank

Korinna Horta

15 Harv. Hum. Rts. J. 227 (2002)

II. Support for Authoritarian Regimes ...

The World Bank [has had] direct involvement in the largest project currently being built on the African continent, the Chad-Cameroon Oil and Pipeline project. The $3.7 billion project—whose principal shareholder, ExxonMobil, is the world's wealthiest corporation—would not have gotten off the ground without World Bank co-financing. The oil companies insisted on Bank participation for two reasons: it provides political risk insurance in a volatile region and it attracts additional financing from other sources such as the European Investment Bank and a host of commercial banks.

The Doba oil fields that the project seeks to exploit are located in the southern part of Chad, which has been in armed conflict with the northern part of the country for over thirty years. Chad's government is run by clans from the northern region, and many southerners feel voiceless and persecuted. According to Amnesty International, the Chadian Government killed hundreds of unarmed civilians in the oil-producing region in the late 1990s at a time when intense project preparations were under way. The U.S. State Department lists both Chad and Cameroon as major abusers of human rights and countries where citizens do not have the power to change their government via the electoral process.

The Chad-Cameroon Oil and Pipeline project provides a stark example of the increasing marginalization of poor rural communities and indigenous peoples. Despite promises of development, local villagers in Chad's oil producing region have had their land and common property resources expropriated without adequate compensation. For example, the oil consortium has taken over fallow fields that are an integral part of local agriculture because they were considered to be empty and un-owned land. There was no proper evaluation of the value of the fruit trees, leaves, and roots that are critical to the survival of local households in order to assess adequate compensation. In cases where one-time compensation payments were made, they were inadequate and left the villagers with the erroneous belief that they would receive these payments on a regular basis. In addition, local organizations warn of an impending water emergency for local communities as oil drilling activities require large amounts of water; some village wells have already begun to dry out....

On the Cameroonian side of the project, the pipeline traverses the Atlantic rainforest, posing serious risks to the indigenous Bakola Pygmy people. Contrary to the World Bank's existing Policy on Indigenous Peoples, the project includes no mechanism for the assessment of the legal recognition of indigenous Peoples' Rights to land and forests. With the construction of the pipeline, the lack of land security will make it difficult to contain land invasions and the pressures on local resources on which the survival of the semi-nomadic Bakola people depends.

Overall, the project might amount to a net loss for the impoverished people of Cameroon. The floating storage and off-loading facility from where the oil will flow onto tankers is to consist of a single-hulled vessel. The dangers of oil spills and leaks will be ever present, and sooner or later are likely to disrupt the delicate marine environment where the pipeline enters the ocean. This is a biologically diverse area where artisanal fisheries provide protein for large numbers of people. A study funded by the World Wildlife Fund calculated that the value of the renewable resources of the coastline directly affected by the pipeline would be about $104 per capita per year in perpetuity, compared with the stated benefits of the pipeline of about $4 per capita per year over the thirty-year operation of the pipeline.

In view of the political repression in Chad, local civil society organizations requested that there be a moratorium on World Bank funding of the project until adequate legal frameworks and other conditions were instituted that would ensure that the oil revenues would benefit the overall Chadian population and that the environment would not be permanently damaged. The request for a moratorium was supported by a broad coalition of NGOs from developed countries, and several of the World Bank's donor governments started raising questions about the serious risks posed by the project. In response to these concerns, the Bank set up what it claimed to be a transparent consultation process with locally affected people, and stated that the consultations had led to a wholehearted endorsement of the project. The Bank failed to mention that the oil company staff sent out to conduct these consultations were accompanied by armed military guards whose services were responsible for the recent massacres in the region....

A rights-based approach by the World Bank would have prevented the institution from descending into the quagmire that the Chad-Cameroon project presents. Such an approach would have called for careful consideration of the courageous voices of civil society organizations in both countries, and may have required the Bank to limit its role to helping create the legal framework necessary for democratic change before helping to launch a multi-billion dollar project that engenders further human repression and marginalization.

III. Marginalizing the Poor and Favoring the Rich ...

A rights-based approach to development would go a long way toward overcoming some of these shortcomings. Perhaps recognizing this, some of the European multilateral and bilateral aid agencies have taken steps in recent years to include democratization and human rights criteria in their decisions on aid flows. Yet these steps may be of limited value as long as the institution at the head of the current development juggernaut fails to incorporate a right-based dimension into its decision-making.

To Lend or Not to Lend: Oil, Human Rights, and the World Bank's Internal Contradictions

Genoveva Hernández Uriz
14 Harv. Hum. Rts. J. 197

The Chad-Cameroon project reflects an unprecedented collaborative effort between the Bank Group, the consortium of private companies and the two governments. While some may still have doubts, I believe that the hard work of specialists from the Bank Group, the private companies and the two countries, combined with the strong participation of civil society within Chad and Cameroon and around the world, have made this a better, stronger project.... —James D. Wolfensohn, President of the World Bank Group

I. INTRODUCTION

Oil exploitation and human rights have traditionally had an uneasy relationship. Human rights organizations and journalists have denounced oil companies for complicity in human rights violations throughout Africa, and this negative publicity has prompted some companies to look for ways to improve their image and ensure that their investments comply with minimum human rights standards. In this context, the World Bank has agreed to participate as a lender and moral guarantor in the Chad/Cameroon project, an oil drilling and pipeline construction project undertaken by an international consortium of Exxon, Petronas, and Chevron.

Why is the Chad/Cameroon project considered a turning point in the Bank's relationship to human rights and to private sector-led development? This project is not the first pipeline investment the Bank has helped to finance. In this case, however, private investors, under growing media, consumer, and NGO pressure, have declared themselves ready to abide by a certain set of standards. The involvement of an international financial institution reduces the companies' political risks and facilitates their access to credit. Exxon announced publicly that it would not move forward without World Bank participation. From the Bank's point of view, the pipeline achieves its goal of attracting private capital for large-scale energy projects.

In the Chad/Cameroon context, the Bank will be a lender, development promoter, and risk mitigator. Although the Bank's financial participation in the investment only amounts to six percent of the project's total cost, the Bank's involvement may set a benchmark for future corporate behavior. Due to the commitment of World Bank funds, the investment must comply with the Bank's policies concerning compensation, resettlement, indigenous peoples, and the environment. If the policies are genuinely respected, the project could mark an important beginning for the establishment of human rights standards for multinational corporations....

The safeguards prescribed by the Bank for the pipeline reflect the strides the Bank has taken in its commitment to responsible investment in the Chad/Cameroon context. The safeguards adopted to ensure state accountability are distinctive because they establish a high degree of transparency vis-á-vis the international community. Under pressure from the World Bank, the government of Chad has adopted revenue management measures, described by the Bank as the first of their kind.

Yet, the Bank only took steps to address human rights concerns after a massive civil society campaign against the pipeline project. A diverse coalition of local and international environmental organizations, human rights NGOs, churches, universities, and public celebrities steadily denounced the appalling human rights conditions in Chad and forced the Bank to respond. Well-known figures such as Archbishop Desmond Tutu and Ethel Kennedy endorsed the campaign, and the controversy even reached the U.S. Congress and the European Parliament. Project opponents argued that taxpayers' money would be used to finance a new Ogoniland, the internationally known oil development disaster in Nigeria. Critics unsuccessfully advocated a moratorium to allow Chad to address environmental, good governance, and human rights concerns.

The Chad/Cameroon project forced the Bank to consider human rights questions, despite previous refusal on the grounds that such issues were outside its mandate....

II. HUMAN RIGHTS AND THE WORLD BANK'S MANDATE ...

D. The Influence of International Pressure on Bank Policies

Although internal formulations of Bank policies have only cautiously taken into account borrowing countries' domestic political situations, donors and NGOs have pressured the Bank to change its lending policies with respect to major human rights violators. While the Bank's best clients have included some repressive regimes, international outrage in the wake of massive human rights abuses has prompted the Bank to freeze its loans in certain cases....

Following the Tienanmen Square massacre in Beijing, China, the World Bank and the Asian Development Bank decided to freeze several loans and to suspend consideration of new loans to China....

External pressure has also influenced the World Bank's lending policies in Africa. In Nigeria, for example, the Bank changed its lending policies in the wake of grave human rights abuses. Shortly after the execution of Ken Saro-Wiwa and eight other Ogoni activists in Nigeria in 1995, the International Financial Corporation, the private lending arm of the World Bank, which is also bound by the political prohibition, decided to cancel a $3 billion liquefied natural gas project that Saro-Wiwa had opposed.

In September 1999, the Bank froze an annual $1 billion program loan to Indonesia on the grounds of corruption....

International advocacy campaigns have also led the Bank to reexamine its project-related human rights policies. For example, the Sardar Sarovar Dam campaign targeted a 1985 Bank loan of $450 million for a complex multi-dam project in India. A coalition of local and Western associations challenged the goals and objectives of the project and lobbied legislators, finance ministers, and Bank executive directors. The campaign succeeded in prompting an independent review of the project, which led to the withdrawal of Bank support and to the cancellation of the remaining part of the loan. The controversy underlined the need for greater transparency and accountability in Bank projects and resulted in a general review of the Bank's environmental and resettlement policies. Ultimately, the campaign led the Bank to adopt a new public information policy and to create the World Bank Inspection Panel.

E. The Chad/Cameroon Project and the Bank's Inconsistent Approach to Human Rights

The Chad/Cameroon project reflects the continuing incoherence of the Bank's approach to human rights considerations. During the project's initial stages, the Bank completely ignored Chad's poor human rights record, despite human rights advocates' protests. The intensification of civil society pressure, however, led the Bank to issue public statements justifying its decision to lend to a government with such a poor human rights record.

The April 5, 2000 online version of the Chad/Cameroon project document displayed the Bank's defensive tone. The document acknowledged that "[m]ilitary incidents ... and the imprisonment of a parliamentarian ... have created concern about the human rights situation in the country," but then noted that the parliamentarian, Ngarléjy Yorongar, was released in 1999. No mention was made of the absence of human rights standards at his trial.

Request for Investigations by the World Bank Inspection Panel
Ngarlejy Yorongar
December 15, 2000, 2001
http://siteresources.worldbank.org/EXTINSPECTIONPANEL/
Resources/RequestEnglishtranslation.pdf

I, Ngarlejy YOROONGAR, Deputy to the National Assembly of the Republic of Chad, [i]n my capacity as representative of the entire country (Article 116 of the Constitution of the Republic of Chad), and on behalf of the persons listed ... who are adversely affected by development of the Doba oil reserves and who live in the vicinity of three oil fields in ... an area in which 300 sampling wells have been drilled by the Consortium....

Assisted by a team of lawyers, states the following:

1. The Bank is financing the design, appraisal, and/or execution of a project for the development of three oil fields in Chad-Cameroon. The project calls for exploitation of 300 sampling wells drilled by the Consortium as part of the development of three oil fields (Komé, Miandoum, and Bolobo) in the Doba region.

An export pipeline more than 1,100 km long with a production capacity of 250 million barrels per day will be built by the Consortium (Exxon, Chevron, and Petronas) through the sub-prefectures of Bébédjia, ... to the terminal of Kribi (Cameroon). The total cost is estimated at U.S. $3.5 billion.

In this scheme, the 300 oil wells will be connected to three pumping stations ... via a complex of pipelines and feeder lines, the dramatic consequences of such an operation being predictable....

3. Our rights and interests will be guaranteed if there is full respect for the directives, rules, ... recommendations, resolutions, and observations of the World Bank, etc. Among other rights and interests are the rights to life, to a healthy environment, to fair and equitable compensation, to resettlement not far from our native soil, to work, to respect for our customs and our burial places, to nature, to land ownership recognized by the laws in force, to social well-being, to public consultation, to access to project-related information, ... to consultation and coordination with our village associations and our representatives, to representation on the entity responsible for monitoring and surveillance of petroleum resources, etc.

4. The Bank has not followed its own rules and procedures, as indicated by the following acts. We allege that the World Bank participates in, indeed even encourages, violations of its own policies and procedures by the Consortium and the Government, as evidence of which we list certain carefully selected facts:

It has ridden roughshod over legislation governing expropriation and the uprooting [of communities]; the laughably small quota assigned to the production zone bears little or no relation to the magnitude of the needs of this region and the size of its population. (A barrel of oil for a barrel of Chadian blood!)

The compensation and indemnification plan fails to take account of [the loss of] medicinal plants. Directive 4.30, which deals with environmental impact assessments, ignores the 300 sampling wells drilled all over the oil production zone (OD [Operational Directive] 4.01). As far as the environmental impact assessment is concerned, the World Bank, the Government, and the Consortium have focused all their attention on the Chad-Cameroon pipeline. Consider the plight of the Ogoni people of Nigeria: the problems they have been left to face are those created by pipelines that link oil wells to pumping stations. It is at this level, and only this level, that the human, material, and environmental damage has been least bearable. Since the World Bank, the Government, and the Consortium refuse to carry out an environmental impact assessment at this level, the danger is inevitable. Because the danger exists all along the entire 1,100-km route of the Chad-Cameroon pipeline, the environmental impact assessment is unsatisfactory. No [cumulative] environmental impact assessment; no compensation plan.

The geological map shows that petroleum in the Doba basin is found from the border of Cameroon to the borders of the Central African Republic and Sudan.... This is precisely the region that feeds Chad and the frontier populations of the neighboring countries. The breadbasket of Chad, this zone is the most densely populated, etc. The slightest pollution of surface water sources will inevitably lead to pollution of water tables, rivers, marshes, and watercourses down to Lake Chad.... However, this lack of transparency regarding the environmental impact of the 300 oil sampling wells drilled by the Consortium ... does not conceal the great ecological danger posed by the exploitation of Chadian oil....

OD 4.20, on notification of native inhabitants and their representatives, was never complied with....

Directive OP [Operational Policy] 17.57, on public consultation, has been honored only with a crude image.... The requirement for participation by grass-roots NGOs in projects financed by the World Bank has not been met; the only NGOs consulted were, for the most part, either created for the purpose in hand or commanded no allegiance in the production region. The obligation to take into account the observations of the people affected by the project when preparing and carrying out the environmental impact assessment was never met, etc.

OP 17.50, on disclosure of operational information, has generated no more than a haphazard, uni-directional release of information, for the sole purpose of deceiving both the World Bank and international public opinion.

Directive OD 4.30, on problems of involuntary displacement and resettlement of people who are adversely affected by projects, has not been complied with yet.

Directive OD 4.04, on respect for native peoples, their nature, usages and customs, sacred sites, burial places, etc. has been completely ignored.

Directives on respect for human rights have been ignored since 1990....

Directives on compensation of persons adversely affected by pipeline routes have been treated as nothing more than an excuse for fraud....

5. We consider that our rights and interests have been, or are likely to be, directly harmed as a result of the Bank's action. This causes, or is likely to cause, the following types of damage, among others: pollution and degradation of the environment, expropriation without compensation, lack of respect for our usages and customs, nature, etc., violation of our human rights, bad governance reflected in the recent misappropriation of a premium of U.S. $2.5 million (CFAF 19 billion) and its use for the purchase of weapons with which to massacre us....

6. We hold the Bank accountable for what it has done and/or omitted to do in this case. If the Bank had taken our observations into account, we would not be in the present mess.

7. We have submitted evidence in our regular correspondence addressed to the President of the World Bank himself and various Bank departments to draw their special attention to the problems described above....

Except for vague responses from aides to World Bank President James D. Wolfensohn, all memoranda, letters, observations, and evidence presented in the course of these seminars and meetings were ignored. Instead, the World Bank concentrated on using its reputation and influence to ensure the project went ahead, to the detriment of the local communities affected and of Chad itself.

9. We have taken the following steps to resolve the problem: Since the World Bank, the Government, and the Consortium have failed to recognize the validity of our position, we have decided to appeal to the Inspection Panel so that justice will be done by halting oil field development works in the Doba basin until all World Bank directives and policies are put into effect and scrupulously respected by those responsible....

Chad-Cameroon Petroleum and Pipeline Project

World Bank Inspection Panel Investigation Report

(Loan No.4558 CD July 17, 2002)

http://siteresources.worldbank.org/EXTINSPECTIONPANEL/

Resources/ChadInvestigationReporFinal.pdf

Executive Summary

Introduction

The Request for inspection (the "Request") was submitted on March 22, 2001, by Mr. Ngarlejy Yorongar, a Member of Parliament in Chad's National Assembly and an active opposition leader, who was acting for himself and on behalf of more than 100 residents (the "Requesters") in the vicinity of three fields of the Pipeline Project area. The Requesters alleged that the Pipeline Project constituted a threat to local communities, their cultural property and the environment and that people in the oil field region (in the Doba Basin area) were being harmed, or were likely to be harmed, because of the absence, or inadequacy, of environmental assessment and compensation; and that proper consultation with and disclosure of information to the local communities had not taken place....

After reviewing Management's response to the allegations (and following a visit to Chad) the Panel recommended an investigation to the Board of Executive Directors. The Board approved the Panel's recommendation on October 1st 2001.

Environmental Compliance

General Environmental Concerns

The Panel notes the substantial effort that has been made in the assembling of the 19-volume Environmental Management Plan (EMP), which followed the preparation of an Environmental Impact Assessment (EIA) in 1997. It also notes the exceptional operational and managerial demands in implementing this plan in a challenging physical and political environment....

Evidence collected by the Panel both at the Bank's headquarters and during field visits indicates that oil and other economic development activities are already taking place outside of the scope addressed in the approved EMP. In reviewing the documentation contained in the EMP, however, the Panel cannot find any indication that any cumulative effects assessment was completed. The Panel finds this a serious omission, particularly when one of the objectives of the Petroleum Sector Capacity Management Project is to assist the Government of Chad to manage the development of its petroleum resources in an environmentally and socially sound manner, "*including the need for cumulative/regional/sectoral environmental assessments.*" The Panel finds that in failing to require a cumulative effects assessment, Management is not in compliance with OD 4.01.

The scale of the now proposed development will impact on the lives of all the people living in the Region as a whole. In failing to require the preparation of a Regional Environmental Assessment, which would adequately assess the nature, and extent of broader environmental and social concerns resulting from the Project, the Panel finds that Management is not in compliance with paragraph 5 of OD 4.01.

OD 4.01 makes specific reference to the importance of engaging an independent advisory panel of international experts. The need for an Expert Advisory Panel is particularly acute *"for major, high risk or contentious projects with serious, multidimensional concerns,*" and is clearly evident in the case of the Pipeline Project. The Panel noted that the Government of Chad (GOC) retained independent experts on environmental assessment but, to its surprise, it was unable to find any relevant records reflecting their work or the conclusions. The Inspection Panel finds this disturbing. Moreover, the Panel cannot understand why or how Management was unable to followup and monitor the work of such an important part of the EA process. The Panel, therefore, finds Management not in compliance with paragraph 13 of OD 4....

The Panel notes the significant efforts made by the Consortium to collect baseline information about the Project. Apart from the additional baseline data collected in response to previous reviews of the 1997 EA, significant site-specific information in the form of environmental baseline assessment has also been collected in areas scheduled for Project development. The Panel finds, however, that this data has not been properly utilized to support the EA process. There is no direct reference of data gaps in the 1999 EMP and those embodied in the 1997 EA. Consequently it is not clear how each specific management action is related to specific impacts or how these impacts relate to relevant data in Management's actions. The Panel, therefore, finds that Management is not in compliance with Paragraph 2 of Annex C of OD 4.01....

A key objective of the Capacity Building Project, and a major rationale for the Bank's involvement in the Project, was to develop and strengthen the institutional capabilities of the Government to a level where it could manage the petroleum sector in environmentally and socially sound manner. This included increasing the Government's capacity to the point where it could begin to monitor the Project effectively before the revenues start to flow. This objective has not been achieved and raises questions about the Project's ability to realize several of its social objectives.

The largest component of the Capacity Building Project involves the development of the capacity of the Committee for Monitoring and Evaluation of the Pipeline Project (CTNSC), which up to January 2002 had limited field staff, was not in position to execute its mandate.... In the light of the above ... the Panel finds that Management is not in compliance with the institutional/capacity requirements of OD 4.01, in respect to CTNSC....

Specific Environmental Concerns

Oil spills

Concerning possible oil spills, the Panel has noted that, apart from a Hazardous Operation assessment and risk assessment that had been already performed and would be repeated at least yearly, the oil field facilities have been designed to conform to international standards, including corrosion prevention and leak detection. An Area Specific Oil Spill Response Plan (ASOSRP), which includes immediate shut off protection and containment and clean-up provisions, is also expected to be in place and operational three months before the first oil is transported. The plans will be subject to audit and approved by outside experts. In. the Panel's view, however, Management 'must require that the Area Specific Oil Spill Response Plans reflect adequate consultation with affected stakeholders and civil society within the geographical area covered by each plan....

Contamination of Lake Chad and Groundwater

With respect to pollution of surface water sources and Lake Chad, the Panel was able to confirm the assertion that the Project EA includes a Comprehensive Ground Water Quality Monitoring Program, which is planned to be in place before the commencement of oil production. Among other measures, flow-lines and production pipelines are buried as safeguard against third party damage....

Although the Consortium has incorporated a number of mitigation measures in the Project design to avoid contamination of regional water supplies, the institutional mechanism for regional water management has not been developed to a similar extent. In the Panel's view, it is imperative that Management ensures that the Regional Development Plan and those responsible for its implementation give priority to the provision of safe and clean water to those living in the Project area. It is also imperative that such Area Specific Oil Spill Plans contain a review of the response to a spill to watercourses that form part of the watershed of Lake Chad.

Given the current status of Project implementation, and the cyclical nature of water shortages and availability in southern Chad, the Panel was unable to find any conclusive evidence that Management is in violation of OD 4.01 in connection with this issue. In the Panel's view, however, it requires continuing observation and monitoring by Management, perhaps through the International Advisory Group (IAG)....

Consultation

The Requesters allege that the obligation to take the views of affected groups and local NGOs fully into account in Project design and implementation, and particularly in the preparation of the EA was never fulfilled. Management maintains that consultation of the affected population was extensively undertaken. The Panel finds that, at least prior to 1997, the consultations were conducted in the presence of security forces, which is incompatible with Bank's policy requirements. As the Panel has said on previous occasions, full and informed consultation is impossible if those consulted perceive that they could be penalized for expressing their opposition to, or honest opinions about, a Bank financed project. At the same time, the Panel recognizes that, since 1999, Management has made significant efforts to achieve compliance with paragraph 19 of OD 4.01, by encouraging frequent consultations with local communities and civil society in an environment more conducive to an open exchange. In these circumstances, the Panel would commend these efforts and urge that they continue.

Disclosure of Information

On disclosure of information, the Panel concludes that adequate and timely release of documents was the norm rather than the exception in the context of the Pipeline Project. In fact, key Project documents (in particular the multi-volume EMP) appear to have been made routinely available on a continuous basis to the local population through specific events and the existence of "reading rooms." The Panel finds, therefore, that Management has complied with BP 17.50 on Disclosure of Operational Information.

Social Compliance

Indigenous Peoples

The Requesters allege that OD. 4.20 on Indigenous Peoples has not been complied with. The Panel finds that the people affected by the Pipeline Project do not constitute an "indigenous people" because they form a majority of the population in southern Chad and share a larger identity with the region as a whole. On the basis of the above considerations, the Panel concludes that OD 4.20 is not applicable to the present case....

Governance and Human Rights

The Requesters allege violations of Directives on proper governance and human rights. Management maintains that improving governance is one of the key objectives of the

Bank's Assistance Strategy to Chad and instances of poor governance are of great concern to it. As for human rights, Management states that the Bank is concerned about violations of human rights in Chad as elsewhere while respecting the Bank's Articles of Agreement but that, in this case, it believes that the Project can achieve its developmental objectives.

It is not within the Panel's mandate to assess the status of governance and human rights in Chad in general or in isolation, and the Panel acknowledges that there are several institutions (including U.N. bodies) specifically in charge of this subject. However, the Panel felt obliged to examine whether the issues of proper governance or human rights violations in Chad were such as to impede the implementation of the Project in a manner compatible with the Bank's policies.

As far as "good" or "proper" governance is concerned, the Panel recognizes that this is an evolving process in Africa and elsewhere in the developing world and that several Bank-supported Projects, including the Capacity Building Project which is the subject of this investigation, have components designed to improve the country's governance record and performance.

As for human rights, the Panel has examined several reports addressing the situation in the country and the extensive exchange of correspondence between Bank Management and NGOs in Chad and abroad. The Panel takes note of the fact that on more than one occasion when political repression in Chad seemed severe, the Bank's President personally intervened to help free local opposition leaders, including the representative of the Requesters, Mr. Yorongar, who was reported as being subjected to torture. During its visit to Chad, the Panel did not seek out the other opposition leaders in N'Djamena who had been arrested. In the field, however, several local leaders and organizations mentioned to the Panel that, while at times feeling harassed by the authorities, they have expressed their opinions about the Project without incurring physical violence. The Panel observes that the situation is far from ideal. It raises questions about compliance with Bank policies, in particular with those that relate to informed and open consultation, and it warrants renewed monitoring by the Bank....

Economic Compliance

Economic Evaluation

The discussion of *Sustainability and Risks* is very brief. This is significant because of the acknowledged complexity of the project's design and the recognition that to avoid the failure associated with development of oil or mineral resources in other SubSaharan African countries, Chad must put in place before 2004 the essential building blocks of its strategy for the management of the petroleum economy. In the Panel's view, therefore, a more thorough appraisal of sustainability and risks would have been required in order to ensure proper compliance with paragraphs 5 and 6 of OP 10.04.

OP 10.04 states that the main purpose of the analysis of risk is *"to identify the scope for improving project design, increase the project's expected value, and reduce the risk of failure."* Given the identified weakness in implementation capacity in the Ministries of Environment and of Energy and Petroleum, and the importance of timely implementation of the rapid intervention measures, the Regional Development Plan and the pilot development fund (FACIL), the Panel finds that Management is not in compliance with OP 10.04 in respect of the analysis of sustainability and risk issues....

Poverty Reduction ...

The Panel recognizes Management's intention to comply with the broad provisions of OD 4.15, and its awareness of the challenges to effectively reduce poverty in Chad. Nevertheless, the Panel has concerns on whether some components of OD 4.15 have been fully met and whether Management has succeeded to put in place sufficient measures to ensure the sustained delivery of poverty reduction outcomes, and hence future compliance with OD 4.15.

The Panel's investigation revealed serious concerns about the failure to develop and strengthen the institutional capabilities of the Government of Chad to a level where it could begin to monitor the Project effectively before the revenues start to flow. In this regard, it is vital that the operations of the dedicated special account be subject of continuing monitoring, review and assessment by an independent body such as the IAG [International Advisory Group].

During the Panel's visits to Chad, several local leaders expressed deep reservations on whether Chadians would be the ultimate beneficiaries of the Project. In more specific terms and in relation to the oil-producing region, the Request alleged that "the laughably small quota assigned to the production zone bears little or no relation to the magnitude of the needs of this region and the size of its population." This refers to the 5% of royalties from oil revenues over the life of the field project for the producing region. While there are no Bank policies and procedures that directly guide the allocation of resource revenues to producing regions, and consequently no question here of non-compliance with OD 4.15, it would appear that no targeted studies were carried out to determine the appropriate share; nor is there any review of material that might underpin the choice of 5 per cent. In the Panel's view, this is a matter of great concern. It is also not clear that Management yet has the information that would enable it to estimate regional shares of planned priority sector expenditures. In the Panel's view, this kind of information is essential if the various stakeholders are to be in a position to debate and argue for appropriate shares in national income and wealth.

The Panel is concerned that activities such as project mitigation measures, establishment of FACIL, the completion of a Regional Development Plan, and the establishment of the College de Controle et de Surveillance des Ressources Petrolieres have been running significantly behind schedule while oil field and pipeline development are running ahead of schedule. In the Panel's view, these delays threaten to compromise the delivery of poverty reduction in the later stages of construction and the early stages of operation of the Pipeline Project. Obviously, Management must renew and invigorate its efforts to ensure that the structures created are fully operational before the expected earnings arrive.

It is obvious to the Panel that neither the Capacity Building Project nor the Petroleum Economy Project have made appropriate provisions to identify and address the above-mentioned types of problems in the areas touched by the Pipeline Project's activities. This is despite their potential to impinge on that Project's potential to attain the poverty reduction envisaged in OD 4. Furthermore, it is not obvious to the Panel that there is sufficient communication and coordination between the two projects to rule out the possibility of their becoming poverty-increasing problems which fall between two stools and fail to be identified and addressed. In the light of this, the Panel finds that the Project is not in compliance with these aspects of OD 4.15....

Questions and Discussion

1. *Allegations.* Did you find the Inspection Panel Report satisfactory? The requesters alleged violations of the right to life, to a healthy environment, to fair and equitable com-

pensation, to public consultation, to access to project-related information, etc. Did the Panel address all these allegations?

2. *Mandate.* The Inspection Panel response addressed several concerns regarding the World Bank's Operational Directive (OD) 4.01 on environmental assessment: lack of cumulative impacts assessment, lack independent advisory panel consultation, lack of consultation with local communities, and the presence of ground water contamination issues. What did the Inspection Panel find regarding the Bank's compliance with 4.01 on each of these issues?

3. *Consultation.* The Requesters allege that the obligation to take the views of affected groups and local NGOs fully into account in Project design and implementation, and particularly in the preparation of the EA was never fulfilled. Management maintains that consultation of the affected population was extensively undertaken. What are the Panel's findings? Is presence of security forces during consultations incompatible with Bank's policy requirements?

4. *Political and civil rights.* The Requesters allege violations of Directives on proper governance and human rights. However, Bank Management maintains that improving governance is one of the key objectives of the project, and poor governance in Chad is its big concern. Regarding human rights, Bank Management states that the Bank is concerned about violations of human rights in Chad as elsewhere while respecting the Bank's Articles of Agreement. It is commonly claimed that the Articles of Agreement separate political and civil rights from economic and social rights through the following clause:

> The Bank and its officers shall not interfere in the political affairs of any member; nor shall they be influenced in their decisions by the political character of the member or members concerned. Only economic considerations shall be relevant to their decisions, and these considerations shall be weighed impartially ... World Bank, *Articles of Agreement*, Article IV Section 10.

The Bank insists that its central mission of reducing poverty contributes to promoting economic and social rights, but that specific consideration of political and civil rights lies outside of its mandate.

5. *Reconsidering the World Bank's position.* Do you agree that the Articles of Agreement prevent the World Bank from including human rights in its consideration beyond project viability? Consider the following:

> An intent to appease the Soviet Union represents the first likely consideration in the 1943 negotiations between the United States and United Kingdom. To the extent that this assertion is correct and Article IV, Section 10, was included with the Soviet Union principally in mind, the obvious concern addressed was a possible Bank bias against Communism. That concern suggests a relatively narrow intent on the part of the drafters to avoid biases against a member nation based on its political form or ideology—Capitalist, Socialist, or Communist. Given the geopolitical backdrop to the 1943 negotiations, such an intent is highly plausible, as British and American leaders already anticipated the postwar polarization between Capitalism and Communism, which would give rise to the Cold War.
>
> If the architects of the World Bank simply intended to protect member nations from biases against Communism or Socialism, the scope of a nation's protected "political character" would be narrow. It would allow a country to select a national ideology and form of governance, but it would not permit unbridled

flaunting of international legal norms. Violations of international human rights law are not inherently tied to any particular form of governance, and intervention taken to protect such rights would not necessarily have a disproportionate impact upon Communist, Socialist, or Capitalist countries. Therefore, to the extent that concern for the Soviet Union drove the inclusion of the political activity prohibition, the drafters did not intend to protect nations from the adverse consequences of human rights violations.

The second suggested motive for Article IV, Section 10, which resonates with the historical accounts of the negotiations, was Keynes' concern for the protection of Britain's postwar economic sovereignty and Commonwealth ties. This intent, like that to appease the Soviet Union, contemplates a definition of "political" activity that does not preclude human rights considerations.… This British concern suggests that the form of "political" insulation contemplated in the IBRD Charter was narrowly focused upon economic policy. Thus, the British desire to preserve economic sovereignty does not imply a desire to protect a sovereign's autonomy regarding human rights considerations.

A final, and relatively undisputed, factor during the 1943 negotiations was Keynes' belief that the Bretton Woods institutions would be most effective if operated by expert economists under conditions of minimal political influence. The rationale for this belief was that decisions would be based on rigorous economic analysis alone.… This intention leaves the door open to human rights considerations whenever they legitimately affect economic performance or ability to repay Bank obligations.

Thus, based upon the available literature, it appears that three major factors drove the inclusion of the political activity prohibition in the IBRD Articles of Agreement.… The important conclusion to be drawn from the *travaux préparatoires* is that none of the three apparent objectives for Article IV, Section 10 leads to an interpretation of a nation's "political character" that would prohibit the Bank from considering a nation's violation of internationally recognized human rights in its lending and credit decisions.…

John D. Ciorciari, *The Lawful Scope of Human Rights Criteria in World Bank Credit Decisions: An Interpretive Analysis of the IBRD and IDA Articles of Agreement*, 33 Cornell Int'l L.J. 331 (2000).

6. *Human rights.* Is the evaluation of the status of governance and human rights, including civil and political, social and economic rights, within the Panel's mandate? Although the inspection panel states that "assessment of human rights in Chad in general" is not part of its mandate, the panel proceeds with a brief synopsis of the conditions. Would the report have been complete without this section? Is it possible to evaluate a project's impact on a country's human rights environment without considering the baseline conditions?

7. *Economic Considerations.* Referring to the 5% of royalties from oil revenues reserved for the producing region, Ngarlejy Yorongar's request alleges that "the laughably small quota assigned to the production zone bears little or no relation to the magnitude of the needs of this region and the size of its population." Does the decision to provide 5% royalties to production zones violate any specific World Bank policies? What is the Inspection Panel's judgment on this? Should royalties be based on the human rights needs of a geographic region, or just the economic impacts of such issues?

III. IFC/MIGA Compliance Advisor and Ombudsman

Democratizing Multilateral Development Banks
Nathalie Bernasconi-Osterwalder & David Hunter
THE NEW "PUBLIC": THE GLOBALIZATION OF PUBLIC PARTICIPATION
(C. Bruch, ed., 2002)

C. Access to Justice and the Accountability Mechanisms ...

2. IFC/MIGA Compliance Advisor/Ombudsman

When the Inspection Panel was created, neither the IFC nor MIGA had any environmental or social policies. Accordingly, the Panel's jurisdiction did not extend to their operations. In 1999, after the IFC adopted its safeguard policies, World Bank President James Wolfensohn announced the creation of an office of the Compliance Advisor and Ombudsman (CAO)....

The CAO has two goals: "first, to help the IFC and MIGA address—in a manner that is fair, objective, and constructive—complaints made by people who have been or may be affected by projects in which the IFC and MIGA play a role; and second, to enhance the social and environmental outcomes of those projects." To achieve those goals, the CAO has three related roles: (i) Responding to complaints by persons who are affected by projects and attempting to resolve issues raised using a flexible, problem solving approach (the ombudsman role); (ii) Providing a source of independent advice to the President and the management of IFC and MIGA. CAO provides advice both in relation to particular projects and in relation to broader environmental and social policies, guidelines, procedures, and systems (the advisory role); (iii) Overseeing audits of IFC's and MIGA's social and environmental performance, both overall and in relation to sensitive projects, to ensure compliance with policies, guidelines, procedures, and systems (the compliance role).

Any individual, group, community, entity, or other party affected or likely to be affected by the social or environmental impacts of an IFC or MIGA project may make a complaint to the Ombudsman's office.

The Ombudsman process tries to resolve the concerns raised by the affected communities through a variety of possible conflict resolution methodologies, including, for example, consultation, dialogue, or mediation. The focus is not necessarily on determining whether the IFC or MIGA have been at fault in the design or implementation of the project. Because IFC and MIGA projects involve private sector companies, the Ombudsman can more easily play an intermediary role using IFC/ MIGA leverage with the project sponsor to address legitimate concerns of affected people.

The CAO may bring the complaint process to a close either when a settlement agreement has been reached or when it has determined that further investigation or problem-solving efforts are not going to be productive. At that point, the CAO will inform the complainant and report to the President of the World Bank Group. The report to the President may include specific recommendations the CAO believes could help to solve problems raised by the complaint. The CAO may also decide to conduct a compliance audit to address non-compliance issues identified in the course of responding to the complaint or may refer any policy issues to the advisory role of the CAO's office.

The CAO's compliance role may be triggered through the ombudsman's process, at the request of management or on the CAO's own initiative. The purpose of a compliance audit is to determine whether IFC, MIGA, or in some cases the project sponsor have complied with the environmental and social safeguard policies of the respective institution. The compliance report may also contain specific recommendations for improving compliance both in the specific project and more generally. A report from each compliance audit is provided to the President.

Given the relatively short period of time in which the CAO has been operating, there is insufficient experience to determine its long-term success in resolving the problems of project-affected people or in improving the IFC's and MIGA's policy compliance. In several cases, however, the affected people have been satisfied with the outcomes of the process or at least the preliminary assessments that have validated their concerns.

According to CAO *Operational Guidelines* "Any individual, group, community, entity, or other party that believes it is affected — or potentially affected — by the social and/or environmental impacts of an IFC/MIGA project may make a complaint to the CAO Ombudsman." The CAO explains that it has three functions:

- Ombudsman role (CAO Ombudsman): Responding to complaints by individual(s), group(s) of people, or organization(s) that are affected by IFC/MIGA projects.... The focus of the CAO ombudsman role is on helping to resolve complaints, ideally by improving social and environmental outcomes on the ground.

- Compliance role (CAO Compliance): Overseeing audits of the social and environmental performance of IFC and MIGA, particularly in relation to sensitive projects....

- Advisory role (CAO Advisor): Providing a source of independent advice to the President of the World Bank Group and the management of IFC and MIGA....

CAO *Operational Guidelines* (April 2007) http://www.cao-ombudsman.org/html-english/documents/WEBEnglishCAO06.08.07Web.pdf.

A complaint to the CAO due to the social and environmental impacts of an IFC funded project could help bring attention to the environmental and human rights problems with the project. However, the CAO does not have the authority to find fault or withdraw a loan. It uses a "flexible, problem-solving approach," which brings the parties together to negotiate a solution. The CAO would not require any specific action from the multinational corporations; it can only make recommendations.

NGOs have historically had some success utilizing the CAO complaint process to safeguard human rights and environmental concerns imperiled by IFC/MIGA funded projects. Often, however, the CAO seems reluctant to make recommendations as to how a project can better account for these important interests, seemingly conceding that a certain degree of privation is an inevitable and acceptable consequence of economic development. As you read the complaint and CAO response below, consider whether you think the CAO has adequately addressed the concerns of the Tanzanian citizens forced to abandon their lives and livelihood to accommodate a major corporate mining operation.

LEAT Bulyanhulu Complaint to IFC/MIGA
Compliance Advisor/Ombudsman

http://www.leat.or.tz/activities/buly/miga.complaint.php
(2001)

We Lawyers' Environmental Action Team ("LEAT") lodge a complaint concerning the Bulyanhulu Gold Mine project. This complaint is made on our own behalf and on behalf of our clients, communities of former small-scale miners and landholders of the Bulyanhulu area organized under the Bulyanhulu Small-Scale Gold Miners' Committee ("the Bulyanhulu complainants"). LEAT is a public interest environmental law organization that has been working with and on behalf of the Bulyanhulu complainants....

Project Description

The Bulyanhulu Gold Mine in Bulyanhulu area of Kahama District, Shinyanga Region is a large-scale underground gold mine that also produces silver and copper.

The Multilateral Investment Guarantee Agency ("MIGA") is involved with the project through the provision of a political risk guarantee in the sum of United States Dollars 172 million approved in August 2000.

The projector sponsor is Kahama Mining Corporation Limited of Dar es Salaam, Tanzania, which is a wholly-owned subsidiary of Barrick Gold Corporation of Toronto, Canada ("the project sponsors").

Background to the Complaint

The Bulyanhulu complainants formerly lived and worked for gain as small-scale miners, small traders, peasant farmers and livestock keepers in an area called Bulyanhulu.... [I]n September 1994, the project sponsors laid a claim over the Bulyanhulu area on the basis of a license granted by the Government of Tanzania on August 5, 1994....

Relying on this license, the project sponsors caused the Canadian High Commission in Tanzania to put diplomatic pressure on the Tanzanian Government to evict the Bulyanhulu complainants....

The project sponsors also commenced judicial proceedings against the Bulyanhulu complainants in the High Court of Tanzania to have the Bulyanhulu complainants evicted by judicial orders....

Following adverse ruling by the High Court of Tanzania, the project sponsors first appealed to the Court of Appeal of Tanzania (Tanzania's highest appellate court) but later withdrew the appeal and reverted to using diplomatic and administrative pressure to evict the Bulyanhulu complainants....

On July 30, 1996, the Tanzanian Government issued orders that the Bulyanhulu complainants should vacate their lands, settlements and property within 24 hours. Paramilitary police units and demolition equipment belonging to the project sponsors and operated by their employees were then stationed in the Bulyanhulu complainants' villages and settlements. The next day the eviction of the Bulyanhulu complainants and the destruction of their settlements and immovable property began and went on for much of August 1996....

In so doing, the project sponsors and the Government of Tanzania went contrary to the order of the High Court of Tanzania....

The Complaint

The Bulyanhulu complainants have been, are being and/or are likely to be affected by social and environmental impacts of the project in the following ways:

Forced Evictions and Displacement When Project Sponsor Took Control of the Mine Site

We believe that potentially hundreds of thousands of the Bulyanhulu complainants were forcibly evicted and displaced from the Bulyanhulu area when the project sponsors illegally and irregularly entered into the Bulyanhulu complainants' lands, settlements and mining areas with the help of the security forces of the Government of Tanzania.

We believe that the project sponsors and the Government of Tanzania failed or neglected to plan, finance and implement any resettlement or relocation plan and to provide alternative lands or settlements or alternative sources of livelihoods for the Bulyanhulu complainants.

We believe that the project sponsors and the Government of Tanzania failed and/or refused to pay any or adequate, fair, just and prompt compensation for loss of agricultural and grazing lands; destruction of settlements including residential and commercial property....

Environmental and Social Impacts Assessments Inaccurate and Inadequate

We believe that the project sponsors failed and/or neglected to carry out any environmental impacts assessment studies and processes prior to their entry into and acquisition of the Bulyanhulu area and prior to the eviction and displacement of the Bulyanhulu complainants;

We believe that the project sponsors failed and/or neglected to carry out adequate and meaningful consultations with the Bulyanhulu complainants prior to their entry into and acquisition of the Bulyanhulu area;

We believe that the project sponsors commissioned, financed, published and submitted to MIGA, the Government of Tanzania and the general public environmental impacts statements, environmental management plan and social development plan that were materially inaccurate; and contained erroneous, false and misleading information and conclusions concerning their acquisition, possession and operation of the Bulyanhulu Gold Mine....

Non-Disclosure of Material Information

We believe that the project sponsors failed to prepare for, and/or disclose to, MIGA, the Government of Tanzania and the general public all material information as to the facts and circumstances pertaining to the acquisition, possession and operation of the Bulyanhulu Gold Mine including all acts and omissions enumerated in the foregoing paragraphs.

We believe that the project sponsors failed to disclose in environmental impacts statements, environmental management plan and social development plan submitted to MIGA, the Government of Tanzania and the general public the existence of the very serious allegations of human rights atrocities implicating the project sponsors and the Government of Tanzania as regards the manner of the project sponsor's acquisition, possession and operation of the project....

MIGA's Inadequate Due Diligence Investigations

We believe that MIGA failed to carry out a thorough and competent due diligence investigation pertaining to the facts and circumstances surrounding the project sponsor's acquisition, possession and operation of the Bulyanhulu Gold Mine in order to establish the veracity of the information submitted and soundness of the conclusions drawn by the project sponsors prior to making the decision to provide political risk guarantee for the project....

MIGA's Violation of its Information Disclosure Policies

We believe that MIGA failed to prepare and/or disclose to the complainants and other interested parties all material information pertaining to the facts and circumstances surrounding the project sponsor's acquisition, possession and operation of the project in spite of repeated requests from the complainants and other interested parties to do so....

We would like to see this complaint resolved in the following way:

Full, fair and just compensation should be paid to all Bulyanhulu complainants who were involuntarily resettled without any resettlement plan.

Full, fair and just compensation should be paid to all Bulyanhulu complainants whose agricultural and grazing lands were expropriated; residential and commercial property and settlements destroyed; investment in mining shafts, machinery and equipment confiscated; and employment opportunities lost....

The CAO should review MIGA's actual process of due diligence investigation, in order to assess whether MIGA properly investigated the foregoing issues, and whether it took the steps necessary to ensure that this project complied with MIGA policies before it approved the political risk guarantee for the Bulyanhulu Gold Mine.

The CAO should review the environmental and social impacts information the project sponsors has submitted to MIGA, and compare it with the information contained in this complaint in order to establish the adequacy and the veracity of the environmental and social impacts information and the soundness of the conclusions drawn in the environmental information submitted to MIGA and the Government of Tanzania....

The CAO should assess whether MIGA has complied with its safeguard policies, particularly its policy on involuntary resettlement, and should assess whether or how MIGA's financing of this project advances its poverty alleviation goals.

The CAO should review MIGA's compliance with its information disclosure policies in responding to requests for information regarding this project and should direct MIGA to fully disclose all documentation save for that protected by the confidentiality clauses to allow for full public participation in the process of resolving this complaint.

The CAO should lend its voice for calls for establishment of an independent commission of inquiry agreeable to the Bulyanhulu complainants as well as to the project sponsors and the Government of Tanzania to independently, transparently and thoroughly inquire into the facts and circumstances pertaining to the acquisition, possession and operation of the project and, where necessary and appropriate, make recommendations for the resolution of this complaint....

MIGA's Guarantee of the Bulyanhulu Gold Mine, Tanzania

CAO Assessment Report Summary
http://www.cao-ombudsman.org/html-english/
documents/bulyfinal.Englishpdf.pdf (2002)

The CAO was unable to find any basis for the allegations of present day intimidation, interference or undermining of the community by the mine. Clearly the development dynamics around an investment of this type and character in an area devoid of other economic opportunities and social services are difficult and the challenges severe. The mine is however stepping up its work in partnership with the community and other NGO partners and with the government in the region.

Conclusions . . .

The CAO is also concerned that MIGA did not carry out a more thorough review of the project following IFC's pre-appraisal visit. Simply reviewing documents without a site visit, especially with changes in the project and with a gap in time between IFC's and MIGA's reviews, is inadequate. In this case MIGA has been well served by a mine and a project sponsor that appear to be committed to best practice. It is for this reason and not as the result of the supervision or due diligence by MIGA that the mine is performing to environmental and social standards that are in line with those expected of an investment of the World Bank Group. . . .

To date no environment or social specialist on contract to MIGA has visited Bulyanhulu. Moreover, in conversations with the mine management and staff there was an expression of interest in other examples of best practice in social development, areas where the World Bank Group positions itself as a leader. MIGA should examine its capacity and willingness to support its clients to replicate and develop best practices and to act a as a source of information and support where clients are inclined to do so.

The CAO does not believe that the project merits a compliance audit and was impressed with the way in which the mine was developing its social and environmental capacity. The questions of revenue management and distribution and the disparities between an investment of the size of Bulyanhulu in one of the poorest regions of Tanzania, and how maximum benefits can be captured for local people is a perennial one for IFC and MIGA.

Once again, there would seem to be room for more coordinated approaches on this issue between MIGA and the World Bank and other agencies active in Tanzania. Without guidance from MIGA, Barrick Gold has established meaningful partnerships with international aid and development organizations to reinforce its social development activities and these should be supported and their development impact monitored.

The CAO does not believe that it can play any further useful role in this case. The CAO respectfully urges the complainants and their international counterparts to assess carefully the way in which they use information and the emphasis they place on substantiation. Advocacy on behalf of local people who may lack the means to make their voices heard to government and international authorities has been a tried and tested method of forcing change. International advocacy NGOs in the environment, development and human rights fields have a proud record of propelling the World Bank Group towards more rigorous approaches to environment and social assessment among other policy initiatives. Similarly, human rights NGOs play an important role in acting as a global conscience and have brought about changes in attitudes in the private sector, including in resource extraction industries. But the CAO believes there is a responsibility that goes with this role.

Questions and Discussion

1. *Whom to believe?* Considering that nobody from MIGA has visited the mine site, does the CAO seem excessively credulous of the mining company in stating that it "appear[s] to be committed to best practice?" Is the NGO law firm's credibility bolstered by the fact that it is subject to the requirements of ethical responsibility in presenting a case?

2. *What substantiation is required?* Recall the language quoted above from the CAO Operational Guidelines: "*Any* individual, group, community, entity, or other party that believes it is affected — *or potentially affected* — by the social and/or environmental impacts of an IFC/MIGA project may make a complaint to the CAO Ombudsman." (emphasis added) Is the CAO's warning to the NGOs about their responsibility in their role as advocates on behalf of "local people who may lack the means to make their voices heard" appropriate? Does the CAO seem exceedingly defensive of its decision not to intervene?

3. *Criminal charges.* Among the consequences of the NGO law firm raising complaints about the events alleged in Bulyanhulu were that criminal sedition charges were filed by the Tanzanian government against some of the NGO lawyers. See discussion in Chapter 11 at page 496.

The Yanacocha Mine, Peru

Consider the following CAO case. Newmont Mining Corporation is a U.S.-based corporation with gold mining operations around the world. It owns a majority share in the world's largest gold mine, the Yanacocha mine in Peru, which produces harmful by-products including mercury. In 2000, over 300 pounds of mercury were spilled into the environment of a small village community. The company did not inform residents about the virulent nature of spill, so, believing it was valuable, the residents collected the mercury. As a result, over 1000 people developed symptoms of mercury poisoning, including blindness, skin rashes, memory loss, muscular pain, and nausea.

Newmont was given a loan by the IFC, which finances 5% of the Yanacocha Mine in Peru. In 2000, an Independent Commission of the CAO conducted an investigation into the mercury spill at the request of the Minera Yanacocha and its shareholders (MYSRL). The findings of the Commission were unfavorable to Newmont and its causation and subsequent handling of the mercury spill. The investigation report included the following:

> Newmont Mining Corporation, as the major shareholder and parent of the manager of the mine, did not apply global standards to the handling and transport of hazardous materials at MYSRL.

> MYSRL did not appear to have a comprehensive procedure in place to identify and record potential environmental hazards....

> Initial response to the spill was slow. Factors contributing to this situation include:

> - MYSRL had no emergency response plan applying to mercury spills off their property.

> - The environmental and human health hazards of inorganic mercury were underestimated.

> - The amount of mercury spilled was underestimated and under reported by MYSRL.

> MYSRL did not provide adequate, nor timely, information on the incident to the public affected, to local authorities in the directly affected communities, the provincial authorities in Cajamarca, and national authorities in Lima.

Investigation into the Mercury Spill of July 2, 2000, in the Vicinity of San Juan, Choropampa, and Magdelena, Peru, Report of the Independent Commission to the Office of Compliance Advisor/Ombudsman of the International Finance Corporation and the Multilateral Investment Guarantee Agency 48–49 (2000). http://www.cao-ombudsman.org/html-english/documents/IndependentCommissionReportInvestigationoftheJune2000MecurySpill.pdf

The Independent Commission report on the mercury spill made several recommendations to the MYSRL, including the following:

> 2. Develop and follow an Emergency Response Plan (EPR) that deals with the transportation of hazardous materials, and spills and transportation incidents/accidents, to and from the mine sites, and on- and off-site, and in incident/accident locations that are distant from the mine site....
>
> 3. Provide additional formal training to MYSRL employees, contractors and subcontractors working on or off-site....
>
> 9. MYSRL should verify that there are no other activities at the mine where the absence of local regulations may have led to procedures or practices of environmental management that are not in line with best practices at the international level.
>
> 10. An Environmental Management Audit of MYSRL should be conducted to assess the capacity of each department and of the company as a whole, to prevent and mitigate the impacts on the environment both on and off the mine site. In the remediation efforts, all monitoring procedures, data, and interpretation should be subject to thorough independent review.

Id.

In addition, in 2001, two complaints were filed to the CAO alleging that the "Yanacocha mine was adversely impacting the water, air, and livelihoods of surrounding villages and that mining development was occurring without adequate community involvement, as required by IFC policies." CAO Press Release *CAO Closes Complaint from* FEROCAFENOP *Regarding Minera Yanacocha* (March 2006) available at http://www.cao-ombudsman.org/html-english/documents/CAOPressRelease-MineraYanacocha3032006English.pdf. In response, the CAO created a "roundtable" dialogue called Mesa, which conducted meetings, workshops, monitoring, etc. since 2001. CAO *Exit Report-Regarding two complaints filed with the CAO in relation to Minera Yanacocha Cajamarca, Peru* (Feb. 2006) available at http://www.cao-ombudsman.org/html-english/documents/Exitreportenglish02-7-06-final.pdf. The complaint was closed in 2006, finding that the problems could be solved with dialogue.

Questions and Discussion

Compare the structure of the CAO to that of the Inspection Panel. Does it appear that one is more likely to provide independent oversight than the other? If so, why? What is your opinion of the reforms proposed for the Inspection Panel, discussed earlier? Would some reforms be advisable for the CAO? Is an in-house body likely to be more effective or less effective than an outside institution, such as a human rights commission or court? What are the arguments on both sides of that question?

Chapter 11

Protecting Environmental Advocates and Defenders

Introduction

Environmental and other human rights defenders—the citizen or lawyer advocates who try to defend the human rights of others to a healthy environment—are often at risk of having their own rights infringed because of their work. The risk can be starkly physical.

Elpidio "Jojo" de la Victoria, a Philippine activist who was trying to bring illegal fishing operators to account, was assassinated in April 2006, on the front steps of his home. In May 2007, the youthful sons of Ildefonso Zamora, an indigenous campesino-activist who had filed complaints about illegal logging in the Lagunas de Zempoala National Park in Mexico, were ambushed. The attackers killed Aldo, 21 years old, and seriously wounded his 16-year old brother, Misael. Previously, Mexican campesinos Rodolfo Montiel Flores and Teodoro Cabrera Garcia, who protested illegal logging of old-growth forests, were arrested, tortured, and imprisoned. In 1995, Nigerian author and activist, Ken Saro-Wiwa, who led protests by the Ogoni people against environmental contamination by Shell Oil Company, was hanged by the Nigerian military government. (Environmental harms in Nigeria are discussed in cases in Chapter 2 at page 55 and Chapter 12 at page 575 The list grows ever more lengthy. Some of the cases were presented in a report by Amnesty International and the Sierra Club: *Environmentalists under Fire: 10 Urgent Cases of Human Rights Abuses* (2000), available at http://www.sierraclub.org/human-rights/amnesty/report.pdf. Other cases can be found in Romina Picolotti, Lewis Gordon, & John Cheverie, *Brief Amicus Curiae: Teodoro Cabrera Garcia and Rodolfo Montiel Flores v. The State of Mexico,* filed before the Inter-American Commission on Human Rights (2002), available at http://www.earthrights.org/legaldocs/rodolfo_montiel_and_teodoro_cabrera_v._mexico.html.

Lawyers as well as activists place themselves at risk with their defense of environmental advocates and activists. The life of Jojo de la Victoria's friend and colleague, Philippine environmental lawyer Antonio Oposa (whose most famous case is in Chapter 3 at page 79) has been threatened. Famed Indian environmental lawyer, M.C. Mehta (one of whose cases is in Chapter 8 at page 94) regularly receives death threats. In October 2001, Digna Ochoa, a lawyer who was a winner of Amnesty International's Enduring Spirit Award and who represented environmentalists jailed for protesting illegal logging, was shot to death in her office in Mexico City. A note found next to her body warned former colleagues that they could be next. As far back as the late 1970s, famed Argentine environmental and human rights lawyer Alberto Kattan was among the "disappeared" in what became known as the "dirty war" waged by the military dictatorship in Argentina. He was tortured with electrical shock and his wrists broken. U.S. President Jimmy Carter managed to convince the generals to release him and flew him to the U.S. for medical treatment. He returned to Argentina while the military was still in power and filed suits against the government to protect penguins and dolphins.

Governments, individual politicians, or private individuals and corporations may also use the legal system to persecute an environmental advocate. Malaysian environmental lawyer Meenakshi Raman was arrested and held in solitary confinement under the Internal Security Act of Malaysia in 1988 after taking a case to court for villagers affected by radioactive dumping by a company co-owned by Mitsubishi Corporation and the Malaysian Government. The tactics used to discourage environmental advocates range from arrests and criminal charges to the use of civil court litigation charging defamation or unlawful interference with business and trade.

This chapter will first examine mechanisms available for those seeking to protect "human rights defenders" through the United Nations system or regional human rights systems. The bulk of the chapter will discuss human rights defenders in national legal systems—the criminal and civil suits filed against them, as well as available responses and remedies.

I. International Protections for Defenders

A. The United Nations Declaration and Special Representative

The General Assembly, after 13 years of discussion by a working group of the Commission on Human Rights, adopted a Declaration on Human Rights Defenders (DHRD) in 1998.[a] Article 1 of the Declaration states, "Everyone has the right, individually and in association with others, to promote and to strive for the protection and realization of human rights and fundamental freedoms at the national and international levels." Article 6 states that everyone has the right "to draw public attention" to matters involving human rights and fundamental freedoms. Article 8 asserts that everyone has the right "individually and in association with others, to submit to governmental bodies and agencies and organizations concerned with public affairs criticism and proposals for improving their functioning" and to "draw attention" to shortcomings. Article 9 affirms that everyone has the right "to benefit from an effective remedy and to be protected in the event of the violation of those rights." Furthermore, according to Article 9, paragraph 3(c), anyone may "offer and provide professionally qualified legal assistance or other relevant advice and assistance in defending human rights and fundamental freedoms." Governments are expected to assist. "The State shall conduct a prompt and impartial investigation or ensure that an inquiry takes place whenever there is reasonable ground to believe that a violation of human rights and fundamental freedoms has occurred in any territory under its jurisdiction." Article 9, para-

---

a. The formal title is Declaration on the Right and Responsibility of Individuals, Groups and Organs of Society to Promote and Protect Universally Recognized Human Rights and Fundamental Freedoms, U.N. Doc. No. A/RES/53/144 (8 March 1999).

graph 5. In addition, The State shall take all necessary measures to ensure the protection by the competent authorities of everyone, individually and in association with others, against any violence, threats, retaliation, de facto or *de jure* adverse discrimination, pressure or any other arbitrary action as a consequence of his or her legitimate exercise of the rights referred to in the present Declaration." Article 12, paragraph 2.

The advocacy group Human Rights First (formerly the Lawyers Committee for Human Rights), made these observations shortly after adoption of the Declaration:

> The slow process in finalizing the Declaration can be attributed to two major factors: 1) from its inception, there has been friction between those governments genuinely interested in strengthening the position of human rights defenders, and those who used this drafting exercise to further restrict and hamper their work; and 2) the need for consensus allowed a small group of participating governments to veto any real progress in the finalization of the declaration. Key contentious issues in the Working Group were; (i) the role of national law in the implementation of the Declaration; (ii) the extent to which human rights defenders have special responsibilities or duties; (iii) the right of human rights defenders to obtain resources for their work; (iv) the right to observe trials; (v) the right to act on behalf of victims; and (vi) the ability of human rights defenders to freely choose which human right issues to work on. A consensus on the text of the Declaration was required before the declaration could go to the Commission on Human Rights, the Economic and Social Council, and, finally, to the General Assembly.

Mireille Hector, *Protecting Human Rights Defenders: Analysis of the newly adopted Declaration on Human Rights Defenders* (January 1999), http://www.humanrightsfirst.org/defenders/hrd_un_declare/hrd_declare_1.htm.

The Declaration contains provisions about domestic law and about individual responsibility that were the subject of extensive negotiations in the working group. Article 3 states:

> Domestic law consistent with the Charter of the United Nations and other international obligations of the State in the field of human rights and fundamental freedoms is the juridical framework within which human rights and fundamental freedoms should be implemented and enjoyed and within which all activities referred to in the present Declaration for the promotion, protection and effective realization of those rights and freedoms should be conducted.

Article 17 further provides:

> In the exercise of the rights and freedoms referred to in the present Declaration, everyone, acting individually and in association with others, shall be subject only to such limitations as are in accordance with applicable international obligations and are determined by law solely for the purpose of securing due recognition and respect for the rights and freedoms of others and of meeting the just requirements of morality, public order and the general welfare in a democratic society.

Regarding these provisions, Mireille Hector further reported:

> Another contentious issue in the negotiations leading to the final Declaration was the role of national law in the implementation of the Declaration. In the Working Group, some States held the position that the rights in the Declaration would only be guaranteed insofar as they conform with national laws and regulations. NGOs and many governments opposed the inclusion of such a provi-

sion and argued that the application of the rights in the Declaration should not be subordinated to national legislation, which will differ from state to state and may restrict the rights of human rights defenders. Instead, national legislation should be brought into conformity with the international standard.

The Declaration does include a reference to the role of national law, but with an important safety clause; it states that in order to provide the "juridical framework" of implementation of the Declaration, domestic law must be "consistent with the Charter of the United Nations and other international obligations of the State in the field of human rights and fundamental freedoms." Many participants in the Working Group have argued that "international obligations" would cover all treaty based and customary law obligations of the State, as well as the human rights standards adopted within the United Nations system and by regional human rights bodies....

Also, it is important to see this provision in the context of other articles in the Declaration. As domestic law is feared to have a more restrictive approach to the rights of human rights defenders, it is particularly important to apply article 3 in accordance with the provision that deals with limitations on the exercise of rights. According to this provision, any limitation on the enjoyment of rights and freedoms has to be in accordance with international obligations and determined by the law solely for the purpose of: (a) securing due recognition and respect for the rights and freedoms of others, and (b) meeting the just requirements of morality, public order and the general welfare in a democratic society. Therefore, if a domestic law pertains to a limitation of a right in the Declaration, it needs to satisfy the above-mentioned criteria.

Mireille Hector, *Protecting Human Rights Defenders, supra.*

In 2000, the U.N. Commission on Human Rights established the mandate of the Special Representative of the Secretary-General on Human Rights Defenders (Special Representative). The Secretary General fulfilled the Commission's request and appointed Hina Jilani, a lawyer from Pakistan. Ms. Jilani, together with her sister and other women, had established the first women's law firm in Pakistan in 1981. Ms. Jilani's mandate has since been renewed twice, once in 2003, and again in 2006. The latter extension allowed the newly created Human Rights Council (HRC) to "review and, where necessary, improve and rationalize all mandates, mechanisms, functions and responsibilities of the Commission on Human Rights in order to maintain a system of special procedures, expert advice and a complaint procedure...."

The High Commissioner on Human Rights previously outlined the mandate of the Special Representative:

(a) To seek, receive, examine and respond to information on the situation and the rights of anyone, acting individually or in association with others, to promote and protect human rights and fundamental freedoms;

(b) To establish cooperation and conduct dialogue with Governments and other interested actors on the promotion and effective implementation of the Declaration;

(c) To recommend effective strategies better to protect human rights defenders and follow up on these recommendations....

Office of the High Commissioner for Human Rights, "Submission of allegations to the Special Representative of the Secretary-General on human rights defenders," http://www.unhchr.ch/html/menu2/7/b/mdefguide.htm.

The Special Representative's ability to respond to individual complaints, protecting the "rights of anyone, acting individually or in association with others" is of paramount importance to defenders, who are increasingly in great danger as they challenge sometimes terrifying State practices. The Special Representative receives information from various sources, which may include States, NGOs, U.N. agencies, the media, and individuals. If the information "falls within the mandate" of the Special Representative, the OHCHR staff helps the Special Representative validate the information. *Id.* The Special Representative then contacts the State that is in alleged violation of the human right(s), usually through an "Urgent Action" or "Allegation" letter. Urgent action must be taken for ongoing or pending violations, whereas an allegation letter will be sent if the violation is over, as in the death of a defender.

The Special Representative on Human Rights Defenders works with the Special Representative or Special Rapporteur responsible for the relevant country or theme. In both cases, the Special Representative asks the State "to take all appropriate action to investigate and address the alleged events and to communicate the results of its investigation and actions to the Special Representative."

The Special Representative gives the States an opportunity to respond as quickly as possible. This initial process should take no longer than several days for "the most serious and urgent cases." Governments are required to respond under the mandate of the Special Representative. However, States do not always consider themselves bound by the mandate, but with the increasing connectivity of the international community, such States are sometimes at least attempting to give the appearance of a respect for human rights.

If resources are available, the Special Representative follows up with the State, often conducting country visits. The Special Representative reports the country visits to the next session of the Human Rights Council. The victim's identity must be included in the communication with the State, so that the State can rectify or prevent the violation. However, the victims may request that their names be withheld from any subsequent publication, and the complainant need not be identified.

In addition to responding to individual complaints, the Special Representative compiles allegations and analyzes the result for patterns of violations, according to the mandate. The process goes one step further, as the Special Representative, Special Rapporteurs, and OHCHR staff devise methods to alleviate problem areas.

Report of the Special Representative of the Secretary-General on Human Rights Defenders
Hina Jilani
U.N. Doc. A/62/225 (13 August 2007)
http://ue.eu.int/uedocs/cmsUpload/GuidelinesDefenders.pdf

I. Introduction

The present report is the seventh annual report submitted to the General Assembly by the Special Representative of the Secretary-General on the situation of human rights defenders. It is submitted pursuant to General Assembly resolution 60/161.

This report focuses on the right to protest in the context of freedom of assembly....

III. Human rights defenders and the right to protest: interventions and positions of the Special Representative

A. Main trends

Between 2001 and 2006, approximately 200 (13 per cent) of the over 1,500 communications sent by the Special Representative dealt with the right to protest in the context of freedom of assembly. Communications on the right to protest were sent to 54 countries....

H. Protests linked to land rights and environmental claims

The Special Representative issued two press releases and sent some 25 cases to 15 countries regarding human rights defenders engaged in protests over land rights or environmental claims. The regions concerned by this kind of protests are Latin America and Asia. The highest number of communications on protests related to environmental issues and land rights were sent to China and Brazil.

As the Special Representative pointed out in her report to the Human Rights Council, "land rights and natural resources is an area where a large part of the defenders come from indigenous populations and minority groups. These populations are often working to secure their right to utilize and live on the land they consider to be theirs." Communications sent included cases of arrests, detentions, threats and, in some cases, killings of human rights defenders protesting over environmental issues and land rights.

In the report on her visit to Brazil, the Special Representative pointed out that violence against defenders "is committed in order to punish the leaders for their protest against illegal acquisition of land, or for their support of landless poor people occupying vacant and non-productive land." "Human rights defenders working for the preservation of the environment become even more vulnerable because of the remoteness of the areas in which they are active. It was reported that many defenders who denounce illegal logging and largescale fishing and those working to preserve wildlife habitats in the Amazon region and in the south and north-east regions of the country face attacks and threats against their lives."

In 2004 the Special Representative sent several communications to the Government of Chile concerning the matriarchal leader of a Mapuche community. Both the defender and members of her family had been victims of physical attacks because of her work to defend the human rights of her community and for protesting against illegal logging. In May 2004, the Mapuche leader, who was pregnant, was allegedly beaten by policemen, causing her to miscarry. In August and October 2006, communications were sent concerning the arrest of her son who has been charged under "anti-terrorism" legislation.

The criminalization of social movements working on land rights and environmental issues is another concern pointed out by the Special Representative on previous occasions, when she stated that "farmers have been prosecuted in anti-terrorist courts for protesting attempts by State security forces to evict them from land. Villagers demonstrating against mega-projects that threaten their environment and livelihood have been charged with conducting anti-State activities." ...

IV. Conclusions and recommendations

The right to protest is a fully fledged right and entails the enjoyment of a set of rights internationally recognized and reiterated in the Declaration on Human Rights Defenders....

Judiciaries have a particular role in the protection of the right to protest through interpretation and application of national laws that are conducive to the realization of the right to freedom of assembly, and by ensuring that human rights defenders are not penalized for using this right for the promotion and protection of human rights.

Questions and Discussion

1. *Value of U.N. efforts.* What value do you see in the Declaration on Human Rights Defenders and the investigative and reporting role of the Special Representative, given

the lack of effective, formal power to protect advocates and human rights defenders? Given the physical violence that is not uncommon toward human rights advocates, would you recommend that individuals or organizations rely on this mechanism in the absence of a broader, sophisticated campaign of protection? Would you recommend that they ignore the Declaration and the Special Representative entirely?

2. *Ms. Jilani's troubles.* During the state of emergency declared by General Pervez Musharraf of Pakistan in late 2007, the Punjabi government issued an order to place the Special Representative, Ms. Jilani, under house arrest. At the same time, her sister, Ms. Asma Jahangir, a human rights lawyer and United Nations Special Rapporteur on freedom of religion or belief, was put under house arrest. The 90 days preventive detention order (SO (IS-I)3-24/2007), was issued by the Home Department of the Government of Punjab, finding her activities to be "prejudicial to public safety and maintenance of public order" and to prevent her from making "inflammatory speeches."

3. *The Americas.* In June 1999, the General Assembly of the Organization of American States (OAS) adopted a resolution, "Human Rights Defenders in the Americas," stating the intention of governments to implement the U.N. Declaration on Human Rights Defenders. O.A.S. Doc. AG/RES. 1671 (XXIX-O/99). In June 2001, another OAS General Assembly resolution "urge[d] member states to step up their efforts to adopt the necessary measures, in keeping with their domestic law and with internationally accepted principles and standards, to guarantee the life, personal safety, and freedom of expression of human rights defenders." O.A.S. Doc. AG/RES. 1818 (XXXI-O/01). On June 4, 2002, the OAS General Assembly asked the Inter-American Commission on Human Rights to "continue to pay due attention to the situation of human rights defenders in the Americas and to consider, inter alia, preparing a comprehensive study on the matter and to give due consideration to this situation at the level it may judge appropriate and continue the dialogue and cooperation with the United Nations, in particular with the office of the Special Representative of the U.N. Secretary-General to Report on the Situation of Human Rights Defenders, through the Inter-American Commission on Human Rights and the Permanent Council." O.A.S. Doc. AG/RES. 1842 (XXXII-O/02).

B. European Union Guidelines

Ensuring Protection—European Union Guidelines on Human Rights Defenders
Council of the European Union
June 2004
http://ue.eu.int/uedocs/cmsUpload/GuidelinesDefenders.pdf

I. Purpose

1. Support for human rights defenders is already a long established element of the European Union's human rights external relations policy. The purpose of these Guidelines is to provide practical suggestions for enhancing EU action in relation to this issue. The Guidelines can be used in contacts with third countries at all levels as well as in multilateral human rights fora, in order to support and strengthen ongoing efforts by the Union to promote and encourage respect for the right to defend human rights. The Guidelines also provide for interventions by the Union for human rights defenders at risk and suggest practical means to support and assist human rights defenders. An important element of the Guidelines is support for the Special Procedures of the U.N. Commission on Human

Rights, including the U.N. Special Representative on Human Rights Defenders and appropriate regional mechanisms to protect human rights defenders. The Guidelines will assist EU Missions (Embassies and Consulates of EU Member States and European Commission Delegations) in their approach to human rights defenders.

II. Definition

3. Human rights defenders are those individuals, groups and organs of society that promote and protect universally recognised human rights and fundamental freedoms. Human rights defenders seek the promotion and protection of civil and political rights as well as the promotion, protection and realisation of economic, social and cultural rights. Human rights defenders also promote and protect the rights of members of groups such as indigenous communities. The definition does not include those individuals or groups who commit or propagate violence.

III. Introduction

4. ... Although the primary responsibility for the promotion and protection of human rights lies with states, the EU recognises that individuals, groups and organs of society all play important parts in furthering the cause of human rights. The activities of human rights defenders include:

- documenting violations;
- seeking remedies for victims of such violations through the provision of legal, psychological, medical or other support; and
- combating cultures of impunity which serve to cloak systematic and repeated breaches of human rights and fundamental freedoms.

5. The work of human rights defenders often involves criticism of government's policies and actions. However, governments should not see this as a negative.... Human rights defenders can assist governments in promoting and protecting human rights....

IV. Operational Guidelines

Monitoring, reporting and assessment

8. EU Heads of Mission are already requested to provide periodic reports on the human rights situation in their countries of accreditation.... Missions should address the situation of human rights defenders in their reporting, noting in particular the occurrence of any threats or attacks against human rights defenders....

Role of EU Missions in supporting and protecting human rights defenders

10. In many third countries EU Missions (Embassies of EU Member States and European Commission Delegations) are the primary interface between the Union and its Member States and human rights defenders on the ground.... EU Missions should therefore seek to adopt a proactive policy towards human rights defenders. They should at the same time be aware that in certain cases EU action could lead to threats or attacks against human rights defenders. They should therefore where appropriate consult with human rights defenders in relation to actions which might be contemplated. Measures that EU Missions could take include:

- co-ordinating closely and sharing information on human rights defenders, including those at risk;
- maintaining suitable contacts with human rights defenders, including by receiving them in Missions and visiting their areas of work, consideration could be given to appointing specific liaison officers, where necessary on a burden sharing basis, for this purpose;

- providing, as and where appropriate, visible recognition to human rights defenders, through the use of appropriate publicity, visits or invitations;

- attending and observing, where appropriate, trials of human rights defenders.

Promotion of respect for human rights defenders in relations with third countries and in multilateral fora

11. The EU's objective is to influence third countries to carry out their obligations to respect the rights of human rights defenders and to protect them from attacks and threats from non-state actors.... Actions in support of these objectives will include:

- where the Presidency, or the High Representative for the CFSP or EU Special Representatives and Envoys, or European Commission are making country visits they will, where appropriate, include meetings with, and raising individual cases of, human rights defenders as an integral part of their visits to third countries;

- the human rights component of political dialogues between the EU and third countries and regional organisations, will, where relevant, include the situation of human rights defenders. The EU will underline its support for human rights defenders and their work, and raise individual cases of concern whenever necessary....

Support for Special Procedures of the U.N. Commission on Human Rights, including the Special Representative on Human Rights Defenders

12. The EU recognises that the Special Procedures of the U.N. Commission on Human Rights (Special Rapporteurs, Special Representatives, Independent Experts and Working Groups) are vital to international efforts to protect human rights defenders because of their independence and impartiality; their ability to act and speak out on violations against human rights defenders worldwide and undertake country visits....

Practical supports for Human Rights Defenders including through Development Policy

13. Programmes of the European Community and Member States aimed at assisting in the development of democratic processes and institutions, and the promotion and protection of human rights in developing countries are among a wide range of practical supports for assisting human rights defenders.... Practical supports can include the following:

- ... the promotion and protection of human rights in developing countries by, inter alia, supporting human rights defenders through such activities as capacity building and public awareness campaigns; ...

- assisting in the establishment of networks of human rights defenders at an international level, including by facilitating meetings of human rights defenders;

- seeking to ensure that human rights defenders in third countries can access resources, including financial, from abroad....

Questions and Discussion

1. *Critical thinking.* Note that the Guidelines state that governments should not view criticism of their policies by their citizens in a negative manner. What does such a comment seek to achieve? Is it realistic?

2. *Audience and scope.* Who is the audience for these European Union Guidelines—countries around the world, EU governments, or the defenders themselves? Are the Guide-

lines worded in a manner that will force EU member states to comply? Or are they more likely to be used to "tilt the balance" during arguments between civil servants or policy-makers within those governments who favor helping defenders and those who do not? Can defenders in a developing country use these guidelines to persuade or shame an EU government into supporting their rights?

II. Criminal Charges against Advocates

The most extreme use of the legal system against environmental and other human rights advocates is the filing of criminal charges. Sometimes the charges involve standard criminal laws alleging corruption, murder, exposing state secrets, and the like. At other times, special legislation is used that is specifically intended to limit the range of expression and advocacy in a country. Such special legislation includes punishing "criminal sedition," "criminal libel," and instigating "insult or contempt" toward a government or a president of a country.

A. Treason and Disclosure of Official Secrets

Nikitin v. Russia

European Court of Human Rights
No. 50178/99, ECHR 2004-VIII, 41 E.H.R.R. 10 (2004)

THE FACTS

I. The circumstances of the case

In February 1995, the applicant, a former naval officer, joined the environmental project of a Norwegian non-governmental organisation, "Bellona," to work on a report entitled "The Russian Northern Fleet—Sources of Radioactive Contamination".... On October 5, 1995 the Murmansk office of Bellona was searched by the Federal Security Service ("the FSB"). The FSB seized the draft report, interrogated the applicant and instituted criminal proceedings on suspicion of treason, as the draft report allegedly contained information about accidents on Russian nuclear submarines classified as officially secret....

[After various decisions and appeals] ... the Supreme Court of the Russian Federation upheld the [applicant's] acquittal. The Court found the charges based on secret and retroactive acts incompatible with the Constitution....

On May 30, 2000, the Prosecutor General lodged a request with the Presidium of the Supreme Court to review the case ... On September 13, 2000, the Presidium of the Supreme Court dismissed the prosecutor's request and upheld the acquittal....

On July 17, 2002, the Constitutional Court of the Russian Federation examined the applicant's challenge to the laws which allow supervisory review of a final acquittal. In its ruling of the same date, the Constitutional Court declared incompatible with the Constitution the legislative provisions permitting the re-examination and quashing of an acquittal on the grounds of a prejudicial or incomplete investigation or court hearing, or on the grounds of a wrong assessment of the facts of the case, save in cases where there had been new evidence or a fundamental defect in the previous proceedings....

II. Relevant domestic law

A. Applicable legislation

Section VI, Ch. 30, of the Code of Criminal Procedure 1960, in force at the material time, allowed certain officials to challenge a judgment which had entered into force and to have the case reviewed on points of law and procedure....

1. Entry into force of a judgment

Pursuant to Art. 356 of the Code of Criminal Procedure, a judgment enters into force and is subject to execution as of the day when the appeal (cassation) instance pronounces its judgment or, if it has not been appealed against, when the time-limit for appeal has expired....

5. The effect of a supervisory review on acquittal

According to Arts. 374, 378 and 380 of the Code of Criminal Procedure, the request for supervisory review was to be considered by the judicial board (the Presidium) of the competent court. The Court could examine the case on the merits, and was not bound by the scope and grounds of the extraordinary appeal....

On July 1, 2002, a new Code of Criminal Procedure entered into force. According to its Art. 405, the application of supervisory review is limited to the cases where it does not involve changes to the detriment of the convicted person. The acquittals and decisions to terminate prosecution cannot be the subject of a supervisory review....

JUDGMENT

I. Alleged violation of Article 4 of Protocol No. 7 to the Convention

The applicant contends that the supervisory review proceedings which took place after his final acquittal constituted a violation of his right not to be tried again in criminal proceedings for an offence of which he had been finally acquitted.... He invokes Art. 4 of Protocol No. 7 to the Convention which, in so far as relevant, provides:

1. No one shall be liable to be tried or punished again in criminal proceedings under the jurisdiction of the same State for an offence for which he has already been finally acquitted or convicted in accordance with the law and penal procedure of that State.

2. The provisions of the preceding paragraph shall not prevent the reopening of the case in accordance with the law and penal procedure of the State concerned, if there is evidence of new or newly discovered facts, or if there has been a fundamental defect in the previous proceedings, which could affect the outcome of the case.

A. The parties' submissions

The Government considers that, for the purposes of Art. 4 of Protocol No. 7, the supervisory review proceedings did not constitute a second trial ...

The applicant contests the Government's position and submits that ... [a]lthough the outcome remained unchanged, he was effectively prosecuted twice for the same offence....

B. The Court's assessment

The Court notes that the protection against duplication of criminal proceedings is one of the specific safeguards associated with the general guarantee of a fair hearing in criminal proceedings. It recalls that the aim of Art. 4 of Protocol No. 7 is to prohibit the repetition of criminal proceedings that have been concluded by a final decision....

1. Whether the applicant had been "finally acquitted" prior to the supervisory review

Protocol No. 7 to the Convention, which itself refers back to the European Convention on the International Validity of Criminal Judgments, a "decision is final if, according to the traditional expression, it has acquired the force of *res judicata*. This is the case when it is irrevocable...."

The Court has ... found that the quashing of a judgment on supervisory review can create problems as to the legal certainty to be afforded to the initial judgment. [See *Brumărescu v. Romania* [GC]: (2001) 33 E.H.R.R. 35 at [62]; *Ryabykh v. Russia*: (2005) 40 E.H.R.R. 25 at [56]–[58]] ...

   2.   Whether the applicant was "tried again" in the proceedings before the Presidium

[T]he Presidium did not accept the application for review, and the final decision remained that of April 17, 2000.

It follows that the applicant was not "tried again" within the meaning of Art. 4(1) of Protocol No. 7 of the Convention in the proceedings by which the Presidium of the Supreme Court rejected the Prosecutor General's request for supervisory review of the applicant's acquittal.

   3.   Whether the applicant was "liable to be tried again"

The Court has next considered whether the applicant was "liable to be tried again," as he alleges.... Importantly, the Presidium was not empowered to make a new determination on the merits in the same proceedings, but merely to decide whether to grant the Prosecutor General's request or not....

[T]he crucial point in this case is that supervisory review could not in any event have given rise to a duplication of criminal proceedings, within the meaning of Art. 4(1) of Protocol No. 7, for the following reasons.

The Court observes that Art. 4 of Protocol No. 7 draws a clear distinction between a second prosecution or trial which is prohibited by the first paragraph of this Article, and the resumption of a trial in exceptional circumstances, which is provided for in its second paragraph. Article 4(2) of Protocol No. 7 expressly envisages the possibility that an individual may have to accept, in accordance with domestic law, prosecution on the same counts where a case is reopened following the emergence of new evidence or the discovery of a fundamental defect in the previous proceedings....

II. Alleged violation of Article 6(1) of the Convention

The applicant maintains that the supervisory review proceedings conducted after his final acquittal constituted a violation of his right to a fair trial. He invokes Art. 6(1) of the Convention which, in so far as relevant, provides:

> In the determination of ... any criminal charge against him, everyone is entitled to a fair ... hearing ... by [a] ... tribunal....

A. The parties' submissions

In its post-admissibility submissions, the Government states that the supervisory review proceedings did not constitute a new examination of the applicant's criminal charge because the request to quash the acquittal lodged by the Prosecutor General was dismissed by the Presidium of the Supreme Court without entering into the merits.... It also claims that, since the supervisory review proceedings had no negative impact on the applicant's final acquittal, they cannot constitute a violation of the applicant's right to a fair hearing within the meaning of Art. 6(1)....

The applicant, on the contrary, maintains that the very possibility to challenge the final and enforceable acquittal violates his right to a fair trial. He states that, although the supervisory review complied with the formal requirements imposed by law at the material time, it was not necessary. He claims that, in the circumstances of the case, the prosecutor's call for supervisory review proceedings was clearly abusive and incompatible with the Convention principles.

B. The Court's assessment

[T]he Court recalls that it has previously held that the institution of supervisory review can give rise to problems of legal certainty....

The Court, moreover, observes that the requirements of legal certainty are not absolute. In criminal cases, they must be read in conjunction with, for example, Art. 4(2) of Protocol No. 7 which expressly permits a state to reopen a case due to the emergence of new facts, or where a fundamental defect is detected in the previous proceedings, which could affect the outcome of the case....

A mere possibility to reopen a criminal case is therefore *prima facie* compatible with the Convention, including the guarantees of Art. 6.... the Court has to assess whether, in a given case, the power to launch and conduct supervisory review was exercised by the authorities so as to strike, to the maximum extent possible, a fair balance between the interests of the individual and the need to ensure the effectiveness of the system of criminal justice.

The prosecutor's request could itself be criticised as being arbitrary and abusive. However, it had no decisive impact on the fairness of the procedure for reopening as a whole....

As for the proceedings before the Presidium of the Supreme Court, their outcome was favourable for the applicant and therefore, in respect of these proceedings, he cannot claim to be a victim of violation of his right to fair hearing. Moreover, according to the established case law of the Convention organs, Art.6 does not apply to proceedings concerning a failed request to reopen a case. Only the new proceedings, after the reopening has been granted, can be regarded as concerning the determination of a criminal charge. [See, *inter alia*, App. No.7761/77, *X v. Austria*, Comm. Dec. 08.05.1978; App. No. 24469/94, *José Maria Ruiz Mateos v. Spain*, Comm. Dec. 02.12.1994].

Accordingly, the Court finds no violation of Art. 6(1) of the Convention.

Questions and Discussion

1. *Secret, retroactive laws.* Nikitin was convicted on the basis of secret laws that were passed *after* he disclosed information about radioactive contamination. Note that the Supreme Court of Russia ruled such laws to be unconstitutional.

2. *Reasons for appeal and decision.* After winning in the Supreme Court and Constitutional Court of Russia and after the legislation was changed, why would Nikitin continue his appeal to the European Court of Human Rights? If the European Court took note of all that, why would it nonetheless express its opinion on the issues of retroactivity?

3. *Precedent.* Is the European Court correct in finding that the applicant's right to a fair hearing was not impaired? Does the fact that the Presidium of the Russian Supreme Court ruled in his favor eliminate the potential for abuse in the future?

4. *New legislation.* The Constitutional Court of Russia declared the legislation allowing supervisory proceedings to be incompatible with the Russian Constitution. Why does the Government use that as support for its position? Does the existence of a new law that disallows the government from bringing supervisory proceedings for parties who are acquitted in future criminal cases eliminate the circumstances in the instant case?

5. *Official secrets laws.* Many countries have laws prohibiting citizens or news media from publishing "official secrets." On the other hand, the U.S. Supreme Court ruled unconstitutional an attempt by the U.S. Government to prevent publication of the "Pentagon Papers," a secret history of the Vietnam War that the New York Times had acquired from an unknown government informant. *New York Times v. Sullivan*, 403 U.S. 714 (1970).

B. Sedition

In April 2001, the Barrick Gold Corporation (Canada) started operating the Bulyanhulu mine under a subsidiary, the Kahama Mining Corporation. A consortium of commercial banks, the World Bank's Multilateral Investment Guarantee Agency (MIGA), and Canada's Export Development Corporation (EDC) provided $345 million in political risk guarantees.

Although small-scale (so-called artisanal) miners had discovered gold at Bulyanhulu in 1975, in 1996 the Tanzanian government ordered the artisanal miners to vacate the area. Another company, Sutton Resources (later bought by Barrick Gold), sued the miners, allegedly claiming they were illegal squatters. Sutton lost in the High Court of Tanzania. However, the Tanzanian government ordered the artisanal miners out. According to Tanzanian environmental attorney Tundu Lissu:

> Within days, serious allegations of a massacre of artisanal miners hit the press. The miners were allegedly trapped inside the mineshafts when the company and administration officials decided to bulldoze the shafts to make them inoperable by miners who continued to sneak in at night. These allegations were vehemently denied by the government, the companies, the World Bank/MIGA, and the Canadian authorities, but have dogged the Bulyanhulu Gold Mine ever since.

Tundu A. M. Lissu, *Tanzania: Human Rights Advocacy and the Bulyanhulu Gold Mine*, available at http://www.eli.org/pdf/advocacytoolscasestudies/casestudy.tanzania.final.pdf.

The Lawyers' Environmental Action Team (LEAT) took up the cause. LEAT published an open letter to the President of Tanzania on the same day that the President officially opened the mine in July 2001, calling for an investigation. http://www.leat.or.tz/about/pr/2001.07.16.president.letter.php. In November 2001, police raided the LEAT office and also searched the homes of two LEAT lawyers. In May 2002, the Tanzanian government filed criminal charges against two of the LEAT lawyers, including charges of criminal sedition. The government charged Rugemeleza Nshala with "Statement of Offence Publishing Words with a Seditious Intention, contrary to Section 31(1)(a) and 32(1)(c) of the Newspapers Act No. 3 of 1976." Tanzania charged Tundu Lissu with "Uttering Words with Seditious Intention," contrary to Section 31(1)(a) and 32(1)(b) of the Newspapers Act No. 3 of 1976. LEAT, *Statement of Charges Against Rugemeleza Nshala and Tundu Lissu*, available at http://www.leat.or.tz/activities/buly/sedition.charges.php. The chairman of the opposition Democratic Party (DP), Rev. Christopher Mtikila, was also charged with uttering "seditious words with intention to bring into contempt and excite dissatisfaction against lawful authorities" and with the reproduction and distribution of "seditious publications."

A coalition of NGOs, journalists, and academics traveled to Tanzania in 2002 to investigate the claims of artisanal miners being buried alive, but were prevented from traveling to the mine area. A few villagers did manage to come to meet with them. The team came to the conclusion that "an independent, impartial, transparent and comprehensive inquiry into the allegations of uncompensated mass evictions of miners and mine owners, and killings of miners at Bulyanhulu during the summer of 1996, is warranted, desirable and urgent." Mining Watch, *Report of the International NGO Fact-finding Mission to Tanzania*, April 16, 2002, available at http://www.miningwatch.ca/index.php?/Tanzania_en/Report_of_the_Intern.

After being requested by LEAT to investigate, the Compliance Advisor/Ombudsman (CAO) for the Multilateral Investment Guarantee Agency and the International Finance Corporation, however, did not find reason to continue its investigation, closing its file in October 2002. (The CAO report is discussed in Chapter 10 of this book on International Financial Institutions, at page 477.)

Two weeks after arriving back in Tanzania from a trip abroad, and after a visit to the Bulyanhulu area to gather evidence, Tundu Lissu was arrested, spent the night in jail, and a week later sent the following message to environmental law colleagues around the world.

View from the Accused

E-mail from Tundu Lissu

Date: Mon, 30 Dec 2002
From: Lawyers' Environmental Action Team — LEAT

Hi friends,

It's quite a week ... What a time to get arrested as all the big guns at LEAT were out of town on holidays.... On the way [to police headquarters] I called my attorney ... who soon turned up at the police HQ with all the righteous rage appropriate for the occasion! You've to bear in mind that I was arrested without probable cause, i.e., no warrant duly signed by a magistrate, and of course I was not committing or about to commit any criminal offense when I got out of my house that morning. All the protestations of the illegality of my arrest by my attorney did not go down well with the officers who made us wait for over five long hours while their superiors consulted on what to do with me. They ultimately decided that I'd be taken to the Central Police Station in town for "safe-keeping" as one officer described my impending incarceration.

Central Police Station in Dar has an underground jailhouse infamously known as "The Hole." ... The Hole is not the kind of place one wants to find oneself in. It's a veritable oven, and hell itself could not stink worse on account of there not being any running water to wash out the inevitable by-products of living humans. It also has some of the biggest and fattest mosquitoes I've ever seen and, since one can hardly keep one's clothes on given the elements, the accursed vermin enjoy unfettered access to their harassed prey! ...

Cash is king inside The Hole. With some you can enjoy all the amenities of life under the circumstances, including three meals a day instead of one served at about midday each day. You can also spend the night outside The Hole as there are better quarters elsewhere in the police building but for a price and when senior officers have already gone home for the night! You can therefore be sure that the 30-plus inmates who spent the night with me inside The Hole were all from the lowest rungs of the Tanzanian society, those evidently forced into petty crime by want.... I spent a good deal of the night being entertained by their hilarious tales of trying to survive in the down and out situation they all find themselves in — almost all of them were accused of committing the pettiest of crimes....

I was by no means a lumpen proletarian but then my circumstances were rather different, which meant I was treated with some kind of awe, if not hostile respect, by the officers. Apparently, the Director of Criminal Investigations ... had issued clear and firm orders that I'd not be ill-treated and should be presented to court first thing the next day.... On Tuesday morning I was taken to court and after charges were read to me and an appropriate plea of not guilty entered, I was granted bail and immediately driven out of the court precincts to some "safe-house," there having been rumours that I'd be rearrested outside the court building. Thank goodness the rumours proved false.

So I'm out on bail together with Rugemeleza and Augustine Mrema of the opposition Labour Party. The case comes up for mention January 6 next year. You may remember that this case was months ago referred to the High Court of Tanzania for a ruling on the constitutionality of the sedition law under which we're charged....

We, Vincent Shauri and I, will be in Maputo, Mozambique, for the World Bank's Extractive Industries Review meeting for the Africa Region between January 13–17. Bulyanhulu has been placed on the order of the day as one of the case studies.... I'm reliably informed that we're going to be meeting face to face with the Bank and MIGA bureaucrats, Barrick Gold's operatives, and the CAO team that threw mud at us a couple of months ago. I cannot wait for the inevitable showdown with them! We've asked that we be allowed to bring 3 representatives from the Bulyanhulu community who were directly affected by the events of August '96....

In a related matter, Vincent and I spent about three days at Bulyanhulu a week before I was arrested. We're able to get more affidavits from the witnesses of the '96 events as well as to get additional testimony from eyewitnesses which we videotaped. For me it was a dream-come-true as I was able to finally get to talk to Mr. Mustafa Taslima whose tragic and heart-breaking story some of you may know already. He lies bedridden—for the third year in a row now—suffering from the effects of a brutal beating meted out to him by paramilitary police officers when he went looking for his sons Ibrahim and Hamdani in what had turned into the killing fields of Bulyanhulu that fateful August '96. He can neither sit nor stand, his ankles, knees and back having been targets of choice for the gun-toting and baton-wielding paramilitaries. And, even at over seventy and in his terribly emaciated state, he still breaks down sobbing when he narrates what happened then. I videotaped that interview too. We shall be sending the affidavits as well as the other material to friends in Europe and North America as soon as the videotapes are ready....

Tundu

Environment Lawyer in Court

Alloyce Komba
The Guardian (Tanzania) (December 25, 2002)

The third accused person in the sedition case on uttering of alleged killings of Bulyanhulu small scale miners in Kahama, Shinyanga Region, in 1996, Tundu Anthipas Lissu, yesterday appeared before Principal Resident Magistrate Samuel Karua at Kisutu in Dar es Salaam.

Lissu, a human rights activist, environmental lawyer and member of Lawyers' Environmental Action Team (LEAT) was arrested on Monday morning at his residence in Tegeta, Dar es Salaam and kept under custody at Central Police Station following his arrival from United States of America two weeks ago.

Other accused persons in the case, Criminal Case No.374 of 2002, who appeared for the first time on April 25, 2002, are Chairman of opposition political party, Tanzania Labour Party (TLP), Augustine Mrema and LEAT Executive Director, Rugemeleza Nshala, who are listed as first and the second accused person respectively.

The prosecution represented by Assistant Superintendent of Police Willy Mlulu told the fully packed magistrate's chamber that Lissu was joined in the four-count charge sheet as the third accused in the fourth count of "uttering words with seditious intention" contrary to the Newspaper Act No. 3 of 1976.

ASP Mlulu read particulars of the charge which alleged that on the 19th day of November 2001 ... with intention to bring into contempt or to excite disaffection against the lawful authority of the United Republic or the Government thereof did utter [certain] words [in the Kiswahili language].... The words literally meant that the Bulyanhulu mining project had for five years been embroiled in serious allegations of killings of small scale miners by the Police Force, the Government and Canadian mining companies and that there was evidence of people having been buried or covered in pits. That there are pictures (video) showing dead bodies being exhumed from the pits and being eaten by dogs.

Lissu pleaded not guilty to the charge. His defence counsel, Melkizedeck Lutema, applied for bail which the magistrate granted as there was no objection from the prosecution.

The Court issued the same bail conditions as were imposed on the first and the second accused persons. The conditions stipulate that the accused was to have three sureties with immovable properties who were to sign a [one million Tanzanian shillings] bond each....

Questions and Discussion

1. *Sedition charges.* As of 2008, the criminal sedition charges were still pending, but the case seemed to be on the back burner.

2. *Colonial influences.* One scholar recently noted:

> Across common law Africa, sedition, criminal libel, and other such laws enacted by authoritarian regimes for purposes of political repression remain on the books. Some of these laws date as far back as the colonial period. This state of affairs arises from the continued recourse to the practice, first used in the transition from colonialism to sovereign statehood, of inserting a "savings" clause in each new constitution to hold over and presume valid all laws from the old regime until they are challenged and found unconstitutional on a case-by-case basis.

H. Kwasi Prempeh, *Marbury in Africa: Judicial Review and the Challenge of Constitutionalism in Contemporary Africa*, 80 Tul. L. Rev. 1239, 1297–1298 (2006).

3. *Sedition in U.S. law.* A law against seditious utterances was passed by the U.S. Congress just a few years after adoption of the U.S. Constitution. As explained by one scholar, the Sedition Act was

> enacted in 1798 to insulate the Federalist administration of John Adams from criticism by the Republican supporters of Thomas Jefferson. The Act made it a crime to publish "any false, scandalous and malicious writing" against the government, Congress, or President of the United States, "with intent to defame [them] or to bring them ... into contempt or disrepute; or to excite against them ... the hatred of the good people of the United States." [1 Stat. 596, 2

(1798)] In concessions to libertarian doctrine, the Act made truth a defense and provided that the jury should have power to determine both law and fact.

Nevertheless, the Act was soon denounced as unconstitutional by the Republican-dominated legislatures of Kentucky and Virginia. In a report on behalf of the Virginia Resolutions, James Madison set forth the Republican case.... Madison ... traced the difference between the two conceptions to the "essential difference between the British Government and the American Constitutions." In Great Britain, the protections of the Magna Carta and Bill of Rights were aimed only at the king, while the people's representatives in the legislature were regarded as unlimited in their power and "sufficient guardians of the rights of their constituents." "Under such a government as this," Madison reasoned, "an exemption of the press from previous restraint, by licensors appointed by the king, is all the freedom that can be secured to it." In America, by contrast, the people's rights were secured not merely by laws but by constitutions, and were protected against violation by the legislature as well as the executive. It followed that in America the liberty of the press was protected not merely against prior restraint by executive officials, but also against subsequent punishment under legislative enactments.

Steven J. Heyman, *Righting the Balance: An Inquiry into the Foundations and Limits of Freedom of Expression*, 78 B.U.L. Rev. 1275, 1292–1293 (1998).

C. Insult and Defamation

1. Insult

The Dutch and Portuguese colonized Indonesia starting in the early 1500s. They left behind laws that have been used by various Indonesian governments to limit dissent on human rights, environmental, and political matters. The Constitutional Court of Indonesia has recently examined these laws. As reported by Amnesty International:

> On 6 December 2006, the Constitutional Court voted to scrap Articles 134, 136 and 137 of the country's Criminal Code (*Kitab Undang-undang Hukum Pidana*, KUHP) which punished "insulting the President or Vice-President" with up to six years' imprisonment.

Amnesty International News Service No: 318 (December 8, 2006). Other provisions of the law that provide penalties for expressing "feelings of hostility, hatred or contempt towards the Indonesian Government in public" were ruled unconstitutional in the following case.

Dr. R. Panji Utomo, Petitioner (Indonesia)
Constitutional Court of the Republic Of Indonesia
Decision No. 6/PUU-V/2007 (17 July 2007)

For the Sake of Justice under the One Almighty God

3. Legal Considerations

[a.] *Legal Standing of the Petitioner*

Considering whereas in petitions for judicial review of laws against the 1945 Constitution, for the legal standing of an individual or a party to be accepted as a Petitioner before the Court, Article 51 Paragraph (1) of the Constitutional Court Law provides that the Petitioners shall be the parties which deem that their constitutional rights and/or authority are impaired by the coming into effect of a law....

Considering whereas the Petitioner, Dr. R. Panji Utomo, is an Indonesian citizen who has been tried and convicted with 3-month imprisonment based on the Decision of Banda Aceh Court of First Instance Number 232/Pid.B/2006/PN-BNA dated December 18, 2006 because he is proven to have committed a criminal offense as regulated in Articles 154 and 155 of the Indonesian Criminal Code. In respect of the Decision of the Court, the Petitioner does not attempt for an appeal and hence the Decision has had binding legal force (*inkracht van gewijsde*)....

Considering whereas the constitutional rights of the Petitioner granted by the 1945 Constitution as specifically and actually deemed impaired by the Petitioner due to the coming into effect of Article 154 and Article 155 of the Indonesian Criminal Code, are the rights to legal certainty and freedom of expression, as regulated in Article 28, Article 28D Paragraph (1), and Article 28E Paragraph (2) and Paragraph (3) of the 1945 Constitution....

[b.] *Principal Issue of the Petition ...*

[T]he Court will only consider the principal issue of the petition for a review of the constitutionality of legal norms contained in Articles 154 and 155 of the Indonesian Criminal Code which respectively read as follows:

Article 154 of the Indonesian Criminal Code reads:

Whosoever declares feelings of hostility, hatred or contempt towards the Indonesian Government in public, shall be subject to a maximum imprisonment of seven years or a maximum fine of four thousand five hundred rupiah,

Article 155 of the Indonesian Criminal Code reads:

Whosoever broadcasts, presents or attaches writings or drawings in public containing statements of feelings of hostility, hatred or contempt towards the Indonesian Government, in the intention of publicly declaring their contents, shall be subject to a maximum imprisonment of four years and six months or a maximum fine of four thousand five hundred rupiah....

[T]he Court is of the following opinion: ...

The primary element or characteristic of a constitutional state is constitutionalism which demands the constitution, *in casu* the 1945 Constitution, be truly realized and enforced in practice.... Therefore, a law shall not be contrary to the 1945 Constitution.... In addition, a constitutional state is also characterized by the guaranteed protection of the human rights.... Therefore, one of the reasons which may cause a law to be declared contrary to the constitution, *in casu* the 1945 Constitution, is that the intended law violates the human rights which ... are included in the definition of constitutional rights of citizens; ...

Considering whereas one of the main arguments of the Petitioner in the petition for judicial review of Articles 154 and 155 of the Indonesian Criminal Code is based on the historical review where the Indonesian Criminal Code is a product of Dutch colonial rule, namely the *Wetboek van Strafrecht voor Nederlandsch-Indie* (*Staatsblad* 1915 Number 732), and hence no longer conforms to the spirit of the state of Indonesia as an independent state as well as a democratic constitutional state....

Following the independence of Indonesia, the *Wetboek van Strafrecht voor Nederlandsch-Indie* was put into effect based on the provision of Article II of the Transitional Provision to the 1945 Constitution ... which reads, "All laws which are still in existence shall remain applicable insofar as there are no new laws according to this Constitution." ... [T]he *Wetboek van Strafrecht voor Nederlandsch-Indie* was affirmed by Law Number 1 Year 1946 regarding Criminal Code Regulation.... [H]ence there are two governing penal laws in Indonesia....

Both penal laws were actually derived from the same source, namely the *Wetboek van Strafrecht* of the Netherlands which was subsequently, based on the principle of concordance, put into effect in Netherlands East Indies since 1918 under the name of *Wetboek van Strafrecht voor Nederlandsch-Indie* toward all social classes (*unificatie*), namely the Natives, foreign Orientals, and the Europeans, each group being previously governed by its own Criminal Code....

[I]t is vital to observe the provision of Article V of the Law Number 1 Year 1946 which reads, "Penal provisions which are presently entirely or in part, unenforceable or *contrary to the position of the Republic of Indonesia as an independent state* or which no longer bear any meaning, must be deemed invalid in its entirety or in part." In other words, since 1946 the legislators had in fact been aware that there were provisions in the Criminal Code which could no longer be applied because they no longer conformed to the position of the Republic of Indonesia as an independent state....

[T]he formulation of the two criminal articles may allow power abuse to occur because they may be easily interpreted according to the will of the authority. A citizen whose intention was to express his criticism or opinion against the Government, which is a constitutional right guaranteed by the 1945 Constitution, would be easily qualified by the authority as expressing a statement of "feelings of hostility, hatred and contempt" towards the Government as a result of the lack of certainty of the criteria in the formulation of both Articles 154 and 155 of the Indonesian Criminal Code to distinguish between criticism or opinion and the feelings of hostility, hatred and contempt....

Articles 154 and 155 of the Indonesian Criminal Code may also be said as irrational, because it is impossible for a citizen of an independent and sovereign state to hold contempt towards his own independent and sovereign state and government, except in the case of subversive acts.... In the *Wetboek van Strafrecht* of the Netherlands itself, as previously mentioned to be the source of the Indonesian Criminal Code, there is no such provision as formulated in Articles 154 and 155 of the Indonesian Criminal Code.

In fact, when the idea to include such provision in the Criminal Code of the Netherlands in the 19th Century emerged, the incumbent Minister of Justice of the Netherlands explicitly expressed his refusal against such an idea by stating, "The regulation below, is automatically declared as applicable for the needs of the colonized society; it is clearly not intended for European states." ...

History shows that the provisions in Articles 154 and 155 of the Indonesian Criminal Code were adopted by the colonial government of the Netherlands East Indies from Article 124a of the British Indian Penal Code Year 1915.... Hence, it is evident that Articles 154 and 155 of the Indonesian Criminal Code, according to its history, were indeed intended to snare prominent figures of the independence movement in the Netherlands East Indies (Indonesia), so that it is also evident that both provisions are contrary to the position of Indonesia as an independent and sovereign state, as intended in Article V of Law Number 1 Year 1946 regarding the Penal Law Regulations.

[T]he Court has also declared its stand in the Review of Articles 134, Article 136 bis, and Article 137 of the Indonesian Criminal Code, as reflected in Decision Number 013-022/PUUIV/ 2006.

In the legal considerations of the intended decision, it is stated that, among other things,

> Indonesia as a democratic constitutional state in the form of a republic, the sovereignty of which is held by its people, and that highly respects human rights as stated in the 1945 Constitution, it is not relevant to have articles such as Article 134, Article 136 bis, and Article 137 in its Criminal Code that negate the principle of equality before the law and decrease the freedom to express ideas and opinions, the freedom to obtain information, and the principle of legal certainty. Therefore, the Draft Indonesian Criminal Code constituting an effort to reform the Indonesian Criminal Code colonially inherited must not contain any articles the provisions of which are identical or similar to Article 134, Article 136 bis, and Article 137 of the Indonesian Criminal Code;

It shows that there has been a change and simultaneously a renewal of the politics of the penal law towards an offence formulation which is not contrary to the spirit of realizing Indonesia as a democratic constitutional state and a democratic state based on the law which is the spirit (*geist*) of the 1945 Constitution.

4. Concluding Opinion

Based on all of the above, it is clear to the Court that the provisions of Articles 154 and 155 of the Indonesian Criminal Code, on the one hand, do not guarantee legal certainty and hence are contrary to Article 28D Paragraph (1) of the 1945 Constitution, on the other hand, as a consequence, disproportionally hinder the freedom to express thoughts and the freedom to express opinions and hence are contrary to Articles 28 and 28E Paragraph (2) and Paragraph (3) of the 1945 Constitution. Therefore, the Petitioner's argument insofar as it relates to the contradiction between Articles 154 and 155 of the Indonesian Criminal Code and Article 28 and 28E Paragraph (2) and Paragraph (3) of the 1945 Constitution must be declared as grounded....

5. Rulings

Passing the Decision:

To grant the petition of the Petitioner in part;

To declare that Article 154 and Article 155 of the Indonesian Criminal Code are contradictory to the 1945 Constitution of the Republic of Indonesia;

To declare that Article 154 and Article 155 of the Indonesian Criminal Code have no binding legal effect; ...

To order the proper promulgation of this decision in the Official Gazette of the Republic of Indonesia....

CHIEF JUSTICE, Jimly Asshiddiqie, JUSTICES, Harjono, I Dewa Gede Palguna, H.A.S Natabaya, H. M Laica Marzuki, Soedarsono, H. Abdul Mukthie Fadjar, H. Achmad Roestandi, Maruarar Siahaan

Questions and Discussion

1. *Comparing laws.* Note how the Court used comparative law techniques, by observing that the Netherlands itself no longer has in its law a provision similar to the one that was left behind in the code for its former colony, Indonesia. Note also how the Court traced the history of the provision from the British Indian Penal Code Year 1915 and observed that the Supreme Court of India had ruled the provision unconstitutional as interfering with freedom of expression in the Constitution of India.

2. *Politics.* The Court's previous December 2006 decision on Articles 134, 136, and 137 of the Criminal Code had been rendered by a 5–4 vote. In this later case, the vote was unanimous. The Court noted that the Government had informed it that a new draft of the Criminal Code would modify Articles 154 and 155 of the Indonesian Criminal Code. Might this have made it politically easier for the Court to rule the current articles unconstitutional?

It's a Crime: How Insult Laws Stifle Press Freedom
Marilyn J. Greene
World Press Freedom Committee (2007)
http://www.wpfc.org/site/docs/pdf/It's_A_Crime.pdf

The good news is … that progress has begun in several countries, either through absolute repeal of insult and criminal defamation laws, or at least in removing imprisonment as a penalty. Reforms have been contemplated or completed in Argentina, Bosnia-Herzegovina, Chile, Costa Rica, Ghana, Kenya, Panama, Paraguay, Slovakia, South Africa and Sri Lanka. Romania, unfathomably, was reversing its decision to decriminalize defamation in early 2007.

Directives stating that such laws should be repealed or reformed abound. International human rights experts from the OSCE (Organization for Security and Cooperation in Europe), the Council of Europe, the United Nations and the Organization of American States have repeatedly stressed that insult and criminal defamation laws are an infringement on freedom of expression and should be replaced with appropriate civil laws....

The notions behind "insult laws" are so vague and subject to broad interpretation that the laws themselves become convenient vehicles for use by authoritarian leaders and governments to silence questions and criticism. Insult can be found against a monarch, a flag or other national symbol, a religion or race, or against someone's honor and dignity. The fact that such laws exist in democracies is no excuse. They remain as models—excuses—for other nations wanting to continue using such laws energetically.

2. Defamation

A study for a Council of Europe committee concerning criminal liability for defamation or similar offenses in Europe found that 42 countries—from Albania and Austria to the United Kingdom—have provisions making defamation a criminal offense in some instances. In several countries, truth is not a defense to a prosecution. Furthermore, criticism of governments or officials is often treated more harshly than criticisms of private persons, contrary to the position taken by the European Court of Human Rights nearly two decades ago:

> [T]he limits of permissible criticism are wider with regard to the Government than in relation to a private citizen, or even a politician. In a democratic system the actions or omissions of the Government must be subject to the close scrutiny not only of the legislative and judicial authorities but also of the press and public opinion.

Castells v. Spain, Application No. 11798/85, judgment of 23 April 1992, Series A no. 236 (Eur. Ct. H.R.), 14 EHRR 445 (1992).

According to the study mentioned above, defamation had been decriminalized in Bosnia and Herzegovina, Cyprus, Georgia, and Ukraine. As for other countries:

In all, it would appear that about half of the Council of Europe member states have taken concrete action or are considering steps to either decriminalise defamation or alleviate the sanctions that can be imposed in its respect....

In practice, the vast majority of Council of Europe member states do not apply criminal sanctions for defamation. In some countries it is stipulated that recourse to criminal law provisions for defamation only be had if remedies are not suitable. However, in several Council of Europe member states, criminal charges continue regularly to be brought for defamation, in particular against journalists, and a few countries continue to imprison media professionals.

In some countries, including in those that have decriminalised defamation, journalists appear often to be confronted with civil litigation which, in certain cases, results in the award of very high or disproportionate damages....

Secretariat, Steering Committee on the Media and New Communication Services, *Examination of the alignment of the laws on defamation with the relevant case-law of the European Court of Human Rights, including the issue of decriminalisation of defamation,* C.O.E. Doc. CDMC(2005)007 5–11 (Strasbourg, 15 March 2006).

Other studies include a comprehensive database on criminal and civil defamation provisions and court practices compiled by the Representative on Freedom of the Media of the Organization for Security and Cooperation in Europe (OSCE), *Libel and Insult Laws: A Matrix on Where We Stand and What We Would Like to Achieve* (2005), available at http://www.osce.org/documents/rfm/2005/03/4361_en.pdf.

One result of this research is that the Parliamentary Assembly of the Council of Europe made the following recommendation in 2007.

Towards Decriminalisation of Defamation, Resolution 1577 (2007)
Parliamentary Assembly of the Council of Europe
adopted 4 October 2007 (34th Sitting)
http://assembly.coe.int/Main.asp?link=/Documents/
AdoptedText/ta07/ERES1577.htm#1

1. ... Where there is no real freedom of expression, there can be no real democracy....

4. As established in the case law of the European Court of Human Rights (the Court), Article 10 of the European Convention on Human Rights (ETS No. 5) guarantees freedom of expression in respect not only of "information" or "ideas" that are favourably received or regarded as inoffensive or as a matter of indifference, but also of those that offend, shock or disturb.

5. The Assembly notes that freedom of expression is not unlimited and that it may prove necessary for the state to intervene in a democratic society, provided that there is a solid legal basis and that it is clearly in the public interest, in accordance with Article 10, paragraph 2, of the European Convention on Human Rights.

6. Anti-defamation laws pursue the legitimate aim of protecting the reputation and rights of others. The Assembly nonetheless urges member states to apply these laws with the utmost restraint since they can seriously infringe freedom of expression. For this reason, the Assembly insists that there be procedural safeguards enabling anyone charged with defamation to substantiate their statements in order to absolve themselves of possible criminal responsibility.

7. In addition, statements or allegations which are made in the public interest, even if they prove to be inaccurate, should not be punishable provided that they were made without knowledge of their inaccuracy, without intention to cause harm, and their truthfulness was checked with proper diligence....

11. [The Assembly] notes with great concern that in many member states the law provides for prison sentences for defamation and that some still impose them in practice—for example, Azerbaijan and Turkey....

13. The Assembly consequently takes the view that prison sentences for defamation should be abolished without further delay. In particular it exhorts states whose laws still provide for prison sentences—although prison sentences are not actually imposed—to abolish them without delay so as not to give any excuse, however unjustified, to those countries which continue to impose them, thus provoking a corrosion of fundamental freedoms.

14. The Assembly likewise condemns abusive recourse to unreasonably large awards for damages and interest in defamation cases and points out that a compensation award of a disproportionate amount may also contravene Article 10 of the European Convention on Human Rights....

16. Lastly, the Assembly would reaffirm that protection of journalists' sources is of paramount public interest. Journalists prosecuted for defamation must be allowed to protect their sources or to produce a document in their own defence without having to show that they obtained it through lawful channels.

17. The Assembly accordingly calls on the member states to:

17.1. abolish prison sentences for defamation without delay;

17.2. guarantee that there is no misuse of criminal prosecutions for defamation and safeguard the independence of prosecutors in these cases;

17.3. define the concept of defamation more precisely in their legislation so as to avoid an arbitrary application of the law and to ensure that civil law provides effective protection of the dignity of persons affected by defamation; ...

17.5. make only incitement to violence, hate speech and promotion of negationism punishable by imprisonment;

17.6. remove from their defamation legislation any increased protection for public figures, in accordance with the Court's case law, and in particular calls on:

17.6.1. Turkey to amend Article 125.3 of its Criminal Code accordingly;

17.6.2. France to revise its law of 29 July 1881 in the light of the Court's case law;

17.7. ensure that under their legislation persons pursued for defamation have appropriate means of defending themselves, in particular means based on establishing the truth of their assertions and on the general interest, and calls in particular on France to amend or repeal Article 35 of its law of 29 July 1881 which provides for unjustified exceptions preventing the defendant from establishing the truth of the alleged defamation; ...

17.9. provide appropriate legal guarantees against awards for damages and interest that are disproportionate to the actual injury....

Questions and Discussion

1. *Repeal?* Does Resolution 1577 of the Parliamentary Assembly call for repeal of criminal libel laws? Note paragraphs 5, 6, and 13, among others. Are they consistent with the

title of the Resolution? What would be the rationale for continuing to allow criminal fines while removing the possibility of prison?

2. *Public figures.* Does paragraph 17.6 do all that the court case, *Castells v. Spain,* advocates? Would higher penalties still be allowed for defamation of the government, so long as it was not defamation of a particular "public figure"?

3. *Truth.* Should truth always be a defense to a criminal defamation charge? Is there potential harm to public respect for others even when truthful but insulting things are stated publicly?

4. *Reform in criminal defamation in Tanzania.* In 2007, a draft Tanzanian government bill regulating the media defined defamation as a civil, not a criminal wrong. It also provided that all publications regarding public officials are matters of public concern and that the burden of proof in all cases involving public officials is on the official to establish that the statements were false. Compare this draft legislation to the proposals in Europe.

5. *Insult and criminal libel in the U.S.* Many countries have criminal libel laws, which provide remedies for insult—even for insults based in truth. Such a law was overturned by the U.S. Supreme Court in *Garrison v. Louisiana,* 379 U.S. 64, 74 (1964), as conflicting with the constitutional guarantee of freedom of expression. The Court applied the same rationale that it gave in overturning a civil libel law in *New York Times v. Sullivan,* 376 U.S. 254, 279–280 (1964). In *Sullivan* it held that a public official could not sue a newspaper critic for a false statement unless there was "knowledge that it was false or with reckless disregard of whether it was false or not."

6. *Japan.* In Japan, by comparison, hundreds of persons are convicted every year for criminal libel. Truth is not a defense except for criticism of public officials or matters of public interest. Salil K. Mehra, *Post a Message and Go to Jail: Criminalizing Internet Libel in Japan and the United States,* 78 U. Colo. L. Rev. 767, 780 (2007) ("A person who injures the reputation of another by publicly alleging facts shall, regardless of whether such facts are true or false, be punished with penal servitude or imprisonment for not more than three years or a fine of not more than five hundred thousand yen." Keiho [Criminal Code], art. 230.) Even when truth is a defense, however, the defense is limited by the burden being placed on the defendant. *Id.,* citing *Ex parte Kawachi,* 23 Keishu 975, 996 (Sup. Ct. of Japan, June 25, 1969) ("in the context of a defamation case, proof of truth of statement is the defendant's burden").

7. *Canada.* Canada also does not go so far as the United States in choosing freedom of expression over protection of reputation. Although section 2(b) of the Canadian Charter of Rights and Freedoms (essentially, the Bill of Rights of Canada), guarantees freedom of expression, section 1 of the Charter provides that all Charter rights are subject to "reasonable limits prescribed by law as can be demonstrably justified in a free and democratic society." As one Australian author explains, this has led to less protection for defamatory speech than in the U.S. cases:

> The Supreme Court of Canada has given detailed treatment to each of the key phrases in section 1: "limit," "prescribed by law," and most importantly, "demonstrably justified in a free and democratic society." The Supreme Court elaborated upon this last phrase in *R. v. Oakes* [[1986] S.C.R. 103], establishing a test that continues to form the basis for section 1 analysis: a law violating a Charter right must serve a "pressing and substantial objective" and use means that are "reasonably and demonstrably justified." The second requirement, that the law be "reasonably and demonstrably justified," in turn requires that the law be "rationally connected" to that objective; "minimally impair" the protected

right; and that there is "a proportionality" between the restrictions imposed and the objective pursued.

The *Oakes* test provides a flexible framework for the assessment of Charter claims.

Adrienne Stone, *Defamation of Public Figures: North American Contrasts*, 50 N.Y.L. Sch. L. Rev. 9 (2005–2006).

8. *Comparisons.* Compare the position in Europe to that in Indonesia, Japan, Canada, the U.S., and other countries, previously discussed. Is it important that governments have the right to bring criminal charges, rather than leaving the persons who allege harm to file civil lawsuits for damages? Is there also a significant danger for environmental advocates from civil lawsuits?

III. Civil Charges and Remedies — SLAPPs

Civil lawsuits can be brought not only by governments but by private parties as well, seeking to limit criticism and protect economic interests. These suits are known as Strategic Lawsuits Against Public Participation — SLAPP suits. Companies achieve their goal of silencing public opposition by testing the financial and emotional limits of the defendants. Most do not have the time nor the money to spend defending themselves against SLAPPs. It has been argued that SLAPP suits are not only an affront to free speech but a violation of a person's constitutional right to petition the government for redress of grievances if the courts hear such suits.

A. Introduction to SLAPPs

SLAPP: Getting Sued for Speaking Out (1996)

George Pring & Penelope Canan

Great discoveries often come from an unexpected shock. Our discovery of SLAPPs came when they dropped—like Newton's apple—on our own heads in the late 1970s. For the environmental lawyer in Denver, it was the shock of having the tables turned and his environmental clients sued by the governments and polluters they opposed. For the sociologist then in Hawaii, it was the shock of having herself and her university threatened with a lawsuit for criticizing a publicly funded research program.

As it turned out, these were not unique experiences. We discovered case after case in which people were being sued just for talking to government, circulating a petition, writing a letter to the editor, speaking at a school board meeting, or testifying in a public hearing....

Recognizing a SLAPP

SLAPPs normally do not advertise themselves as such. Filers do not usually sue people for "exercising their First Amendment rights" or "petitioning the government" or "speaking out politically" (although some unsophisticated complaints actually are that blatant). Instead, to gain and maintain access to the court, filers must recast or camouflage the targets' political behavior as common personal injuries or legal violations. They need to mask the nature of the dispute and present it as personal and legal, not public and political.

Two litmus tests can determine whether a case is a SLAPP: defendants' actions, and plaintiffs' claims.

1. Defendants' actions: To begin with, exactly what activities of defendant-targets are described in the fact section of the filer's complaint? Do any of those activities involve communicating with government officials, bodies, or the electorate, or encouraging others to do so? Are government hearings, complaints, appeals, letters, reports, or filings mentioned? If so (and regardless of how many non-government activities are also mentioned), the case is a SLAPP. Even if no government-connected actions are mentioned, however, one must ask: Are targets politically active citizens and groups? Are they involved in speaking out for or against some issue under consideration by some level of government or the voters? If so, there is a high likelihood that a suit against them is a disguised SLAPP, regardless of the facts alleged.

2. Plaintiffs' claims: SLAPPs repeatedly use six very predictable tort or other legal categories to mask their real purpose. They are, in order of frequency, (1) defamation (libel, slander, business libel, product disparagement, and so on), (2) business torts (interference with business, with contract, with prospective economic advantage; antitrust, restraint of trade, or unfair competition), (3) conspiracy (planning and acting together with others for any illegal purpose), (4) judicial or administrative process violations (malicious prosecution, abuse of process), (5) violation of constitutional or civil rights (denial of due process or equal protection, taking of property, discrimination), and (6) other violations (nuisance, trespass, invasion of privacy, outrageous conduct, falsifying tax-exempt status, and so on). If any of these categories are specified, suspect a SLAPP.

Three other filer tactics are further indicators:

1. Unrealistically high dollar demands: Large claims of monetary injury, out of proportion to any real harms done, are a hallmark of SLAPPs. Small claims do occur, but filings in the $100,000, $1,000,000, or even $100,000,000 range are not unusual. (In states that have a rule against specifying dollar amounts, the complaints bear the ominous phrase "damages in an amount to be determined at trial"). The key is that the dollar figures demanded are huge but typically bear no relationship to the amount of any actual damages the filer could have suffered, even if the complaint were 100 percent true.

2. "Does": The inclusion of unnamed John or Jane Doe defendants—a blank check device used only occasionally in other litigation—is frequent in SLAPPs. It is a highly effective way of creating "ripple effects" among citizens and officials who support or might support the targets' campaign. We have found whole communities chilled by the inclusion of Does, fearing "they will add my name to the suit."

3. Naming individuals but not the organizations they represent: When the League of Women Voters of Beverly Hills led an election campaign to block a condo development, the $63,555,000 SLAPP was filed only against the individual leaders—the league was not named—and the same thing has happened to Sierra Club volunteers. This "divide and conquer" technique seems designed to isolate the individuals (for greater chilling effect) and cut them off from organizational financial support, since some groups' rules or insurance may not permit them to cover a legal defense unless the group is actually named.

Given any of the foregoing indicators, targets should scrutinize the complaint with special care. In judging whether the case is really a SLAPP, search for any mention of Petition Clause-protected activity by defendants. Some complaints are embarrassingly blatant. Even if the complaint avoids mentioning protected government communications and focuses instead on seemingly nongovernmental communications such as letters to the editor, media statements, or leaflets to the community, look to see whether the actions complained of are (1) part of an overall petitioning strategy or (2) too minor to support the massive dollar damages demanded; in either case, other unmentioned activity is probably provoking the filing. The target attorney should carefully probe all target activities in the previous year that involved or affected the filer, whether mentioned in the complaint or not. If any of those activities are either direct government communications or indirectly government-connected or designed to influence others to communicate with government, the attorney should proceed on the basis that this is a bona fide SLAPP. Then the attorney can "pierce the veil" of the camouflage claims and use the Petition Clause defense.

Questions and Discussion

1. *Recognizing a SLAPP Suit.* Go back and look over *Nikitin v. Russia*, earlier in this chapter. Does it show the signs of a SLAPP suit?

2. *Limit defenses?* Do Pring and Canan limit the defenses against SLAPP suits too much, by basing the arguments for protection on the Petition Clause of the U.S. Constitution? Are other arguments equally valid? Should protections exist only for public statements that are, directly or indirectly, addressed to a government body?

3. *Broaden defenses?* Do Pring and Canan broaden the defenses against SLAPP suits too much, by allowing potentially defamatory or otherwise tortious material to be distributed any time that an activist can tie it to the Petition Clause?

B. Legal Claims Against Appeals and Litigation

SLAPP: Getting Sued for Speaking Out (1996)

George Pring & Penelope Canan

The Sierra Club: First and Foremost

Among its distinctions, the Sierra Club can count itself the nation's leading SLAPP target, with at least 10 suits against it, yet a very atypical one: Instead of the local environmentalists and small groups usually targeted, these SLAPPs have taken on a real Goliath. The Sierra Club, with its multimillion-dollar annual budget, hundreds of thousands of members, 100-year existence, extensive courtroom experience, and even its own law firm (the Sierra Club Legal Defense Fund [now an independent organization named Earthjustice]) would seem "unchillable"—and indeed it has won dismissal of all SLAPPs filed against it. Yet despite all its resources, even its volunteers can be intimidated, its funds diverted, and its campaigns lost in the real world, just like those of the smallest, poorest neighborhood group.

The spectacular wilderness areas of California have been a battleground between the Sierra Club and timber/mining/ranching interests since the nineteenth century. One of the great modern battles triggered what we believe is the first officially reported eco-

SLAPP and one of the best reasoned to date—*Sierra Club v. Butz*. In 1965, the U.S. Forest Service opened for logging a virgin 3,500-acre area near what was to become the Salmon-Trinity Alps Wilderness in the far northwest corner of California. The contract was awarded to Humboldt Fir, the largest employer in the region, but it did not begin logging immediately. In 1970, the Sierra Club awoke, began objecting to the Forest Service that the proposed logging was "illegal," and requested that the area be kept in wilderness. The government denied the request, and in 1972 the club appealed, filing a federal court challenge to overturn the government's decision.

Three days later Humboldt Fir filed a counterclaim demanding an injunction, $750,000 in actual damages, and $1,000,000 in punitive damages against the Sierra Club. Humboldt claimed to have been driven into bankruptcy and—in an unashamedly literal attack on the Petition Clause—charged "interference with contract" because the Club "orally and by letter and by administrative appeal proceedings and by the complaint herein, engaged in a calculated course of conduct to induce the Forest Service ... to refuse to continue its performance of the said contract." The club promptly filed a motion to dismiss, plainly worried about the "drastic monetary liability," and objecting strenuously to the violation of its political rights:

> [Humboldt's] claim is that the presence of a timber sale contract ... chokes off [the Sierra Club's] freedom to address the Government with their views as to the best use of the public lands in question. If such a fanciful notion bore any resemblance to the law, it would stifle any effective effort to remedy the myriad environmental abuses that spring from government projects.... It would mean that any citizen who beseeched the Government to end oil drilling in the Santa Barbara Channel or to halt the SST project would be subject to the same kind of potential liability to Union Oil or Boeing.... It would be difficult to imagine a cruder attempt to deprive ordinary citizens of their right ... to communicate with their Government and petition it for redress of grievances."

The Sierra Club's decision to focus on political-constitutional issues rather than the breach-of-contract camouflage was quickly rewarded: The U.S. District Court dismissed Humboldt's counterclaim in a near-record four months. One of the very first federal court opinions to rule SLAPPs unconstitutional, *Sierra Club v. Butz* remains a landmark precedent today:

> The First Amendment provision guaranteeing the right of the people to petition the government for a redress of grievances ... is a basic freedom in a participatory government, closely related to freedom of speech and press; together these are the "indispensable democratic freedoms" that cannot be abridged if a government is to continue to reflect the desires of the people.

The court saw clearly the risk of such suits and its own critical role in controlling or perpetuating them:

> This court cannot be too careful in assuring that its acts do not infringe this right.... [The U.S. Supreme Court has said that] "fear of damage awards ... may be markedly more inhibiting than the fear of prosecution under a criminal statute.... Erroneous statement is inevitable in free debate, and ... it must be protected if the freedoms of expression are to have the 'breathing space' that they 'need ... to survive.'" Under a less strict rule, the [Supreme Court] feels: "would-be critics of official conduct may be deterred from voicing their criticism, even though it is believed to be true and even though it is in fact true, because of

doubt whether it can be proved in court or fear of the expenses of having to do so.... [This would] dampen the vigor and limit the variety of public debate. It is inconsistent with the [U.S. Constitution]." ...

Since then, the Sierra Club or its members have been targets in at least nine other eco-SLAPPs, not always ending so well. The club has been twice sued for opposing logging: by a timber company on the Mission Indian Reservation east of Los Angeles; and by an Alaskan Native Corporation in the nation's largest forest reserve, the magnificent coastal rain forest of Alaska's Tongass archipelago. Its efforts to protect rivers provoked two more: a commercial river rafting company SLAPPed the club over a new river management plan for the Grand Canyon in 1978; Oregon water interests sued the club in 1994 for trying to remove a dam from the Rogue River. Fighting residential, resort, and road developments in wilderness areas triggered three more.... Just publishing a book, *Environmental Justice and Communities of Color,* got it sued by New Mexico landfill operators for libel. Finally, even opposing a small expansion of an existing seaside hotel in Mendocino got the club sued for $3,250,000. Seeing the litigious Sierra Club itself as the target of lawsuits raises a very important point. We are often asked, "If targets can file a lawsuit, what's wrong with filers doing it?" The answer lies in the relief sought by the suit. Our study includes as SLAPPs the countersuits and counterclaims filed against an initial lawsuit brought by the target—but only when the target's original lawsuit can be classed as pure "government petitioning": in short, a suit seeking to change a government policy, action, decision, or plan, not to acquire money damages. The countersuit or counterclaim is classified as a SLAPP because it has completely different goals or effects—not a government result or outcome but monetary compensation from the target. It thus injects a collateral issue, changes the stakes, and diverts attention and resources from the real public dispute needing resolution.

Litigation is protected under the Petition Clause, but pure lobbying, nonmonetary, public-interest cases merit greater solicitude than private-interest money cases because they involve the very kind of "private attorney general" citizen participation in government that is at the core of First Amendment concern and of Congressional policy in the health, safety, and welfare area. Targets petition courts to alter another government authority's decision. SLAPP countersuits and counterclaims seek to cut off citizens' access to courts to petition government outcomes, just as other SLAPPs seek to cut off access to achieve outcomes from our legislatures and agencies.

Questions and Discussion

1. *Companies vs. citizens.* Pring and Canan, in defining SLAPP suits, distinguish between citizen suits brought against companies involved in a government action from suits brought by companies against citizens which allege that they are interfering with their contract rights. Is there really a difference between the companies' right to sue and the citizens' right to sue under the Petition Clause?

2. *Free speech in Australia.* A few democratic countries, such as Australia, do not have a constitutionally based right to free speech, and may not have the equivalent of the U.S. Constitution's Petition Clause. In fact, Australian courts balance business interests against free speech interests. If a similar action were brought in Australia against an environmental organization attempting to stop logging, would the court be able to dismiss the action based on the Sierra Club's defense in *Sierra Club v. Butz*? See *Gunns v. Marr* (No. 2) [2006] VSC 329 (28 August 2006).

C. Demonstrations and Economic Boycotts

Fighting the Big Gunns in Tasmania
Tom Price
CorpWatch (March 14, 2005)

Along a narrow dirt road, about 90 minutes from Tasmania's provincial capital of Hobart lies the small, residential community of Lucaston. It's an area of rugged, natural beauty that draws people looking to live a quiet life.

"A couple hundred acres of bush, wet forest thick with ferns and the like. Splendid, it is," says Lou Geraghty as she describes her homestead near the top of a slope along a rolling valley. Along with her fisherman husband, this grandmother has dreamt of setting up an ecotourism retreat here. Ideally, this would mean little more than building a few small cabins out in the bush and allowing city folk to come traipse through the primordial old growth forests that carpet this Ireland-sized isle off the southern tip of Australia.

So when a few years ago the timber conglomerate Gunns Limited announced plans to clear-cut the slopes below her house and run massive haul rigs right past her home, Geraghty did what most concerned residents would do; she talked to elected officials, she went to meetings, and eventually she showed up at protests to wave banners and stand in the way of logging trucks. But while her response may have been typical, the timber company's was not.

Two weeks before Christmas, on December 14, 2004, Gunns stunned Australia's conservation community by filing a 216 page, $6.3 million (AU) claim against a group of activists and organizations, including Geraghty. Gunns, the world's largest woodchip exporter, claimed that the group had cost the company millions and demanded their money back. The most costly allegation: environmentalists conspired to pressure Japanese buyers out of doing business with Gunns. "The demands were to be accompanied by threats express and implied," reads the writ, "of adverse publicity, consumer boycotts, and direct action against the Japanese customers and all of their operations." For corporate campaign activists, all those tactics are fairly standard fare. Gunns, however, is asking the courts to declare such activity illegal....

As another of the defendants, Dr. Bob Brown, an Australian Senator for the Greens Party representing Tasmania, explains, "The implications are enormous. If Gunns is successful, it would echo through all the legal systems of the English-speaking world. It would mean that criticizing a corporation could land you in bankruptcy."

Yet keeping quiet isn't an option for Brown or Geraghty, who have seen firsthand the negative impacts of widespread clear-cutting....

Gunns ships five million tons of shredded trees to Japan annually. This business, and others including a small winemaking business, earn the company a revenue of $674 million, of which $105 (AU) million is profit.

Founded in 1875, by brothers John and Thomas Gunn, Gunns, Ltd. also has a great deal of political influence in Tasmania. As is often the case in areas rich in natural resources, the connection between industry and government is exceptionally close. For example Robin Gray, one of Tasmania's former Premiers, sits on the Gunns Ltd. board....

And now the playing field is tilted even further in their favor. "Gunns already has legal protection—if the roads are blockaded they can and do call the police," Beder says, but their December SLAPP suit "goes way beyond the company exercising its legal rights to protect its property. It's using the civil court for the purpose of intimidating protestors, and shifting the forum from public debate to private court action—a situation where the corporation has far more resources." Unlike criminal cases where a defendant has a legal right to representation, activists have few such rights during a civil matter. Even if the ruling goes in their favor the defendant may still end up on the hook for 20–40% of their legal fees....

It's not just activists and politicians who are getting sued—Gunns is also going after doctors who complain about potential health risks. In 2002, Dr. Frank Nicklason raised concerns about the possible contamination in massive woodpiles left on a harbor wharf, and called for an independent analysis. What he got instead was a letter from Gunns saying he had "recklessly, irresponsibly and negligently" misused his position as a medical practitioner to draw attention to "supposed health risks existing in the local community." He has also now been SLAPPed with a potentially large fine, raising alarm in the medical community. As Australian Medical Association's president told the Australian Financial Times: "Our Hippocratic oath demands we investigate any possible cause of disease, whatever that may be—tobacco, asbestos or any other concerns. It would be a dangerous development if doctors faced legal action any time they raised concerns." ...

While many of the small-time activists have been quieted down, at least one is staying vocal—Senator Bob Brown of the Greens Party. "If the idea was to put the conservation movement out of action, and it has had an enormous effect, they've picked on the wrong person." Although he was not among those traveling to Japan before the lawsuit to influence Gunns' customers, he has since "made it [his] business to go" for the recent Kyoto protocol meetings. There he takes advantage of the opportunity to distribute press kits and DVDs decrying Gunns' logging. "Gunns has let us know just how successful we've been in Japan," he explains, noting the writ claims some $3 million in damages. By continuing to speak out, he's likely putting his savings and home on the line, but the veteran campaigner—who's been shot at for his views before—won't be silenced....

True to their reputation, the Australian activists are maintaining a cheeky sense of humor about most things, even deforestation. Car bumpers all over the province, which have had a "Save Tasmania's Forests" sticker on them, now have a new addition aimed right at Gunns: "So Sue Me."

But for Lou Geraghty, who's fighting for her children and grandchildren to have a safe place to play, finding the humor is a bit tough some days. She's at once resigned and defiant. Her personal liability is $30,000, enough to cost her both the dream of a tourist retreat and the home along the ridge. "The only thing we've got to fight this with is the media," she says, "because there're a lot of little communities like this one in Tasmania that the same things are happening to, or will happen to."

Sipping a mug of tea on a cool March morning at her home in the forest, Geraghty can't know when the next blow will come. "We don't know when or if they're coming back," she says. "We won't ever be given any information." Nor does she know how the decades-long fight over Tasmania's forests will end. One thing, however, is certain: if Gunns' trucks do return to the quiet dirt road along Baker's Creek, "I'll be down there with my banner again, yelling and screaming and blocking the road."

Questions and Discussion

1. *Background.* The original allegations, grouped as "logging operations disruption campaigns" and "corporate vilification," began at 216 pages, growing to 360 pages by July

of 2005. *Gunns v. Marr* [2005] VSC 251 at 2 [2], 3 [6], 5 [10]. "The torts relied upon include interference with trade or business by unlawful means, wrongful interference with contractual relations, conspiracy to injure, and defamation." *Id.* at 5 [11].

2. *Gunns's claims.* After years of filing amended claims—at one point Judge Bongiorno told Gunns that the "defects in the pleading are such that to salvage those parts which are not objectionable" would likely "result in greater confusion" than just to start over, *Gunns v. Marr* [2005] VSC 251 at 21 [63], 18 [58]—the plaintiffs dropped their claims against five of the original defendants. *Gunns v. Marr* [2007] VSC 91 at [6] (3 April 2007). Claims dropped included those "in respect of business losses" concerning "their Japanese business interests [influencing shareholders and woodchip buyers] ... various alleged defamations and associated torts and, most importantly, a claim in respect of an overarching conspiracy...." *Id.* In August of 2007, Gunns also settled claims against Russell Hanson, CEO of the Wilderness Society at the time of the claims. Hanson "denied liability, did not have to pay damages or Gunns costs and agreed not to undertake certain activities in relation to Gunns." *Id.* Gunns dropped one claim against Dr. Nicklason, but filed another one, which on September 17, 2007, was stricken out by Master Evans of the Victoria Supreme Court. The action started with a Gunns request to strike the part of the defense claiming that what Dr. Nicklason stated was true. Instead, Master Evans struck the Gunns claim. Friends of Forest and Free Speech, Gunns, Media Releases, *Gunns Case Against Hobart Doctor Struck Out!* Sep. 17, 2007.

Daishowa, Inc. v. Friends of the Lubicon (Canada)
Ontario Court of Justice
[1998] 39 O.R. (3d) 620 (Can.)

MACPHERSON, J.

Introduction

In this action, the plaintiff Daishowa Inc. seeks to restrain permanently the consumer boycott activities of the defendant Friends of the Lubicon and of some of its individual members, the defendants Kevin Thomas, Ed Bianchi and Stephen Kenda. The action raises novel and important questions about the relationship between, on the one hand, ordinary citizens seeking to participate in and influence debate on a public issue and, on the other hand, corporations and consumers who are directly affected by the manner in which the citizens choose to express their views. The factual touchstones for these questions are a consumer boycott organized by the defendants and their choice of picketing as the ultimate weapon in the boycott.

Factual Background ...

Daishowa is a subsidiary of Daishowa Forest Products Ltd.... This subsidiary negotiated a Forest Management Agreement ("FMA") with the Government of Alberta in 1988. It built a large pulp mill in Peace River and anticipated that it would supply the mill with wood harvested from the area covered by the FMA....

The defendant Friends of the Lubicon ("Friends") is a small public interest group based in Toronto.... Its mission is to draw attention to the sad plight, as it perceives it, of the Lubicon Cree Nation in Alberta and to put pressure on governments to take steps to overcome the problems faced by the Lubicon Cree. The Friends try to achieve these objectives through a variety of activities, including letter writing campaigns to governments, public speaking in schools and universities, and the organization of conferences and symposia. The majority of the Friends' activities are strictly educational in nature....

In simple terms, the FMA negotiated between Daishowa Canada Company Ltd. and the Government of Alberta covered a substantial portion of land claimed by the Lubicon Cree. The agreement gave the company the right to cut trees in an area which the Lubicon Cree regarded as central to its economic and spiritual history and future.

The Lubicon Cree took steps to protect its interests. One of those steps was participation in a demonstration organized by the United Native Nations at the Vancouver office of Daishowa Canada Company Ltd. on March 7, 1988.

On the day of the demonstration, representatives of the company and the Lubicon Cree met to discuss the situation.... Unfortunately, the results of the meeting have haunted the participants for a decade, and are a major source of this litigation. In bald terms, the Lubicon Cree Nation thought that the company agreed at the meeting not to log on disputed lands until the rights of the Lubicon had been finally settled in negotiations among the Lubicon and the federal and Alberta Governments. The company, on the other hand, regarded the outcome of the meeting as a useful and hopeful introduction, a promise to meet again, and nothing more....

The Lubicon Cree was concerned that the company or its subsidiaries would log in its "area of concern" in the 1991–1992 winter season....

On November 6, 1991 Kevin Thomas wrote to Mr. Tom Hamaoka at Daishowa Canada Company Ltd.... This letter represented the first direct contact between Daishowa and the Friends. In his letter Mr. Thomas set out the commitment the Friends were seeking from Daishowa and presaged the Friends' plan if the commitment was not made....

For three years, from late 1991 to late 1994, the Friends continued their boycott campaign. They approached about fifty companies which purchased Daishowa paper products....

The results of the Friends' campaign against Daishowa from 1991 to 1994 were, in a word, stunning. Approximately fifty companies which purchased paper products (mostly paper bags) from Daishowa were approached by the Friends.... Every one of the companies approached by the Friends joined the boycott of Daishowa products. All but two did so at stage one of the Friends' campaign, that is before their stores were picketed. Some of the companies who joined the boycott did so willingly; they appeared to agree with the Friends' position and wanted to help. However, the vast majority of companies joined the boycott with great reluctance. They were satisfied with the Daishowa products, including quality, price and service, and would not have stopped using them but for the Friends' threat to proceed with stage two of the campaign, namely picketing outside their stores....

On January 11, 1995 Daishowa issued its Statement of Claim in this action. On March 20, 1995 the defendants filed their Statement of Defence....

Legal Issues

The principal relief sought by the plaintiff is a permanent injunction restraining the defendants' conduct....

The plaintiff claims an entitlement to permanent injunctive relief on six bases:

(1) the tort of interference with economic and contractual relations, including inducing breach of contract;

(2) the tort of intimidation;

(3) the tort of conspiracy;

(4) the tort of misrepresentation;

(5) the tort of defamation; and

(6) the use and threatened use of unlawful means, including unlawful secondary picketing, watching and besetting, nuisance, injurious falsehood, as well as the aforementioned torts.

Analysis

I propose to consider the six bases on which the plaintiff seeks injunctive relief. I have decided to consider the sixth ground first....

(1) Unlawful Secondary Picketing

Daishowa has refused to give the Friends what they have been seeking since November 6, 1991, namely "a clear, firm and public commitment to not cut and not to purchase any wood cut on unceded Lubicon territory until after a settlement of Lubicon land rights and negotiation of a harvesting agreement with the Lubicon people that takes into account Lubicon wildlife and environmental concerns." (see Thomas-Hamaoka letter, November 10, 1991).

In response to Daishowa's refusal to make this commitment, the Friends have engaged at various times in picketing activities outside Daishowa's corporate office in Toronto and its paper products manufacturing plant in Winnipeg. Daishowa does not contest the Friends' legal right to engage in such activities. Daishowa says that if the Friends have a dispute with its corporate practices, the Friends are entitled in law to convey their message to Daishowa at its business locations. Daishowa does not oppose, in labour law parlance, primary picketing of its business sites.

However, the Friends have not limited their protest activities to primary picketing. They have taken their message to Daishowa's customers, the many companies in Ontario which buy paper products from Daishowa. The Friends have approached those companies, by personal visits, telephone calls and letters. Their message to these customers has been simple: please stop using Daishowa paper products in your business because of the effects of Daishowa's corporate activities on the Lubicon Cree in Alberta. If the customer agreed with this request the Friends would take no further action. However, if the customer refused to discontinue its use of Daishowa products, the Friends would take their campaign one step farther. They would personally attend at the customer's stores and engage in informational picketing. Their goal at this second stage would be to educate the customers of the customers of Daishowa about the plight of the Lubicon Cree and the perceived connection of Daishowa to that plight with a view to enlisting their support to persuade Daishowa's direct customers to change their minds....

Daishowa contends that the Friends' picketing and boycott activities directed at the customers of the customers of Daishowa ... is unlawful. It articulates this contention in a lucid and sophisticated fashion at paragraph 83 of its factum:

> The common law prohibition against secondary picketing of customers in order to force them to stop dealing with the primary target of the picketers, aims to strike a balance between the rights of protesters to express their views by, for example, directly picketing parties with whom they have a legitimate dispute and the right to pursue one's legitimate economic interests without unlawful interference. Our courts have long recognized and still recognize that the act of picketing involves more than the dissemination of information but, rather, that it aims to send a "strong and automatic signal" and to create a barrier which people often refuse to cross regardless of their views.... The freedom to pursue one's economic interest is a value to be considered just as much as other values, such as the right to protect one's reputation, which must be balanced in the private

law context against the values embodied in the [Canadian] Charter [of Rights and Freedoms]....

The first and most important case cited by Daishowa on the picketing issue is *Hersees of Woodstock v. Goldstein*, [1963] 2 O.R. 81 (C.A.)....

In *Hersees*, a retail store was picketed by a union for buying clothing products from a manufacturer which did not employ union labour. Thus the chain of connection was union-retailer-manufacturer. The Court of Appeal concluded that the union's picketing activity was unlawful for several reasons. Three of the reasons are found in the judgment of Aylesworth J.A.; they have anchored the jurisprudence relating to secondary picketing in a labour relations context for several decades, not just in Ontario but in other common law jurisdictions as well.

The first of these reasons is what has come to be known as the "signalling" effect of picketing. As expressed by Aylesworth J.A. at p. 85:

> In this day and age the power and influence of organized labour is very far indeed from negligible. "Loyalty to the picket line" is a credo influencing a large portion of any community such as the City of Woodstock ... [T]he employees of more than one employer whose premises had been picketed refused out of "loyalty to the picket line" to cross that line. In this and in several other cases in Canadian Courts judicial notice has been taken of "the rule" so far as employees are concerned.

The second reason has come to be identified as the "neutrals" argument, namely that secondary picketing implicates third parties in a dispute that is not theirs. As expressed by Aylesworth J.A., at p. 85:

> [D]oubtless for many private citizens not directly interested in the labour movement the presence of pickets before business premises is a powerful deterrent to doing business at those premises.

The third reason for restraining secondary picketing is that it can have a substantial detrimental effect on a business....

In recent cases, some Canadian courts have articulated a fourth reason for prohibiting secondary picketing in a labour context, namely that such activity has as its primary objective the infliction of economic harm on a business rather than the dissemination of information about the labour dispute....

The question which must be considered in this trial is whether the reasons in favour of the prohibition against secondary picketing in a labour relations context support a prohibition against picketing in a consumer boycott context. In my view, they do not. I will consider each of the four reasons in turn.

The "signaling" reason is, in my view, distinctively located in its labour relations context. In *B.C.G.E.U. v. British Columbia (Attorney General)*, [1988] 2 S.C.R. 214, Dickson C.J. said, at p. 231:

> Picketing sends a strong and automatic signal: do not cross the line lest you undermine our struggle; this time we ask you to help us by not doing business with our employer; next time, when you are on strike, we will respect your picket line and refuse to conduct business with your employer.

The Friends do not have any kind of similar relationship with the customers they try to persuade not to purchase Daishowa products. Nor do they have the power or clout of the organized union movement. Any community of interest with Daishowa's customers ...

will be established solely by the content of their message and the means by which they convey it....

It is reasonable to restrain picketing so that the conflict will not escalate beyond the actual parties. While picketing is, no doubt, a legislative weapon to be employed in a labour dispute by the employees against their employer, it should not be permitted to harm others.

There is no collective bargaining relationship between the Friends and Daishowa. Rather the Friends have identified what they perceive to be an important social and political issue—the plight of the Lubicon Cree. They believe that Daishowa's corporate activities have contributed, and will continue to contribute, to the worsening of that plight. Accordingly, they speak to Daishowa and ask it to change its conduct....

The third reason for restraining picketing in *Hersees* and other labour cases is its detrimental effect on business. In the passage from Aylesworth J.A.'s judgment set out earlier, he refers explicitly to a "right to trade." ...

[I]t strikes me that this component of Aylesworth J.A.'s reasoning is anachronistic today. The fact that freedom of expression is protected in the Charter of Rights and Freedoms, coupled with the absence of any economic rights, except for mobility to pursue the gaining of a livelihood, in the same document, is a clear indication that free speech is near the top of the values that Canadians hold dear. As expressed by *MacIntyre J. in Dolphin Delivery*:

> Freedom of expression ... is one of the fundamental concepts that has formed the basis for the historical development of the political, social and educational institutions of western society. Representative democracy, ... is in great part the product of free expression and discussion of varying ideas, depends upon its maintenance and protection....

The fourth reason for the prohibition against secondary picketing in the labour cases is that the primary purpose of the picketing is the infliction of economic harm on an employer, rather than the dissemination of information about the labour dispute.... [T]he parties must fight each other with their own economic weapons; they should not be able to engage unwilling third parties in the dispute....

The Friends say that their picketing activities at the business locations of Daishowa's consumers is speech concerning public affairs. I agree. The essential subject matter of everything the Friends say and do is the plight of the Lubicon Cree in Alberta....

[T]he expression engaged in by the Friends relates directly to a very important public issue. As such, it deserves respect, protection and a forum. It is precisely the type of expression that the Supreme Court of Canada has declared as lying at the heart of the fundamental freedom protected by the Charter....

I agree that the Friends' message has a strong and direct economic content.... The message is also a vigorous attempt to persuade Daishowa to change its position. However, the message goes even farther—it invites consumers of Daishowa products to become informed about Daishowa's position and to participate in the debate on the issue by refusing to purchase Daishowa products unless Daishowa changes its position. In short, an important part of the Friends' message, and certainly the most effective part, is the attempt, through speech in a picketing context, to enlist consumers in a boycott of Daishowa products.

Is there anything unlawful about such a consumer boycott? And do those who conceive and organize it violate any law? I think not....

In my view, the answer is clear; there is no reason, in logic or in policy, for restraining a consumer boycott....

For these reasons, my conclusion is that if the Canadian Constitution protects a corporation's expression where the context is largely economic, and where one of the consequences of the expression, if accepted by the listener, might well be economic harm to competitors, then the common law should not erect barriers to expression by consumers where the purpose and effect of the expression is to persuade the listener to use his or her economic power to challenge a corporation's position on an important economic and public policy issue. The plight of the Lubicon Cree is such an issue, as is Daishowa's connection to it....

[T]he manner in which the Friends have performed their picketing and boycott activities is a model of how such activities should be conducted in a democratic society....

[The Court dismisses plaintiffs claims 2 through 5 for the tort of interference with economic and contractual relations, including breach of contract, the tort of intimidation, the tort of conspiracy to injure, and combines the tort of misrepresentation with the tort of defamation.] ...

Disposition

The principal relief sought by Daishowa, namely, a permanent injunction restraining the picketing activities of the Friends at the stores of Daishowa customers, is refused....

[In addition, under defamation law, the Court did issue an order restraining the Friends from claiming that the Lubicon Cree Nation had reached an agreement concerning Daishowa's exercise of logging rights and from using the word "genocide" in its campaign.]

Questions and Discussion

1. *Picketing.* The Court distinguishes between primary and secondary picketing, what exactly is the difference between these two actions? Should the court distinguish between labor picketing and political picketing?

2. *Proper dismissal.* Canada's Charter of Rights and Freedoms states:

Everyone has the following fundamental freedoms: (a) freedom of conscience and religion; (b) freedom of thought, belief, opinion and expression, including freedom of the press and other media of communication; (c) freedom of peaceful assembly; and (d) freedom of association.

Constitution Act, 1982, Canadian Charter of Rights and Freedoms, Part 1, Sch. B. Ch. 11. Based on these rights, should Daishowa's claim against the Friends of Lubicon have been dismissed? Does the tort of "unlawful secondary picketing," conflict with the fundamental freedoms expressed in the Charter?

3. *Lubicon's Action.* The boycott against Daishowa was part of the Lubicon's larger struggle to reclaim their land from the Canadian government since 1939. The Canadian government had leased 10,000 square kilometers, virtually all of their traditional lands to Daishowa just seven months after the Lubicon had applied for interim protection from the U.N. *Lubicon Lake Band v. Canada*, [Decision on] Communication to the Human Rights Committee, No. 167/1984, (26 March 1990), U.N. Doc. Supp. No. 40 (A/45/40) at 1 (1990). In 1990 the U.N. Human Rights Committee held that Canada's actions against the Lubicon violated Article 27 of the International Covenant on Civil and Political Rights. *Id.* In 2005 the Lubicon appealed once again to the U.N. because Canada had allegedly

not followed through on their obligation to negotiate the land dispute with the Lubicon. The Commitee reaffirmed its concerns over the situation. Human Rights Committee, *Consideration of Reports Submitted by States Parties Under Article 40 of the Covenant, Concluding observations of the Human Rights Committee*, U.N. Doc. CCPR/C/CAN/CO/5 (October 27–28, 2005).

4. *Daishowa's Action.* Daishowa appealed the Court's decision, meanwhile the Lubicon continued their boycott. On May 4, 2000, the day before the appeal hearing, Daishowa agreed to a settlement including that they would not log until the Lubicon reached a land rights settlement with the Canadian government. Friends of the Lubicon, *Background on the Lubicon Lake Indian Nations's Struggles*, http://www.tao.ca/~fol/pa/luback.htm.

D. Campaigns, Criticisms, Defamation

One of the main weapons turned against human rights or environmental advocates has been the use of national defamation laws. Those laws may, however, be subject to examination under human rights standards. Consider the following examples.

1. European and Inter-American Courts of Human Rights

In applying article 10 of the European Convention, the European Court of Human Rights has held that a state may not extend defamation laws to restrict dissemination of environmental information of public interest. *Bladet Tromsö and Stensaas v. Norway* (ECHR, May 20, 1999); *Thoma v. Luxembourg* (ECHR, March 29, 2001). In the first case, the editor and publisher of a newspaper were sued and found to have committed defamation by publishing a series of articles that accused seal hunters of illegal and cruel hunting methods. The European Court said that most careful scrutiny is called for when the measures taken or sanctions imposed on journalists by the national authority are capable of discouraging the participation of the press in debates over matters of legitimate public concern. It found that the crew members' undoubted interest in protecting their reputation was insufficient to outweigh the vital public interest in ensuring an informed public debate over a matter of local and national as well as international interest. Thus, the reasons for imposing liability relied on by Norway, although relevant, were not sufficient to show that the interference with freedom of speech was "necessary in a democratic society." Accordingly, the Court held that there had been a violation of Article 10 of the Convention. The Thoma case involved a journalist's accusations of self-dealing by officials engaged in reforestation projects in Luxembourg. Numerous forest wardens and engineers sued for defamation and the journalist was fined a nominal amount. The European Court again found the action incompatible with the requirements of freedom of expression, in part because the subject was one of public concern, but also because the Court noted that public officials must accept a greater amount of scrutiny and criticism than private persons.

Dinah Shelton & Alexandre Kiss, JUDICIAL HANDBOOK ON ENVIRONMENTAL LAW 28 (2005).

The Inter-American Court of Human Rights is a court charged with analyzing human rights violations in the Americas similar to the ECHR in Europe.

The Inter-American Court positively influenced international jurisprudence in the area of criminal defamation in 2005. The Inter-American Court decided three criminal defamation cases in which the applicant had been convicted in domestic courts of defaming a public official or person who was involved in activities of public interest. The Court ruled in each case that criminal defamation was not the least restrictive means of limiting freedom of expression so as to protect other rights and, therefore, the State had violated the rights of the person convicted domestically of criminal defamation. [For example,] [i]n *Herrera Ulloa v. Costa Rica*, also known as La Nación Newspaper Case, ... the Court held that requiring a journalist to prove the truth of statements made by third parties was an excessive restriction on the journalist's right to freedom of expression, and that there is a higher standard of protection for statements made about persons whose activities are within the domain of public interest.

Jo M. Pasqualucci, *Criminal Defamation and the Evolution of the Doctrine of Freedom of Expression in International Law: Comparative Jurisprudence of the Inter-American Court of Human Rights* 39 J. Transnat'l L. 379 (2006).

2. Australia

Chapman v. Conservation Council of South Australia

Supreme Court of South Australia
[2002] SASC 4

Williams, J.

1. An overview of the plaintiffs' case

The plaintiffs' claim damages for libel in respect of eleven individual publications....

It is the plaintiffs' case that the Conservation Council and its officers in the course of a campaign against the building of the Hindmarsh Island bridge were party to attacks upon the reputation of the plaintiffs as persons known to be the developers of a marina and real estate project which would be serviced by the Bridge. The plaintiffs' contend that the campaign was designed to influence public opinion and to persuade those with an immediate commercial interest to withdraw from the project or to abandon the bridge construction and continue to rely upon ferries to provide access to the Island.... It is the plaintiffs' case that there were aspects of the anti-bridge campaign (to which the defendants were party) which went beyond the bounds of justifiable debate or lawful protest; the 11 publications now in issue are claimed to be instances of these excesses in the course of "the struggle." ...

The plaintiffs' allege that defamatory attacks were made through media releases and by publication of articles in Environment South Australia—a periodical produced by the Conservation Council for circulation amongst its member organisations and the conservation movement more generally....

The defendants deny the alleged defamatory imputations.... The defendants also plead fair comment upon a matter of public interest and they further assert that the publications were made on occasions of qualified privilege (in accordance with common law principles and as these were extended by *Lange*—see below). In order to make out this last mentioned defence the defendants assert that their conduct as publishers was reasonable with respect to discussion of "Government or political matters" (see *Lange v. Australian Broadcasting [Corporation]* (1997) 189 CLR 520 at 574). There is an issue as to whether these defences are available but in any event the plaintiffs reply that any defence of fair comment or qualified privilege which might otherwise be available to the defendants is defeated because the defendants were actuated by malice.

In respect of some publications and to some imputations the defendants purport to plead truth as a defence but in each case the supposed justification is a false plea in that the defendants purport to deal with imputations which the defence puts forward rather than the imputations relied upon by the plaintiffs....

To the extent that the defendants claim to have published (on occasions of privilege) material which is defamatory of a plaintiff it becomes important to examine the motivation for the publication....

The legal principles

(a) The nature of libel

The gist of the tort of libel is the publication of material ... conveying a defamatory imputation.... The issue is whether the words in their particular context impinge adversely upon the reputation of the particular plaintiff....

Words or matter which merely injure the feelings of the plaintiff or cause annoyance but without in any way reflecting on character or reputation or tend to cause the plaintiff to be shunned or avoided are not actionable as defamation [*Gatley* supra at par 2.9].... Words which tend to cause inference with a person's business are not as such defamatory unless they tend to injure the plaintiff's reputation....

(b) The defence of qualified privilege

Qualified privilege at common law was described by Lord Atkin in *Adam v. Ward* [1917] AC 309 at 334:

> [A] privileged occasion is, in reference to qualified privilege, an occasion where the person who makes a communication has an interest or a duty, legal, social, or moral, to make it to the person to whom it is made and the person to whom it is so made has a corresponding interest or duty to receive it. This reciprocity is essential.

Qualified privilege is defeated if the plaintiff proves that the defendant was activated by "express" or "actual" malice. The plaintiff must prove that the defendant's dominant motivation was something not directly connected with the privilege so as to constitute an abuse of the privilege of the occasion. The usual motive is a desire to injure the plaintiff.

This defence has been "extended" by the High Court in *Lange v. Australian Broadcasting Corporation* (1997) 189 CLR 520....

The High Court said at 571:

> [T]his Court should now declare that each member of the Australian community has an interest in disseminating and receiving information, opinions and arguments concerning government and political matters that affect the people of Australia.... The interest that each member of the Australian community has in such a discussion extends the categories of qualified privilege. Consequently, those categories now must be recognised as protecting a communication made to the public on a government or political matter.

and at 574:

> ... [T]he reputations of those defamed by widespread publications will be adequately protected by requiring the publisher to prove reasonableness of conduct. The protection of those reputations will be further enhanced by the requirement that the defence will be defeated if the person defamed proves that the publication was actuated by common law malice to the extent that the elements of malice are not covered under the rubric of reasonableness....

(c) The defence of fair comment on a matter of public interest

It is of the essence of this defence that the published material is an honest expression of opinion. An imputation of corrupt or dishonourable motives will render the comment unfair unless such imputation is warranted by the facts truly stated. The essential elements of the defence are:

    (a) the words are an expression of opinion (as opposed to a statement of fact).

    (b) the opinion is with respect to a topic of public interest.

    (c) the comment was fair; this requires the opinion to be expressed on a matter of fact (or on privileged material such as the judgment of a court or the proceedings of Parliament) and to be expressed honestly (see Tobin and Sexton—Australian Defamation Law par 13010).

This defence will also be defeated by malice (the onus of proving which lies on the plaintiff)....

The identification of defamatory imputations (and consequential issues thereby raised on the pleadings) ...

The first step is to decide whether the words in question were written of or concerning the plaintiffs (or any of them) and whether any of the alleged imputations arise and, if so whether any such imputation is defamatory....

Synopsis of conclusions

[The court summarises 11 different publications which plaintiffs allege are defamatory. The court dismisses all but three of the alleged publications as non-defamatory. However, publication 6, 7, and 11 are found to be defamatory.]

Defamatory imputations

In respect of the three defamatory publications I find that the following imputations arise:

Publications No 6 and 7 impute motive and conduct which the ordinary person would treat as dishonourable. Publication No 11 attributes to developers a cavalier attitude (at the least) in the discharge of their professional responsibilities....

In my judgment each of these imputations would tend to "lower Tom or Wendy Chapman (as the case may be) in the estimation of right thinking members of society generally." They are statements which if false bring discredit upon the reputation of the persons about whom they are written....

Upon a fair reading of the pleadings ... I do not consider that a defence of truth (or justification as it is often called) is properly raised....

Conclusion ...

The defendants rely upon claims of qualified privilege and fair comment but I am satisfied that each of the personal defendants was activated by malice which would defeat any such defence. I impute malice to the Conservation Council by reason of the state of mind of the person or persons responsible for publishing in its name....

In the present case the evidence as to motivation for Publications No 6, 7 and 11 is strong. The plaintiffs have produced clear and cogent evidence of motivation which satisfies the civil standard of proof and discharges the onus which Mrs. Chapman (together with her husband in two instances) bears....

The Conservation Council of SA [South Australia] is liable for these publications made in its name and on its behalf by its officers.

Each of the publications was made in the course of and for the dominant purpose of a campaign to attack those associated with the building of the bridge. The defendants claim that that they were only interested in preventing the bridge from being built. However, the means adopted was to coerce the Chapmans and their interests and also to seek to demonstrate to others that the Chapmans were not the sort of people with whom they should be associated in business. The defendants' statements were not the honest expressions of their real opinions and they did not have an honest belief in the truth of the facts which they asserted.

The personal defendants ... claim to be acting to protect the wetlands of the Lower Murray from further degradation by an influx of visitors; they also condemn the urban sprawl which they anticipate from the development of the Island as a suburb of the Town of Goolwa. For these environmental reasons (amongst others) they sought to ensure that the bridge project was abandoned ... Although the personal defendants in their own minds justify their conduct by reference to their environmental concerns, I am satisfied that their immediate object in publishing Publications No 6, 7 and 11 has been to coerce the Chapmans to give way.

In my opinion the conduct of the defendants in the circumstances is not reasonable. I do not consider that the defendants had reasonable grounds for believing that the imputations (for which they respectively were responsible) were true; they did not take proper steps to verify the accuracy of the material; they were (at least) recklessly indifferent as to the truth of what they published....

In fixing damages I have brought to account the effect of § 11 of the *Wrongs Act* 1936.... I have had regard to the fact that each of the tortious acts appears to have occurred in the course of a concerted campaign in which each blow which was delivered must have had some cumulative effect. Each blow must have had the effect of besmirching the reputation of Tom or Wendy Chapman....

In fixing damages I have had regard to the important position of influence occupied by the Conservation Council with regard to public affairs. Liability having been established, the damages to be awarded must reflect the unique and responsible position occupied by the Conservation Council and the authority which will be seen by the ordinary person as attaching to its statements. The result is as follows:

Publication No. 6, September 1994

The President's message "Suppression of Free Speech" written by Professor Shearman carries the imputation that Wendy Chapman was party to the commencement of Court proceedings for the purpose of stopping the Conservation Council (and others) from engaging in legitimate expression of opinion regarding the Hindmarsh Bridge issue....

This article was written on an occasion of qualified privilege (at common law) but any claim to privilege is defeated by malice. Professor Shearman's history discloses his preparedness (using his own expression) to "target" the developers and their financiers in order to apply improper pressure. This is what happened on this occasion. This publication is part of a campaign designed to injure the Chapmans in terms of reputation.

Publication No. 7, December 1994

"A Win for Freedom of Speech" was written by Ms Bolster and Mr. Owen. It carries the imputation that Tom and Wendy Chapman are oppressing the people of Goolwa in relation to the Bridge issue.

The publication did not occur on a privileged occasion. In any event the publication was malicious. The publication is part of the campaign to which Mr. Owen and Ms Bolster are party to coerce Tom and Wendy Chapman to withdraw from the Bridge project and to denigrate them in the eyes of others.

Publication No. 11, September 1995

"Hindmarsh Island-Not so secret political business" is published by the Conservation Council over the name "Kumarangk Coalition." It reflects adversely upon the way in which Tom and Wendy Chapman as developers carried out the planning process for the bridge and the way in which thereafter they gave effect to consultative obligations with respect to the bridge building.

I consider that this publication was dealing with a topic of "government or political information" and has the potential to attract the *Lange* defence. However, the conduct of the publisher was not reasonable. No proper steps were taken to verify the accuracy of the information. The publication was for the purpose of the campaign as abovementioned and the subject matter of complaint was published without any honest belief in the truth of the imputation on the part of the person responsible for the publication. The publication was actuated by malice.

There is a public interest in encouraging bodies such as the Conservation Council to participate in public debate but within limits; individual reputations must be protected. The principles which I have discussed achieve a balance between these considerations.

In the result:

(1) Professor Shearman and the Conservation Council are jointly and severally liable to Mrs. Chapman in respect of Publication no 6 in respect of which I award her $20,000 as damages.

(2) Ms. Bolster and Mr. Owen and the Conservation Council are jointly and severally liable to Mr. Tom and Mrs. Wendy Chapman respectively in respect of Publication no 7 in respect of which I award each of them $25,000 as damages.

(3) The Conservation Council is liable to Mr. Tom and Mrs. Wendy Chapman respectively in respect of Publication no.11 in respect of which I award each of them $30,000 as damages.

(4) The claims made by all plaintiffs are otherwise dismissed.

Questions and Discussion

1. The *Chapman case.* The case was part of a string of similar defamation suits in Australia that led to reforms in the defamation law. The New South Wales Defamation Act of 2005 states as one of its objects, "to ensure that the law of defamation does not place unreasonable limits on the publication and discussion of matters of public interest and importance." Defamation Act 2005, [1](3)(b) (Austl.) The act denies corporations with 10 or more employees a cause of action under defamation law. *Id.* at section [2](9)(2)(b). However, the act still would not have prevented the *Chapman* suit because the plaintiffs sued the defendants as individuals rather than through their corporation. What other reforms do you think are necessary in order to protect defendants like the Conservation Council from being sued as a result of their political campaign activities?

2. *Malice generally.* In Australian common law, defamation defenses, including qualified privilege and fair comment on a matter of public interest can be defeated with proof that the defendant acted with malice. The dominant motivation must be something not directly connected to the statement that gives rise to the libel suit. In *Chapman*, what ev-

idence did the court point to in order to establish malice? Was the Defendants' motivation to publish the statements separate from their overall goal to prevent the bridge from being built? What evidence did the court point to in its finding that the defendant's did not have an honest or reasonable belief in the truth of the statements that they made?

3. *Malice requirements.* What does malice mean? Isn't there always a certain amount of malice toward the people allegedly violating human rights? Do the courts set too high a bar by requiring that citizens be pure of mind and thought in order to have their speech protected?

E. Judicial Remedies in the U.S. and Europe

Defendants have attempted several strategies to make it more difficult for a SLAPP suit to be tried in court. One of the first successful strategies was to "SLAPP back" with a countersuit or motion to dismiss. Judges will often side with the defendant in a SLAPP suit if it is obvious from the complaint that the suit is an abuse of process. However, it is not always so easy for courts to dismiss a SLAPP suit. As you read this next section, think about what court reforms might make it easier for a judge to recognize the difference between a legitimate claim and one meant to stifle an individual's free speech and public participation rights.

1. U.S. "SLAPPback"

SLAPP: Getting Sued for Speaking Out (1996)

George Pring & Penelope Canan

Judicial Cures—Managing the SLAPPback

What chance does a big corporation [filing a SLAPP] have against a family farmer ... or a humongous developer against an environmentalist? The plaintiffs will have a field day [with a SLAPPback]. —Attorney defending a real estate developer in a SLAPPback

The most promising prevention and cure for the SLAPP phenomenon, we find, is what we call the "SLAPPback": a countersuit in which targets turn the tables and sue the filers for the injuries and losses caused by the SLAPP .

SLAPPbacks are exercises in irony. The first irony is, as one target put it, that "the cure is a dose of the same disease." It is true that they fight fire with fire, one lawsuit with another, but each of the two stands on a quite different footing. The SLAPP, the dismissals tell us, is an abuse of the courts, a violation of constitutional rights, and an unconstitutional effort to quell public participation in government. The SLAPPback, on the other hand, is an accepted use of the courts, a vindication of constitutional rights, and an effort to hold persons accountable for the injuries they cause individuals and the body politic. A second irony is that SLAPPbacks are really conventional personal injury actions, with more similarities to a vehicle accident or medical malpractice suit than to a constitutional test case. A third irony is that SLAPPbacks "recycle" the SLAPP filers' original charges. Malicious prosecution and abuse of process head the list, followed by defamation, interference with business, conspiracy, and other familiar complaints. A final irony is that whereas SLAPPs are usually losers, SLAPPbacks tend to be winners in court. The filer's attorney quoted above is correct: plaintiffs and juries do have a "field day" in many

SLAPPbacks. Jury verdicts of $5,000,000, $9,000,000, $13,000,000, and even a staggering $86,000,000 have been handed down against SLAPP filers in the 1980s and 1990s.

Those ironies are not lost on filers. As consumer-advocate Ralph Nader observes, real estate developers, polluters, public officials, and others who just a few years ago might have unthinkingly SLAPPed their opposition are now "thinking twice." Even though SLAPP-backs are not a panacea, the risk of having to defend against them may prove the most effective SLAPP deterrent of all. . . .

Leonardini: The First Multimillion-Dollar Verdict

A megacorporation, Shell Oil Company, has the distinction of being the first to lose a multimillion-dollar SLAPPback. In *Shell v. Leonardini*, Shell sued a consumer advocate and union attorney for reporting to a state health agency that there were cancer-causing substances in a Shell product used in home plumbing. Target Ray Leonardini took the SLAPP to Sacramento trial attorney John M. Poswall; the two attorneys immediately saw the Petition Clause aspects of the case and lashed back with a dismissal motion charging constitutional rights violations. Shell first pressed its lawsuit and then, in a turnabout, voluntarily dismissed it, claiming that a codefendant's settlement was vindication. Now truly outraged, the Leonardini-Poswall team filed their SLAPPback, charging malicious prosecution to violate Leonardini's constitutional rights.

The case went to trial in 1986, and Shell lost badly. Poswall hammered away at the constitutional issues, arguing that Shell's suit had been groundless and designed to keep Leonardini from testifying to the government against its product:

This case is not about chemicals. . . . The issues . . . are more fundamental to our society than the dangers posed to millions of Californians by toxic chemicals in their drinking water. . . .

Ray Leonardini advocated that the public bodies charged with the responsibility for health and safety independently test and examine the polybutylene pipe system before exposing millions of Californians to the unknown consequences of such use. In the midst of the ongoing public debate regarding the policies that California governmental bodies should follow, the Shell Oil Company sued its most effective political "opponent."

Shell pursued the standard SLAPPback defense strategy, denying that its suit had anything to do with constitutional rights and portraying it instead as an ordinary, defamation action "based on Leonardini's circulation of false, incomplete, and misleading statements concerning Shell's polybutylene resin . . . result[ing] in irreparable and unquantifiable harm to Shell. . . . Shell requested injunctive relief . . . to stop the continued dissemination of false statements about its product." The five-week case put Shell's product, truthfulness, mental state, and politics on trial.

Malicious prosecution, the core charge in virtually all SLAPPbacks, is not an easy charge to prove. Some courts even call it "a disfavored action," because the Petition Clause and public policy favor giving everyone open access to the courts for redress of grievances. Even though no one has an absolute right to sue (one does not have a right, for example, to file an unconstitutional suit), strict proof requirements are customary to justify suing someone for suing you—state-of-mind proofs like "malice" and "lack of probable cause." Nonetheless, after both sides had presented their evidence, Judge Lloyd A. Phillips Jr. of Sacramento County Superior Court found the evidence so one-sided that he decided the issue of probable cause himself, issuing a directed verdict that Shell had no reasonable, good-faith grounds to regard its suit against Leonardini as proper. The jury unanimously found that Shell had been malicious and awarded Leonardini $175,000 in actual damages for intimidation, $22,000 in attorneys' fees, and a whopping $5,000,000 in punitive damages (damages designed not to compensate victims but to punish perpetrators, and therefore based less on the magnitude of the wrong than on the perpetrator's net worth).

Shell appealed the $5,197,000 verdict, but the state appeals court upheld it in full in 1989 in a detailed 32-page opinion, the first published SLAPPback opinion of which we are aware. The court clearly saw the case as one involving an attempt "to influence government" in a "public debate ... being aired before a branch of state government ... of great [importance]."

2. Fair Trial and Disproportionate Damages

While the SLAPPback has been used successfully by savvy SLAPP defendants in the United States, some SLAPP defendants have no recourse other than to defend themselves on the merits and continue through the appeals process until either their rights are recognized or their remedies are exhausted. The *Steel & Morris* case demonstrates how arduous a battle it can be for SLAPP defendants to work their way through the judicial system if they are acting *pro se* or if they have quite limited legal representation. Does it establish a general right in Europe to legal aid for SLAPP defendants of limited means?

Steel & Morris v. United Kingdom

European Court of Human Rights
No. 68416/01, ECHR 2005-II, 41 E.H.R.R. 22 (2005)

I. The Circumstances of the Case

A. The leaflet

The applicants, Helen Steel and David Morris, were born in 1965 and 1954 respectively and live in London....

Ms Steel was at times employed as a part-time bar worker, earning approximately 65 pounds sterling (GBP) per week.... Mr. Morris, a former postal worker, was unwaged and in receipt of income support. He was a single parent ... of his son, aged 4.... At all material times the applicants were associated with London Greenpeace....

In the mid-1980s London Greenpeace began an anti-McDonald's campaign. In 1986 a six-page leaflet entitled "What's wrong with McDonald's?" ("the leaflet") was produced and distributed as part of that campaign....

The first page of the leaflet showed a grotesque cartoon image of a man, wearing a Stetson and with dollar signs in his eyes, hiding behind a "Ronald McDonald" clown mask. Running along the top of pages 2 to 5 was a header comprised of the McDonald's "golden arches" symbol, with the words "McDollars, McGreedy, McCancer, McMurder, McDisease ..." and so forth superimposed on it....

B. Proceedings in the High Court ...

Between October 1989 and January or May 1991, UK McDonald's hired seven private investigators from two different firms to infiltrate the group with the aim of finding out who was responsible for writing, printing and distributing the leaflet and organising the anti-McDonald's campaign. The inquiry agents attended over forty meetings of London Greenpeace, which were open to any member of the public who wished to attend, and other events such as "fayres" and public, fund-raising occasions. McDonald's subsequently relied on the evidence of some of these agents at trial to establish that the applicants had attended meetings and events and been closely involved with the organisation during the period when the leaflet was being produced and distributed.

On 20 September 1990 McDonald's Corporation ("US McDonald's") and McDonald's Restaurants Limited ("UK McDonald's"), together referred to herein as "McDonald's," issued a writ against the applicants and three others, claiming damages of up to GBP 100,000 for libel caused by the alleged publication by the defendants of the leaflet. McDonald's withdrew proceedings against the three other defendants, in exchange for their apology for the contents of the leaflet....

The applicants applied for legal aid but were refused it on 3 June 1992, because legal aid was not available for defamation proceedings in the United Kingdom. They therefore represented themselves throughout the trial and appeal. Approximately GBP 40,000 was raised by donation to assist them (for example, to pay for transcripts: see paragraph 20 below), and they received some help from barristers and solicitors acting pro bono: thus, their initial pleadings were drafted by lawyers, they were given some advice on an ad hoc basis, and they were represented during five of the pre-trial hearings and on three occasions during the trial, including the appeal to the Court of Appeal against the trial judge's grant of leave to McDonald's to amend the statement of claim (see paragraph 24 below). They submitted, however, that they were severely hampered by lack of resources, not just in the way of legal advice and representation, but also when it came to administration, photocopying, note-taking, and the tracing, preparation and payment of the costs and expenses of expert and factual witnesses. Throughout the proceedings McDonald's were represented by leading and junior counsel, experienced in defamation law, and by one or two solicitors and other assistants....

The trial took place before Bell J between 28 June 1994 and 13 December 1996. It lasted for 313 court days, of which 40 were taken up with legal argument, and was the longest trial (either civil or criminal) in English legal history. Transcripts of the trial ran to approximately 20,000 pages; there were about 40,000 pages of documentary evidence; and, in addition to many written witness statements, 130 witnesses gave oral evidence — 59 for the applicants, 71 for McDonald's. Ms. Steel gave evidence in person but Mr. Morris chose not to....

When all the evidence had been adduced, Bell J deliberated for six months before delivering his substantive 762-page judgment on 19 June 1997.

The judge awarded U.S. McDonald's GBP 30,000 damages and UK McDonald's a further GBP 30,000....

C. The substantive appeal

The applicants appealed to the Court of Appeal on 3 September 1997. The hearing ... lasted 23 days, and on 31 March 1999 the court delivered its 301-page judgment....

The applicants ... challenged a number of Bell J's findings about the content of the leaflet, and the Court of Appeal found in their favour on several points, summarised as follows:

> On the topic of nutrition, the allegation that eating McDonald's food would lead to a very real risk of cancer of the breast and of the bowel was not proved....

> In addition to the charges found to be true by the judge — the exploiting of children by advertising, the pretence by the respondents that their food had a positive nutritional benefit, and McDonald's responsibility for cruel practices in the rearing and slaughtering of some of the animals used for their products —

the further allegation that, if one eats enough McDonald's food, one's diet may well become high in fat etc., with the very real risk of heart disease, was justified. . . .

The Court of Appeal therefore reduced the damages payable to McDonald's, so that Ms Steel was now liable for a total of GBP 36,000 and Mr. Morris for a total of GBP 40,000. It refused the applicants leave to appeal to the House of Lords.

On 21 March 2000 the Appeal Committee of the House of Lords ... refused the applicants leave to appeal.

II. Relevant Domestic Law and Practice

A. Defamation

Under English law the object of a libel action is to vindicate the plaintiff's reputation and to make reparation for the injury done by the wrongful publication of defamatory statements concerning him or her.

The plaintiff carries the burden of proving "publication." ...

A defence of justification applies where the defamatory statement is substantially true. The burden is on the defendant to prove the truth of the statement on the balance of probabilities. It is no defence to a libel action to prove that the defendant acted in good faith, believing the statement to be true. English law does, however, recognise the defence of "fair comment," if it can be established that the defamatory statement is comment, and not an assertion of fact, and is based on a substratum of facts, the truth of which the defendant must prove.

As a general principle, a trading or non-trading corporation is entitled to sue in libel to protect as much of its corporate reputation as is capable of being damaged by a defamatory statement. There are certain exceptions to this rule: local authorities, government-owned corporations and political parties, none of which can sue in defamation, because of the public interest that a democratically elected organisation, or a body controlled by such an organisation, should be open to uninhibited public criticism ...

B. Legal aid for defamation proceedings

Throughout the relevant time, the allocation of civil legal aid in the United Kingdom was governed by the Legal Aid Act 1988. Under Schedule 2, Part II, paragraph 1 of that Act, "[p]roceedings wholly or partly in respect of defamation" were excepted from the scope of the civil legal aid scheme. . . .

The normal rule in civil proceedings in England and Wales, including defamation proceedings, is that the loser pays the reasonable costs of the winner. This rule applies whether either party is legally aided or not. An unsuccessful privately paying party would usually be ordered to pay the legal costs of a successful legally aided opponent. However, an unsuccessful legally aided party is usually protected from paying the costs of a successful privately paying party, because the costs order made against the loser will not usually be enforceable without further order of the court, which is likely to be granted only in the event of a major improvement in the financial circumstances of the legally aided party. . . .

D. Damages

The measure of damages for defamation is the amount that would put the plaintiff in the position he or she would have been in had the wrongdoing not been committed. The plaintiff does not have to prove that he has suffered any actual pecuniary loss: it is for the jury (or judge, if sitting alone) to award a sum of damages sufficient to vindicate the plaintiff's reputation and to compensate for injury to feelings.

THE LAW

I. Alleged Violation of Article 6 § 1 of the Convention

The applicants raised a number of issues under Article 6 § 1 of the Convention, which provides:

> In the determination of his civil rights and obligations..., everyone is entitled to a fair ... hearing ... by [a] ... tribunal....

The applicants' principal complaint under this provision was that they were denied a fair trial because of the lack of legal aid....

A. Legal Aid ...

2. The Court's assessment

The Court reiterates that the Convention is intended to guarantee practical and effective rights. This is particularly so of the right of access to a court in view of the prominent place held in a democratic society by the right to a fair trial. It is central to the concept of a fair trial, in civil as in criminal proceedings, that a litigant is not denied the opportunity to present his or her case effectively before the court and that he or she is able to enjoy equality of arms with the opposing side (see, among many other examples, *De Haes and Gijsels v. Belgium*, judgment of 24 February 1997, Reports of Judgments and Decisions 1997-I, p. 238, § 53).

Article 6 § 1 leaves to the State a free choice of the means to be used in guaranteeing litigants the above rights. The institution of a legal aid scheme constitutes one of those means but there are others, such as for example simplifying the applicable procedure.

The question whether the provision of legal aid is necessary for a fair hearing must be determined on the basis of the particular facts and circumstances of each case and will depend, inter alia, upon the importance of what is at stake for the applicant in the proceedings, the complexity of the relevant law and procedure and the applicant's capacity to represent him or herself effectively.

The right of access to a court is not, however, absolute and may be subject to restrictions, provided that these pursue a legitimate aim and are proportionate. It may therefore be acceptable to impose conditions on the grant of legal aid based, inter alia, on the financial situation of the litigant or his or her prospects of success in the proceedings. Moreover, it is not incumbent on the State to seek through the use of public funds to ensure total equality of arms between the assisted person and the opposing party....

The Court must examine the facts of the present case with reference to the above criteria.

First, as regards what was at stake for the applicants ... it must be recalled that the applicants did not choose to commence defamation proceedings, but acted as defendants to protect their right to freedom of expression, a right accorded considerable importance under the Convention. Moreover, the financial consequences for the applicants of failing to verify each defamatory statement complained of were significant....

Against this background, the Court must assess the extent to which the applicants were able to bring an effective defence despite the absence of legal aid....

The present applicants appear to have been articulate and resourceful; in the words of the Court of Appeal, they conducted their case "forcefully and with persistence," and they succeeded in proving the truth of a number of the statements complained of....

The Government have laid emphasis on the considerable latitude afforded to the applicants by the judges of the domestic courts, both at first instance and on appeal, in recognition of the disadvantages the applicants faced. However, the Court considers that, in an action of this complexity, neither the sporadic help given by the volunteer lawyers nor the extensive judicial assistance and latitude granted to the applicants as litigants in person was any substitute for competent and sustained representation by an experienced lawyer familiar with the case and with the law of libel.... Finally, the disparity between the respective levels of legal assistance enjoyed by the applicants and McDonald's was of such a degree that it could not have failed, in this exceptionally demanding case, to have given rise to unfairness, despite the best efforts of the judges at first instance and on appeal....

In conclusion, therefore, the Court finds that the denial of legal aid to the applicants deprived them of the opportunity to present their case effectively before the court and contributed to an unacceptable inequality of arms with McDonald's. There has, therefore, been a violation of Article 6 § 1 of the Convention.

II. Alleged Violation of Article 10 of the Convention

The applicants also complained of a breach of Article 10 of the Convention, which provides:

1. Everyone has the right to freedom of expression. This right shall include freedom to hold opinions and to receive and impart information and ideas without interference by public authority and regardless of frontiers....

2. The exercise of these freedoms, since it carries with it duties and responsibilities, may be subject to such formalities, conditions, restrictions or penalties as are prescribed by law and are necessary in a democratic society, in the interests of national security, territorial integrity or public safety, for the prevention of disorder or crime, for the protection of health or morals, for the protection of the reputation or rights of others, for preventing the disclosure of information received in confidence, or for maintaining the authority and impartiality of the judiciary....

The Court's assessment

It was not disputed between the parties that the defamation proceedings and their outcome amounted to an interference, for which the State had responsibility, with the applicants' rights to freedom of expression.

It is further not disputed, and the Court finds, that the interference was "prescribed by law." The Court further finds that the English law of defamation, and its application in this particular case, pursued the legitimate aim of "the protection of the reputation or rights of others."

The central issue which falls to be determined is whether the interference was "necessary in a democratic society." The fundamental principles relating to this question are well established in the case-law and have been summarised as follows (see, for example, *Hertel v. Switzerland*, judgment of 25 August 1998, Reports 1998-VI, pp. 2329–30, § 46):

(i) Freedom of expression constitutes one of the essential foundations of a democratic society and one of the basic conditions for its progress and for each individual's self-fulfilment. Subject to paragraph 2 of Article 10, it is applicable not only to "information" or "ideas" that are favourably received or regarded as inoffensive or as a matter of indifference, but also to those that offend, shock or disturb. Such are the demands of pluralism, tolerance and broadmindedness without which there is no "democratic society." As set forth in Article 10, this freedom is subject to exceptions, which … must, however, be construed strictly, and the need for any restrictions must be established convincingly.…

(ii)   The adjective "necessary," within the meaning of Article 10 § 2, implies the existence of a "pressing social need." The Contracting States have a certain margin of appreciation in assessing whether such a need exists, but it goes hand in hand with European supervision, embracing both the legislation and the decisions applying it, even those given by an independent court. The Court is therefore empowered to give the final ruling on whether a "restriction" is reconcilable with freedom of expression as protected by Article 10.…

In its practice, the Court has distinguished between statements of fact and value judgments. While the existence of facts can be demonstrated, the truth of value judgments is not susceptible of proof. Where a statement amounts to a value judgment the proportionality of an interference may depend on whether there exists a sufficient factual basis for the impugned statement, since even a value judgment without any factual basis to support it may be excessive.

The Court must weigh a number of factors in the balance when reviewing the proportionality of the measure complained of. First, it notes that the leaflet in question contained very serious allegations on topics of general concern, such as abusive and immoral farming and employment practices, deforestation, the exploitation of children and their parents through aggressive advertising and the sale of unhealthy food. The Court has long held that "political expression," including expression on matters of public interest and concern, requires a high level of protection under Article 10 (see, for example, *Thorgeir Thorgeirson v. Iceland*, judgment of 25 June 1992, Series A no. 239, and also *Hertel*, cited above, p. 2330, § 47).

The Government have pointed out that the applicants were not journalists, and should not therefore attract the high level of protection afforded to the press under Article 10.

The Court considers, however, that in a democratic society even small and informal campaign groups, such as London Greenpeace, must be able to carry on their activities effectively and that there exists a strong public interest in enabling such groups and individuals outside the mainstream to contribute to the public debate by disseminating information and ideas on matters of general public interest such as health and the environment (see, *mutatis mutandis, Bowman v. the United Kingdom*, judgment of 19 February 1998, Reports 1998-I, and *Appleby v. the United Kingdom*, no. 44306/98, ECHR 2003 VI).

Nonetheless, the Court has held on many occasions that even the press "must not overstep certain bounds, in particular in respect of the reputation and rights of others and the need to prevent the disclosure of confidential information.…" The safeguard afforded by Article 10 to journalists in relation to reporting on issues of general interest is subject to the proviso that they act in good faith in order to provide accurate and reliable information in accordance with the ethics of journalism, and the same principle must apply to others who engage in public debate. It is true that the Court has held that journalists are allowed "recourse to a degree of exaggeration, or even provocation," and it considers that in a campaigning leaflet a certain degree of hyperbole and exaggeration is to be tolerated, and even expected. In the present case, however, the allegations were of a very serious nature and were presented as statements of fact rather than value judgments.

The applicants ... stress that they genuinely believed the leaflet's content to be true. They claim that it places an intolerable burden on campaigners such as themselves, and thus stifles public debate, to require those who merely distribute a leaflet to bear the burden of establishing the truth of every statement contained in it. They also argue that large multinational companies should not be entitled to sue in defamation, at least without proof of actual financial damage....

The Court further does not consider that the fact that the plaintiff in the present case was a large multinational company should in principle deprive it of a right to defend itself against defamatory allegations or entail that the applicants should not have been required to prove the truth of the statements made.... [I]n addition to the public interest in open debate about business practices, there is a competing interest in protecting the commercial success and viability of companies, for the benefit of shareholders and employees, but also for the wider economic good. The State therefore enjoys a margin of appreciation as to the means it provides under domestic law to enable a company to challenge the truth, and limit the damage, of allegations which risk harming its reputation.

If, however, a State decides to provide such a remedy to a corporate body, it is essential, in order to safeguard the countervailing interests in free expression and open debate, that a measure of procedural fairness and equality of arms is provided for. The Court has already found that the lack of legal aid rendered the defamation proceedings unfair, in breach of Article 6 § 1. The inequality of arms and the difficulties under which the applicants laboured are also significant in assessing the proportionality of the interference under Article 10. As a result of the law as it stood in England and Wales, the applicants had the choice either to withdraw the leaflet and apologise to McDonald's, or bear the burden of proving, without legal aid, the truth of the allegations contained in it. Given the enormity and complexity of that undertaking, the Court does not consider that the correct balance was struck between the need to protect the applicants' rights to freedom of expression and the need to protect McDonald's rights and reputation. The more general interest in promoting the free circulation of information and ideas about the activities of powerful commercial entities, and the possible "chilling" effect on others are also important factors to be considered in this context, bearing in mind the legitimate and important role that campaign groups can play in stimulating public discussion. The lack of procedural fairness and equality therefore gave rise to a breach of Article 10 in the present case.

Moreover, the Court considers that the size of the award of damages made against the two applicants may also have failed to strike the right balance. Under the Convention, an award of damages for defamation must bear a reasonable relationship of proportionality to the injury to reputation suffered. The Court notes on the one hand that the sums eventually awarded in the present case (GBP 36,000 in the case of the first applicant and GBP 40,000 in the case of the second applicant), although relatively moderate by contemporary standards in defamation cases in England and Wales, were very substantial when compared to the modest incomes and resources of the two applicants. While accepting, on the other hand, that the statements in the leaflet which were found to be untrue contained serious allegations, the Court observes that not only were the plaintiffs large and powerful corporate entities but that, in accordance with the principles of English law, they were not required to, and did not, establish that they had in fact suffered any financial loss as a result of the publication of the "several thousand" copies of the leaflets found by the trial judge to have been distributed....

[T]he Court finds that the award of damages in the present case was disproportionate to the legitimate aim served.

In conclusion, given the lack of procedural fairness and the disproportionate award of damages, the Court finds that there has been a violation of Article 10 of the Convention....

FOR THESE REASONS, THE COURT UNANIMOUSLY

1. Holds that there has been a violation of Article 6 § 1 of the Convention;

2. Holds that there has been a violation of Article 10 of the Convention;

3. Holds

    (a) that the respondent State is to pay the applicants, within three months from the date on which the judgment becomes final according to Article 44 § 2 of the Convention, the following amounts, to be converted into pounds sterling at the rate applicable at the time of settlement:

        (i) EUR 20,000 (twenty thousand euros) to the first applicant and EUR 15,000 (fifteen thousand euros) to the second applicant in respect of non-pecuniary damage;

        (ii) EUR 47,311.17 (forty-seven thousand three hundred and eleven euros seventeen cents) in respect of costs and expenses;

        (iii) any tax that may be chargeable on the above amounts....

Michael O'Boyle, Registrar

Matti Pellonpää, President

Questions and Discussion

1. *Time considerations.* If Helen Steel and David Morris had SLAPPed-back with a libel or malicious prosecution claim, would the case have lasted as long as it did? (Note, however, that in some instances, malicious prosecution can be filed only after the original case has ended.) Would they have been able to avoid the drawn out legal proceedings if legal aid was available for defamation defendants? Even if Steel and Morris had legal aid, would they have had fair representation against the attorneys representing McDonald's?

2. *Significance of truth.* Was the major difference between the *Leonardini* case, where the defendant SLAPPed-back against Shell, and the *Steel and Morris* case the level of representation available to the defendants, or was it the difference between the United States defamation law and English defamation law? In England, it is not a defense to libel that a statement was made with a good faith belief in its truth. Rather, the defendant must prove that the statement was "substantially true." In U.S. defamation law, where the plaintiff is a public figure, the burden is on the plaintiff to prove that the defendant published statements with knowledge that the statements were false and a reckless disregard for the truth. See *New York Times v. Sullivan*, 376 U.S. 254 (1964).

3. *Deterrent effect.* The negative press that McDonald's received over this case ultimately made Steel and Morris heroes in the activist community. Does that seem likely to deter other corporations from suing individuals exercising their rights to free expression? Should corporations have as much a right as individuals to sue for defamation?

4. *Lost income.* In their appeal to the European Court of Human Rights, Morris and Steel asked for pecuniary damages as a result of the United Kingdom's violations of articles 6 and 10. The court denied their claim because Morris and Steel could not present any evidence that the time they spent preparing for trial and defending themselves resulted in any loss because they did not lose any income (being unemployed).

F. Legislative Remedies in the U.S. and Australia

1. Anti-SLAPP Legislation

Baker v. Parsons (USA)

Supreme Judicial Court of Massachusetts, Middlesex
434 Mass. 543, 750 N.E.2d 953 (2001)

Present (Sitting at Northampton): MARSHALL, C.J., GREANEY, SPINA, COWIN, SOSMAN, & CORDY, JJ.

Cordy, J.

The plaintiff, a property owner in Plymouth, appeals from the decision of a Superior Court judge granting the defendants' special motion to dismiss his lawsuit, pursuant to G.L. c. 231, § 59H, commonly known as the anti-SLAPP statute.... We conclude that to defeat a special motion to dismiss made pursuant to G.L. c. 231, § 59H, the nonmoving party (the plaintiff here) must show by a preponderance of the evidence that the moving party's petitioning activities were devoid of any reasonable factual support or any arguable basis in law. Because this standard was not met in the present case, we affirm the decision allowing the defendants' special motion to dismiss.

Background. Between 1979 and 1991, John W. Baker (Baker) purchased various parcels of land on the northern end of Clark's Island in Plymouth. In 1987, he placed a portion of his acreage in a forestry trust on which he has since operated a tree farm. The defendants, Manomet Bird Observatory and Dr. Katherine C. Parsons, now a senior staff scientist for Manomet, studied bird populations on the island from 1975 to 1989. Manomet had once owned land on the island that was ultimately purchased by Baker. Baker allowed Parsons and Manomet to continue using his property for research purposes until he learned that they were seeking to have the island classified as an "area of critical environmental concern," which Baker believed would severely restrict his use of his land. He alleges that his decision to deny access to his property to the defendants "resulted in a smear campaign" by them against him.

In 1991, Baker applied for a license from the Massachusetts Department of Environmental Protection, and for a Federal permit from the United States Army Corps of Engineers (Army corps), to construct a pier on the northern end of his property. In response to his application, the Army corps solicited comment from various agencies including the natural heritage and endangered species program (natural heritage program), a division of the Massachusetts division of fisheries and wildlife, which has as one of its purposes the review of Army corps permit applications. In reviewing the application, Jay Copeland, an environmental reviewer for the natural heritage program, solicited comments from Parsons....

On October 23, 1991, Parsons wrote a letter to Copeland that included the following statements:

> In sum, the Clark's Island site provided unique and rare nesting habitat to several species of colonial birds until 1986 when the site changed hands and no longer benefited from protective ownership. The present owner's activities in the heronry clearly have diminished and perhaps decimated a once robust and viable heronry.

> The significance of the site and its value to the state's avifauna cannot be overestimated. Located within a sheltered harbor within easy commute of extensive

marshes to the north and south, Clark's Island provides a predator-free habitat not easily replaced.

Habitat loss is the primary cause of loss in biodiversity at virtually any scale examined. It is my fervent hope that the state and federal agencies charged with protecting the region's natural resources will act to halt the continued degradation of this important site and restore Clark's Island to the prominence it held only recently in providing nesting habitat to aquatic birds. Thank you for this opportunity to comment.

Baker characterizes this letter as containing "defamatory allegations ... known by Parsons to be false and devoid of any reasonable factual support," and alleges that these statements caused ten citizens to petition the Executive Office of Environmental Affairs to require an environmental impact review of the proposed pier construction.

Last, Baker asserts that Parsons, when contacted in 1991 by Christopher Dowd, an officer with the United States Fish and Wildlife Service, falsely accused Baker of destroying heron nests on Memorial Day in 1989, by cutting his grass with a "brush hog," so that Baker would be criminally prosecuted for violating the Migratory Bird Treaty Act (MBTA), see 16 U.S.C. §§ 703–712 (2000), and so that his pier permit application would be denied....

Procedural history. In June, 1993, Baker brought various claims against the defendants, including a claim for tortious interference with his pier permit application. The defendants unsuccessfully sought summary judgment, asserting that the protection provided by the First Amendment to the United States Constitution to their petitioning activities immunized them from civil liability for injuries alleged by the plaintiff.

While the case was pending, the anti-SLAPP suit statute was enacted by the Legislature and made applicable to pending cases. The defendants then filed a special motion to dismiss.... A judge in the Superior Court allowed the motion, concluding that Parsons's statements constituted petitioning activity under the statute, and that Baker "failed to show that Parsons's alleged petitioning activity was devoid of any reasonable factual support or any arguable basis in law." ... Baker took an appeal from the allowance of the special motion to dismiss. We transferred the case here on our own initiative.

The amenability of this action to the statute.... Baker argues that a review of [recent] decisions, *McLarnon v. Jokisch*, 431 Mass. 343 (2000)(McLarnon), and *Duracraft Corp. v. Holmes Prods. Corp.*, 427 Mass. 156, 160 (1998)(*Duracraft*), makes it clear that the Superior Court erred in allowing the defendants' special motion to dismiss, because his claims against the defendants contain none of the indicia of a "typical" SLAPP suit. We do not agree.

In essence Baker maintains that because he is not a "developer," but just "an individual operating an environmentally friendly tree farm," while the defendant Manomet is a "wealthy and politically well-connected environmental organization," his lawsuit is not one to which the anti-SLAPP suit procedures of G.L. c. 231, § 59H, apply. Even if we were to accept these characterizations of the parties as true, this would not, without more, foreclose a special motion to dismiss pursuant to the statute....

In addition to its legislative history, the plain language of the statute, which is not limited in the manner suggested by Baker, squarely encompasses the facts of this case. Parsons, a biologist, responded to inquiries from State and Federal environmental officials.... As a result of her responses, Baker eventually sued Parsons and the nonprofit organization for which she works, thus, according to the defendants, "chilling" any further participation by the defendants in assisting State and Federal agencies gathering information on the merits of Baker's application.[12] ...

The special motion to dismiss.... In order to safeguard the rights of all parties, we required [in *Duracraft*] the special movant seeking the protection of the anti-SLAPP statute "to make a threshold showing through the pleadings and affidavits that the claims against it are "based on" the petitioning activities alone and have no substantial basis other than or in addition to the petitioning activities." [*Duracraft*] at 167–168.

Although she ruled before our decision in *Duracraft*, the motion judge evaluated the motion in a manner that demonstrates it met the threshold requirement set forth in that case. The judge writes:

> ... Parsons' communications with Copeland and Dowd fall squarely within the definition of petitioning activity as defined by the statute because they pertained to consideration by governmental agencies of Baker's application to construct a pier.

This initial showing by the defendants that the claims against them were based on their petitioning activities alone is not defeated by the plaintiff's conclusory assertion that "certain statements made by the [d]efendants [in petitions to government officials] constitute defamation." See Barker, *Common-law and Statutory Solutions to the Problem of SLAPPS*, 26 Loy. L.A. L.Rev. 395, 402 (1993) (defamation most popular SLAPP cause of action). Baker argues that the "libellous" statements of Parsons in her letter to Copeland were all directed at his tree farming activities on Clark's Island, and his tree farming activities were never under review by the natural heritage program. But, according to Copeland, Parsons was not asked to comment simply on the habitat value of the island, but to give "her impressions ... about the effect of the activities on the site."

Also, the judge correctly concluded that even if Parsons had made statements or taken actions to cause ten citizens to write to a State agency to petition for environmental review of Baker's pier proposal, as Baker alleges, such statements or actions would have constituted legitimate petitioning activity. Parsons's allegedly "false statements" to the citizens would have constituted "statement[s] reasonably likely to enlist public participation in an effort to effect such consideration." G.L. c. 231, § 59H.

Once the defendants established through pleadings and affidavits that the claims against them were based on petitioning activities..., the burden shifted to the nonmoving party to show ... that "(1) the moving party's exercise of its right to petition was devoid of any reasonable factual support or any arguable basis in law and (2) the moving party's acts caused actual injury to the responding party." G.L. c. 231, § 59H. See *McLarnon*, supra at 348–349. The judge found that Baker failed to meet this burden, reasoning that Parsons, a biologist who had studied bird populations on Clark's Island for many years, and had observed a decline in bird populations following Baker's activities, was not without a factual basis in projecting that an escalation of activities associated with the construction and use of a pier on the north end of the island would adversely affect the bird population.

---

12. Seen in this light, Baker's actions do in fact present a "typical" SLAPP suit, which often targets individuals for "reporting violations of law, writing to government officials, attending public hearings, testifying before government bodies, ... [and] filing agency protests or appeals." *Duracraft*, supra at 161–162, 691 N.E.2d 935, quoting G. Pring, *SLAPPs: Strategic Lawsuits Against Public Participation*, 7 Pace Envtl. L.Rev. 3, 5 (1989). "[SLAPP suits] are a response by detrimentally affected parties to the activities of citizens who petition the government. SLAPPs are intended to silence those citizens. In doing so, SLAPPs effectively deny vocal citizens their constitutional right to petition the government." (Footnotes omitted.) *Comment, Strategic Lawsuits Against Public Participation: An Analysis of the Solutions*, 27 Cal. W.L.Rev. 399, 399–400 (1991).

Neither the Legislature nor this court in our cases interpreting the anti-SLAPP statute has indicated what evidentiary standard is to be applied by a judge in weighing conflicting factual allegations in order to determine whether a party has met its burden of showing that an opposing "party's exercise of its right to petition was devoid of any reasonable factual support or any arguable basis in law." G.L. c. 231, § 59H....

[W]e conclude that the party opposing a special motion to dismiss is required to show by a preponderance of the evidence that the moving party lacked any reasonable factual support or any arguable basis in law for its petitioning activity. This standard places the burden on the nonmoving party, as the Legislature intended, but without creating an insurmountable barrier to relief.

We conclude that there was no abuse of discretion or other error of law in the judge's decision to grant the defendants' special motion to dismiss pursuant to G.L. c. 231, § 59H.

Judgment affirmed.

Questions and Discussion

1. *Burden of proof.* The Court was concerned about striking the right balance between the plaintiff's and the defendant's rights to petition. Did the court strike the right balance by requiring the plaintiff to prove by a preponderance of the evidence that defendant's action was devoid of any reasonable factual or legal support and that plaintiff suffered actual injury? What is the defendant's burden of proof in seeking the protection of the Anti-SLAPP statute?

2. *Anti-SLAPP in the U.S.* As of 2007, 25 states have passed Anti-SLAPP legislation, and nine states have pending legislation. See *The California Anti-SLAPP Project* at www.casp.net for links to State Anti-SLAPP statutes.

3. *Availability of "SLAPP-back" suits.* Some Anti-SLAPP statutes have created ambiguity as to whether a defendant that invokes its protections is then barred from SLAPPing-back with a claim for malicious prosecution. In 2005, California amended its statute to specifically allow relief through a SLAPP-back provision. See. Cal. C.C.P. § 425.16(b)(3) (2005).

2. Changes in Australian Legislation

Gunning for Change:
The Need for Public Participation Law Reform
Greg Ogle
The Wilderness Society, Inc., Australia (2005)

Part 1: The Problem

The Gunns Case, and More

In December 2004 the Tasmanian forestry giant, Gunns, Ltd., sued The Wilderness Society, five of its staff, and 14 other conservation groups and individuals (including Green Members of Parliament, Bob Brown and Peg Putt). Gunns claimed some $6.3m damages alleging that the defendants had interfered with the company's trade and business and contractual relations, and that the conservationists had conspired to injure Gunns by illegal means. There were nine discrete actions in the claim which include media statements, what Gunns claim was unlawful lobbying of shareholders, customers and governments, and protest actions in the forests and at woodchip mills. And overlaying all these actions has been the notion of a broad campaign (or conspiracy) against Gunns which makes all defendants liable for all actions — even where no direct involvement in particular actions is alleged.....

Part 2: Towards a Solution

The Need for Law Reform

There is no doubt that lawsuits against community activists can and do have a chilling effect on freedom of speech and the rights and ability of the community to engage in political action. As one U.S. judge said, "short of a gun to the head, a greater threat to [free] expression can scarcely be imagined." *Gordon v. Marrone* 155 Misc. 2d 726, 736 (NY Sup. Ct. 1992)....

The U.S. Examples

The United States already has had considerable law reform activity. Pring and Canan, who first described the problem with SLAPP suits also proposed legislation to protect public participation based on the U.S. First Amendment. Many jurisdictions [in the United States] have now introduced anti-SLAPP legislation in various forms. This legislation ranges from limited models which allow for summary dismissal of actions brought for an improper purpose (British Columbia), or dismissal of actions with no prima facie merit (California), to more far-reaching laws like the Rhode Island, Massachusetts and Minnesota statutes where cases which relate to reasonable public participation can be dismissed regardless of the merits of the case. The differences in these models are discussed below in relation to potential legislation.

In Australia, there is no such legislation to protect public participation in the political process. However, law reform is on the agenda — albeit somewhat timid reform from the perspective of guaranteeing the community's right and ability to participate in public debate and political activity....

Defamation Law Reform

In November 2004, nearly 25 years after the Australian Law Reform Commission recommended the adoption of uniform defamation laws, the State Attorneys-General agreed to a model set of defamation provisions which each state would enact by 2006. This agreement was itself prompted by the Commonwealth threatening to use its powers in relation to media and telecommunications to legislate new laws over the top of the states if the states did not act. The driver for these reforms was the need for uniformity in laws across Australia rather than the need to grant additional protections for free speech. Nonetheless, there are a variety of provisions in the new uniform laws which do promote freedom of speech and have been welcomed by a range of stakeholders.

Arguably the most important initiative of the new laws is the removal of the rights of corporations to sue for defamation. The arguments for and against corporations' rights to sue for defamation have been summarized elsewhere, and were key to the debates in various parliaments. Suffice to say here that the imbalance of resources when a corporation sues a community group or activist has long been identified as fundamentally unfair and one of the key things which makes defamation law a vehicle for chilling public participation.

However, on the one hand the removal of a corporation's right to sue in defamation is a fairly blunt instrument for dealing with the problem of SLAPP suits because it stops all defamation actions, not just those relating to genuine acts of public participation. But on the other hand, this reform by no means guarantees the safety of a community member in criticising corporate behaviour. Private corporations employing less than 10 people can still sue in defamation, and the reform would have done nothing to prevent the litigation in the Hindmarsh Island bridge cases where the party bringing the cases was not the development company but was the individual directors of the company.

More than that, as the SA [South Australia] Attorney-General was keen to emphasise, corporations retain ample legal instruments to defend themselves from erroneous claims and attacks, namely actions in tort (injurious falsehood) or misrepresentation under the Trade Practices Act. For the individual and community activist, the end result of the new defamation laws may simply be a change in the types of actions brought against them (although even this might be an advance in that these other actions may be harder to sustain as they usually require evidence of actual harm, whereas defamation law simply assumes damage to reputation).

The major winner from the abolition of the corporation's right to sue in defamation would appear to be the big media players who are now assured that when a defamation case is litigated, they are the only major corporates at the table. However, a free commercial media is part of a vibrant democracy, and if investigative journalists and community activists get more speaking space in that media without the sword of defamation hanging overhead, the abolition of the corporate right to sue for defamation will be a welcome advance.

The uniform defamation laws also contain other provisions which will enhance the space for public debate, including:

- the limitation of the time period for bringing actions to 12 months;
- the ability to stop litigation or have a defence by making a reasonable offer to make amends prior to litigation;
- the extension of the defence of truth to all jurisdictions.

The defence of innocent dissemination being extended, including to cover internet service providers, will also help as legal threats aimed at ISPs in the past have been successful at getting material removed from campaign websites.

However, in terms of a broad free speech agenda and community level politics, some of the changes, while going in the right direction, are simply tinkering at the edges. Abolishing exemplary damages (which have rarely been awarded) and capping damages payouts at $250,000 is fine, but the cost is still scarily high for ordinary people. Many of the other modifications will need an engaged (and expensive) legal brain to be utilised for free speech.

Technical changes to already complex defences are not likely to give the community confidence in speaking out. Moreover, as noted above, defamation is only one area of civil law threat to free speech, and increasingly the cases being brought against community activists are not defamation cases....

The Next Step ...

A model needs to be developed which begins from the premise that public participation is one of the most fundamental rights in a democratic society and needs to be protected by strong legislation.

One proposal which fits this model has been put forward by Bover and Parnell in a paper released by the South Australian Environmental Defenders Office.... They define public participation widely:

communication or conduct aimed, in whole or in part, at influencing public opinion, or promoting or furthering action by the public or corporations or by any government body, in relation to an issue of public interest, but does not include communication or conduct that:

1. constitutes vilification based on race, sex, sexuality, ethnicity, nationality or creed [per relevant State and Commonwealth legislation],

2. causes or threatens physical injury,

3. causes damage to property,

4. attempts to incite others to cause or threaten physical injury or damage to property.

This is clearly a wider definition than the Walters/Greens' bill in that it lacks exclusions for such things as trespass (although criminal and property damage remains suable), and perhaps more importantly, it explicitly includes influencing corporate behaviour as a legitimate and protected activity.

The Bover-Parnell model establishes public participation as a positive right and effectively provides three mechanisms to protect that right:

1. a court declaration as to public participation (§ 5);

2. summary dismissal of claims relating to public participation (§ 6);

3. the introduction of a statutory tort of Improper Interference with the Right to Public Participation (§ 7).

In the first instance, if a person is threatened with legal action which they believe is inconsistent with their right to public participation, then that person can apply to a Magistrate's court for a declaration that the conduct complained of was an act of public participation. Such a declaration would carry substantial moral and political weight. Given that such an order would be accompanied by a costs order, and would open the door to summary judgement if proceedings were brought, it is hoped that this provision would provide a substantial disincentive to bring SLAPP type actions.

If however legal actions were brought, a defendant would have a right to bring an application to dismiss the action—with the defendant having only to prove that their conduct was an act of public participation and it was reasonable in the circumstances. The intention of those bringing the case is irrelevant here. The logic is simply that if the conduct complained of is a genuine act of public participation, then it should be protected. It is a much more realistic task for a defendant to establish prima facie that their own conduct was reasonable than to have to try to establish that the motive of the person bringing the case was improper. This would make the summary dismissal provision usable and provide a level of protection for public participation, both through the court process and also because community activists could be more confident that a case would not go forever and that they could put their side at an early stage.

Potential Problems

Given the objection of many (mainly Liberal [Australian political party]) politicians around the country to the removal of corporations' right to sue for defamation, it is important to note that the aim of the bill proposed by Bover and Parnell is not to give a carte blanche to all attacks on corporate behaviour. For instance, in the defamation debate in the South Australian parliament, an MP raised an example of the need to protect a corporation where a competitor or someone with a grudge claimed that the food from a particular restaurant had given customers food poisoning. This should still be actionable, although Bover and Parnell's definition of the public participation which is to be protected may be problematic here. Arguably even this type of attack on a corporation by a competitor is still be aimed at "influencing public opinion" or promoting particular actions by corporations and might therefore come under the definition of public participation to be protected. However, this is clearly not the intention as the authors suggest that:

> The complete test for whether an instance of public participation constitutes an acceptable exercise of the right and is therefore exempt from litigation would require the defendant to demonstrate that there were honestly held and sufficiently arguable reasons behind the public participation and that the public participation was motivated in whole or in part by the aim of influencing public opinion or promoting or furthering action by the public or by any government body.

Following the Californian model, the onus is on the defendant to prove their act is one of public participation, but this can be established through a showing of facts in pleadings, affidavit evidence and, if necessary, in testimony at a summary hearing. Again, this is an easier threshold for defendants than having to prove that those bringing the case acted improperly, but it does provide some level of protection against malicious claims masquerading as public participation. Thus, by showing their record of genuine concern for the environment, an environmentalist could be protected when criticising a development's environmental impact, but the protection would not apply if they had launched into an attack on the sexual politics of a developer.

Overall, the effect of the bill proposed by Bover and Parnell would be to make paramount and to protect the rights of public participation, even when there is a clash with an individual's economic right. While this may appear radical, the fact that legislatures in the United States have introduced similar anti-SLAPP legislation might suggest it is not as radical as first thought.

Abuse of Process

The third arm to the Bover and Parnell bill provides for a statutory tort of Improper Interference with the Right to Public Participation to enable defendants to sue if an action is brought or is maintained against them for the purpose of interfering with their right to public participation.

This formalises and arguably extends the existing tort of collateral abuse of process. This existing abuse of process tort allows for action where a court process is instituted for purposes beyond the purpose of the original tort. Thus, for instance, bringing a trespass claim should be about recovering damages or preventing future trespasses, not to punish, silence or harass political opponents who may have trespassed during the course of a protest. While this tort looks superficially attractive as an "anti-SLAPP cause of action, it has proved largely unhelpful. Beyond the difficulty of proving the intention of those originally bringing any action, until recently it was necessary to prove not just that a case was brought predominantly for improper motive, but that there was no proper motive at all. The courts have also required that special damages need to be proven — ie. the ordinary legal costs are not enough to found the claim.

Animal Liberation is South Australia has pleaded a counterclaim based on a SLAPP suit being an abuse of process, and while this counterclaim survived a strike out application, it remains to be seen what final approach the court will take. However, there appears little doubt that, where a defendant can prove that an original action was brought to improperly prevent or limit political participation, then the Bover-Parnell bill would clearly overcome the barriers of the common law tort and make such an abuse of process actionable.

More Generic Solutions

Beyond the above types of laws specifically designed to protect public participation from the effects of civil litigation, there are also more general laws which may have a role. Human Rights legislation and a Bill of Rights are key possibilities here.

In response to issues raised by The Wilderness Society about the Gunns case, ACT [Australian Capital Territory] Chief Minister, Jon Stanhope, pointed to the fact that the ACT Human Rights Act would guarantee freedom of speech. In its relevant parts, the Act says:

> Everyone has the right to freedom of expression. This right includes the freedom to seek, receive and impart information and ideas of all kinds, regardless of borders, whether orally, in writing or in print, by way of art, or in another way chosen by him or her.

This is a fairly general statement of principle and it is unclear whether it would have legal teeth if it ran counter to other laws. The Human Rights Act itself provides that rights may be subject to reasonable limits set by Territory laws. This reflects the type of qualification made in the International Covenant on Civil and Political Rights, the cornerstone of international human rights law, which allows for the right of freedom of speech to be constrained by laws necessary for the protection of the rights and reputation of others, or for national security, public order, public health or morals. Such qualifications render broad statements of human rights meaningless because the argument becomes about appropriate balance rather than right to free speech. Indeed, the ACT Chief Minister made no claims that this Act would prevent "Gunns-type" litigation.

However, some assistance could be gained from legislating to clarify where to draw such legal lines — in effect, qualifying the qualification. This is proposed in the New Matilda's proposal for a national Human Rights Bill — the second qualification being that the restrictions on free speech allowed for in the law "shall not be interpreted so as to prevent participation of members in the public in issues of public interest where they do so without malice."

In theory these limitations could also be overcome by a constitutional guarantee of free speech, such as a bill of rights, which would trump other laws where they became oppressive. Of course the Australian constitution is not a document of lofty ideals. The main freedom guaranteed in the constitution is the freedom to trade between states. The only freedom of speech to be found in it, the right the High Court found to be implied by a system of representative government, is severely constrained and pales in comparison to the robust sentiments of the U.S. constitution's First Amendment (admittedly often honoured in the breach). Importantly though, even this robust First Amendment right was not in itself sufficient in the U.S. to deal with the silencing effects of civil litigation — hence the need for anti-SLAPP legislation in the various jurisdictions there.

Ultimately, the human rights paradigm is probably limited by its traditional focus on asserting rights against government interference, rather than on cases involving civil litigation. Even where the state is held responsible for its failure to establish a fair civil court processes (as in the European Court's McLibel judgement) this is only at the end of a long legal process which is little use if the process has already silenced debate. Thus, whatever the merits of an Australian Bill of Rights, any such bill would probably still need to be supplemented by purpose built legislation of the types discussed above.

NSW Defamation Act (2005)-Sect 9

New South Wales Consolidated Acts (Australia)

9. Certain corporations do not have cause of action for defamation

(1) A corporation has no cause of action for defamation in relation to the publication of defamatory matter about the corporation unless it was an excluded corporation at the time of the publication.

(2) A corporation is an excluded corporation if:

(a) the objects for which it is formed do not include obtaining financial gain for its members or corporators, or

(b) it employs fewer than 10 persons and is not related to another corporation,

and the corporation is not a public body....

(5) Subsection (1) does not affect any cause of action for defamation that an individual associated with a corporation has in relation to the publication of defamatory matter about the individual even if the publication of the same matter also defames the corporation.

(6) In this section:

"corporation" includes any body corporate or corporation constituted by or under a law of any country (including by exercise of a prerogative right), whether or not a public body.

"public body" means a local government body or other governmental or public authority constituted by or under a law of any country.

Questions and Discussion

1. *Proposed Protection of Public Participation Bill.* In addition to changes in defamation law, other reforms are afoot. The Legal Affairs Committee for the Australian Capital Territory (ACT) began receiving submissions and taking evidence, with the aim of creating a new law. A proposed *Protection of Public Participation Bill 2006* is:

An Act to protect and encourage participation in public debate and matters of public interest, and discourage people and corporations from bringing or maintaining legal proceedings that interfere with another person's right to engage in public participation.

Standing Committee on Legal Affairs, Court Procedures (Protection of Public Participation) Amendment Bill 2005 ii, (May 2007).

A 96-page report recommended that a bill be introduced to protect public participation. The bill should:

• contain a positive right to public participation;

• provide for a declaration that actions are public participation (and only public participation) and therefore protected. This will not, for instance, protect one from a truly defamatory statement;

• provide for exemplary and punitive damages.

Standing Committee on Legal Affairs, Court Procedures (Protection of Public Participation) Amendment Bill 2005 v, 41 [6.18–6.20] (May 2007).

The Committee cited *Gunns*, and quoted the Wilderness Society:

> Free speech and robust public debate, together with the ability to participate in community and political activity without fear of litigation, are fundamental rights in a democratic society. The increasing and widespread use of defamation law, trade practices laws and economic torts laws against public participation must be wound back.

Id.

2. *Overview/looking back.* Of the many legislative solutions proposed in this section, which are the most likely to protect the right to petition and the right to speech? What are the most important elements of an Anti-SLAPP statute? How will the different burdens of proof discussed above affect the defendant's chances of getting the SLAPP suit dismissed?

Chapter 12

Human Rights and Climate Change

Introduction

We, the human species, are confronting a planetary emergency—a threat to the survival of our civilization that is gathering ominous and destructive potential.... But there is hopeful news as well: we have the ability to solve this crisis and avoid the worst—though not all—of its consequences, if we act boldly, decisively and quickly.

Speech by Al Gore on the Acceptance of the
Nobel Peace Prize, December 10, 2007

Does human rights law have a role to play in dealing with climate change by limiting greenhouse gas emissions? This chapter asks you to consider each of the types of human rights, institutions, and possibilities for relief (both substantive and procedural) studied earlier in the book. Can some of them be used to deal with climate change? Can some of them help spur judicial or political action to limit emissions of greenhouse gases? Can some of them be used to spur action to help people adapt to changes in the climate caused by human activities? Can some of them provide compensation that will help redress harms from human-caused climate change and cause industries to take actions to limit future liability?

As we mentioned in Chapter 1, the Human Rights Council in its resolution of March 26, 2008, "Human rights and climate change," emphasized that "climate change poses an immediate and far-reaching threat to people and communities around the world and has implications for the full enjoyment of human rights." It noted that

> the world's poor are especially vulnerable to the effects of climate change, in particular those concentrated in high-risk areas, and also tend to have more limited adaptation capacities, ... that low-lying and other small island countries, countries with low-lying coastal, arid and semi-arid areas or areas liable to floods, drought and desertification ... are particularly vulnerable to the adverse effects of climate change.

The Human Rights Council decided to undertake "a detailed analytical study of the relationship between climate change and human rights ... and thereafter to make available the study ... to the Conference of Parties to the United Nations Framework Convention on Climate Change for its consideration." A/HRC/7/L.21/Rev.1 (26 March 2008).

The resolution, initiated by the island state of the Maldives, in the Indian Ocean, received broad support, in particular by vulnerable countries, although Russia said that it was not effective or productive for the Human Rights Council to deal with climate change. Many delegations emphasized the impact of climate change on human rights and right to life itself.

I. Climate Change, Its Effects, and International Obligations

In 1988 two United Nations bodies, the World Meteorological Organization and the United Nations Environment Programme, created the Intergovernmental Panel on Climate Change (IPCC). The IPCC was given the task of assessing the scientific, technical, and socioeconomic information necessary for understanding the risk of human-induced climate change. The IPCC strives for scientific integrity, objectivity, openness, and transparency. It does not endorse particular policy, yet instead focuses on providing scientific information for policy makers to consider. The IPCC's first assessment report in 1990 led to the United Nations Framework Convention on Climate Change (UNFCCC). Since then, three other IPCC assessment reports have been made. Below, the fourth assessment report published in 2007 outlines some of the most recently observed effects of human-induced climate change.

Climate Change 2007: Synthesis Report (4th Assessment Report)
Intergovernmental Panel on Climate Change
(November 2007)

Summary for Policymakers

This Synthesis Report is based on the assessment carried out by the three Working Groups of the IPCC. It provides an integrated view of climate change as the final part of the IPCC's Fourth Assessment Report.

1. Observed changes in climate and their effects

Warming of the climate system is unequivocal, as is now evident from observations of increases in global average air and ocean temperatures, widespread melting of snow and ice, and rising global average sea level.

Eleven of the last twelve years (1995–2006) rank among the twelve warmest years in the instrumental record of global surface temperature (since 1850)....

Rising sea level is consistent with warming.... Global average sea level has risen since 1961 at an average rate of 1.8 [1.3 to 2.3] mm/yr and since 1993 at 3.1 [2.4 to 3.8] mm/yr, with contributions from thermal expansion, melting glaciers and ice caps, and the polar ice sheets....

Observed decreases in snow and ice extent are also consistent with warming.... Satellite data since 1978 show that annual average Arctic sea ice extent has shrunk by 2.7 [2.1 to 3.3] % per decade, with larger decreases in summer of 7.4 [5.0 to 9.8] % per decade. Mountain glaciers and snow cover on average have declined in both hemispheres.

2. Causes of change

Global GHG[a] emissions due to human activities have grown since pre-industrial times, with an increase of 70% between 1970 and 2004....

Carbon dioxide (CO_2) is the most important anthropogenic GHG. Its annual emissions grew by about 80% between 1970 and 2004.

Global atmospheric concentrations of CO_2, methane (CH_4) and nitrous oxide (N_2O) have increased markedly as a result of human activities since 1750 and now far exceed pre-industrial values determined from ice cores spanning many thousands of years....

Most of the observed increase in globally-averaged temperatures since the mid-20th century is *very likely*[b] due to the observed increase in anthropogenic GHG concentrations. It is *likely* there has been significant anthropogenic warming over the past 50 years averaged over each continent....

Human influences have:

- *very likely* contributed to sea level rise during the latter half of the 20th century
- *likely* contributed to changes in wind patterns, affecting extra-tropical storm tracks and temperature patterns
- *likely* increased temperatures of extreme hot nights, cold nights, and cold days
- *more likely than not* increased risk of heat waves, area affected by drought since the 1970s and frequency of heavy precipitation events.

Anthropogenic warming over the last three decades has *likely* had a discernible influence at the global scale on observed changes in many physical and biological systems....

3. Projected climate change and its impacts

There is *high agreement* and *much evidence* that with current climate change mitigation policies and related sustainable development practices, global GHG emissions will continue to grow over the next few decades....

Continued GHG emissions at or above current rates would cause further warming and induce many changes in the global climate system during the 21st century that would *very likely* be larger than those observed during the 20th century.

For the next two decades a warming of about 0.2°C per decade is projected for a range of SRES [Special Report of Emission Scenarios] emission scenarios. Even if the concentrations of all GHGs and aerosols had been kept constant at year 2000 levels, a further warming of about 0.1°C per decade would be expected. Afterwards, temperature projections increasingly depend on specific emission scenarios.

---

a. Greenhouse gas. This includes CO_2 as well as several other gases emitted from human industry and other activities.

b. *Very likely* means more than 90% likelihood, *likely* means more than 66% likelihood, and *more likely than not* means more than 50% likelihood. Le Treut, H., R. Somerville, U. Cubasch, Y. Ding, C. Mauritzen, A. Mokssit, T. Peterson and M. Prather, *Historical Overview of Climate Change*, in *Climate Change 2007: The Physical Science Basis. Contribution of Working Group I to the Fourth Assessment Report of the Intergovernmental Panel on Climate Change* (Solomon, S., D. Qin, M. Manning, Z. Chen, M. Marquis, K.B. Averyt, M. Tignor and H.L. Miller, eds., 2007). The concept of giving specific, probability-based definitions to the terms originated in Moss, R.H. and Schneider, S.H., *Uncertainties in the IPCC TAR: Recommendations to lead authors for more consistent assessment and reporting*, in R. Pachauri, T. Taniguchi and K. Tanaka, eds., World Meteorological Organization, Geneva, 2000), pages 33–51.

There is now higher confidence than in the TAR [Third Assessment Report by the IPCC, 2001] in projected patterns of warming and other regional-scale features, including changes in wind patterns, precipitation, and some aspects of extremes and sea ice....

Regional-scale changes include:

- warming greatest over land and at most high northern latitudes and least over Southern Ocean and parts of the North Atlantic Ocean, continuing recent observed trends....

- contraction of snow cover area, increases in thaw depth over most permafrost regions, and decrease in sea ice extent; in some projections using SRES scenarios, Arctic late-summer sea ice disappears almost entirely by the latter part of the 21st century

- *very likely* increase in frequency of hot extremes, heat waves, and heavy precipitation

- *likely* increase in tropical cyclone intensity; less confidence in global decrease of tropical cyclone numbers

- poleward shift of extra-tropical storm tracks with consequent changes in wind, precipitation, and temperature patterns

- *very likely* precipitation increases in high latitudes and *likely* decreases in most subtropical land regions, continuing observed recent trends.

Questions and Discussion

1. *Global warming and human rights.* The IPCC report suggests that global warming will increase the intensity and duration of major tropical storms. Warming also can severely increase rain in some areas while causing drought in others. New diseases may emerge. Will such a warming world result in adverse consequences to human rights? What, if any, human rights claims might be attached to such consequences? What would be the legal sources of such claims? Who are possible defendants? Based on issues studied in other chapters of this book, are there any human rights obligations to which the United States, China, India, Russia, the European Union countries, or other major emitting countries are bound? What about individual corporations that emit greenhouse gases or have done so in the past? We will discuss these and other questions below in this chapter.

2. *International redress.* Are there human rights institutions at the international level, or courts at the national level, that an injured party might approach for relief? Recall discussions from Chapter 4 about the limited power of international human rights tribunals. For example, does the Inter-American human rights system have the power to order redress for injuries suffered by persons whose rights might be violated? Could the European Court of Human Rights order effective relief? Would the International Court of Justice have the jurisdiction or power? What kinds of redress might be obtained?

3. *National redress.* Can the consequences of global warming be redressed by judicial or quasi-judicial decisions at the national level? Do some institutions have the power to order limitations in emissions? Do they have jurisdiction over either governments or private companies? Some domestic litigation seeks to force government to take action. In 2007 the Supreme Court rejected the U.S. Environmental Protection Agency's claim that it had no authority to regulate greenhouse gas emissions from new motor vehicles. See *Massachusetts v. E.P.A.*, 549 U.S. __, 127 S. Ct. 1438, 1446–47 (2007). However, there is a big difference between telling the EPA that, contrary to its legal arguments, it is *allowed* to regulate greenhouse gases and demanding that it *must* create an effective regulation scheme.

EPA may also stand in the way of others creating strong regulations. In early 2008, EPA refused to grant the State of California the waiver of federal preemption that is needed under the Clean Air Act for it and other states to regulate such vehicle emissions. California State Motor Vehicle Pollution Control Standards; Notice of Decision Denying a Waiver of Clean Air Act Preemption for California's 2009 and Subsequent Model Year Greenhouse Gas Emission Standards for New Motor Vehicles, 73 Fed. Reg. 12156 (March 6, 2008). California and other states went to court to seek to overturn EPA's refusal. The case was pending at press time for this book.

4. *Procedural relief.* Can claims of violations of procedural rights lead to new methods of decisionmaking that might elevate the political power of those who want to control emission of greenhouse gases? What sources of law might provide the basis for a procedural rights claim?

5. *Political change.* Is obtaining judicial redress the only reason for making a claim before a court? Professor Eric Posner has written that "the main purpose of litigation may not be to persuade courts to determine greenhouse gas emission policy, but to attract public attention and pressure governments to reach political solutions, including treaties and domestic laws." However, he concludes that "the assumption that it can drive global greenhouse gas policy at all, or in the right direction, is doubtful." Eric A. Posner, *Climate Change and International Human Rights Litigation: A Critical Appraisal*, 155 U. Pa. L. Rev. 1925 (2007). Others would argue that citizens are more likely to pressure governments to reach a political solution to global warming if they view the atmosphere as a trust *res* and the government as a trustee. Mary Christina Wood, *Nature's Trust: A Legal, Political and Moral Frame for Global Warming*, 34 B.C. Envtl. Aff. L. Rev. 577 (2007).

6. *Who is responsible?* Are there problems with attributing causation of global warming to specific business entities? What about joint and several liability of corporations? What about suing a particular country or a group of countries for failure to regulate emissions? Could that accomplish something worthwhile? How should a court or tribunal assess responsibility to take actions or pay damages? Should responsibility be based on total emissions? Emissions per capita? Emissions per unit of gross domestic product?

International Agreements and Climate Change

In 1992 at the United Nations Conference on Environment and Development (UNCED) in Rio de Janeiro, the UNFCCC was signed. U. N. Doc. A/AC.237/18 (Part II) (Add. 1), May 9, 1992, 1771 U.N.T.S. 107, 31 I.L.M. 849. Its objective is the "stabilization of greenhouse gas concentrations in the atmosphere that would prevent dangerous anthropogenic interference with the climate system." Article 2. Nations have "common but differentiated responsibilities" and respective capabilities. Accordingly, the developed country Parties should take the lead in combating climate change and its adverse effects." Article 3. Nearly 200 countries are Parties to the UNFCCC, including the United States.

At the third Conference of the Parties, held in Kyoto, Japan, in 1997, Parties adopted the "Kyoto Protocol" to the UNFCCC. U.N. Doc. FCCC/CP/1997/L.7/Add.l, 10 December 1997, 37 I.L.M. 22 (1998). It aimed to reduce greenhouse gas emissions to 5% below 1990 levels. Nearly all parties to the UNFCCC have become Parties to the Kyoto Protocol, with the conspicuous exceptionsof the United States. (Australia became a Party at the end of 2007 after a national election.)

The Conference of the Parties to the UNFCCC, serving as a Meeting of the Parties of the Kyoto Protocol, met in Bali, Indonesia, in December 2007 and started comprehensive and inclusive negotiations intended to lead to a new multilateral framework to deal with climate change. The new period will cover the period beyond 2012—the end of the first commitment period of the Kyoto Protocol. However, the United States persuaded the others to leave out any firm goal for reductions in emissions. According to the New York Times:

> The targets sought by Europe and others remain in the action plan—including the need for rich countries to cut emissions by 2020 up to 40 percent below 1990 levels, and a 50 percent cut in emissions globally by 2050. But they are now a footnote to the nonbinding preamble, not a main feature of the plan.

Thomas Fuller & Andrew C. Revkin, *Climate Plan Looks Beyond Bush's Tenure*, New York Times, December 16, 2007. In the words of the Los Angeles Times:

> Nonetheless, for the first time, it enrolled the developing world in efforts to reduce global emissions and pushed those nations to consider ways to limit their output of greenhouse gases. More important, the agreement kept the United States—long considered the biggest roadblock to unified action in curbing global warming—at the negotiating table and offered hints that the country might finally be willing to join international efforts....
>
> Negotiators, particularly the Europeans, were looking beyond the current American administration to the next one, and insisted that the next two years of talks proceed on two tracks. The second would build on the Kyoto Protocol that requires emissions reductions in major industrialized nations, but has been rejected by the United States. The United States team in Bali was demanding that a new agreement encompass the world's major polluters and have sufficient flexibility, and no hard targets, to do that. But in the end the United States had to agree to two tracks to avoid a total breakdown of the talks.

Alan Zarembo & Thomas H. Maugh II, *Bali Climate Keeps World at Table*, Los Angeles Times, December 16, 2007.

II. Human Rights Litigation and Climate Change

This section focuses on the question whether human rights litigation has a role in efforts to limit GHG emissions and slow climate change. First, we explore different litigation theories. Next, we look at claims to international human rights bodies, specifically the 2005 Inuit petition to the Inter-American Commission on Human Rights. Then, we consider the value of domestic human rights litigation. Finally, we turn to procedural rights.

A. Litigation Theories

A Moral Imperative: The Human Rights Implications of Climate Change
Sara C. Aminzadeh
30 Hastings Int'l & Comp. L. Rev. 231 (2007)

IV. The Impacts of Climate Change on Human Rights

The protection of the environment is ... a vital part of contemporary human rights doctrine, for it is a sine qua non for numerous human rights such as the right to health and the right to life itself. There are arguably three viable strategies for constructing a human rights-based approach to climate change: 1) the application of procedural rights found in international human rights law to climate change litigation; 2) the recognition of a distinct right to environmental well-being; and 3) the re-interpretation of existing human rights in the environmental context. This note adopts the third approach, arguing that existing human rights law should be expanded to encompass climate change impacts when appropriate....

The following identifies some of the human rights that have been implicated by environmental issues in the past and suggests that the consequences of climate change for certain communities may similarly warrant consideration under human rights law....

B. Right to Property

The UDHR [Universal Declaration of Human Rights] defines the right to property as follows: "1) Everyone has the right to own property alone as well as in association with others; 2) No one shall be arbitrarily deprived of his property." ...

In the near future, small island nations may also face the loss of property as low-lying territories become inundated from sea level rise. For example, some homes in Papua New Guinea's Cataret Islands have already been washed away as a result of rising sea levels. At this point, authorities see resettlement as "the only action available." In the Indian Ocean, the Maldives' 1,200 coral islands lie so low that a tsunami briefly swamped the islands....

C. Right to Life

The right to life is increasingly understood to include the traditional protection against intentional or arbitrary deprivation of life, as well as the state's obligation to ensure that every individual within its boundaries has access to means of survival....

In 2004, the European Court of Human Rights decided *Öneryildiz v. Turkey*, its first environmental case involving the loss of life. The applicant lived in a poor area of Istanbul built around a garbage dump under the authority of the City Council. An expert report observed that no measures had been taken to prevent a possible explosion of methane gas from the dump and such an explosion subsequently occurred. The explosion caused to bury eleven houses, including the home of the applicant, who lost nine members of his family. The applicant based his claim on the right to life provision of Article 2 of the ECHR [European Convention on Human Rights], arguing that the relevant authorities' negligence caused the accident. The Court found that the authorities had committed a procedural violation of Article 2's right to life, and violated other rights espoused in Protocols to the European Convention.

When a nation fails to take reasonable measures to prevent environmental damage, and the result of such non-action is climate change, those harmed may seek redress for violations of their right to life. For example, Alaskans affected by sea level rise or the melting of polar ice caps may assert a right to life claim against the United States for failing to take action. However, the damage at issue must reach serious proportions in order to invoke the right to life. Additionally, when climate change directly threatens the right to life, it may be too late to seek redress....

V. The Utility of a Human Rights Based Approach to Climate Change Litigation

A human rights-based approach to climate change would integrate the theoretical and advocacy approaches of international environmental law and human rights law....

Current international environmental law does not adequately protect human life and dignity from the threats associated with environmental degradation. Victims of environmental harm can benefit from a human rights-based approach to environmental litigation because "international human rights law provides a basis for intervention when harm occurs solely within another state's borders while international environmental law generally does not." Reformulating existing human rights in the environmental context would garner more effective environmental protection by taking advantage of existing international and regional monitoring and enforcement mechanisms, which are more developed in the human rights arena than they are in the environmental arena....

Another reason to pursue a human rights-based approach is that environmental governance on climate change, primarily the United Nations Framework Convention on Climate Change (UNFCCC) and the Kyoto Protocol, do not provide remedies for injured parties. Though international foras will not likely issue injunctive relief to restrict GHG emissions, they can issue monetary relief to help underwrite the cost of climate-change-related weather damage (e.g., the cost of building seawalls) or establish special funds to build coastal defenses, protect fresh water supplies, and develop new forms of agriculture....

States could bring claims against other states in the International Court of Justice. Individuals could also bring complaints against states in the European Court of Human Rights, the IACHR [Inter-American Commission on Human Rights], and possibly the OECD [Organisation for Economic Co-operation and Development]. Furthermore, indigenous and other displaced peoples could bring complaints to the World Bank Inspection Panel.

The claims of indigenous peoples may be well-suited for consideration by the World Bank Inspection Panel, particularly since the Bank's two-pronged internal policy focuses on indigenous peoples and displacement issues.... The World Bank Inspection Panel could serve as a venue for indigenous peoples to give input on projects such as coal plants, pipelines, and other matters that have direct links to increasing GHG emissions....

[T]he characterization of the problem as human, rather than merely environmental, would subject states' activities to increased international scrutiny.... Ideally, increased visibility of the human rights implications of climate change would spark new cooperation in climate change diplomacy....

VI. A Response to Possible Criticisms Regarding a Human Rights-Based Approach to Climate Change ...

One theoretical problem to a human rights approach to climate change is that it may require subjective valuation of some rights over others. While climate change will seriously threaten the basic human rights of some individuals and groups, it may actually be beneficial for others. Climate change jeopardizes the lives and livelihoods of the Inuit and SIDS [small island developing states] such as the Maldives and Tuvalu. However, the melting of sea ice could open up new sea routes for Russia, Iceland, and Canada, and parts of Russia might benefit from an increase in crop yields. In other words, if the Inuit have a human right to health and life, do not the people of Russia and Iceland have an equal right to development? ...

Others worry that emphasizing environmental aspects of human rights may divert attention from more important human rights objectives. Characterizing certain climate change impacts as human rights issues might weaken the protection of "real" human rights issues such as genocide and crimes against humanity. There are two responses to this point. First, the diversion of efforts to more so-called important objectives is not a legitimate concern because the consequences of climate change range from quite serious to catastrophic. Second, an approach that utilizes the human rights framework to address climate change would not undermine other environmental and human rights efforts. Instead, a human rights-based approach would aid the development of jurisprudence in both areas by encouraging debate and drawing new linkages between the two fields.

Questions and Discussion

1. *Connecting climate change to the right to life.* Can one argue that climate change causes a violation of the right to life? Would jurisprudence from India, Pakistan, and the Philippines (from Chapter 3) be useful?

2. *Litigation venues.* Taking into account the European Court of Human Rights decision in *Öneryıldız v. Turkey*, might it be possible to apply to that court for alleged violations of the right to life caused by climate change? Could the Inuit people living in Russia apply?

3. *Environmental refugees.* It has been suggested that "environmental refugees" might bring legal claims. Is the definition of refugee under the Convention Relating to the Status of Refugees broad enough to include environmental refugees and therefore provide protection for them? Do environmental refugees satisfy the "persecutions" requirement of the refugee definition? Can they argue that they belong to a "social group" of persons who lack the political power to protect their own environment, and that the lack of power forces them to migrate? If this is not a viable argument, is there a need for a new treaty giving status and protection to environmental (including climate change) refugees? To what international bodies can environmental refugees apply?

4. *Procedural rights.* Could procedural rights be used to combat climate change? Is public participation an effective procedural right, in particular, in the environmental impact assessment (EIA) of a project, plan, or policy that is likely to have significant impacts on climate change through GHG emissions? Procedural rights are more thoroughly addressed later in the chapter.

B. Litigation in International Human Rights Bodies — The Inuit Petition

1. Background

Petitioning for Adverse Impacts of Global Warming in the Inter-American Human Rights System
Donald M. Goldberg & Martin Wagner
http://www.ciel.org/Publications/Petitioning_GlobalWarming_IAHR.pdf

III. SEEKING REDRESS IN THE INTER-AMERICAN HUMAN RIGHTS SYSTEM ...

Unchecked, global warming threatens to destroy [Arctic people's] culture, render their land uninhabitable and rob them of their means of subsistence. At present, it may not be possible to fully redress these harms through the Inter-American system. The Commission does not have the authority to force countries to curtail their emissions, nor can it compel states to compensate individuals for human rights violations. The Inter-American Court does have such power, at least in theory, but two barriers bar access to the Court by Arctic inhabitants seeking to sue the United States. First, the Convention does not permit a private citizen to submit a case directly to the Court. Second, because the United States has not ratified the Convention, it is not subject to the jurisdiction of the Court.

Nevertheless, a report by the Commission examining the connection between global warming and human rights could have a powerful impact on worldwide efforts to address global warming. It would demonstrate that the issue is not merely an abstract problem for the future, but is instead a problem of immediate concern to all people everywhere. Recognition by the Commission of a link between global warming and human rights may establish a legal basis for holding responsible countries that have profited from inadequate greenhouse gas regulation and could provide a strong incentive to all countries to participate in effective international response efforts.

A. Procedural Issues Arising Under the Rules of the Inter-American Commission

1. General Requirements

Anyone alleging a human rights violation by the government of a nation that is a member of the OAS may submit a petition to the Inter-American Commission. If the accused state is party to the American Convention, that document, the Commission's Statute and its Rules of Procedure establish jurisdiction and procedure. If, like the United States, the accused state is not a party to the American Convention, but is a member state of the OAS, the Commission's Rules of Procedure and past practice recognize that the obligations of the Declaration apply and the Commission may hear claims asserting violations by that state: "Pursuant to the [OAS] Charter, all member states undertake to uphold the fundamental rights of the individual, which, in the case of non-parties to the Convention, are those set forth in the American Declaration, which constitutes a source of international obligation." [Report No. 109/99, Case 10.951, *Coard v. United States*, Sept. 29, 1999, at para. 36.]

Petitioners may be the victims themselves, third parties, or any "non-governmental entity legally recognized in one or more of the member states of the OAS." The petition must identify the state responsible, "by act or omission," for the violations of any of the applicable human rights, and describe the acts or situation leading to the violations....

2. Claims of Extraterritorial Causes of Human Rights Violations

The Arctic region includes parts of the United States, Canada, Greenland/Denmark, Iceland, Norway, Sweden, Finland, and Russia. An important question is whether all inhabitants of the Arctic have rights to bring claims against the United States in the Inter-American system, no matter which country they reside in. Article 1 of the American Convention suggests that a nation has a human rights obligation only with respect to individuals subject to its jurisdiction.... The American Declaration of the Rights and Duties of Man contains no similar limitation. Arctic peoples residing in Alaska clearly are subject to the jurisdiction of the United States, and the obligations of the United States under the Convention and Declaration apply to them without question. There are important reasons to extend these protections to inhabitants of other regions of the Arctic as well. Unlike the types of violations anticipated when the basic international human rights agreements were drafted, violations arising out of the effects of global warming are clearly not limited to the territory of the nations responsible for those effects. The impacts of U.S. greenhouse gas emissions on Siberian, Canadian, and Scandinavian Arctic communities are fundamentally the same as those on Alaskan Arctic communities. Because the primary contributors to anthropogenic global warming are few (the United States being the primary culprit), and the victims of global warming effects are residents of nations all around the globe, it is important that those nations responsible for global warming not be shielded from responsibility for impacts outside their territory by outmoded limitations on human rights.

Fortunately, the Inter-American Commission is one of several international institutions that have recognized that responsibility for human rights is not circumscribed by national borders. The Commission has interpreted the notion of jurisdiction broadly....

B. Relevant Rights Protected by the Declaration

The rights that apply to OAS member states, like the United States, that are not parties to the Convention are those that are contained in the American Declaration. The Commission and the Inter-American Court on Human Rights have recognized, however, that related rights in the Convention or other human rights documents, even those in other systems, may be used to elaborate the rights in the Declaration, as well as to understand the human rights obligations of OAS member states.... Many rights contained in the Declaration may give rise to complaints based on the adverse impacts of global warming. These include the right to life (Art. I), the right to residence and movement (Art. VIII), the right to inviolability of the home (Art. IX), the right to the preservation of health and to well-being (Art. XI), the right to the benefits of culture (Art. XIII), and the right to work and to fair remuneration (Art. XIV). The Commission has applied several other rights that would be relevant to our petition, including the non-derogable right of all peoples to their own means of subsistence and the right to freely dispose of natural resources. In addition, the Commission has recognized that indigenous peoples are entitled to special protections, especially in the case of threats to the environment on which their physical and cultural lives depend....

C. Remedies

The Commission cannot force the United States to take any particular action, whether to reduce the causes of global warming or compensate for the effects. However, a favorable outcome to a claim based on those effects could contribute significantly to global efforts to address global warming. In the best case, the Commission would accept the claim and encourage the parties to negotiate a solution. Assuming the United States and the petitioners would not agree to a mutually satisfactory remedy..., the Commission likely would undertake an independent investigation of the facts underlying the claim, probably including site visits to affected regions, and would then issue a report on the petition. The report would set out the Commission's conclusions concerning the relationship between global warming and human rights.

Each significant phase of the Commission's consideration of the claim would provide an opportunity to raise public awareness concerning the human rights implications of global warming. A Commission report finding that global warming results in human rights violations would be important. As an authoritative interpretation of international law, such a finding would help bring a rights-based approach to global warming discussions. Governments or private individuals wishing to pressure the United States and other governments to take meaningful action to address the causes of global warming would welcome the ability to cite the Commission's findings. Plaintiffs in domestic judicial proceedings could use the findings to supplement their claims (or, in some judicial systems, as an independent basis for a claim), and domestic tribunals could use them to justify favorable decisions.

IV. Conclusion ...

Formal recognition by an international authority like the Inter-American Commission of the connection between global warming and human rights would have a powerful impact on worldwide efforts to address global warming. Such recognition would demonstrate that the issue is not an abstract problem of degrees per decade and statistical probabilities, but is instead a vital concern of all people everywhere. It would bring to the global warming discourse a basis for holding responsible those who have profited from poorly regulated greenhouse gas emissions, and for placing limits on such emissions in the future. And it would be consistent with the growing international recognition that a healthy environment is fundamental to the enjoyment of nearly all of the most fundamental human rights.

Questions and Discussion

1. *United States accountability.* Is the United States accountable for the violation of the rights listed in the American Convention? The United States is not a Party to the American Convention. How could reference instead to the American Declaration seek to sidestep this problem in a Petition to the Inter-American Commission on Human Rights?

2. *Redress.* What sorts of remedies can the Inter-American Commission offer? Given the widespread scientific consensus regarding global warming, but the relatively slow political reaction, would recognition of a link between global warming and human rights have "a powerful impact on worldwide efforts"?

3. *Disposition of natural resources.* The authors mention a right "to freely dispose of natural resources." Does this right apply only to the Inuit people or also to those in the United States who are cutting down forests and disposing of coal and oil through combustion in industries and automobiles? How should the Commission balance conflicting rights to use resources?

4. *International Covenant on Civil and Political Rights.* The article focuses on the Inter-American system for three reasons. First, the Inter-American Commission on Human Rights has the authority to receive petitions by private citizens directed at member states. Second, the Commission's history and case law suggests it would be receptive to allegations linking human rights to environmental impacts. Third, the Commission has the flexibility to look at new developments in human rights law. But what about other human rights mechanisms to which the United States is subject, such as the ICCPR? What analogous rights in this document are implicated by United States' climate change policy? Are remedies available for violations of the ICCPR?

5. *Law or politics?* The authors talk about how the Commission's public hearing procedures could lead to raising public awareness, how favorable Commission findings would help bring a rights-based approach to discussions and contribute to "global warming discourse," and how governments or individuals who wanted to pressure the U.S. government to take action could cite the Commission's findings. They also talk about how Commission findings could be used to supplement claims in domestic litigation or even provide independent claims and, at a minimum, that courts could use the findings to justify favorable decisions. Which of these seems most likely? Do all of them justify filing a human rights complaint?

2. Does Climate Change Violate Recognized Human Rights Law?

Petition to the Inter-American Commission on Human Rights

Sheila Watt-Cloutier with the Support of the Inuit Circumpolar Conference
(7 December 2005)

IV. Facts: Global Warming is Harming Every Aspect of Inuit Life and Culture ...

Global warming has already visibly transformed the Arctic. Inuit observations and scientific studies are consistent in documenting substantial and lasting alterations in the physical environment of the Arctic due to global climate change....

Because the Arctic is especially vulnerable to the effects of global climate change, the "[a]nnual average arctic temperature has increased at almost twice the rate as that of the rest of the world over the past few decades." The rising temperature has set in motion an ever-escalating series of changes in the arctic climate and environment. Some of the more observable changes include deteriorating ice conditions, decreasing quantity and quality of snow, unpredictable and unfamiliar weather, and a transfigured landscape.

Commonly observed ice changes include thinner ice, later freezes, and earlier, more sudden thaws. In the past, sea ice and lake ice froze hard enough for safe travel earlier in the year. Now the freeze comes later, and once the ice freezes it is generally thinner than in the past....

"Over the past 30 years, the annual average sea-ice extent has decreased by about 8%, or nearly one million square kilometers, an area larger than all of Norway, Sweden and Denmark combined, and the melting trend is accelerating."

The quality, quantity and timing of snowfall have changed dramatically due to global warming. For example, snow falls later in the year, and the overall quantity has diminished in most areas. Average snow cover over the region has decreased ten percent over the last three decades, and climate-modeling projections predict a further loss of another ten to twenty percent in coming decades....

Global warming is also altering land conditions. Permafrost, which holds together unstable underground gravel, is melting at an alarming rate, causing slumping and landslides. Severe erosion is also increasing dramatically. The loss of sea ice that used to prevent the creation of large waves has resulted in increasingly violent sea storms, resulting in coastal erosion. The erosion exposes more coastal permafrost to the warmer air, resulting in faster permafrost melt. The accelerating loss of ice can only be expected to aggravate this problem in the future.

The weather of the Arctic has become increasingly unpredictable. Inuit elders, who have long experience in reading the weather, report various changes in weather patterns in different areas of the Arctic.... Shifts in the prevailing wind direction and intensity have added to the unpredictability of the weather. Sudden changes in wind direction and speed have rendered traditional weather forecasting methods useless.

The combination of these changes further alters the arctic environment. Lack of snowfall, early thaws, increased erosion, melting permafrost, melting ice caps and changing wind conditions have combined to decrease water levels in lakes and rivers. In addition, the sudden spring thaw fills rivers with more water at one time than in the past, which erodes the banks and straightens the river paths. Because the water flows more intensely during a shorter period of time, the water level is unusually low once the spring flood is over. Water levels are further reduced by the longer warm season and increased temperatures, which evaporate more water than in the past.

Observers have also noted changes in the location, characteristics and health of plant and animal species caused by changes in climate conditions. The harder snow pack, lower water levels, unusual vegetation, changing seasons and deteriorating ice conditions have altered the quantity, quality, behavior and location of the Inuit's sources of harvested game....

Using conservative projections based on current conditions and likely continued emissions, scientists have determined that climate change in the Arctic will continue, with devastating consequences. Arctic temperatures will probably rise at least another 2.5 degrees Celsius by the middle of this century. By the end of this century, arctic temperatures will have risen five to seven degrees Celsius.

In addition to temperature increases, precipitation is likely to increase, perhaps by as much as thirty five percent over current levels by the end of this century. Snow and sea-ice cover over the most of the Arctic will decrease dramatically as well. Some models show that the polar ice cap will be virtually nonexistent by 2100. [Ed. note: Predictions in 2007 by some models moved this date to mid-century.] In particular, fall and winter in the Arctic will become warmer and wetter. Moreover, the changes that have already occurred will continue to accelerate, along with their impacts on the environment, landscape, and people of the region....

V. VIOLATIONS: THE EFFECTS OF GLOBAL WARMING CONSTITUTE VIOLATIONS OF INUIT HUMAN RIGHTS, FOR WHICH THE UNITED STATES IS RESPONSIBLE ...

B. The Effects of Global Warming Violate Inuit Human Rights

    1. The Effects of Global Warming Violate the Inuit's Right to Enjoy the Benefits of their Culture

        a. The American Declaration guarantees the Inuit's right to the benefits of culture.

The American Declaration guarantees the Inuit's right to the benefits of culture. The Charter of the Organization of American States places cultural development and respect for culture in a position of supreme importance.... Cultural rights are also protected in other major human rights instruments including the Universal Declaration of Human Rights the ICCPR, and the International Covenant on Economic, Social and Cultural Rights (ICESCR)....

In the *Awas Tingni* case, the Inter-American Court, in discussing the right to property, acknowledged the link between cultural integrity and indigenous communities' lands....

In its *Yanomami* decision, the Commission noted that the State had an obligation under the OAS Charter to give priority to "preserving and strengthening ... the cultural heritage" of indigenous peoples, and determined that the granting of concessions to sub-soil resources on indigenous land....

The Inuit's human right to enjoy the benefits of their unique culture is thus guaranteed under the American Declaration and affirmed by other sources of international law. In the global and Inter-American human rights systems, indigenous peoples' right to culture is inseparable from the condition of the lands they have traditionally occupied. The United States thus has a clear duty not to degrade the arctic environment to an extent that infringes upon the Inuit's human right to enjoy the benefits of their culture.

        b. The effects of global warming violate the Inuit's right to enjoy the benefits of their culture ...

The subsistence way of life central to Inuit cultural identity has been damaged by, and may cease to exist because of, climate change. Traditional Inuit knowledge, passed from the Inuit elders in their role as keepers of the Inuit culture, is becoming less useful because of the rapidly changing environment....

The United States government itself has recognized the importance of the subsistence way of life to the continued survival of the Inuit culture. In granting preference to subsistence uses of fish and wildlife in Alaska, the United States Congress noted that "the continuation of the opportunity for subsistence uses ... is essential to Native physical, economic, traditional, and cultural existence." ...

The loss of this form of traditional knowledge further undermines Inuit culture. Predicting the weather, a crucial part of planning safe and convenient travel and harvest, as well as an important role for the Inuit elders, has become much more difficult because of changes in weather patterns. As a result, the elders can no longer fulfill one of their important roles, nor can they pass the science of weather forecasting to the next generation....

The elders' roles as educators have been compromised because the changing conditions have rendered inaccurate much of their traditional knowledge about weather, ice, snow, navigation and land conditions. The Inuit educational system, passing on and building upon knowledge from one generation to the next, is critical to Inuit cultural survival....

> 2. The Effects of Global Warming Violate the Inuit's Right to Use and Enjoy the Lands they Have Traditionally Used and Occupied
>
> > a. The American Declaration guarantees the Inuit's right to use and enjoy the lands they have traditionally occupied

The American Declaration includes the human right to "own such private property as meets the essential needs of decent living and helps to maintain the dignity of the individual and of the home." The Commission acknowledged the fundamental nature of this right when it stated, "[v]arious international human rights instruments, both universal and regional in nature, have recognized the right to property as featuring among the fundamental rights of man." Similarly, the American Convention declares that "[e]veryone has the right to the use and enjoyment of his property.... No one shall be deprived of his property except upon payment of just compensation, for reasons of public utility or social interest, and in the cases and according to the forms established by law." The Inter-American Court and this Commission have long recognized that indigenous peoples have a fundamental international human right to use and enjoy the lands they have traditionally occupied, independent of domestic title. The Inter-American Court affirmed the independent existence of indigenous peoples' collective rights to their land, resources, and environment in the *Awas Tingni* case. The Court held that the government of Nicaragua had violated the Awas Tingni's rights to property and judicial protection when it granted concessions to a foreign company to log on their traditional lands without consulting them or getting their consent.

In its recent *Belize Maya* decision, the Commission found that Belize violated the Maya people's right to use and enjoy their property by granting concessions to third parties to exploit resources that degraded the environment within lands traditionally used and occupied by the Maya people. Indigenous people's international human right to property, the Commission noted, is based in international law, and does not depend on domestic recognition of property interests....

The Inuit's human right to protection of their land is thus guaranteed by the American Declaration and general international law. The United States government has an obligation not to interfere with the Inuit's use and enjoyment of their land through its acts and omissions regarding climate change.

> > b. The effects of global warming violate the Inuit's right to use and enjoy the lands they have traditionally occupied

The "land" that the Inuit have traditionally occupied and used are the landfast winter sea ice, pack ice, and multi-year ice. The Inuit have traditionally spent much of the winter traveling, camping and hunting on the landfast ice. They have used the summer pack ice and multi-year ice to hunt seals, one of their primary sources of protein. Because the international human right to property is interpreted in the context of indigenous culture and history, the Inuit have a human right to use and enjoyment of land and ice that they have traditionally used and occupied in the arctic and sub-arctic regions of the United States, Canada, Russia, and Greenland. Inuit have also secured domestic property rights through the conclusion of four agreements with the Government of Canada and in Alaska by the legislated 1971 Alaska Native Claims Settlement Act....

Global warming violates the Inuit's human right to use and enjoy their land.... Climate change has made the Inuit's traditional lands less accessible, more dangerous, unfamiliar, and less valuable to the Inuit. The disappearance of sea ice, pack ice, and multi-year ice is affecting the very existence of Inuit land. In the last thirty years, about eight percent of the total yearly sea ice has ceased to exist, with more dramatic losses more recently, and further acceleration of the trend expected in the future. Summer sea ice has decreased fifteen to twenty percent, and is projected to disappear completely by the end of this century. The ice that remains is less valuable to the Inuit because the later freezes, earlier, more sudden thaws, and striking loss of thickness have made use of the ice more dangerous and less productive. Sea ice, a large and critical part of coastal Inuit's property, is literally melting away....

The loss of sea ice has another effect on the Inuit's use and enjoyment of their property ... contributed to alarming coastal erosion because sea storms and wave movement are so much greater without the breakwater effect of the ice. The erosion threatens the Inuit's homes and villages, forcing them to move their homes, which are expensive, arduous, and inconvenient, or lose them. Coastal campsites, a traditional use of land while traveling and harvesting, have been washed away. The erosion in turn exposes coastal permafrost to the warmer air and water, causing it to melt as well....

The United States' acts and omissions regarding climate change have violated their right to use and enjoy their ancestral lands and their rights of property in those lands....

4. The Effects of Global Warming Violate the Inuit's Right to the Preservation of Health

a. The American Declaration guarantees the Inuit the right to the preservation of health

The American Declaration provides that "[e]very person has the right to the preservation of his health through sanitary and social measures relating to food, clothing, housing and medical care, to the extent permitted by public and community resources." This guarantee is interpreted in the Additional Protocol to the American Convention on Human Rights in the Area of Economic, Social and Cultural Rights ("Protocol of San Salvador") as ensuring "the enjoyment of the highest level of physical, mental and social well-being." ...

This Commission has acknowledged the close relationship between environmental degradation and the right to health, especially in the context of indigenous peoples. In the *Yanomami* case, the Commission recognized that harm to people resulting from environmental degradation violated the right to health in Article XI of the American Declaration.... The Inter-American Commission found that "by reason of the failure of the Government of Brazil to take timely and effective measures [on] behalf of the Yanomami Indians, a situation has been produced that has resulted in the violation, injury to them, of the ... right to the preservation of health and to well-being." Additionally, in the *Belize Maya* case, the Commission noted that the right to health and well-being in the context of indigenous people's rights was so dependent on the integrity and condition of indigenous land that "broad violations" of indigenous property rights necessarily impacted the health and well-being of the Maya.

b. The effects of global warming violate the Inuit's right to the preservation of health

Climate change caused by the U.S. government's regulatory actions and inactions is harmful to the Inuit's health and well-being. Disappearing sea-ice and changing environmental conditions have diminished populations, accessibility, and quality of fish and game upon which the Inuit rely for nutrition. The Inuit's health is also adversely affected by changes in insect and pest populations and the movement of new diseases northward. The quality and quantity of natural sources of drinking water has decreased, exacerbating the already damaging effects on Inuit health. In addition to physical health issues, the Inuit's mental health has been damaged by the transformation of the once familiar landscape, and the resultant cultural destruction. These increases in health risks, caused by the United States' acts and omissions, violate the Inuit's right to the preservation of health....

Climate change has subjected the Inuit to a higher risk of diet-related diseases....

The less healthy and more expensive store-bought food the Inuit must use to supplement the subsistence harvest increases dietary health risks such as cancer, obesity, diabetes, and cardiovascular diseases....

The United States' acts and omissions with respect to climate change have degraded the arctic environment to the point that those acts and omissions violate the Inuit's fundamental human right to the preservation of their health.

> 5. The Effects of Global Warming Violate the Inuit's Right to Life, Physical Integrity and Security

>> a. The American Declaration protects the Inuit's right to life, physical protection and security

Under the American Declaration, "[e]very human being has the right to life, liberty and the security of his person." The right to life is the most fundamental of rights, and is contained in all major international human rights conventions. The United States has repeatedly bound itself to protect this fundamental right by ratifying the OAS Charter and the ICCPR, adopting the American Declaration, and signing the American Convention on Human Rights. The right to life is also a general principle of law that is contained in the constitutions of many nations, including that of the United States.

This Commission has made clear that environmental degradation can violate the right to life. In the *Yanomami* case, the Commission established a link between environmental quality and the right to life. The Commission found that, among other things, the government's failure to protect the integrity of Yanomami lands had violated the Yanomami's rights to life, liberty and personal security guaranteed by Article 1 of the American Declaration.

In its [1997] Report on the Situation of Human Rights in Ecuador, the Commission stated that "[t]he right to have one's life respected is not ... limited to protection against arbitrary killing."

> The realization of the right to life, and to physical security and integrity is necessarily related to and in some ways dependent upon one's physical environment. Accordingly, where environmental contamination and degradation pose a persistent threat to human life and health, the foregoing rights are implicated.

The United States has an obligation to protect the Inuit's human rights to life and personal security. This obligation includes the duty not to degrade the arctic environment to such an extent that the degradation threatens the life and personal security of Inuit people.

>> b. The effects of global warming violate the Inuit's right to life, physical protection and security ...

Changes in ice and snow jeopardize individual Inuit lives, critical food sources are threatened, and unpredictable weather makes travel more dangerous at all times of the year....

The thinner ice and new, unpredictable areas of open water cause hunters and other travelers to fall through the ice and be injured or drowned....

The U.S. Congress has acknowledged that, for many Inuit, "no practical alternative means are available to replace the food supplies and other items gathered from fish and wildlife which supply rural residents dependent on subsistence uses." [Alaska National Interest Lands Conservation Act, 16 U.S.C. 3111(2).] Damage to the Inuit's subsistence harvest violates their right to life.

The inability of elders to predict the weather accurately increases the risk that hunters and travelers will be caught unprepared, with life-threatening consequences in the harsh arctic climate. Stranded travelers can no longer rely on the abundance of snow from which to construct emergency shelters. This lack of shelter has contributed to deaths and injuries among hunters stranded by sudden storms. In addition, the decrease in summer ice has caused rougher seas and more dangerous storms, increasing hazards to boaters. Formerly familiar and common activities are now laden with unavoidable and unpredictable threats to human life because of the unpredictable weather.

Climate change has damaged the arctic environment to such an extent that the damage threatens human life. The United States has breached its duty under the American Declaration to protect the Inuit's right to life and personal security.

6. The Effects of Global Warming Violate the Inuit's Right to Their Own Means of Subsistence

a. The American Declaration protects the Inuit's right to their own means of subsistence

A people's right to their own means of subsistence is inherent in and a necessary component of the American Declaration's rights to property, health, life, and culture in the context of indigenous peoples. The ICESCR and ICCPR both provide that all peoples "may freely dispose of their natural wealth and resources," but that "[i]n no case may a people be deprived of its own means of subsistence." In the context of indigenous peoples, the rights to self-determination and one's own means of subsistence have become recognized principles of international human rights law....

Other human rights bodies have acknowledged the right of a people to control over their own means of subsistence.... [I]n response to Canada's failure to implement recommendations for aboriginal land and resource allocation, the Human Rights Committee emphasized Canada's obligations under Article 1 of the ICCPR and the ICESCR, stating, "peoples ... may not be deprived of their own means of subsistence." [*Concluding Observations: Canada 07/04/99,* U.N. HRC, 65th Sess., at ¶8, U.N. Doc. CCPR/C/79/Add.105 (1999) (citing ICCPR, art. 1(2)).]

The Inuit's right to their own means of subsistence is protected under international law and is an intrinsic part of the rights established in the American Declaration. The United States has an international obligation not to deprive the Inuit of their own means of subsistence.

b. The effects of global warming violate the Inuit's right to their own means of subsistence

Arctic climate change is making the Inuit's subsistence harvest more dangerous, more difficult and less reliable. In fact, climate change is gradually and steadily destroying the Inuit's means of subsistence. Changes in ice, snow, weather, seasons and land have combined to deprive the Inuit of their ability to rely exclusively on the subsistence harvest, violating their right to their own means of subsistence. Continuing changes in the arctic climate will further interfere with the Inuit's right to their own means of subsistence....

The harvest of ice-dependent animals has also become less fruitful because the animals' habitat, food sources, and living space are disappearing. The animals are suffering a loss in numbers and decline in overall health that is expected to accelerate in the coming years. The remaining animals are changing location and habits, making them less accessible, harder to find and, because of impacts on the ability to travel, sometimes impossible to hunt.

As a result of the problems with travel and food sources due to climate change, the Inuit are no longer able to rely exclusively on the subsistence harvest for their survival.... The United States' acts and omissions with regard to climate change, done without consultation or consent of the Inuit, violate the Inuit's human rights to self-determination and to their own means of subsistence.

7. The Effects of Global Warming Violate the Inuit's Rights to Residence and Movement and Inviolability of the Home

a. The American Declaration guarantees the Inuit's right to residence and movement and inviolability of the home

The American Declaration guarantees every person "the right to fix his residence within the territory of the state of which he is a national, to move about freely within such territory, and not to leave it except by his own will." The American Declaration also guarantees every person "the right to the inviolability of his home." Like the right to life, the rights to residence and movement and inviolability of the home are established in all major human rights instruments, including the Universal Declaration of Human Rights, the ICCPR, the American Convention on Human Rights, the European Convention on Human Rights and the African Charter on Human and Peoples' Rights. Many constitutions also guarantee the right to movement and residence.

In the *Yanomami* case, this Commission found a violation of the right to residence and movement where some Yanomami people had to leave their traditional lands because of a series of adverse changes caused by government development projects. The Commission noted that the construction of a highway through the territory of the Yanomami Indians, "compelled them to abandon their habitat and seek refuge in other places." ...

Other human rights tribunals have recognized the significant link between environmental quality and the right to the inviolability of the home. In *López Ostra v. Spain*, the European Court of Human Rights held that Spain's failure to prevent a waste treatment plant from polluting nearby homes violated this right. Similarly, in *Guerra and Others v. Italy*, the Court held that severe environmental pollution may affect individuals' well-being and adversely affect private and family life, and as a result held Italy liable for its failure to secure these rights. The European Court recently reaffirmed this concept in *Fadeyeva v. Russia*, in which the failure of the State to relocate the applicant away from a highly toxic area constituted violation of the right to respect for the home and private life.... The connection between the home, private life and the environment is thus well established in international law....

b. The effects of global warming violate the Inuit's right to residence and movement, and inviolability of the home

The United States' acts and omissions that contribute to global warming violate the Inuit's right to residence and movement because climate change threatens the Inuit's ability to maintain residence in their communities. Furthermore, the Inuit's right to inviolability of the home is violated because the effects of climate change adversely affect private and family life. In particular, climate change harms the physical integrity and habitability of individual homes and entire villages. Coastal erosion caused by increasingly severe storms threatens entire coastal communities. Melting permafrost causes building foundations to shift, damaging Inuit homes and community structures. The destruction is forcing the coastal Inuit to relocate their communities and homes farther inland, at great expense and distress.

This forced relocation goes to the heart of the rights to residence and movement and inviolability of the home. The destruction of Inuit homes due to climate change "compel[s the Inuit] to abandon their habitat and seek refuge in other places," affecting their family and private lives....

C. The American Declaration Should Be Applied in the Context of Relevant International Norms and Principles ...

3. International Environmental Norms and Principles Are Relevant to the Interpretation and Application of the American Declaration

a. The United States is violating its obligations under the United Nations Framework Convention on Climate Change and the Kyoto Protocol.

The United States ratified the U.N. Framework Convention on Climate Change (FCCC) on October 15, 1992.... The objective of the Framework Convention is to "achieve ... stabilization of greenhouse gas concentrations in the atmosphere at a level that would prevent dangerous anthropogenic interference with the climate system." To further this objective, Article 4.1(b) of the Convention requires Parties to formulate and implement national programs for mitigating anthropogenic greenhouse gas emissions.

Article 4.2(b) is more specific: each Annex I Party (developed country) must communicate information on its polices and measures to limit emissions and enhance removals of greenhouse gases, and on the resulting projected emissions and removals through 2000, "with the aim of returning individually or jointly to [its] 1990 levels these anthropogenic emissions of [GHGs]."

Although the year 2000 has passed, this obligation is not moot. In light of the Framework Convention's objective of avoiding dangerous atmospheric concentrations of greenhouse gases, mooting the obligation would make no sense. Indeed, were Article 4.2(b) to be read as applying only during the period before 2000, the objective would be have been unachievable from the start. It is clear that U.S. climate policy must aim at returning U.S. emissions to 1990 levels as quickly as possible.

Judging by its most recent report to the Framework Convention secretariat, which forecasts U.S. GHG emissions increasing markedly for the foreseeable future, as well as statements by President Bush and numerous other government officials, the United States has abandoned the aim of returning its emissions to 1990 levels, in violation of its obligation to implement the Framework Convention in good faith and in light of the Convention's objective. Although the U.S. government has acknowledged its obligation to reduce emissions, it has not taken mandatory steps to remedy the defects identified by the secretariat in its first review of U.S. climate policy, in 1999....

[T]he U.S. Government predicts that U.S. emissions will increase 42.7% by 2020, from 1562 MMTC in 2000 to 2088 MMTC in 2020. As if to confirm its complete rejection of Article 4.2, the United States' latest report to the secretariat makes no mention of ever returning to 1990 emissions levels, instead identifying the U.S. goal as the 18% carbon intensity reduction proposed by President Bush in 2001. The U.S. plan to reduce greenhouse gas intensity by 18% in ten years exceeds by only 4% the 14% reduction in greenhouse gas intensity expected in the absence of the President's additional proposed policies and measures. This goal, which is to be met in 2012, will allow *actual* emissions to *increase* by 12% over the same period, a rate of growth that is nearly the same as at present....

D. By Its Acts and Omissions, the United States Violates the Human Rights of the Inuit ...

1. The United States Is the World's Largest Contributor to Global Warming and its Damaging Effects on the Inuit ...

[T]he United States has contributed more than any other nation to the rise in global temperature. U.S. emissions of energy-related CO_2 are also vastly out of proportion to its population size. On a per-person basis, U.S. emissions in 2000 were more than five times the global average, nearly two-and-a-half times the per capita emissions in Europe, and nine times those in Asia and South America. Among the countries with significant emissions, the United States had the highest level of per capita emissions....

4. The United States Has Failed to Cooperate with International Efforts to Reduce Greenhouse Gas Emissions ...

Beginning with its rejection of the Kyoto Protocol in 2001, the United States has hindered attempts by other nations even to agree on the need for coordinated action to deal with global warming....

Although the United States concedes the fact that climate change is occurring and is caused in large part by anthropogenic greenhouse gases, it refuses to take meaningful action to tackle global warming. The result is that temperatures in the Arctic continue to rise unabated, with dire consequences for the Inuit.

IX. REQUEST FOR RELIEF

For the reasons stated above, Petitioner respectfully requests that the Commission:

1. Make an onsite visit to investigate and confirm the harms suffered by the named individuals whose rights have been violated and other affected Inuit;

2. Hold a hearing to investigate the claims raised in this Petition;

3. Prepare a report setting forth all the facts and applicable law, declaring that the United States of America is internationally responsible for violations of rights affirmed in the American Declaration of the Rights and Duties of Man and in other instruments of international law, and recommending that the United States:

   a. Adopt mandatory measures to limit its emissions of greenhouse gases and cooperate in efforts of the community of nations—as expressed, for example, in activities relating to the United Nations Framework Convention on Climate Change—to limit such emissions at the global level;

   b. Take into account the impacts of U.S. greenhouse gas emissions on the Arctic and affected Inuit in evaluating and before approving all major government actions;

   c. Establish and implement, in coordination with Petitioner and the affected Inuit, a plan to protect Inuit culture and resources, including, inter alia, the land, water, snow, ice, and plant and animal species used or occupied by the named individuals whose rights have been violated and other affected Inuit; and mitigate any harm to these resources caused by U.S. greenhouse gas emissions;

d. Establish and implement, in coordination with Petitioner and the affected Inuit communities, a plan to provide assistance necessary for Inuit to adapt to the impacts of climate change that cannot be avoided;

e. Provide any other relief that the Commission considers appropriate and just.

Questions and Discussion

1. *Right to the benefits of culture.* The petition listed a number of ways that global warming is diminishing the ability of the Inuit to enjoy cultural traditions. While perhaps few people have a greater association with cold temperatures than the Inuit, the cultural impact of global warming is widespread. Many countries and peoples are forced to alter their way of life to deal with volatile weather patterns, diminished access to resources, the spread of disease, etc. In comparison with the Inuit, are there distinct and valued aspects of American culture that would be threatened by global warming?

2. *Right to use and enjoy lands traditionally occupied.* When the petition makes its case for the violation of this right, do you see the same strong connection between the indicted state action and the rights violation that the other cases demonstrate? Most applications of this right, including the *Belize Maya* and *Dann* cases in Chapter 5 on Indigenous Rights, pages 193 and 198, involve direct invasion or taking of land. Is the "land" really "taken" from the Inuit in this case? Does the lack of a material invasion by a third party (or the state itself) weaken the argument? What do you think of the argument that the ice traditionally used by the Inuit is part of their traditional "land"?

3. *Right to the preservation of health.* The petition makes a good case for specific ways that global warming affects Inuit health, from sustenance deprivation to hazardous living conditions to changes in sunlight. On a global scale, consider the impacts of even slight warming as it regards our knowledge of disease. Might a change in temperature trigger the evolution of new and as-yet-untreatable bacteria and viruses? What about the vectors that carry this disease—will they be able to travel to new places?

4. *Right to life.* The petition described ways in which the effects of climate change have taken and will take the lives of Inuit people. This is perhaps the strongest arrow in the human rights quiver for combating climate change, for it is the most universally accepted right and it is the easiest to link to health. Beyond the Inuit condition, what about the millions displaced by rising seas in Bangladesh or stricken by floods and drought in China? As the link between global warming and extreme weather events grows stronger, will the United States consider that the tragedies associated with Hurricane Katrina can be partially attributed to global warming? Do you think that the link between global warming and deaths caused by heat waves has already been acknowledged in recent years? The right to life has also been expanded in ways that increase its applicability to global warming. Remember how Indian courts found the right to life violated on account of the degradation of the quality of life. Considering ways in which climate change directly takes life, is it evident that climate change can also have a subtle impact on the quality of life?

5. *Right to subsistence.* Subsistence farmers throughout the world will suffer acutely due to global warming. The IPCC report found it very likely (>90% certainty) that hot extremes, heat waves, and heavy precipitation events will continue to become more frequent. All three are closely linked to successful crop production, especially among less-developed societies. The changing conditions can also affect the migratory patterns of important species and, in some cases, destroy habitats altogether. Lake Chad, a 20,000 year old body of water in Africa, was once 9,700 square miles and provided important fish-

eries and crop irrigation to the 20 million nearby residents. Today it is nearly 1/20 that size, and much of the shrinkage has occurred in the past 40 years. Complicating matters, the lake is bordered by four countries: Chad, Cameroon, Niger, and Nigeria.

6. *Right to residence, movement, and inviolability of the home.* This is another particularly useful tool for combating climate change in the human rights arena. Consider threatened pacific islands, low and flat countries like Bangladesh, cities actually *below* sea level like New Orleans, and rising tides in general. Does not every inch that the oceans claim violate the property rights of somebody? Remember another part of the IPCC report, where it is stated that future tropical cyclones (typhoons and hurricanes) will likely become more intense, with larger peak wind speeds and heavier precipitation. In 2005 Hurricane Katrina devastated the Southeast, ultimately leaving behind a damage bill that may reach into the hundreds of billions of dollars. As the link between global warming and extreme weather events grows stronger, will this particular right move to the forefront? In early 2008, a District Court decision found the United States government immune from liability in a suit brought by Hurricane Katrina victims. See *In re Katrina Canal Breaches Consol. Litigation*, 533 F.Supp.2d 615, 2008 WL 314396 (E.D. La. 2008). The court, after acknowledging that the Army Corp of Engineers failed in its task of securing the levees around New Orleans, concluded, "It is not within this Court's power to address the wrongs committed. It is hopefully within the citizens of the United States' power to address the failures of our laws and agencies. If not, it is certain that another tragedy such as this will occur again."

7. *Application and interpretation of the American Convention.* Article 29 of the Convention states that the Convention must not be interpreted as "restricting the enjoyment or exercise of any right or freedom recognized by virtue of the laws of any State Party or by virtue of another convention … ; precluding other rights or guarantees that are inherent in the human personality or derived from representative democracy as a form of government; or excluding or limiting the effect that the American Declaration of the Rights and Duties of Man and other international acts of the same nature may have." Does it mean that the Inter-American Commission may apply the ICCPR, ILO Convention 169, European Convention of Human Rights, or U.S. law? Or that the Commission and the Court can use official interpretations of these instruments by human rights bodies? In the Inuit case, should the Commission take into account not only the specific rights provisions in the American Convention on Human Rights, but also other relevant obligations the United States has assumed under international treaties and customary international law?

8. *The role of multiple agreements.* Do you agree that the American Declaration of Rights and Duties of Man and the American Convention on Human Rights should be read in light of other international treaties and customs to which the United States has not become a party? What is the purpose of signing individual agreements if they all should be considered when enforcing one? The U.S. specifically embraced the ICCPR, but rejected the ICESCR. When enforcing the ICCPR against the United States, would it be appropriate or inappropriate to read it "in light of" the ICESCR and other human rights documents?

9. *Utilizing multiple human rights courts.* Is it possible and viable to apply, with claims similar to those in the Inuit petition, to other regional human rights courts—European and African? In particular, can the Russian Inuit population apply to the European Court of Human Rights? What articles of the European Convention on Human Rights and Fundamental Freedoms can be used? If using Article 8, who has arbitrarily deprived the Inuit of their rights to private and family life? The Russian Federation? The U.S. government? Corporate actors within the United States?

10. *The UNFCCC and the Kyoto Protocol.* One item that often fails to be mentioned during discussions of the Kyoto Protocol is the fact that the UNFCCC, which the United States *has* ratified, is a binding document. The United States pledged to "achieve … stabilization of greenhouse gas concentrations in the atmosphere at a level that would prevent dangerous anthropogenic interference with the climate system." Has the United States failed to do so? Have anthropogenic emissions originating in the U.S. "interfered" with climate systems in a legally cognizable way? Does the IPCC report have enough confidence to make this case? The most cited reason for the U.S.'s decision not to join the Kyoto Protocol has been the fact that China and India, both among the top greenhouse gas emitting countries, currently do not have mandatory obligations to reduce their emissions. Does it make sense that some countries should bear less of a burden than others? At what point is a country sufficiently *developed* to begin contributing to the effort to reduce greenhouse gases? Can you make the case for inclusion of China and India in the group of developing countries, despite their burgeoning economies? If so, and the U.S. is thus persuaded to join, nearly 50% of the world's greenhouse gas emissions could be brought into regulation under a post-Kyoto treaty.

11. *The power of the Commission.* Could the petition establish a precedent for holding countries liable for profiting from not regulating greenhouse gas emissions? Could a report or ruling by the Inter-American Commission of Human Rights provide an incentive for countries to ratify the Kyoto Protocol and to participate in good faith in post-Kyoto negotiations?

12. *Procedural hurdles.* What are possible procedural obstacles for the Inuit petition? The IACHR gives standing to any NGO legally recognized by an OAS Member State. It has allowed the Center for International Environmental Law and Earthjustice, for example, to have standing to submit petitions. The Inuit argued that any group, regardless of national citizenship or residence, is able to petition for redress by an OAS member state. Is jurisdiction problematic, taking into account that the United States is not party to the American Convention?

3. The Next Step?

In 2006, the Inter-American Commission on Human Rights rejected the Inuit Petition, but not with a decision on the merits of the legal claims. The IACHR found, "Specifically, the information provided does not enable us to determine whether the alleged facts would tend to characterize a violation of rights protected by the American Declaration." In other words, there was insufficient proof. Does this mean that the IACHR found the scientific facts surrounding climate change questionable? Or, does this mean that the IACHR did not see the United States as legally accountable for specific violations of protected rights? Or might it appear that the Commission simply found a convenient means of sidestepping a politically dangerous issue?

In early 2007, the IACHR granted the petitioners a hearing, although not on the petition that it had dismissed. This did not reopen the door for accepting the petition. It did, however, allow the petitioners to appear before the IACHR and provide testimony about the connection of global warming and human rights. During the rest of 2007, the United Nations Intergovernmental Panel on Climate Change issued its Fourth Assessment in various stages, comprising hundreds of pages of newly documented scientific evidence and conclusions.

On June 3, 2008, the General Assembly of the Organization of American States approved a resolution, "Human Rights and Climate Change in the Americas." The resolution instructed the Inter-American Commission on Human Rights to contribute to efforts "to determine the possible existence of a link between adverse effects of climate change and the full enjoyment of human rights." OEA/Ser.P AG/doc.4886/08 (2008).

C. International Court of Justice

Treading Deep Waters
Substantive Law Issues in Tuvalu's Threat to Sue the United States in the International Court of Justice

Rebecca Elizabeth Jacobs
14 Pac. Rim L. & Pol'y 103 (2005)

II. Global Warming Endangers a Unique Island and Its Brave People

The island nation of Tuvalu is located in the Pacific Ocean halfway between Hawaii and Australia. It is part of the Oceania island group, one of nine atolls in the South Pacific. The sinking of volcanic islands formed the atolls, leaving a ring of coral islands around a lagoon. When Polynesians first arrived on the island approximately 200 years ago, they found it difficult to adapt to the sandy soil and sparse local food sources.

More threatening, however, than the lack of resources, was the danger of the tropical storms and cyclones that struck the island once or twice a decade. During the fiercest of these storms, the inhabitants would protect themselves from being blown into the Pacific by tying themselves to coconut palms, hoping the wind was not forceful enough to take the rooted trees as well.

Although the Tuvaluans were largely successful in protecting themselves from these natural disasters, there is a modern and unnatural disaster against which they are largely impotent—global warming. The high tides and floods that briefly overwhelmed the islands every February now occur frequently from November through March. The heavy storms that formerly hit the island once or twice a decade struck Tuvalu seven times in the 1990s, likely due to the effects of global warming. Scientists predict that with sea levels expected to increase up to eighty-eight centimeters in the next century, the future of the island above water is rather grim. Further, the rising floods and waves have increased the salt water table, harming agricultural efforts which were already difficult due to Tuvalu's sandy island soil. During the last century, the sea level has risen at an alarming rate. An outer reef now protects the island from the constant beating of the waves, but the growth of coral cannot keep pace with the ascending sea level. Approximately 11,000 Tuvaluans live on a mere twenty-six square kilometers of land. Remarkably, the island's highest point is only five meters above sea level. As Koloa Talake, an elder statesman, puts it plainly: "We don't have hills or mountains. All we have is coconut trees. If the industrial countries don't consider our crisis, our only alternative is to climb up in the coconut trees when the tide rises."

Realizing that the people of Tuvalu will soon have to follow their island to a salty demise or move to higher ground, the Prime Minister has requested environmental refugee status for its citizens from both Australia and New Zealand. While New Zealand responded to the plea by allowing seventy-five Tuvaluans to relocate annually to their country, Australia has refused to make any such offer. At a rate of seventy-five Tuvaluan relocations a year, the island would hypothetically be uninhabited in 140 years—ninety years after scientists predict it will be under water. As Tuvalu environment official Paani Laupepa remarked in a conversation with the British Broadcasting Company: "While New Zealand responded positively in the true Pacific way of helping one's neighbors, Australia on the other hand has slammed the door in our face." Further angering the Tuvaluan people, the Australian government has asked Tuvalu and its fellow South Pacific islands nations to allow Middle Eastern asylum seekers to live there. Panapa Nelesone, a Tuvaluan Government spokesman responded to the request by saying: "We ask them for space and now they're sending us their own people."Without support from their neighbors, Tuvaluans face a not-so-distant demise.

In 2002, in response to the United States' refusal to ratify the Kyoto Protocol, the Pacific island nation of Tuvalu, vulnerable to submersion due to the rising sea level, threatened to bring a lawsuit against the United States in the International Court of Justice for damages to its island. Outside of various jurisdictional issues that may preempt the suit, Tuvalu's suit will likely have a number of substantive law problems. Tuvalu must show not only that the United States is unlawfully causing the island damage, but also that it has a right to future damages that have yet to occur. Tuvalu might succeed by arguing principles of intergenerational rights and the precautionary principle....

Two major obstacles Tuvalu may face in a suit against the United States are proving that 1) the release of GHGs causes the sea level to rise; and 2) in particular, the United States' release of GHG's will cause the submersion of their island...."Tuvalu could request an I.C.J. advisory opinion through certain bodies of the United Nations.... As evidence of current damage, Tuvalu would likely point to the increased storm activity causing damage to above-island buildings and vegetation and to rising water tables that erode the island's beaches and destroy local crops.... In petitioning to the I.C.J. for damages in the 1995 Nuclear Test Case, New Zealand relied on the precautionary principle to request that the Court impose on France the burden of proving that no harm would result from its activities.

Tuvalu is not and will not be the only island affected by global warming. Regardless of whether Tuvalu is successful in the international arena, contemplating the issues Tuvalu may face in a possible suit will provide guidance for prospective actions by other nations that will surely face a similarly dire future.... Tuvalu's case presents a unique opportunity to address international environmental law issues that will likely arise in future cases brought by victims of global warming.

Questions and Discussion

1. *Tuvalu.* The situation in Tuvalu appears to be as imminent as and perhaps even graver than that of the Inuit. Based on the conditions described by Rebecca Jacobs, what human rights are violated or threatened? Tuvalu's highest point is only five meters above sea level and at its widest point it is a mere couple hundred meters across. With seas rising at the rate suggested in the IPCC report, most of Tuvalu may well disappear entirely within this century. What human rights are implicated when an entire country is swept away? Would this be a clear enough violation of the right to life to bring a major GHG-emitting state before the International Court of Justice? Or would causation issues persist that would doom a lawsuit?

2. *Better standing?* Walking through the standing issues presented in the Inuit Petition and the Goldberg-Wagner article, will Tuvalu have the same hurdles? Does their injury appear any more particularized? Will their legal cause be aided by the fact that the victims all hail from the same country? Does Massachusetts v. EPA, page ____ have any rel-

evance? Does this help open the door to the International Court of Justice (I.C.J.) for Tuvalu? Note that only 1/3 of countries, not including the U.S., recognize the compulsory jurisdiction of the I.C.J. What difficulties of application to the I.C.J. do you expect? Compare with the 1995 Nuclear Test Case, when the I.C.J. rendered a decision on atmospheric nuclear testing alleged to have adverse impacts on New Zealand current and future generations.

3. *Where will they go?* Tuvalu has struck a bargain with New Zealand to allow immigration, but only for seventy-five Tuvaluans each year and only if they are able to work. Australia's former opposition party, now in power, proposed in 2006 that Australia establish an international coalition of Pacific Rim counties willing to accept climate change refugees. See, e.g., Human Rights and Equal Opportunity Commission (Australia), *Human Rights and Climate Change, Background Paper* (2008). The issue of environmental refugees displaced by climate change is certainly not limited to Tuvalu. Bangladesh, already one of the poorest nations in the world, also has many citizens near sea level and vulnerable to rising seas and stronger storms. Some reports suggest that already nearly one million people are displaced each year, and that the one meter sea level rise predicted by IPCC could displace as many as 13 million. Keep in mind a situation closer to home—Hurricane Katrina not only killed thousands and left huge amount of economic and physical damage, but it also forced over 200,000 people to move permanently out of Louisiana into neighboring states.

D. Substantive Rights in National Courts

Jonah Gbemre v. Shell Petroleum (Nigeria)
Federal High Court of Nigeria. Benin Judicial Division
14th Day of November, 2005
Suit No: FHC/B/CS/153/05

JUDGMENT

On the 21st of July 2005 this Court granted leave to the Applicants to apply for an order enforcing or securing the enforcement of their fundamental rights to life and dignity of human person as provided by Sections 33(1) and 34(1) of the Constitution of Federal Republic of Nigeria, 1999, and Arts 4, 16, and 24 of the African Charter on Human and Peoples Rights....

The Reliefs claimed by the Applicants in their subsequent Motion on Notice filed on 29th July, 2005 include:

1. A declaration that the Constitutionally guaranteed fundamental rights to life and dignity of human person provided in Sections 33(1) and 34(1) of the Constitution ... inevitably includes the right to clean poison-free, pollution-free and healthy environment.

2. A declaration that the actions of the 1st and 2d Respondents in continuing to flare gas in the course of their oil exploration and production activities in Applicant's Community is a violation of their fundamental rights to life (including healthy environment) and dignity of human person guaranteed by Sections 33(1) and 34(1) of the Constitution....

5. An order of Perpetual Injunction restraining the 1st and 2d Respondents by themselves or by their agents, servants, contractors or workers or otherwise howsoever from further flaring of gas in the Applicants said Community.

It is the case of the Applicants (as shown in the itemized grounds upon which the above-mentioned Reliefs are sought) that:

a. By virtue of the provisions of Sections 33(1) and 34 (1) of the Constitution ... they have a fundamental right to life and dignity of human person.

b. Also by virtue of Arts 4, 16 and 24 of the African Charter on Human and Peoples Procedure Rules ... they have the right to respect for their lives and dignity of their persons and to enjoy the best attainable state of physical and mental health as well as right to a general satisfactory environment favourable to their development.

c. That the gas flaring activities in their Community in Delta State of Nigeria by the 1st and 2d Respondents are a violation of their said fundamental rights to life and dignity of human person and to a healthy life in a healthy environment....

It is also, in the case of the Applicants (as summarized in their Affidavit in verification of all the above-stated facts) that they are bonafide citizens of the Federal Republic of Nigeria....

7. That burning of gas by flaring [in their] community gives rise to the following:

a. Poisons and pollutes the environment as it leads to the emission of carbon dioxide, the main green house gas; the flares contain a cocktail of toxins that affect their health, lives and livelihood.

b. Exposes them to an increased risk of premature death, respiratory illness, asthma and cancer.

c. Contributes to adverse climate change as it emits carbon dioxide and methane which causes warming of the environment, pollutes their food and water.

d. Causes painful breathing chronic bronchitis, decreased lung function and death.

e. Reduces crop production and adversely impacts on their food security.

f. Causes acid rain....

9. That no Environmental Impact Assessment (E.I.A) whatsoever was undertaken by any of the 1st and 2d Respondents to ascertain the harmful consequences of their gas flaring activities to the environment, health, food, water, development, lives, infrastructure, etc....

14. That the constitutional guarantee of right to life and dignity of human person available to them as citizens of Nigeria includes the right to a clean, healthy, poison-free and pollution-free air and healthy environment conducive for human beings to reside in for our development and full enjoyment of life, and that these rights to life amid dignity of human person have been and are being wantonly violated and are continuously threatened with persistent violation by these gas flaring activities.

15. That unless this Court promptly intervenes their said fundamental rights being breached by the 1st and 2d Respondents will continue unabated and with impunity while its members will continue to suffer various sicknesses, deterioration of health and premature death.

16. And that the 1st and 2d Respondents have no right to continue to engage in gas-flaring in violation of their right to life and to a clean, healthy, pollution-free environment and dignity of human person....

Now, before I consider the Counter-Affidavit and other processes of the 1st and 2d Respondents, it is necessary for me to reproduce some of the statutory provisions mentioned so far and other relevant enactments for the Court's case of reference.

Section 46(1) of the Constitution states that

Any person who alleges that any of the provisions of this Chapter has been, is being or likely to be contravened in any state in relation to him, may apply to a high Court in that State for redress.

Section 33(1) [of the Constitution] states that:

Every person has a right to life, and no one shall be deprived intentionally of his life save in execution of the sentence of a court in respect of a criminal offence of which he has been found guilty in Nigeria.

Section 34(1) of the Constitution ... states:

Every individual is entitled to respect for the dignity of his person and accordingly....

Article 4 of the African Charter on Human Procedure Rules states:

Human beings are inviolable. Every human shall be entitled to respect for his life and the integrity of his person. No one may be arbitrarily deprived of this right....

Article 24 of the Charter:

All peoples shall have the right to a general satisfactory environment favorable to their development....

On the 30th of August, 2005 and 16th of September, 2005 the 1st and the 2d Respondents filed two separate Counter-affidavits in opposition to the depositions of the Applicants' Affidavit in support of their claims in this suit and I wish to summarize the case of the Respondents contained there as follows....

4. That the activities of the Respondents in relation to gas exploitation and processing has not caused any pollution of the air, or any respiratory disease, endanger or impaired the health of anybody including the Applicant or those whom he purports to represent.

5. That the Respondents' gas operation is carried out in accordance with the Laws, Regulations and Policy of the Federal Government and in conformity with International Standards and Practices and these standards have no ruinous or adverse consequences to either health or lives as alleged or at all....

7. That the incidents of death, respiratory illness, asthma, cancer, adverse climate change corroded corrugated house roofs, painful breathing chronic bronchitis, decreased lung functions, pollutions of food and water, are not the result of any of the Respondents oil and gas exploration activities and their gas and oil exploration activities have no causal connection with any of the alleged incidents....

11. That their operations have in no way affected the fundamental rights of the Applicant as alleged and that these oil and gas exploration activities are carried out in compliance with good oil field practice and as permitted by the Laws of the Federal Republic of Nigeria.

12. That their operations have not in any way affected the health, air or environment, life or dignity of the Applicants to entitle them to bring this action under the 1999 Constitution or any International Convention....

In his submission, the Learned SAN [Senior Advocate of Nigeria] for the Applicants stated that his application was brought under Order 2 Rule (1) of the Fundamental Right Enforcement Procedure Rules 1979 pursuant to the Leave granted by this Honourable Court on the 21st of July, 2005. He restated the 5 Reliefs as contained in the Motion paper, and said that there is a Verifying Affidavit in support of the motion and the statement filed along with the application for leave and relies on all those processes.

He submitted further that Section 33(1) of the Constitution guaranteed the right to life and proceeded to the Black's Law Dictionary for a definition of life since there is nowhere in the Constitution the word "Life" is defined. Neither did the interpretation Act define Life in any of its provisions. That therefore the definition of Life in the 6th Edition of Blacks Law Dictionary at pages 923–924 stress that life means:

    a.   the sum of all the forces by which death is resisted;

    b.   the state of the humans in which its organs are capable of performing their functions;

    c.   all personal rights and their enjoyment of the faculties.

He submits that this definition shows the wide scope of the right to life as it does not just portray a narrow meaning of the right—that is not just to have one's head cut or guillotined, but also more significantly, included the right of a human being to have his organs function properly and to the enjoyment of all his faculties [a]nd refers to the relevant evidence before the Court....

In clarifying this submission, the Learned SAN said that the inconsistency lies in the fact that the Constitution, having guaranteed right to life (which includes right to a healthy environment), same cannot be whittled down by an Act of National Assembly, which allows for a continuation of gas flaring which pollutes the air, water and food. And that both statutes cannot stand side by side....

Mr. B.E.I. Nwofor, SAN finally submitted that the Applicants prayer for an injunction is a consequential relief which flows logically from the other prayers and also urged me to hold that Gas Flaring has contributed to global warming of the Environment and depletion of the OZONE Layer. That I should grant all the Applicants reliefs and consequently dismiss objections of the 1st and 2d Respondents....

In his response the Learned Lead Counsel for the 1st and 2d Respondents, Chief T.J. Okpoko, SAN submitted that this action is for the enforcement of the fundamental rights of one person (representing a community) and that Fundamental Rights Enforcement Proceedings are applicable to an injured individual, and not to a person that is well and healthy....

Upon a thorough evaluation of all the processes, submissions, judicial and statutory authorities as well as the nature of the subject matter, together with the urgency which both parties through their Counsel have observably treated the weighty issues raised in the substantive claim, I find, myself able to hold as follows: (after a thoroughly painstaking consideration)

    1.   That the Applicants were properly granted leave to institute these proceedings in a representative capacity for himself and for each and every member of the Iweherekan Community in Delta State of Nigeria.

    2.   That this Court has the inherent jurisdiction to grant leave to the Applicants who are bonafide citizens and residents of the Federal Republic of Nigeria, to apply for the enforcement of their fundamental rights to life and dignity of the

human person as guaranteed by Sections 33 and 34 of the Constitution of the Federal Republic of Nigeria, 1999.

3. That these constitutionally guaranteed rights inevitably include the rights to clean poison-free, pollution-free healthy environment.

4. The actions of the 1st and 2d Respondents in continuing to flare gas in the course of their oil exploration and production activities in the Applicant's Community is a gross violation of their fundamental right to life (including healthy environment) and dignity of human person as enshrined in the Constitution.

5. Failure of the 1st and 2d Respondents to carry out Environmental Impact Assessment in the Applicants Community concerning the effects of their gas flaring activities is a clear violation of Section 2(2) of the Environmental Impact Assessment Act ... and has contributed to a further violation of the said fundamental rights.

6. That Section 3(2)(a) and (b) of the Associated Gas Re-Injection Act and Section 1 of the Associated Gas Re-Injection (Continued Flaring of Gas) Regulations. Section 1.43 of 1984 under which continued flaring of gas in Nigeria may be allowed are inconsistent with the Applicant's rights to life and/or dignity of human person enshrined in Sections 33(1) and 34(l) of the Constitution ... and Articles 4, 16 and 24 of the African Charter on Human and Peoples Rights ... and are therefore unconstitutional, null and void by virtue of Section 1(3) of the same Constitution.

Based on the above findings, the Reliefs claimed by the Applicants as stated in their motion paper as 1, 2, 3, 4 are hereby granted as I make and repeat the specific declarations contained there as the Final Orders of this Court.

1. DECLARATION that the Constitutionally guaranteed fundamental rights to life and dignity of human person provided in Sections 33(l) and 34(1) of the Constitution ... and reinforced by Arts 4, I 6 and 24 of the African Charter on Human and Peoples Rights ... inevitably includes the right to clean poison-free, pollution-free and healthy environment.

2. DECLARATION that the actions of the 1st and 2d Respondents in continuing to flare gas in the course of their oil exploration and production activities in the Applicant's Community is a violation of their fundamental rights to life (including healthy environment) and dignity of human person guaranteed by Sections 33(1) and 34(1) of the Constitution ... and reinforced by Arts 4, 16 and 24 of the African Charter on human and Peoples Rights....

3. DECLARATION that the failure of the 1st and 2d Respondents to carry out environmental impact assessment in the Applicant's Community concerning the effects of their gas flaring activities is a violation of Section 2(2) of the Environment Impact Assessment ... and contributed to the violation of the Applicant's said fundamental rights to life and dignity of the human person.

4. DECLARATION that the provisions of Section 3(2)(a), (b) of the Associated Gas Re-injection Act ... and Section 1 of the Associated Gas Re-Injection (continued flaring of gas) Regulations Section 1.43 of 1984, under which the continued flaring of gas in Nigeria may be allowed are inconsistent with the Applicant's Right to life and/or dignity of human person enshrined in Sections 33(1) and 34(1) of the Constitution ... and Arts. 4, 16, and 24 of the African Charter on Human and Peoples Right ... and are therefore unconstitutional, null and void by virtue of Section 1(3) of the same Constitution.

5. I HEREBY ORDER that the 1st and 2d Respondents are accordingly restrained whether by themselves, their servants or workers or otherwise from further flaring of gas in Applicant's Community and are to take immediate steps to stop the further flaring of gas in the Applicant's Community.

6. The Honourable Attorney-General of the Federation and Ministry of Justice, 3d Respondent in these proceedings who regrettably did not put up any appearance, and/or defend these proceedings is HEREBY ORDERED [to] immediately set into motion, after due consultation with the Federal Executive Council, necessary processes for the Enactment of a Bill for an Act of the National Assembly for the speedy amendment of the relevant Sections of the Associated Gas Regulation Act and the Regulations made there under to quickly bring them in line with the provisions of Chapter 4 of the Constitution, especially in view of the fact that the Associated Gas Regulation Act even by itself also makes the said continuous gas flaring a crime having prescribed penalties in respect thereof. Accordingly, the ease as put forward by the 1st and 2d Respondents as well as their various preliminary objections are hereby dismissed as lacking merit.

C.V. NWOKORIE

JUDGE

Questions and Discussion

1. *Creative interpretation?* The *Gbemre* case is one of the first where a national court held that climate change may implicate human rights. What human rights are alleged to be violated in the Nigerian gas flaring case? Could the interpretation of the constitutional rights to life and a healthy environment be interpreted in other creative ways to combat climate change in other contexts? Do you agree with the interpretation of "life" by plaintiff? What components does it include?

2. *Obeying the order.* The Court ordered that gas flaring must stop in the Niger Delta community as it violates guaranteed constitutional rights to life and dignity. However, Shell continues to flare gas in the Niger Delta to this day. In April 2006, the judge ordered the managing director of Shell Nigeria to appear in court. There, Shell was granted a stay of execution by the court to continue gas flaring until April 2007. When this deadline was reached, the Nigerian government shifted the deadline to the end of December 2007. A week into 2008 the government shifted the deadline again to December 31, 2008. The new deal appears to take a stronger stance by fining oil companies for gas flaring during 2008 and threatening to shut down any oil field that flares gas in 2009. How do you think Shell and the Nigerian government are able to maneuver around a High Court ruling that human rights are being violated? If judicially recognized constitutional human rights are not enforced, where else can afflicted parties turn?

3. *Gas flaring.* Nigeria flares more gas than any other country in the world, which in turn releases more GHG than all other emission sources in sub-Saharan Africa combined. Gas flaring is the process of burning off the natural gas that is released during oil production. Nigeria is the eighth largest oil exporter in the world and the fifth largest exporter to the United States. The oil sector makes up 90% of Nigeria's total exports and is the largest contributor to its economic growth. The World Bank estimates that Nigeria loses about US$2.5 billion annually to gas flaring, while about 2/3 of the country lives on less than US $1 a day. Capturing natural gas and transporting it to market, instead of flaring it, would en-

tail large infrastructure costs. Are there any legal claims available against those who waste a natural resource? Why would someone not take advantage of a potential profit source?

4. *Strong precedent?* Another court refused to allow a similar case against gas flaring to proceed, ruling that the persons in the community who were injured had not been named individually as plaintiffs. *Barrister Ikechuckwu Okpara v. Shell Petroleum Devel. Corp. of Nigeria,* Suit No. FHC/PH/CS/518/2005 (Sept. 29, 2006). Could there be reasons other than the stated procedural grounds that the court dismissed the case? Recall that the plaintiff in the main case, Jonah Gbemre, was said to represent an entire community.

In early 2008, a tort lawsuit claiming "public nuisance" was filed in United States District Court. The village of Kivalina, Alaska is being forced to relocate because of rapid erosion. The sea ice that normally protects the village from fall and winter storms is no longer forming because of global warming. The U.S. Army Corp of Engineers and the Government Accountability Office estimate that it will cost between $95 and $400 million to relocate the village. The village sued nine oil companies (including ExxonMobil Corp., Chevron Corp., and Shell Oil Corp.), fourteen power companies, and one coal company.

The suit claimed damages due to the defendants' contributions to global warming and invokes the U.S. federal common law of public nuisance. Is this pending suit likely to have more success than the Inuit petition, discussed earlier in this chapter? Are private corporations, as opposed to the U.S. government, a better target when fighting climate change, as in the Nigeria case? Does suing on the grounds of public nuisance, as opposed to international human rights violations, trivialize climate change litigation in any way? Or does it package human rights claims in a form that has a greater chance of success before judges in a traditionally conservative profession? Is its purpose likely to be compensation, pressure for change in future corporate behavior, or political change?

Climate Change and International Human Rights Litigation: A Critical Appraisal
Eric A. Posner
155 U. Pa. L. Rev. 1925 (2007)

Litigation seems attractive to many people mainly because the more conventional means for addressing global warming—the development of treaties and other international conventions such as the Kyoto Accord—have been resisted by governments. A rational treaty system would require states to reduce greenhouse gas emitting activities in their territory or, in some versions, to purchase the privilege from other states. The treaty approach has obvious appeal: it would permit states to design a system that creates the most efficient incentives for reducing greenhouse gases, while taking account of differences in local capacity and economic development, international equity, and other relevant factors. Nearly everyone agrees that a treaty system would be better than litigation. But treaty negotiations have stalled, and there are numerous reasons for pessimism about international cooperation in the face of global warming, so lawyers concerned about global climate change have been searching for other approaches.

These approaches all involve the creative use of litigation on the basis of existing domestic and international law.... A handful of treaties and, possibly, norms of customary international law imply that states are liable for emitting pollution that injures people living in other states, and one could argue that if these rules do in fact prohibit such pollution, they apply to greenhouse gases as well. These legal claims could potentially be pursued before domestic courts or international tribunals....

Liability [of companies in the United States] based on American activities alone would have only a marginal effect on the climate, especially if, as seems likely, it would mainly cause industry to migrate overseas. Congress would not permit this to happen, and would modify tort law that placed American industry at such a profound global disadvantage.

Litigation targeting the U.S. government for failing to regulate greenhouse gas emissions is even less likely to succeed because of sovereign immunity. Litigation against foreign states based on international law is likely to fare poorly in domestic courts because of foreign sovereign immunity and other doctrines that limit the liability of foreign states and individuals. This barrier is compounded by the weakness of international environmental treaties and customary law. The weakness of the law also makes litigation before international tribunals largely pointless, except perhaps as a way of attracting attention; further, international tribunals have no power to coerce states to comply with their judgments.

But if international environmental law is weak, international human rights law is, by comparison, robust. Scholars have therefore argued that international environmental law claims are more likely to succeed if they can be reconceptualized as international human rights claims. Most states belong to human rights treaties, and many of the obligations embodied in these treaties have become norms of customary international law. Human rights treaties potentially give individuals (as opposed to foreign governments) claims against states — both the state of which the individual is a citizen and any given foreign state implicated in an alleged rights violation. In theory, individuals or groups could bring human rights claims against their own state and foreign states in certain international tribunals, and prevail if they can show that failure to regulate greenhouse gas emissions has resulted in a violation of their human rights. Because international tribunals generally have very limited powers, the most promising avenue lies with domestic litigation in the United States. The Alien Tort Statute (ATS) allows non-Americans to bring claims in American courts based on torts that violate treaties and customary international law. Litigants can bring these claims against American and foreign corporations and government officials, even if sovereign immunity bans claims against most states. ATS litigation has been distinctive because it has produced awards and even payment of damages (in settlements), so today it is the most prominent and effective means for litigating international human rights claims. If a plausible claim can be made that the emission of greenhouse gases violates human rights, and that these human rights are embodied in a treaty or customary international law, then American courts may award damages to victims....

American courts would be, in effect, setting up a regime of sanctions, under which American markets would be effectively closed to foreign corporations that do not comply with the emissions standards established by the courts.... Although nominally directed at foreign corporations, these sanctions would effectively be a challenge to the economic, environmental, and development policies of other nations on the ground that those policies are insufficiently sensitive to the dangers of climate change.

This would be odd. There is no reason to think that American courts could or should develop greenhouse gas policy for Australia, Ecuador, Sweden, and Chad....

Foreign states object when American courts try to control activities on their territory, and so we would have to expect a reaction from affected individuals, groups, and states if this ATS litigation were to succeed. As noted above, a simple way for multinational corporations to avoid paying damages in ATS litigation is to remove attachable assets from the United States.... Many corporations would continue to be able to serve the American market by manufacturing goods abroad and exporting them.... ATS liability would serve as a tax on doing business in the United States—one that, because of the collective nature of the climate problem, would have little or no effect on global warming. Furthermore, we would have to expect some American industry to move overseas in order to avoid this tax.

Conclusion: Political Ramifications

Having said all this, I should acknowledge again that the main purpose of litigation may not be to persuade courts to determine greenhouse gas emission policy, but to attract public attention and pressure governments to reach political solutions, including treaties and domestic laws. Supporters of the recent decision in *Massachusetts v. E.P.A.* no doubt believe that, even if EPA regulation by itself would not affect global warming, a victory might lead other countries and their regulatory agencies to take global warming more seriously. If this is correct, then there is nothing objectionable about the litigation. But it is a gamble, and an odd one at that. If the courts take this and similar litigation seriously, and plaintiffs prevail, we may be in a worse world unless governments act, and governments might not act.

In the United States, litigation drives policy to a greater extent than it does in other countries. Consider how tort litigation has driven smoking policy, for example, or how constitutional litigation has driven policy on schools, prisons, and abortion. That litigation can be effective for changing policy cannot be denied; that litigation leads to better policy than can be achieved through politics is hotly contested. American lawyers concerned with human rights and climate change understandably look toward this litigation experience as they try to develop ways to circumvent the recalcitrant political branches of the national government and the ineffectual state legislatures. Whatever the merits of policy-driven litigation in the domestic arena, however, the assumption that it can drive global greenhouse gas policy at all, or in the right direction, is doubtful.

Questions and Discussion

1. *Tort claims.* What are your views about the likely effects of tort-based lawsuits (making claims of injury on the basis of either international human rights violations or violations of rights under ordinary domestic tort law)? Prof. Posner said that if such suits are taken seriously by courts, "we may be worse off unless governments act, and governments might not act." Do you agree? In what ways specifically would the U.S. be worse off?

2. *ATS litigation.* If ATS liability would serve as a tax on doing business in America, should policy makers consider tort reform to free up markets? What would such reform look like? Can you imagine legislators standing by while court decisions challenge U.S. business?

E. Procedural Rights in International and National Fora

Procedural rights provide another possible route for combating climate change and another form of climate change litigation. They are a vital aspect of modern democracy. Consider the following as an introduction to the issue of procedural rights and climate change.

U.N. Framework Convention on Climate Change
U.N. Doc. A/AC.237/18 (Part II) (Add. 1), May 9, 1992,
1771 U.N.T.S. 107, 31 I.L.M. 849

Article 6

In carrying out their commitments..., the Parties shall:

(a) Promote and facilitate at the national and, as appropriate, subregional and regional levels, and in accordance with national laws and regulations....

(ii) Public access to information on climate change and its effects;

(iii) Public participation in addressing climate change and its effects and developing adequate responses....

1. Access to Information

"Public access to information on climate change and its effects" is necessary for uncovering the truth. "Public participation in addressing climate change and its effects and developing adequate responses" pressures legislature to adopt necessary laws and helps lobby government for adoption of executive regulations that combat climate change.

A national case with international dimensions provides an example of using the right to information to address acts or omissions by governmental agencies related to climate change. On June 15, 2004, two German non-governmental organizations (NGOs) commenced the first European case to enforce a law in the interest of combating climate change. The NGOs claim that the federal Environmental Information Act grants citizens the right to information about the extent to which Euler Hermes AG, an export credit agency, provides political and economic risk insurance to projects that produce GHGs. Still pending adjudication, the case aims to force the German government to disclose this information and is essentially a means for civil society to gain leverage against the credit agency.

In *Öneryıldız v. Turkey,* discussed in Chapter 2 at page 49, the Grand Chamber of the European Court of Human Rights said broadly that where dangerous activities are concerned, "public access to clear and full information is viewed as a basic human right" in Europe. The Court cited Resolution 1087 and said that the resolution "makes clear that this right must not be taken to be limited to the risks associated with the use of nuclear energy in the civil sector." The Grand Chamber went further, noting that such a human right to information had previously been found by the Court to be part of the right of private and family life under Article 8 of the European Convention on Human Rights where pollution was concerned, citing the decision in *Guerra v. Italy*. The Grand Chamber said that this same right to information "may also, in principle, be relied on for the protection of the right to life, particularly as this interpretation is supported by current developments in European standards." Only with information, the Grand Chamber said, could government "take all appropriate steps to safeguard life for the purposes of Article 2."

Would the European court be willing to take this right concerning access to information on pollution risks and apply it as well to information relevant to the pollution causing global warming? Can *Öneryıldız*, or at least its line of reasoning, be used in the cases where access to information on decisions related to climate change is denied to the public? Kyoto flexibility mechanisms, cap and trade, and green investments projects all require transparency and public access to information.

2. Public Participation

Gray v. Minister for Planning (Australia)

New South Wales Land and Environment Court

[2006] NSWLEC 720

PAIN J.

The applicant is challenging decisions made under Pt 3A of the *Environmental Planning and Assessment Act 1979* (NSW) (the EP&A Act) by the Director-General of the Department of Planning in relation to the proposal to build a large coal mine known as the Anvil Hill Project by Centennial Hunter Pty Ltd (Centennial), the third respondent. The Minister (the first respondent) has filed a submitting appearance.

The applicant is seeking a declaration that the Director-General's view that an environmental assessment prepared by Centennial adequately addressed the Director-General's environmental assessment requirements was void and without effect. He seeks an order that the decision to place the environmental assessment on public exhibition be set aside....

The area of land which constitutes Anvil Hill has a deposit of approximately 150 million tonnes of thermal coal. The proposed open cut mine will produce up to 10.5 million tonnes of coal per annum. The mine is intended to operate for 21 years. The intended use of this coal is for burning as fuel in power stations in New South Wales and overseas.... About half the coal is intended for export for use as fuel in power stations to produce electricity generally in Japan. There is no dispute that burning of coal will release substantial quantities of greenhouse gases into the atmosphere.

On 16 January 2006 Centennial applied to the Minister for major projects approval under Pt 3A of the EP&A Act in respect of the Anvil Hill Project in the Hunter Valley....

Part 3A is headed "Major Infrastructure and Other Projects" and provides a process for the consideration and approval of projects described in § 75B(2) as major infrastructure or other development that in the opinion of the Minister is of State or regional significance....

Section 75H is headed "Environmental assessment and public consultation" and provides:

(1) The proponent is to submit to the Director-General the environmental assessment required under this Division for approval to carry out the project.

(2) If the Director-General considers that the environmental assessment does not adequately address the environmental assessment requirements, the Director-General may require the proponent to submit a revised environmental assessment to address the matters notified to the proponent.

(3) After the environmental assessment has been accepted by the Director-General, the Director-General must, in accordance with any guidelines published by the Minister in the Gazette, make the environmental assessment publicly available for at least 30 days.

(4) During that period, any person (including a public authority) may make a written submission to the Director-General concerning the matter....

Section 75X is headed "Miscellaneous provisions relating to approvals under this Part" and provides:

(2) The following documents under this Part in relation to a project are to be made publicly available by the Director-General:

(a) applications to carry out projects,

(b) environmental assessment requirements for a project determined by the Director-General or the Minister,

(c) environmental assessment reports of the Director-General to the Minister,

(d) approvals to carry out projects given by the Minister,

The Director-General's report under section 75I of the Act in relation to a project is to include the following matters (to the extent that those matters are not otherwise included in that report in accordance with the requirements of that section):

(a) an assessment of the environmental impact of the project,

(b) any aspect of the public interest that the Director-General considers relevant to the project,

(c) the suitability of the site for the project,

(d) copies of submissions received by the Director-General in connection with public consultation under section 75H or a summary of the issues raised in those submissions....

The Environmental Assessment must take into account relevant State government technical and policy guidelines. While not exhaustive, guidelines which may be relevant to the project are included in the attached list. The attached list refers under Air Quality to "Approved Methods for the Modelling and Assessment of Air Pollutants in NSW (DEC)."

The parties agreed that greenhouse gases are not one of the pollutants to which this document refers. In other words no relevant State government technical or policy guidelines in relation to the assessment of greenhouse gases was referred to in the EAR. The EAR were advised to Centennial as provided by § 75F(3).

On 26 August 2006 Centennial lodged the assessment with the Director-General as required under § 75H(1). The assessment is a very large and detailed document. It contains, at Appendix 11, a section headed "Energy and Greenhouse Assessment." ...

The assessment of scope 1, 2 and 3 emissions.

These are defined as follows.

Scope 1: Direct GHG emissions

Direct GHG emissions occur from sources that are owned or controlled by the company, for example, emissions from combustion in owned or controlled boilers, furnaces, vehicles, etc.; emissions from chemical production in owned or controlled process equipment.

Direct CO_2 emissions from the combustion of biomass shall not be included in scope 1 but reported separately....

GHG emissions not covered by the Kyoto Protocol, e.g. CFCs, NOx etc. shall not be included in scope 1 but may be reported separately....

Scope 2: Electricity indirect GHG emissions

Scope 2 accounts for GHG emissions from the generation of purchased electricity consumed by the company....

Scope 3: Other indirect GHG emissions

Scope 3 is an optional reporting category that allows for the treatment of all other indirect emissions. Scope 3 emissions are a consequence of the activities of the company, but occur from sources not owned or controlled by the company.

Some examples of scope 3 activities are extraction and production of purchased materials; transportation of purchased fuels; and use of sold products and services. Scope 1 and 2 emissions were assessed and included in the environmental assessment but not scope 3 emissions which could include an analysis of the potential greenhouse gas emissions from the burning of coal by third parties outside the control of the proponent....

In regard to greenhouse emissions, the EA includes an assessment of the direct greenhouse gas emissions likely to be generated by the mine itself (e.g methane escaping from the coal seams and diesel emissions from the mining fleet), but does not include an assessment of the indirect emissions associated with the use of the resource either in Australia or overseas....

Consequently, while it is recognised that the burning of coal extracted from coal mines produces significant amounts of greenhouse gases, and that increasing greenhouse gas levels in the atmosphere have implications for global warming and climate change, the Department does not believe it is either necessary or appropriate ... to examine the implications of the project on climate change....

The process of assessment under § 75H has continued since proceedings were commenced. Section 75H(6)(a) provides that the Director-General may require the proponent to submit to him a response to the issues raised in submissions, and this was done by letter to Centennial dated 16 October 2006. A partial response to submissions received during the public exhibition of the assessment dated 30 October 2006 was provided by Centennial to the Director-General.

That response included an assessment of greenhouse gas emissions resulting from the burning of the coal intended to be recovered from the Anvil Hill mine (scope 3 emissions)....

The applicant conceded that if this material had been part of the assessment and placed on public exhibition pursuant to § 75H(3) he would not be before the Court. He argued his case still has utility because the failure to publicly exhibit the environmental assessment with this information is a failure to comply with an important part of the Pt 3A process so that members of the public can be properly informed in order to determine if they wish to make submissions.

It is also clear from documents tendered that a large number of submissions raising concerns about the greenhouse implications of burning coal from the Anvil Hill project were received before and during the exhibition period for the environmental assessment....

APPLICANT'S CASE

Issue 1: Assessment did not comply with EAR

Section 75F(1) empowers the Minister to issue guidelines for the purpose of approving projects under Pt 3A including guidelines as to "levels of assessment." No such guidelines have been issued.

The EAR issued by the Director-General included a requirement that Centennial's environmental assessment include an assessment of as a "key" issue "Air quality—including a detailed greenhouse gas assessment."

The EAR necessitated "a detailed greenhouse gas assessment" as an aspect of Centennial's environmental assessment. It follows that whatever else the "detailed greenhouse gas assessment" was to be, it was to be an "environmental assessment." This follows from § 75H(1) which required Centennial to submit an "environmental assessment" and the EAR.

Issue 2: Failure to take into account ESD principles

The EP&A Act includes in its objects at § 5(a)(vii) the encouragement of ecologically sustainable development ("ESD")....

The two ESD principles most relevant are the precautionary principle and intergenerational equity. There is no reference to either of these in the Director-General's documents at all, including at the stage of deciding whether the assessment "adequately addressed" EAR....

[Director-General's Submissions]

Issue 2: Failure to take into account ESD principles

The Director-General did have regard to ESD principles. The fact that an assessment of GHG emissions alone was required demonstrates that regard was intended to be had to the future impacts of GHG. The problem of climate change/global warming is an increasing problem which is recognised by the Director-General in taking into account the environmental concern about GHG emissions by requiring an analysis of these and that must include the effect on future generations....

Centennial's Submissions ...

Issue 2: Failure to take into account ESD principles

ESD principles are not mandatory relevant considerations as determined in *Minister for Aboriginal Affairs v. Peko-Wallsend* (1986) 162 CLR 24 for any decision under Pt 3A and certainly not the intermediate decision under review.... The applicant has not established that they were not taken into account....

Finding

Issue 1: Assessment did not comply with EAR ...

Firstly, the Director-General argued that Pt 3A does not have the effect of requiring that an environmental assessment be produced by a proponent for development under that part. Environmental assessment by the proponent is required under Pt 3A, contrary to the arguments of the Director-General. That is clear from the nature of the projects which are likely to come under Pt 3A....

Thirdly, according to the Director-General's submissions, an environmental assessment may be accepted for public exhibition by the Director-General even if it does not adequately address the EAR. The provisions of Pt 3A do not bear out this interpretation....

This is further confirmed by the second reading speech for the Reform Bill which states:

Prior to exhibiting the environmental assessment the director-general must be satisfied that the assessment meets the specified requirements....

I have already decided that the environmental assessment must be held to have complied with the EAR before it can be publicly exhibited it is difficult to accept that submission. Further, the decision to allow the environmental assessment to be publicly exhibited cannot act as an implied modification of the EAR because that is not a process contemplated in the division....

As the environmental assessment provided did not contain a detailed analysis of GHG in conformity with the EAR it was clear that the Director-General did not ask himself the first question and he therefore fell into legal error. This submission was made on the basis that a detailed GHG assessment could only comply with the EAR if the conduct of the mine did not have the effect of causing carbon dioxide emissions when the coal is burnt because that caused an environmental impact, meaning an impact on all aspects of the surrounding of humans "whether affecting any human as an individual or in his or her social groupings." ...

Causation of environmental impact ...

The applicant proposed ... that a common sense test applies to causation of environmental impact....

Given the quite appropriate recognition by the Director-General that burning the thermal coal from the Anvil Hill Project will cause the release of substantial GHG in the environment which will contribute to climate change/global warming which, I surmise, is having and/or will have impacts on the Australian and consequently NSW environment it would appear that Bignold J's test of causation based on a real and sufficient link is met. While the Director-General argued that the use of the coal as fuel occurred only through voluntary, independent human action, that alone does not break the necessary link to impacts arising from this activity given that the impact is climate change/global warming to which this contributes....

The Director-General's test that the effect is significant, is not unlikely to occur and is proximate also raises issues of judgment. Climate change/global warming is widely recognised as a significant environmental impact to which there are many contributors worldwide but the extent of the change is not yet certain and is a matter of dispute. The fact there are many contributors globally does not mean the contribution from a single large source such as the Anvil Hill Project in the context of NSW should be ignored in the environmental assessment process. The coal intended to be mined is clearly a potential major single contributor to GHG emissions deriving from NSW given the large size of the proposed mine. That the impact from burning the coal will be experienced globally as well as in NSW, but in a way that is currently not able to be accurately measured, does not suggest that the link to causation of an environmental impact is insufficient. The "not likely to occur" test is clearly met as is the proximate test for the reasons already stated....

I consider there is a sufficiently proximate link between the mining of a very substantial reserve of thermal coal in NSW, the only purpose of which is for use as fuel in power stations, and the emission of GHG which contribute to climate change/global warming, which is impacting now and likely to continue to do so on the Australian and consequently NSW environment, to require assessment of that GHG contribution of the coal when burnt in an environmental assessment under Pt 3A....

Issue 2: Did the Director-General fail to take ESD principles into account?

The applicant's Points of Claim challenge the Director-General's opinion that the environmental assessment prepared by Centennial was adequate because he failed to take into account ESD principles, particularly the precautionary principle and the principle of intergenerational equity....

[T]he precautionary principle is now given statutory recognition not only in the *Water Management Act* but in numerous NSW Statutes ... it is a central element in the decision making process and cannot be confined. It is not merely a political aspiration but must be applied when decisions are being made under the *Water Management Act* and any other Act which adopts the principles....

Prior environmental impact assessment and approval are important components in a precautionary approach. The precautionary principle is intended to promote actions that avoid serious or irreversible damage in advance of scientific certainty of such damage. Environmental impact assessment can help implement the precautionary principle in a number of ways including:

(a) enabling an assessment of whether there are threats of damage to threatened species, populations or ecological communities; ...

(d) shifting the burden of proof (evidentiary presumption) to persons responsible for potentially harmful activity to demonstrate that their actions will not cause environmental harm....

The requirement for prior environmental impact assessment and approval enables the present generation to meet its obligation of intergenerational equity by ensuring the health, diversity and productivity of the environment is maintained and enhanced for the benefit of future generations....

Intergenerational equity

The key purpose of environmental assessment is to provide information about the impact of a particular activity on the environment to a decision maker to enable him or her to make an informed decision based on adequate information about the environmental consequences of a particular development. This is important in the context of enabling decisions about environmental impact to take into account the various principles of ESD including the principle of intergenerational equity. Intergenerational equity has received relatively little judicial consideration in this Court in the context of the requirements for environmental assessment under the EP&A Act....

Preston J refers in [a law review] article to several decisions in other national courts which have taken intergenerational equity into account, including the landmark decision of the Supreme Court of the Philippines in *Minors Oposa v. Secretary of the Department of Environment and Natural Resources*. This and other cases referred to at pp 180–182 clearly occur in a different legal context to that before me but do underscore the importance of this principle....

There is no failure to consider the issue of GHG. It is clear from the documents that downstream emissions were not included in the inventory calculations of the Anvil Hill Project in the environmental assessment. Those submissions overlook the role the environmental impact assessment process plays in Pt 3A in relation to the implementation of intergenerational equity, particularly the need to assess cumulative impacts. If an important downstream impact is omitted from that assessment it is more difficult for the final decision maker, the Minister, to be informed about all relevant matters.... While the Court has a limited role in judicial review proceedings in that it is not to intrude on the merits of the administrative decision under challenge it is apparent that there is a failure to take the principle of intergenerational equity into account by a requirement for a detailed GHG assessment in the EAR if the major component of GHG which results from the use of the coal, namely scope 3 emissions, is not required to be assessed. That is a failure of a legal requirement to take into account the principle of intergenerational equity.

Precautionary principle

As identified in *Telstra v. Hornsby*, if the two conditions precedent or thresholds are satisfied so that there is a threat of serious or irreversible environmental damage and there is the requisite degree of scientific uncertainty the principle will apply so that the shift in an evidentiary burden will occur meaning that the proponent for the development has to demonstrate that the threat does not exist or is negligible....

That principle requires that if there are "threats of serious or irreversible environmental damage, lack of full scientific certainty should not be used as a reason for postponing measures to prevent environmental degradation." No aspect of the acceptance by the [Director-General] of the EA involved any element of refusing to take into account the GHG issue by reference to a "lack of full scientific certainty." ...

The precautionary principle is part of the bundle of ESD principles identified in §6(2) of the PEA Act such as intergenerational equity and the conservation of biological diversity and ecological integrity. While not all of these were relied on by the applicant I observe that there is a clear connection between climate change/global warming resulting in possibly permanent climatic change and the conservation of biological diversity and ecological integrity which are likely to be impacted upon. I have referred earlier to the principle of intergenerational equity and observe that the approach to environmental assessment required by the application of the precautionary principle requires knowledge of impacts which are cumulative, on going and long term. In the context of climate change/global warming there is considerable overlap between the environmental assessment requirements to enable these two aspects of ESD to be adequately dealt with.

I also conclude that the Director-General failed to take into account the precautionary principle when he decided that the environmental assessment of Centennial was adequate, as already found in relation to intergenerational equity. This was a failure to comply with a legal requirement....

The submission was made by the Director-General that raising climate change/global warming as an issue is enough to satisfy any requirement that intergenerational equity was taken into account, because climate change/global warming was inherently concerned with impacts on future generations. Simply raising an issue such as climate change/global warming is unlikely to satisfy a requirement that intergenerational equity or the precautionary principle has been considered in the absence of any analysis of the impact of activities which potentially contribute in the NSW context in a substantial way to climate change/global warming....

Preston J in *Telstra v. Hornsby* stated that if the precautionary principle did apply so that there was a shifting of the evidentiary burden of proof to a proponent in relation to environmental damage this is but one of the factors a decision maker under the EP&A Act must consider and is not determinative of the outcome of that decision making process. The Minister in this case will decide if the coal mine should be approved at all and if approved, subject to what conditions. For example, if approving the project he could limit the time period for the operation of the mine to a different time period to that sought by the applicant.

Exercise of discretion whether to grant relief

I have held that the applicant is successful on the second ground he has raised, namely that the Director-General failed to take into account ESD principles, in particular the principle of intergenerational equity and the precautionary principle, when he formed the view that Centennial's environmental assessment was adequate. It is necessary that I consider whether I should exercise the broad discretion I have under §124(1) of the EP&A Act to grant the relief sought by the applicant....

I also need to consider if I should set aside the decision of the Director-General to place the environmental assessment, lodged by Centennial, on public exhibition under §75H(3).... The effective result of making such a declaration is that, I surmise, the environmental assessment and the response document with scope 3 emissions now provided by Centennial to the Director-General will be placed on further public exhibition. It is clear that the information the applicant argued should have been exhibited, being an analysis of scope 3 emissions, has been provided in response to submissions received in the public exhibition process and is part of the environmental assessment process....

ORDERS

The Court makes the following declaration:

1. That the view formed by the Director-General on 23 August 2006 that the environmental assessment lodged by Centennial Hunter Pty Ltd in respect of the Anvil Hill Project adequately addressed the Director-General's requirements is void and without effect....

Questions and Discussion

1. *EP&A Act compared with NEPA.* Both environmental assessments in Australia and environmental impact statements in the U.S. purport to help decision makers take the environment into account. However, does either one require decisionmakers to protect the environment? In the United States, NEPA is almost exclusively a procedural requirement with no substantive bite. Thus, EISs need only be considered, after which point a decision maker's choice cannot be overruled based on the findings of an EIS. In reading through the case above, is there a sense that the outcome of an EA has more importance for Australian decision makers, at least in the State of New South Wales? If EAs and EISs lack substantive power, why is there so much litigation surrounding them? Is the public participation that EAs and EISs require enough to make up for any lack of direct substantive power?

2. *Evolving case law in national courts.* Soon after the *Gray* decision, the Land and Resources Tribunal of Queensland took the opposite position. *Re Xstrate Coal Queensland* [2007] QLRT33 (Feb. 2007). That court ruled that an EIA for a coal mine need not assess greenhouse gas emissions and said that regulations would have "no demonstrated impact on global warming or climate changes." In March 2007 the U.S. District Court for the Northern District of California made a decision that the Export-Import Bank (Ex-Im) and Overseas Private Investment Corporation (OPIC) are not automatically exempt from NEPA requirements. Defendants had argued that NEPA does not apply to foreign projects at all. However, the court did not make a decision about whether Ex-Im or O.P.I.C. has enough authority over the projects in which they invest money that their funding must be subject to EIA requirements. The extent of control was to be decided in a further trial. *Friends of the Earth v. Mosbacher*, 488 F.Supp. 2d. 889 (N.D. Cal. 2007). What is the significance of NEPA being expanded to include domestically funded foreign projects? Can this lead to an entire new area of litigation focusing on U.S. investment overseas? Is there a chance government investing agencies (Ex-Im, OPIC) will try to minimize their authority in foreign projects to avoid NEPA requirements?

3. *Public participation under NEPA.* If financial investments made by government agencies Ex-Im and OPIC are recognized by the court as sufficiently controlling, may the court require the government to conduct an EIA? Will it open an opportunity for Friends of the Earth and Greenpeace as well as other members of the concerned public to be involved in the process? Will it allow participation in evaluating the impact of those projects on climate change and require public hearings where public comments are taken into account under NEPA? May the court overrule a decision to finance the project?

4. *ESD principles.* The principle of intergenerational equality and the precautionary principle played a large role in the outcome of the Australian case above. What impacts would these and similar principles have if adopted by more courts and international bodies? Are those principles part of customary law? Can these two principles be adopted as some form of human rights? Consider the right to the benefits of culture brought up in

the Inuit petition—what are similarities and differences between the right to culture and the principle of intergenerational equity?

Similarly, the precautionary principle seems primed for a place in climate change litigation. Are there creative ways to use the precautionary principle to fight climate change not explored in the case above? If courts worldwide accept the science of climate change unquestionably, what would the effect be on the usefulness of the precautionary principle?

5. *Revisiting the Gbemre case.* We placed the *Gbemre* case from Nigeria in the substantive rights portion of this chapter, page 575 However, the court also ruled there had been a violation of Section 2(2) of Nigeria's Environment Impact Assessment Act, which may be considered to be a violation of procedural participation rights.

III. United Nations Security Council: Right to Security

The Universal Declaration of Human Rights declares the fundamental "right to life, liberty and security of person." The American Declaration contains the "right to life, physical protection and security." Both treaties treat the right to personal security as related to the right to life, as a part of the right to life. The American Convention on Human Rights contains a separate "right to personal liberty and security."

Is global warming a threat to personal security? Might global warming affect international and national security? Global warming will result in scarce water and food resources. Global warming impacts such as flooding, melting permafrost, and desertification will lead to loss of agricultural lands and water supplies. Flooding, disease, and famine as a result of climate change may lead to unprecedented migration. Drought and crop failure will intensify competition for food, water and energy, and increase the potential for economic disruption. Scarcity of water and food may spark violence, political and international conflicts, and even wars.

In 2007, the United Nations Security Council held a groundbreaking debate on the effect of climate change on peace and international security. The British Foreign Minister, Margaret Beckett, said, " … An unstable climate will exacerbate some of the core drivers of conflict, such as migratory pressures and competition for resources." *See* "Security Council Holds Landmark Debate On Climate Change," Agence France Press, April 17, 2007. Most industrial countries, including the EU, as well as some developing nations such as Peru, Panama, and a group of small island states, agreed with Britain. So did U.N. Secretary General Ban Ki-moon. On the other hand, Russia, China, Qatar, Indonesia, South Africa and Pakistan—on behalf of 130 developing nations—argued that the Council was encroaching on more democratic bodies, such as the 192-member U.N. General Assembly.

The U.N. Security Council is composed of five permanent members and ten rotating members. All U.N. members have expressly vested the Security Council with the power to maintain international peace and security (as found in Chapter VII of the U.N. Charter). This power includes binding legal authority to require state action when international peace and security are at risk. Substantive Security Council decisions require nine affirmative votes and no veto by any of the five permanent members.

Consider the power of the Security Council and the security threats of climate change discussed above. Professor Christopher K. Penny has suggested that the Security Council has the power to force states into action combating climate change. He notes, "While potentially coercive, Security Council Chapter VII enforcement measures nonetheless rest upon the prior legal consent of all Members, including the target state(s), as expressed through their voluntary ratification of the U.N. Charter." Christopher K. Penny, *Greening the Security Council: Climate Change as an Emerging "Threat to International Peace and Security,"* Human Security and Climate Change — An International Workshop (Oslo, 23–25 June 2005), available at http://www.gechs.org/downloads/holmen/Penny.pdf. He argues:

> Article 39 establishes the substantive threshold criteria for invoking the Security Council's Chap. VII enforcement authority, providing that:
>
> > [t]he Security Council shall determine the existence of any threat to the peace, breach of the peace, or act of aggression and shall make recommendations, or decide what measures shall be taken in accordance with Articles 41 and 42, to maintain or restore international peace and security....
>
> Traditional understandings of "threats to international peace and security" focused on cross-border security issues, in particular actual or threatened interstate armed conflict....
>
> However, invocation of Chapter VII is not limited to international armed conflicts.... Starting in the late 1990s, the Security Council began to address broad issues relating to conflicts in general, including threats to children and civilians, though without specifically invoking Chap. VII or imposing mandatory enforcement measures following such characterizations.
>
> The Security Council has also recently turned itself to the potential security implications of other non-traditional threats, signaling its willingness to further expand the concept of "threat to international peace and security." In particular, although it has not invoked Chap. VII in this context, it has already noted that the HIV/AIDS pandemic might in future constitute a threat to international peace and security. As with international terrorism and WMD proliferation, the Security Council response to this threat is not limited by clear geographical or temporal restrictions, though it has focused on Africa....
>
> In summary, while the Security Council has shown increasing willingness to intervene in the domestic affairs of U.N. Members in a wide variety of circumstances, it has continued to justify its invocation of Chap. VII enforcement authority on direct or indirect international security ramifications, albeit broadly defined. Interventionism on this basis has been generally accepted by U.N. Members and appears to rest on a solid legal foundation. Recent practice indicates a further willingness to address global security threats in the absence of clearly defined geographical or temporal parameters, and a nascent trend toward acceptance of non-traditional soft security issues as "threats to international peace and security" within the meaning of Chap. VII.

Id.

Questions and Discussion

1. *Realism about the Security Council.* How realistic is the idea that the permanent members of the Security Council would authorize action if they are having a hard time agreeing upon actions to combat global warming? If the nations of the world *do* agree

on joint action to reduce greenhouse gas emission sharply in post-Kyoto negotiations, under what situations can you imagine the Security Council becoming, in effect, the enforcement arm of such an agreement?

2. *Self-imposed limitation.* Climate responsibility "is first of all a matter of self-limitation on the part of high-emitting nations and social groups," according to Wolfgang Sachs, CLIMATE CHANGE AND HUMAN RIGHTS (2006). Is it possible that after high-emitting nations achieve self-limitation, perhaps through transition to a post-carbon world economy, the Security Council could agree on coercive action against "rogue" nations that refused to join that transition?

3. *U.N. Security Council authority.* It is easier to imagine the role of the U.N. Security Council using its authority to manage national or international conflicts over scarcity of water, food, and other resources or environmental refugees caused by climate change. What would be its recommendation and enforcement measures in the case of Lake Chad or Darfur? What kind of measures might the U.N. Security Council use to help resettlement of the populations of small island states like Tuvalu?

4. *UNDP Report.* The security threats posed by climate change have also been spelled out in a report of the United Nations Development Programme. UNDP, Human Development Report 2007/2008, *Fighting Climate Change: Human Solidarity in a Divided World,* p. 186.

5. *Other theories.* One of the best collections of legal documents and legal theories for forcing action on greenhouse gas emissions, including human rights approaches, is *Climate Justice: Enforcing Climate Change Law*, website hosted by the Environmental Law Alliance Worldwide (ELAW), available at http://www.climatelaw.org.

In this book, we have suggested that environmental harms often raise significant human rights issues. This may be nowhere as apparent as in the looming disaster of catastrophic climate change. In our view, such catastrophic change will produce human rights violations of almost unimaginable magnitude. In turn, this calls for new kinds of thinking. Some of that thinking has begun and is reviewed in Svitlana Kravchenko, *Right to Carbon or right to Life: Human Rights Approaches to Climate Change*, 9 Vermont J. Envir. L. 515 (2008).

Does a broadened concept of human rights law have a role to play in trying to limit climate change, as well as to help the world adapt to those aspects of climate change that cannot be held back? It is up to a new generation of environmental lawyers and human rights lawyers to decide.

Table of Authorities

Cases

I. INTERNATIONAL CASES

Aarhus Convention Compliance Committee

Findings and Recommendations with Regard to Compliance by Albania, *278*
Findings and Recommendations with Regard to Compliance by Belgium, *343*, 351
Findings and Recommendations with Regard to Compliance by Ukraine, *270*
Findings and Recommendations with Regard to Compliance by Kazakhstan, *228*

African Commission on Human and Peoples' Rights

Communications 25/89, 47/90, 56/91, 100/93 (Joined) against Zaire, 116
Social and Economic Rights Action Center v. Nigeria, *55, 189*
Union des Jeunes Avocats /Chad, 58

Compliance Advisor/Ombudsman

Exit Report-Regarding Minera Yanacocha Cajamarca, Peru, 482
MIGA's Guarantee of the Bulyanhulu Gold Mine, Tanzania, *479*

European Commission on Human Rights

José Maria Ruiz Mateos v. Spain, 495
X v. Austria, 495

European Court of Human Rights

Appleby v. the United Kingdom, 534
Bladet Tromsö and Stensaas v. Norway, 521
Bowman v. the United Kingdom, 534
Brumârescu v. Romania, 494
Castells v. Spain, 504, 507
De Haes and Gijsels v. Belgium, 532
Fadeyeva v. Russia, *43*, 47, 48, 567
Giacomelli v. Italy, 30
Guerra v. Italy, *31*, 36, 37, 38, 40, 41, 42, 43, 52, *251*, 567, 584
Hatton v. United Kingdom, *37*, 41, 42, 43, 47, 52
Hertel v. Switzerland, 533, 534
Katsoulis v. Greece, 41

Kyrtatos v. Greece, 30
Ledyayeva v. Russia, 48
López Ostra v. Spain, *26*, 36, 37, 38, 40, 41, 43, 52, 115, 140
Nikitin v. Russia, *492*, 510
Öneryildiz v. Turkey, 35, *49*, 555
Powell & Rayner v. United Kingdom, 35, 38, 42
Ryabykh v. Russia, 494
Steel & Morris v. United Kingdom, 363, 364, *529*, 536
Thoma v. Luxembourg, 521
Thorgeir Thorgeirson v. Iceland, 534
X and Y v. Fed. Rep. of Germany, 24
X and Y v. Netherlands, 58, 189
Zander v. Sweden, 115

European Court of Justice

Stichting Greenpeace Council v. European Commission, 336

Inter-American Commission on Human Rights

Maya Indigenous Communities of the Toledo District v. Belize, 193, 563, 564, 570

Inter-American Court of Human Rights

Advisory Opinion OC-11/90, 361
Advisory Opinion OC-16/99, 362
Awas Tingni Community v. Nicaragua, 115, *174*, 178, 179, 182, 190, 197, 562, 563
Claude Reyes v. Chile, *239*
Herrera Ulloa v. Costa Rica, 522
Mayagna (Sumo) Awas Tingni Community, Provisional Measures (2007), 179
Moiwana Community v. Suriname (I), *180*
Moiwana Community v. Suriname (II), *181*
Saramaka People v. Suriname, 185
Saramaka People v. Suriname, *186*
Velàsquez Rodríguez v. Honduras, 58, 189
Yakye Axa Indigenous Community versus Paraguay, 183, 186
Yanomami Case, 5, *61*, 63, 140, 562, 564, 565, 567

International Court of Justice

Gabčíkovo-Nagymaros, 18, 115
New Zealand v. France, 575

International Centre for Settlement of Investment Disputes

Aguas del Tunari v. Republic of Bolivia, 128

United Nations Human Rights Committee

Anni Äärelä & Jouni Näkkäläjärvi v. Finland, 156
Bernard Ominayak and the Lubicon Lake Band v. Canada, *149*, 155, 190, 520
Concluding Observations: Canada 07/04/99, 566
Kitok v. Sweden, 155

Länsman II, 156, 157
Länsman III, 157
Länsman v. Finland, *154*

World Bank Inspection Panel

Chad-Cameroon Petroleum and Pipeline Project, *468*

II. NATIONAL CASES

Argentina

Case of Alberto Sagarduy, 84
Irazu, Margarita v. Copetro SA, 84
Kattan, Alberto v. National Government, 84
Menoris Comunidad Paynemil/s accion de amparo, 132
Sociedad De Fomento Barrio Félix v. Camet, 85

Australia

Adam v. Ward, 523
Australian Conservation Foundation, 328, 329
Chapman v. Conservation Council of South Australia, *522*
Gray v. Minister for Planning, *585*
Gunns v. Marr, 512
Lange v. Australian Broadcasting Commission, 522, 523
Mabo v. Queensland, 196, 200
Minister for Aboriginal Affairs v. Peko-Wallsend, 588
Ogle v. Strickland, 332
Onus v. Alcoa of Australia Ltd, 329
Telstra v. Hornsby, 590, 591
Truth About Motorways v. Macquarie Infrastructure Management, *324*

Bangladesh

Dr. Mohiuddin Farooque v. Bangladesh, 86, 98, 99

Belgium

Judgment 133.834 of 13 July 2004, 344, 345
Judgment 135.408 of 24 September 2004, 344

Belize

Aurelio Cal v. Atty. Gen. of Belize, *193*

Canada

B.C.G.E.U. v. British Columbia, 518
Calder v. AG of British Columbia, 200
Daishowa, Inc. v. Friends of the Lubicon, *515*
Delgamuukw v. British Columbia, 200, 201
Haida Nation v. British Columbia, 201, 202
Haida Nation v. British Columbia, *201*
Hersees of Woodstock v. Goldstein, 518
Port Hope Case, 115
R. v. Oakes, 507

Chile

Comite de Desarrollo de Putre y CODEFF v. Ministro de Obras Publicas, 340
Comunidad de Chañaral v. Codeco División el Saldor, 70, 109, 321, 340
Pedro Flores v. Corporación del Cobre, 71, *105,* 108, 109,
Trillium Case, 71, 108

Colombia

Fundepublico v. Mayor of Bugalagrande, 140
Unconstitutionality of the General Forestry Act, *168*
Victor Ramon Castrillon Vega v. Federacio Nacional de Algodoneros, 70

Costa Rica

Carlos Roberto Mejía Chacón contra el Ministerio de Salud, 86, 322

Ecuador

Decision No. 054-2000-TP, 167

Hungary

Balaton Highway Case, 336
Magyar Kozlony Case, 79, 339

India

AP Pollution Control Board-II v. Prof. MV Nayudu, *139,* 141
Attakoya Thangal v. Union of India, 130
Bandhua Mukti Morcha v. Union of India, 140
Garg v. State, 130
Kharak Singh v. State of UP, 89
L.K. Koolwal v. Rajasthan, 96
M.C. Mehta v. Kamal Nath, 114
M.C. Mehta v. Union of India, AIR 1987 SC 1086, *322*
M.C. Mehta v. Union of India, AIR 1992 SC 382, *94*
M.C. Mehta v. Union of India, AIR 1988 SC 1037, 89
M.C. Mehta v. Union of India, AIR 1988 SC 1115, 89
Narmada Bachao Andolan v. Union of India, 139
People's Union for Democratic Rights v. Union of India, 323
Rural Litigation & Entitlement Kendra v. State of UP, 89
S.P. Gupta v. Union of India, 323
Satyapal v. CPIO, TCIL, 249
Shajimon Joseph v. State of Kerala, *142*
Subhash Kumar v. State Of Bihar, 90, 130
Vishala Kochi Kudivella Samrakshana Samithi v. State of Kerala, 143

Indonesia

Dr. R. Panji Utomo, Petitioner, *500*

Japan

Ex parte Kawachi, 507

Korea

Forests Survey Inspection Request Case, *244*
Records Duplication Request Case, 247

Malaysia

Kerajaan Negeri Selangor v. Sagong Bin Tasi, 195, 200
Superintendent Of Land & Surveys v. Madeli Salleh,, 200
Superintendent Of Land & Surveys v. Nor Anak Nyawai, 200

Nepal

Dhungel v. Godawari Marble Industries, *96*

Netherlands

Reinwater case, 334

Nicaragua

Consultation on Law 364, *432*

Nigeria

Barrister Ikechuckwu Okpara v. Shell Petroleum Devel. Corp. of Nigeria, 581
Jonah Gbemre v. Shell Petroleum, *575*, 593

Norway

Alta case, 337

Pakistan

Shehla Zia v. WAPDA, *87*

Philippines

Oposa v. Factoran, 69, 71, *79,* 85, 86, 87, 90, 93, 99, 140, *317,* 321, 322, 340, 590

Privy Council

Amodu Tijani v. The Secretary, Southern Nigeria, 195, 200
Jeffs v. New Zealand Dairy Production and Marketing Board, 299

South Africa

Earthlife Africa (Cape Town) v. Dept. of Envt'l Affairs & Tourism & Eskom Holdings, *297*
Gov't of the Republic of South Africa v. Grootboom, 139
Minister of Health v. Treatment Action Campaign, 138
Residents of Bon Vista Mansions v. So. Metropolitan Local Council, *134*
S. v. Makwanyane, 135

Turkey

Senih Özay v. Ministry of the Environment and Eurogold Madencilik, *90*

United Kingdom

Englebert Ngcobo v. Thor Chemicals, *417*
Boyce v. Paddington Borough Council, 328, 329
Evan v. Avon Corporation, 329
Ex parte Richard Dixon, 338
Gouriet v. Union of Post Office Workers, 325

Marcic v. Thames Water Utilities, 24
Spiliada Maritime Corporation v. Cansulex Ltd., 419, 420, 421
Stockport District Waterworks Company v. Mayor of Manchester, 325
Thorp Nuclear Case, 338, 339

Ukraine

Stanovych v. Drohobych City Council, 145

United States

Aguinda v. Texaco, 410, 412, 413, 414, *415*, 424
Anderson v. Evans, 309
Arizona v. California, 213, 214
Associated Industries v. Ickes, 325
Baker v. Parsons, *537*
Banco Nacional de Cuba v. Sabbatino, 386, 396
Beanal v. Freeport-McMoran, *399*, 402, 403, 407
Bennett v. Spear, 326
Bering Strait Citizens for Responsible Resource Development v. U.S. Army Corps of Engineers, 309
Black and White Taxicab & Transfer Co. v. Brown and Yellow Taxicab & Transfer Co, 389
Bremner v. City & County of Honolulu, 90
Brown & Williamson Tobacco Corp. v. F.T.C., 248
Butte Community Union v. Lewis, 75
Calvert Cliffs' Coordinating Committee v. U. S. Atomic Energy Commission, 308
Cape-France Enterprises v. Estate of Peed, 109
Cherokee Nation v. Georgia, 203
Choctaw Nation v. United States, 203
Clark Fork Coalition v. DEQ, 79
Coard v. United States, 558
Confederated Tribes of the Umatilla Indian Reservation v. Alexander, 204
Delgado v. Shell Oil Co., 425
Doe I v. Exxon Mobil Corp. (USA), 397
Doe I v. Unocal, 380, 409, *393*
Dole Food Company Inc. v. Walter Antonio Gutierrez, 439
Dow v. Calderon, *437*
Duracraft Corp. v. Holmes Prods. Corp, 538
Ely v. Velde, 71
Environmental Defense Fund v. Corps of Engineers, 71
Erie R.R. Co. v. Tompkins, 384, 389, 391
Federal Election Commission v. Akins, 326
Filartiga v. Pena-Irala, 387, 389, 391, 405, 406
Flores v. Southern Peru Copper, *401*
Foster & Elam v. Neilson, 385
Friends of the Earth v. Mosbacher, 592
Garrison v. Louisiana, 507
Garza v. Lappin, 406
Georgia v. Tennessee Copper Co., 102
Gideon v. Wainwright, 362
Glisson v. City of Marion, 78

Gordon v. Marrone, 541
Griswold v. Connecticut, 84
Gulf Oil Corp. v. Gilbert, 416
Hilton v. Guyot, 384
Illinois Pure Water Committee v. Director of Public Health, 79
In re Agent Orange Product Liability Litigation, 407
In re Katrina Canal Breaches Consol. Litigation, 571
In re Union Carbide Corp. Gas Plant Disaster at Bhopal, 410
Jackson v. Metropolitan Edison Co., 100
Jota v. Texaco, 414
Just v. Marinette County, 103
Kadic v. Karadzic, 394
Kellas v. Department of Corrections, *332*
Khulumani v. Barclay Nat. Bank Ltd., 397
Laguna Lake Development Authority v. Court of Appeals, 105
Liu v. Republic of China, 396
Lujan v. Defenders of Wildlife, 322, 326, 332
Marbury v. Madison, 384
Mary and Carrie Dann v. United States, 198, 570
McCready v. Virginia, 102
McLarnon v. Jokisch, 538
Memphis Light, Gas & Water Division v. Craft, 136
Merlin Myers Revocable Trust v. Yellowstone County, 105
Michigan Citizens for Water Conservation v. Nestle Waters North America, 340
Missouri v. Holland, 385
Missouri v. Illinois, 102
Montana Environmental Information Center v. Dep't of Environmental Quality, *73*, 90, 109
Munn v. Illinois, 89
New York Times v. Sullivan, 248, 496, 507
Pennsylvania v. National Gettysburg Battlefield Tower, *100*
Phelps v. Western Mining Corporation, 324
Piper Aircraft Co. v. Reyno, 415
Presbyterian Church of Sudan v. Talisman Energy, 392
Prosecutor v. Furundzija, 395
Richmond Newspapers v. Virginia, 248
Roe v. Wade, 84
Sarei v. Rio Tinto (C.D. Cal. 2002), *407*
Sarei v. Rio Tinto (9th Cir. 2007), *408*
Save Our Ecosystems v. Clark, 309
Shell v. Leonardini, 528
Sierra Club v. Butz, 511, 512
Sohappy v. Hodel, 203
Sosa v. Alvarez-Machain, *388,* 398, 408
State of Washington v. Washington State Commercial Passenger Fishing Vessel Association, 213, 214, 217
Steel Co. v. Citizens for a Better Environment, 326
Stop H-3 Ass'n v. Dole, 71
Tellez v. Dole, *438*

The Paquete Habana, 384, 390

U.S. v. Washington (9th Cir.1982), 212

U.S. v. *Sioux Nation of Indians*, 203

U.S. v. *Smith*, 390

U.S. v. Washington (Phase I), (W.D. Wash. 1974), 203, 204, 205, 206, 207, 208, 212

U.S. v. Washington, (W.D. Wash.) (Phase II, Culverts), *210*

U.S. v. Washington, (W.D. Wash. 1980) (Phase II), 204, 205, 212

U.S. v. Washington, (9th Cir. 1985) (Phase II appeal), 205, 212

U.S. v. Washington, Civil No. C70-9213, Subproceeding 01-01 (Phase II, Culverts), 208, 210, 216

U.S. v. Winans, 204, 216

U.S. v. Yousef, 402

Wadsworth v. State, 75, 77

Worcester v. Georgia, 203

Conventions and Treaties

Aarhus Convention on Access to Information, Public Participation in Decision-Making and Access to Justice in Environmental Matters, 4, 16, 20, 220, 228, 238, *254*, 287, 290-293, 295, 304, 313-316, 356
  Article 1, 4, 5, 9, 10, 15, 20, 270
  Article 2, 223, 229, 230, 343, 346
  Article 3, 231, 256, 267, 278, 335, 343, 345, 349
  Article 4, 221, 223, 224-227, 229, 230, 231, 255, 269, 273, 275, 341
  Article 5, 223, 254, 255, 257
  Article 6, 229, 266, 268, 270, 271, 275, 278, 281-285, 341, 346, 347
  Article 7, 266, 275, 276, 281-285
  Article 8, 267, 275-277, 310
  Article 9, 224, 229, 231, 334, 340, 341-355, 357, 359
  Article 15, 270, 313
  Preamble, 4
  U.K. limiting declaration, 5
Africa Convention on the Conservation of Nature and Natural Resources in Africa, 295
African Charter on Human and Peoples' Rights, 53, 188
  Articles 4, 5, 188, 190
  Article 9, 219
  Article 16, 53, 57, 58, 60
  Article 17, 189, 190
  Article 21, 189, 190
  Article 24, 4, 7, 8, 10, 15, 16, 53, 57-59, 294, 577
  Article 30, 53
  Article 45, 53
  Article 55, 54
  Article 59, 53, 54
  Protocol on the Establishment of the African Court on Human and Peoples' Rights, 54
American Convention on Human Rights, 3, 20, *62*, 64, 147, 171, *172*, 184, 228, 234, 361, 362, 404, 428, 558, 560, 563-567, 571, 572, 593
  Article 1, 172-174, 188, 239, 242, 243
  Article 2, 172-174, 177, 239, 242-244
  Article 4, 5, 7, 63, 172, 219, 242
  Article 5, 173
  Article 21, 115, 173-179, 180-183, 186, 188
  Article 22, 180, 182
  Article 25, 174, 182, 186, 239, 243
  Article 29, 176
  Article 50, 239
  Article 61, 239
  Article 62, 174
  Article 63, 173, 177, 183
  Article 67, 181
  San Salvador Protocol, 8, 16, *63*, 65, 564
    Article 11, 4, 7, 10, 15, 63, 64
    Article 19, 64

Basel Convention, 314
Cartagena Protocol on Biosafety, 170, 264, 315
Convention against Torture and other Cruel, Inhuman, or Degrading Treatment or
    Punishment, 20
Convention on Biological Diversity, 170, 264
Convention on Persistent Organic Pollutants, 220
Convention on the Elimination of all Forms of Discrimination Against Women, 20
Convention on the Elimination of all Forms of Racial Discrimination, 20, 197
Convention on the Prevention and Punishment of the Crime of Genocide, 20, 385
Convention on the Rights of the Child, 16, 20, 118, 404
Convention on the Status of Refugees, 182
Convention on the Transboundary Effects of Industrial Accidents, 220, 264
Convention to Combat Desertification, 264
Espoo Convention on Environmental Impact Assessment in a Transboundary Context,
    264, 274, 285, 315
    Protocol on Strategic Environmental Assessment (SEA Protocol), 275, 285, *286*, 287
European Convention on Human Rights, 3, 20, *24*
    Article 2, 5, 24, 25, 31-37, 48, 50-52, 252-555, 584
    Article 3, 25, 29, 34
    Article 6, 363-365
    Article 8, 5, 24-48, 52, 252, 253, 571, 584
    Article 10, 25, 31-35, 219, 251-253, 363, 505, 506, 521, 533-536
    Article 13, 25
    Article 19, 25
    Article 27, 25
    Article 34, 26
    Article 41, 46
    Article 50, 33
European Social Charter (1961), 20
Hague Convention on the Taking of Evidence Abroad in Civil or Commercial Matters,
    428
IAEA Convention on the Safety of Spent Fuel Management and on the Safety of Ra-
    dioactive
Waste Management, 220
ICJ Statute, 402, 406
ILO Convention No. 107, 160
ILO Convention No. 169 concerning Indigenous and Tribal Peoples in Independent
    Countries, 16, 22, 147, 155, 156, 160-164, 165, 166-170, 191, 217, 571
*ILO Convention No. 169 Concerning Indigenous and Tribal Peoples in Independent
    Countries*, 161
    Article 1, 161
    Article 2, 161, 167
    Article 4, 162
    Article 6, 162-164, 167-169
    Article 7, 162, 167
    Article 13, 162, 166
    Article 14, 163, 166
    Article 15, 163, 167
    Article 16, 163

International Bill of Rights, 19, 20
International Covenant on Civil and Political Rights, 3, 5, 13, 19-21, 115, 116, 122,
     147, 197, 228, 390, 404, 545, 560
     Article 27, 61, 149, 151, 153-157, 192, 520
     Optional Protocol, 149-151, 153-156, 312, 314
International Covenant on Economic, Social and Cultural Rights, 3, 6, 8, 13, 19, 20,
     58, 122, 129, 131, 135, 404, 562, 566, 571
     Article 11, 119-121
     Article 12, 119-121
Kyoto Protocol to the UNFCCC, 315, 553-556, 568, 569, 572, 574, 586
Memorandum of Understanding between the Republic of Kenya and the United Re-
     public of Tanzania and the Republic of Uganda, 265, 296
North American Agreement on Environmental Cooperation, 265
North American Free Trade Agreement, 265
Paris Convention on the North-East Atlantic, 220
Protocol on Heavy Metals to the Convention on Long-Range Transboundary Air Pollu-
     tion, 264
Protocol on Pollutant Release and Transfer Register, 257
Protocol on Water and Health to the Convention on the Protection and Use of Trans-
     boundary Watercourses and International Lakes, 118, 264, 316
Rome Statute of the International Criminal Court, 380
Rotterdam Convention on the Prior Informed Consent Procedure for Certain Haz-
     ardous Chemicals and Pesticides in International Trade, 220
San Salvador Protocol, see American Convention on Human Rights
Treaty 8 of 21 June 1899 (Aboriginal Rights, Canada), 150, 152, 154
Treaty Establishing the European Community, 336
Treaty with the Nisqualli, Puyallup, etc. (Treaty of Medicine Creek), *202*, 209
U.N. Charter, 21, 148, 385
U.N. Framework Convention on Climate Change, 220, 264, 549, 550, 553, 556, 572,
     584
U.N. Convention on the Law of the Sea, 407-409
UNESCO Convention concerning the Protection of the World Cultural and Natural
     Heritage, 184
UNESCO Convention for the Safeguarding of the Intangible Cultural Heritage, 184
UNESCO Convention on the Protection and Promotion of the Diversity of Cultural
     Expressions, 184
Vienna Convention on the Law of Treaties, 345, 348
Water Charter of the Senegal River, 119
World Charter for Nature, 13, 405

Declarations, Guidelines, Resolutions, Standards, & Voluntary Codes

Agenda 21, 13, 263, 453
American Declaration on the Rights and Duties of Man, 5, 20, 60, 62, 172, 197, 238, 405, 558-572, 593
Arab Declaration on Environment and Development and Future Perspectives, 219
Declaration of Cartagena (1984) (refugees), 183
Declaration of Mexico (2004) (refugees), 183
Declaration of Principles of Freedom of Expression (IACHR), 234
Declaration of San José (1994) (refugees), 183
Declaration of the Third World Water Forum, 118
Draft Principles on Human Rights and the Environment, 7, *13*, 21
Dublin Statement on Water and Sustainable Development, 124, 126, 128
Equator banks principles, 377, 378
European Union Guidelines On Human Rights Defenders, 489
Extractive Industries Transparency Initiative, 376, 377
Fair Labor Association standards, 377-379
Global Reporting Initiative, 378
ILO Tripartite Declaration of Principles Concerning Multinational Enterprises and Social Policy, 368, *371*, 375
Inter-American Strategy for the Promotion of Public Participation in Decision-Making for Sustainable Development (ISP), 287-293, 295
Kimberley Process Certification Scheme, 376, 377
Millennium Declaration, 116
Ministerial Declaration on Environmentally Sound and Sustainable Development in Asia and the Pacific, 219
OECD Guidelines for Multinational Enterprises, 368, *369*, 371, 376, 378
PACE Resolution 1087, Consequences of the Chernobyl disaster (1996), 33, 254, 584
PACE Resolution 1577, Towards Decriminalisation of Defamation (2007), *505*
Rio Declaration, 4, 13, 15-17, 88, 89, 263, 400-403, 406, 453
Social Accountability 8000, 378
Sofia Guidelines on Public Participation in Environmental Decisionmaking, 225
Stockholm Declaration, 3, 6, 8, 13, 15, 67, 70, 89
U.N. Commission on Human Rights, Resolution 2005/60 on human rights and environment 21
U.N. Declaration on the Rights of Indigenous Peoples, 147, *157*, 186, 198, 199
U.N. Draft Code of Conduct on Transnational Corporations, 367
U.N. Draft Norms on the Responsibilities of Transnational Corporations, *372*, 379
U.N. General Assembly Declaration on Human Rights Defenders, 484, 488, 489
U.N. General Assembly Resolution 45/94, 4
U.N. General Assembly Resolution 60/251, 21, 374
U.N. Global Compact, *369*, 371, 374, 377, 378
U.N. Human Rights Council resolution on human rights and climate change, 21
U.N. Human Rights Council resolution on water, 123
Universal Declaration of Human Rights, 3, 5, 6, 8, 13, 18-20, 24, 115, 119, 129, 172, 219, 371, 374, 375, 378, 385, 390, 403, 405, 555, 562, 567, 593

U.S. House of Rep., Joint Resolution 1205, 67
U.S. House of Rep., Joint Resolution 1321, 67
Voluntary Principles on Security and Human Rights, 376, 377

Constitutional Provisions

Constitution of Argentina, 84
Constitution of Australia, 324-327
Constitution of Belize, 193-199
Constitution of Canada, 520
    Charter of Rights and Freedoms, 506, 520
Constitution of Chad, 465
Constitution of Chile, 70, 106-109
    Article 8, 240, 244
    Article 19, 70
    Article 20, 70
Constitution of Colombia, 70
Constitution of Costa Rica, 427
Constitution of Ecuador, 166, 167, 288, 291
Constitution of Greece (1975), 337
Constitution of Hungary, 339
Constitution of Illinois, 78, 79
Constitution of India, 68, 111, 112, 142, 145, 503
    Article 21, 69, 89, 90, 95, 130, 139, 140-144, 323
    Article 32, 90, 94, 322, 323
    Article 51A, 94
Constitution of Indonesia, 499, 500-502
Constitution of Korea, 245, 248
Constitution of Michigan, 340
Constitution of Montana, 73-79, 109
Constitution of Nepal - Interim Constitution 2007, 99
    Constitution of Nepal 2019, 96
    Constitution of Nepal 2047 (1990), 96, 99
Constitution of Nicaragua, 176, 432-435
Constitution of Nigeria, 575, 579
Constitution of Oregon, 333
Constitution of Pennsylvania, 101-105, 322
Constitution of Portugal, 352
Constitution of Russia, 45, 492, 495
Constitution of Slovenia, 338
Constitution of South Africa, 130, 134, 247
    Section 7, 134-138
    Section 27, 134-138
    Section 35, 134
    Section 39, 134
Constitution of Spain, 27
Constitution of Thailand (1997), 303, 305
Constitution of the Philippines, 69, 319
    Section 16, 320
Constitution of the Province of Buenos Aires (Argentina), 291
Constitution of Turkey, 91
Constitution of U.S., 67, 71, 84, 204, 248, 325, 326, 327, 383, 499, 510, 512, 541

Constitution of Ukraine, 145, 257
Constitution of Venezuela, 288

Statutes

Albania: EIA Law, 284
Australia: ACT: Human Rights Act, 545
Australia: ACT: Protection of Public Participation Bill 2006 (proposed), 546
Australia: NSW: Environmental Planning & Assessment Act, 331, 585-592
Australia: NSW: *NSW Defamation Act (2005)*, 526, *546*
Australia: NSW: PEA Act, 591
Australia: NSW: Water Management Act, 589
Australia: Consumer Protection Act, 324, 325
Australia: Trade Practices Act, 542
Australia: Wrongs Act 1936, 525
Belgium: Right of Action Relating to the Protection of the Environment Act of 1993, 335
Belize: National Lands Act, 196, 199
Bolivia: Public Participation Law, 292
Canada: Indian Act of 1970, 150
Chile: Act No. 19,653 of 1999 on Administrative Probity of the Body of the Administration, 240
Chile: Administrative Procedure Act, 240
Chile: Decree Law No. 600 (the Foreign Investment Statute), 242
Chile: Supreme Decree No. 26 of the Ministry-General Secretariat of the Presidency, 241
China: Law on Environmental Impact Assssment, 300
China: Law on the Protection of Women's Interest and Rights, 305
Colombia: Act 1021 of 2006 (General Forestry Act), 168
Colombia: Act 21 of 1991 (approving ILO 169), 169
Colombia: General Environmental National System Law, 291
Costa Rica: Law for Searching, Seizing and Evaluating Private Documents, 427
Dominica: Transnational Causes of Action Act, 426
Ecuador: Hydrocarbons Act, 167
France: Code Napoleon, 120
India, Kerala: Kerala Water Supply and Sewerage Act, 145
India: Environment Protection Act of 1986, 110, 111
India: Irrigation Acts, 131
India: *Right To Information Act, 2005, 249,* 256
India: Water Act 1974, 111, 141
Indonesia: Constitutional Court Law, 501
Indonesia: Criminal Code, 501-504
Italy: Law no. 349 of 1986, 335
Italy: Presidential Decree No. 175 of 18 May 1988, 31
Korea: Act on Disclosure of Information by Public Agencies), 247
Korea: Administrative Appeals Act, 246
Korea: Constitutional Court Act, 246
Korea: Governmental Records rules (Presidential decree no. 11547), 246
Malaysia: Internal Security Act, 484
Mexico: Federal Transparency and Access to Government Information Law, 233–237
Nepal: Environmental Impact Evaluation Law, 97

Nepal: Industrial Enterprises Act 2049-B.S., 96
Nepal: Minerals Act 2042 (1985), 98
Netherlands: Environmental Protection Act, 334
Netherlands: General Administrative Law Act, 334
Netherlands: Wetboek van Strafrecht voor Nederlandsch-Indie, 501, 502
New Zealand: Local Government Act 2002, 128
New Zealand: Resource Management Act, 305
Nicaragua: *Law No. 364*, 430, *432*, 433-437, 442
Nicaragua: Law of Amparo, 433
Nigeria: Associated Gas Regulation Act, 580
Nigeria: Associated Gas Re-Injection Act, 579
Pakistan: Environment Protection Act of 1997, 110
Philipines: Civil Code (Human Relations), 81, 319
Philippines: Presidential Decree (P.D.) No. 1151, 81, 319
Rome: Institutes of Justinian, 114
Russia: Decree no. 1161, 44
Slovenia: Environmental Protection Act, 339, 352
South Africa: EIA Law, 297
South Africa: Environment Conservation Act 73 of 1989, 297, 298
South Africa: Water Services Act 108 of 1997, 135-137
South Africa: Workmen's Compensation Act 1941, 418
South Africa:National Water Act of 1998, 133
Spain: Siete Partidas, 120
Sri Lanka: National Environmental Protection Act, 110
Sweden: Environmental Code, 354
Switzerland: Environmental Protection Act of 1983, 335
Switzerland: Federal Nature and Heritage Conservation Act of 1966, 334
Switzerland: Trails and Footpaths Act of 1987, 335
Tanzania: Newspapers Act No. 3 of 1976, 496
Thailand: Environment Act of 1992, 305
Turkey: Law No. 2709, 91
Turkey: Law on the Environment No. 2872, 91
U.K.: Legal Aid Act 1988, 531
UK: Access to Justice Act 1999, 365
Ukraine: Law on Information, 257
Ukraine: Law On Local Government, 145
USA: Calif.: Cal. C. C. P. §425.16(b)(3) (2005), 540
USA: Mass.: G.L. c. 231, §59H, 537, 538, 539, 540
USA: Mich.: Michigan Environmental Protection Act of 1970, 109, 340
USA: Mont.: §75-5-303, MCA (1995), 73, 74, 77, 79
USA: Mont.: §75-5-317, MCA (1995), 73, 74, 77
USA: Mont.: Water Quality Act, 73, 74, 78, 79
USA: Oregon: ORS 183.400, 332, 333
USA: *Administrative Procedure Act, 310*
USA: Alaska National Interest Lands Conservation Act, 566
USA: Alaska Native Claims Settlement Act, 564
USA: Alien & Sedition Act, 499
USA: Alien Tort Claims Act, 381, 382, 383, 387, 388-409, 412, 414, 582
USA: Civil Rights Attorney Fees Award Act, 360

USA: Clean Air Act, 109, 226, 340, 360, 553
USA: Endangered Species Act, 206, 209, 401
USA: Equal Access to Justice Act, 360, 361
USA: Freedom of Information Act, 225-227, 249-251, 360, 456
USA: Freedom of Information Act Amendments of 2007, 251
USA: Migratory Bird Treaty Act, 538
USA: *National Environmental Policy Act of 1969*, 300, 301, 303, *306,* 308, 309, 401, 407, 592
USA: Privacy Act, 250
USA: Puget Sound Salmon Management Act, 207
USA: Trade Act of 1974, 436

Reports

Australian Law Reform Comm., *Beyond the Door-Keeper: Standing to Sue for Public Remedies*, 330

CEQ, *Environmental Quality: 25th Anniversary Report*, 309

Council of Europe, *Examination of the alignment of the laws on defamation*, 505

Hague Academy of Intl. Law, *Water Resources and International Law*, 117

IACHR, *Access to Justice as a Guarantee of Economic, Social, and Cultural Rights*, 361

IACHR, *Report on the Situation of Human Rights in Ecuador*, 62, 63, 115, 565

IPCC, *Climate Change 2007: Synthesis Report (4th Assessment Report)*, 550

IPCC, *Fourth Assessment Report of the Intergovernmental Panel on Climate Change*, 21, 550, 551

Jilani, *Report of the Special Representative of the Secretary-General on Human Rights Defenders*, 487

Ksentini Report, 6, 7, 8, 12, 13, 15

Le Treut, et al., *Historical Overview of Climate Change*, 551

Moss, et al., *Uncertainties in the IPCC TAR: Recommendations to lead authors for more consistent assessment and reporting*, 551

OHCHR, *Report on safe water*, 122

OSCE, *Libel and Insult Laws: A Matrix on Where We Stand and What We Would Like to Achieve*, 505

OUSTR, *2007 National Trade Estimate Report on Foreign Trade Barriers*, 436

Ruggie, *Mapping International Standards of Responsibility and Accountability for Corporate Acts*, 374, 379, *380*

Survival International, *Isolated Indians in Peru*, 180

UNHCR, *Global Consultations on International Protection*, 183

Vera, et al., *Summary Report on the Inventory of EU Member States' Measures on Access to Justice in Environmental Matters*, 351

Water & Health Protocol, *Report of the Meeting of the Parties*, 316

World Bank, *About Us: Articles of Agreement*, 446

World Bank, *Multilateral Development Banks*, 445

Books

Alston, Peoples' Rights, 11

Anaya, Indigenous peoples in International Law, 148

Blacks Law Dictionary, 578

Blackstone, Commentaries on the Laws of England, 389

Bodansky, Brunée, & Hey, The Oxford Handbook of International Environmental Law, 265

Boyle & Anderson, Human Rights Approaches to Environmental Protection, 9, 10

Bruch, The New 'Public': Globalization of Public Participation, 288, 293, 453, 457, 475

Carson, Silent Spring, 3

Coggins & Glicksman, Public Natural Resources Law, 309

de Sadeleer, Roller, & Dross, Access to Justice in Environmental Matters, *356*

de Schutter, Transnational Corporations and Human Rights, 367, 374

Dejeant-Pons & Pallemaerts, Human Rights and The Environment, 10

Eide, Krause & Rosas, Economic, Social and Cultural Rights: A Textbook, 6

Gwin, U.S. Relations With The World Bank, 446

Kapur, The World Bank: Its First Half Century, 445

Kimmerling, Amazon Crude, 411, 412

Malone & Pasternack, Defending the Environment, *164*

O'Brien, The Public's Right to Know: The Supreme Court and the First Amendment, 248

Picolotti & Taillant, Linking Human Rights and the Environment, 9, 63

Pring & Canan, SLAPP: Getting Sued for Speaking Out, *508, 510, 527*

Razzaque, Public Interest Environmental Litigation in India, Pakistan, and Bangladesh, 324

Robb, Human Rights And Environment, 19, 105

Rodgers, Environmental Law in Indian Country, 209

Routledge Encyclopedia Of International Political Economy, 446

SACEP, Compendium of Summaries of Judicial Decisions in Environment Related Cases, 19

Sachs, Climate Change and Human Rights, 595

Salman, et al., The Human Right To Water, 117

Sands, Principles Of International Environmental Law, 400

Sarmiento, Las acciones populares en el derecho privado Colombiano, 321

Sax, Defending the Environment: A Strategy for Citizen Action, 340

Scanlon, Cassar, & Nemes, Water as a Human Right?, *114*

Schrijver & Weiss, International Law and Sustainable Development — Principles and Practice, 287, 300

Sheldon & Squillace, NEPA Litigation Guide, 309

Shelton & Kiss, Judicial Handbook on Environmental Law, 220, 521

Stec & Casey-Lefkowitz, The Aarhus Convention: An Implementation Guide, *223, 255, 266, 276*, 343

Stec, Handbook on Access to Justice, 334

Sunstein, Laws of Fear: Beyond the Precautionary Principle, 374

Tananbaum, THE BRICKER AMENDMENT CONTROVERSY: A TEST OF EISENHOWER'S POLITICAL LEADERSHIP, 385

UNEP, 2000 GLOBAL ENVIRONMENTAL OUTLOOK, *304*

UNEP, COMPENDIUM OF JUDICIAL DECISIONS ON MATTERS RELATED TO ENVIRONMENT: NATIONAL DECISIONS, 19, 417

Wade & Forsyth, ADMINISTRATIVE LAW, 329

Weiss , et al., FRESH WATER AND INTERNATIONAL ECONOMIC LAW, 119

Zillman, Lucas, & Pring, HUMAN RIGHTS IN NATURAL RESOURCE DEVELOPMENT, 260, 262

Articles & Book Chapters

Acevedo, *The Intersection of Human Rights and Environmental Protection in the European Court of Human Rights*, 35

Aminzadeh, *A Moral Imperative: The Human Rights Implications of Climate Change*, 554

Amnesty International and Sierra Club, *Environmentalists under Fire: 10 Urgent Cases of Human Rights Abuses*, 483

Anderson, *Forum Non Conveniens Checkmated?*, 425

Anderson, *Human Rights Approaches to Environmental Protection: An Overview*, 9, 10

Asenjo, *Innovative Environmental Litigation in Chile: The Case of Chañaral*, 340

Assaf, et al., *Water as a Human Right: The Understanding of Water in Arab Countries of the Middle East—A Four Country Analysis*, 117

Banisar, *Freedom of Information Around the World 2006*, 247, *249*

Pontin, *Environmental Rights under the UK's "Intermediate Constitution,* 24

Bernasconi-Osterwalder & Hunter, *Democratizing Multilateral Development Banks*, *453, 457,* 475

Beth, *The Public's Right to Know: The Supreme Court as Pandora?*, 248

Bluemel, *The Implications of Formulating a Human Right to Water*, 129

Bogado, et al., *The Federal Institute for Access to Information & A Culture of Transparency—Follow Up Report*, 237

Bonine, *Removing Barriers and Providing Incentives for Citizen Enforcement of Environmental Laws*, 357

Bonine, *The Construction of Participatory Democracy in Central and Eastern Europe*, 262

Bonine, *The New Private Public Interest Bar*, 358

Bonine, *The Public's Right to Enforce Environmental Law*, 334

Breger: *Defending Defenders: Remarks on Nichol and Pierce*, 326

Caillaux, et al., *Environmental Public Participation in the Americas, 288*

Ciorciari, *The Lawful Scope of Human Rights Criteria in World Bank Credit Decisions*, 474

Circi, *The World Bank Inspection Panel: Is It Really Effective?*, 458, 459

Clark, *The World Bank and Human Rights*, 459

Cohen, *Bretton Woods System*, 446

Comment, *Strategic Lawsuits Against Public Participation: An Analysis of the Solution*, 539

Dam & Tewary, *Is A "Polluted" Constitution Worse Than a Polluted Environment?, 110*

Daschbach, *Where There's a Will, There's a Way, 429*

de Schutter, *Challenge of Imposing Human Rights Norms on Corporate Actors, 367,* 374

de Vos, *Pious Wishes or Directly Enforceable Human Rights?: Social and Economic Rights in South Africa's 1996 Constitution*, 139

Diskin, *Note: The Historical and Modern Foundations for Aiding and Abetting Liability under the Alien Tort Statute*, 397

Dommen, *Claiming Environmental Rights: Some Possibilities Offered by the United Nations' Human Rights Mechanism*, 21

Ebbesson, *Public Participation*, 265

Emerson, *The Affirmative Side of the First Amendment*, 248

Fabra & Arnal, *Background Paper No. 6: Review of jurisprudence on human rights and the environment in Latin America*, 85

Feller, *Public Participation under NEPA*, 309

Fletcher, *International Human Rights in American Courts*, 393

Francis, *Water Justice in South Africa: Natural Resources Policy at the Intersection of Human Rights, Economics, and Political Power*, 133

Gatmaytan, *The Illusion of Intergenerational Equity: Oposa v. Factoran as Pyrrhic Victory*, 86, 87

Gleick, *The Human Right to Water*, 118

Goldberg & Wagner, *Petitioning for Adverse Impacts of Global Warming in the Inter-American Human Rights System*, 557

Greene, *It's a Crime: How Insult Laws Stifle Press Freedom (2007)*, 504

Grote, *On The Fringes Of Europe: Europe's Largely Forgotten Indigenous peoples*, 191

Handl, *Human Rights and the Protection of the Environment*, 6

Hardberger, *Whose Job Is It Anyway?: Governmental Obligations Created by the Human Right to Water*, 129

Hart, *Comment [on Hatton]*, 41

Hart, *Environmental Rights and the Public Interest: Hatton*, 43

Hassan & Azfar, *Securing Environmental Rights Through Public Interest Litigation in South Asia*, 99, 110

Head, *For Richer or For Poorer: Assessing the Criticisms Directed at the Multilateral Development Banks*, 446

Hector, *Protecting Human Rights Defenders: Analysis of the newly adopted Declaration on Human Rights Defenders*, 485, 486

Herz, *Litigating Environmental Abuses Under the Alien Tort Claims Act: A Practical Assessment*, 398

Heyer, *Latin American State Secrecy and Mexico's Transparency Law*, 233

Heyman, *Righting the Balance: An Inquiry into the Foundations and Limits of Freedom of Expression*, 500

Hill, et al., *Human Rights and the Environment: A Synopsis and Some Predictions*, 68

Horta, *Rhetoric and Reality: Human Rights and the World Bank*, 462

Jacobs, *Treading Deep Waters*, 573

Kamb, *Boldt Decision 'Very Much Alive' 30 Years Later*, 205

Kaur, Note: *Global Warming Litigation under the Alien Tort Claims Act*, 398

Kidd, *Not a Drop to Drink: Disconnection of Water Services for Nonpayment and the Right of Access to Water*, 138

Kimerling, *Transnational Operations, Bi-National Injustice*, 410

Koester, *Review of Compliance under the Aarhus Convention: a Rather Unique Compliance Mechanism*, 316

Koh, *Transnational Public Law Litigation*, 382

Komba, *Environment Lawyer in Court*, 498

Kravchenko, *The Aarhus Convention and Innovations in Compliance with Multilateral Environmental Agreements*, 227, 313

Kravchenko, *Right to Carbon or Right to Life: Human Rights Approaches to Climate Change*, 9 Vermont J. Envir. L. 515 (2008).

Kreimer, *Allocational Sanctions: The Problem of Negative Rights In A Positive State*, 93

Langewiesche, *Jungle Law*, 421

Linde, *The State and the Federal Courts in Governance: Vive La Différence!*, 333

Lissu, *View from the Accused*, 497

Manguiat & Yu, *Maximizing the Value of Oposa v. Factoran*, 86, 87

Marcus, *The Normative Development of Socioeconomic Rights through Supranational Adjudication*, 42, 52

McCaffrey, *The Human Right to Water*, 119

McClellan, *Access to Justice in Environmental Law: An Australian Perspective*, 327

McClure & Stiffler, *Sound's Salmon Carry High PCB Levels*, 209

McKaskle, *The European Court of Human Rights: What it is, how it works, and its future*, 52

McManus, *Sovereignty, Self-Determination, and Environment-Based Cultures: The Emerging Voice of Indigenous Peoples in International Law*, 172

Mehra, *Post a Message and Go to Jail: Criminalizing Internet Libel in Japan and the United States*, 507

Moorman & Ge, *Promoting and Strengthening Public Participation in China's Environmental Impact Assessment Process: Comparing China's EIA Law and U.S. NEPA*, 300

Mushkat, *The Principle of Public Participation: An Asia-Pacific Perspective*, 287, *300*

Nichols, *Justice Scalia, Standing, and Public Law Litigation*, 326

Odote & Makoloo, *African Initiatives for Public Participation in Environmental Management*, 293

Ogle, *Gunning for Change: The Need for Public Participation Law Reform*, 540

Olsen, *Orcas on the Edge*, 209

Pallemaerts, *The Human Right to a Healthy Environment as a Substantive Right*, 10

Pasqualucci, *Criminal Defamation and the Evolution of the Doctrine of Freedom of Expression in International Law*, 522

Pejan, *The Right to Water: The Road to Justiciability*, 139

Penny, *Greening the Security Council: Climate Change as an Emerging "Threat to International Peace and Security,"*, 594

Picolotti, *The Right to Water in Argentina*, 132

Popovic, *In Pursuit of Environmental Human Rights: Commentary on the Draft Declaration of Principles on Human Rights and the Environment*, 15

Popovic, *Pursuing Environmental Justice with International Human Rights and State Constitutions*, 71

Posner, *Climate Change and International Human Rights Litigation: A Critical Appraisal*, 553, *581*

Prempeh, *Marbury in Africa: Judicial Review and the Challenge of Constitutionalism in Contemporary Africa*, 499

Price, *Fighting the Big Gunns in Tasmania*, 513

Pring & Noé, *The Emerging International Law of Public Participation Affecting Global Mining, Energy and Resources Development*, 260

Pring, *SLAPPs: Strategic Lawsuits Against Public Participation*, 539

Rodriguez-Rivera, *Is the Human Right to Environment Recognized under International Law? It Depends on the Source*, 8

Saint Dahl, *Forum Non Conveniens, Latin America and Blocking Statutes*, *426*, 430, 432

Salzman, *Thirst: A Short History of Drinking Water*, 123

Santoyo, *Comment, Bananas of Wrath: How Nicaragua May Have Dealt Forum Non Conveniens a Fatal Blow Removing the Doctrine as an Obstacle to Achieving Corporate Accountability*, 430

Scalia, *The Doctrine of. Standing as an Essential Element of the Separation of Powers*, 332

Schwartz, *$2.5 million in punitive damages awarded to banana workers*, *442*

Secretariat, CBD, *The Convention on Biological Diversity, from Conception to Implementation*, 170

Shelton, *Environmental Rights*, *11*

Shipman, *Steel & Morris v. United Kingdom: Legal Aid in the European Court of Human Rights*, *363*

Smith & Green, *Free basic water in Msunduzi, KwaZulu-Natal*, 134

Stein, *Water Law in a Democratic South Africa*, 139

Stone, *Defamation of Public Figures: North American Contrasts*, 508

Sunstein: *What's Standing after Lujan? Of Citizen Suits, Injuries, and Article III*, 326

Swepston & Tomei, *Indigenous and Tribal Peoples: A Guide to ILO Convention No. 169*, 164

Swepston, *A New Step in the International Law on Indigenous And Tribal Peoples: ILO Convention No. 169 of 1989*, 161, 164

Taillant, *Environmental Advocacy and the Inter-American Human Rights System*, *9*, *63*

Udombana, *Toward the African Court on Human and Peoples' Rights: Better Late Than Never*, 54

UNEP, *Policy Responses—Asia and Pacific*, *304*

Univ. of Arizona, *Boletín Informativo El Caso Awas Tingni v. Nicaragua*, 179

Uriz, *To Lend Or Not To Lend*, *463*

Vasak, *A 30-Year Struggle*, 19

Viljoen & Louw, *State Compliance with the Recommendations of the African Commission on Human and Peoples' Rights*, 54, 60

Wiessner, *Rights and Status of Indigenous peoples: A Global Comparative and International Legal Analysis*, 148

Wood, *Nature's Trust: A Legal, Political and Moral Frame for Global Warming*, 553

World Bank, *The World Bank Group Historical Chronology*, 446

Wright, *Finding an Impetus for Institutional Change at the African Court on Human and Peoples' Rights*, 55

Young, *Regulatory and Judicial Responses to the Possibility of Biological Hazards from Electromagnetic Fields generated by Power Lines*, 88

Zarembo & Maugh, *Bali Climate Keeps World at Table*, 554

Other Authorities

Aarhus Convention, Meeting of the Parties, *Decision I/7, Review of Compliance*, 229, 231, 270, 274, 314, 316, 349

CAO, *Operational Guidelines*, 476

CESCR, *General Comment 12*, 135

CESCR, *General Comment 15*, 21, 119, 120, 121, 122, 128, 129

EPA, *California State Motor Vehicle Pollution Control Standards; Notice of Decision Denying a Waiver of Clean Air Act Preemption*, 553

ILO, *Constitution of the International Labour Organization*, 164, 165, 166, 371

LEAT, *Bulyanhulu Complaint to IFC/MIGA Compliance Advisor/Ombudsman*, 477

Mining Watch, *Report of the International NGO Fact-finding Mission to Tanzania*, 497

OHCHR, *Introduction to the Human Rights Committee*, 312

OHCHR, *Meeting of Experts on Human Rights and the Environment*, 16

Picolotti, et al., *Brief Amicus Curiae: Garcia and Flores v. The State of Mexico*, 483

Plenum of Supreme Court of Russian Federation, 48

The California Anti-SLAPP Project, 540

Yorongar, *Request for Investigations by the World Bank Inspection Panel*, 465

Index

A

access to information. *See generally* Chapter 6,
   See also Freedom of speech & expression; *see also* various statutes in TABLE OF AUTHORITIES
active duty, 251–57
American Convention
   right to receive information, 219
countries
   Canada, 247
   Chile, 239
   India, 249, 256
   Korea, 244
   Mexico, 237, 233–38
   New Zealand, 247
   South Africa, 247
   Sweden, 221, 247
   Ukraine
      Chernobyl, 253, 257
      Constitution, 257
      Law on Information, 257
   United States
      19th century, 221
      Constitution, 248
      FOIA, 249–51
environmental information, 223
Europe, Caucasus, & Central Asia
   Aarhus Convention. See Aarhus, Articles 4 & 5, in TABLE OF AUTHORITIES
   Council of Europe, 254
   European Convention on Human Rights, 251–53
   PRTR Protocol, 257
international declarations, 219
Latin America, 233, 239
multilateral environmental agreements, 220

national constitutions, 247
passive duty, 221–51
purposes, 223
Access to justice. *See generally* Chapter 8,
   See also Financial barriers to justice; Standing to sue

B

Banks & financial institutions, *See generally* Chapter 10
in general
   critiques, 446–53
   information & participation, 453–56
   review bodies
      IFC/MIGA Compliance Advisor & Ombudsman, 475, 476, 475–76, 479, 480, 481, 482, 497, 498
      World Bank Inspection Panel, 457–61
international development banks
   International Bank for Reconstruction & Development (IBRD), 446, 447, 457, 474
   International Development Association (IDA), 446, 447, 457
   International Finance Corporation (IFC), 376, 377, 378, 445, 446, 454, 455, 475, 476, 480, 481, 482, 497
   International Monetary Fund (IMF), 123, 126, 450, 451
   Multilateral Investment Guarantee Association (MIGA), 446, 475, 476, 477, 478, 479, 480, 481, 496, 498
   World Bank, 22, 44, 123, 126, 261, 279, 280, 304, 457, 458, 459, 460, 461, 462, 463, 464, 465, 466, 467,

Banks & financial institutions *continued*
  473, 474, 475, 476, 480, 496, 498,
    556, 580
  EIA requirement, 279
  history, 445–46
  regional development banks
    Asian & African Development Banks,
      445–56
    European Bank for Reconstruction &
      Development (EBRD), 279–81,
      447–51
    European Investment Bank (EIB),
      279
    Inter-American Development Bank
      (IADB), 445, 447, 450, 455

C

Climate change. *See generally* Chapter 12
  environmental refugees, 557, 575, 595
  human rights approach
    benefits, 555–56
    critiques, 556–57, 556–57
  intergenerational equity, 574, 590
  international agreements, 553–54, 572
  litigation
    approaches, 554–57
    critiques, 581–83
    human rights bodies, 557–72,
      581–83
    ICJ, 573–75
    national courts
      procedural, 585–93
      substantive, 575–81
  political change, 553
  precautionary principle, 574, 590
  procedural rights
    access to information, 583–84
    public participation, 585–93
  science, 552, 560–62
  substantive rights
    culture, 562–63, 570
    food & subsistence, 566–67, 570
    health, 564–65, 570
    home, 567–68, 571
    life, 555, 565–66, 570, 576
    property, 555, 563–64, 570
  security, 593–95
  sustainable development, 551, 588

conventions. *See* Treaties, etc.; *see also*
  Sources of international law; TABLE
  OF AUTHORITIES
Corporate accountability. *See generally*
  Chapter 9
  Alien Tort Claims Act. See TABLE OF AU-
    THORITIES and torts below
  anti-forum non conveniens legislation,
    425–37
  crimes abroad, 382
  forum non conveniens, 407, 410–21,
    443
  liability under international law, gener-
    ally, 375
  self-regulation, 377–79
  soft law, 367–72, 375–77, 379
  torts
    Alien Tort Claims Act, 382–410
      Act of State doctrine, 386, 396,
        409
      aiding and abetting liability, 381,
        395–96, 397
      law of nations, 382–410
    ordinary litigation
      Ecuador, 421–25
      United States, 437–43
  transnational litigation, 382–88
  voluntary codes, 367–72
  courts, international. *See* International
    bodies
Courts, national
  Australia
    New South Wales
      Supreme Court, 329
    South Australia
      Supreme Court, 522
  Bangladesh
    Dhaka High Court, 98
    Supreme Court, 86
  Belgium
    Council of State, 335, 343–50, 356
    Supreme Court, 344
  Belize
    Supreme Court, 193
  Canada
    Ontario
      Court of Justice, 515
      Supreme Court, 200, 201, 507,
        519

Chile
    Supreme Court, 70, 71, 105, 108,
        208, 216, 352, 392
Colombia
    Constitutional Court, 70, 140, 163,
        168
Costa Rica
    Supreme Court, 86
Ecuador
    Constitutional Court, 166, 167
    Supreme Court, 413
England
    High Court, 339
Greece
    Council of State, 336, 337
Hungary
    Constitutional Court, 79, 338
    Supreme Court, 336
India
    Supreme Court, 69, 89, 90, 94, 96,
        114, 139, 141, 322, 323, 426, 503
Indonesia
    Constitutional Court, 500
Kazakhstan
    Supreme Court, 232
Korea
    Constitutional Court, 244
Nepal
    Supeme Court, 96, 99
Nicaragua
    Supreme Court, 175, 432
Norway
    Supreme Court, 337
Pakistan
    Supreme Court, 87
Philippines
    Supreme Court, 71, 79, 140, 317
Russia
    Constitutional Court, 492
    Supreme Court, 492
Slovenia
    Constitutional Court, 338, 339
South Africa
    Constitutional Court, 138, 139
South Asia
    Supreme Courts
        criticism, 110–12
        praise, 110
United States

Illinois
    Supreme Court, 78
Michigan
    Supreme Court, 340
Montana
    Supreme Court, 73
U.S. Supreme Court, 84, 203, 204,
    213, 248, 322, 326, 332, 333, 362,
    396, 398, 406, 496, 507, 511, 552
criminal insult. *See* SLAPP
criminal libel. *See* SLAPP
customary international law. *See* Sources
    of international law

D
defamation. *See* SLAPP
defenders of human rights. *See generally*
    Chapter 11

E
Environmental impact assessment (EIA)
    China's law compared to United States,
        300–302
    EIA as property of developer, 272, 274,
        275
    Espoo EIA Convention, 264, 315
    notification of public, 284
    procedural rights, 30
    public participation, 274, 275, 282, 284,
        287, 291, 296, 297, 300, 301, 354,
        592
    specific disputes
        Albania, 278–84
        Italy, 30
        South Africa, 297–99
        Ukraine, 271–74
    strategic environmental assessment
        (SEA), 285–87, 301
    transboundary impacts, 264, 268, 271,
        285, 315
    United States (NEPA), 306–9, 592
Events
    Earth Day 1970, 3
    U.N. Conference on Environment and
        Development, 4, 17, 170, 220, 264,
        403, 553
    U.N. Conference on the Human Envi-
        ronment, 3, 13, 67, 88, 451

Events *continued*
U.N. World Summit for Sustainable Development, 118

F
Financial barriers to justice
attorney fees (costs)
American Rule, 359, 360
loser pays rule, 358, 359, 531
modified American Rule, 360
constitutions, international law, 360
court fees, 29, 356, 357, 360
equal access and agency decisions, 361
equality of arms, fair trial, 361–65, 532, 535
foundation funding, 359
government funding, 358
legal aid, 363–65
number of law suits, 356
number of lawyers, 358
prohibitively expensive (Aarhus), 357
forum non conveniens. See Corporate accountability
Freedom of assembly, 192, 488
Freedom of speech & expression, 545,
See also SLAPP
basis for right to information, 242–44, 244–47, 248
American Convention, 234
constitutions
France, India, Israel, Japan, Pakistan, Sweden, 247
Korea, 245
Mexico, 234
United States, 248
European Convention, 25, 35, 219, 252, 363
criminal defamation
Inter-American Court of Human Rights, 522
decriminalization of defamation, 505
defamation, 504–8, 535
Canada Charter of Rights & Freedoms, 507
European Convention, 533
margin of appreciation, 534
reform (Australia), 526, 540–47
human rights defenders, 489
ILO Tripartite Declaration of Principles, 371

insult and hostility toward government, 504
McLibel Case, 532
SLAPP suit defense, 541
Canada, 519
European Court of Human Rights, 521
Norway, 521
United States, 511
unconstitutionality of restrictions
India, 503
Indonesia, 500–504
United States, 507

I
Indigenous peoples
Amahuaca, 180
Cree (Lubicon), 149, 150, 151, 152, 153, 149–54, 155, 160, 190, 515–21
Haida, 201, 202
Inuit, 62, 191, 192, 209, 557–73, 574, 581, 592
Mashco-Piro, 180
Maya, 193, 194, 195, 196, 197, 199, 200, 193–200, 563, 564
Mayagna, 174–80, 182, 197
N'djuka, 180, 181, 182, 183, 185
N'djuka, 180–85
Nisqually, 202, 206, 210
Ogoni, 55, 56, 57, 55–60, 190, 465, 466, 483
Puyallup, 202, 210
Saami or Sami, 154–57, 191–92
Saramaka, 185, 186, 187, 188, 185–88, 188
Shuar, 166
Temuan, 200
Tuvaluan, 573
Western Shoshone, 198
Yakye Axa, 183
Yora, 180
Indigenous rights. *See also* Rights to culture, fish, & property, *See generally* Chapter 5
compensation, 159
consent, free, prior and informed, 158, 159, 160, 163, 171, 174, 182, 187, 197, 199, 201, 202, 563, 567
conservation and protection of environment, 159

consultation and participation, 160, 162, 163, 164, 166, 168, 169, 174, 181, 182, 185, 186, 187, 197, 201
cultural identity, 153, 155, 156, 158, 159, 162, 169, 183
demarcation and titling of lands, 159, 162–63, 174–78, 181–85
institutions and systems, 158
mechanisms for redress, 160
metajuridical reflection, 184
natural resources, 163
relationship to environment, 147, 169, 181, 183, 186
restitution, 159
return, voluntary and sustainable, 183, 184
self-determination, 150, 172
spiritual, 158, 162
spiritual relationship, 159
water, 113
information. *See* Access to information
insult. *See* SLAPP
Intergenerational equity, 69, 179, 588, 589, 590, 591, 592, 590–92
International bodies. generally, 20–22, *See also* Banks & financial institutions
African Commission on Human and Peoples' Rights, 53, 54, 53–54, 55, 58, 59, 60, 55–60, 116, 122, 189, 190, 189–90, 294, 311
  case, 55–59
  structure, 22
African Court on Human and Peoples' Rights, 54, 55, 294, 311
  standing of individuals, 55
  structure, 22
Committee Against Torture, 21
Committee on Elimination of Racial Discrimination, 21, 191, 197
Compliance Advisor/Ombudsman
  case, 479–80
Compliance Committee of the Aarhus Convention, 227, 228, 229, 232, 270, 274, 275, 278, 285, 313, 316, 343, 350, 351, 355
  cases, 228–32, 270–74, 278–84, 343–50
  standing of individuals, 22

European Court of Human Rights, 25, 251, 529, 557
  cases, 26–35, 37–41, 43–48, 48–52, 251–54, 492–95
  exhaustion of remedies, 30
  jurisprudence, 24, 35–37, 41–43, 52, 58, 192, 202, 363–65, 375, 504, 521, 567, 584
  jurisprudence cited by others, 115, 135, 140, 189, 406, 505, 555
  standing of individuals, 22, 26, 55, 311, 314, 316, 556
  structure, 25
European Court of Justice, 336
ILO Committee on Multinational Enterprises, 371
Implementation Committee of the Espoo EIA Convention, 315
Implementation Committee of the Montreal Protocol, 315
Inter-American Commission on Human Rights, 61, 62, 177, 179, 180, 193, 194, 198, 234, 239, 241, 311, 361, 375, 483, 489, 554, 558, 559, 560, 564, 571, 572, 573
  case, 61–62
  jurisprudence, 5
  jurisprudence cited by others, 135, 140
  standing of individuals, 55, 61–62, 316, 556
  structure, 22, 62, 174
Inter-American Court of Human Rights, 58, 174, 179, 180, 181, 182, 186, 189, 311, 375, 521, 522
  cases, 174–78, 180–85, 186–88, 239–44
  standing of individuals, 55, 316
  structure, 22, 174
International Centre for Settlement of Investment Disputes, 128, 446
International Court of Justice, 18, 402, 406
International Criminal Court, 311, 380, 381, 385
International Labour Organization, 16, 22, 147, 155, 156, 160, 161, 163, 164, 165, 166, 167, 168, 169, 170, 191,

International bodies. *continued*
217, 368, 369, 371, 372, 375, 378,
379, 571
Organization for Economic Cooperation
and Development (OECD), 306, 368,
369, 371, 374, 376, 378
standing of individuals, 556
U.N. Commission on Human Rights,
21, 149, 374, 379, 484, 485, 486, 490,
491
U.N. Committee on Economic, Social
and Cultural Rights, 21, 119, 120,
121
U.N. Economic Commission for Europe, 118, 264
U.N. General Assembly, 4, 21, 22, 24,
65, 157, 186, 198, 312, 371, 374, 405,
484, 485, 487, 489, 593
U.N. High Commissioner for Human
Rights, 15, 16, 21, 122, 312, 486
U.N. Human Rights Committee, 20, 21,
115, 116, 122, 149, 153, 154, 156,
157, 228, 312, 520, 566
cases, 149–53, 154–56
U.N. Human Rights Council, 21, 122,
149, 157, 374, 486, 487, 488, 549,
550
U.N. Intergovernmental Panel on Climate Change, 550, 551, 552, 570,
571, 572, 574, 575
U.N. Security Council, 198, 250, 593,
594, 595
U.N. Special Representative on Human
Rights and Transnational Corporations, 374, 379
U.N. Special Representative on Human
Rights Defenders, 486–89, 491
World Bank Inspection Panel
case, 468–72
World Health Organization, 119
international financial institutions. *See*
Banks & financial institutions; *see*
generally Chapter 10

L
law of nations. *See* Sources of international law:customary international
law
Lawyers, public interest

Bonine, John E., 262, 334, 357, 358
Caillaux, Jorge, 288
Casey-Lefkowitz, Susan, 223, 255, 266,
343
Fajardo, Pablo, 421–25
Farooque, Mohiuddin, 86, 98, 99
Hassan, Parvez, 99, 110
Kattan, Alberto, 84, 484
Kravchenko, Svitlana, 227, 313, 595
Lissu, Tundu, 496, 497
Makoloo, Maurice O., 293
Mehta, M.C., 89, 94, 95, 111, 112, 114,
130, 322, 483
Oposa, Antonio, 87, 483
Sarmiento, German, 321
Shauri, Vincent, 498
Stec, Stephen, 223, 255, 266, 276, 343
legal aid. *See* Financial barriers to justice
libel. *See* SLAPP
linkages. *See* Rights

M
multilateral development banks. *See*
Banks & financial institutions

N
NGOs
Alliance for the Protection of the Vlora
Gulf (Albania), **278**
Bond Beter Leefmilieu Vlaanderen (Bel-
gium), 343
Center for International Environmental
Law, 572
Confederación Ecuatoriana de Organi-
zaciónes Sindicales Libres (CEOSL),
166
Conservation Council of South Aus-
tralia, 522, 524
Earthjustice, 510, 572
Earthlife Africa (Cape Town), 297
Ecopravo-Lviv [Ecology-People-Law]
(Ukraine), 270
Environmental Law Alliance Worldwide
(ELAW), 359
European ECO Forum, 264
Friends of the Earth, 592
Friends of the Lubicon (Canada, First
Nations), 515
Green Salvation (Kazakhstan), 228

Greenpeace, 336, 338, 339, 529, 534, 592

Human Rights First, 485

Independent Federation of the Shuar People of Ecuador (FIPSE), 166

Lawyers' Environmental Action Team (Tanzania), 477, 496, 497, 498, 499

Montana Environmental Information Center, 73

Pro Public (Nepal), 99

Social and Economic Rights Action Center (Nigeria), 55

Society for Preservation of Environment and Quality Life (India), 141

The Wilderness Society (Australia), 515, 540, 545

Truth About Motorways (Australia), 324

P

participation. *See* Public participation

People. See also Lawyers, public interest

Carson, Rachel, 3

Ken Saro-Wiwa, 55, 465, 483

Ksentini, Fatma Zohra, 6, 7, 8, 13, 15

Nelson, Sen. Gaylord, 67

Nikitin, Alexandre, 492–95

Stevens, Gov. Isaac, 202, 208

Trindade, Judge Cançado, 174, 177, 182, 185, 188, 200

Precautionary principle or approach

Australia, 588–91

climate change, 593

criticisms, 374

draft Norms on Responsibility of Transnational Corporations, 373

India, 141

International Court of Justice, 574

nuclear testing, 574

Pakistan, 88

Rio Declaration Principle 15, 88

U.N. Global Compact, 369

U.N. Human Rights Committee, 157

procedural environmental rights. *See* Access to information; Public participation; Access to justice

Public participation. *See generally* Chapter 7, See also Environmental impact assessment (EIA)

Africa, 293–99

East Africa MOU, 265

South Africa, 297–99

Americas

NAFTA, 265

Asia, 300–306

benefits & results, 261, 266

China, 300–302

constitutional right or duty, 288, 303–4

criticisms, 262

early stage, 187, 268, 269, 282, 284, 285, 286, 291, 293, 303, 450

Eastern Europe (history), 262–63

Europe, Caucasus, & Central Asia

Aarhus Convention, 265–87

Espoo EIA Convention, 264

in international forums, 265

Latin America, 287–93

multilateral environmental agreements, 264–65

NEPA, 592

plans, programs, policies, regulations, 285

projects, 267–75

purpose, 289

rationales, 260

Rio Declaration, Principle 10, 263

strategic environmental assessment, 285–87

sustainable development, 289, 292, 295, 454

Thailand, 303–4

time for comments, 273

United States

APA, regulations, 309–10

NEPA, EISs, 306–9

Public trust

Argentina, 131

Australia, 329

global warming, 553

India, 69, 130

Institutes of Justinian, 114

responsibilities of trustee, 105

South Africa, 133, 139

United States, 114

Pennsylvania, 103

water supply, 114, 124

R

regional development banks. *See* Banks & financial institutions

Right to culture
  African Commission, 189–90
  American Convention (humane treat-
    ment), 173
  climate change, 562, 592
  Colombia Constitutional Court, 169
  Declaration of Rights of Indigenous
    Peoples, 158
  ICCPR, 116, 149, 153, 155–57
  ILO Convention No. 169, 162
  Inter-American Court, 183–85
  UNESCO Conventions, 184
Right to fish, 202–17
  as necessary to existence as air, 204
  Boldt decision, 203, 205
  culverts, diminishment by, 211
  proportion of harvest, 203
  religious importance, 203
  Stevens Treaties, 205, 211
  survival of fish, 202
right to freedom of speech & expression.
    See Freedom of speech & expression
Right to health, 405
  African Charter, 57
  American Declaration
    environmental degradation, 564
  climate change, 554, 556
  constitutions
    Philippines, 82, 83, 320
  customary international law, 401, 403
  ESC Covenant, 120
  ICJ case, 115
  implied right to water, 120
  linkage to environmental protection, 18
  substantive rights, 83
  Universal Declaration, 405
Right to healthy, safe environment
  aspiration, 5
  history, origin, 3–4
  linkages between environment & rights,
    6, 17, 18, 36, 564
  satisfactory environment (African Char-
    ter), 294, 576, 577
  self-executing, 10, 68, 69, 85, 90, 101,
    102, 103, 104, 114, 386, 390
  standing. See Standing to sue, legal
    tests:environmental right
  substantive right

  international law, 6–10, See generally
    Chapter 2
  national law, 17, See Chapter 3
  U.S. Constitution proposal, 67
  variations
    balanced and healthy ecology (Con-
      stitution of Philippines), 69, 83
    environment free of contamination
      (Constitution of Chile), 70
    healthy environment (Colombia
      court), 70
    healthy or satisfactory environment
      (San Salvador Protocol), 10, 15,
      16
    live in harmony with nature (Rio De-
      claration), 15
    quality environment (Stockholm De-
      claration), 3, 6, 15, 67, 88
    satisfactory environment (African
      Charter), 4, 10, 15, 53, 57, 58
    secure, ecologically sound environ-
      ment (Draft Principles), 14
right to information. *See* Access to infor-
    mation
Right to isolation, 180
right to justice. *See* Access to justice
Right to life
  African Charter, 190
  American Convention, 63, 404
  American Declaration, 5, 60, 62, 559
  climate change, 555, 557, 565–66, 570,
    574
  constitutions
    implied environmental rights
      Bangladesh, 98
      Chile, 70
      Colombia, 70
      India, 69, 90, 95, 96, 98, 130, 140,
        142, 144, 323
      Nepal, 99
      Nigeria, 576, 577
        Black's Law Dictionary, 578
      Pakistan, 90
    implied indigenous rights
      Belize, 197
  cultural identity, 184
  customary international law, 401, 403
  environmental contamination and
    health, 115, 190, 404

European Convention, 25, 33, 34, 35
  failure to inform of pollution, 34
  serious risk to life, 34, 48–52
first generation right, 19
generally, 9, 12, 24
ICCPR, 404
ICJ case, 115
implied environmental right, 5
implied information right, 584
implied right to security, 593
Inter-American Commission
  environmental contamination and
    health, 62
linkage to environmental protection, 18
low corporate recognition, 378
positive obligations of government, 51
Stockholm Declaration, 70
substantive right, 18
U.N. Human Rights Committee, 122
Universal Declaration, 405
right to participate. *See* Public participation
Right to private and family life, 23, 24,
  25, 33, 115, 140
as environmental right, 5, 202
  beginnings & growth, 26–37
  decline, 37–43
  reestablishment, 37–43
climate change, 567, 568, 571
domestic law violation, 28, 36, 40, 42,
  43–48, 43–46, 52
exhaustion of remedies, 30
fair balance, 28, 36
implied information right, 33, 584
margin of appreciation, 28, 29, 35, 37,
  39, 37–41, 46, 48, 52
positive obligations of government, 33,
  46
protection of health, 34
public participation, 39
Right to property
American Convention, 173
drinking water (well), 115
global warming, 555, 564
indigenous rights, 175–79, 180–83,
  185–88, 193–202
right to security. *See* Climate change
Right to water. *See generally* Chapter 4
constitutional basis

Argentina, 131–32
India (implicit), 130–31, 139–45
South Africa, 114, 129–30, 134–39
Ukraine (implicit), 145–46
privatization, 123–28
property, water well, 115
public trust, 114, 124
scope & content, 119–23
sources of law, 114–19
thirst, right of, 123–27
virtual water, 121, 122
Rights
generations, 19–20
linkages between human rights & environment, 12–20

S

sedition. *See* SLAPP
SLAPP. *See also* Freedom of speech & expression, *See generally* Chapter 11
criminal libel, 499, 506, 507
defamation, 504–8, 529–47
  decriminalization, 505–7
insult, 500–504
right to appeal and litigate, 510–12
right to boycott and picket, 513–21
right to campaign and criticize, 521–27
right to petition, 508, 512
sedition
  colonial law origin, 499
  Tanzania, 481, 496, 498, 499
  United States, 496–500
SLAPPback, 529
soft law. *See* Sources of international law
Sources of international law
customary international law
  abstention when no consensus, 386,
    387
  aiding and abetting, 397
  Alien Tort Claims Act, 401–9
  arbitrary arrest not included, 391
  as law of nations, 402
  constitutional tool of interpretation
    (South Africa), 134
  Convention on Law of the Sea, 408
  corporate liability, 393, 399
  environmental harms, 399
  environmental rights, 4, 6, 8
    Colombia, 140

Sources of international law *continued*
    evidence, 402
    forced labor, 394
    human rights, 6
    improper general federal common
        law, 391
    indigenous rights to land and re-
        sources, 198
    judicial creativity, 409
    murder, rape, and torture, 387, 396
    right of self-determination, 148
    right to health, 401, 403
    right to life, 401, 403
    right to sustainable development, 401
    right to water, 114, 119, 129
    Stockholm Declaration, 6
    Universal Declaration, 6, 375
    soft law, 4, 302, 369, 374, 375, 376, 377,
        379
    treaties, conventions, & covenants, 4,
        23, 141, 148, 402, 403, 405
Standing to sue
    Aarhus Convention, 231, 340–56
        information, 231
    acciones difusas, 321
    actio popularis, 321, 323, 334, 338, 340,
        351, 352
    administrative proceedings, 290
    based on participation, 334, 354, 355
    by state government, 322
    cause of action, 317, 319, 335, 340
    citizen suit
        Clean Air Act, 109
        Mich. Envir. Prot. Act of 1970, 109
        U.S., 326
    common law, 338
    concept, 321
    countries
        Australia, 324, 327, 328, 329, 330,
            331, 324–32
        Bangladesh, 98
        Chile, 71, 109, 340
        Colombia, 321
        Costa Rica, 321
        European countries, 334–40, 351–55
        India, 69, 323
        Indonesia, 500
        Nicaragua, 433
        Philippines, 85, 320

        South Asia, 323
        U.K., 329, 330
        United States, 316, 322, 325, 326, 340
            Michigan, 109, 340
            Oregon, 332
            Pennsylvania, 322
            tribal rights, 211
    duties versus rights, 338
    epistolary (India), 323
    ICCPR Optional Protocol, 150
    informational, 326
    international courts or bodies
        African Commission, 54
        African Court on Human Rights, 311
        European Court of Justice, 336, 339
        Inter-American Comm. On Human
            Rights, 572
        Inter-American Court of Human
            Rights, 311
        U.N. Human Rights Committee, 312
    legal personality, 353
    legal tests
        case or controversy, 333
        constitutional rights, 319–20, 338,
            340, 501
        diffuse interest, 352, 353
        direct interest, 336, 337, 344, 347,
            352, 353
        environmental concern, 339
        environmental right, 17, 319–21,
            336, 337, 339, 340
        future generations, 320, 321, 322
        generalized grievances, 322
        genuine interest, 338
        geographical area of NGO, 344
        injury, 574
        legal interest or right, 319, 334, 336,
            337, 338, 342, 343, 344, 351
        personal and direct interest, 335, 344,
            345, 347
        sufficient interest, 334, 335, 342
        wide access to justice (Aarhus Con-
            vention), 341, 342, 343, 346, 350
    legislated, 324–33, 334, 339, 344
    neighbors, 352, 353
    NGO standing, 232, 311, 334, 336, 337,
        339, 340, 342, 343, 344, 346, 348,
        350, 351, 353, 354, 355, 572

open standing, 321, 324, 330, 331, 332, 333, 340
private Attorneys General, 326
private defendants, 340
public interest, 336
reasons, 321
Substantive environmental right
compared to procedural, 18
international law, 6–10
  Africa, 52–60
  Americas, 60–65
  Europe, 24–52
national law, 17
  constitutions, 68–72
    overturning executive action, 79–93
    overturning legislation, 73–79
    private defendants, 100–109
    requiring affirmative programs, 93–99
    role of courts, 110–12
possible sources, 18
Sustainable development
African Charter, 58
attitude of MDB staffs, 448, 450
climate change, 21, 551
Constitution of India, 69
Convention on Biological Diversity, 170
corporate responsibilities, 370
customary international law, 401, 406
Draft Principles on Human Rights and the Environment, 14
EBRD Charter, 448, 451
environmental governance, 297
EP&A Act (New South Wales, Australia), 588
Inter-American Commission, 239
Inter-American Strategy (ISP), 289
IPCC 4th Assessment Report, 551
Kampala Declaration, 295
OECD Guidelines, 370
public participation, 289, 292, 295, 454
right to water, 116
Rio Declaration, 4, 406
SADC Treaty, 296
Supreme Court of India, 69
U.N. Draft Norms on Transnational Corporations, 373
U.N. Human Rights Council, 21

Water Charter of Senegal River, 119
World Bank, 459

T

Treaties, conventions, & covenants. *See also* Sources of international law; *see generally* TABLE OF AUTHORITIES
direct application (self-executing), 10, 24, 230, 231, 273, 385, 390, 404